THE HANDBOOK OF FORECASTING

A Manager's Guide

THE HANDBOOK OF FORECASTING

A Manager's Guide

Edited by
SPYROS MAKRIDAKIS
INSEAD, Fontainebleau, France

and

STEVEN C. WHEELWRIGHT
Stanford University, Stanford, California

1807 1982

175 YEARS OF PUBLISHING

A Wiley-Interscience Publication
JOHN WILEY & SONS
New York   Chichester   Brisbane   Toronto   Singapore

Library of Congress Cataloging in Publication Data
Main entry under title:

The Handbook of forecasting.

  "A Wiley-Interscience publication."
  Includes indexes.
  1. Business forecasting. I. Makridakis,
Spyros III. Wheelwright, Steven C., 1943–
HD30.27.H36   658.4'0355   81-16269
ISBN 0-471-08435-2   AACR2

Printed in the United States of America

10 9 8 7 6 5 4 3 2

———— PREFACE ————

The past decade has seen a number of major developments in the field of forecasting and planning. These have included an increasing number of sophisticated methodologies for preparing forecasts, experience in using such methodologies in a broader range of planning situations, and a deeper understanding of the psychological and organizational considerations that determine forecasting's impact on planning and decision making.

In addition, the events and environmental changes of the late 1970s and 1980s have presented managers with both significant challenges and significant opportunities in the field of forecasting. Some of the critical challenges have included:

1. Increasing economic uncertainty, not just in relation to basic factors like inflation, interest rates, and unemployment, but in the underlying relationships among economic factors.

2. Increasing complexity of econometric and time series forecasting techniques, requiring more data, better expertise, and more computations for their application.

3. Recognition that management judgment applied to problem identification and problem formulation must be matched with analytical skills if forecasting is to be effective.

Some of the developments that provide significant opportunities for dealing with these challenges include:

1. Technical and data communication advances that provide better access to improved data bases in several areas important to forecasting.

2. Better and cheaper access to computing power through time sharing, minicomputers, and "home" computers.

3. Increasing numbers of management students trained in the analytical techniques of forecasting who are eager and willing to work with experienced managers in forecasting and planning jobs.

In forecasting, as in all fields of systematic endeavor, applications in practice have lagged behind the development of both theory and technique. However, in the past 5 years a number of organizations and managers have gained solid experience in what seems to work and why. The purpose of this book is to bring together that knowledge and experience in a manner that will be most helpful to managers.

Three main guidelines have been used by the editors in preparing this volume. First, it is intended to be a handbook; that is, it is meant to serve as a reference book—to provide broad coverage, to be up to date, to be easy to read, and to be organized in a manner that makes it easy for the reader to find information. The Glossary, the detailed Subject Index, and the basic structure of the book were developed with this "handbook" role in mind.

A second major aspect of the book, highlighted by the title, is its intended audience. Not only have chapters been outlined and included on the basis of what managers need, but the individual orientation, topic coverage, and presentation of materials have all been geared to a management audience. The style of writing, the coverage of organizational issues and decision-making processes as they interact with forecasting, and the use of numerous practical illustrations, for example, are all in keeping with the needs of a management audience.

Finally, as the title makes clear, the book is about forecasting. However, in keeping with both the handbook role of the volume and the management audience, the definition that the editors have given to forecasting is much broader than that provided in most books on forecasting. It is the editors' view that forecasting is not solely a staff function, separable from the management tasks of planning and decision making. Rather it is an integral part of those tasks, and while it often involves the use of staff to complement the manager's time and abilities, the successful impact of forecasting is tied directly to the manager's involvement, understanding, and need for forecasts. Unless managers are directly involved in preparing the forecasts, the chances that these forecasts will be incorporated into planning or decision making are slim. Thus several of the chapters in this book highlight the context within which forecasting must be applied and what both the manager and forecaster need to understand about each other's roles to have the greatest impact on the organization's performance.

This volume could not have been prepared even just a few years ago because of the lack of sufficient integrated experience among practitioners, analysts, and academics. Significant advances in the field, however, now make this handbook possible. The editors are the first to admit that several major limitations still exist, as highlighted in Chapter 33. Nonetheless, we do anticipate continued progress at an increasing pace during the next few years. If that assessment is correct, a second edition of this handbook will be able to report on the next generation of developments and provide further support to management needs and efforts. This specific forecast by the editors is intended both to encourage those who don't find all the answers in this edition and to express our commitment to the field and its future.

The editors would like to give special thanks to the many authors who contributed to this handbook both in their individual chapters and in the overall structure and philosophy. We also appreciate the work of many managers who were willing to review the concepts in specific materials included in the handbook and hope that their efforts will make the book much more useful to its intended audience.

SPYROS MAKRIDAKIS
STEVEN C. WHEELWRIGHT

Fontainebleau, France
Stanford, California
January 1982

CONTENTS

PART 2.   APPROACHES TO FORECASTING

PART 3.   FORECASTING CHALLENGES

PART 4. MANAGING THE FORECASTING FUNCTION

THE HANDBOOK OF FORECASTING

A Manager's Guide

1

ROLE AND APPLICATION OF FORECASTING IN ORGANIZATIONS

CHAPTER

1

INTRODUCTION TO MANAGEMENT FORECASTING

Status and Needs

SPRYOS MAKRIDAKIS
European Institute of Business Administration—Insead

STEVEN C. WHEELWRIGHT
Graduate School of Business Administration, Stanford University

While forecasting has always been an integral part of virtually all types of management decision making, as a discipline it has grown tremendously during the past two decades. Forecasting became a full-fledged field for both practitioners and academicians by the late 1970s as its importance to all forms of planning and decision making became apparent in such diverse areas as business, government, nonprofit institutions, and military organizations.

It is the editors' belief that forecasting is not just a statistical area, but the domain of psychology, sociology, politics, management science, economics, and other related disciplines. A major goal of this handbook is to provide an up-to-date summary of these perspectives and the progress that has been made in the forecasting field in recent years. These developments have been impressive, and their consequences for organizational decision making are of significant importance to managers and forecasters alike.

The purposes of this introductory chapter are three: First is to provide an overview of some of the major perspectives on forecasting that have appeared in the literature in the past two decades. These perspectives can serve as useful reference points for practitioners seeking to broaden their understanding of available approaches to forecasting and the challenges and issues being addressed at the present time. A second purpose is to provide an overview of the various sections of this handbook and to suggest some of the interrelationships among individual chapters. Finally, the management role in recognizing forecasting needs and developing procedures for meeting them in a manager's own organization is highlighted.

ALTERNATIVE PERSPECTIVES ON FORECASTING

It is perhaps ironic that during the 1960s, when economic and political conditions were relatively stable for the industrialized countries of the world, there was little interest in forecasting among practitioners. In contrast, in the turbulent environment of the early 1980s, the need for forecasting has become widely recognized. The irony is that when forecasting is accurate, the need for it is limited, and few praise its successes. On the other hand, when forecasting is inaccurate, everyone complains about it; its potential usefulness is substantial, but its performance is less than satisfactory.

Formal forecasting started as a technical area dominated by statistical methods applied solely to historical data. In recent years, this emphasis has shifted, and while statistics and quantitative data still play important roles, the psychological and organizational aspects of forecasting have become increasingly important. In addition, it has become clear that many standard methodologies are not adequate for dealing fully with such areas as political forecasting, new product forecasting, long-term environmental forecasting, or with special events. In the 1980s, this set of circumstances has made the forecasting field particularly frustrating for practitioners seeking sound advice about which methods will give the best results for their specific needs. There is no single answer to such questions. However, an understanding of some of the alternative frameworks useful in viewing the forecasting field can help managers to develop their own guidelines. One such framework is summarized in Chart 1-1.

While Chart 1-1 simply summarizes examples of various combinations of these two dimensions of forecasting possibilities, understanding the pros and cons of each is one way to develop a reference point for planning forecasting applications. Let us first examine the rows in Chart 1-1. "Intuitive" forecasting refers to processes that are internal to the planner(s) or decision maker(s). Thus, while the same person may do the

CHART 1-1. Categorizing Forecasting Possibilities

	Implicit	Explicit
Intuitive	Estimating the sales of Product A for the coming month in an intuitive, ad hoc manner.	Using a monthly meeting of senior management to develop forecasts for Product A for the next month.
Formal	Predicting the sales of Product A for the coming month using a statistical forecasting method.	Obtaining monthly forecasts for each major product group on a specified date for use in production planning.

forecasting, he or she may be subject to many of the biases reported in the psychological literature with regard to such subjective and judgmental estimating procedures. This literature also suggests that such intuitive forecasting may be less accurate than very simple, formal techniques.

The approaches in Chart 1-1 referred to as "formal" forecasting methods are those whose steps can be written down and which, when applied by different individuals, provide a similar forecast. Thus, an important distinction between intuitive and formal approaches is the degree to which forecasts can be replicated.

The major characteristic of "implicit" forecasts (see first column) is that the forecasts are not integrated into plans and decisions being made. Thus, even if a formal forecast procedure were used to arrive at a forecast, with an implicit approach, the forecast would not be systematically recorded or incorporated into a specific plan of action or decision. "Explicit" forecasting procedures, on the other hand, seek to clearly delineate the value of that forecast and the time at which it is obtained, and to use it directly (possibly after having applied some consistent adjustment process) for planning or decision-making purposes.

As suggested in the final section of this chapter, most forecasting applications start out being intuitive and implicit in nature. However, research in the field of forecasting indicates that moving to more explicit procedures, and eventually to formal explicit procedures, tends to lead to significant improvements in forecasting performance. Managing the movement from the upper left-hand corner of Chart 1-1 to the lower right-hand corner is addressed further in the final section of this chapter.

A second reference point for the practicing manager looking at the forecasting field is understanding what existing techniques can and cannot do, so that realistic expectations can be developed and used in evaluating performance. Many of the major problems currently attributed to forecasting can be tied directly to inappropriate expectations as to what formal explicit techniques can deliver.

What a manager can expect from forecasting depends in large part on the type of method being used and the time horizon of the forecast. In terms of methodologies, there are two major types or categories of formal techniques. One of these consists of time series methods. Approaches of this type seek simply to extrapolate past data patterns into the future. The basis for such methods is that momentum exists in a time series and that momentum will carry the series for at least the time horizon to be forecast. Generally, this momentum is assumed to be largely independent of external factors. In one sense, such time series approaches can be viewed as "fatalistic," assuming that things will not change but that "history will repeat itself."

The other major type of formal forecasting techniques can be called causal or explanatory and includes regression and econometric methods. Techniques in this category attempt to discover causal or at least explanatory factors that link two or more series together. Such methods seek to answer questions like "What will happen to B if A occurs?" This approach is very popular in the natural sciences, and it is one that certainly has inherent appeal to managers. An important aspect of such regression or econometric methods is understanding the relationship between various series and how the variable in question interacts with other variables. For example, if it can be determined that price increases will decrease sales, then a planned price increase can be linked directly to anticipated sales forecasts.

One of the problems with both time series and regression/econometric approaches is that the patterns on which they are based are computed using historical data. As these patterns or relationships change, the accuracy of forecasting deteriorates. Unfortunately, in most business and economic environments, such patterns and relationships are continually changing, and it is simply the rate of change that varies. Thus, it is the rate of change that determines the relative effectiveness of formal forecasting approaches in general.

This fluidity of patterns and relationships is further accentuated by the goals and actions of managers that influence the future course of events. Like self-fulfilling prophecies, the things that management seeks to accomplish often become determinants of changes in patterns and relationships and thus affect the accuracy and applicability of various forecasting methods. Not only is this a micro concern (within the individual organization), but it can be a macro concern as well. For example, when several companies in an industry forecast a certain business cycle for their product or have similar forecasts of the market potential for a new technology, the result for the entire industry may be changed simply because of the consistency of those expectations and projections.

This makes it particularly important for the management user of forecasting to ask what expectations are appropriate in judging forecasting performance, and to determine how much of the goal will be achieved through increased accuracy versus reaching a better understanding of the environment. Generally speaking, it is of little value to talk about forecasting accuracy without first understanding the complex processes that determine the future and the role of management in affecting those processes.

When the main purpose of forecasting is to provide a better understanding of the environment and causal factors that affect it, accuracy becomes of secondary importance. Unfortunately, understanding the causal factors affecting an organization raises many of the same problems as extrapolating past patterns to predict the future. Relationships, like patterns, do not remain constant, and the ability to understand complex phenomena is limited. However, simply identifying the factors that affect change and the direction of causality can be very helpful in many planning or decision-making situations.

A third perspective on forecasting, its role, and its current status relates to the issue of uncertainty in planning and decision making. As should be apparent from the paragraphs above, the ability of forecasting to reduce future uncertainty is often very limited, either because uncertainty may exist independent of what planners and decision makers do, or because the perception of uncertainty changes with the amount of forecasting. Ideally, managers would prefer that the more forecasting that is done, the lower the resulting uncertainty. However, there are many situations where simply spending more time on forecasting often has the opposite effect. That is, the very process of exploring the future through forecasting may open many new possibilities and lead to the consideration of more alternatives (and thus more uncertainty), rather than fewer alternatives.

From this perspective, the main purpose of forecasting is to enable decision and policy makers to understand the uncertainties in the future and to force decisions about the level of risk that is appropriate. Planners and decision makers have a number of choices in dealing with future uncertainty. One possibility is to buy insurance against possible undesirable events. Alternatively, guidelines might be developed to prevent the organization from venturing into situations involving certain kinds of high risks. However, high returns often are associated with high risks. This poses a dilemma—to operate in a risky and potentially high-reward environment or to operate in a less risky and lower-reward environment. A major role of forecasting is to aid in assessing various future alternatives and the levels of risk and return that are associated with each of them, so that managers can effectively address this dilemma.

A fourth perspective on the range of forecasting approaches discussed in this handbook centers on forecasting accuracy. The basic reference point here is to consider the performance of forecasting methodologies over the past two decades and then to extrapolate that performance into the future. The time horizon of the forecasts has been shown to be closely tied to the accuracy of different methods, as outlined below. (For more detail, see Hogarth and Makridakis.[6])

Long-Range Forecasting

Forecasts that cover a period of two years or more are typically very inaccurate. After examining the predictive accuracy of forecasting in such fields as population, economics, energy, transportation, and technology, Ascher[2] reached some very pessimistic conclusions. He found systematic biases, as well as errors that varied from a few percentage points to a few hundred percentage points. He also concluded that one could not specify beforehand which forecasting approach or forecaster would have been right or wrong. Furthermore, because policy makers tended to be supplied with so many different forecasts, the problem of "choosing" a forecast appeared to be as difficult as preparing one's own forecast. Since the fields examined by Ascher tended to be characterized by substantial experience and expertise in forecasting, as well as readily available data, one might well postulate that in other fields with data less suitable for forecasting (less aggregation and greater fluctuations) and less forecasting experience, the results would be even worse.

Ascher's conclusions are echoed by opinions expressed in the long-term forecasting literature (e.g., Gold[5]). It is difficult to assess beforehand the size of forecasting errors—unforeseen changes in trend can occur, discontinuities can arise, and new events or conditions can emerge. Moreover, past data can provide contradictory clues to future trends (see Dhalla and Yuspeh[4]). For instance, while growth of certain products in an industry can occur in one way, others may follow very different patterns (Brown and Rozeff[3]). Furthermore, even in the early 1970s, few imagined the possibility of an oil embargo, a quadrupling of oil prices, severe shortages of raw materials, stagflation, high unemployment accompanied by high inflation and high interest rates, a near collapse of the stock market, and two recessions in less than five years. All of this supports the conclusion that historically, long-term forecasts have not been very accurate, and there is little reason to believe that their accuracy will improve in the future.

Medium-Term Forecasting

Forecasts covering three months to two years are typically derived from long-term forecasts or from a buildup of short-term forecasts. A number of misconceptions exist concerning the ability of economists and business forecasters to predict important changes, either in the general level of economic activity or in the level of such activity for a specific industry, firm, or product over the medium term. Turning points in the business cycle, in particular, are extremely difficult to forecast (see Chapter 15 and Chapter 18) with any degree of accuracy.

The medium-term forecasting problems faced by economists and forecasters are twofold. One problem is that unanticipated recessions can and do occur. The other is that predicted recessions and accelerations are frequently difficult, if not impossible to forecast. Finally, with medium-term forecasts, as with long-term forecasts, numerous approaches and resulting forecasts are available, and most managers tend to choose those that best fit their preconceptions and personal biases.

Short-Term Forecasting

Because there is considerable inertia in most economic and natural phenomena, the current status of many variables is a good predictor of their near-term future status. This is especially true when the time horizon is three months or less. Mechanistic methods such as time series forecasting techniques often can make relatively accurate short-term forecasts and even outperform more theoretically elegant and elaborate approaches such as econometric techniques (see Armstrong[1] and Makridakis and Hibon[7]).

Short-term forecasting and planning are an integral part of several operations essential to the basic functions of a business. These include establishment of schedules for production, distribution, and employment, the development of cash management budgets, and the allocation of sales and promotion budgets. For such short-term needs, forecasting tends to be reasonably accurate, and the gains to be made from going from the intuitive/implicit to the formal/explicit mode of forecasting tend to be consistently positive. However, because the management procedures typically used to cope with short-term uncertainty are an integral part of the business (excess resources and inventories, extra cash balances, and some leeway in budget levels), these applications often receive less forecasting attention than they probably deserve.

Each of the foregoing perspectives should provide the reader with a better understanding of forecasting and the range of information provided on it in this handbook. It is the editors' conclusion that, while this can do much to help the manager who is not systematically addressing forecasting opportunities in the business, the field as a whole is not likely to see substantial gains in the accuracy of the best applications. It is our position that managers should not expect or try to eliminate inaccuracies or uncertainty from forecasts. Although this is particularly true in the long term, it also applies in the medium term. Rather, they should seek to understand the limits of the forecasting approaches being used, to select those that best fit their own needs, and to seek understanding of the items being forecast, instead of searching for a specific number that meets their immediate decision requirements.

What is extremely important to understand, in addition, is that whatever the problems and difficulties with formal forecasting methods, all other alternatives (notably intuitive, judgmentally based forecasts) produce results that are even worse. At the same time, obtaining these forecasts can be substantially more expensive.

HANDBOOK OVERVIEW

In developing the outline and contents for this handbook, the editors sought to provide a comprehensive yet practical guide for managers. It was decided that four major areas needed coverage in order to accomplish this goal.

Part 1, "Role and Application of Forecasting in Organizations," considers the perspective of the manager in the business organization and his or her view of forecasting needs. The chapters in this section are organized around management planning and decision making concerns, rather than around forecaster concerns. Thus, chapters taking a functional point of view—sales and marketing, operations and control, capacity and facilities, and finance—are included. In addition, general management concerns with medium- and long-term issues, and particularly with long-range and strategic planning, are also covered. The final chapter in this part addresses the relationship of forecasting methodologies to this range of management issues and concerns.

In Part 1, the management reader should be able to identify closely with the chapter structures, yet learn from the identified forecasting applications in each of those areas of management. The forecaster, on the other hand, will recognize many of the individual applications, yet find the broad discussion of management concerns of primary benefit. These chapters should form a good reference base for managers and forecasters to enhance their communication and understanding of each other's perspectives.

Part 2, "Approaches to Forecasting," deals with approaches to forecasting. It covers all of the major classes of forecasting techniques ranging from smoothing methods to decomposition methods, and on to regression and econometric methods. This part also describes some of the more subjective approaches, such as Bayesian techniques, that can be used to complement the more statistical quantitative methods. The final chapter of Part 2 goes beyond obtaining initial forecasts and looks at the problems and challenges of updating forecasts and maintaining tracking and adjusting procedures.

The chapters in Part 2 describe techniques that are in common use in the early 1980s. These are also likely to form the basis of most of the techniques to be used throughout the decade. While the chapters are structured in a manner familiar to forecasters, their contents include numerous applications and highlight the limitations and concerns most likely to be on the minds of practitioners.

Part 3, "Forecasting Challenges," takes a topical view of several critical issues facing forecasting, planning, and decision making in the decade of the 1980s. Thus, rather than taking either the traditional view of the manager or the traditional view of the forecaster, the chapters in Part 3 are organized around topics that are of mutual concern. Thus, such special problems as forecasting in a rapidly changing environment, life-cycle forecasting, dealing with recessions, and the uncertain macro-economic scene are addressed. These issues have been of concern during the past couple of decades, and they have yet to be put to rest. A number of issues are also addressed that have come of age only in the last five years. These include the forecasting of political risks and forecasting in the energy field. Finally, Part 3 concludes by considering other classes or problems that are likely to receive increased attention in the coming decade. Such topics as special events, new products, industrial and service product concerns, and the overall long-term environment, are covered in the chapters that round out Part 3.

Part 4, "Managing the Forecasting Function," looks at the task of managing the forecasting function. In contrast to the first three parts, which should be of concern to anyone having a specific forecasting requirement, the final part is concerned with those who have repetitive forecasting requirements and who must handle a range of forecasting applications.

Part 4 includes chapters dealing with the evaluation of forecasting models, the selection and maintenance of external data sources, and the use of third-party forecasting services. In addition, internal issues of concern to those charged with improving organization forecasting are covered in chapters dealing with determining what needs to be forecast, integrating forecasting with decision making, the organizational aspects of forecasting, and auditing and evaluating the forecasting function. The final chapter summarizes the editors' views regarding major concerns of both forecasters and decision makers in the decade ahead.

As two further aids to the management audience for whom this handbook is intended, each of the chapter authors was asked to prepare a problem-solving index for their chapter and a glossary of terms. The problem-solving index has been integrated into the handbook index to provide a more detailed reference source for managers seeking answers to specific problems and concerns. For ease of reference, the glossaries of forecasting terms prepared for the individual chapters have been combined into a single glossary at the end of the handbook. However, the source chapter for the definition of each term is identified so that readers seeking additional detail can easily locate the chapter in which that term is addressed in depth.

REFERENCES

1. Armstrong, J. Scott, "Forecasting with Econometric Methods: Folklore versus Fact," *Journal of Business*, Vol. 51, No. 4, pp. 549–564, 1978.

2. Ascher, W., *Forecasting: An Appraisal for Policy Makers and Planners*, John Hopkins University Press, Baltimore, 1978.

3. Brown, L. D. and Rozeff, M. S., "The Superiority of Analyst Forecasts as Measures of Expectations: Evidence from Earnings," *The Journal of Finance*, Vol. 33, No. 1, pp. 1–16, 1978.

4. Dhalla, N. K. and Yuspeh, S., "Forget the Product Life Cycle Concept," *Harvard Business Review*, Vol. 54, No. 1, pp. 102–112, 1976.

5. Gold, B., "From Backcasting towards Forecasting," *OMEGA*, Vol. 2, No. 2, pp. 209–224, 1974.

6. Hogarth, R. M. and Makridakis, S., "Forecasting and Planning: An Evaluation," *Management Science*, Vol. 27, No. 2 (February 1981), pp 115+.

7. Makridakis, S. and Hibon, M., "Accuracy of Forecasting: An Empirical Investigation," *Journal of the Royal Statistical Society A*, Vol. 142, Part 2, pp. 97–125, 1979.

CHAPTER

2

SALES FORECASTING
REQUIREMENTS*

G. DAVID HUGHES

Burlington Industries, Professor of Business Administration
University of North Carolina

A company considering the development of sales forecasts will need to answer a variety of questions before it can design a sales forecasting method to meet its needs. Who needs a sales forecast? What should we forecast? What are the determinants of sales? How do we determine the functional relationships between these determinants and sales? What are the sources of data for these determinants? Which direction do we forecast? From the aggregate to the small unit—the breakdown method? Or do we forecast from the smallest unit to the aggregate—the buildup method? Who participates in the forecast? How do we evaluate a forecast? This chapter will help executives answer these questions when they are developing a sales forecasting procedure.

---

*An expanded version of this discussion may be found in G. David Hughes and Charles H. Singler, *Strategic Sales Management* (Reading, MA: Addison-Wesley Publishing Co., 1983), Chapter 17.

WHO NEEDS A SALES FORECAST?

Strategic corporate planning operates in an environment of uncertainty. Sales forecasting attempts to reduce some of this uncertainty by predicting *what* will be sold to *whom* and *when*. This information regarding what (products and services), whom (market segments), and when (time patterns) is necessary input for planning in all functional areas of the firm. It is useful to classify these needs as long-run and short-run needs for sales forecasts.

Long-Run Needs

Chart 2-1 shows graphically where the long-run sales forecast fits into the corporate strategic planning process. This forecast is needed for organizational changes such as divisional decentralization, changing the sales force organization, opening new territories, acquiring new companies, developing new channels, and changing advertising agencies. Adding new products, product line extensions, and dropping old products require long-run sales forecasts. The capital budgeting process and changes in the production facilities will require a long-run sales forecast.

Short-Run Needs

The left-hand side of Chart 2-1 shows how the annual sales forecast is used in the short-run planning process. First, a forecast for next year may help to evaluate the current strategy. The success or failure of the present strategy may be explained as the forecaster examines the trends in the determinants of sales. What looked like an outstanding strategy may have been simply that we underestimated the growth of the market last year. Conversely, a great strategy may have been buried in a declining market.

The short-run forecast is needed for each of the elements in the marketing mix. *Product planning* requires a forecast for estimating inventories that will be required at various times throughout the year and at geographic locations. Timing *price* changes, channel discounts, and promotional deals requires good sales forecasts. Estimates of sales potential for market segments are a prerequisite for the *advertising* decisions that include copy themes and media strategies. A sales forecast may reveal the need for expanding the *sales force*, which will require plans for recruiting, hiring, training, and deployment. A change in the location of potential sales may require altering the *channel* strategy. All of these marketing strategies will appear in the cash budget as marketing expense items.

The sales forecast is needed for planning the production of a product. Scheduling, purchasing raw materials, inventory planning, hiring and

CHART 2-1. The Role of the Sales Forecast in Corporate Strategic Planning

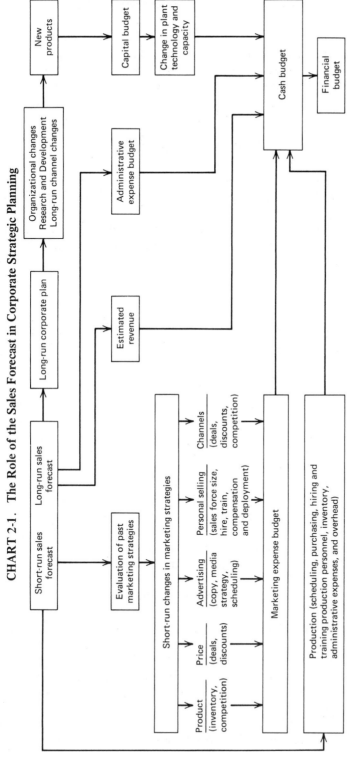

training personnel, and estimating overhead charges require estimates of the timing and magnitudes of company sales.

In summary, virtually all departments have some need for the annual sales forecast. Production, finance, personnel, accounting, and all of the marketing functions use the sales forecast in their planning activities.

WHAT SHOULD WE FORECAST?

Because the term "sales" can have different meanings, there can be many different kinds of sales forecasts. To prevent confusion, the terms market capacity, market potential, company potential, company forecast, sales goals, and sales quota will be defined in this section. The next section will explain how each of these forecasts requires a different set of variables.

Market Capacity

Market *capacity* is the number of *units* of a product or service that could be absorbed by a market at a given time irrespective of prices of products or the marketing strategies of suppliers. *Capacity* includes unmet needs for which a product or service does not exist. Thus, an analysis of market capacity could be the first step in developing a new product.

Market capacities could be expressed in terms of the total market or disaggregated segments of the market that have similar needs or buying styles. For example, we may forecast the total need for automobiles, or we may forecast the economy segment, the sporty segment, the luxury segment, and the fleet segment. Each segment would have different demographic, economic, educational, and social–psychological profiles. The needs of a person within one segment would be similar to those of others within the segment, but quite different from those of persons in other segments. The capacity of each of these segments is the *market segment capacity*. The total market capacity is simply the sum of all of these market segment capacities.

Market Potential

Market *potential* is the sales, expressed in the number of products and the dollar volume, that an entire industry expects to sell, given a known mix of products, prices, and market strategies. Thus, a sales forecast for the automobile industry may be stated in the number of luxury, compact, sporty, and economy cars that will be sold next year, given estimates of manufacturers' prices and their usual marketing strategies. The market potential differs from the market capacity because it speaks in terms of products instead of needs. Potential also introduces the concept of the *ability to buy a product* by introducing price and income. The term potential also recognizes the effect that the total industry marketing strategy can have on translating a capacity into a potential. Potentials may be expressed in terms of segments and industry totals.

Company Potential

A *company potential* is the *maximum* that a company could sell at a given price, irrespective of the capacities of its production and marketing facilities. This measure of company potential would be used to decide whether to add production and marketing capacities, whether to subcontract for production and perhaps marketing capacities, or whether to let some of the market go to competitors.

Company Forecast

The *company forecast* is a company's estimated sales, in units and dollars, for a brand, given a price and a marketing strategy. The forecast will reflect the capacity limitations of the firm, so generally it will be *lower* than the company potential.

Company forecasts are frequently expressed in absolute units and dollars and in the industry *share* of these units and dollars. Share estimates must consider competitive efforts regarding product attributes, pricing, promotion, and channel strategies.

Sales Goals

Sales goals are a hoped for sales level for a company, a division, or a product. They are generally *higher* than a forecast to provide motivation, especially for the sales force. Goals must be within reach, however, or they will be discouraging and therefore demotivating.

Sales Quotas

A *sales quota* is a goal that has been broken down into smaller units, such as a region, a district, or a specific representative's territory to provide a management objective. The quota is generally part of a motivation plan that is linked to compensation plans for sales managers and representatives.

WHAT DETERMINES SALES?

After the two previous questions have been answered, the sales forecaster must identify those variables that determine sales. Note again that we face the problem of how we want to define sales. For this section we shall examine what variables are needed to forecast market capacity, market potential, and company sales. By examining these three definitions of sales we shall see how each forecast requires different variables.

Variables to Forecast Market Capacity

Market capacity represents the total number of units that could be absorbed, regardless of persons' ability to pay. For many products and services there are limitations. There is a limit to how much one can eat. One haircut per person per week may be the upper limit for that service. One automobile per person may be the market capacity for that industry.

Identifying this capacity is necessary before making a commitment to a product. But there have been some classic cases in underestimating the market. When the first adding machine was developed, the market capacity was estimated to be 9000 units—one for each bank branch in the United States and Canada. Fifty years later the computer industry made a similar underestimate when it estimated that the capacity for computers was one for each major university and governmental agency.

Marketing capacities are based on the needs of individual consumers and firms. The needs of individuals may be defined in broad terms such as the need for food, shelter, safety, clothing, socialization, self-esteem, and self-actualization. A company has needs associated with its basic mission. For example, a manufacturing company will need machinery, materials, capital, trained labor, and management.

The magnitude of a need is measured by variables that are known as *market factors*, which are variables that either cause or are associated with the magnitude of the need. For example, a consumer's age will be related to food, clothing, and social needs. By knowing the number of persons in different age groups we can estimate the market capacity for baby food, soft drinks, and geriatric foods. Additional market factors for individual consumers include birth rates, marriage rates, education, geographic location, and the ages of children in the family. Sources of data for these market factors include the U.S. Census of Population and the "Survey of Buying Power," published annually by *Sales & Marketing Magazine*. (See Chapter 28.)

Market factors for a manufacturer may be the number of units sold, the dollar volume of services delivered, the number of employees in a company, or value added. The U.S. Censuses of Manufacturing, Transportation, Retailing, and Wholesaling and the "Survey of Industrial Buying Power," published annually by *Sales & Marketing Magazine*, provide data for estimates of industrial market capacity.

Variables to Forecast Market Potential

The market potential forecast is a refinement of the market capacity forecast because it includes the additional variables of price, economic capacity to buy, and the effect of the marketing strategies within the industry. Here we are trying to answer questions such as, "How much would sales increase if we lowered price 1%?" or "How much will sales drop if disposable personal income drops 1%?" These are concepts of price and income elasticity, as developed by economists.

Market factors for the ability to buy include not only income levels, but employment rates, the availability of credit, inflation rates, and consumers' expectations for the future. Market factors for a firm's ability to buy include the gross national product, inflation, the availability of capital, government policies, and executives' expectations for the future. Consumers' and business executives' expectations for the future are reported by The Conference Board, *Business Week*, and the Survey Research Center of the University of Michigan.

Additional variables will be needed to forecast potentials for specific market segments. These variables reflect psychological needs and life styles. Market factor variables that are used to identify market segments include variables such as beliefs, attitudes, heavy user/light user, and life style variables such as stylish, worrisome, economical, and sporty. These variables are not generally collected by public sources, so the researcher will need to conduct primary research using survey research methods.

Variables to Forecast Company Sales

The forecast of a company's sales reflects the variables that go into a forecast of the market potential, the capacities of the company, and the effectiveness of its marketing strategy relative to its competitors. Thus, to forecast company sales we need to know the comparative advantages and disadvantages of the company's product, its relative price, and the relative effectiveness of its advertising, personal selling, and channel strategies.

One approach to forecasting company sales is to forecast the market potential and then multiply this potential by a forecast of the percentage of this potential that will be captured by the company. This percentage, which is known as the *market share*, will be determined by the cumulative effect of previous marketing strategies for the company and the industry as well as planned changes in strategy by the company and other companies in the industry. This approach is known as the *breakdown method* of forecasting company sales.

Three frequently used approaches for forecasting company share are econometric models, brand preference models, and brand switching models. Each of these will be explained in nontechnical terms.

Econometric models reflect several relationships simultaneously. The forecaster may have one equation that predicts the market potential for a product. This market potential equation would have demographic and economic variables. A second equation, to forecast market shares, would have variables that reflect product attributes and marketing strategies relative to the entire industry. The share equation may also reflect the cumulative effect of previous promotions or the carryover effect of a previous advertising blitz. This system of equations would be solved to estimate the effect of a change in a company's marketing strategy. (See Chapter 19).

Brand preference models are based on the fact that people do not buy products; they buy a bundle of attributes that will meet their needs. Some needs are more important than others, which is reflected in a choice model by weighting procedures. Buyers perceive brands as possessing different amounts of these attributes. These perceptions are measured as attitudes toward the brands. Various metric and nonmetric methods have been devised for measuring these attitudes. These measures are reported in the form of attitude profiles, brand maps, and models. One of the difficulties with brand preference models is the fact that they are weak predictors of behavior. Their strength would seem to be as a diagnostic tool for developing better strategies. For instance, misperceptions regarding product attributes may be corrected with an advertising strategy. Correctly perceived product weaknesses may require further product research and development.

Brand switching models are based on the assumption that behavior patterns will be repeated. A matrix of the proportion of the market that has switched among brands can be multiplied using matrix multiplication to predict market shares in the future if certain mathematical assumptions have been met. One of the most difficult assumptions to meet is that people are homogeneous with regard to their probabilities of switching. One market segment may be loyal to a single breakfast cereal, for example, while another segment may be loyal to three or four cereals, switching for the sake of variety. This loyalty to a group of brands makes it difficult to identify switching patterns. Another limitation is that the basic model does not fully describe consumer behavior. Refinements in the basic switching model must be made to include the effects of learning that may occur from using a brand or from advertising.

The brand switching model is a better predictor of market shares than the brand preference model because it uses behavioral variables, those of brand switching, to predict behavior. The switching model is inferior to the preference models in diagnosing problems and developing better promotional strategies because it does not explain why consumers behaved as they did.

HOW DO WE DETERMINE THE FUNCTIONAL RELATIONSHIPS?

After we have decided who needs the forecast, defined the kind of sales that we want to forecast, and identified the variables that either cause or are associated with these sales, we are ready for the next forecasting question, "How do we determine the functional relationships between these variables and sales?" Generally we depend on empirical answers to this question.

In the strict definition of the philosophy of science, there are no theories of consumer or buyer behavior, but some empirical regulatories have been so labeled. *Price theory*, for example, states that generally more products will be sold as the price is lowered, except in those cases where there is a snob appeal for high-priced products. Price theory, therefore, states only that the sign of the price–sales relationship is generally negative—that as one goes down the other goes up. The degree of change is an empirical question.

Some relationships can be described in terms of empirical probabilities. For example, market capacity (MC) may be defined as the product of the number (N) of persons who have a given need, their probability (P) of using the product in question to meet the need, and the rate (R) at which they use the product during time period t. This relationship may be expressed algebraically as follows:

$$MC_t = N_t P_t R_t$$

For example, if there are 50,000 fans at a football game, N equals 50,000. If the product category is soft drinks, we need an estimate of the probability that a fan will drink at least one cup of a soft drink during the game. We may express this event as either a probability for a single fan or the proportion of the total fans; the outcome is identical. This probability will vary according to the date of the game and its geographic location, both of which will determine the temperature. If it is cold weather, soft drinks may not sell well. Let's assume that this probability is 0.20. Finally, we need to know the rate or number of cups of soda that will be consumed during an average game, given the expected temperature. If we assume that the average number of cups per consumer is 2.25, we may calculate the market capacity for all soft drinks during the game as follows:

$$MC = 50,000 \times 0.20 \times 2.25$$

$$= 22,500 \text{ cups of soft drinks}$$

The *market potential*, however, may be considerably less than this number because of the price charged and the distribution system. Perhaps the price is too high. Perhaps the vendors working the isles of the stadium are more interested in the game than selling soda. Thus, estimates of price elasticity and salespersons' motivation are needed to forecast the market potential.

What will be the market share for a given brand of soft drink? That will depend on consumers' past buying patterns, which reflect the cumulative effect of past strategies and current marketing strategies. Perhaps we generally get a share of 0.15, but we sold the vendor on using our cups, which show our brand name on one side of the cup and the name of the home team on the other side. From previous experience we have found that this increases the share to 0.20. Thus, in this case we may expect a market brand potential of 4500 cups (0.20 × 22,500).

Empirical relationships may be established with existing data, which is frequently the case with econometric models, or controlled experiments may be used to establish cause and effect relationships. Experimental data are scientifically more acceptable and generally more expensive to collect.

IN WHICH DIRECTION DO WE FORECAST?

The two basic approaches to sales forecasting are the breakdown method and the buildup method. The breakdown approach, as we have seen above, begins with an estimate of the market potential and breaks it first into a company potential that may be divided further into district, region, and territory potentials.

RCA uses the breakdown approach to forecast color television sales (ref. 1, pp. 119–25). It begins with an econometric model that forecasts gross national product (GNP) in constant dollars by using variables to reflect the current supply of money, government expenditures during periods of full employment, a price deflator, and dummy variables to reflect seasonality and periods when strikes occur. The color television model uses this forecasted estimate of GNP in constant dollars as one input along with estimates of the money supply in constant dollars (which would reflect the availability of consumer credit), a dummy variable for strike conditions (segments that would be temporarily off of the market for major purchases), and the position of color television in its product life cycle, expressed as an S curve. The total model includes 85 variables. (See Chapter 17 for another example of forecasting color television.)

The Timken Company makes bearings for railroad freight cars. It forecasts its sales using the breakdown method (ref. 7, pp. 110–14). Timken uses two equations to derive the demand for new and rebuilt freight cars. The first equation derives the demand for railroad ton-miles per day by first estimating the total intercity ton-miles for the next year. This estimate is multiplied by railroads' estimated share of the market to produce the railroad ton-miles for the coming year. This yearly estimate is divided by 365 to produce a daily demand.

The second Timken Company equation estimates the supply of freight service that is available, expressed in terms of ton-miles per serviceable freight car. The size of the fleet that will be required during the coming year is derived by dividing the projected railroad ton-miles per day by the ton-miles per serviceable freight car. Because only 85% of the cars are available for service at one time, this estimated fleet size must be divided by 0.85 to yield the total fleet that is required for the forecasted year. To this figure the Timken Company adds the number of cars that will be retired next year and subtracts the size of the fleet at the end of the previous year. The net result of this computation is the market capacity for new and rebuilt freight cars.

The Cummins Engine Company uses a breakdown and a buildup approach to forecast the sales of its diesel truck engines (ref. 1, pp. 114–19). The breakdown approach uses an econometric model and an estimate of Cummins's market share to derive a company forecast. The buildup forecast is based on a detailed study of the needs of each Cummins account. This analysis includes market factors such as the account's present engine inventory and back orders as well as the account's marketing program that may increase its truck sales. The resulting forecast is reported by account, model, and month. These individual account forecasts are added to produce a company forecast, which is then reconciled with the company forecast that is derived by the breakdown method.

Which is better, the breakdown or the buildup method? There are no theoretical answers to this question. The breakdown method tends to be less expensive when it can use aggregate forecasts that have been made by others, such as the government, universities, or consulting firms. The buildup method generally requires the forecaster to collect more data. With regard to reliability, Cummins reports that the breakdown method is more reliable for six months and beyond, while the buildup method tends to be more reliable for shorter periods. Thus, the planning horizon seems to determine the appropriateness of the sales forecasting method.

The introduction of the planning horizon requires that we ask, "How far into the future are we forecasting?" If we are making a one-year forecast, variables such as birth rates and geographic shifts in population are not important because there would be only slight changes. If, however, we are making a 10-year forecast, these demographic variables become extremely important.

WHO PARTICIPATES IN SALES FORECASTING?

The broadening of the base for strategic marketing planning has also broadened the base for forecasting. Individual sales representatives are frequently involved in forecasting the needs for specific accounts, as illustrated in the Cummins Engine Company example. Market and product planners will provide input for changes in the general market, changes in competitive activities, and changes in the company's marketing strategies. The legal and government relations departments will provide estimates of regulatory and legislative changes that will affect sales. The Jones & Laughlin Steel Corporation has broad involvement in sales forecasting, including the sales managers, marketing managers, operations personnel, market planners, economics and sales analysts, and a general manager for steel planning (ref. 1, pp. 35–39).

HOW DO WE EVALUATE A SALES FORECAST?

It is harder to answer this question than it is to answer the question, "How do we evaluate a weather forecast?" Because we cannot control the weather, we can evaluate weather forecasting methods according to their reliability and validity. Reliability means simply will the method give similar results over time. Validity, in this case, means did it rain as predicted. (See Chapter 27.)

To understand the problem of validating a sales forecast, we must consider the concepts of self-fulfilling forecasts and nonfulfilling forecasts. A rumor of a run on a bank may produce a run on a bank, which is a self-fulfilling forecast. In contrast, a sales forecast for a bad year may provide a motivation for creating better marketing strategies, and it may stimulate higher selling productivity, thereby increasing sales and invalidating the forecast. This is a happy ending for the company, but it ruins the forecaster's record. Thus, the ultimate test of a sales forecast is whether it made the marketing strategy a better strategy.

CONCLUSION

The sales forecasting requirements of a company will be unique to each company. To design a forecasting system, the company must answer the questions that are asked in this chapter. Subsequent chapters will provide more detail and techniques for answering these questions and for developing an operational forecasting system.

REFERENCES

1. Hurwood, David L., Elliot S. Grossman and Earl L. Bailey, *Sales Forecasting*, Report No. 730, The Conference Board, New York, 1978.

CHAPTER

3

FORECASTING REQUIREMENTS FOR OPERATIONS PLANNING AND CONTROL

BAYARD E. WYNNE
Principal and Director of
Modeling and Quantitative Techniques
Arthur Andersen & Co.

DAVID A. HALL
Internal Consultant
Inland Steel Company

THE OPERATIONS FUNCTION

The fundamental issues in operations planning and control (OP&C) are what to make, how much to make, and when to make it. Marketing presumably converts its assorted customer and competitive intelligence into some form of estimated demand. Facilities management decisions on physical capacity limits are similarly defined externally for OP&C. All these factors are integrated into the financial program which will be one of the measures used to evaluate OP&C performance.

Within those limits OP&C has the task of balancing the many tradeoffs among material availability, labor efficiency, capacity utilization, and finished goods inventory balance or customer service.

This chapter treats both the inputs and outputs of a typical OP&C model, their sources, screening, and application. This chapter's references are a good source for more detailed information on OP&C systems and the associated forecasts. In addition, *Journal of the American Production and Inventory Control Society* provides a wealth of applications articles.

MODEL INPUTS

General Requirements

OP&C models are demand driven, receiving their key inputs in the form of demand forecasts from the marketing department and order backlog status reports from the order entry system. This demand for gross products is then exploded[11, 19] into indivisible net subcomponent, labor, capital, facilities, and transportation requirements. In turn these are compared against exogenously given working constraints: capital availability, plant capacity, personnel availability, raw materials inventory, and order lead times and finished goods storage and transportation constraints in order to determine desired feasible production and product mix.

Chart 3-1 illustrates this context for forecasting as related to the OP&C function. Implicit in the interrelationships shown in Chart 3-1 is the critical necessity of insuring that a complete adaptive management information system[4] is in operation to deal with all issues, regardless of the particular organization structure which exists.

Screening

All incoming data should be screened for three key factors: *timeliness, accuracy,* and *sensitivity.* Timely data are both current and available early enough to allow production changes to meet the new projections.

Screening for accuracy is a three-part test. First, is the variable correct? For example, has nominal plant capacity been substituted for peak capacity, and so on? Second, are the data consistent? Have data been correctly entered and do the projected inputs and outputs seem appropriate? Third, have the inputs been intentionally altered, misprojected, or skewed? An example of this inaccuracy occurs when a marketing department with a compensation plan based on exceeding quotas is allowed to set sales forecasts.

Finally, the sensitivity of both inputs and outputs should be considered. How sensitive are current projections for sales or labor costs to

CHART 3-1. OP&C Forecasting Context

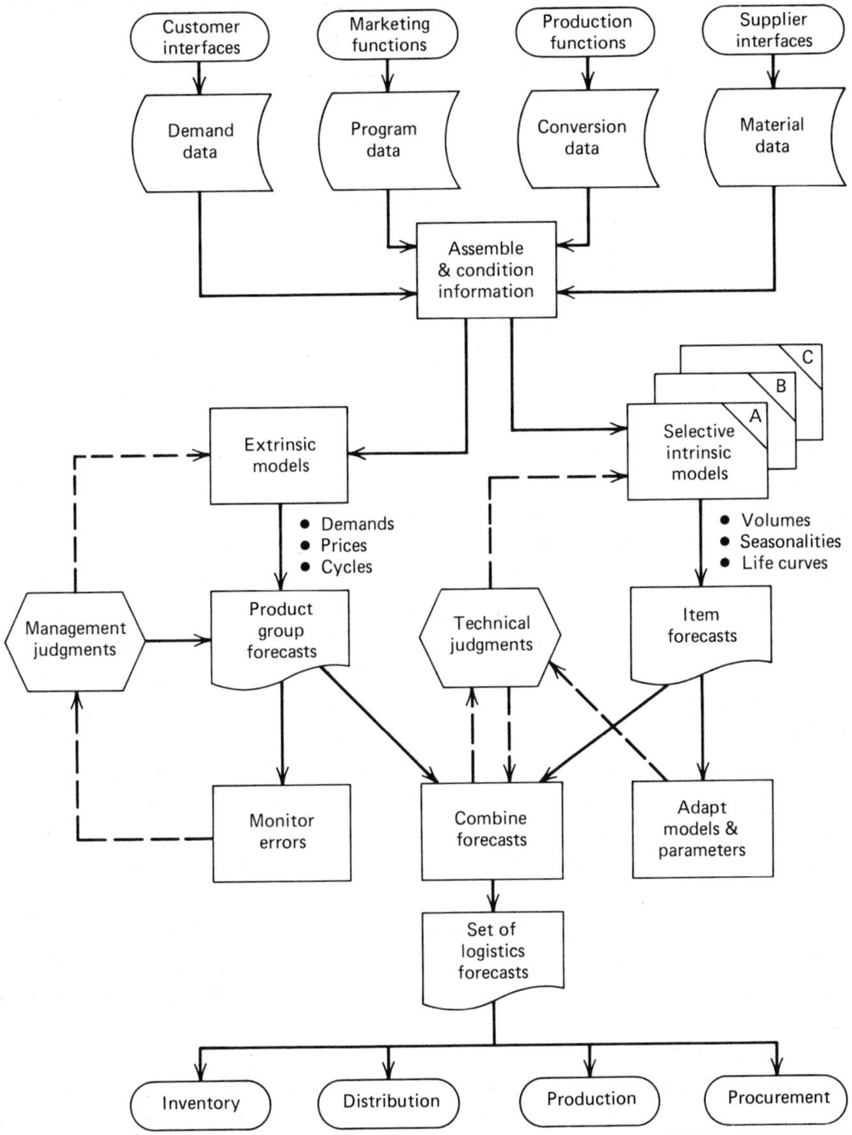

changes in competitive strategies, the environment, or anticipated wage increases? How sensitive is the resulting production schedule to variations in these inputs? Output sensitivity to input parameters will highlight those variables requiring the most screening for management purposes.

In actual practice you normally find that several problems must be dealt with as you define tasks related to the top cluster of elements in Chart 3-1. Perhaps new potential data sources must be formalized to improve accuracy, reduce bias, or to synchronize data in time. It is vital that a methodical approach be taken in this design of data screening. For example, clear user manuals are required if this foundation of the target OP&C system is to be accomplished successfully.

Specific Input Requirements

Demand Information Treatment

Real demand is not merely backlogged orders and sales forecasts. Rather, it is the required number of shippable units by expected need dates. The discrepancy between orders and real demand can be traced to several key factors.

Order cancellations are a primary cause of this difference and can play a major role in production misscheduling in the face of an economic downturn or in a capital-intensive technological market. While backlogged orders can be aged and weighted to better approximate demand, inappropriate production allocation can arise as a result of customer volatility. This volatility is often a function of how expensive a product is and how technologically sensitive the market for a firm's product is. Witness IBM's dilemma during the introduction of their 3300 series as the market failed to buy and cancelled standing orders in anticipation of the introduction of their 4300 series computer.[18]

In actual practice, you will frequently have to take competitor's behavior into account. Imagine the difficulty of attaining useful demand forecasts if IBM'S competitors failed to include data about IBM actions in making their own demand forecasts. The left side of Chart 3-1 encompasses such issues.

Promotional activities contribute unpredictably to the divergence between orders and demand. Sales promotions can provide both an unpredictable increase in sales and an increase in order cancellation rates because of indecisive marginal trial customers.

Disasters, whether they be natural or economic, that affect the market can further influence this divergence. Examples of these factors would include the near-collapse of the construction market in 1980 caused by spiraling interest rates, and the shift to imported economy automobiles in the period 1973–1980 in response to OPEC-generated energy price increases.

Finally, the relationship between orders placed and demand may be seasonal in nature. Parker-Hannifin Corp. has successfully used a pragmatic cycle forecasting technique[15] to approximate demand well enough with sufficient lead time to program integrated sales and production activities by product line in advance of swings in the segments of the economy that affect its businesses.

Motivational differences further complicate demand forecasts. Marketing targets that include sales objectives, quotas, and executive bias due to compensation plans all motivate one group while OP&C is driven primarily by shipping requirements. The costs of associated errors in demand estimation also differ between the two functional areas where stockout costs or carrying costs can far exceed marketing's cost of error.

This difference between motivation- and error-associated costs requires a clarification of cross-functional demand estimation. Who is to make the estimates, and how are those people motivated? How are errors tracked and utilized in updating flexible budgets and testing model accuracy? And, finally, how well do extrinsic and intrinsic demand estimates track real demand?[14] A forecast system must have systematic feedback if organizational learning is to take place and performance is to improve.[7]

Capacity Information Issues

Physical plant capacity, both nominal and peak as defined by plant engineering, is a basic given to the OP&C manager. While plant capacity is usually assumed fixed, it must be subject to periodic updating because of the effects of: capital expenditures, replacement or overhaul of equipment, increase in downtime due to plant aging, changes in product production, and the impact of moving along the learning curve.

Manning levels and shifts are one decision variable to the OP&C manager. Shift decisions are long-run in nature. Manning levels within a shift are used to "fine tune" production and provide flexibility to meet discrepancies between forecast and actual demand. (See Chapter 11 for an example of one approach to these issues.)

Varying final production mix by scheduling is another decision variable. By changing the number of shifts, the staffing level of shifts, or responsibilities within shifts, product mix within the physical plant capacities can be adjusted.

Key questions concerning capacity constraints include: How are shift changes planned? What constraints are imposed by the union? How much flexibility is provided within shifts by responsibility reassignment with the constraints of the union? Should peak periods be handled by overtime or an additional shift? Who varies manning levels? How much power should be vested in the foreman? Which product should be run when, and in what quantity, taking into consideration demand, capacity, and setup or additional tooling costs?

In actual practice, you will want to include these production planning/ scheduling algorithms and heuristics in your systems analysis diagram. They would appear in conjunction with the bottom cluster of elements in Chart 3-1. The practical reason for including them on your detailed version of Chart 3-1 is to insure that you provide for any desirable feedbacks between the several schedules and their predecessor forecasts.

Financial Planning Matters

Marketing shipments are the driving force of OP&C models, and both additions to accounts receivable and marketing expenses are implicit in the model. By assuming inventory buffers as a safety factor, the stock-piling of both raw materials and finished goods to satisfy demand, the minimization of costs via forward buys, and given a targeted customer service level or aggregate inventory level, fluctuation should be plannable. These anticipated fluctuations in inventory in coordination with marketing expenses and additions to accounts receivable allow the forecasting of financial requirements. These requirements will be on a cash basis enabling the firm to quickly assess the feasibility of various production strategies with respect to cash demands and funding requirements. These production demands assist the firm in capital budgeting by providing a calendar of net cash flows with respect to operations covering both expenses and capital outlays.

Operating budgets represent combined functional decisions and are cross-functional agreements concerning allocation of a firm's limited financial resources. The cash flow calendar provided by the OP&C model enables the manager to readily identify those future periods of cash flow problems; it also may suggest replanning of capital expenditures or reallocation rather than demanding budget cuts as an emergency procedure.

These links between the OP&C forecasting system, the derivative planning systems, and the trailing financial planning tools are not shown in Chart 3-1. However, they will be an integral part of the bottom symbol cluster of your detailed version of Chart 3-1.

OUTPUTS

Efficient production planning is the basic goal of all OP&C models, including material requirement planning, machine/work center loading, and shop floor control.[6]

Material procurement is one derivative of the OP&C model. By exploding finished goods demand to yield raw material requirements, and analyzing each input by quantity discount factors and order lead times, an Economic Order Quantity (EOQ) can be derived. This EOQ will minimize total costs by balancing stockout costs, carrying costs, quantity order discounts, desired buffer stocks, anticipated demand, and order placement costs. While no one EOQ method is universally best, the dynamic Silver-Meal algorithm[12] has had a demonstrated widespread success.

A family of forecasts are produced by the model.

Procurement Leadtimes. When orders of size EOQ must be placed to maintain buffer and satisfy demand.

In-Process Leadtimes. When production must begin and in what quantity to satisfy anticipated demand.

Uncertainty. The buffer level that should be maintained to be sure of satisfying demand at the confidence interval stipulated by the firm's desired level of customer service.

Stockpiles. When and to what levels should inventory be allowed to increase in order for the firm to satisfy demand when demand is anticipated to be greater than production capacity.

Forward Buys. Forecasting of price series can be used to size and time advance buying against expected consumption levels. Decision rules have been constructed which attain expected returns on investments from investment in commodity futures for consuming organizations.

Labor Productivities. Depending on the labor content leverage, learning curve forecasts, for example, can have a major impact both on product costs—and therefore demand—and on effective production capacity.

Process Yields. Long-term drift in mean process yields has high impact on all cost elements as well as on salable output capacity.

Shipping Times. Time lost in outbound transit is a severe restraint on higher market share and production economies through more stable product mixes that might otherwise be obtained.

These illustrative forecasts, as they relate in a comprehensive OP&C model, are shown in Chart 3-2.

The particular linkages, of course, depend on the business situation you face in your practice. Chart 3-2 should be regarded as a graphic checklist to be specifically structured in your design context.

FORECAST SYSTEM MANAGEMENT

Three primary issues exist in managing the development and use of forecasting systems. These are: (1) careful mutual consideration of the criteria to be satisfied, (2) a focus on systems rather than techniques, and (3) the conduct of forecasting implementation studies or projects.

Management's Forecast Criteria

General management seeks to have a combination of benefits from an OP&C forecasting system. The particular relative importance attached to each component benefit will vary among organizations. The importance of each will also vary in time within an organization.

Therefore, a good forecasting system will be constructed so that expected tradeoffs among these benefits in response to policy variable

CHART 3-2. Linkages Among
Operations and Control Forecasts

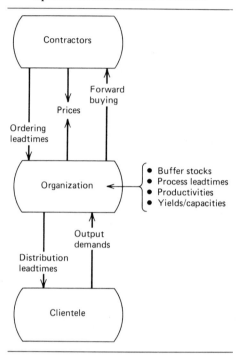

changes can readily be portrayed. As a corollary, a good forecast system
will also be driven by settable parameters through which management
can "tune" the forecast system to their desired benefit mix.

The three major component benefits are:

Reasonable customer service.

Inventories controllable to targets.

Attainment of procurement, conversion, and delivery economics.

These benefits have been listed in order of generally perceived importance. It is fundamental to the business organization's survival that it be
aware of and potentially responsive to customer service requirements.
Within that constraint there must be a capability to control aggregate
inventory investments. Then, it is also necessary to be cost efficient.

Brown[3] has codified one good approach (his indifference curve analyses) to providing general management control over the tradeoffs among
these benefits. Peterson and Silver[12] provide an excellent coverage of
the cost efficiency techniques. Some combination of both objectives
(each offers such) is required in the good OP&C forecast system.

Selection of specific techniques to use to meet the management criteria leads to a consideration of the technical criteria of forecast systems. An important trio of criteria are:

Forecast accuracies.

Forecasting costs.

Forecast comprehension.

Generally, the more forecast accuracy, the better. However, small forecast inaccuracies make essentially no difference in the complex aggregate operation of a typical industrial organization. Too many time lags and buffers as well as countervailing pressures exist to enable small forecast errors to have significant impact. Increased forecast accuracy is normally attained only at higher expense.

Therefore, what is usually sought is a robust forecast technique that operates at reasonable cost with tolerable errors. The technical design issue therefore is to structure the forecasting system so that it effectively uses adequate techniques.

This design perspective will usually satisfy the third technical criterion, making forecasts comprehensible to the user. System forecasts must be intuitively acceptable to the user or an alternative informal forecast system will evolve. Again, a well-structured combination of robust techniques with periodic human judgmental interaction coupled with adaptive or learning feedbacks for both the models and the humans is appropriate most often.[20]

Systems Versus Techniques

The preceding section emphasized that good forecasting systems are based on their architectural design specifying the techniques, rather than permitting "best" forecast techniques to dictate the system design. This theme and related topics are covered in J. Scott Armstrong's Chapter 32, "The Forecasting Audit."

Here, only some basic reminders are given:

Even the most accurate forecasts are wrong.

Error feedback and exception handling are keys to results.

Forecast frequency, period, and horizon are system design variables.

Incorporation of human judgment in the forecast process is vital.

Technical simplicity is most desirable.

Behavior aspects of forecast users are crucial and can be dealt with only at the system level.

Managing Forecast Studies

The last five chapters of this handbook deal with managing the forecasting function. In contrast we deal here simply with the management of forecast studies—a development project and the ensuing maintenance task. In the interest of brevity, however, this material is presented as a checklist. Expanded discussion of the context and implications are to be found in the chapters in Part 4.

Specifying the Task

Three steps are involved in project definition and preliminary design. Each is essentially concerned with an external interface with the organization.

1. *Situation Diagnosis.* What is the problem to be overcome or opportunity to be systematically exploited?

2. *Forecasting Strategy.* What inputs are to be converted to what outputs for use in what way and how often?

3. *Acceptance Criteria.* What target standards are to be met by the as yet unknown system?

Organizational Participation

Successful forecasting systems are the product of joint technical and user/management development. How is that to be attained?

1. *Working Assignments.* Which specific individuals are to do each task? How do these tasks interrelate in time and sequence or dependency?

2. *Steering Committee Role.* Who is on the steering committee? How is task coordination accomplished? Where does system design authority rest?

3. *User Endorsement/Ownership.* Are there programmed milestones or checkpoints at which (1) technicians must attain user signoff, (2) users must attain technician signoff, and (3) the study team must obtain management signoff or redirection?

"Annual Physicals" for Forecasts

This concept is not farfetched. Forecasting systems must be like living things in the sense that they must cope with change and adapt or evolve. To some extent and at some expense this adaptability can be built in, but never to the extent necessary under current technology at afford-able prices. Therefore, the question is how to externally assist in attaining adequate adaptation.

1. *Reading Continual "Vital Signs."* As shown in Chart 3-1, both management and technical judgment points are contained in the general OP&C forecasting system design. An automatic part of the forecasting system should be the tracking of mean average deviation (MAD) signals on system operation at a number of levels. And this (or comparable indices) should be monitored on both technical and managerial judgments.

2. *Control System Error Propagation.* After some experience is gained with the system, periodic physicals should be given. That is, a study should be made of the impact of the forecast system on adjacent organization systems as a result of various levels of forecast errors. Simulation is often helpful here. A frequent result is further training of the humans whose judgment is an integral part of the forecasting system so that they can better understand how to constructively interact as a contributing portion of the overall system.

REFERENCES

1. Anderson, O. D., *Time Series Analysis and Forecasting,* Butterworths, London, 1976.
2. Armstrong, J. Scott, *Long-Range Forecasting,* John Wiley, New York, 1978.
3. Brown, Robert G., *Materials Management Systems,* John Wiley, New York, 1977.
4. Chambers, John C., Satinder Mullick, and Donald Smith, "How to Choose the Right Forecasting Technique," *Harvard Business Review,* July-August, 1971, pp. 45–74.
5. Gilchrist, Warren, *Statistical Forecasting,* John Wiley, New York, 1976.
6. Johnson, R. A. *Operations Management: A Systems Concept,* Houghton Mifflin, Boston, 1972.
7. Linstone, Harold A. and Murray Turoff, eds., *The Delphi Method,* Addison-Wesley, Reading, MA, 1975
8. Makridakis, Spyros, Steven C. Wheelwright, and Victor E. McGee, *Forecasting Methods and Applications,* 2nd ed., John Wiley, New York, 1982.
9. Montgomery, Douglas C. and Lynwood A. Johnson, *Forecasting and Time Series Analysis,* McGraw-Hill, New York, 1976.
10. Nelson, Charles R., *Applied Time Series Analysis,* Holden-Day, San Francisco, 1973.
11. Orlicky, Joseph, *Material Requirements Planning,* McGraw-Hill, New York, 1975.

12. Peterson, Rein and Edward A. Silver, *Decision Systems for Inventory Management and Production Planning,* John Wiley, New York, 1979.

13. Plossl, G. W. and O. W. Wight, *Production and Inventory Control,* Prentice-Hall, Englewood Cliffs, NJ, 1969.

14. Smith, Bernard T., *Focus Forecasting: Computer Techniques For Inventory Control,* CBI Publishing Co., Boston, 1978.

15. Sommer, Dale W., "Cycle Forecasting Spots Trends," *Industry Week,* April 25, 1977, pp 25+.

16. Sullivan, William G. and W. Wayne Claycombe, *Fundamentals of Forecasting,* Reston Publishing Company, Reston, VA, 1977.

17. Tursine, Richard J., *Materials Management and Inventory Systems,* Elsevier North-Holland Publishing Co., New York, 1976.

18. *The Wall Street Journal* (1) 1/31/79, 2:2, "IBM Introduces . . . "; (2) 5/17/79, 47:3, "Amerada Hess . . . "; and (3) 9/10/79, 21:1, "Uncalculated Risk: . . . ."

19. Wight, Oliver W., *Production & Inventory Management in the Computer Age,* Cahners Books, Boston, 1974.

20. Woolsey, Robert E. D. and Huntington S. Swanson, *Operations Research for Immediate Application: A Quick & Dirty Manual,* Harper & Row, New York 1975.

CHAPTER

4

CAPACITY PLANNING FORECASTING REQUIREMENTS

STEVEN C. WHEELWRIGHT
Graduate School of Business
Stanford University

Planning for capacity requirements is one of the most important decision areas addressed by all but the most stable of organizations. This is especially true when such planning involves new facilities or major changes in existing facilities, as is common in both service and manufacturing industries.

As will be discussed in this chapter, forecasting plays an important role in such capacity decisions for a number of reasons. One of these is simply because of the lead time involved in altering the physical assets and resources associated with capacity. Another reason is that the cost of such assets is usually a major portion of a company's balance sheet. Finally, the fact that most organizations must live with their capacity decisions for several decades makes the development of accurate forecasts for the amount, type, and location of capacity extremely important.

This chapter is divided into three main sections. The first deals with a general framework for capacity planning and its tie to other forms of both short- and long-range planning. This section also examines the process by which forecasts are incorporated into typical capacity planning procedures and some of the key issues that arise in connection with those forecast requirements. The second section then looks at some of the specific forecasting tasks and the approaches that have been found to be useful in handling them in a variety of settings. This second section also includes three examples, illustrating how forecasting for capacity planning purposes requires a combination of knowledge of forecasting methodologies, knowledge of the specific problem being addressed, and the judgment needed to appropriately fit existing methodologies to situation requirements. In the third section of this chapter, the task of integrating forecasting into capacity planning is addressed, and specific guidelines for doing that effectively are provided.

A GENERAL FRAMEWORK FOR CAPACITY PLANNING AND DECISION MAKING

While every situation is somewhat different, a nine-step procedure for tackling capacity planning and facilities decisions has been observed to have practical application in a wide range of situations. These nine steps, outlined in Chart 4-1, can serve as a checklist to guide capacity planning and to reduce the chances of major opportunities being missed.

In thinking about the forecasting requirements for capacity planning, a cursory review of Chart 4-1 might suggest that the forecaster really need only be involved in step 3, estimating required capacity. While that is clearly a major focal point for integrating forecasting into capacity planning, almost every other step of the process also involves significant requirements for forecasting. For example, in the first step of assessing the company's situation and environment, the forecaster can play a very useful role in forecasting the economic environment and its impact on demand for the company's products and services. That first step might also involve the "forecasting" of the competitive environment and the likely capacity plans of other competitors.

CHART 4-1. Capacity Planning: Nine-Step Procedure

1. Assess company situation and environment.
2. Audit and analysis of existing capacity.
3. Forecast and analysis of required capacity.
4. Definition of alternatives to achieve required capacity.
5. Quantitative and financial analysis of alternatives.
6. Analysis of qualitative issues for each alternative.
7. Selection of alternative to be pursued.
8. Implementation of chosen alternative.
9. Audit and review of actual results.

In the second step, determining available capacity, the forecaster can contribute by preparing estimates of usable capacity and the relationship of cost to capacity utilization. The concept of capacity is not a precise scientific measure, but involves estimating sustainable levels of output that fall within the cost constraints set by management and the market.

In the fourth step, developing alternative plans for matching required and available capacity, forecasting can contribute by estimating the costs of each option. This links directly to the fifth step and the thorough quantitative evaluation of the alternatives. This would include forecasting lead times for new construction and relocations, as well as predicting major cost elements such as construction costs, interest rates, and operating costs.

While the remaining four steps of this procedure involve significant amounts of management judgment, a forecaster who understands the capacity issues facing the firm and has been involved in the first five steps of the planning process can make significant contributions to management in these remaining steps.

In the final step, auditing and reviewing the results of the selected plan, the forecaster has the opportunity to upgrade existing forecasting procedures for capacity planning purposes, as well as to develop personal skills and knowledge with regard to the company's needs in this important area.

Expanding the View of Capacity Planning

In the nine-step procedure outlined in Chart 4-1, the implicit assumption is that the firm has recognized a specific need for a project that will alter its capacity. While such project formats are the normal approach for approving capital appropriations for capacity expansions, alterations, or contractions, in most organizations, capacity planning is also given annual or periodic attention as well. In this context, capacity planning can be viewed as a major subsegment of a company's long-range business plan and annual budget plan. Charts 4-2 and 4-3 summarize capacity planning in this context as it commonly arises in both manufacturing and service businesses.

As illustrated in Chart 4-2, capacity planning is often broken into a long-range segment (covering more than one year) and an annual segment which becomes a major part of the budget. There are then two short-term aspects of planning related to overall capacity, but these are generally referred to as scheduling (covering one to 12 months) and dispatching (covering the very near-term horizon). As also suggested in Chart 4-2, capacity planning must not only provide for physical space and equipment but must also provide for the human resources and materials required by the organization. A final aspect of Chart 4-2 is

CHART 4-2. Capacity Planning and the Time Horizon in Operations[a]

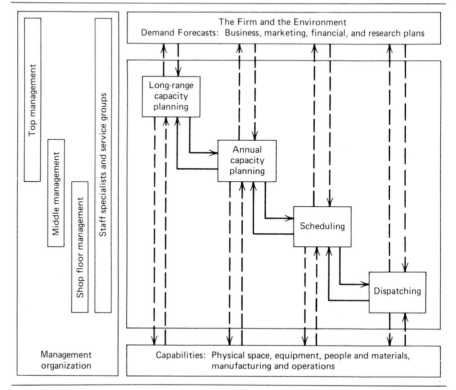

[a]See "Note on Capacity Planning" (9-674-081), Harvard Business School, Boston, 1974. *Capacity Planning and Facilities Choice* (5-979-001), by S. C. Wheelwright, Harvard Business School, Boston, 1979.

the level of the organization taking primary responsibility for each of these various segments of capacity planning. These are shown on the left-hand side of the exhibit and involve overlaps to ensure that shorter-term plans in the operating area are integrated with longer-term plans in the other functions and for the total business.

Many of the typical decisions associated with the primary resources of physical space and equipment, people, and materials are aligned in Chart 4-3 with the time horizon or major subsegment of capacity planning. When forecasters consider their inputs broadly enough to recognize the interaction of the various levels, functions, and resources they can greatly leverage their contribution to capacity planning.

The remainder of this chapter emphasizes long-range capacity planning and annual capacity planning, but not the two shorter time horizon categories. These are covered in Chapters 3 and 11 of this handbook. There are, however, several other chapters in this handbook that relate

CHART 4-3. Capacity Planning Decisions in Operations[a]

Capacity Determining Resources	Types of Decisions—by Time Horizon			
	Long-Range Capacity Planning	Annual Capacity Planning	Scheduling	Dispatching
Acquiring and deploying physical space & capital equipment	Selection of capabilities Location decisions Timing decisions Quantity Capital spending	Minor additions Subcontracting Product Mix	Allocation of facilities to products in specific time periods	
Acquiring and deploying human resources	Hiring & layoff policies Skill requirements Timing Quantity Training & development	Number of shifts Overtime Hire-fire Line balancing	Overtime, allocation of manpower to products (jobs) in specific time periods	Rescheduling Expediting, and detailed coordination of all three factors of production
Acquiring and deploying materials	Material requirements Long-term contracts Vendor selection Warehouse requirements Timing Quantity	Short-term purchase commitments Shipping schedules Inventory planning	Ordering materials Marshalling materials Inventory control Allocation of materials	

[a]See "Note on Capacity Planning" (9-674-081), Intercollegiate Case Clearing House, Boston, 1974; and *Capacity Planning and Facilities Choice* (5-979-001), by Steven C. Wheelwright, Harvard Business School, Boston, 1979.

41

directly to the topic of capacity planning forecasting requirements. In Chapter 16, some of the environmental issues related to picking the right forecasting approach and recognizing the assumptions inherent in that approach are reviewed. In Chapter 17, the impacts of product and market life cycles on demand forecasting and capacity planning are outlined. Finally, Chapter 2 details what is shown in Chart 4-2 as demand or sales forecasts.

TOOLS AND TECHNIQUES FOR HANDLING THE SPECIFIC FORECASTING REQUIREMENTS ASSOCIATED WITH CAPACITY PLANNING

In the previous section, the topic of capacity planning was viewed from an overall perspective. However, in most companies, when the issue of capacity planning arises, it is split up into a number of separate decisions. These include: How much capacity? When to alter capacity? Where to alter capacity? What form of capacity is required? How to accomplish the capacity plan?

One way to view the forecasting requirements associated with capacity decisions is to take each of the questions above and examine the tools and techniques commonly used in deciding them. Chart 4-4 summarizes these, and the bibliography at the end of this chapter provides additional detail on each.

As illustrations of how these techniques can be applied, it is useful to consider the range of applications included in the reference publication, *Capacity Planning and Facilities Choice*. This publication contains detailed descriptions of six capacity planning situations. Since the fore-

CHART 4-4. Tools and Techniques for Capacity Decisions

Management Decisions	Tools and Techniques for Forecasting, Analysis and Planning
1. How much capacity?	Demand forecasting, economies of scale, learning curves, and decision analysis.
2. When to alter capacity?	Economic cycle forecasting, competitive analysis, economics of over vs. under capacity.
3. Where to alter capacity?	Transportation analysis, site selection.
4. What form of capacity develop?	Technological forecasting, production planning, facilities focus.
5. How to accomplish the capacity plan?	Project management.

casting task in capacity planning is often very situation-specific, each of these is reviewed briefly below, and comments are provided on the specific nature of the key forecasting inputs.

1. *Litton Microwave Cooking Products.*   In this situation the Microwave Oven Division of Litton Industries must decide how best to expand its capacity in a very uncertain but rapidly growing market. An analysis of this situation indicates that the cost of carrying excess capacity is relatively low compared to the cost of having insufficient capacity. As a result, the forecasting task is to estimate the likelihood of a wide range of capacity requirements and to use a technique, such as decision analysis (see Chapter 13), to arrive at an optimal capacity plan.

2. *Distrigas Corporation.*   A firm is being established in the Boston area to distribute liquefied natural gas, brought in by large ships, to help cover peak load requirements in the winter months. The seasonality of demand for such gas during the winter and the arrival rates of the ships are key factors in determining the appropriate mix of storage tanks and the best operating plan for conveying the gas from the storage farm to the local utilities.

3. *Town of Belmont Payson Park School.*   This application is set in the public environment but involves many of the same capacity planning issues found in the private sector. In this particular instance, an elementary school district must determine how best to plan its long-term classroom needs in the face of declining school enrollments. The forecast of school-age children by elementary grade for the next two decades is not only a critical input to the development of the community's school capacity plan, but also becomes the focal point for many political arguments and pressures from special-interest groups. Thus, in this instance, the forecaster is in the middle of a very heated debate that intertwines both the issues of the forecast and how best to cope with declining enrollments.

4. *FMC Crane and Excavator Division.*   This business unit manufactures heavy equipment and is faced with long-term expansion needs to maintain its existing market position and support the aggressive marketing and business strategies recently developed within the corporation. The major forecasting requirement is of the long-term operating and investment costs associated with a variety of alternatives ranging from expanding an existing facility to building a completely new facility in a "green field" site. Thus, while marketing has provided some basic demand forecasts, the options open to manufacturing, which is doing the basic capacity planning, are very diverse in their cost implications and the resulting profitability of the integrated business plan.

5. *Carborundum Inc.*   In this application, capacity planning takes on a major competitive strategy role because as the market leader,

Carborundum may be able to preempt other competitors by picking a particular site for a new facility and carefully timing the announcement of that site. The major forecasting requirements in this situation are twofold. One involves predicting the costs associated with various capacity alternatives and relating those to the likely actions and reactions of competitors in terms of prices and their capacity changes. The other deals with integrating all of the cost elements into an overall projection of delivered cost for each of the possible capacity alternatives. Such things as material cost, operating cost, and transportation cost all have to be forecast to meet this second requirement.

6. *Trus Joist Corporation.* In this company, the major capacity planning situation involves expanding the components end of the business and timing that to fit with an upturn in the depressed housing and construction market. The forecasting task includes predicting the construction industry turnaround and its speed. It is interesting that this particular example describes the situation in 1975, but in 1980/1981 this company faced the identical situation because of the swing in the business cycle.

The above examples illustrate the range of situations for which capacity planning forecasting is required. It is also useful to consider the range of approaches that can be used effectively in such situations. As suggested previously, these often require the modification of existing techniques in order to fit the available data and circumstances of the given situation. Three very different forecasting approaches, each associated with a different situation, are described below.

Forecasting for Capacity Planning When the Learning Curve Applies

In many situations, it has been observed empirically that labor hours per unit and even operating costs per unit often follow what is referred to as the *learning curve*. When the rate of growth is rapid, and the rate of learning is also fairly rapid, the effect of the learning curve on capacity planning can be dramatic—the labor required per unit produced declines significantly as additional cumulative production experience is gained. The result is that, over several years, the labor input per unit may become only a fraction of what it was initially. Thus, in forecasting floor space requirements as well as human resource requirements, forecasting the learning curve may be an important first step.

In one manufacturing fabrication firm, the approach taken to forecasting the labor required per unit was that summarized in Chart 4-5. The initial step was to identify historical data on the product in question and on several products that were felt to exhibit similar behavior with regard to labor hours per unit and learning rates. The technique

CHART 4-5. Forecasting Labor Requirements/Unit Using the Learning Curve

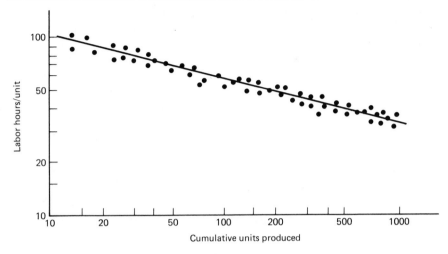

A. Graphical Approach for Estimating the Rate of Learning

1. Fit a straight line to actual data plotted on log-log paper.

2. Identify two levels of cumulative production, where one is twice the other (i.e., $J/I = 2.0$).

3. Identify the cost/unit for each of these two cumulative production volumes (i.e., Y_J and Y_I).

4. Compute the ratio Y_J/Y_I and convert to a percentage. This is the rate of learning.

5. Forecast future labor required for unit J by reading, from the fitted line, the the labor/unit that corresponds to that cumulative production unit.

B. Regression Analysis Approach for Estimating the Rate of Learning

1. Convert the learning curve equation $Y_I = AI^{-B}$ to a linear form by taking logs of both sides [i.e., $\log Y_I = \log A + (-B) \log I$].

2. Transform the actual observed data to $\log Y_I$ and $\log I$ data.

3. Apply regression analysis to estimate a and b in $y = a + bx$ where $y = \log Y_I$ and $x = \log I$.

4. Transform the regression estimates of a and b to obtain $A = \log^{-1} a$ and $B = -b$.

5. Convert B to a rate of learning by computing 2^{-B}.

6. Forecast labor requirements, Y_J, for some future unit, J, by computing $Y_J = Y_I (J/I)^{-B}$.

applied to these data was simply to use a graphical method to estimate the historical learning curve and to project that into the future.

Once a number of different sets of data had been analyzed in this manner, it was determined that a more precise approach was needed. For all subsequent analysis and forecasting of learning, they shifted to the use of regression analysis. That had the advantage of allowing them to use a programmable hand-held calculator, and thus to easily estimate the sensitivity of the forecasts to variations in the rate of learning and the rate of growth in cumulative production units.

Capacity Planning at a Capital-Intensive Electric Utility

An important dimension which has a major impact on the forecasting requirements for capacity planning is the capital intensity of the business. While the preceding example dealt with a parts assembly and fabrication business, in the case of Duke Power, an electric utility, the economics of capacity were very different. Like other major process industries (steel, paper, oil, and food processing), electric utilities deal with significant capital requirements any time they consider capacity expansion.

In this particular application, Duke Power had historically found itself on what is described in Chart 4-6 as the left-hand side of the U-shaped cost curve. That is, prior to the early 1970s, the characteristics of new capacity in the electric utility business were that the capital cost per unit of capacity had been decreasing, average cost per unit of electricity had been decreasing, and marginal cost per unit of electricity had been decreasing.

Since marginal cost was lower than average cost, and since rate setting agencies had traditionally set rates (prices) based on average cost, it was in the utilities' best interest to continually expand demand and capacity. As a consequence of this environment, the emphasis in forecasting for capacity planning at Duke Power (and most other major utilities) had generally been on avoiding mistakes that would result in not enough capacity. This tended to bias forecasts toward the high side.

Unfortunately, as a result of several environmental changes in the 1970s—rapidly increasing oil prices, increased government regulation, and spiraling increases in construction costs—the characteristics of capacity expansion in the utility industry changed dramatically. As shown in the right-hand side of Chart 4-6, utilities like Duke Power found that the capital cost per unit of capacity was increasing (new capacity was more expensive than old capacity), average cost was increasing, and marginal cost was increasing. With the marginal cost exceeding the average cost, when rates (prices) were based on average cost, the utility and its stockholders seemed to be the losers. As a consequence, the emphasis in capacity planning started to shift toward

CHART 4-6. U-Shaped Cost Curves

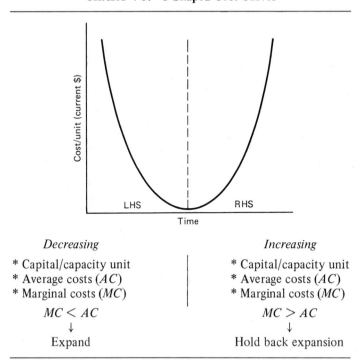

Decreasing	*Increasing*
* Capital/capacity unit	* Capital/capacity unit
* Average costs (*AC*)	* Average costs (*AC*)
* Marginal costs (*MC*)	* Marginal costs (*MC*)
$MC < AC$	$MC > AC$
↓	↓
Expand	Hold back expansion

holding back expansion and waiting as long as possible before providing new generating capacity. This shift dramatically changed the role of the forecaster, putting a premium on accuracy and a more objective recognition of the tradeoffs associated with overcapacity versus undercapacity. Increasingly, forecasters found themselves on the witness stand during rate-setting hearings in which increasing pressure was being brought to bear by special-interest groups to cut down on excess capacity while still providing adequate levels of service to all customers.

Some of the implications of this type of a shift from a declining cost capacity planning environment to an increasing cost capacity planning environment are highlighted in Chart 4-7. These implications are not only for management but for forecasters and planners as well. The referenced article by Leone and Meyer provides further details on the forecasting and planning requirements associated with this shift in capital intensive, maturing industries.

Tennis Court Capacity at Sea Pines Racquet Club

While the public utility cited above is an example of a service business, it has many of the same characteristics as capital-intensive manufacturing

CHART 4-7. Implications of U-Shaped Cost Curves

A. Implications for Management Strategy and Policy

Past	*Future*
Build large scale	Build small scale
Build before demand	Build to match (or lag) demand
Use new capacity first	Use new capacity last
Promote demand	Manage (limit) demand
Avoid stockout	Avoid excess capacity
Compete on price	Compete on service
Expand with new capacity	Expand by revising old capacity

B. Implications for Staff Forecasters/Planners

1. Forecasting accuracy required
2. Forecasting accuracy available
3. Basic data for forecasting
4. Cost of over/under errors
5. Time horizon for planning
6. Relating forecasting to actions

---

businesses. However, at Sea Pines Racquet Club, many of the more typical characteristics of capacity planning in the service environment were highlighted during the development of a capacity plan for tennis courts. Like many of the major resort locations in the southeastern United States, in the early 1970s Sea Pines was primarily a real estate venture. Such amenities as golf and tennis were viewed primarily as ways to attract potential real estate investors. However, as the company approached the need for capacity planning and tennis courts in 1973, it quickly found that even rough forecasts of requirements indicated that eventually half the property might be covered by tennis courts if all peak demands were to be met. At that point, a much more systematic approach to forecasting tennis capacity requirements and fitting that with overall business plans was developed.

As a starting point, the manager of the tennis facilities followed the procedure outlined in Chart 4-1. It was determined that during the peak months (July and August), the total daylight hours available for any single tennis court were 319. However, it was felt that only about 80% of those hours were actually "usable" because of the high humidity and heat during midday. In addition, the tennis manager had estimates of total guest nights for three years based on overall business plans for the resort. Finally, records had been kept indicating the court hours required per guest night in 1972 and in 1973. This information is summarized in Chart 4-8.

**CHART 4-8. Forecasting for Tennis Capacity Planning
at Sea Pines Racquet Club**

	Court Hours/Guest Night		
	1972	1973	1973/1972
March	.040	.068	1.70
April	.061	.082	1.34
May	.046	.084	1.83
		Average	1.62

	Hours Available per Court	Guest Nights (in 1000s)	Court Hours per 1972 Guest Night	Court Hours Needed	Courts Required		
					Base	1.62 Adj.	÷ .80
July 1973	319	83.9	.056	4700	15	24	30
August 1973	319	86.5	.056	4840	15	25	37
July 1974	319	130.7	.056	7320	23	37	46
August 1974	319	129.1	.056	7230	23	37	46
July 1975	319	168.8	.056	9450	30	48	60
August 1975	319	166.3	.056	9310	29	47	59

From this information, a forecast of court hours needed could be prepared, as shown in Chart 4-8. That could then be converted into courts required, initially assuming that 100% of the time was usable and that 1972 usage rates per guest night applied. With that as a base point, an adjustment could be made to reflect the fact that court usage (per guest night) was running 62% higher in 1973 than in 1972. Finally, an additional adjustment could be made to reflect the manager's estimate that only 80% of the available court time was usable.

At that point, the manager of the tennis facilities determined that there was such a wide range of potential court requirements that it made more sense to think about managing demand in this service business rather than simply trying to provide capacity for all possible demand. This was further reinforced by an economic analysis of the cost of a tennis court that is used in only one or two peak months of the year. As a result of this, the facilities manager decided to plan for an intermediate level of capacity and to work with some of the other amenities (golf, swimming, hiking, sailing, etc.) to provide ample opportunity for all guests, but not necessarily to provide tennis for any guest who happened to desire to play at the peak hour in the peak month.

This situation illustrates what is often the case not only in service businesses but in many manufacturing businesses: seasonal peaks not only need to be forecast, but the possibilities for managing those peaks and spreading them need to be studied.

INTEGRATING FORECASTING, CAPACITY PLANNING, AND BUSINESS PLANNING

As suggested at the outset of this chapter, one of the overriding considerations in forecasting for capacity planning is understanding the context in which that capacity plan is being prepared and the issues that it must address. One approach for thinking about the levels of activity involved in business planning, and the corresponding levels involved in capacity planning, is summarized in Chart 4-9.

As highlighted in Chart 4-9, there are a number of specific types of forecasting inputs that can be made at various levels of capacity planning. While Chart 4-1 highlighted the capital project request level of such capacity plans, the subsequent sections have indicated the role that forecasting can and should play at higher levels. Other chapters in this handbook, as well as the bibliography at the end of this chapter, should enable the forecaster to more effectively contribute to capacity plans and strategies.

CHART 4-9. Integrating Capacity Planning and Business Planning

Operations strategy	Corporate strategy
Capacity strategy	Business strategy
Capacity plan	Business plan
Capital project requests	Capital plan
Department budgets	Budget

Forecasting Inputs to a Capacity Plan or Project

Unit volume requirements
Space requirements
Manpower requirements
Material requirements
Capital requirements
Operating cost requirements
Technology requirements

BIBLIOGRAPHY

Atkins, Robert J. and Richard H. Shriver, "New Approach to Facilities Location," *Harvard Business Review,* May-June, 1968.

"Duke Power Company—Revised," (9-677-147), Intercollegiate Case Clearing House, Boston MA, 1977.

Erlenkotter, Donald, "Preinvestment Planning for Capacity Expansion: A Multi-Location Dynamic Model," Stanford University, Ph.D. Dissertation, 1970.

Francis, Richard L. and John A. White, *Facility Layout and Location: An Analytical Approach*, Prentice-Hall, Englewood Cliffs, NJ, 1974.

Hayes, Robert H. and Steven C. Wheelwright, *Manufacturing Strategy*, John Wiley, New York, 1982.

Hiller, Frederick S. and Gerald J. Lieberman, *Operations Research,* 3rd ed., Holden-Day, San Francisco, 1980.

Holloway, Charles, *Decision Making Under Uncertainty,* Prentice-Hall, Englewood Cliffs, NJ, 1979.

Leone, Robert A. and John R. Meyer, "Capacity Strategies for the 1980's," *Harvard Business Review*, November-December, 1980.

Makridakis, Spyros, Steven C. Wheelwright, and Victor E. McGee, *Forecasting Methods and Applications,* 2nd ed., John Wiley, New York, 1982.

Manne, Alan S., ed., *Investments for Capacity Expansion: Size, Location, and Time-Phasing,* George Allen & Unwin Ltd., London, 1967.

Maynard, H. B., *Handbook of Modern Manufacturing Management*, McGraw-Hill, New York, 1970.

"Note on Capacity Planning," (9-674-081), Intercollegiate Case Clearing House, Boston, MA, 1974.

Sasser, W. Earl, "Match Supply and Demand in Service Industries," *Harvard Business Review,* November-December, 1976.

Scherer, F. M. and A. Beckenstein, *The Economics of Multiplant Operation,* Harvard University Press, Cambridge, MA, 1975.

Schmenner, Roger, "Before You Build a Big Factory," *Harvard Business Review,* July-August, 1976.

Skinner, Wickham, "Manufacturing—Missing Link in Corporate Strategy," *Harvard Business Review,* May-June, 1969.

Skinner, Wickham, "The Focused Factory," *Harvard Business Review,* May-June, 1974.

Stallworthy, E. A., *The Control of Investment in New Manufacturing Facilities*, Gower Press, Essex, England, 1973.

Stobaugh, Robert B., "Where in the World Should We Put That Plant?" *Harvard Business Review*, January-February, 1969.

Vatter, Paul, *Quantitative Methods in Management*, Richard D. Irwin, Homewood, IL, 1978.

Wheelwright, Steven C., "Reflecting Corporate Strategy in Manufacturing Decisions," *Business Horizons*, February, 1978.

Wheelwright, Steven C., *Capacity Planning and Facilities Choice*, Division of Research, Harvard Business School, Cambridge, MA, 1979.

Wheelwright, Steven C. and Spyros Makridakis, *Forecasting Methods for Management.* 3rd ed., John Wiley, New York, 1980.

CHAPTER

5

FINANCIAL FORECASTING

Requirements and Issues

KENNETH S. LOREK
College of Business
The Florida State University

I. INTRODUCTION

The investment and financial analysis literature is replete with citations that emphasize the importance of earnings forecasts to the valuation process.* Cross-sectional valuation models typically include parameters for future earnings numbers, yet little attention is usually directed to the specific manner in which these earnings forecasts are generated. In many cases, simplistic averaging and other mechanical ad hoc methods are invoked. Furthermore, the statistical association between unexpected earnings and security prices or returns which has recently been established in efficient market research provides empirical support for the importance of earnings forecasting.† Finally, the existence of financial forecasting intermediaries such as financial analysts as well as financial forecasting services such as *Value Line* and Standard and Poor's

---

*See Bernstein[6] (p. 494) for a succinct statement regarding the importance of earnings forecasts to financial statement analysis.
†Gonedes et al.[14] and Patell[25] provide examples of market research in conjunction with earnings forecasts.

Earnings Forecaster provides an economic justification for the marginal utility of the forecast function.

The foregoing factors interact to provide a convincing justification for management involvement or concern with detailed financial forecasting requirements. We note that many firms have voluntarily disclosed their own forecasts of earnings publicly via stockholders' meetings or financial releases to the press. However, it is very surprising that very few firms have provided forecasts on a continuing, year-to-year basis.* The norm in management earnings forecasting amounts to haphazard disclosure with little continuity. We might infer from such behavior that such actions might be at least partially due to the unstable environment and the complex set of operational problems confronting the financial forecaster. Recent promulgations by the Securities and Exchange Commission (SEC) regarding earnings forecast disclosures indicate a trend toward possible, mandatory earnings forecasts for all New York Stock Exchange firms in the 1980s. Of course, these comments represent speculations on our part regarding perceived trends and attitudes of the SEC in this highly controversial area. With this background in mind, we will provide a discussion of financial forecasting requirements which should prove useful to managers who are interested in generating more accurate earnings forecasts for internal or external consumption. Although the primacy of earnings forecasting will be emphasized within this chapter, forecasts of alternative financial variables such as sales revenues and expenses will also be addressed indirectly.

II. ALTERNATIVE FORECAST METHODS

Surveys have been conducted which have attempted to ascertain what forecast methods are being employed by financial forecasters.† It is our opinion that most published management *earnings* forecasts are still subjectively determined by some sort of group decision making process. However, a diversity in forecast methods, which runs the entire spectrum of quantitative state-of-the-art methodologies, has been reported in the financial literature. Recently, the financial research literature has been dominated by applications of univariate Box–Jenkins time series analysis in the prediction of annual earnings numbers. The appendix (Section VII) provides the structure of the autoregressive integrated moving average (ARIMA) model, which has proven very successful in financial forecasting situations. Alternative time series approaches such as moving average models, autoregressive models,

---

*See McDonald[22] for descriptive statistics regarding the number of firms that provided earnings forecasts each year throughout the 1966–70 period.

†Pan et al.[24] provide data on sales forecasting practices of large U.S. industrial firms.

weighting schemes of varying sorts, and exponential smoothing have also been tested with somewhat less degrees of accuracy.* Econometric approaches in which functional relationships are established between the dependent variable of interest, say, earnings, and endogenous, firm-specific and exogenous, industry- and economy-wide independent variables have received much less attention at the firm level. Of course, this is in marked contrast to econometric applications on wide sets of macroeconomic variables.

Our discussion will emphasize univariate time series analysis because of its wide range of applicability in financial earnings forecasting. Our viewpoint is simply that time series analysis is a necessary starting point in the development of an overall management forecasting schema. It might be coupled with econometric methods such as in the forecasting of future values of the independent variables which are then structurally linked to the dependent variable. Time series forecasts might also serve as quantitative inputs or benchmarks for a judgmental management forecast developed by such approaches as the delphi method or perhaps cross-impact analysis.

III. DATA CONSIDERATIONS

The data problems faced by a financial earnings forecaster who employs univariate time series models are significant. Some data issues are readily apparent to the causal observer, while others are very subtle albeit potentially troublesome. Five specific data considerations are addressed in this section: (1) data frequency, (2) data base length, (3) object of prediction, (4) generally accepted accounting principles (GAAP), and (5) level of aggregation. Operational decisions in these areas significantly affect the forecasting environment.

Data Frequency

The major consideration of the data frequency problem concerns the use of annual data versus interim data. Since our primary focus is forecasting earnings, the forecaster must decide to employ time series data bases comprised of annual earnings or interim (quarterly or monthly) earnings for model estimation purposes. Results from financial research suggest that annual earnings numbers are randomly distributed. For example, Little and Rayner[19] have reported that earnings growth occurs in an almost purely random fashion. Ball and Watts[4] reported that net earnings, as currently reported, is a submartingale or some very similar

*Lorek[21] provides a comparative analysis of univariate time series models versus several sets of simplistic models.

process.* More recent studies by Watts and Leftwich[29] and Albrecht et al.[2] report similar "random walk" tendencies for annual earnings. The last two studies are particularly germane since they employed Box–Jenkins time series models in an attempt to predict annual net earnings. It appears that little serial correlation is exhibited in time series data bases of annual net earnings. However, interim data provide markedly different results. Specifically, quarterly earnings data do *not* exhibit "random walk" characteristics.

Substantial research efforts have been undertaken recently to specify the time series properties of quarterly earnings data. Two major findings have emerged from the work of Foster,[13] Griffin,[15] and Brown and Rozeff.[8] First, seasonality is an important characteristic of quarterly earnings data. Seasonality may be described generally as a quarter *by* quarter movement in the data such that similar quarters in successive years are serially correlated. For example, the quarterly earnings data of toy manufacturers are greatly affected by the increase in demand for toy products in the last quarter of the calendar year. Second, statistical dependencies between adjacent quarters in the same year have also been detected. In fact, the foregoing studies suggest that the time series properties of quarterly earnings may be characterized as a multiplicative combination of quarter *by* quarter (seasonal) effects and quarter *to* quarter (adjacent) effects. Simply stated, serial correlation, while absent from annual earnings data, is present across two dimensions in quarterly earnings data. It is our contention that these patterns can be used effectively for predictive purposes.

We recommend that quarterly earnings data be employed in the development of an earnings forecast model using time series analysis. Monthly, weekly, or even daily data may also prove worthwhile, especially when the object of prediction is sales revenue or expenses rather than net earnings. However, we must caution users that the manner in which income numbers are generated is dependent upon the reporting period. Annual data are prepared with great care and attested to by external auditors, while interim data are typically generated using estimation techniques and approximations not usually subject to the scrutiny of auditors.

Data Base Length

Time series modeling of quarterly earnings data bases has been greatly influenced by the 50 observations rule of thumb mentioned by Box and Jenkins.[7] This specific number of observations represents a supposed compromise between working with lengthy data bases in which

*The submartingale model includes the random walk and random walk with drift models.

structural change is a possibility or data bases which are so short that small sample bias is a problem. Although it is difficult to provide an optimal tradeoff between structural change and small sample bias, research by Lorek and McKeown[21] suggests that 32 quarterly earnings numbers is a reasonable minimum target. Note that this represents eight years of time series data. Of course, this limits the applicability of time series forecasting to firms that have been in existence for this time period.

Empirical evidence suggests that levels of numerous financial variables such as net earnings, sales revenue, and expenses are nonstationary.* Prior to the estimation of a descriptively valid time series forecast model, stationarity must be induced on the data set. Various combinations of consecutive and/or seasonal differencing are typically employed to accomplish this objective. On rare occasions, logarithmic transformations might be required in addition to differencing; however, our experience suggests that differencing is almost always sufficient.†

Object of Prediction

Up to this point we have employed the term "net earnings" as if it were the single operational index for income on which there was general agreement in the financial community. In actuality, the forecasting literature has concentrated on both undeflated (net earnings, earnings per share) and deflated versions (rate of return) of income. Financial analysts have also directed attention to numerous income statement items such as net operating earnings, net earnings before or after extraordinary items, net earnings available to common shareholders, and even cash flow surrogates. The operational question is what particular earnings concept should management be interested in predicting. Unfortunately, no single answer to this question is possible. If management is primarily concerned with normal, recurring operations, then net operating earnings might be appropriate. If overall firm performance is stressed, then perhaps the final net earnings number on a net of tax basis would be relevant. If individual share holder returns are dominant, then primary or fully diluted earnings per share might be the object of prediction. Alternative scenarios could easily be constructed for different objects of prediction dependent upon top management goals and objectives.

The financial research literature suggests that undeflated annual earnings numbers appear to follow a submartingale (random walk with

---

*A stationary process is one in which the joint distribution of any set of observations is invariant through time.

†Although a logarithmic transformation might be valuable in certain settings, it is inappropriate whenever the data may take on negative values.

or without drift), while deflated earnings numbers follow a moving average process. Alternatively, quarterly deflated and undeflated earnings concepts appear to follow a multiplicative ARIMA process.* We recommend that the financial forecaster concentrate on undeflated quarterly earnings numbers. If other earnings concepts are deemed important by management, earnings predictions may be deflated by estimates of stockholders' equity to derive rate of return or number of shares outstanding to derive earnings per share numbers.

Generally Accepted Accounting Principles

Regardless of data base length or the object of prediction, the financial forecaster faces a subtle data problem not normally recognized by nonaccountants. This problem concerns the particular rules that accountants must follow in generating financial statements. These "generally accepted accounting principles" (GAAP) are promulgated by the Financial Accounting Standards Board. Chart 5-1 shows the relationship of GAAP to financial forecasting.

The financial accounting reporting system transforms the raw input data about production, marketing, and administrative decisions into financial statements which are used as financial scorecards for management performance. The rules (GAAP) by which this transformation process is governed are exceedingly complex and subject to change. The output data are then used routinely by financial forecasting models. We note that different forecast models make statistical assumptions regarding such items as the independence of the data and its normality. Can the output data set fulfill assumptions like these when there has been a change from one generally accepted accounting procedure to another? Is the prechange series similar to the postchange series, or has there been an intervention of the time series properties? Very little work has been done in this area on microeconomic GAAP data.†

Dopuch and Watts[11] did conduct a study which examined a sample of steel firms that switched from straight-line depreciation to accelerated methods of depreciation with the passage of the 1954 tax law. They attempted to assess the impact of a GAAP change on the reported earnings numbers. Although studies similar to theirs are critical to further refinements in financial forecasting, no other research has been directed toward this objective. Yet, accounting gymnastics such as inventory switches from LIFO to FIFO and changing definitions of extraordinary items affect the output data relied on by the financial forecaster. Varying GAAP rules induce nonhomogeneous characteristics

---

*See Griffin[15] for a thorough description of this multiplicative ARIMA process.

†Deakin[10] has examined the normality assumption with respect to a host of financial ratios typically employed in financial statement analysis.

CHART 5-1. Relationship of GAAP to Financial Forecasting

on financial data. Alternative GAAP procedures also destroy interfirm data comparisons as well as intertemporal comparisons for the same firm. Perhaps time series data bases should be adjusted for major changes in GAAP during the examination period so that all data are stated on a comparable basis. Unfortunately, these problems represent a "fact of life" in financial forecasting that should be recognized rather than ignored by forecasters.

Arbitrariness in the allocation process inherent in the historical cost model itself may also induce certain unspecified biases in the data. Beaver[5] argues that depreciation and amortization techniques induce serial dependencies in net earnings numbers which are an artifact of the allocation process. Moreover, Ronen et al.[27] have suggested that management could conceivably manipulate GAAP to achieve certain objectives.* Perhaps these sources of potential bias and manipulation partially explain the greater success which has been achieved in predicting sales revenues versus net earnings numbers, since the former series is less subject to the allocation procedures and potential manipulations inherent in GAAP.†

Level of Aggregation

The employment of univariate time series analysis on consolidated net earnings data of a multidivision firm implies that each division's contribution to aggregate results is proportional through time. If the composition of consolidated net earnings varies substantially from year to year, it might prove advantageous to build separate time series models for each division and then aggregate the divisional forecasts to obtain overall firm results. Kinney[18] and Collins[9] describe forecasts generated from segmental earnings and sales data which reduced uncertainties in predicting overall firm results for the test companies. Multidivision firms with widely varying divisional contributions should consider working with segmental data in the derivation of consolidated earnings forecasts.

Another satellite issue concerns time series analysis of net earnings data versus analysis of the subcomponents of the income statement.

---

*This flexibility in GAAP is generally referred to as "income smoothing."
†Abdulkader[1] reports on the superiority of revenue predictions versus predictions of net earnings.

Specifically, analysis of the sales revenue, cost of goods sold, selling expenses, and other expense series could be undertaken, and then a net earnings forecast could be generated by subtracting the summation of the expense forecasts from the sales revenue forecast. An initial attempt at such derived earnings forecasts was undertaken by Kee[17] with moderate success. From a statistical viewpoint the homogeneity of the input series is greater when working with separate sales and expense series as opposed to net earnings numbers. This is manifested by the higher levels exhibited in the autocorrelation functions for sales as compared to net earnings.

IV. PARSIMONIOUS BOX–JENKINS MODELS

Univariate time series models for quarterly earnings data may be identified using two distinct approaches. The first is the firm-specific approach which develops a unique model for each firm based on patterns exhibited by the sample autocorrelation function. Alternatively, parsimonious models may be identified by a process in which we assume that a particular structure is appropriate for all firms. Diverse factor input and product output markets appear to signal underlying differences across firms, thus favoring the firm-specific approach. Yet, predictive ability results tend to favor the parsimonious models.* Since the generation of the parsimonious models is more cost effective and less time consuming than the firm-specific approach, considerable work has been done in this potentially fruitful area of financial forecasting.

Foster[13] and Griffin[15] suggest that *ex post* differences in firm-specific models may simply be induced by sampling variation, noise in the data, parameter redundancy, and model overfitting. The apparent implication is that the financial forecaster becomes mesmerized by firm-specific oscillations of the autocorrelation function. Proponents of the parsimonious models have developed several reasonable candidate models for quarterly earnings data. The major parsimonious models for quarterly earnings that have been suggested in the literature are the Griffin–Watts (011) × (011) model, the Foster (100) × (010) model with drift, and the Brown–Rozeff (100) × (011) model.† These models were originally developed by analyzing autocorrelation functions cross-sectionally for large samples of firms. A single autocorrelation function is constructed

---

*See Brown and Rozeff[8] and Lorek[20].

†We are employing the customary $(pdq) \times (PDQ)$ Box–Jenkins notation in which p = number of autoregressive parameters, d = number of consecutive differences, q = number of moving average parameters, P = number of seasonal autoregressive parameters, D = number of seasonal differencing, and Q = number of seasonal moving average parameters.

for an entire sample of firms by aggregating the corresponding lags of the function across the sample and then dividing these cumulative values by the number of sample firms. In essence, a single function of arithmetic means is obtained which attempts to capture the time series behavior of each sample firm. In summary, the parsimonious approach identifies a singular best-fitting ARIMA structure for the entire sample of firms, and then the parameters of the model are identified on an individual firm basis. This varies from the firm-specific approach which allows the structure of the ARIMA model as well as its parameters to vary firm by firm. Thus, without previous experience in time series analysis, the financial forecaster can simply apply one of the set of efficient parsimonious models for quarterly earnings without a considerable investment of time and resources and expect relatively attractive predictive performance.

Although it is customary to present Box–Jenkins ARIMA models in $(pdq) \times (PDQ)$ notation, the precise nature of these models is more readily interpretable if we plug the parameter values back into the generalized ARIMA framework presented earlier. After suitable transformations, the three parsimonious models may be stated as follows.

Griffin–Watts (GW) Model

$$(1 - B)(1 - B^4)Z_t = (1 - \theta_1 B)(1 - \overline{\theta}_1 B^4)a_t \qquad (5\text{-}1)$$

or

$$Z_t = Z_{t-4} + (Z_{t-1} - Z_{t-5}) + a_t - \theta_1 a_{t-1} \\ - \overline{\theta}_1 a_{t-4} + \theta_1 \overline{\theta}_1 a_{t-5} \qquad (5\text{-}2)$$

Equation (5-2) suggests that the GW model relates current earnings (Z_t) to quarterly earnings received four periods ago (Z_{t-4}), plus the most recent quarter's growth in earnings $(Z_{t-1} - Z_{t-5})$, a current disturbance term (a_t), and disturbance terms one, four, and five periods removed.

Foster (F) Model

$$(1 - \phi_1 B)(1 - B^4)Z_t = a_t \qquad (5\text{-}3)$$

or

$$Z_t = Z_{t-4} + \phi_1(Z_{t-1} - Z_{t-5}) + a_t + \theta_0 \qquad (5\text{-}4)$$

Equation (5-4) suggests that the F model also relates current earnings to quarterly earnings received four periods ago. It too contains the most recent quarter's growth in earnings, but this growth is multiplied by an autoregressive parameter (ϕ_1). The F model contains the current disturbance term (a_t) but lacks the sequence of lagged disturbance terms present in the GW model. Finally, it contains a deterministic trend constant (θ_0) or drift term.

Brown–Rozeff (BR) Model

$$(1 - \phi_1 B)(1 - B^4)Z_t = (1 - \bar{\theta}_1 B^4)a_t \qquad (5\text{-}5)$$

or

$$Z_t = Z_{t-4} + \phi_1(Z_{t-1} - Z_{t-5}) + a_t - \bar{\theta}_1 a_{t-4} \qquad (5\text{-}6)$$

The BR model is identical to the F model with two exceptions. It contains a seasonal moving average parameter with a lagged disturbance term ($\bar{\theta}_1 a_{t-4}$), and it does not contain a deterministic trend constant. In conclusion, the F model appears to be the simplest of the parsimonious models, followed by the BR model and then the GW model.

The main advantage of the parsimonious model approach is that the relatively time-consuming and potentially subjective identification stage of the model building process is entirely bypassed. In its place one of the parsimonious models described above is used. This approach is a very attractive alternative to firm-specific modeling for those firms without forecasting personnel who are very familiar with the Box–Jenkins process. We recommend that all three parsimonious models be estimated, and the one which provides the best descriptive fit by using either the Box–Pierce Q statistic or residual mean square error should be used for forecasting purposes.* Alternatively, the relative predictive power of the three models could be assessed over time with the best model in this trial period being selected for operational forecasting purposes. For those firms which have personnel with expertise in Box–Jenkins, we also recommend that the firm-specific approach be considered.

V. ILLUSTRATIVE EXAMPLE OF PARSIMONIOUS MODELS

Chart 5-2 presents the quarterly earnings numbers for General Mills Corporation from the first quarter, 1962, until the fourth quarter, 1975.† Inspection of the quarterly earnings data reveals highly seasonal

---

*The Box–Pierce Q statistic is a goodness of fit measure which is distributed as a chi-square distribution.

†The data were obtained from the Compustat 360/370 general quarterly industrial tape, Standard and Poor's *Corporate Records*, and the *Wall Street Journal Index*.

CHART 5-2. Quarterly Net Earnings for General Mills Corporation, 1962–75 (in millions)

Year	1st Quarter	2nd Quarter	3rd Quarter	4th Quarter
1962	3.592	4.392	3.324	3.602
1963	4.013	4.604	3.472	5.096
1964	4.671	5.992	4.249	5.472
1965	5.994	7.778	5.906	8.047
1966	6.592	8.365	6.483	7.016
1967	7.879	11.130	6.140	7.085
1968	9.490	11.600	7.579	9.465
1969	10.200	12.450	8.159	9.799
1970	11.470	13.500	8.726	10.160
1971	13.350	17.070	11.720	14.480
1972	16.250	21.660	13.750	14.480
1973	18.990	25.000	15.300	15.830
1974	19.230	26.560	14.730	15.690
1975	24.630	34.300	21.200	20.460

earnings with a marked increase occurring in the second quarter of almost every year in the data base. We also note an increasing trend in earnings over the 56-observation data base.

Chart 5-3 presents the autocorrelation function for the 56-observation data base. Panel A provides the function for the raw series. We observe the data are apparently nonstationary as evidenced by the relatively high values for longer lags of the function. Second, seasonality in the

CHART 5-3. Autocorrelation Function—General Mills Corporation

Panel A: Raw Data							
1-8	.77	.63	.61	.72	.55	.47	.45	.55
St.E.| .13	.20	.23	.26	.29	.31	.32	.33
9-16	.40	.31	.28	.35	.23	.16	.12	.18
St.E.| .35	.36	.36	.37	.37	.37	.38	.38

Panel B: Regular First Difference							
1-8	-.24	-.43	-.24	.78	-.21	-.29	-.21	.64
St.E.| .13	.14	.16	.17	.23	.23	.24	.24
9-16	-.15	-.25	-.19	.52	-.11	-.17	-.18	.41
St.E.| .27	.27	.27	.28	.29	.29	.30	.30

CHART 5-4. Estimation and Forecasting Information—General Mills Corporation

Foster Model: (100) × (010) with drift		Forecasting Results			
			P	A	% Error
Regular autoregressive parameter	.660				
Trend constant	.624	1976-1	28.400	31.593	-.101
Box–Pierce Q statistic	16.327	1976-2	37.415	39.675	-.057
Residual mean square error	1.810	1976-3	23.879	23.828	.002
		1976-4	22.856	21.297	.073

Griffin–Watts Model: (011) × (011)		Forecasting Results			
			P	A	% Error
Regular moving average parameter	.231				
Seasonal moving average parameter	.230	1976-1	30.190	31.593	-.044
Box–Pierce Q statistic	20.490	1976-2	39.776	39.675	.003
Residual Mean Square Error	2.246	1976-3	26.674	23.828	.119
		1976-4	25.938	21.297	.218

Brown–Rozeff Model: (100) × (011)		Forecasting Results			
			P	A	% Error
Regular autoregressive parameter	.845				
Seasonal moving average parameter	.008	1976-1	28.662	31.593	-.093
Box–Pierce Q statistic	21.294	1976-2	37.710	39.675	-.050
Residual mean square error	2.025	1976-3	24.079	23.828	.011
		1976-4	22.897	21.297	.075

quarterly earnings data is apparent by observing spikes at lags 4, 8, and 12 (.72, .55, and .35). Panel B provides the autocorrelation function for the differenced data. Since the original series appeared nonstationary in its levels, consecutive differencing was used to induce stationarity. We now observe strong seasonal patterns at lags 4, 8, 12, and 16 (.78, .64, .52, and .41). Along with the spikes at nonseasonal lags, this demonstrates the quarter *by* quarter and quarter *to* quarter patterns exhibited by the data.

Chart 5-4 provides the parameter values, Box–Pierce Q statistics, residual mean square errors, and forecasting information for all three parsimonious models. We will concentrate on the Foster model for exposition purposes. The estimated model is:

$$Z_t - Z_{t-4} = .660 \,(Z_{t-1} - Z_{t-5}) + \theta_0 \qquad (5\text{-}7)$$

For forecasting purposes this model becomes:

$$E(Z_t | Z_{t-1} \cdots) = Z_{t-4} + .660(Z_{t-1} - Z_{t-5}) + \theta_0 \qquad (5\text{-}8)$$

Thus, a one step ahead forecast for the 1976 first quarter earnings number is generated in the following manner:

$$E(Z_{1976,1}) = Z_{1975,1} + .660(Z_{1975,4} - Z_{1974,4}) + \theta_0 \qquad (5\text{-}9)$$
$$= 24.63 + .660(20.46 - 15.69) + .624$$
$$= 28.40$$

This agrees with the 1976-1 prediction listed in Chart 5-4. The remaining forecasts are generated in an analogous fashion.

Chart 5-4 also presents the quarterly earnings predictions for all four quarters of 1976 using the three parsimonious models which have been suggested in the literature. The actual values of the 1976 quarterly earnings numbers and the percentages of forecast errors are also provided. We stress that these are *ex-ante* predictions conditional on the 56-observation data base listed in Chart 5-2. Although it is difficult to discriminate among the parsimonious models, it appears that the Foster and Brown–Rozeff models outperform the Griffin–Watts model on the quarterly earnings data for General Mills Corporation. It is also apparent that all three models have incorporated seasonal patterns in the predictions and that the percentages of forecast errors appear reasonably attractive for financial forecasting purposes.

VI. A CONCLUDING REMARK

Although the financial literature reports high predictive ability for univariate time series models, we do *not* recommend that firms simply employ Box–Jenkins forecasts without modifications. Time series models simply extrapolate past trends into the future without incorporating unusual or nonrecurring events. Firm-specific and macroeconomic factors could conceivably alter the time series forecasts. It is incumbent upon management to make fine-tuning adjustments to the time series forecasts.* In this manner, the time series forecasts are simply viewed as inputs into a more complex forecasting schema.

VIII. APPENDIX

The particular structure of the autoregressive integrated moving average (ARIMA) model employed in the literature is presented below. Nelson[23]

---

*One interesting methodology which incorporates expert management opinion into the forecast process is the delphi method reported on by Dunn and Hillison.[12] A fusion of time series forecasting and the iterative delphi approach appears to be a promising avenue to pursue.

and Box and Jenkins[7] provide detailed discussions of the underlying concepts in this area. The customary Box–Jenkins notation of $(pdq) \times (PDQ)$ is employed here, where (p, P) are regular and seasonal autoregressive parameters, (d, D) are regular and seasonal differences, and (q, Q) are regular and seasonal moving average parameters.

$$(1 - \bar{\phi}_1 B^s - \ldots - \bar{\phi}_P B^{sP})(1 - \phi_1 B - \ldots - \phi_p B^P)(1 - B^s)^D (1 - B)^d Z_t$$
$$= \theta_0 + (1 - \bar{\theta}_1 B^s - \ldots - \bar{\theta}_q B^{sQ})(1 - \theta_1 B - \ldots - \theta_q B^q) a_t$$

where

Z_t = observation of data at time t
B = backshift operator $BZ_t = Z_{t-1}$
S = seasonal span (S = 4 for quarterly data)
$\bar{\phi}$ = seasonal autoregressive parameter
ϕ = regular autoregressive parameter
$\bar{\theta}$ = seasonal moving average parameter
θ = regular moving average parameter
θ_0 = deterministic trend constant
a_t = current disturbance term.

REFERENCES

1. Abdulkader, A. *An Empirical Investigation of the Time Series Properties of Accounting Numbers at the Industry Level*, unpublished dissertation, 1979, The Florida State University.

2. Albrecht, W. S., L. Lookabill and J. C. McKeown, "The Time Series Properties of Annual Earnings: An Analysis of Individual Firms," *Journal of Accounting Research*, Autumn 1977, pp. 226–44.

3. Ang, J., J. Chua and R. Sellers, "Generating Cash Flow Estimates: An Actual Study Using the Delphi Technique," *Financial Management*, Spring 1979, pp. 64–67.

4. Ball, R. and R. Watts, "Some Time Series Properties of Accounting Income," *The Journal of Finance*, June 1972, pp. 662–81.

5. Beaver, W. H., "The Time Series Behavior of Earnings," *Empirical Research in Accounting: Selected Studies, 1970*, Supplement to *Journal of Accounting Research*.

6. Bernstein, L. P., *Financial Statement Analysis*, Irwin, Homewood, IL, 1974.

7. Box, G. E. P. and G. M. Jenkins, *Time Series Analysis: Forecasting and Control*, rev. ed., Holden-Day, San Francisco, 1976.

8. Brown, L. and M. Rozeff, "Univariate Time Series Models of Quarterly Accounting Earnings Per Share: A Proposed Model," *Journal of Accounting Research*, Spring, 1979, pp. 179–189.

9. Collins, D. W., "Predicting Earnings with Sub-Entity Data: Some Further Evidence," *Journal of Accounting Research*, Spring 1976, pp. 163–77.

10. Deakin, E. "Distributions of Financial Accounting Ratios: Some Empirical Evidence," *The Accounting Review*, January 1976, pp. 90–96.

11. Dopuch, N. and R. Watts, "Using Time Series Models to Assess the Significance of Accounting Changes," *Journal of Accounting Research,* Spring 1972, pp. 180-94.

12. Dunn, M. and W. Hillison, "The Delphi Technique—Adapted for the Management Accountant," *Cost and Management,* May-June 1980, pp. 32-37.

13. Foster, G., "Quarterly Accounting Data: Time Series Properties and Predictive Ability Results," *The Accounting Review,* January 1977, pp. 1-21.

14. Gonedes, N., N. Dopuch and S. Penman, "Disclosure Rules, Information Production, and Capital Market Equilibrium: The Case of Forecast Disclosure Rules," *Journal of Accounting Research,* Spring 1976, pp. 89-137.

15. Griffin, P. A. "The Time Series Behavior of Quarterly Earnings: Preliminary Evidence," *Journal of Accounting Research,* Spring 1977, pp. 71-83.

16. Johnson, T. and T. Schmitt, "Effectiveness of Earnings Per Share Forecasts" *Financial Management,* Summer 1974, pp. 64-72.

17. Kee, R. *An Empirical Investigation of the Time Series Properties of Quarterly Revenue and Expense Data,* unpublished dissertation, 1980, Florida State University.

18. Kinney, W. R., "Predicting Earnings: Entity versus Subentity Data," *Journal of Accounting Research,* Spring 1971, pp. 127-36.

19. Little, I. M. D. and A. C. Rayner, *Higgledy Piggledy Growth Again,* Blackwell, Oxford, England, 1966.

20. Lorek, K. S., "Predicting Annual Net Earnings with Quarterly Earnings Time Series Models, *Journal of Accounting Research,* Spring 1979, pp. 190-204.

21. Lorek, K. S. and J. C. McKeown, "The Effect on Predictive Ability of Reducing the Number of Observations on a Time Series Analysis of Quarterly Earnings Data," *Journal of Accounting Research,* Spring 1978, 204-14.

22. McDonald, C., "An Empirical Examination of the Reliability of Published Predictions of Future Earnings," *The Accounting Review,* July 1973, pp. 502-10.

23. Nelson, Charles R., *Applied Time Series Analysis for Managerial Forecasting,* Holden-Day, San Francisco, 1973.

24. Pan, J., D. Nichols and O. Joy, "Sales Forecasting Practices of Large Industrial Firms," *Financial Management,* Fall 1977, pp. 72-76.

25. Patell, J., "Corporate Forecasts of Earnings per Share and Stock Price Behavior: Empirical Tests," *Journal of Accounting Research,* Autumn 1976, pp. 246-76.

26. Ricketts, D. and M. Barrett, "Corporate Operating Income Forecasting Ability," *Financial Management,* Summer 1973, pp. 53-60.

27. Ronen, J., S. Sadan and C. Snow, "Income Smoothing: A Review," *The Accounting Journal,* Spring 1977, pp. 11-26.

28. Stone, B. and R. Wood, "Daily Cash Forecasting: A Simple Method for Implementing the Distribution Approach," *Financial Management,* Fall 1977, pp. 40-50.

29. Watts, R. and R. Leftwich, "The Time Series of Annual Accounting Earnings," *Journal of Accounting Research,* Autumn 1977, pp. 253-71.

CHAPTER

6

FORECASTING IN
STRATEGIC PLANNING

PHILIPPE LASSERRE
INSEAD

HEINZ T. THANHEISER
INSEAD

INTRODUCTION

Corporate strategic planning is a creative process. In contrast to other planning processes (e.g., long-range planning, marketing, production planning, and budgeting) within the firm, it is not primarily concerned with the time sequence and coordination of specific future actions of various parts of the organization, but with the choice of a competitive posture and with the formulation of the major policies for the corporation as a whole and, in diversified firms, for each strategic business unit. The interface between firms and their environment is complex, particularly in the case of large manufacturing or service organizations. The variables inside the firm (people, structure, procedures, physical and financial resources, etc.) and outside factors such as economic, social, and political forces are numerous, subject to more or less rapid change, and linked by interdependencies so complicated and uncertain that systematic optimization is not a feasible approach to determining strategy. The creative discovery of viable options is needed, based on as much systematic analysis and forecasting as the firm can afford to carry out.

The identification of certain critical causalities—the key factors for success—between the firm's resource deployment and selected environmental factors (opportunities and risks) poses forecasting challenges of many kinds. The analytical tools which are considered fundamental in the current practice of strategic planning are reviewed below. Given the limited space available in this overview chapter, more emphasis is placed on the analysis of the immediate competitive environment of the firm than on the broader economic, social, and political dimensions. These latter areas are addressed in detail in later chapters.

ANALYTICAL TOOLS FOR STRATEGIC PLANNING

Industry Analysis

Until quite recently, understanding the market and consumer and customer needs—and, therefore, demand forecasting and focus on market share—were given such excessive priority in strategic thinking that competitive interaction between suppliers was too often overlooked. Witness, for example, the business plans of the major competitors in the U.S. appliance industry, covering the five-year period from 1965 to 1970: the sum of planned sales and market shares amounted to 160% of the total market forecast.

The lesser and more uncertain growth rates of the late 1970s have shifted the strategic planning focus to competitive analysis and, more particularly, to the analysis of entry barriers, competitive cost performance, and strategic segmentation aimed at avoiding head-on competitive collision across entire industries.

Barriers to Entry

The traditional measures of entry barriers such as capital intensity, economies of scale, proprietary know-how, brands, and distribution channels need not be elaborated here; they are useful for analysis and pose no particular forecasting problems. Some recent examples of successful challenges to industry leaders in fields protected by formidable barriers of this kind show, however, that additional measures are needed.

The Swiss watch industry had dominated most world markets until a few years ago. Its strengths were technology, distribution, service, brand names, and quality image. And yet, in segment after segment, leadership was taken from them by American and Japanese manufacturers.

The U.S. beer industry was firmly in the hands of two leading brands, Budweiser and Schlitz, until Philip Morris acquired the third strongest brand, Miller, and made it a major challenger for overall market leadership against, a priori, unlikely odds in terms of scale economies in manufacturing, distribution, and advertising.

The concept which helps us explain these and other shifts in competitive positions is that of the "experience effect" in long-term cost behavior.

The Experience Effect

Documented first by statistical analysis of long-term price behavior and later extended to costs, the experience effect consists of the apparently unlimited unit cost reduction potential for manufactured goods. The value added costs, that is, total costs less purchases, tend to decline by 20–30% every time cumulative production volume doubles. (See Chapter 4.)

The implications for competitive strategy of the experience effect are easy to see. If one competitor is able to grow his volume faster than others he should achieve, over time, a significantly lower cost position. The size of the cost advantage and the time it will take to achieve it can be forecast readily: if competitor A grows at 5% and competitor B at 15% per annum and both operate on a 70% experience curve, B will double his cumulative output approximately every five years while A will take 15 years. Therefore, over a span of approximately 10 years, B should achieve a cost reduction of about 50% while A would have reached only 20%.

Clearly, the cost reduction described as the experience effect is not automatic. It has to be managed by exploiting the full panoply of cost saving measures available such as scale economies, product redesign, substitution of raw materials, and exploiting technological advances in manufacturing and other activities. In practice, this often means making investments in R&D and fixed assets and, consequently, acceptance of higher risks and less flexibility.

Recent examples of the successful application of high investment–cost reduction strategies are those of semiconductor manufacturers (e.g., TI in electronic watches) and of Japanese competitors who achieved world dominance, for example, in motorcycles and photographic equipment.

Companies which outgrow their competitors over long periods of time may achieve market dominance and, unless they make serious strategic mistakes, it is unlikely, particularly after market growth has slowed down, that any smaller competitor can catch up with their overall low cost position unless he is able to inject into the business funds earned in other markets or to significantly alter the value added structure of the business by a technological breakthrough. This conclusion, based on the experience effect, would lead one to forecast a tendency toward a stable competitive equilibrium condition. In a variety of branches of manufacturing industries this seems indeed to be borne out by historical fact. For example, automobiles, steel, tires, home appliances, and cigarettes are industries where, in the United States, there have been few successful challenges of market leaders. Yet, it would be wrong to consider low cost strategies as necessarily the best in terms of risk and return.

Recent findings on other key variables for success put the experience effect and the cost dimension of strategy into perspective.

Empirical Evidence on Key Variables for Success

The PIMS (Profit Impact of Market Strategy) project which originated in the General Electric Company consists of a continuing analysis of information on a large sample of companies. The PIMS data bank currently contains about 100 items of information on the strategic experiences of over 1500 businesses. The research conducted with this data base has been aimed at discovering the empirical "laws" that determine which strategy, under which conditions (e.g., market trends, industry competition, cost structure) produces what results in terms of return on investment and cash flows irrespective of the nature of products or services. To date, PIMS research has identified nine major strategic factors influencing return on investment; the nine account for almost 80% of the variation in profitability across businesses in the data base. The three most important factors are:

1. *Investment Intensity.* Technology and the chosen way of doing business govern how much fixed capital and working capital are required to produce a dollar of sales. Investment intensity, contrary to common expectations, has a negative impact on both return on investment and sales (see Chart 6-1). The major reason lies in the changed competitive climate produced by heavy investments in an industry: that is, competitors eager to keep their capacity loaded engage in price wars or marketing wars which reduce profitability. Rising cost of capital in an inflationary environment, strong cyclicality, and price controls would tend to aggravate the situation.

2. *Market Position.* Businesses with a high share of their served markets (both absolute and relative to their largest competi-

CHART 6-1. As Investment Intensity Rises, ROI Declines[a]

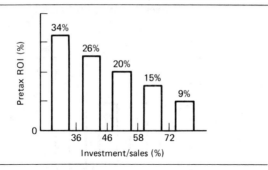

[a]Source: PIMS Letters Nos. 2 and 3.

tors) are often considerably more profitable than those with a low share (see Chart 6-2). Three effects account for this: the possibility for the high share business to benefit from economies of scale, the greater bargaining power vis-à-vis its suppliers and distributors, and the accumulated "experience" which gives a cost advantage over competitors.

3. *Quality of the Products or Services Offered.* Businesses selling high quality products or services are generally more profitable than those with low quality offerings. (See Chart 6-3.) This relationship holds for almost all kinds of products and market situation. High quality producers tend to command a price premium over competitors. (Quality is defined as the customers' of the business product/service package as compared to that of competitors.)

CHART 6-2. As Relative Market Share Increases, ROI Rises[a]

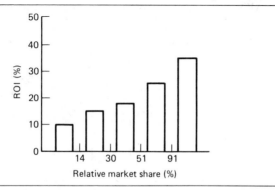

[a]Source: PIMS Letters Nos. 2 and 3.

**CHART 6-3. High Quality Products and
Services Are Most Profitable**[a]

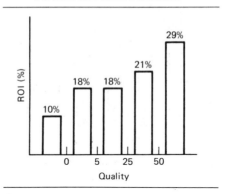

[a]Source: PIMS Letters Nos. 2 and 3.

Other major factors which PIMS shows to have a positive impact on profitability are: productivity increase, growth of served market, innovation, and differentiation.

The operation of the major strategic influences, according to the PIMS model, is complex. Sometimes, they tend to offset each other (e.g., greater investment intensity which tends to reduce earnings often goes along with greater productivity which tends to increase earnings). Sometimes they reinforce each other (e.g., strong market position and high quality usually go together), and a cumulative effect occurs. The model, therefore, leads to the conclusion that when formulating strategy, it would be dangerous to focus on one or the other factor in isolation. It suggests a useful way of visualizing interdependencies in cross tabulations, such as the examples, based on recent PIMS findings, shown in Charts 6-4 and 6-5.

CHART 6-4. Quality, Market Share, and Return on Investment[a]

Average ROI (%)		Market share		
			13%	28%
	Low	11	17	23
Product quality	Average	11	17	26
	High	20	26	35

[a]Source: PIMS Letters Nos. 4 and 5.

CHART 6-5. R&D/Sales, Market Share, and Return on Investment[a]

	Total R&D/sales		
ROI (%)	1%	3%	
	17	14	5
12%			
Market share	21	24	13
27%			
	31	32	28

[a]Source: PIMS Letters Nos. 4 and 5.

BASIC STRATEGIC MODES

A fundamental strategic choice faces many large firms, namely whether to compete (1) across the board, in all segments of an industry/market or (2) only in certain segments of the industry/market.

In product/markets at the early stages of the life cycle, this choice is typically less clear-cut than in mature industries. Technology may evolve so fast, and enough new market segments may emerge, that there is room, for many years, for several successful competitive postures. This is certainly still true today in some industries based on electronics technology such as automation and "office of the future," and in the "new energies" field. Yet, these markets will eventually mature just as yesterday's high growth markets (photocopiers, entertainment electronics, telecommunications, aerospace, etc.) are now beginning to mature.

One of the major strategic "blind spots" is the failure to forecast the emergence of more price sensitive (as opposed to quality and feature sensitive) segments in product/markets based on sophisticated technology. Typical examples of this are the segments left to competition by IBM in the computer industry and by Xerox in copiers. Clearly, the opposite is also occasionally true, that is, that a low-cost oriented industry leader fails to exploit emerging differentiated product segments. Such was the famous case of Ford's Model T strategy which opened the road to GM's success.

If we expect slower and more erratic growth in the 1980s and if relatively free trade allows the continuation of international competition, there will be few industries in which unfocused technology and the marketing based "go-go" strategies of past decades will be relevant for success. A clear choice will have to be made by many firms between pursuing a high volume, low cost leadership strategy across entire industries or focusing on a few market segments which can be defended by offering customers meaningful product differentiation for which they are willing to pay. The former competitive posture is, clearly, available only to a few, large industry leaders. Simple emulation of leaders' strategies by smaller competitors will lead to more of the type of failure which Chrysler suffered against GM.

The latter strategy, the "segment and differentiate" option, a priori open to many firms, will require the kind of sustained technological and marketing capabilities that firms like Daimler-Benz (Mercedes cars), Seiko (watches), and Michelin (radial tires) have been demonstrating. A critical issue in the pursuit of differentiation strategies is the maintenance of a cost position that is not too far above the low cost leader. When the costs of the differentiator get too high, will be unable to defend his business volume and will get backed into the tiny "Rolls Royce" segment of the market. This is the risk that such firms as Leitz (producers of Leica cameras) and BMW (for motorcycles) are exposed to.

Finally, in a few exceptional instances, segment leaders may also achieve overall industry leadership (e.g., Caterpillar in construction equipment, Honda in motorcycles). Philip Morris is employing such simultaneous (low cost and differentiation) strategies in cigarettes and beer. Michelin has been instrumental in changing the tire market from traditional belted tires to higher cost, higher quality radials and finds itself confronted with the American and Japanese industry leaders.

As these examples show and as confirmed by trends in other industries—steel, aircraft, telecommunications, to name a few—the choice between a low cost leadership strategy and a segmentation/differentiation posture will increasingly have to be made on an international scale. Forecasts of worldwide demand shifts (international product life cycle) and of labor cost in, and technology transfers to, the developing world will be more and more essential inputs to strategic planning, together with predicting energy and raw materials supplies, and political risks.

DIVERSIFIED BUSINESS STRATEGY

The top management of the diversified firm has to cope with one further level of complexity in its strategic planning. In addition to the choice of competitive postures for each business, it needs to combine all of them into a coherent whole. There are some analytical tools to assist corporate management in structuring this type of problem and in forecasting financial results in a more meaningful way than by simple aggregation of divisions' or subsidiaries' balance sheets and profits. They have been entering the strategic planning practice of many firms over the last several years.

Strategic Portfolio Analysis

Following the work done in the mid-1960s at the General Electric Company, several analytical approaches, using an analogy with an investor's portfolio, consider diversified companies as a portfolio of businesses having a different strategic posture and hence contributing differently over time to the achievement of long-term corporate objectives. Various tools, known as strategic portfolio methods, are proposed: the growth-share matrix (Boston Consulting Group), the directional policy matrix (Shell Chemical), the ABC matrix (McKinsey), and the strategy centers approach (Arthur D. Little), to name the best known. These methods have in common an approach consisting of three steps.

1. The classification of each business (generally called strategic segments or strategic business units) according to its competitive position on the one hand, and to the long-term attractiveness of the sector on the other hand (see Chart 6-6).

This classification is usually visualized in a matrix in which each cell represents a different strategic situation. The measures applied to the axes vary from method to method. In the growth–share matrix, industry attractiveness is measured by a single indicator, the industry's expected future growth rate; competitive position is measured by relative market share, that is, the company's market relative to the share of the largest competitor in the segment. The high share–low growth businesses, known as "cash cows," are the cash providers for

CHART 6-6. Common Framework Used by Various Strategic Portfolio Approaches

Industry future attractiveness		Business competitive posture	
		Weak	Strong
	Strong	These businesses are very risky. They need careful corporate attention and "go or no go" investment decisions.	These businesses are very promising. They warrant full corporate support and investment priority.
	Weak	These businesses are candidates for disinvestment or, at the most, limited support.	These businesses should be capable of generating more resources than needed for reinvestment and can, therefore, support investments in the other businesses.

CHART 6-7. Example of a Growth Share Matrix

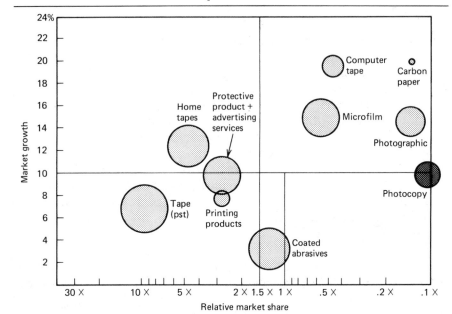

the investment needed in the high share–high growth businesses, "stars," or in selected low share–high growth businesses "question marks." The fourth category, low share–low growth, are natural candidates for divestment or for stringent cost control (see Chart 6-7). Other approaches use multiple criteria to assess these positions, but the recommendations remain similar (Chart 6-8).

2. Comparison of the actual strategic performance of each business with the normative strategic behavior expected from the position in the matrix: for example, check if a high growth–high share business is growing at a rate which improves, keeps, or diminishes its relative position; check if the cash generated by the high share–low growth business exceeds, in fact, the cash absorbed, or if excessive reinvestments were made, and so forth.

3. Consolidation of the various business strategies into a corporate plan which needs to be balanced in terms of financial and human resources.

These approaches raise a certain number of forecasting challenges for the corporation that attempts to use them. The two major ones are:

1. The validity of the assumptions behind each system of classification: expected rate of growth, expected financial profile

CHART 6-8. Example of a Directional Policy Matrix (Multiple Criteria)

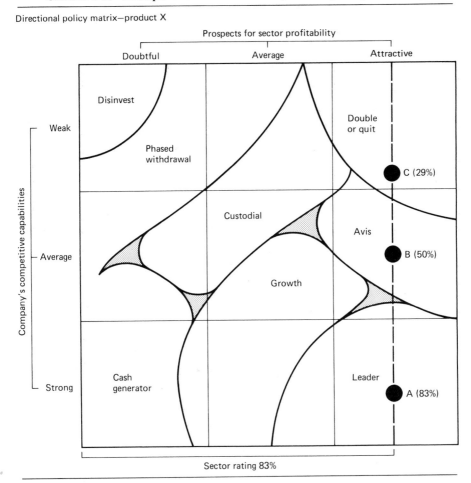

Directional policy matrix—product X

Prospects for sector profitability

Doubtful | Average | Attractive

Company's competitive capabilities

Weak

Disinvest

Double or quit

Phased withdrawal

C (29%)

Average

Custodial

Avis

B (50%)

Growth

Strong

Cash generator

Leader

A (83%)

Sector rating 83%

of each "ideal" position, expected stability of competitive advantages, actual possibility of implementing "independent" strategies, ... In answering these questions, historical data have to be used with great caution. The nature of change may be such that the relationships underlying past data become obsolete. This calls for sophisticated use of the various forecasting methods described elsewhere in this book.

2. The adaptability of the organizational context (planning and control systems, power structure, reward and evaluation of managers, . . .) to implement a business portfolio strategy. The differentiated strategies call for differentiated management styles. Usually large corporations have developed management systems stressing uniformity; change will be difficult.

CHART 6-9. Forecasting Methods for Strategic Planning

Forecasting Methods	Focus of the Method	Advantages and Disadvantages
Econometric models		
Trend analysis	Growth rate of sectors	Short-term accuracy often good
Causal models	Size of potential markets	Inability to forecast large discrete changes ("surprises")
Business survey		
General (economic outlook type)	Routine input in planning cycles	Useful for short-term Too aggregate
Specific (industry type and market research)	Industry and competitive analysis	Most useful for major one-shot decisions (investments, mergers, diversifications, divestment, new products, etc.)
Environmental scanning	Systematic review of structural change in the social, political, and economical environment	Still in infancy problem of definition of the relevant variables to monitor
Social and Technological forecasting	Search for major change in either technology or social environment—combine quantitative and qualitative assessment	Most useful to subparts of organization Methodology for integration with strategic planning still in infancy
Scenario building	Elaboration of alternative futures (optimistic, pessimistic, median) often at global level	Very sensitive to assumptions and to methodology Useful for contingency planning if explicitly linked to company's immediate environment
Country risk analysis	Assessment of political and economical risk for foreign investors	Ratings procedures often too general One-shot studies are more often appropriate

CONCLUSION

This chapter has reviewed certain analytical tools useful for strategic planning. Much of the data needed for their application will be generated by forecasting methods discussed elsewhere in this book (see Chart 6-9). However, in addition to the uncertainty of various forecasts, the top manager dealing with strategy faces the truly unknowable. The factors which influence the success or failure of a firm in a competitive environment are so many and varied, and capable of such unpredictable combinations, that forecasting strategic outcomes on the basis of past relationships is rarely relevant.

Strategic focus and flexibility are useful approaches and particularly necessary in the complex diversified enterprise. To achieve both, top management is confronted with an apparent dilemma. Strategic focus, on the one hand, calls for the definition of a clear competitive posture, understandable and motivating to the managers in charge of its implementation. To make a strategic focus credible, adequate resources have to be made available for implementation. Flexibility, on the other hand, calls for keeping options open as long as possible before making specific resource commitment. This means delays or commitment by small increments. The challenge to top managers is to resolve the dilemma without confusing the organization.

BIBLIOGRAPHY

Abell, Derek F., *Defining the Business: The Starting Point of Strategic Planning,* Prentice-Hall, Englewood Cliffs, NJ, 1980.

Ansoff, H. Igor, *Corporate Strategy,* McGraw-Hill, New York, 1965.

Ansoff, H. Igor, "Managing Strategic Surprise by Response to Weak Signals," *California Management Review,* Vol. 18, No. 2, Winter 1975, pp. 21–23.

_____, *Strategic Management,* Macmillan, London, 1979.

The Boston Consulting Group, *Perspectives on Experience* and *Perspectives on Strategy,* The Boston Consulting Group, 1968, 1970 and 1972.

Bower, Joseph L., *Managing the Resource Allocation Process,* Harvard University Press, Cambridge, MA, 1970.

Corey, E. Raymond, "Key Options in Market Selection and Product Planning," *Harvard Business Review,* September-October 1975, pp. 119–128.

Doz, Yves L., *Government Control and Multinational Strategic Management: Power Systems and Telecommunications Equipment,* Praeger, New York, 1979.

Dyas, Gareth and Heinz Thanheiser, *The Emerging European Enterprise,* Macmillan, London, 1977.

Emshoff, James R. and Ian I. Mitsoff, "Improving the Effectiveness of Corporate Planning," *Business Horizons,* October 1978, pp. 49–60.

Galbraith, Jay R., and Daniel A. Nathanson, *Strategy Implementation: The Role of Structure and Process,* West Publishing Co., St. Paul, MN, 1978.

Hall, William K., "Changing Perspectives on the Capital Investment Process," *Long Range Planning,* Vol. 12, No. 1, February 1979, pp. 37–40.

Hofer, Charles W. and Dan Schendel, *Strategic Management: A New View of Business Policy and Planning,* Little, Brown, Boston, 1979.

Lorange, Peter, *Corporate Planning: An Executive Viewpoint,* Prentice-Hall, Englewood Cliffs, NJ, 1980.

Mintzberg, Henry, "The Manager's Job: Folklore and Fact," *Harvard Business Review,* July-August 1975, pp. 49–61.

Norman, Richard, *Management for Growth,* John Wiley, New York, 1977.

Porter, Michael E., "How Competitive Forces Shape Strategy," *Harvard Business Review,* March-April 1979, pp. 137–145.

Scott, Bruce R., "Old Myths and New Realities," *Harvard Business Review,* March-April 1973, pp. 135–148.

Unterman, Israel, "Three Views of Strategy," *Journal of General Management,* Vol. I, No. 3, 1974, pp. 39–47.

Vancil, Richard F., "Better Management of Corporate Development," *Harvard Business Review,* September-October 1972, pp. 53–62.

Wrapp, H. Edward, "Good Managers Don't Make Policy Decisions," *Harvard Business Review,* September-October 1967, pp. 91+.

CHAPTER

7

FORECASTING

The Issues

ROBERT FILDES
Manchester Business School
University of Manchester

OVERVIEW

This chapter argues that an organization must be concerned with a much wider set of issues than just the technical problem of selecting a forecasting procedure when it examines its forecasting performances. An overview of the wider aspects of forecasting is presented in the introduction. That is not to say that the problem of selecting an appropriate procedure should be neglected. The various commonly used methods of forecasting are described and an evaluation offered of their strengths and weaknesses. Unfortunately in many important applications even the most accurate of methods leaves the organization trying to cope with too high a level of residual uncertainty. Organizations have to develop ways of limiting the impact of forecast error, and some possible approaches are described here. In the end, most of the alternatives to forecasting cost money. The chapter concludes that because of the increasingly low growth likely to be expe-

R. Michael Jalland was particularly helpful in commenting on earlier drafts of this chapter.

rienced in the industrialized world, all aspects of forecasting—the technical, the organizational, the information system on which the forecasts are based—require careful consideration, but the major benefits from such an evaluation will accrue from improvements in design of the organization's information about its environment.

A FORECASTING FRAMEWORK

Who makes forecasts? Who needs forecasts? How are they used? What is the best forecasting method to use? In the first part of this chapter I describe a framework that highlights the areas of forecasting which demand attention by the practical forecaster. The aspect that has been best researched is the forecasting methods themselves. In the second part of the chapter I examine those mostly widely used, concentrating on their advantages and disadvantages. The aim is to show where resources can best be employed by the organization intending to improve its forecasting performance. It turns out that the organization can improve the forecasting techniques it employs quite easily. Of more importance is the context in which forecasting takes place, the information on which it is based, and the organization's response to a forecast.

Chart 7.1 presents a framework for understanding the process of organizational forecasting and the issues we need to understand. In this model the forecaster is advising the decision maker on the predicted consequences of a proposed set of plans. To do this he or she uses selected information available about the environment. The information might be available through a management information system (MIS)—but as likely as not it will be collected on an ad hoc informal basis. To produce the forecasts the forecaster will adopt a particular procedure by considering the cost of the various possibilities, the time available before the forecast is needed, and some rough guesses of the likely accuracy of those methods he or she is competent to perform. The forecaster also has to take into account the value of improving forecast accuracy.

These criteria are not defined in a vacuum. The forecaster has the professional expertise that has taken so long to develop and his or her personal career goals, which I have labeled the forecaster's values. But the forecaster's organizational masters have their values too, and they may well not match. The forecaster is influenced by the decision maker's values but does not necessarily share them. In fact, as Wheelwright and Clarke[20] show, the forecaster and decision maker are usually at odds. The forecaster is too technical, does not understand the manager's problems, and rarely performs cost effectively. To the

CHART 7-1. The Forecasting System[a]

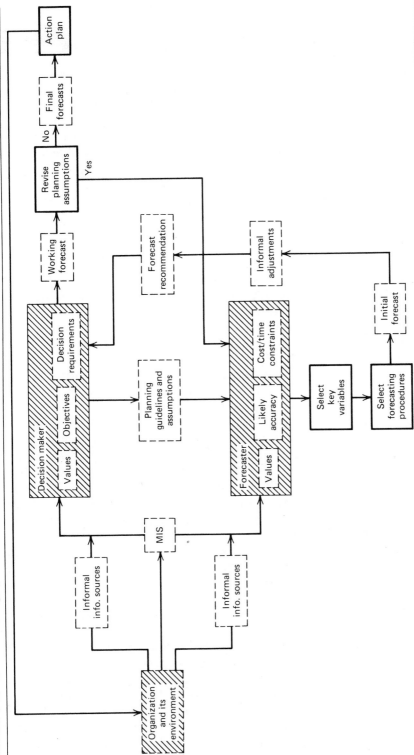

[a] Direct influences or flows. The shaded boxes represent the major components of the forecasting system. The bold-outlined boxes represent actions taken by the participants—the forecaster and the decision maker. The broken boxes represent information and assumptions.

forecaster, the decision maker hardly understands anything at all about the technical aspects of forecasting.

However, the forecaster will do his or her best. And if after carrying through a chosen approach the forecaster does not like the result he or she will modify it; so will the decision maker when the forecast reaches him or her, this time using alternative sources of information. The resulting forecast (the working forecast as labeled in Chart 7.1) may still not please when contrasted with the decision maker's initial values and objectives. Therefore the planning guidelines and assumptions that formed an input to the initial set of forecasts have to be revised. Round one of the planning process has just been unsuccessfully completed.

Perhaps the most obvious omission from this model of the interrelationship between the forecaster and the decision maker is that it fails to include the organizational framework in which the two protagonists (or participants) work. Hidden assumptions in different parts of the organization will influence what variables are considered crucial and what modifications take place. The harsh contrast between the forecaster's forecast based on the selected planning assumptions and the decision maker's optimistic hopes and objectives for those plans is often alleviated by their personal relationship.

A second omission is that in many organizations, forecasting of the same variables is done in different parts of the organization and is therefore subject to differing pressures toward bias and inaccuracy. Thus it is often argued that marketing staff tend to produce optimistic forecasts due to their need to believe sales are likely to improve from a better marketing effort. Likewise accountants' sales forecasts are often seen as pessimistic for this allows them to argue either "I told you so" or alternatively "We've done better than expected." By this argument the accountants protect themselves from criticism. These two examples lead to contrasting sales forecasts with different errors implicit in them.

What parts of the process shown in Chart 7-1 are important—the process of producing information, generating forecasts, and responding to forecasts?

A Link between the Forecasting and Decision Making Systems

The links between the forecasting and decision making function are weak in many organizations. This arises because decision makers and forecasters differ in their priorities. What are the most productive organizational designs which link the two? Fildes et al.[8] and Wheelwright and Clarke[20] suggest some solutions. The key to evaluating the organization's forecasting performance is to examine how forecasts are used—not just how they are produced.

The Quality of the Management Information Systems (MIS)

Most forecasting procedures are premised on the assumption that there is readily available information useful to the organization. Unfortunately in our experience many firms do not keep adequate records, nor have they thought through a consistent approach to their information, so for example volume and price figures for homogenous product groups are often not available. It is true that before advanced techniques are used suitable information must be collected over a number of years. However, careful forecasting should not be delayed until a suitable data base is developed. Instead the data base should be designed with a number of alternative forecasting procedures in mind.

It might be objected that MIS should not be the concern of an article surveying forecasting problems. However, the slow adoption of quantitative forecasting techniques can perhaps be explained only by reference to an often ill-developed information system. The routine collection of data is an elementary aid to decision making. Good forecasting demands a good data base and a good data base management system.

Selecting Key Variables

There are two ways of looking at the selection of key variables—how it is done and how it should be done. Casual empirical evidence collected by Jalland and Fildes and reported in Fildes et al.[8] suggests that many managers are confused by the differences among forecasts, budgets, plans, and targets. The effect of this confusion is that items which should be treated as variable and subject to forecasting are assumed to be constant. Consider for example an item such as "time taken by a debtor to pay," which is an input into a monthly cash flow forecast. Historically it may well have been treated as fixed. For debtors, however, the time taken to pay creditors will depend on their cash flow position and therefore in a recession the time is likely to lengthen. Thus, just at the time when it is most important to be realistic about the organization's cash flow, the assumption that the "time taken by a debtor to pay" is fixed is least likely to be valid.

A related issue is when two interdependent items, for example, sales volume and margin on sales, are treated separately. While margin on sales *may* be decided by the administrative fiat of the finance director as an input into the annual corporate plan, to neglect the effect of this assumption on sales volume would very likely undermine the revenue forecasts in the plan.

These two simple examples point to the importance of identifying those items that should be treated as variable. The interrelationships

CHART 7-2.   The Firm's Forecasting Needs

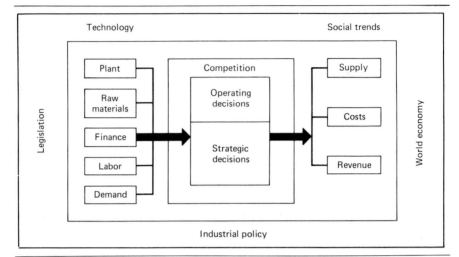

of assumptions and variables that are forecast also need to be systematically considered.

In Chapter 29 of this handbook Kappauf and Talbott propose a method for evaluating which variables require careful attention. Their argument is that for an organization to operate in a competitive environment, buying and transforming resources such as labor, finance, and raw materials into a supply of products (as shown in Chart 7-2), particular types of information are needed.

As the time scale of decision making lengthens it becomes increasingly necessary to look at those variables—social, legislative, technological—that can reasonably be regarded as constant in the short term. By considering a checklist of variables and their likely impact on the decisions being currently contemplated, it becomes possible to identify those variables that most require attention. The sensitivity of the decisions to forecast error also places an upper limit to expenditure on forecasting. For example, if an error of 10% in a product sales forecast leads to increased costs (and loss of revenue) of $100,000, it is worth spending up to $100,000 to eliminate that 10% forecast error.

Cost and Benefits of Improving Forecasting

The value of eliminating forecasting error is only one consideration in evaluating forecasting procedures. A second aspect requires the forecaster to take a view on likely improvements in accuracy as a function of expenditure on forecasting. Put more formally, improved accuracy is a function of expenditure on forecasting (hopefully increasing) while the benefit from forecasting is also a function of improved accuracy. This argument leads us to the truism that there is an upper limit on *profitable* expenditures on forecasting. It also highlights what we would like to know—the relationships between expenditure and accuracy, and between accuracy and benefits.

Fortunately the cost element in an organization's forecasting is relatively simple to calculate for any chosen approach. Later in this chapter I will examine in some detail what is known about the accuracy of the various methods employed in forecasting. The remaining element in the equation is the estimation of likely benefits derivable from improvements in accuracy. This is done by calculating the consequences of various levels of forecast error and comparing the result with what would have obtained if perfectly accurate information had been available.

The above paragraphs describe the economic costs and benefits of improved forecasting. But these are not the only considerations—the forecaster and the decision maker each have their individual preferences for one particular approach or another. Often enough these preferences seem to dominate the economic arguments and lead to the neglect of the more rational analysis described above. This neglect can be costly. It is important that organizations estimate the economic consequences of inaccurate forecasting and, where necessary, try to move toward a more cost-effective forecasting system.

Selecting a Forecasting Procedure

Earlier writers in forecasting have speculated on which methods are most accurate; for example, see Wheelwright and Makridakis.[21] If one turns to these works, well known in the mid-1970s, one finds that the evaluations offered boil down to the principle "increased sophistication is good," leaving aside questions of cost.

Even in their own terms this begs the question: if we want to forecast a particular variable, how do the various methods perform? Since these early publications the prescriptions offered have been subject to empirical criticism which, in particular circumstances, showed them to be misleading (Fildes and Howell[7] and Makridakis and Hibon[16]). As we enter the 1980s we are left with the uncomfortable feeling that the empirical support for many generalizations is weak.

The search for simple rules by which a forecaster would select that method (within the cost constraints) which would attain the desired accuracy level is difficult. Nor do I expect that the analyst will search through all the alternative methods, comparing and evaluating. Such an approach is ruled out for any except the most important project. Instead choices are made based on a range of considerations, as follows:

Prior Beliefs of the Forecaster. If only one method is known, that is the one that will be used. If a long time has been spent learning a complicated method, that effort is likely to unduly influence the choice. Previous experience and related research by the forecaster will also be important influences.

How the Forecast Is to Be Used. If the decision maker requires an evaluation of the impact of, say, advertising as a part of the market forecast, the approach selected will have to answer that question.

Complexity and Comprehensiveness. If a model is too complex for the decision maker to understand it is unlikely to be used. On the other hand if a model fails to include those elements the decision maker regards as important this will again lead to the model being rejected.

Comparative Testing. If the job of selection is being taken seriously, a few of the more plausible methods will be developed in parallel and tested for their forecasting performance. As pointed out above this search will not include all the possible alternatives.

Important decisions sensitive to forecast inaccuracy require a careful search through a range of alternatives. The all too likely mistake is to limit consideration to a narrow range of forecasting methods. Armstrong[2] has persuasively argued that there are invariably advantages to trying more than one approach—the more disparate the better. Organizations therefore need to have a forecasting procedure that on important problems permits the easy comparison of a range of alternatives. This means that the information system should be well developed, and historical records of previous forecasting performance should be kept. The ongoing costs of such record keeping are small, and once complete, allow time to be spent on forecasting rather than data collection. A wide range of alternative statistical, economic, and marketing models should also be available for easy use with the data base.

Adjusting the Forecasts

Both forecaster and decision maker allow themselves to alter the forecasts to suit their own beliefs. Armstrong comments on this practice in Chapter 32 of this handbook. The adjustments take place for a number of reasons: to make the results more "plausible"; to better meet the expectations of the decision maker; to comply with some prespecified target. In general this practice does not improve the final forecasts. But the evidence is not strong.

Three alternatives exist for integrating prior beliefs into a forecasting procedure: (1) as a formal input into the model; (2) adjustments of the type as discussed above, and (3) interactively, in which the forecaster is able to examine the effects on the forecasts of adopting a particular viewpoint. Examples of the latter are Little's[12] decision support systems, where the user has to specify a number of parameters such as the "advertising effectiveness" parameter. The model can then be adjusted until the forecaster is happy with both the chosen parameter and the resulting forecast.

Unfortunately we just do not know which of these procedures is likely to produce the better forecasts. Both forecasters and decision makers typically believe such adjustments are necessary. It is therefore important to monitor performance both with and without the adjustments.

Revising Plans

The final state of the planning round arises if the conditional forecasts derived from a particular business plan are at odds with the objectives set by the decision maker. The decision maker or planner will then search for alternative courses of action likely to bring the forecasts when revised into line with his set objectives. But we have already widened the scope of forecasting sufficiently, and so discussion of this topic is left to the planners.

A PROBLEM IN ORGANIZATION DESIGN?

What are the important issues in forecasting? The previous section has shown that the technical aspects of forecasting are just a small part of the problem of generating cost-effective forecast information and acting on it. Distortions and inefficiencies creep in from a variety of sources. Leaving aside the technical issues until the next section, the major weakness of the system just described is the system itself. An information system set up by accountants and therefore unconcerned with markets and not future oriented, a technician entranced with the sophisticated statistical hardware of his profession, and a decision maker whose primary concern is saying what his bosses want to hear—a caricature certainly and only one of the many possible. However, it underscores the major theme of this chapter: because we do not know how best to improve the information flow from the environment to the decision maker we have to experiment. To experiment means to evaluate and measure. Information systems can be improved, and (in the British companies we have examined) there is major scope for such improvement. Technical staff can be deployed so that they understand the manager's problems but are not subject to the same political pressure. Decision makers can distinguish between an objective forecast and the political actions they wish to take for their own or their organization's success.

Of course no single solution to the behavioral problems in forecasting can be applied across all organizations. With experimentation and the monitoring of the results of the experiments it is not unreasonable to hope for major improvements in the effective generation and use of forecast information. Analysis of such experiments by researchers should result in a better understanding of how forecasting and information systems best fit with an organization's needs and how the recommended improvements should be implemented. We could then more reasonably move on to worry about those issues most familiar—the technical.

APPROACHES TO FORECASTING

The Methods

Of all the aspects of the forecasting system just described the one most studied is the technicalities of the various forecasting methods. The different methods can be broken down into three classes:

> The judgmental—where individual opinions are processed, perhaps in a complicated fashion.

> The extrapolative—where forecasts are made for a particular variable using only that variable's past history. The patterns identified in the the past are assumed to hold over to the future

> The causal (or structural)—where an attempt is made to identify relationships between variables that have held in the past, for example, volume of brand sales and that product's relative price. The relationships are then assumed to hold into the future.

Most forecasting *procedures* use more than one of these approaches. But before turning to how these approaches fit in with the general questions raised in the first section I describe some of the more common methods under the above headings, and I also offer an evaluation.

Charts 7-3, 7-4, and 7-5 give brief definitions of the most important methods in each class. Later chapters in this handbook take up the topic of how they are used in more detail. For the moment these definitions will suffice.

Extrapolative Forecasting

Two useful surveys exist, Makridakis[14] with further comment by Anderson[1] and Makridakis,[15] and Fildes.[5] Extrapolative methods

Judgmental Forecasting

Chart 7-3 describes the standard judgmental methods of forecasting.

CHART 7-3. Judgmental Methods—the Definitions

Method	Definition
J1 Individual (subjective) forecasts	An individual makes a judgment about the future without reference to any other set of forecasts.
J2 Forecasting by committee/ survey	The committee aspects are only too familiar. A variant of the committee, the "sales force composite," aggregates the opinions of the sales force or "experts" on future prospects. Alternatively customers can be surveyed as to their prospective purchases.
J3 Delphi	Delphi has three attributes which distinguish it from the committee: anonymity, feedback, and group response. Typically, the participants are unknown to each other. The forecasting exercise is conducted in a series of rounds with each participant offered a summary of the opinions expressed earlier, until the group response stabilizes.

only work for quantitative variables, and in the remainder of this section we use Y_t to denote the variable we wish to forecast, measured at time t. Chart 7-4 gives a brief description of the most well-known methods.

Causal and Structural Models

The aim of these models is to link the variable being forecast to the causes that historically have influenced it and to use their established relationship to forecast. Chart 7-5 lists the well-known approaches and offers a brief definition.

We have described in some detail a wide range of forecasting procedures and given up-to-date references for readers interested in extending their knowledge further. It is idle to pretend the list is all-embracing: in particular we have neglected a range of adaptive extrapolative methods (Fildes[5]), leading indicator methods (McLaughlin[13]), and the wide range of ideas that go under the heading "social and technological forecasting." Any method can be employed either badly or well, and a careful analysis of how the organization uses its chosen procedures should usually lead to improvement. However, the major technical issue is how to choose among the competing approaches.

CHART 7-4. Extrapolative Forecasting—the Definitions

Method	Definition
E1 Trend curves	The past observations are described as a function of time, and the identified pattern is then used to forecast ahead. Typical functions are the straight line, the exponential, and the S-shaped curve. Available computer software provides a number of alternative curves. This method is often used for long-term forecasting.
E2 Decomposition	A time series is thought of as having four components, trend (its long-term behavior), cyclical (the longer-term swings around the trend), seasonal, and a random component left over. Once the systematic components are identified they can be reintegrated to generate forecasts.
E3 Exponential smoothing	The forecast is based on a weighted sum of past observations. The weights depend on so-called smoothing parameters. Once the smoothing parameters are selected, the forecasts are simple to calculate. The method can be easily adapted to take into account trend and seasonal factors.
E4 Box–Jenkins (or ARIMA) models	Like exponential smoothing the forecasts are based on a weighted sum of previous observations. However, the choice of weights is much more complex. ARIMA models offer the analyst a range of different models, and the most appropriate is selected for the particular application (Jenkins[11]).
E5 Bayesian	In normal applications Bayesian forecasting is similar to exponential smoothing. However, sudden changes in series behavior can take place that are essentially unpredictable, for example, a strike at a competitor's plant. Regular extrapolative forecasting methods require human intervention to recalibrate after such a change. Bayesian forecasting attempts to allow for these changes by evaluating each new data point to see whether any change has occurred. Once recognized, the forecasts are adjusted automatically. The method can also incorporate subjective information.

CHART 7-5. Causal and Structural Models—the Definitions

Method	Definition
C1 Single equation regression models	The dependent variable Y_t is thought of as determined by a number of "causes," or "exogenous factors," as well as past values of the dependent variable itself. The relationships between Y and its causes are identified by examining past data. To forecast, either assumptions need to be made concerning the values of the exogenous factors in the future, or alternatively these values have in turn to be forecast. Wood and Fildes[22] offer a nonstatistical introduction.
C2 Simultaneous system models	These have a similar structure to the single equation models described above but with more than one dependent variable. The dependent (or endogenous) variables are then forecast by making assumptions about the future values of the exogenous variables.
C3 Simulation models	Like simultaneous system models, simulation models are concerned with a large number of variables and their interrelationships with exogenous factors. Simulation modelers stress model structure (rather than the linear structures of the regression and simultaneous system models). Typically they include a lot more detail of the system being modeled, for example, information flows. Identifying the model is usually much more ad hoc than with the rigorous statistical models first discussed.
C4 Input-output models	Input-output models are based on the idea that to obtain a given output of goods or services requires a fixed set of inputs. Once forecasts are made of consumer demand, input-output techniques allow the calculation of the amount of a particular product needed to sustain that level of demand (Blin et al.[4]).
C5 Cross-impact analysis	A list of events likely to have an impact on the system being analyzed is generated. The probabilities of each of these events happening are then estimated. Second, the conditional probability of event A happening given that event B has happened, for all possible pairs of events A and B, is also estimated. From these assumptions it is possible to define scenarios made up of a mixture of these various events and to calculate the associated probability of each scenario. Those sets of events with low probability are eliminated. (Helmer[9]).

AN EVALUATION OF FORECASTING METHODS

No one method can be relied on to produce the "best" forecasts in all circumstances. Each of the methods has its strengths and weaknesses, and these are summarized in Chart 7-6.

Each of the methods discussed in Chart 7-6 has been evaluated on a set of criteria, and the results are summarized in Chart 7-7. The scores shown correspond quite closely to those given by Makridakis and Wheelwright.[17] The conclusion that stands out from Chart 7-7 is that the problem of selecting a forecasting procedure is far from straightforward. No one method is better than the others on all the dimensions considered.

SELECTING A FORECASTING PROCEDURE REVISITED

In the first section I briefly considered some of the issues involved in selecting a forecasting procedure, concentrating on what could be considered "best practice." Here I discuss the information that should be available to the forecaster in an ideal world. My aim is to show what questions need answering and what compromises have to be made in the meantime.

Ideally the forecaster would be able to describe his problem on a series of dimensions: for example, certain simple statistical characteristics of the variable to be forecast, the forecast lead time, the level of aggregation in the data (is it firm, market, or macroeconomic data?), the type of economic or social system in which the forecast variable is generated, and so on. With a stable relationship existing between these problem categories and the performance of the various alternative forecasting methods the final choice of method only depends on the returns from forecast accuracy. In essence a forecasting model of forecast performance would exist to guide the choice of model.

If this sounds too fanciful certain authors have attempted to do exactly this (Makridakis and Hibon[16]), although with only limited success. Armstrong[2] has also evaluated a wide range of forecasting cases and has attempted to generalize about when to use which method. Fildes et al.[6] have accepted the difficulties of developing a quantitative model to explain forecasting success and produced a large-scale bibliography that describes the success analysts have had in forecasting in a wide range of circumstances. Asher[3] has attempted an evaluation of forecasting success (and failure) for a number of situations, for example, energy, population, transport, and others. These various studies have resulted in increasing our knowledge of predictability and changed our views on the likely success of the different alternative methods. Unfortunately the residual uncertainty is very high, and as we move from the short to the medium term—the situation where

CHART 7-6. The Advantages and Disadvantages of the Forecasting Methods

Method[a]	Advantages	Disadvantages

JUDGMENTAL

Individual (subjective) forecasts

J1 Cheap if you want it to be; flexible, it can forecast anything; anybody can do it.

Accuracy suspect (Armstrong[2]); although perhaps the quality of judgments can be improved by evaluating the forecaster's accuracy, skills are embodied in a person rather than the organization; subject to all the problems of human judgments (Hogarth and Makridakis[10] provide a survey).

Forecasting by committee/survey

J2 Brings different perspectives to bear on the problem; plus the advantages listed above.

One loudmouth can dominate, and he might not be the best forecaster; who wants to disagree with the boss in a hierarchical organization; has the disadvantages of human judgment; more expensive than the individual. No answer to the questions, "How do you select a committee" and "How do you organize the meeting?" A survey may say more about people's *current* attitudes and expectations than future activities.

Delphi

J3 As above, but attempts through anonymity to eliminate the effects of authority and group domination.

Complex; pressure toward consensus as the rounds progress; no necessary convergence to an agreed forecast; not necessarily an improvement on the more straightforward committee. Sackman expands on these.[19]

EXTRAPOLATIVE

Trend curve analysis

E1 Easy to learn, to use, and to understand.

Too easy and therefore encourages thoughtlessness; particularly in the long term why should a curve depending only on time provide a suitable description of the distant future?

Decomposition methods

E2 Intuitively plausible.

No statistical rationale; not ideally suited to forecasting, and suffers from the same problems as trend curves. As a method of identifying trend, seasonal, and cyclical factors it is useful.

CHART 7-6. (Continued)

Method[a]	Advantages	Disadvantages

Exponential smoothing

E3 Easy to computerize for a large number of products. Very cheap to operate. Easy to set up monitoring schemes. Easily understood.

No theoretical base; misses turning points; inaccurate.

Box-Jenkins (or ARIMA) models

E4 The choice of weights is wide allowing the user to identify much more subtle patterns in the data than with the previous methods. More than a technique, the Box-Jenkins approach offers a philosophy of modeling based on the *principle of parsimony*: the simpler the model the better, so long as it passes a range of suitable diagnostic checks.

Complex and difficult to understand; for many users it promises more than it delivers; expensive in its use of computing time.

Bayesian models

E5 Attempts to include the probability of structural change; includes subjective information; can be used with very little data; computationally quite cheap.

Complex; little is known about its performance.

CAUSAL AND STRUCTURAL

Single equation regression models

C1 If models can be developed that are sufficiently reliable they are ideal in that they answer the question "how does the company influence sales?" They are control models as well as forecasting models.

The models are difficult to develop, requiring expert staff and large amounts of data that the organization often fails to collect. There still remains the problem of forecasting the exogenous factors.

Simultaneous system models

C2 Many systems do not naturally fall into the format of a single equation model. In macroeconomic policy, unemployment, output, and inflation are all interdependent. In the firm, it is often argued that sales and advertising are jointly determined. Simultaneous system models capture these interrelationships.

High data requirements; hard to understand; statistically complex; difficult to define model; do not easily allow for nonlinearities; expensive.

Simulation models

C3 If properly implemented such models can offer the decision maker substan-

Expensive; often high data requirements; no clear rationale behind

CHART 7-6. (Continued)

Method[a]	Advantages	Disadvantages
	tial help; they can be designed to be simple to use and understand; they can also solve the "right" problem.	their construction; require careful validation.

Input–Output Models

C4	Unlike many of the techniques described, input-output is ideally suited for forecasting industrial products.	Governmental input-output tables seldom contain sufficient detail for a company concerned with specific product classes; they also tend to be out of date by a number of years; it is unknown how important is the assumption of constant proportionality between input and output. Preparing a product-specific input-output table is expensive. The forecasts depend on the accuracy of the initial forecasts of consumer demand.

Cross-Impact Analysis

C5	Is able to deal with unlikely events which may have a major impact. It can deal with both quantitative and qualitative events.	The probabilities usually have to be estimated through the various judgmental methods already discussed. This may affect which scenarios are given full consideration. The choice of which events to include is also crucial. How good are we at knowing which events could conceivably affect the organization? Finally, is there any evidence that cross-impact has any predictive value?

[a]J1–J3, judgmental methods. E1-E5, extrapolative methods.
C1–C5, causal and structural methods.

increased accuracy probably has the highest payoff—our knowledge decreases to almost zero. For me, the major issue in selecting a forecasting procedure remains how to link simple measures of the forecasting problem to forecast accuracy. Without substantial further progress decision makers and their organizations will have to give more attention to my final topic, the avoidance of forecasting.

AVOIDING FORECASTING

If forecasting with any validity is impossible, what alternatives exist? Of all the issues in forecasting this remains perhaps the least researched.

CHART 7-7. An Evaluation of Various Forecasting Procedures

Criteria for evaluating forecasting procedures

METHOD	Data requirements	Statistical basis	Staff expertise To set up	Staff expertise To use	Comprehensibility	Assessability[a]	Reported effectiveness[b]
Judgmental							
Individual	0[c]	0	0	0	4	2	4
Committee	0	1	1	0	4	1	2
Delphi	0	1	2	0	4	1	2
Extrapolative							
Trend curves	2	2	1	1	4	4	3
Decomposition	2	1	2	1	3	4	3
Exponential smoothing	1	1	1	1	3	4	3
Box–Jenkins	3	3	3	2	1	4	4
Bayesian	1	2	3	2	1	4	1
Causal							
Single equation	3	3	3	2	2	4	3
Simultaneous system	4	4	4	4	1	4	2
Simulation	2–4	2	4	2	2	2	1
Input–output	4	3	4	2	1	4	1
Cross-impact	1	3	4	3	2	1	1

[a] "Assessability" denotes the ease with which the procedure under discussion can be evaluated. It measures whether the procedure is completely specific or not.
[b] "Reported effectiveness" denotes whether many studies have been done comparing and evaluating the procedure with its alternatives.
[c] In the scoring system 0 is equivalent to "low," and 4 to "high."

Most forecasting research has concentrated on the short term. Here techniques have been rigorously examined and their comparative performance analyzed. In rough-and-ready terms the process may be described as (1) choose a plausible forecasting procedure, (2) modify it a little, (3) estimate the likely magnitude of the error, and (4) carry enough stocks or whatever to reduce the impact of forecast uncertainty. We are used to responding to uncertainty in our decision making. Any inaccuracy in our estimate of the error is blamed on God, and for a brief period the forecasting department is inundated by irate telephone calls. But the system settles down after this period of chaos. Stability is restored.

Contrast with this the long-term forecaster's problem. His misestimate of the forecast error can lead to under- (or over-) employed factories. Such poor performance can even lead to bankruptcy or opportunities missed forever. Unlike the inventory control example the mistake will not quickly go away.

A number of answers have been developed that can help the forecaster working to help long-term decision making.

Insurance

Unlike the stock control example, covering the residual uncertainty and riding out its consequences are regarded as too dangerous. Instead the risks are reduced by sharing the consequences of any disasters with an insurance company. The effect, of course, is a reduced return in that insurance always costs money.

A subtler variation of this same idea has been described by Quinn[18] as "logical incrementalism." Simply described, it is the recommendation that where uncertainty is high, only those decisions are contemplated that are viable over a wide range of possible futures. As the forecasting (and planning) lead time reduces, uncertainty is also reduced and finer choices can be usefully analyzed. Decisions here are seen as sequential rather than one-off. The cost, more limited than the straightforward "insure" option, derives from the alternative courses of action being kept open for a longer period than if the decision had been made once and for all. Such an approach also demands sophisticated planning departments. An example of this is the commission of a power station whose power source, coal or oil, is not decided until much of the construction work has been completed.

Portfolio Procedures

It has long been know that if two alternative investments can be found with similar returns but whose outcomes are negatively correlated, a portfolio investment in both decreases the risk level, leaving the return unchanged. The same idea can be used in examining whether diversification (of products or businesses) can lead to decreased risk. In effect the forecaster needs to forecast not just the returns expected from different projects but their inter-relationships as well. Although in some contexts improvements necessarily derive from considering a porfolio rather than its individual components, the problem remains one of identifying alternative investments that are negatively correlated with one's own. The difficulties associated with the portfolio approach do not negate the usefulness of seeking out countercyclical investments. It is a solution that should prove profitable.

Organizational Flexibility

The time horizon of a forecast is made up of a number of distinct times: the time to gain information (the information lead time), the time to plan and execute a course of action (the planning lead time), and the time period during which the action reaps its consequences (the action lead time).

Some of these times are under the control of the organization—the delay in obtaining current information and the time spent in choosing a course of action. By increasing the speed by which internal information is made available and by increasing the organization's responsiveness to a problem, the need to forecast is minimized. Of course for research-based organizations this is only of limited help in that the action lead time is considerably longer than the other two.

Leverage (Gearing)

Forecasting attempts to reduce risk at only a limited cost. But there are a number of alternative structural solutions that the organization can sometimes adopt. For firms funded by both debt and equity an increased proportion of funds deriving from equity (reducing the leverage) has the effect of lowering the degree to which fluctuations in pre-interest profits are amplified in terms of post-interest profit. Low leverage also reduces exposure to interest rate fluctuations.

Leverage is a concept primarily associated with finance, but it also applies to other functions such as purchasing, production, and sales. For example, raw materials (and foreign currency) can be purchased through a futures market so that the amount to be paid for a future need is known now. In marketing, long-term contracts can be made with large purchasers. Of course all these devices cost money (even though the cost is sometimes hidden as an opportunity cost). However, they do meet the aim of lessening the need to forecast.

Forecasting—We Still Cannot Do Away With It

The ideas discussed above do not eliminate the need for forecasting long term. Portfolio procedures shift the emphasis from forecasting for one business to forecasting their joint performance. Insurance shifts the problem to the insurer but at some cost. Organizational flexibility and leverage have only limited applicability. No universal means are thus on offer that would allow an organization to avoid forecasting. Instead two simple questions have to be squarely faced:

How best to forecast?

How to estimate the likely forecast error reliably.

As I have argued, the answers are both technical and organizational. It is the latter solution that has received little attention, and in the longer term it seems to hold the most promise for helping organizations avoid the worst consequences of what is apparently an increasingly malevolent future.

REFERENCES

1. Anderson, O. D., "A Commentary on 'A Survey of Time Series,'" *International Statistical Review*, vol. 45, 1977, pp. 273–97.

2. Armstrong, J. S., *Long-Range Forecasting: From Crystal Ball to Computer*, John Wiley, New York, 1978.

3. Asher, W., *Forecasting: An Appraisal for Policy Makers and Planners*, Johns Hopkins University Press, Baltimore, 1978.

4. Blin, J. M., E. A. Stohr, and B. Bagamery, "Input-Output Techniques in Forecasting," *in Forecasting* (S. Makridakis and S. C. Wheelwright, eds), TIMS Studies in the Management Sciences, vol. 12, North-Holland, Amsterdam, 1979.

5. Fildes, R., "Quantitative Forecasting—the State of the Art: Extrapolative Models," *Journal of the Operational Research Society*, vol. 30, 1979, pp. 691–710.

6. Fildes, R., D. Dews, and S. Howell, *A Bibliography of Business and Economic Forecasting*, Gower, Farnborough, Hants, Great Britain, 1981.

7. Fildes, R. and S. Howell, "On Selecting a Forecasting Model," *in Forecasting* (S. Makridakis and S. C. Wheelwright, eds), TIMS Studies in the Management Sciences, vol. 12, North-Holland, Amsterdam, 1979.

8. Fildes, R., R. M. Jalland, and D. Wood, "Forecasting in Conditions of Uncertainty," *Long Range Planning*, vol. 11, August 1978, pp. 29–38.

9. Helmer, O., "Problems in Futures Research—Delphi and Causal Cross-Impact Analysis," *Futures*, vol. 9, 1977, pp. 71+.

10. Hogarth, R., and S. Makridakis, "Forecasting and Planning— an Evaluation," *Management Science*, vol. 27, no. 2, 1981, pp. 115+.

11. Jenkins, G. M., *Practical Experiences with Modelling and Forecasting Time Series*, A GJP Publication, Jersey, 1979.

12. Little, J. D. L., "BRANDAID: A Marketing Mix Model," *Operations Research*, vol. 23, 1975, pp. 628–73.

13. McLaughlin, R. L., "Leading Indicators: A New Approach for Corporate Planning," *Business Economics*, vol. 6, no. 3, 1971, pp. 7–12.

14. Makridakis, S., "A Survey of Time Series," *International Statistical Review*, vol. 44, 1976, pp. 29–70.

15. Makridakis, S., "Time-series Analysis and Forecasting: An Update and an Evaluation," *International Statistical Review*, vol. 46, 1978, pp. 255–78.

16. Makridakis, S. and M. Hibon, "Forecasting Accuracy and Its Causes: An Empirical Investigation," *Royal Statistical Society* (A), vol. 142, 1979, pp. 97+.

17. Makridakis, S. and S. C. Wheelwright, "Forecasting: Framework and Overview," *in Forecasting* (S. Makridakis and S. C. Wheelwright, eds.), TIMS Studies in the Management Sciences, Vol. 12, North-Holland, Amsterdam, 1979.

18. Quinn, J. B., "Strategic Change: Logical Incrementalism," *Sloan Management Review*, Fall 1978, pp. 7–21.

19. Sackman, H., *Delphi Critique: Expert Opinion, Forecasting and Group Process*, Lexington, MA, Lexington Books, 1975.

20. Wheelwright, S. C. and D. G. Clarke, "Corporate Forecasting: Promise and Reality," *Harvard Business Review*, vol. 54, 1976, pp. 40+.

21. Wheelwright, S. C. and S. Makridakis, *Forecasting Methods for Management*, 3rd ed., John Wiley, New York, 1980.

22. Wood, D. and R. Fildes, *Forecasting for Business: Methods and Applications*, Longmans, London, 1976.

PART

2

APPROACHES TO FORECASTING

CHAPTER

8

SMOOTHING METHODS FOR SHORT-TERM PLANNING AND CONTROL

A. DALE FLOWERS
Weatherhead School of Management
Case Western Reserve University

BASIC CONCEPTS OF SMOOTHING METHODS

Exponential smoothing is a method to systematically revise the estimates of the coefficients of a forecasting model based on each successive actual observation. It is an extremely popular technique which has enjoyed widespread appeal among forecasting practitioners. Its popularity may be traced to the intuitively appealing logic on which the whole of exponential smoothing is based: *If the forecast for a particular period was too high, reduce it for the next period; if it was too low, raise it!* The method by which the adjustment is made is termed the *basic operation of exponential smoothing* and may be stated generally as:

New estimate = old estimate + fraction of error

The *error* is defined as the actual value minus the forecasted value. The fraction must be between zero and one and is termed the *exponential smoothing constant.*

To illustrate how the technique works, consider the following simple example. A beverage store manager estimated that 50 cases of Billy Beer would be sold in a particular week. The manager held a reserve of an additional 25 cases to meet any unexpectedly high demand. During the week 60 cases were actually sold. If the smoothing constant is 0.3, what is next week's forecast?

$$\text{New forecast} = 50 + 0.3(60 - 50) = 53$$

Notice that since the forecast was low, the exponential smoothing operation raised its value. If the situation had been the reverse, that is, a forecast of 60 but only 50 units demanded, the result would be:

$$\text{New forecast} = 60 + 0.3(50 - 60) = 57$$

For greater responsiveness to forecast errors, the smoothing constant value may be increased. However, care should be taken since high values of the smoothing constant may cause overreaction to forecast errors.

The application of the exponential smoothing technique results in an exponentially weighted moving average forecast, in contrast to a simple moving average which assigns equal weights to historical observations. The smoothing process assigns the greatest weight to the most recent demand observation and exponentially decreasing weights to older historical observations. This exponential weighting is the basis for the name exponential smoothing. The logic underlying this process is that each observation reveals more information about the time series in question and therefore should be immediately incorporated into the values of the model coefficients. Furthermore, more recent observations are more important than older ones for forecasting the immediate future; thus the weighting scheme is used.

Exponential smoothing methods have had their greatest application in production/distribution environments, but they have been used in a variety of other situations, including such diverse areas as forecasting expenditure flows for a large state university and forecasting demand for electricity for a large public utility. The reader should not assume such models are appropriate for all situations, however. The strategy of exponential smoothing is to *extrapolate* historical observations into the future. (This is also true of many other time series methods.) Then through the adaptive mechanism, adjustments to the forecast may be made if the demand pattern shifts. Such shifts or turning points will *not*, in general, be forecasted by exponential smoothing methods. Such methods *are* appropriate when:

There are many items to be forecast.

Only a small proportion of the items are critical, but planning is necessary for all.

Only *short-term* forecasts are required (up to a few months).

Reasonable, but not *precise*, accuracy is acceptable.

The past is an acceptable guide to the future for a high proportion of the items.

More sophisticated procedures are not cost/benefit justified.

Forecasts are required for *independent*, as opposed to dependent [Material Requirements Planning (MRP)], demand situations.

For production environments, if production is to stock as opposed to order.

A classic example of such a situation is a large warehouse that stocks a high variety of stock keeping units.

In spite of the precautions listed above for the use of smoothing methods, the reader should not be reluctant to consider them for possible adoption. In the most definitive empirical investigation reported to date of competing forecasting methodologies, Makridakis and Hibon[14] conclude: "Table 1 indicates that if a single user had to forecast for all 111 series, he would have achieved the best results by using the exponential smoothing methods after adjusting the data for seasonality." *Accuracy* was the main criterion used to evaluate the various methods in this study. Reports by Gardner and Dannenbring[12] and Bunn[4] which have appeared after the Makridakis and Hibon study have generally confirmed portions of the more exhaustive earlier study. The Makridakis and Hibon study also provides an excellent review of earlier studies comparing various forecasting methodologies and is therefore recommended to the interested reader. (Also, see Chapter 27.)

In the remainder of this chapter, a *sample* of both technical and managerial considerations for using smoothing methods is presented. [The nontechnical reader may skip over chart sections or subsections having an asterisk (*) to the right of the heading for that section.] The items included in this chapter have been chosen for both their effectiveness and general acceptance by practitioners. For example, only the forecasting models proposed by Winters[21] are detailed in this chapter to illustrate the exponential smoothing technique for *revising* the model coefficients. Brown[2] presents a variety of other models to which smoothing may be applied.

It is assumed throughout this chapter that a computer system is available to the user for implementation of forecasting models. However, the simple versions of the models presented in this chapter are available for smaller applications on the Texas Instruments T1-58 and T1-59 Programmable Calculator through the *Business Decisions* Library.[8] It should finally be noted that some of the examples and diagrams are purposely simplified to clearly communicate the logical concept to the reader.

ADVANTAGES AND DISADVANTAGES OF SMOOTHING METHODS

With the foregoing discussion in mind, the advantages and disadvantages of exponential smoothing forecasting methods (hereafter called ES) can be succinctly listed as follows.

Advantages

Simplicity, ease of understanding.

Reasonable (but by no means precise) accuracy under a wide range of conditions.

Apparently as accurate as other methods, although evidence is conflicting.

Computational efficiency.

Information storage requirements are small.

Adaptiveness, even at different rates for some ES models.

Disadvantages

Generally require man–machine system with manual surveillance and override features.

Lag shifts in demand; do *not* predict turning points.

Apply to short-run forecasting only.

May overreact to randomness, causing destructive oscillations.

Technical problems including:
    a. Choosing the right model.
    b. Choosing smoothing constant values.
    c. Operating discipline *each* time period.

COMPONENTS OF A TIME SERIES

The components of a time series are listed and defined as follows:

Average or Level Component. The long-run average or stable demand base (the other components are defined *relative to* this one).

Trend Component. The per period change in the level component.

Seasonal Component. Systematic variation about the level component through a seasonal period of relatively short duration (one year, for example).

Cyclical Component. Long-run changes in the demand pattern associated with the general business and economic cycles.

Random Component. Chance variations due to unexplained forces in consumption habits, technically referred to as noise.

For short-term forecasting, cyclical components are excluded from explicit considerations for modeling. However, practitioners may intervene in short-term forecasting systems to increase or decrease the rate of response in times of strong cyclical movements or relatively placid times.

The other four components will all be considered in this chapter by the combination of methods presented. The level and random components exist in every time series, while trend and/or seasonal effects may or may not be present. These latter two may be evidenced in different forms as well. For example, a trend effect may be linear (constant per period change in the level) or nonlinear (variable rate of change). Only the linear case is discussed in the following sections since it suffices for the great majority of trend cases.

Similarly, seasonal effects are illustrated as additive or multiplicative. Additive seasonals imply that a constant value should be added to the level component for a particular period (i.e., a month within the year) without respect to changes which may have occurred in the level since the preceding season. A multiplicative seasonal means that the observed demand should be a constant ratio of the level component. Thus, if the level component has increased since the last season, the seasonal effect will be *proportionately* increased rather than increased by a constant amount. Only multiplicative seasonals are included in the sections to follow based on their popularity in use. However, Chatfield[5] points out that the practitioner should experiment to determine which type of seasonal is appropriate given that the data contain seasonal effects.

The section of this chapter entitled "Four Exponential Smoothing Forecasting Systems" contains charts (Charts 8-3 through 8-10) illustrating these components of demand in various combinations. The reader may wish to glance at the charts before proceeding.

EXPONENTIAL SMOOTHING

Simple Exponential Smoothing

For a time series containing only a level or average component of demand along with randomness, the following equation expresses the smoothing operation:

$$A_{t+1} = A_t + \alpha_A (D_{t+1} - A_t) \qquad (8\text{-}1)$$

where A_t = the estimate of the average or level component of demand at time t ($t + 1$, etc.)

D_{t+1} = the actual demand for time $t + 1$

α_A = the smoothing constant used to smooth the level component.

Equation (8-1) may be rewritten as

$$A_{t+1} = (1 - \alpha_A)A_t + \alpha_A D_{t+1} \qquad (8\text{-}2)$$

While many authors write smoothing equations in this second form, they are kept in the prior format in this chapter for ease of understanding and for consistency with the basic operation of exponential smoothing defined earlier.

If we assume that the above model has been correctly fitted to the time series (level, random), then the forecast accuracy subsequently observed will be *critically* dependent on α_A, the smoothing constant. This value may be set at a so-called "robust" value for all time series exhibiting a particular combination of demand components, or it may be "individualized" to fit each particular time series. This problem and several ways to solve it are discussed more thoroughly in a later section.

Double and Higher Forms of Smoothing

Double exponential smoothing could be generally characterized as a second smoothing of the single smoothed level so as to allow for both level and trend components in a time series. If a trend is present, the model implied by equation (8-1) will lag the time series; therefore, some adjustment for the trend is necessary. Double smoothing allows such an adjustment by defining both a single and a double smoothed average and then combining these mathematically to produce estimates of the level and trend components for forecasting. The interested reader is referred to Brown[2] for computational details. Since double smoothing offers no advantage over models that *directly compute and smooth* a trend component, and the latter are more easily understood, only the latter type are detailed in a later section.

In addition to double smoothing, there is also triple and higher forms of smoothing based on the same basic principle of resmoothing the base component. For example, triple smoothing may be used when the forecaster determines that a nonlinear trend exists, that is, a variable change in the level per period. However, in all such cases where higher order smoothing might be used, it is also true that a more appropriate model might simply be chosen to fit the time series more closely. Then single smoothing of the parameters of that model may be sufficient. Nonetheless, the interested reader may examine more technical details of higher order smoothing in Brown[2]. (Also, see Chapter 11.)

Adaptive Exponential Smoothing

Adaptive exponential smoothing, in contrast to simple exponential smoothing discussed above, allows for adaptation of the forecasting model coefficients (components) at a *variable* rather than a fixed rate. Rather than the smoothing constant values being set equal to some constant value, they are redetermined each time period based on how the model is performing compared to the actual time series. While many different adaptive schemes have been proposed, the extent to which they will influence the forecasting chain of events is a function of the *magnitude* and *direction* of forecast errors when viewed on an essentially *cumulative* basis. That is, a larger (in absolute magnitude) forecast error will trigger a larger smoothing constant value. The system assumes that a large error means the model is not tracking demand accurately and it should be adapted at a more rapid rate to center back in on the time series. Similarly, if the forecasts consistently fall on one side or the other of the actual demand values (direction, bias), the rate of adjustment will be increased as opposed to a situation in which the errors are not biased. Finally, the above discussion suggests that errors having opposite signs may essentially cancel each other so that little adjustment to the smoothing constant value will be made when unbiased forecasts are produced.

Adaptive smoothing was introduced to counteract the sudden shifts or nonstationarities in real world time series. There are three different types of such disturbances identified from control theory[7]: the impulse, step, and ramp. The *impulse* disturbance is a single observation that is either unusually large or small as compared to the expected value of the time series. It may correspond to a single large order being lost due to a strike at a customer's plant, for example. Generally, it is not desirable to make substantial changes to a forecasting model based on such one-time occurrences, and therefore lower smoothing constants are preferred.

The *step disturbance* refers to a sudden marked change in the level component of demand to a new level which continues for an extended period of time. A business situation mirroring the step change would be a sudden jump in demand for a particular item due to a competitor dropping that item from his line. It is desirable to respond to such changes quickly so as to capture the new business or, in case of a decrease, to avoid overstocking the inventory.

A *ramp disturbance* indicates the existence of a trend (upward or downward) in a time series not displaying a notable trend previously. The ramp continues over an extended period of time and may be exemplified by a situation in which a product does an average level of business for a while and then suddenly takes off due to increased demand. New recreational products frequently assume such patterns. The forecasting system should adjust quickly to such an occurrence to avoid a constant lagging of actual demand. This will be possible, however, only if a trend component is explicitly represented in the forecasting model.

Brown[3] introduced the concept of a "tracking signal" to monitor the forecasting system and cause adjustments in smoothing rates to be made if the forecast error exceeded a critical value. Later, Trigg and Leach[19] introduced a variation of this tracking signal theme which is very intuitively appealing for both its simplicity and automatic control features. The following section details this latter approach, followed by a brief identification of other adaptive smoothing schemes.

Trigg and Leach Adaptive Smoothing

To evaluate forecasting systems, measures of both accuracy and bias are important. Two such measures are the mean absolute deviation (MAD) of forecast error and the average signed deviation (AD) of forecast error. The latter considers the sign of forecast errors so plus and minus errors may cancel each other. Trigg and Leach observed that the MAD must always be greater than or equal to the AD. Furthermore, if the forecasting system is producing unbiased forecasts, the AD will stay relatively close to zero while the MAD will depend on the randomness (variation) in the time series. If the system is operating properly, the *absolute value* of the AD should be small as compared to the MAD. But if forecast errors become biased, the AD absolute value should grow relative to the MAD. It is exactly when such biased results are occurring that the forecaster would desire a higher smoothing constant. Thus, Trigg and Leach conjectured that setting the smoothing constant equal to the ratio of the absolute value of AD to MAD (which will always be between zero and one) would provide an effective tracking signal which would automatically adapt the rate of response of the forecasting system. The details of this technique are explained in Chapter 14, and are incorporated into the forecasting systems presented later in this chapter.

Other Adaptive Smoothing Schemes

While space does not allow detailed descriptions of other adaptive smoothing schemes, a list of some proposed systems is shown in Chart 8-1.

FOUR EXPONENTIAL SMOOTHING FORECASTING SYSTEMS

As is now apparent, many different ES forecasting systems could be chosen for detailed presentation in this section. Those chosen extend to a wide range of practical situations and illustrate several popular and effective ES concepts in a single combination of models.

CHART 8-1. Adaptive Smoothing Systems

Author	Reference Number
Chow	6
Brown	3
Roberts and Reed	18
Montgomery	16
Whybark	20
Eilon and Elmaleh	9

Components of a Forecasting System

To completely specify a forecasting system requires at least initial conditions, a forecasting equation, and the necessary revision equations to update the model. The initial conditions allow the practitioner to compute initial values of the forecast model coefficients and parameters preparatory to using the model. They are generally used only once. The forecasting equation converts the current model coefficient values into forecasts for the desired number of periods into the future. Finally, the revision equations allow the model coefficients to be updated each period as a new datum becomes available.

The forecasting systems which follow employ the initial conditions equations of Flowers,[10] the forecasting models of Winters,[21] and revision systems based on a combination of the concepts of Winters,[21] Trigg and Leach,[19] and Flowers.[10] (Also see Chapters 11 and 14.) As indicated in the earlier discussion ("Components of a Time Series") only level, linear trend, multiplicative or ratio seasonals, and randomness are addressed by the models which follow. Since level and random components exist in all stochastic time series, the allowable combinations of forecasting systems include:

Level random.

Level trend random.

Level seasonal random.

Level trend seasonal random.

The essential elements of each of these systems are detailed in the following Charts, complete with illustrative graphs and numerical examples. Chart 8-2 defines the variables for all four systems and Charts 8-3 through 8-11 contain the equations and graphs of each. Chart 8-11 contains sample numerical computations for each of the four systems.

CHART 8-2.   Variable Dictionary for All Four Systems

A_t = level component estimate as of time t
T_t = trend component estimate as of time t
S_t = seasonal component estimate as of time t
α = Trigg and Leach computed tracking signal
α_A = level smoothing constant
α_T = trend smoothing constant
α_S = seasonal smoothing constant
α_e = error terms smoothing constant
$LL(\alpha_A)$ = lower limit on α_A
$UL(\alpha_A)$ = upper limit on α_A
$LL(.)$ = analogous lower limits on α_T, α_S, α_e
$UL(.)$ = analogous upper limits on α_T, α_S, α_e
AD_t = smoothed average (signed) deviation as of time t
MAD_t = smoothed mean absolute deviation as of time t
$DF_{t,t+k}$ = demand forecast as of time t, computed for time period $t + k$ so k is the number of periods into the future for which forecasts are desired
m = the number of time periods in a seasonal pattern (i.e., 12 months for a one year seasonal)
D_t = actual demand observed in period t
t = number of periods of historical data available

SUGGESTIONS FOR USING SMOOTHING METHODS

Cleaning up the Data

When examining the historical data to be used to compute initial conditions, the user should "massage" the data to make it as meaningful as possible. This is especially true for the high volume important items in the product line. The replacement of statistical outliers (values widely divergent from those normally experienced) which are due to unusual events should be achieved prior to using the data. Examples of such events are a strike at the forecaster's plant which caused no sales in a particular period, or high sales due to a strike at a competitor's plant. The forecaster should simply change such values to ones more in line with normal expectations.

Unusual operating practices may also have to be examined if they influence the data. For example, accounting and billing cycles as opposed to customer order due dates and shipping dates may cause lags in recording historical data so as to make short-term forecasting lag

CHART 8-3. System I: Level and Random Components

Initial Conditions*

$$A_t = \sum_{i=1}^{t} \frac{D_t}{t}$$

$$MAD_t = \sum_{i=1}^{t} \frac{(|D_i - A_t|)}{t}$$

$$AD_t = (0.1) MAD_t$$

Note AD_t is arbitrarily initialized to one-tenth the MAD_t value so as to set beginning smoothing constants equal to the popular value of 0.1.

Forecasting Equation*

$$DF_{t,t+k} = A_t$$

Revision Equations*

$$AD_{t+1} = AD_t + \alpha_e (e_{t+1} - AD_t)$$

$$MAD_{t+1} = MAD_t + \alpha_e (|e_{t+1}| - MAD_t)$$

$$\alpha = \frac{|AD_t|}{MAD_t}$$

$$\alpha_e = [LL(\alpha_e) : \alpha : UL (\alpha_e)]$$

The above expression and those to follow should be interpreted by setting α_e equal to α, unless α is out of the acceptable limits. In that case, α_e is set equal to either the lower limit or upper limit depending on which limit the computed α is closer to.

$$\alpha_A = [LL(\alpha_A) : \alpha : UL (\alpha_A)]$$

$$A_{t+1} = A_t + \alpha_A (D_{t+1} - A_t)$$

actual demand. The forecaster must decide what the correct information should be and then obtain it.

Another problem which occurs regularly is marketing campaigns or other business practices that introduce artificial as opposed to natural patterns in the data. The forecaster must insure that these practices were consistently used in the historical data base (or the inconsistent data should be eliminated from use) and that they will be continued in the future.

CHART 8-4. Graph Illustrating Forecasting System I.

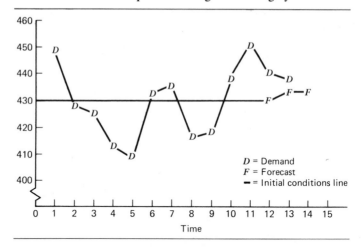

CHART 8-4. Graph Illustrating Forecasting System I.

CHART 8-5. System II: Level, Trend, and Random Components

Initial Conditions*

$$T_t = \frac{(D_t - D_1)}{(t - 1)}$$

$$A_t = \left(\frac{\sum\limits_{i=1}^{t} D_i}{t}\right) + \frac{(T_t)(t - 1)}{2}$$

Forecasting Equation*

$$DF_{t,t+k} = A_t + k\,T_t$$

Revision Equations*
Same as System I; then:

$$\alpha_T = [LL\,(\alpha_T) : \alpha : UL\,(\alpha_T)]$$

$$A_{t+1} = A_t + \alpha_A\,[(D_{t+1} - T_t) - A_t] + T_t$$

$$T_{t+1} = T_t + \alpha_T\,[(A_{t+1} - A_t) - T_t]$$

CHART 8-6.   Graph Illustrating Forecasting System II.

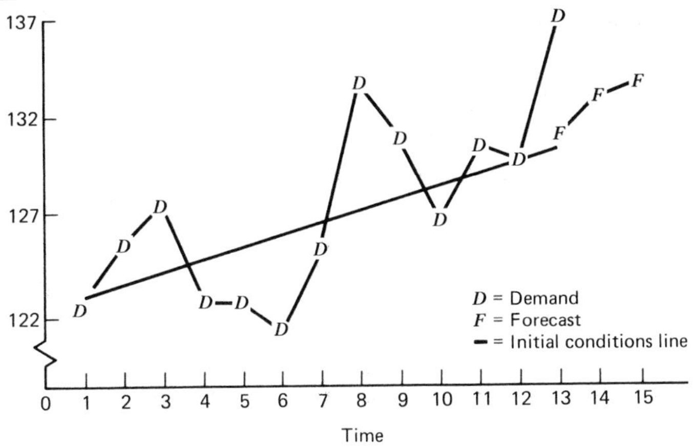

Selecting the Right Model

Selection of the correct model from the four presented earlier is very important to the resulting accuracy. One or a combination of product knowledge, graphing, and experimental simulations may be employed to make this determination. A complete knowledge of the industry and product lines may allow the forecaster to group products into the four systems described above. In addition, simply graphing the data will reveal valuable insights to determine an appropriate model. Such graphing must be done with computer plotters, except for situations with a small number of products. If a plotter is not available, the last of the three approaches may be tried.

The author has developed a series of computer simulation models corresponding to the four forecasting systems which allow the testing of each on a historical time series. The model which yields the smallest forecast error is selected provided that it is reasonable. For example, if a seasonal model is indicated, the seasonal coefficients should be checked for small or zero values as well as very large values (≥ 2). If a model produces the best historical fit but contains inconsistencies or irregularities, it should not be used. Instead, the next most accurate system should be investigated. A final point worth emphasizing is that *when in doubt about model selection, the forecaster should generally opt for the simpler of two competing models.* A model too complex for the time series will introduce irregularities causing larger forecast errors over time.

CHART 8-7. System III: Level, Seasonal, and Random Components

Initial Conditions*

$$A_t = \sum_{i=t-m+1}^{t} D_i/m$$

$$S_j = \frac{D_j}{A_t} \quad \text{for } j = t - m + 1, \cdots, t$$

$$MAD_t = \sum_{i=t-m+1}^{t} \frac{(|D_i - A_t|)}{m}$$

$$AD_t = (0.1)\, MAD_t$$

Forecasting Equations*
$$DF_{t,t+k} = (A_t)(S_{t-m+k}) \quad \text{for } k = 1, \cdots, m$$
$$DF_{t,t+k} = (A_t)(S_{t-2m+k}) \quad \text{for } k = m + 1, \cdots, 2m$$
And so on for $2m + 1, \cdots, 3m, 3m + 1, \cdots, 4m, \cdots$.

Revision Equations*
Same as System I; then:

$$\alpha_S = [LL(\alpha_S) : \alpha : UL(\alpha_S)]$$

$$A_{t+1} = A_t + \alpha_A \left[\frac{D_{t+1}}{S_{t-m+1}} - A_t \right]$$

$$S_{t+1} = S_{t-m+1} + \alpha_S \left[\frac{D_{t+1}}{A_{t+1}} - S_{t-m+1} \right]$$

Historical Simulation and Evaluation

In addition to the simulation models cited above, there are many others available which allow a forecaster to try before he buys. Two precautions should be noted, however, in using such systems. First, the systems should allow for simulating the model on a portion of the time series that was *not* used to fit the model in initial conditions. The results obtained by Makridakis and Hibon[14] suggest that one may "overfit" a model to historical data such that random occurrences may be cemented into the initial model structure. There is no guarantee that a historically good fit will provide accurate *future* forecasts.

Second, the forecaster should have clear objectives with which to

CHART 8.8. Graph Illustrating Forecasting System III.

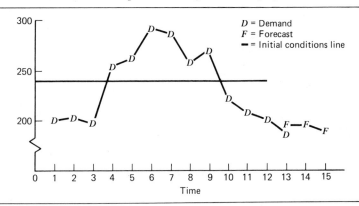

CHART 8-9. System IV: Level, Trend, Seasonal, and Random Components

Initial Conditions*

$$T_t = \left(\frac{\sum\limits_{i=t-m+1}^{t} D_i/m - \sum\limits_{i=1}^{m} D_i/m}{(t-m)} \right)$$

where $t > m$

$$A_t = \sum_{i=t-m+1}^{t} \frac{D_i}{m} + (T_t)(m-1)/2$$

$$S_j = \frac{D_j}{[A_t - (t-j)T_t]} \qquad \text{for } j = t-m+1, \cdots, t$$

MAD_t, AD_t same as in System III.

Forecasting Equation*
$$DF_{t,t+k} = (A_t + kT_t)(S_{t-m+k}) \qquad \text{for } k = 1, \cdots, m$$
$$DF_{t,t+k} = (A_t + kT_t)(S_{t-2m+k}) \qquad \text{for } k = m+1, \cdots, 2m$$
And so forth for $2m+1, \cdots, 3m, 3m+1, \cdots, 4m, \cdots$.

Revision Equations*
Repeat earlier equations from System I and System III; then:

$$A_{t+1} = A_t + \alpha_A \left[\left(\frac{D_{t+1}}{S_{t-m+1}} \right) - T_t - A_t \right] + T_t$$

121

CHART 8-10. Graph Illustrating Forecasting System IV.

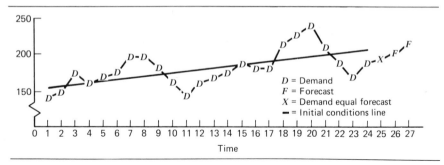

evaluate such experiments. Questions such as accuracy versus bias versus computational efficiency and others should be detailed. The forecaster must also insure that the error measures which are important or meaningful for a particular situation are collected in such runs.

Selecting Smoothing Constant Values

There are no fewer than five methods one may employ to select smoothing constant values for simple smoothing, or smoothing constant limits for certain adaptive systems. These include:

Robust suggestions

Empirical experimentation

Regression analysis

Control theory

Computer search

This selection coupled with the model choice discussed above are the two most critical decisions that will determine the success or failure of smoothing methods. Methods for choosing smoothing constant values may be generally described as "robust" methods or "individualized" methods. Robust methods are those that assign standard values for all items, while individualized approaches determine these values uniquely for each time series. The last four methods listed above are individualized approaches. There is an obvious tradeoff between cost and effectiveness in these two approaches.

Robust suggestions for both simple and adaptive smoothing systems can be found in references 3, 6, 10, 12, and 18. Chatfield[5] criticizes the use of robust suggestions since he found some unusually high smoothing

CHART 8-11. Numerical Examples of the Four Forecasting Systems

System I

t	D_t	t	D_t	t	D_t	t	D_t
1	448	4	411	7	438	10	439
2	428	5	409	8	416	11	453
3	425	6	436	9	418	12	442

t	D_t	$DF_{t-1,t}$	AD_t	MAD_t	α_t	A_t
12	442	—	1.24	12.42	0.10	430.25
13	439	430	2.02	12.08	0.17	431.74

System II

t	D_t	t	D_t	t	D_t	t	D_t
1	123	4	123	7	126	10	127
2	126	5	123	8	134	11	131
3	128	6	122	9	131	12	130

t	D_t	$DF_{t-1,t}$	AD_t	MAD_t	α_t	A_t	T_t
12	130	—	0.43	4.26	0.10	130.52	0.64
13	137	131	0.99	4.43	0.22	132.44	0.92

System III (Note: m = 12)

t	D_t	t	D_t	t	D_t	t	D_t
1	204	4	259	7	293	10	223
2	207	5	264	8	259	11	213
3	203	6	294	9	270	21	205

t	D_t	$DF_{t-1,t}$	AD_t	MAD_t	α_t	A_t	S_t
12	205	—	3.20	32.00	0.10	241.17	0.850
13	188	204	1.28	30.40	0.04	240.41	0.843

Other Seasonals: $S_1 = 0.846$ $S_2 = 0.858$ $S_3 = 0.842$ $S_4 = 1.074$ $S_5 = 1.095$

$S_6 = 1.219$ $S_7 = 1.215$ $S_8 = 1.074$ $S_9 = 1.120$ $S_{10} = 0.925$ $S_{11} = 0.883$

System IV (Note: m = 12)

t	D_t	t	D_t	t	D_t	t	D_t
1	145	7	199	13	171	19	230
2	150	8	199	14	180	20	242
3	178	9	184	15	193	21	209
4	163	10	162	16	181	22	191
5	172	11	146	17	183	23	172
6	178	12	166	18	218	24	194

CHART 8-11.   (Continued)

t	D_t	$DF_{t-1,t}$	AD_t	MAD_t	α_t	A_t	T_t	S_t
24	194	–	2.27	22.66	0.10	209.32	2.24	0.927
25	196	196	2.04	20.39	0.10	211.57	2.24	0.926

Other Seasonals: $S_{13} = 0.926$ $S_{14} = 0.963$ $S_{15} = 1.020$ $S_{16} = 0.946$ $S_{17} = 0.945$

$S_{18} = 1.113$ $S_{19} = 1.161$ $S_{20} = 1.208$ $S_{21} = 1.032$ $S_{22} = 0.932$ $S_{23} = 0.831$

values to be most effective for certain time series, and robust suggestions call for generally low values (≤ 0.3). However, if a user must use at least some robust suggestions, the following ideas seem relevant.

First, if possible, use robust suggestions on class "C" items from an ABC analysis of inventory (see reference 11 for a quick review of ABC analysis). Then consider higher classes A and B more carefully, that is, individually if possible. If time series exhibit low noise (standard deviation of demand to mean demand ratio of 0.05 or less) and high propensity to large shifts or other disturbances, then *higher* smoothing constant values may be desirable. Otherwise, lower values are generally more effective.

If the user has a simulation model for conducting historical simulations, then through simple trial and error smoothing constant values or limits may be obtained for each series. This method will depend heavily on the particular analyst.

For certain models, statistical regression analysis may be used to determine smoothing constant values that cause a minimization of the sum of squared errors for the historical data used to fit the model. Brown[3] describes how such generalized least squares curve fitting may be done.

For specific models and conditions, Brown,[2] Morris and Glassey,[17] and McClain and Thomas[15] have demonstrated how the analytical techniques of control theory[7] may be used to determine smoothing constants that will yield stable forecasting systems. Both this approach and regression analysis may *not* be used in certain situations due to the inability to derive such mathematical results. In those cases, computer search may be used.

Winters[21] suggested the use of grid search to find simple smoothing constant values, while Flowers[10] reports its use in finding adaptive limits. However, Berry and Bliemel[1] and Flowers[10] have demonstrated the superiority of the direct search procedure of Hook and Jeeves[13] over the grid search approach for yielding greater accuracy and more computational efficiency.

Variables Equal to Zero

The forecaster must be careful that certain values are carefully monitored so that they do not assume a value of zero. For example, if α_e in the equations in this chapter should become zero, the AD_t, MAD_t, and resulting α value would never be changed again and the system would revert to simple smoothing rather than adaptive. The entire adaptive procedure would be foiled if α_A, α_T, and/or α_S became and remained at a zero value.

Another problem may occur if a historical demand was zero and a seasonal model is used. This would cause an initial seasonal coefficient of zero, and a subsequent attempt to divide the actual demand by zero (see the next to last equation in Chart 8-7 and the last equation in Chart 8-9). If the coefficient is arbitrarily initiated to a low value, that is, 0.001, to avoid division by zero, and a nonzero demand occurs, very large *unwanted* changes to the level and trend (if included) would result. Thus, some bypassing procedure must be used which leaves the level and trend values alone and changes the seasonal only if a nonzero demand occurs.

In general, the user must carefully examine details of an operational forecasting system to insure totally consistent and complete logic is incorporated to overcome problems such as those above.

New Products

Since no historical data are available for new products, one of two approaches may be used. First, the forecasts may be generated by managers and handled completely independently of the forecasting system until enough data are available for model fitting.

Second, any market survey information and/or analogous product histories may be examined to determine (1) an appropriate model and (2) initial estimates of model coefficients. If this is done, the forecasts should be carefully monitored by management through a stabilization period, and further experimentation for model and smoothing constant selection should be performed when enough data are available.

Other Inputs to the Forecasting System

Some of the necessary inputs to a forecasting system have already been discussed, that is, historical data, managerial override, and new products, but others which would be emphasized are:

Order entry system

Economic information

"Forcing" systems

Obsolete or delisted products

An effective and up-to-date order entry system provides the best basis for forecasting customer desires of any company data base (i.e., sales or shipments). Having such a basis drive the operational system is therefore highly preferred where available. In addition, listing current orders for *future* periods from such a system side by side with forecasts for those same periods provides one excellent source of information for manual overrides of automatic forecasts.

General economic conditions and future expectations of same may make a forecaster want to raise or lower all or part of the item forecasts. An automated mechanism for this process should be provided in a forecasting system. Such a process may allow an *extrapolative* forecasting system to respond as one which would predict turning points due to the combination of the man and computer system efforts.

One technique to achieve the above as well as other adjustments is termed "forcing." Forcing has traditionally referred to mechanisms that cause aggregated forecasts, such as for an entire product group, to be kept consistent with individual item forecasts. This was done by either having one of the two types of forecasts dominate the other or through a compromise procedure. The forcing concept also may be applied to forecasts of the same item from two or more sources. For example, in a recent project, the author developed a routine to allow the automatic forecasts to be scaled up or down to be consistent with the marketing analysts' annual predictions for individual items. This could be done with a simple command for either all products or for a subset specified by the forecaster. This feature is used only when forecasts are to be overridden.

Finally, if the forecasting system is tied to a production scheduling or inventory ordering system, the manager should take care to quickly remove any obsolete or delisted product. Otherwise, more production or inventory may be ordered.

Displaying Forecasting System Output

Care should be paid to the format and readability of reports from a forecasting system. The use of as few abbreviations as possible and the presentation of only the most important information are recommended. For example, users of such reports need the forecasted values, any firm future orders summarized, and an error measure to indicate the reliability of the forecasts. They generally do not need detailed values of model coefficients and smoothing constants. If possible, plots showing the most recent year's actual values with the forecasts for the same periods superimposed, along with the next few future periods, are desirable outputs.

Measuring the Impact of Forecast Accuracy on Operations

An effective forecasting system provides several important contributions to operations. First, there is the generally recognized inventory management effect which is easily illustrated by an example. Assume a company operates on a monthly production and forecasting cycle and desires to maintain sufficient buffer stock to provide a 95% customer service level. This translates into 1.645 standard deviations (SD) of demand given the monthly lead time. The SD is frequently approximated by 1.25 times the MAD. That means for every *one* unit decrease in the average absolute forecast error, we may reduce safety stock by 1.645 times 1.25 or *two* units and maintain the same customer service level.

There are other advantages to an effective forecasting system, however. Customer service should improve in terms of order filling measures due to the proper items being stocked or production in more nearly the proper amounts. Also, in manufacturing environments, disruptions to production schedules should be reduced. While usually not quantified, those who have worked in turbulent production environments will recognize the significance of this benefit.

Finally, a computerized forecasting system operating effectively will save a great deal of managerial and clerical time required to produce routine forecasts for a high volume of Stock Keeping Units (SKU's), as compared to the absence of such a system. This allows such time to be spent exercising a management-by-exception principle to further improve upon the automated forecasts and to invest in other productive efforts for the organization.

REFERENCES

1. Berry, William L. and Friedhelm W. Bliemel, "Selecting Exponential Smoothing Constants: An Application of Pattern Search," *International Journal of Production Research*, vol. 12, no. 4, 1974, pp. 483–99.

2. Brown, R. G. *Smoothing, Forecasting and Prediction of Discrete Time Series*, Prentice-Hall, Englewood Cliffs, NJ, 1963.

3. Brown, R. G., *Decision Rules for Inventory Management*, Holt, Rinehart & Winston, New York, 1967.

4. Bunn, D. W., "A Comparison of Several Adaptive Forecasting Procedures," *OMEGA: The International Journal of Management Science*, vol. 8, no. 4, 1980, pp. 485–91.

5. Chatfield, C., "The Holt–Winters Forecasting Procedure," *Applied Statistics*, vol. 27, no. 3, 1978, pp. 264–79.

6. Chow, W. M., "Adaptive Control of the Exponential Smoothing Constant," *Journal of Industrial Engineering*, vol. 16, no. 5, 1965, pp. 314-17.

7. DiStefano, J. J. III, A. R. Stubberud, and I. J. Williams, *Feedback and Control Systems*, McGraw-Hill, New York, 1967.

8. Dukes, David L. and A. D. Flowers, consulting eds., *Business Decisions*, Texas Instruments, Dallas, 1978.

9. Eilon, S. and J. Elmaleh, "Adaptive Limits in Inventory Control," *Management Science*, vol. 16, 1970, pp. 533-48.

10. Flowers, A. D., "A Simulation Study of Smoothing Constant Limits for an Adaptive Forecasting System," *Journal of Operations Management*, vol. 1, no. 2, 1980, pp. 85-94.

11. Flowers, A. D. and James O'Neill, III, "An Application of Classical Inventory Analysis to a Spare Parts Inventory," *Interfaces*, vol. 8, no. 2, 1978, pp. 76-79.

12. Gardner, E. S. and D. G. Dannenbring, "Forecasting with Exponential Smoothing: Some Guidelines for Model Selection," *Decision Sciences*, vol. 11, 1980, pp. 370-83.

13. Hook, R. and T. A. Jeeves, "Direct Search' Solution of Numerical and Statistical Problems," *Journal of the Association for Computing Machinery*, vol. 8, 1961, pp. 212-29.

14. Makridakis, S. and M. Hibon, "Accuracy of Forecasting: An Empirical Investigation," *Journal of the Royal Statistical Society*, vol. 142, A, 1979, pp. 97-145.

15. McClain, J. O. and L. J. Thomas, "Response-Variance Tradeoffs in Adaptive Forecasting," *Operations Research*, vol. 21, 1973, pp. 554-68.

16. Montgomery, D. C., "Adaptive Control of Exponential Smoothing Parameters by Evolutionary Operation," *AIIE Transactions*, vol. 2, 1970, pp. 268-69.

17. Morris, R. H. and C. R. Glassey, "The Dynamics and Statistics of Exponential Smoothing Operators," *Operations Research*, vol. 11, 1963, pp. 561-69.

18. Roberts, S. D and R. Reed, Jr., "The Development of a Self-Adaptive Forecasting Technique," *AIIE Transactions*, vol. 1, 1969, pp. 314-22.

19. Trigg, D. W. and A. G. Leach, "Exponential Smoothing with an Adaptive Response Rate," *Operational Research Quarterly*, vol. 18, 1967, pp. 53-59.

20. Whybark, D. C., "A Comparison of Adaptive Forecasting Techniques," *Logistics and Transportation Review*, vol. 8, no. 3, 1973, pp. 13-26.

21. Winters, P. R., "Forecasting Sales by Exponentially Weighted Moving Averages," *Management Science*, vol. 6, 1960, pp. 324-42.

CHAPTER

9

A PRACTICAL OVERVIEW
OF ARIMA MODELS FOR
TIME SERIES FORECASTING

DAVID J. PACK

Union Carbide Corporation

I. IN THE BEGINNING

Let us define a *time series* to be an ordered sequence of values of a variable observed at equally spaced time intervals. Chart 9-1 illustrates the monthly time series of U.S. Government three-month treasury bills interest rates from January, 1956 through December, 1978.* Chart 9-2 pictures the highly seasonal monthly time series of the number of enplanements of international airline passengers on U.S. air carriers from January, 1961 through December, 1978.†

Time series forecasting is based on a time series model (implicit or explicit, depending on the approach) that expresses the relationship of current data to historical data. Having seen the enplanements series of

---

*The U.S. government three-month treasury bills interest rates data were obtained from the *Survey of Current Business.*

†The enplanements of international airline passengers on U.S. air carriers data were obtained from the monthly *Civil Aeronautics Board Air Carrier Traffic Statistics.* This series is similar in behavior to an older series used by Box and Jenkins,[2] but it is not from the same source as their series (no longer available) and is apparently differently defined in some way.

CHART 9-1. Interest Rate Time Series

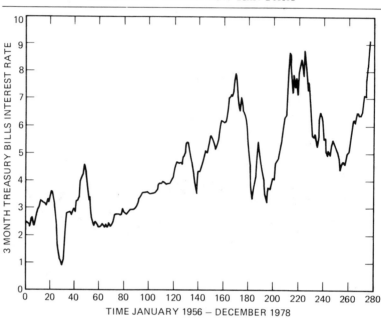

TIME JANUARY 1956 – DECEMBER 1978

Chart 9-2, one might well believe that later values in the series could readily be forecast based solely on earlier values in the series. In other words, a single series model may be quite adequate. The interest rate series of Chart 9-1 does not look very describable by its own history (graphs may, of course, not reveal all)—perhaps motivating one to seek other time series, such as money supply, that may help, and thus a multiple series model. So be it. In principle, time series forecasting (or time series models, or time series analysis) need *not* be limited to a single series, and those who define it with this limitation mislead you.

The decade of the 1970s has seen significant growth of a time series forecasting philosophy and methodology formulated by Box and Jenkins[2] based on autoregressive integrated moving average (ARIMA) time series models. This chapter first illustrates the single series methodology by describing its application to the forecasting of the interest rates data in Chart 9-1 and the enplanements data in Chart 9-2. In both cases, 21 months of data from January, 1979 through September, 1980 have been held in reserve for forecast evaluation. The following commentary then summarizes the Box–Jenkins philosophy and the ARIMA model structure and gives particular emphasis to:

Practical aspects of application.

Forecast interpretation, strengths, weaknesses.

CHART 9-2. Enplanements Time Series

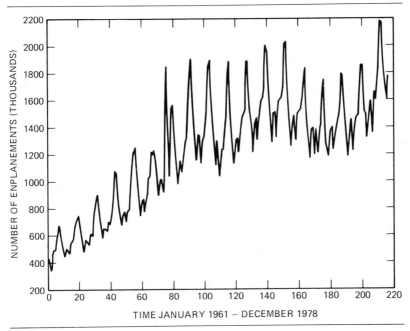

Comparison to other time series forecasting approaches.

The chapter concludes with a brief but strong emphasis on the fact that both the Box–Jenkins philosophy and ARIMA models extend into the multiple series domain. In terms of Chart 9-3, you need not limit your time series forecasting perspective for forecasting the variable Z_1 at time t to the first row of available data, but may employ other variables Z_2, Z_3, . . . at times t, $t - 1$, $t - 2$, ... Recent research has provided practical (admittedly still developing) methodologies for building

CHART 9-3. Available Data Matrix

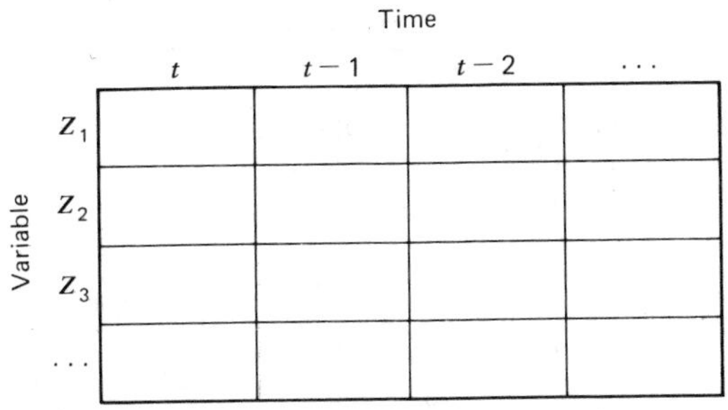

true multiple series ARIMA models—multiple equation models structurally comparable to the typical econometric model—that produce simultaneous forecasts of multiple time series. One can conceive of a long-term ideal in the forecasting discipline where econometric forecasting, which has focused rather heavily on the first column (or two) of available data in Chart 9-3, and time series forecasting, which has focused rather heavily on the first row of available data in Chart 9-3, will merge to become one.

II. THE INTEREST RATES EXAMPLE

What is the best model (i.e., description) of the relationship of a value of the three-month treasury bills interest rate to the values before it? The philosophy of Box and Jenkins says that this model leads immediately to the logical forecasts of future rates, given that information is limited to the forecast series' history. It further says that this model should be built up with the aid of simple summary statistics from the data on hand, rather than be simply assumed, based on abstract theory, or arrived at via relatively uninformed trial and error.

One set of summary statistics is the observed data's autocorrelation function—simply the correlation of the data with itself at time lags 1, 2, 3, ... Chart 9-4 shows the autocorrelation function for lags 1 through 36 of the logarithm* of the 276 observed interest rates in Chart 9-2. Thus .97 is the correlation between the value at time t, say Z_t, and the value at time $t - 1$, say Z_{t-1}, calculated over pairs of times $(2, 1)$, $(3, 2)$, . . . exactly as one would calculate the correlation of two distinct variables X and Y.

The crux of the Box and Jenkins methodology is to be able to identify patterns in summary statistics such as those in Chart 9-4 as being indicative of a particular model. The analysis in this case proceeds as follows:

Chart 9-4 suggests the time series is nonstationary (has no mean), and any model should focus on the first difference series $W_t = Z_t - Z_{t-1}$.

Similar summary statistics for the first difference series given in Chart 9-5 suggest a regression of W_t on some previous W's, although the exact lags to be used are not clearly revealed (combinations of 1 and 2, or 1 and 6, are most likely).

*The reader will note that the interest rate data in Chart 9-2 evidence increasing variability with increasing level—the typical motivation for using logarithms. Actually the logarithmic transformation has little impact on the analysis in this case, as was seen through use of the Box–Cox choice of transformation procedure in Pack's computer program (see footnote on page 205).

CHART 9-4. Interest Rates Autocorrelations

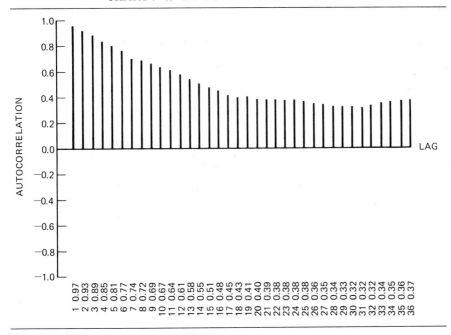

CHART 9-5. Differenced Rates Autocorrelations

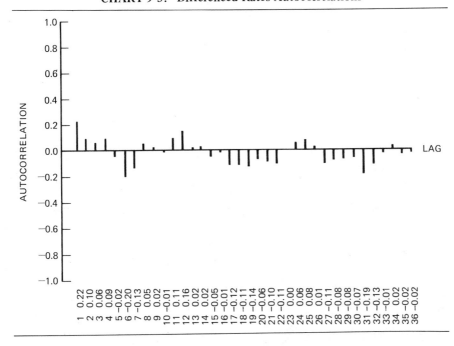

Partial autocorrelations for the first difference series (essentially the estimated coefficients of W_{t-k} in regressions of W_t on $W_{t-1}, \ldots,$ W_{t-k} for lags $k = 1,2, \ldots$) given in Chart 9-6 suggest a regression of W_t on W_{t-1} followed by (compounded by, or multiplied by) a regression of lag 6.

The identified model may be written in terms of W_t as

$$W_t - \phi_1 W_{t-1} - \phi_6' W_{t-6} + \phi_6' \phi_1 W_{t-7} = a_t$$

an autoregression of W_t on W_{t-1}, W_{t-6}, and W_{t-7} involving parameters ϕ_1 and ϕ_6'. The a_t represents the model error term in period t, assumed to follow the usual error term assumptions of zero mean, independence between observations, and so on.

Estimation of the parameters ϕ_1 and ϕ_6' is the next task, and it is accomplished by general-purpose minimization of squared error techniques. Given the parameter estimates, an estimated set of errors (a_t's) can be calculated. The Box–Jenkins philosophy strongly emphasizes a lengthy examination of these estimated errors, and this examination is termed *diagnostic checking*. One asks if the errors appear to be unrelated to each other (i.e., independent), with an average value of zero, con-

CHART 9-6. Differenced Rates Partial Autocorrelations

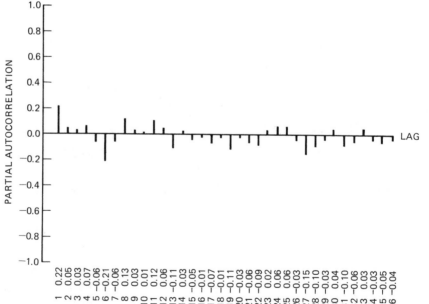

stant absolute size regardless of time, and so on. A primary tool is the determination of the autocorrelation function of the estimated errors, in the same spirit as Charts 9-4 and 9-5, but hopefully in this case containing patternless correlation which is not significantly different from zero. Diagnostic check failures lead iteratively to reidentification, reestimation, and rechecking.

An estimated model that has passed all diagnostic checks is easily turned into a forecasting model. In the estimated interest rates model, the rate at time t is described by

$$Z_t = 1.36Z_{t-1} - .36Z_{t-2} + .24Z_{t-6} - .3264Z_{t-7} + .0864Z_{t-8} + a_t$$

using the estimated $\hat{\phi}_1$ of .36 and the estimated $\hat{\phi}_6'$ of $-.24$. Forecasts for $t = 277, 278, \ldots$ follow by recursive application of this equation, using observed Z's on the right when subscripts are 276 or less, previously calculated forecasts for Z's on the right when subscripts are 277 or more, and the expected value zero for a_t in all cases, since it will always represent future error.

Forecasts for January, 1979 through September, 1980 are shown against the actual three-month treasury bills interest rates in Chart 9-7 (both unlogged). The results are, of course, a disaster! There is no need

CHART 9-7. Forecast (Solid) Versus Actual (Dotted)

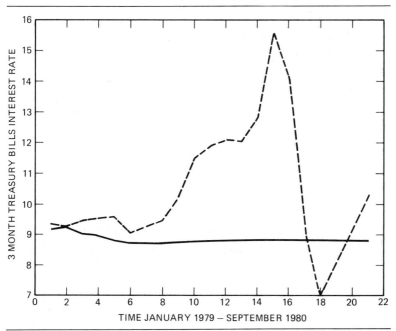

to calculate mean squared errors here to confirm failure! What happened to the interest rate during this period of time *was unprecedented in its history.* Unfortunately this history was the information upon which we based the forecasts.

III. THE ENPLANEMENTS EXAMPLE

The international airline passenger enplanements data of Chart 9-2 present a very hopeful picture for the time series forecaster in that the time series has followed a highly seasonal historical precedent reasonably faithfully for 216 months.

Working with the logarithms of the data,* we can identify a model through the autocorrelation function summary statistics, as follows:

Chart 9-8, like Chart 9-4, suggests one change his or her focus from the nonstationary Z_t values to the hopefully stationary first difference $W_t = Z_t - Z_{t-1}$.

CHART 9-8.   Enplanements Autocorrelations

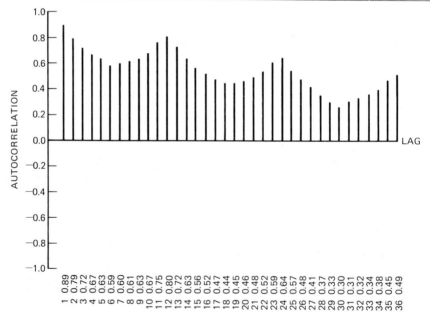

*Logarithms are again introduced, following the line of discussion in the previous footnote. In the case of the enplanements data, the Box–Cox choice of transformation procedure strongly chooses the logarithmic transformation over the original metric.

CHART 9-9. Differenced Enplanements Autocorrelations

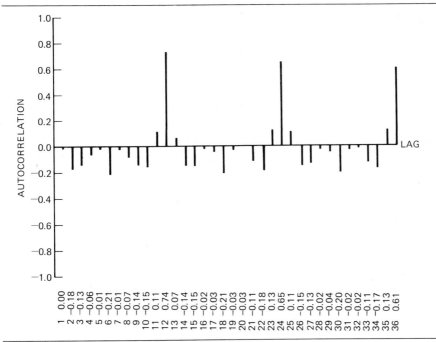

The autocorrelation function for the W_t series in Chart 9-9 implies a further nonstationarity at a 12 period lag suggesting one focus on the further difference $W_t - W_{t-12}$, or, redefining W_t, $W_t = Z_t - Z_{t-1} - Z_{t-12} + Z_{t-13}$.

The autocorrelation function for the latest W_t series in Chart 9-10 contains isolated correlations at lags 1 and 12. This correlation may be most efficiently represented in a model by suggesting that, if W_t is affected by random error a_t, W_t also contains parts of the previous errors a_{t-1} and a_{t-12}.

One experienced with the methodology would probably go slightly beyond the above discussion and identify the model in terms of W_t as

$$W_t = a_t - \theta_1 a_{t-1} - \theta'_{12} a_{t-12} + \theta_1 \theta'_{12} a_{t-13}$$

that is, basically using a product of lag 1 and lag 12 terms with parameters θ_1 and θ'_{12} rather than a simple addition.* The series of W_t's described is loosely seen to be a "moving average" of the random errors.

*The product form is known to produce theoretical autocorrelations for W_t at lags 1, 11, 12, and 13 with the lag 11 and 13 autocorrelations being equal to the product of the lag 1 and 12 autocorrelations. Chart 9-10 agrees reasonably well with this theoretical pattern.

CHART 9-10.   Further Differenced Enplanements Autocorrelations

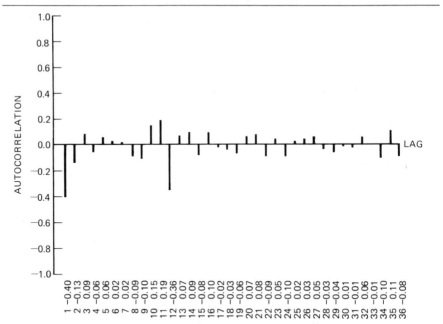

Having estimated the parameters θ_1 and θ_{12}' in the identified model, having diagnostically checked the implied random errors via their auto-correlation function and so on, and having found no problems, we see that the identified model becomes the forecasting model. The number of enplaned passengers in month t (logged) is described by

$$Z_t = Z_{t-1} + Z_{t-12} - Z_{t-13} + a_t - .57a_{t-1} - .96a_{t-12} + .5472a_{t-13}$$

using the estimated $\hat{\theta}_1$ of .57 and the estimated $\hat{\theta}_{12}'$ of .96.

Forecasts for January, 1979 through September, 1980 follow from the forecasting model when $t = 217, 218, \ldots, 237$ as described in the previous example (adding the fact that a's on the right are replaced by calculated errors from the estimation process when the subscripts are 216 or less). Chart 9-11 graphs these forecasts and the actual enplane-ments (both unlogged). In this case the strong historical precedent continued, and the time series forecasts are quite successful. The absolute percent error in the forecasts is 2% over the first 12 months and 4% over the entire 21 month span.

IV. PHILOSOPHY AND STRUCTURE

The Box–Jenkins philosophy of model building for time series fore-casting has been demonstrated through the interest rates and enplane-

CHART 9-11. Forecast (Solid) Versus Actual (Dotted)

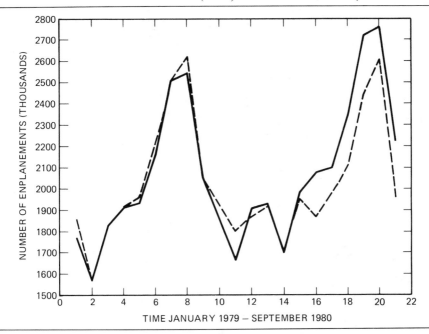

ments examples. This philosophy is expressed generally in Chart 9-12*:

Identify a tentative model using summary statistics (autocorrelations, partial autocorrelations) calculated from available data.

Estimate parameters in the tentative model via minimization of squared error.

Diagnostically check the estimated errors (via their autocorrelation function, etc.). Reidentify, reestimate, and recheck when checks indicate a problem. When the model is adequate, proceed to forecasting.

Chart 9-12 further suggests that the philosophy of model building must be supported by a structure of potential models. Box and Jenkins have employed the general class of autoregressive integrated moving average (ARIMA) models in the building of a forecasting model for a single time series variable. The examples of the previous sections have suggested the three major elements of the ARIMA model:

If the original times series, represented by Z_t in period t, is nonstationary, it may be differenced, say d times, to obtain a new time series, say W_t in period t. This is the integrated element—Z_t may be

---

*Taken from Box and Jenkins.[2]

CHART 9-12. Stages in the Iterative Approach to Model Building

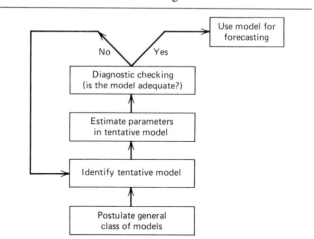

recreated from W_t by a process of "integration" (actually summation in our discrete environment).

The W series (if Z was stationary, define W as the deviation of Z from a mean) value at period t may be autoregressed on $W_{t-1}, W_{t-2}, \ldots, W_{t-p}$, that is, have a pth order autoregressive element.

The W series value at period t may be a moving average of random errors $a_t, a_{t-1}, \ldots, a_{t-q}$, that is, have a qth order moving average element.

If all three elements are simultaneously present, the model would then be expressed as

$$W_t - \phi_1 W_{t-1} - \cdots - \phi_p W_{t-p} = a_t - \theta_1 a_{t-1} - \cdots - \theta_q a_{t-q}$$

where the ϕ_j represent autoregressive parameters and the θ_j represent moving average parameters. This is the ARIMA (p, d, q) model.

The structure represented by the above equation is readily expanded, or limited, in some meaningful ways that should be noted briefly:

Expanded to deal fully with seasonal behavior, essentially by saying the a's from the above equation would follow their own ARIMA (sp', sd', sq') model, with s representing the basic seasonality. The interest rates and enplanements examples both involved this expansion [the former ARIMA $(6, 0, 0)$ where $s = 6$, and the later ARIMA $(0, 12, 12)$ where $s = 12$].

Expanded to imply deterministic trend by insertion of a constant term on the right.

Limited to purely autoregressive models (i.e., $q = 0$). Many people find moving average models nonintuitive, and they can in principle always be reexpressed in a purely autoregressive form. This reexpression, however, often requires additional parameters. Box and Jenkins employ the moving average form because their philosophy emphasizes minimizing the number of model parameters (i.e., seeking parsimony).

V. PRACTICAL ASPECTS OF APPLICATION

The practical problem of applying the time series forecasting approach discussed in this chapter focuses on the suggestion that the user should iteratively build up a forecasting model based on substantial user interpretation of summary statistics from the data—particularly autocorrelation and partial autocorrelation functions like those in Charts 9-4 through 9-6 and Charts 9-8 through 9-10.

The practical requirements imposed by ARIMA model building are summarized in Chart 9-13—with certain qualifications to follow. First, it is perhaps obvious that this forecasting approach cannot be undertaken without appropriate computer software. Such software is widely available for in-house installation, either as a separate package,* or as a component of the latest versions of the major statistical packages (BMDP, SAS, SPSS). It also appears in most time-sharing systems. Computationally, this time series forecasting approach is more demanding than a

CHART 9-13. Practical Requirements for
the ARIMA Model Building Time Series
Forecasting Approach

ARIMA model building computer software	M.S. statistician or a mathematical equal
50 observations per series minimum; 100 observations desirable	100 or fewer separate series to forecast in a short period

*David J. Pack, "A Computer Program for the Analysis of Time Series Models Using the Box–Jenkins Philosophy," available through Automatic Forecasting Systems, P.O. Box 563, Hatboro, PA, 19040 (May, 1978). This computer program has capabilities in multiple series transfer function modeling and intervention modeling, which are discussed later in the chapter, as well as in single series modeling.

number of alternatives, but the demands are very ordinary in terms of today's computers and the broad range of mathematical demands made of these computers.

The ARIMA model building requirement that should be emphasized most strongly is that of having an observed time series of 50 or more observations. In practice, thus, one will rarely use the approach on yearly data—demanding instead observations on at least a quarterly basis. This requirement is motivated by the identification process (*not* the estimation process, where something less would suffice)—getting estimates of autocorrelations and partial autocorrelations of sufficient quality to maintain the integrity of patterns such as those in Charts 9-4, 9-5, 9-6, 9-8, 9-9, and 9-10.

What need one require of the actual forecaster as an individual analyst? Subjectivity abounds in answering this question, but it is clear that this time series forecasting approach does contain a need for the analyst's interpretation of a number of calculated statistics, focusing upon, but not limited to, autocorrelations and partial autocorrelations. Certainly the approach is not for the mathematically naive. Neither does it require a Ph.D. statistician. The description in Chart 9-13 serves as a good compromise—but let no one dwell on a heavy defense of it.

Another practical concern is for the manager or organization that must produce forecasts for numerous products, regions, and so on in a short period of time. ARIMA model building properly done does take time. It is not realistic to think that one can apply the methodology fully to hundreds of time series in a short period of time—unless they are really very similar series (i.e., follow the same ARIMA model). You may survive 100 series, but more . . . ?

There is an important qualification to be added to the requirements suggested by the last two paragraphs (the right side of Chart 9-13)—beyond the subjectivity already implied. In principle, the process of identification, that is, interpretation of autocorrelation and partial autocorrelation functions, can be turned over to the computer, lessening the demands for the analyst's training and time. "Automatic" modeling computer software internalizing the identification process does exist.* While this "checking your brains at the door and letting the computer do it" philosophy is strongly disavowed by Box and Jenkins, it has clear practical value for the manager or organization that hopes to produce forecasts for numerous *similar* products, regions, and so on in a short period of time.

Finally, the practical manager is wisely cautioned to be sure that he or she sees the trees as well as the forest in this time series forecasting approach. The initial graphing and calculation of autocorrelation and

---

*It is available from David P. Reilly, Automatic Forecasting Systems, Statistical Consultants, at the address given in the preceding footnote.

partial autocorrelation summaries of available time series data are simple and informative—whether or not followed by the full-blown ARIMA model building effort. Simply structured autocorrelation might suggest a less sophisticated time series forecasting approach to a manager worried about the complexities of ARIMA model building. Total lack of auto-correlation implies that no time series forecasting approach (at least not a single series approach) will produce useful forecasts, and thus it directs the forecaster to other methods.

VI. FORECAST INTERPRETATION, STRENGTHS AND WEAKNESSES

How does one interpret the time series forecasts produced by the ARIMA model building approach? Let us discuss the forecasts and the models that produced them—with the understanding that, until other-wise noted, the discussion concerns a series of forecasts like those in Charts 9-7 and 9-11, a series of forecasts from *one* time origin that involve no known data beyond that time origin.

The interest rates forecasting model suggested that

$$Z_t = 1.36Z_{t-1} - .36Z_{t-2} + .24Z_{t-6} - .3264Z_{t-7} + .0864Z_{t-8} + a_t$$

Mathematically, the forecasted value at time t is strongly related to the forecast (or observed) value at time $t - 1$, mildly related to values at times $t - 2$, $t - 6$, and $t - 7$, and weakly related to the value at time $t - 8$. The autoregressions present in this model, a "regular" auto-regression through the estimated $\hat{\phi}_1 = .36$ and a "seasonal" autoregression through the estimated $\hat{\phi}_6' = -.24$, are both relatively weak.* Thus, the model is dominated by the first difference $W_t = Z_t - Z_{t-1}$, and the primary influence in the time t value is the time $t - 1$ value. Chart 9-7 showed one property of a first difference forecasting model—the fore-casts approach a constant level for longer lead times. This pattern ob-viously bears little resemblance to the observed interest rate behavior.

The enplanements forecasting model described the number of en-planements in period t as

$$Z_t = Z_{t-1} + Z_{t-12} - Z_{t-13} + a_t - .57a_{t-1} - .96a_{t-12} + .5472a_{t-13}$$

This model includes an extremely strong monthly seasonal component through two elements—differencing between the same month in con-

---

*Each autoregressive parameter in the model is restricted to be less than 1 in abso-lute value to guarantee a stationary system. Absolute values of the estimated parameters close to 1 would be indicative of strong autoregression.

secutive years, and the strong seasonal moving average element represented by the estimated $\hat{\theta}'_{12} = .96$. The first 13 forecasts from a given time origin are influenced by one or more of the random error terms on the right. Thereafter, one can see (by subtracting Z_{t-12} from both sides) that this month's change from last year is forecast to be the same as last month's change from last year. In essence, each month is forecast by a trend line with an intercept equal to the first forecast of that month and a slope that is the same for all months equal to the difference between the 13 periods ahead forecast and the 1 period ahead forecast. As demonstrated in Chart 9-11, this pattern matches the observed enplanements behavior very closely.

The forecast models for ARIMA model time series forecasting should not be interpreted as saying that observations at time t are *caused by* previous observations and/or random errors. The time series history serves as a surrogate for exogenous variables that one might include in a model to represent a cause for changes in the forecast variable (cause can never really be proven in an uncontrolled environment). The potential strength of this removal of exogenous variables is that no forecasts are required for these variables to produce a forecast for the one variable of interest. The weaknesses of this removal are potentially that (1) the surrogate simply contains little or no information and (2) the exogenous variable patterns change so that the time series history is no longer the meaningful surrogate it might once have been. The interest rate forecasts certainly suffer the first weakness, and there is evidence that they suffer the second weakness as well. On the other hand, the enplanements forecasts are derived from a strong and unchanging surrogate.

ARIMA model time series forecasting is particularly suited to short-term forecasting and to forecasting highly seasonal variables. The utilization of quarterly or more frequent observations in model building tends to dictate the short-term nature of the approach. Even in the interest rates example, if one focused on one or two month lead times the forecasts would be reasonably good (if uninteresting because they were not too different from the last observation). The enplanements example was highly seasonal. The ARIMA approach captures not only what the eye sees—the 12 month cyclical upward trend of Chart 9-2 described by $Z_t = Z_{t-1} + Z_{t-12} - Z_{t-13}$—but the potential for momentary change in the trend also present in Chart 9-2 and allowed for in the model by the moving average elements. Almost by definition, the surrogate (time series history) contains substantial information in highly seasonal situations and may allow us to extend the "short term" to 3 or 4 years.

A final set of strengths and weaknesses focuses on the fact that this time series forecasting approach is based on a statistical model. Assuming the estimated model is the true model, one is readily led to the following:

CHART 9-14. Updated Forecasts of September 1980 Enplanements

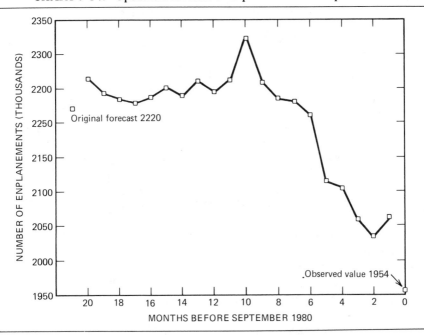

A strength in one's ability to calculate justifiable ranges within which the observed values will fall with a particular certainty (i.e., confidence limits). These limits are presumably conservative in that the estimated model is assumed to be the true model.

A weakness in the fact that forecast errors are often significantly correlated—usually in the positive direction.* Thus, one sees the pattern of Chart 9-11 where the forecasts go above (below) the observations and stay above (below) them for a sequence of lead times (lead times 15–21 in Chart 9-11).

A strength in one's ability to easily and meaningfully update the original forecasts when one or more new observations become available. New observations give you information on random errors (a's) that were originally set equal to their expected value of zero. Chart 9-14 shows the September, 1980 enplanements forecast made based on data through December, 1978 and the sequence of *updated* forecasts as each new month of data becomes available. There is little change for about 12 months. Then the updates begin to trend down toward the finally observed value.

---

*Box and Jenkins[2] discuss correlation of forecast errors in forecasts of various lead times from the same time origin. See p. 129 and pp. 159–160.

VII. COMPARISON TO OTHER TIME SERIES FORECASTING APPROACHES

The previous section's discussion of ARIMA model time series forecasts' interpretation, strengths, and weaknesses should provide some indirect guidance in the choice of a forecasting methodology. This choice would be further aided by more direct general comparisons of the ARIMA model approach with other specific approaches. This section provides some brief general comparisons with a few specific time series forecasting approaches. This section also makes some summary comments on published empirical comparisons of time series forecasting approaches.

Exponential Smoothing, Census II Method, and Other Approaches

There are innumerable time series forecasting approaches, simple exponential smoothing and the census II method* being only two of the more common ones, where the forecasts are produced by exactly the same sequence of mathematical steps on *every* forecasting problem. This is equivalent to the implicit assumption of the *same* "model" (explicit models are usually ignored in these approaches) for *all* forecasting problems irrespective of the evidence in the data. The very appealing logic of the ARIMA approach model identification—that the model should be built up with the aid of simple summary statistics from the data on hand—is ignored in all of these approaches.

Function of Time

Expressing observations as functions of time, such as linear trends, polynomials, sine and cosine curves, and so on, is an often employed time series forecasting approach. Some have termed such a model "deterministic." While from one viewpoint the model can still be called "stochastic" (i.e., it includes an error term), the forecasts produced by the model are deterministic in nature as compared to the adaptable ARIMA model forecasts.

Consider the enplanements example. The original ARIMA model forecasts of Chart 9-11 follow the pattern diagrammed by solid lines in Chart 9-15—individual month trend lines with common slope but individual intercepts. One or more new observations lead to updated forecasts (as discussed at the end of the previous section) which follow a similar overall pattern, but with a potentially different common slope

---

*See the book by Makridakis and Wheelwright.[6] It contains summaries of the two methods explicitly mentioned and many others of the same spirit in terms of the discussion at this point.

CHART 9-15. Original and Updated Enplanements Forecast Pattern

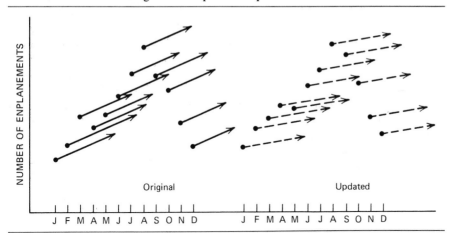

and a potentially different set of individual month intercepts—as suggested by the dotted lines in Chart 9-15. Alternatively, if enplanements were forecast by some sine–cosine curve combination, new observations could not change the forecasts unless one elected to totally reestimate the curve parameters (and even this change would typically be very small in the face of very much historical data).

Regression Analysis

One frequently encounters applications of regression analysis to time series forecasting problems. While regression analysis as usually defined involves two or more variables, and thus is not comparable to the ARIMA model approach as discussed to this point in an overall sense, there is one point of contrast that must be emphasized here.

The ARIMA model approach is directed toward fully dealing with any pattern of autocorrelation (i.e., dependence) that may exist in a set of time series observations. Regression analysis in its raw form does *not* permit *any* dependence between observations of the dependent variable—a dependence that usually exists in time series observations. This dependence leads to autocorrelated errors. Particular procedures, such as applying differencing or autoregression to the observations, have been used to deal with particular autocorrelation patterns. However, general patterns of observation dependence are not well dealt with in a regression analysis framework.*

*There are those who suggest doing a full ARIMA model analysis on the residuals of the raw form regression analysis. (See Pindyck and Rubinfeld.[9]) This would in principle speak to the problem under discussion but it leaves other problems not under discussion here untouched (choice of time lags on independent variables).

Published Empirical Comparisons

In principle, the ARIMA model approach is a generalization of a number of other time series forecasting approaches. Simple exponential smoothing, for example, is known to be equivalent to the utilization of one specific model from the ARIMA class of models. Empirical comparisons, however, have often shown the ARIMA model approach to produce forecasts that are no better than those of the (in principle) less general approaches (see Makridakis and Hibon[5]).

How is this seeming contradiction to be explained? It is explained through examples like this chapter's interest rate example. The reality that all time series forecasters must admit is that many business and economic variables cannot be forecasted adequately with *any* single series approach. When the variable's own history is relatively informationless, as in our interest rate example, ARIMA model building and a less general approach (e.g., exponential smoothing) are going to look the same—*bad*! Informationless series are common members of empirical comparison samples since financial time series tend to be informationless (in the above sense) and they are among the most readily available time series. Know that the ARIMA model building approach is inherently more capable of using information in a single variable's time series history. Know also that there is often little information in this history, and one must turn to a multiple time series approach or a non–time series methodology.

VIII. MULTIPLE SERIES ARIMA MODELS FOR TIME SERIES FORECASTING

The principle emphasis of time series forecasting is on the reasoned utilization of time lagged data in the forecasting process. Those who practice time series forecasting have no inherent desire to deal with a single series, and certainly they do not believe that they can always produce a successful forecast in a single series environment.

Just as the discipline of regression analysis developed over the years through a logical progression of research from simple regression to multiple regression to using dummy variables to nonlinear forms to simultaneous linear relationships to today's complex econometric models, so is the discipline of time series analysis and forecasting developing. Speaking of ARIMA model building specifically, published practical methodology dates from 1970–the publication date for the Box–Jenkins time series analysis book.[2] Logically, published applied research in the 1970's has focused on single series applications, and several additional books have limited themselves to single series methodology.[1,7] Do not be deceived, however. Significant practical methodology beyond the single series case exists today, and continued research is constantly expanding the ARIMA model building scope.

ARIMA models for time series forecasting beyond the single series model exist under the following labels:

Transfer function models.

Intervention models.

Multiple time series models.

While all three of these models involve "multiple" time series, that is, more than one time series, note that the title "multiple time series models" is reserved for a particular model form which is in fact a generalization of the other two forms.

Transfer function models are comparable to simple or multiple regression models in that the model focuses on one dependent (or endogenous, or output) time series to be forecast as a function of one or more independent (or exogenous, or input) time series. The dependent time series' history may naturally also play a part in the forecast. The model form, however, presumes that the dependent series does not influence subsequent values of the independent series—thus permitting a single equation representation. The 1970 Box–Jenkins book provided practical methodology for the one input case (multiple inputs are a straightforward extension if one can presume some sort of independence). This methodology follows the identification, estimation, and diagnostic checking philosophy of Chart 9-12. Identification must logically focus on cross correlation of series with each other—with care being exercised to adjust what is cross correlated to avoid confusion of within-series dependence and between-series dependence. The author has written a tutorial on the methodology,[8] and it may be observed as applied to a sales-advertising relationship in an article by Helmer and Johansson.[3]

Intervention models allow one to represent the effects of identifiable isolated events such as strikes, wars, boycotts, price changes, and so on within the overall ARIMA model structure. Could the slope changes in the enplanements data of Chart 9-2 be associated with airline industry decisions? Could some of the interest rate movements of Chart 9-1 be associated with specific monetary policy decisions? The event is represented by a "dummy" time series assuming 0–1 values corresponding to times of nonoccurrence or occurrence of the event. Structurally, the model is a transfer function model with a dummy input series. The single series model identification, estimation, and diagnostic checking methodology is still employed in principle. However, model identification is complicated in proportion to the magnitude of the effects of events represented, and identification and representation of specific event effects in the model largely rest on graphical or theoretical hypotheses. Wichern and Jones provide a practical illustration in their assessment of the impact of the American Dental Association's 1960 endorsement of Crest tooth paste on the Crest tooth paste market share.[11]

Multiple series models which involve a simultaneous equation structure are placed under the "multiple time series model" label. Suppose, for example, that having seen the failure of the single series interest rate model in this chapter, you determined that a money supply time series might help. Further presume that you wanted your ARIMA model to permit each series' past behavior to affect the other series, that is, to treat both series as dependent (or endogenous, or output). If Z_1 and Z_2 represent the two series, with W_1 and W_2 being respective stationary differences, a model allowing this joint dependence representing an expansion of a single series model with an autoregressive element of order 1 (i.e., $p = 1$) would look like

$$W_{1t} = \phi_{11} W_{1,t-1} + \phi_{12} W_{2,t-1} + a_{1t}$$
$$W_{2t} = \phi_{21} W_{1,t-1} + \phi_{22} W_{2,t-1} + a_{2t}$$

These equations clearly express the dependence of current values of each series on past values of the other series (as well as its own past values) using the arbitrarily assumed order 1 autoregressive element. If $\phi_{12} = 0$ or $\phi_{21} = 0$, there is a one-directional relationship between the two series; this special case has been discussed above under the label "transfer function model."

Extending the class of ARIMA models into the simultaneous equation domain is much easier than extending the philosophy of identification, estimation, and diagnostic checking into that domain. While the latter extensions are still active research subjects, two practical methodologies do exist, each supported by the required computer software. Tiao and Box illustrate their methodology in a 1979 technical report which contains three interesting examples.[10] Jenkins illustrates his methodology in a 1979 book which contains two extensive examples as part of a sequence of examples of single series, transfer function, intervention, and multiple time series model building.[4] The two methodologies differ most importantly in terms of what they elect to cross correlate during the identification step.

IX. CONCLUSION

In conclusion, let us simply and briefly enumerate the major highlights of our practical overview of ARIMA models for time series forecasting:

The single series methodology was seen to work well on one example and poorly on another. Never let yourself be convinced that any one methodology always works.

ARIMA model building for time series forecasting is supported by a very logical philosophy and structure. It possesses a degree of generality and a potential beyond that of many other time series forecasting approaches—but it can look just as bad as much simpler approaches when applied to informationless time series.

The practical requirements of Chart 9-13.

Simple and informative graphing of time series data, and calculation of their autocorrelation and partial autocorrelation summaries—whether or not a full-blown ARIMA modeling effort is to follow.

ARIMA model time series forecasting is particularly suited to short-term forecasting and to forecasting highly seasonal variables.

Because the approach is based on an explicit statistical model, one can determine justifiable confidence limits for forecasts, and the forecasts are readily adapted to new data; on the same basis, one knows that forecasts for various lead times from the same time origin are correlated.

The absence of exogenous variables in the single series methodology is a weakness in that patterns in these variables may never have been captured in the surrogate history, or may change at some point. It is also a strength because these exogenous variables do not have to be forecast themselves.

ARIMA models are not limited to a single series horizon (nor is time series forecasting). Practical methodology exists for building transfer function, intervention, and full multiple time series models.

REFERENCES

1. Anderson, Oliver D., *Time Series Analysis and Forecasting—The Box–Jenkins Approach*, Butterworth, London, 1975.
2. Box, George E. P. and Gwilym M. Jenkins, *Time Series Analysis, Forecasting and Control*, Holden–Day, San Francisco, 1970.
3. Helmer, Richard M. and Johny K. Johansson, "An Exposition of the Box–Jenkins Transfer Function Analysis with Application to the Advertising-Sales Relationship," *Journal of Marketing Research*, vol. 14, May 1977, pp. 227–39.
4. Jenkins, Gwilym M., *Practical Experiences with Modeling and Forecasting Time Series*, Gwilym Jenkins & Partners (Overseas) Ltd., St. Helier, Jersey, Channel Islands, 1979.
5. Makridakis, Spyros and Michele Hibon, "Forecasting Accuracy and Its Cause: An Empirical Investigation," *Journal of the Royal Statistical Society, Series A*, vol. 142, part 2, 1979, pp. 97–145.

6. Makridakis, Spyros and Steven C. Wheelwright, *Forecasting Methods and Applications,* John Wiley, New York, 1978.

7. Nelson, Charles R., *Applied Time Series Analysis for Managerial Forecasting,* Holden–Day, San Francisco, 1973.

8. Pack, David J., "Revealing Time Series Interrelationships," *Decision Sciences,* vol. 8, April 1977, pp. 377–402.

9. Pindyck, R. S. and D. L. Rubinfeld, *Econometric Models and Economic Forecasts,* McGraw-Hill, New York, 1976.

10. Tiao, George C. and George E. P. Box, "An Introduction to Applied Multiple Time Series Analysis," Technical Report No. 582, Department of Statistics, University of Wisconsin-Madison, October 1979.

11. Wichern, Dean W. and Richard H. Jones, "Assessing the Impact of Market Disturbances Using Intervention Analysis," *Management Science,* vol. 24 November 1977, pp. 329–37.

CHAPTER

10

DECOMPOSITION METHODS FOR MEDIUM-TERM PLANNING AND BUDGETING

BERNARD E. MAJANI
Director of Corporate Planning
Aussedat-Rey

INTRODUCTION

Decomposition methods represent the oldest and most commonly used approach to forecasting. They employ simple mathematical formulas to separate the four components of a time series: seasonality, cycle, trend, and randomness. Removing seasonality and randomness gives the trend-cycle curve which, in the author's opinion, is the most important element in business forecasting. The popularity of the methods is reflected in the fact that they are widely used in the business world today.

The trend-cycle curve not only allows the present situation to be visualized within a historical perspective, but it also extends to the user the facility of incorporating his or her own knowledge and intuition into the formulation of a forecast. Other methods, such as Box–Jenkins, may in fact be more accurate; but they tend not to be used by management because their results are difficult to interpret and integrate into the decision making process.

Several publications[1-6] describe in detail the various methods available to decompose a time series. The classical decomposition method is very simple, and all calculations can be carried out manually by a hand calculator. The census II method (and its many variations[7-9]) is much more elaborate, requiring a computer, and is used on a wide scale by governmental and business organizations.

THE CLASSICAL DECOMPOSITION METHOD

To separate a time series into its four components, the simplest procedure is as follows:

1. Calculate a moving average based on the length of seasonality: 12 terms moving average for yearly seasonality, three terms for quarterly data, and so on.

2. Divide the actual data by the corresponding moving average value. This provides the seasonality ratios.

3. Remove randomness from the seasonality ratios by averaging corresponding values. Thus, all January ratios are averaged together, all February ratios are averaged together, and so on. These averages represent the coefficients of seasonality.

4. Divide the original data by the coefficient of seasonality to obtain the deseasonalized series. Such series still include the three other components: trend, cycle, and randomness.

5. Remove randomness. This is accomplished by computing a three or five terms moving average of the deseasonalized values. This moving average series is called the *trend-cycle series*.

These few steps suffice to obtain a fairly smooth curve of the trend-cycle components. Two additional operations will improve it:

1. Center the moving average (i.e., put it in the middle of the averaged N data values) in step 1 above, when the number of average terms is even. When the length of seasonality is odd, the average is automatically "centered."

2. Use a medial average ratio in step 3. This is done simply by removing the highest and the lowest value before averaging the ratio of seasonality. Removing the outliers will result in greater stability of the seasonality coefficient.

THE CENSUS II METHOD

The census II method was developed in 1955 by the Bureau of Census of the U.S. Department of Commerce. Drawing on the empirical evidence accumulated through tens of thousands of deseasonalized series, the Bureau of Census has greatly improved the classical decomposition method, designing tests to verify the accuracy of the decomposition process.

To improve on the classical method, the Bureau of Census discovered a means of separating one by one the four components of a time series—seasonality, trend, cycle, and randomness—and recommended a method of correcting the original series for trading days.

Trading Days Adjustment

Excluding the month of February, any month can have as many as five, or as few as four, Saturdays and Sundays. This can represent an additional variation in the data of up to 10% and has to be corrected prior to deseasonalization. To adjust for trading days, the original data are multiplied by the ratio between the number of trading days corresponding to each month, and the average of trading days is found for the same month throughout the years.

Removal of Randomness

The deseasonalized series include trend, cycle, and some randomness. To avoid removing randomness at this stage, the census method calculates a very smooth trend-cycle series from the deseasonalized values. This is generally achieved using a Henderson weighted moving average. The original data are subsequently divided by the Henderson series. This operation removes the trend cycle components from the original series, leaving only seasonality and randomness in the data. Randomness can, at this point, be removed with greater accuracy as the data are not encumbered by the presence of the trend-cycle component.

Other Improvements

Several other steps are incorporated in the census method in order to secure better seasonality coefficients. These include a procedure to replace extreme values in the ratio of actual to moving average values and a method to replace the lost data at the beginning and end of the series.

Testing the Accuracy of Decomposition

To determine whether or not the decomposition process has been successful, the Bureau of Census has devised three tests: the adjacent month test, the January test, and the equality test.

The Adjacent Month Test

The census method calculates the ratio between the deseasonalized values and their adjacent months' average. Empirical evidence shows that the overall average of these ratios for a given month should be between 95 and 105 for the deseasonalization process to be adequate.

The January Test

This test, which was conceived to ensure that the deseasonalized data do not include any intra-year seasonality, involves computing the ratio between each month of any given year and the corresponding January value. A plot of these monthly ratios will reveal that there is no seasonality if the ratios are random. If there is a pattern in the ratios, it will be shown from one year to the next, as is the case in Chart 10-1. This graph represents the January test values for the years 1974 and 1975 for electricity consumption in France. This widely used time series experienced a major seasonality change after the 1973 oil price rise, which was easily detected by the January test (see Chart 10-1).

The Equality Test

The purpose of this test is to detect any overadjustment arising from the census process itself. Such a discrepancy may occur in the final deseasonalized series. A ratio of the final to the preliminary deseasonalized series will reveal whether or not the data were overadjusted. Experience has shown that these ratios should neither fall below 90, nor rise above 110.

Statistics

The census II method of decomposition provides many interesting and useful statistics, of which the percentage change figures are of particular benefit to the forecaster. The monthly percentage change is calculated for the four major series: the original, deseasonalized, trend-cycle, and randomness series. A browse through these percentage change series will reveal the largest percentage changes, which can then be rectified after detection of the reason for the discrepancy. The overall percentage changes for these four series, which measure the magnitude of each component, are also available.

For the French printing paper series shown in Chart 10-4, these average percentage changes are:

Original series, 25.13%

Seasonally adjusted series, 5.96%

Randomness component, 5.71%

The percentage change in randomness (5.71%) indicates the maximum

CHART 10-1. French Consumption of Electricity—Ratios to Preceding January

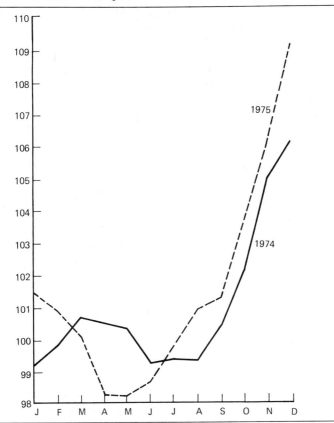

accuracy to be anticipated with this series. The percentage change difference between the seasonally-adjusted series (5.96%) and the original one (25.13%) measures the improvement derived from deseasonalization. This difference is 19.17 (25.13% − 5.96%); thus the seasonality factor represents 76.3% of all variations in the data. The trend cycle variations represent 0.25% (5.96% − 5.71%). Seasonality is therefore the most important factor. It explains the significance and appropriateness of decomposition, as well as the interest of practitioners in this approach.

The Months for Cyclical Dominance Trend-Cycle Curve

As the number of terms included in a moving average series increases, the curve obtained becomes smoother. Conversely, if more terms are included in a moving average series, then a corresponding number of terms are lost at the end of the series.

According to the census method, the number of terms in the moving average trend-cycle series should be the minimum required to permit the trend-cycle to "dominate" the randomness component. The number of months for cyclical dominance (MCD) is obtained simply by dividing the percentage change average of the Henderson weighted moving average series by the percentage change average of the randomness component. More often than not, the number of months for cyclical dominance will be comprised between 3 and 5, and only one or two terms will have to be filled in at the end of most series.

TREND AND CYCLE ANALYSIS

Past events are in fact recorded in time series, but most of them are fleeting changes linked to seasonality and randomness. These must be removed from the series in order to analyze the recent past. When this has been accomplished, the trend-cycle and trend curve are obtained. These curves, together with a thorough cycle analysis, provide a sound basis for making forecasts.

The Trend-Cycle

The trend-cycle curve, obtained from decomposition methods, is a great improvement over the original series, as original data do not provide a good description of the actual state of business. The reason for this is that they are affected by such factors as seasonality and randomness, which thus makes their interpretation difficult. In Chart 10-2, the original monthly values of newsprint consumption in France have been plotted. Seasonality and randomness dominate the pattern and render it incomprehensible. Chart 10-3, on the other hand, exhibits the trend-cycle series which was obtained from the same original data used to plot Chart 10-2. Such a curve illustrates the evolution of the business, and it can become the basis for forecasting the cycle of newsprint consumption in France.

The use of other approaches, in the attempt to understand the recent past, can often be misleading. A common practice, for instance, is to compare a particular month's outcome with its equivalent value from the preceding year. This procedure attempts to elicit a measure of past events that is unaffected by seasonality, but such an approach is both incomplete and unsound. For example, the previous year's results may have been affected by a high degree of randomness, or the figure might have been a high or low point in a short-lived cycle; similarly, the equivalent months of two consecutive years may not have the same number of working days; and so forth.

Another inadvisable approach, which is often used to avoid deseason-

CHART 10-2. French Newsprint Consumption (Original Data)

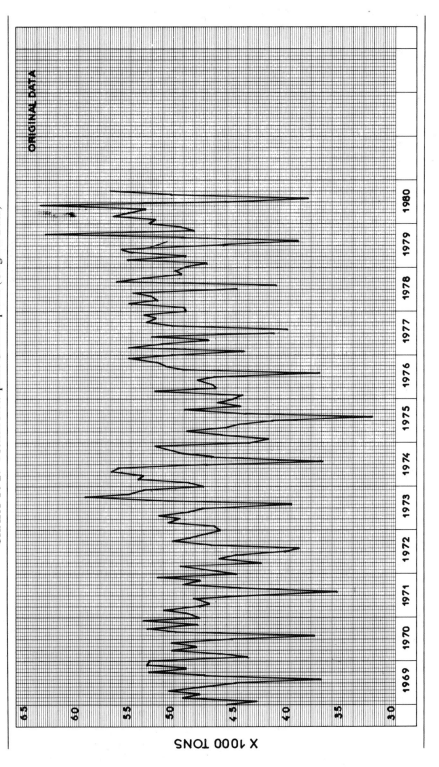

159

CHART 10-3. French Newsprint Consumption (Trend Cycle)

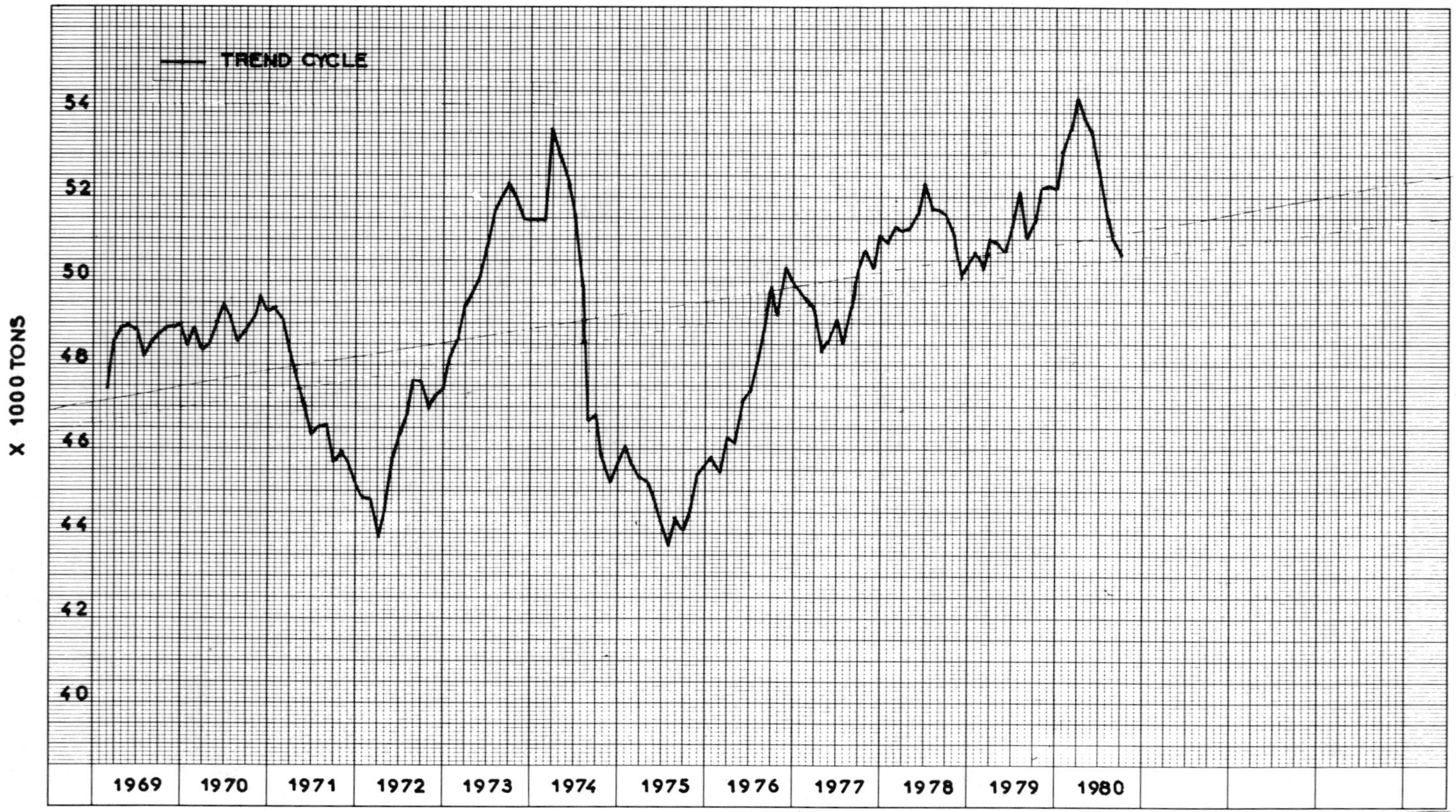

alization, is to prepare a 12 month moving average of, say, the monthly series to be analyzed. Such a procedure deseasonalizes the data but lags the actual data by about 6 months, since the moving average—by definition—refers to the middle value of the data.

The Trend

To complete the decomposition process, it is possible to separate the trend-cycle series into its two components: trend *and* cycle. The trend is usually calculated separately and plotted on the same graph along the trend-cycle curve. This is done in Chart 10-4 for the French printing paper industry. The trend curve indicates the prevailing direction of the series, and the cycle can then be seen more clearly.

Mathematically, many formulas can be used to represent theoretical trends. In practice, linear and exponential trends are, as far as business data are concerned, the most common. Exponential trend fitting is, in the author's experience, the most frequently used, as it is more natural to express growth in percentage terms to allow comparison between series. Great care should be taken in calculating the trend of a series. Any error in this process will repeat itself from period to period, becoming increasingly prominent with exponential trends.

Chart 10-4 illustrates the monthly trend in the French printing paper industry. The exponential trend curve has been calculated over the 1964–72 period and extrapolated thereafter.

It appears that the French printing paper business has experienced three recessions. These were: mild in 1969, serious in 1974–75, and just starting in 1980. In all cases, the recessions were preceded by a boom comparable in intensity to the recession itself when assessed in terms of the area formed by the trend cycle curve above and below the exponential trend. There is no mathematical principle that requires symmetry between the areas above and below the exponential trend each time there is a recession, or that states that the recession should follow a boom, and not vice versa. But this is nevertheless an economic fact, and it is believed that the forecaster who acknowledges it will be in a much better position than those who do not take it into account.

It is up to the forecaster to choose the period that is most representative, in terms of calculating the trend. Obviously, to calculate the trend curve of Chart 10-4, both the boom and recession of 1974–75 must be either included or, as was done, excluded altogether. Furthermore, if this trend curve is supposed to be representative of the whole 1968–80 period, both boom and recession should fluctuate clearly above and below the trend curve. Otherwise, a change in trend would be indicated.

Unfortunately, there can be no certainty that the trend will not change, and straight extrapolation may prove quite erroneous. On the

CHART 10-4. French Printing Paper Industry

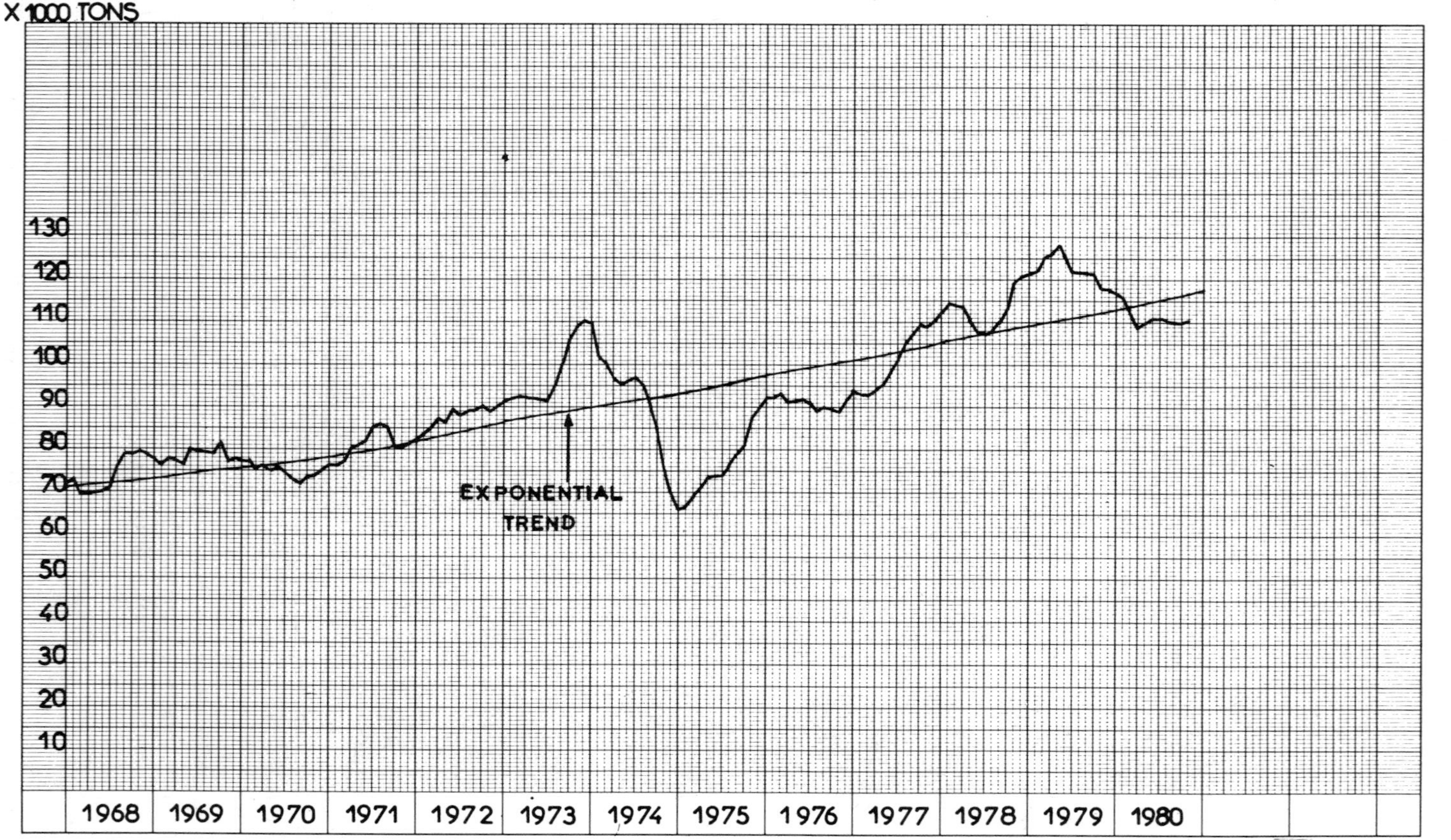

EXPONENTIAL
TREND

X 1000 TONS

1968 1969 1970 1971 1972 1973 1974 1975 1976 1977 1978 1979 1980

130 120 110 100 90 80 70 60 50 40 30 20 10

other hand, the approach just described will allow the forecaster to detect when a change in trend is taking place—the earlier he can do so, the more effective the process will be.

Chart 10-5 presents the French gasoline consumption trend-cycle curve. Three very distinct trends were recorded between 1968 and 1980, the first of these being the old historical trend, which was very regular until the 1973 Kippur War. The sharp price increase that followed this event had two results: an immediate and radical drop in gasoline consumption, and the evolution of a new lower trend. Before the Kippur War, gasoline consumption in France achieved a growth of 7.7% per year. The new trend, right after the war, attained only 5.6%. After further price increases, in 1977, a third trend materialized, and gasoline consumption is now expanding at a rate of only 1.9% per year. Recent price increases indicate a further drop between 0 and 1%. No mathematical means exists that could forecast this abrupt change in trend, unless one were able to forecast the price increase and the events leading up to it.

On the other hand, right from the start, the decomposition method was able to pick up the new trend fairly rapidly. It should be stressed that during 1974, many people continued to measure the growth of gasoline consumption on a monthly basis by comparing it to the previous year—a procedure that was argued to be incorrect. Each month they determined that the drop in consumption (see chart 10-5) was increasing. This, of course, was incorrect since most of the drop occurred during the last quarter of 1973; throughout the whole of 1974, gasoline consumption increased steadily at a yearly rate of 5.5%. This example demonstrates the importance of choosing the proper period to calculate the trend. Furthermore, it would be meaningless to calculate a trend of gasoline consumption in France for the entire 1972–80 period.

CYCLE ANALYSIS

The phenomenon of the business cycle is well established. Between 1854 and 1945, 30 cycles were recorded in the United States, and since 1945 another eight have followed. There is no doubt as to the fact that they follow a recurrent pattern, but unfortunately, it has also been proven that no two business cycles are ever alike. For example, the expansion phase of the American economic cycle has been known to last from 25 to 105 months, and the contraction period from 7 to 65 months. During the postwar period, a full cycle covered from 34 to 117 months.

Business cycles do, however, exhibit some analogy. Chart 10-6 presents a reproduction from "Business Conditions Digest"[10] of the evolution of the 1975, 1958, 1954 business cycles, as measured by the

CHART 10-5. French Gasoline Consumption

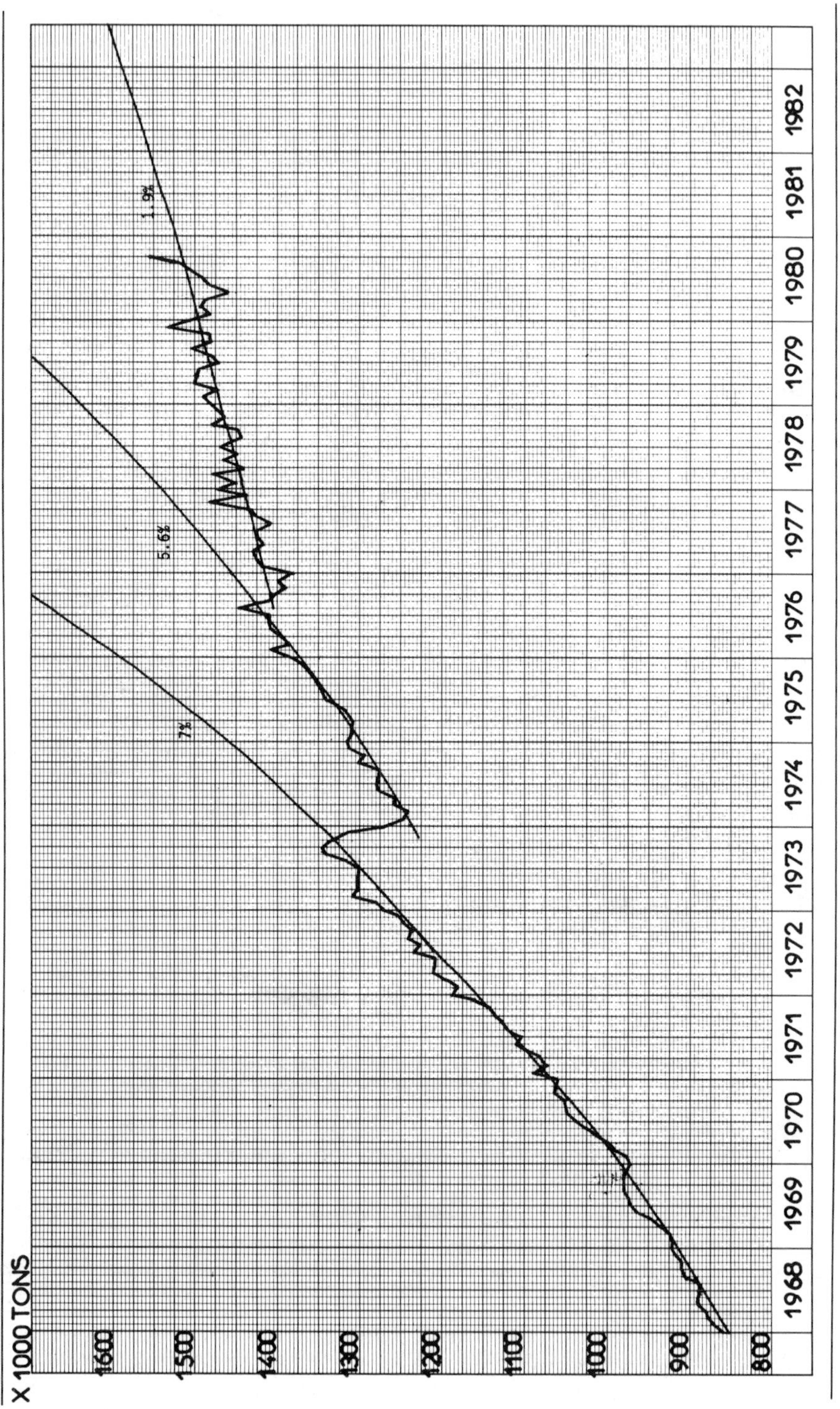

CHART 10-6. Cycles of Industrial Production Index

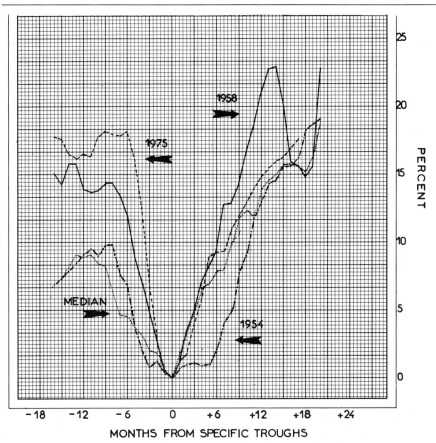

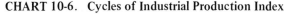

Index of Industrial Production. The median behavior of all business cycles since the war has also been included. Their similarity may be used to analyze business cycles.

Cycles have been extensively studied in the areas of both macroeconomics and business. It has more recently been necessary to step up this research because of the staggering consequences for business life—from both human and profitability standpoints—which are brought about by the switch from expansion to contraction, and vice versa. A forecaster's primary objective is to forewarn the advent of a recession, and he or she should be looking out for signs of this throughout the whole expansion phase.

Even a sophisticated method, such as that of Box and Jenkins, is not able to predict turning points. Makridakis and Wheelwright[1] have reported errors of 5.22% and 5.55% in the mean absolute percentage error (MAPE) of a monthly sales series connected with the French writing paper industry. These MAPE errors were obtained with the Box–Jenkins and generalized adaptive filtering methods for the period prior to the 1974 recession.

When sales started to drop in September 1974, the MAPE increased considerably, as shown in the accompanying table.

		Box–Jenkins %	Generalized Adaptive Filtering %
1974	September	+3.3	+4.4
	October	-7.9	-4.59
	November	-26.97	-19.13
	December	-41.08	-28.87
1975	January	-80.56	-72.42
	February	-88.39	-81.56

Sophisticated methods did *not* pick up this change in the cycle, as is obvious from the large errors during the November–February recession period.

Five years afterwards, a new recession came along; and the same method applied to the same series committed the same type of errors. These models were not able to forecast the major turning points of the series in 1974, and they are still unable to do so in 1980. This time the errors were smaller, but only because the recession was not as steep. They reached 40% with both models, which is much too high a level to allow managers to trust these methods.

To predict a turning point in a cycle, decomposition methods are useful—not so much because of their accuracy, but because of the trend-cycle curve derived from them. As has been shown, it is easy, using the graphs, to determine the position at any given time with regard to the trend and trend-cycle curves. In Chart 10-4, it was clear that in 1973 a boom had taken place, which should have been acknowledged as a warning of an impending recession. In 1979, the boom was less clearly defined, but the trend-cycle curve was well above the historical trend. Furthermore, the expansion phase in 1979 lasted for 4 years—a span of time long enough to provide some hint of a recession.

BUSINESS FORECASTING

It is well known that forecasting is not an exact science. This fact has escaped the attention of neither seasoned forecasters nor business managers. The sole reason for forecasting is to assist managers in making better decisions. It is not surprising that many businessmen are reluctant to use a purely mathematical approach to forecasting, mainly because many managers do not fully understand the advantages and limitations involved.

Forecaster and Manager Symbiosis

Mintzberg[11] contends "that a great deal of the manager's inputs are soft and speculative—impressions and feelings about other people, hearsay, gossip and so on." Mintzberg further suggests that "the very analytical inputs, reports, documents, and hard data in general seem to be of relatively little importance to many managers."

If this assertion is correct, forecasters should actively look for methods that can be easily understood by managers. To be successful in a company, forecasters must be not only accurate but also convincing. The decomposition methods, and the forecasts based on them, have a strong appeal to executives. They are simple to understand and easy to interpret; furthermore, executives can relate their knowledge to past events as recorded in the trend-cycle curve. Finally, executives can incorporate their intuition and knoweldge of forthcoming events into the extrapolation of the trend-cycle. Thus, it is believed that the census method is capable of creating a true symbiosis between managers and forecasters. This is a most relevant factor, which should always be considered when choosing a forecasting method.

BUDGET FORECASTING

Forecasting plays a vital role in the formulation of budgets. Forecasting accuracy, however, is not necessarily the most important element in the budgeting process; management aspirations, optimism, and the political concerns always enter the picture. It is therefore the task of the forecaster to introduce objectivity into the budgeting procedure—to the extent that this is possible.

A frequent ploy is to incorporate an optimistic element into a budget, which serves as a psychological driving force, motivating people to achieve better results. Forecasters, however, must resist the temptation to promote unwarranted optimism; their function is to *forecast* the future, not improve it.

In the opinion of the author, the budgeting process should begin with the presentation of a forecast that takes the following into account:

National economy.

International environment, when relevant to the company.

Demand of the sectors in which the company is involved.

Volume of sales.

Market share.

Price of goods sold.

An elaboration of the information required for each of the above points is given below.

Many companies today regularly subscribe to forecasting services. At the same time, the forecasting department within the organization makes its own predictions for the most important company series. In the particular company with which the author is concerned, the forecasting group produces trend-cycle curves and forecasts—on both a monthly and quarterly basis—of all major series. The budget forecasting analysis includes a separate section for the incorporation of the forthcoming year into the current cycle, from which an attempt can be made to predict the next turning point—even if it is not expected to affect the forthcoming budget year.

This same approach is adopted when dealing with the international environment. A good trend-cycle analysis is generally produced by a combination of the forecaster's intuition and the scientific tools available to him. It should also incorporate the experience and judgment of the company managers, for it is they, rather than the forecasters, who have the most complete knowledge of the business.

It is often difficult to persuade managers to become involved with forecasting. They would perhaps be surprised to learn, however, how easily the problem can be overcome, with the simple use of a pencil, graph paper, and the trend-cycle curve. The author believes that he has persuaded the management of his company that quantitative forecasting is not mystical, nor is it something they cannot do.

The following example illustrates how the trend-cycle approach advocated in this chapter made a significant contribution to the company for which the author is working.

At the end of 1979, the forecasting department of Aussedat-Rey concluded that 1980 would be a negative growth year and predicted a 3.8% drop in the French printing paper industry. The preceding years' growth was as follows:

1979/1978	+9.1%
1978/1977	+12.9%
1977/1976	+9.0%
1976/1975	+22.0%

Average of the four years: 13%

In early October, 1979, when the budget was under discussion, the sales department acknowledged a drop in growth. They suggested a 6%

growth for 1979, based on an average obtained from regional sales managers. At that point, the forecasting department prepared the graph shown in Chart 10-7 (no 1980 data were available at the time). The two solid lines in the year 1980 show the average levels corresponding to the two forecasts (the upper line shows the 6% growth, while the lower one shows the 3.8% decline). On this evidence alone, it was argued that a 6% growth was unattainable. It appeared also, in further discussion, that the sales department did not, in fact, anticipate a much better year in 1980 than the forecasting department. Their estimate was strongly influenced by the fact that during the previous 4 years the average growth had been about 13%. With regard to such a figure, 6% represented a sharp drop for 1980.

The forecasting department later sent the sales trend-cycle curve shown in Chart 10-7 (data for 1980 were not, however, included as this was done in late 1979) to a dozen of their sales offices, asking them simply to pencil in their own estimate of the curve for the coming year. From the resulting graphs, the forecasting department then calculated an average curve. This Delphi-type approach proved very useful and resulted in an average estimated growth of –1%. The method has since been institutionalized, and, in the opinion of all concerned, constitutes a considerable improvement in the forecasting of the company. (Incidentally, the actual decline for 1980 was a little more than 4%.)

Perhaps the most important advantage of this approach is that it brings together managers and forecasters. Both are now able to express their ideas in a vernacular language, to assimilate—with greater ease—each other's reasoning, and finally, to benefit from each other's intuition and knowledge. This factor is of great help in the endeavor to compensate for the less than perfect accuracy of available forecasting methods.

Trend-cycle analysis has also been effectively used in price forecasting. *Economie Papetière,* [12] a monthly French publication aimed at the paper industry, published the graph in Chart 10-8, showing the historical price movement of paper up until 1980. The 1981 forecast (prepared in 1980) is represented by the dotted lines. The bottom line retraces the classical behavior of paper prices during a recession, based on the many factors affecting them. Giving reasons for the decision, *Economie Papetière* forecasts that prices in 1981 will divert from their classical behavior pattern. This use of the trend-cycle curve clearly expresses the opinion of the editors in a visual form and the reader can decide whether or not he or she wants to accept it.

Once the budget and corporate plans are set, they must be monitored on a continuous basis, and time series decomposition is one of the best available methods for that purpose. Presenting the trend-cycle curves from the budget and the actual data on the same graph is the most striking way of measuring what has already been accomplished and what has still to be achieved.

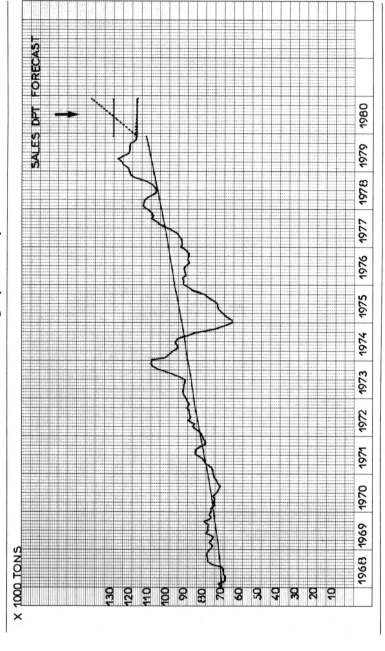

CHART 10-7. French Printing Paper Industry—1980 Forecast

CHART 10-8. Paper Prices Forecast

1970=100

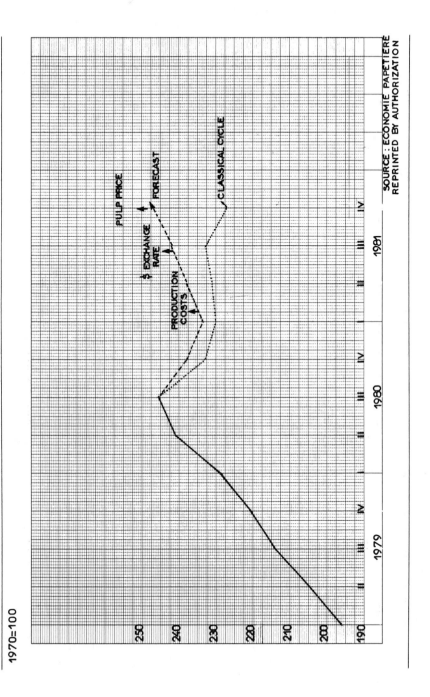

SOURCE : ECONOMIE PAPETIERE
REPRINTED BY AUTHORIZATION

SUMMARY

This chapter has presented decomposition methods and has argued that, as far as business forecasting is concerned, these methods are highly relevant and of extreme value. In the experience of the author, no other quantitative forecasting method can give management the information provided by decomposition methods, which in addition are simple to use, intuitive, and can be used as a means to bring together managers and forecasters.

REFERENCES

1. Makridakis, S., S. C. Wheelwright, and V. E. McGee, *Forecasting Methods and Applications* 2nd Edition, John Wiley, New York, 1982.

2. Burman, J. P., 1979. "Seasonal Adjustment—A Survey," *TIMS Studies in the Management Sciences,* 12, 1979, pp. 45–57.

3. Nullau, B., 1969. *The Berlin Method—A New Approach to Time Series Analysis* German Institute for Economic Research, Berlin, 1969.

4. McLaughlin, R. L., "Time Series Forecasting," Marketing Research Technique, Series No. 6, American Marketing Association, 1962.

5. McLaughlin, R. L. and J. J. Boyle, "Short-term Forecasting," American Marketing Association Booklet, 1968.

6. Organization for Economic Cooperation and Development (OECD), "The X-II Variant of U.S. Census Method II," *Sources and Methods*, No. 15, December 1972.

7. Shiskin, J., "Electronic Computers and Business Indicators," National Bureau of Economic Research, Occasional Paper 57, 1957.

8. Shiskin, J., "Tests and Revisions of Bureau of the Census Methods of Seasonal Adjustments," Bureau of the Census, Technical Paper No. 5, 1961.

9. Shiskin, J., A. H. Young, and J. C. Musgrave, "The X-II Variant of the Census II Method Seasonal Adjustment Program," Bureau of the Census, Technical Paper No. 15.

10. "Business Condition Digest," U.S. Government Printing Office.

11. Mintzberg, H., "Planning on the Left Side and Managing on the Right," *Harvard Business Review,* July-August, 1976, pp. 49–58.

12. Communication Conseil International (France), *Economie Papetière*, No. 4, 1980, pp. 8–11.

11

HIGH ORDER SMOOTHING METHODS FOR SHORT- AND MEDIUM-RANGE PLANNING

JAMES R. FREELAND

*The Colgate Darden Graduate School
of Business Administration
University of Virginia*

Forecasts are useful for planning activities in the operations, marketing, and financial functions. In a recent survey[6] of the Fortune 500 companies, 64% of those responding said that forecasting was critical to the success of their companies. Twenty-eight percent said it was important to their success, while only 8% said it was relatively unimportant.

There are many uses of forecasts in today's business environment. Chart 11-1 illustrates some possible uses for different functions as well as typical time horizons. The *time horizon* of a forecast is how far into the future it must predict. The required time horizon is one of the determinants of the approach to use in forecasting.

This chapter focuses on the use of time series forecasting methods for planning when the horizon is 6 to 12 months. In planning it is important that one distinguish between a forecast and a goal. A *forecast* is an estimate, based on the available information, of what will happen, for example, number of units of product demanded, whereas a *goal* may be an expression of what management would like to have happen.

CHART 11-1. Uses of Forecasts

Type	Use	Function	Time Horizon
Market forecast	Guide R&D planning and facilities planning	Top management Corporate planning	1–20 years
Financial forecast	Estimate future profits, cash flow, and capital requirements	Finance Accounting	1 month–3 years
Sales forecast	Plan sales campaigns, promotions, and other market strategies	Marketing	1 month–1 year
Operations forecast	Plan capacity utilization and inventory levels, schedule production, and determine workforce size and number of shifts	Operations	1 day–1 year

Goals are sometimes used for motivational purposes. However, since a plan should be based on the forecast and typically involves the commitment of resources, it should be based on estimates of what really is to happen rather than what one desires to happen.

Finally, it is important to distinguish between a plan and a forecast. A *plan* is based on three factors: the forecast, the likelihood of the forecast being wrong, and the consequences of over and under forecasting. As an example consider a manufacturer of electronic games who is trying to decide a production plan to satisfy the Christmas demand. Based on historical sales and current economic conditions, an estimate of sales of 100,000 units is made. This is the forecast. The actual demand will, of course, differ from this. Suppose based on historical performance the error in the forecast is felt to be normally distributed with a standard deviation of 20,000 units. If the cost of underestimating (primarily the lost profit margin) is $10, and the cost of overestimating is $30, then the plan chosen should be such that the chance of demand exceeding the production plan equals $10/(30 + 10)$. That is, the area under the normal curve to the right of the planned amount should be .75. The optimal plan is then:

$$\text{Plan} = 100{,}000 - z_{.25}(20{,}000)$$
$$= 100{,}000 - (.675)(20{,}000) = 86{,}500$$

This amount is considerably less than the expected demand because the cost of overforecasting is greater than the cost of underforecasting.

STRUCTURE OF A TIME SERIES FORECASTING SYSTEM

Chart 11-2 shows the conceptual structure of a time series forecasting system. Using previous sales data, the forecaster applies some time series technique to generate a forecast. Since time series methods simply extrapolate the past into the future, it is important that forecasts be modified by managerial judgment to reflect any subjective information that is not contained in the historical data. This can be accomplished by implicitly accounting for new information and manually altering the forecast. (Typically the level of the demand or amount of trend is changed). Alternatively, formal procedures like Bayesian techniques (discussed in Chapters 13 and 14) can be used.

An important and often neglected component of any forecasting system is the continual monitoring of forecast performance. This is done by comparing the actual demand with the predicted demand. The amount and direction of error become important elements for adjusting the forecast generation process as well as for applying managerial judgment.

TIME SERIES APPROACHES FOR PLANNING

The process of developing a time series forecast is given in Chart 11-3. The process begins with the analysis of representative historical data.

CHART 11-2.   Structure of a Forecasting System

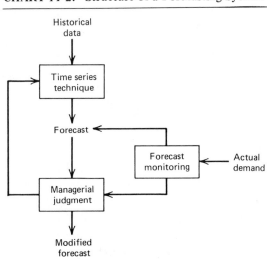

CHART 11-3. Time Series Methodology

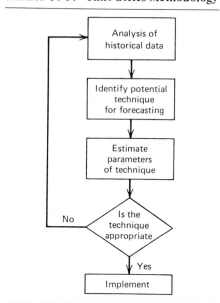

One key to the successful use of time series analysis is to identify the underlying components of the demand pattern. Those components include trend and seasonal variation.

Analysis of historical data assists in hypothesizing the form of the process generating the demand, and thus in the selection of the correct time series method. This analysis is typically done by plotting the data and studying it for trends and seasonal patterns. There are more sophisticated techniques such as autocorrelation analysis (see Makridakis and Wheelwright[5]) which can also be used. These sophisticated methods are especially useful when the generation process has components other than linear trend or periodic seasonality. Trends in the data are consistent increases or decreases in the demand over time. Seasonal patterns can often be identified by noting if the time series repeats itself in some fashion, for example, December having high demand and June having low demand.

Based on the initial examination of data, one hypothesizes a model (or several possible models) of demands, and this suggests a particular method or methods to try. For example, if the historical data suggest there is an upward trend with no seasonality, one might select a technique such as double order exponential smoothing.

The third step is to estimate the parameters (the values) in the formula for the technique to be tested. This is done using the historical data (or maybe only a portion of the history.)

Finally, forecasts are prepared using the technique, and these forecasts are compared to actual demands for some or all of the historical data. Measures of the error such as the mean percentage error or the standard deviation can be computed. Based on this comparison, a decision is made regarding the appropriateness of the chosen method.

There are many time series techniques available. Most of them can be divided into four classes: (1) decomposition, (2) regression, (3) smoothing, and (4) Box–Jenkins.

The Box–Jenkins method[1] is one that is very powerful for forecasting when little is known about the underlying pattern. Whereas in simple exponential smoothing one begins with an assumption that there is a horizontal process working, the Box–Jenkins method starts with a very general family of models and selects the best model on the basis of fit to the data. However, it will also be more expensive to use and requires more sophisticated handling. While presentation of this approach is beyond the scope of this chapter, it can serve in problems for which the methods presented here are inadequate. (See Box and Jenkins[1] and Mabert[4] for more detailed explanations.)

The first three classes are discussed in other chapters of this handbook. One smoothing method which was only mentioned in Chapter 8 and which is often used in practice is Winters' three factor procedure.[7]

Winters' method is an exponential smoothing procedure which can handle situations when trend and seasonality are present. This technique assumes the underlying process generating the demand is given by:

$$\text{Demand} = (\text{level} + \text{trend})(\text{seasonal index})$$

Each of the three factors in this expression is updated by exponentially smoothing new information as it becomes available. At time period t when the actual demand, x_t, is known, estimates for the three factors are updated using

$$\text{level}_t = a\frac{x_t}{I_{t-L}} + (1-a)(\text{level}_{t-1} + \text{trend}_{t-1})$$

$$\text{trend}_t = b(\text{level}_t - \text{level}_{t-1}) + (1-b)\text{trend}_{t-1}$$

$$I_t = c\left(\frac{x_t}{\text{level}_t}\right) + (1-c)I_{t-L}$$

where a, b, and c are the smoothing constants (numbers between 0 and 1), I_t is the seasonal factor for period t, and L is the length of the seasonal cycle. The forecast equation computed at the end of period t for k ($k = 1, 2, \ldots$) periods into the future is

$$\text{Forecast}_{t+k} = (\text{level}_t + k\,\text{trend}_k)\,I_{t-L+k}$$

Typical ranges for the smoothing constants will vary depending on the nature of the demand being forecast. For each smoothing constant the larger the value, the more weight that is placed on the most recent observation. For example, Winters[7] found the following weights gave the best results:

Item Being Forecast	a	b	c
Cooking utensils	.2	.2	.6
Paint	.2	.4	.4
Prefab homes	.4	.0	.0

In general, if the best value of a or b is greater than .5, one should probably question the validity of using Winters' model. Higher values for c are not unexpected since the seasonal factors are revised only once per season.

For an example, consider an insurance company that is interested in forecasting the number of claims of a particular type that will be filed during each quarter. It is believed that there is both linear trend and seasonality in the generating process. Historical data have been used to estimate the seasonally adjusted average, $level_0$, as 65; the trend, $trend_0$, as 3; and the seasonal factors for quarters one, two, three, and four as 1.26, .93, .54, and 1.27. The smoothing constants—a, b, and c—are set equal to .45, .05, and .05 respectively. It has been decided to set the present as $t = 0$; therefore forecasts for quarters one through four would be given by

$$F_1 = (level_0 + trend_0)I_{1-4} = (65 + 3)1.26 = 85.68$$
$$F_2 = (level_0 + 2\ trend_0)I_{2-4} = [65 + (2)3].93 = 66.03$$
$$F_3 = (level_0 + 3\ trend_0)I_{3-4} = [65 + (3)3].54 = 39.96$$
$$F_4 = (level_0 + 4\ trend_0)I_{4-4} = [65 + (4)3]\ 1.27 = 97.79$$

Suppose the demand in quarter one is actually 80. Each of the three factors would be updated in the following manner:

$$level_1 = a\frac{x_1}{I_{1-4}} + (1 - a)(level_0 + trend_0) = .45\frac{80}{1.26} + .55(65 + 3)$$
$$= 66$$

$$trend_1 = b(level_1 - level_0) + (1 - b)trend_0$$
$$= .05(66 - 65) + .95(3) = 2.9$$

$$I_1 = c\frac{x_1}{level_1} + (1 - c)I_{1-4}$$

$$= .05\frac{80}{60} + .95(1.26) = 1.26$$

Thus, if one were to forecast for the next four quarters at the end of quarter one, one obtains

$$F_2 = (\text{level}_1 + \text{trend}_1)I_{2-4} = (66 + 2.9).93 = .64$$
$$F_3 = (\text{level}_1 + 2\ \text{trend}_1)I_{3-4} = 38.77$$
$$F_4 = (\text{level}_1 + 3\ \text{trend}_1)I_{4-4} = 94.87$$
$$F_5 = (\text{level}_1 + 4\ \text{trend}_1)I_{5-4} = (66 + 42.9)1.26 = 97$$

The reader should note that by setting the initial factors and smoothing constants at appropriate values, one can make Winters' method the same as single or trend adjusted exponential smoothing.

AN APPLICATION OF TIME SERIES METHODS IN PLANNING

In this section an application of time series forecasting to the problem of aggregate planning is discussed. The aggregate planning problem is an important one to many companies that face a seasonal demand for their products. The problem is to determine what mix of production strategies (regular time, overtime, hiring and layoffs, and inventory) to use in order to satisfy demands over the next 6–12 months.

The Carswell Cabinet Company[3] produces a variety of kitchen cabinets for the remodeling and new construction markets. The demand for their products has historically shown a regular seasonal pattern, with high demand in April and in July to October and low demands in the winter months. Using 5 years of historical demand Winters' technique was used to generate a forecast of aggregate cabinet demand. Chart 11-4 shows the monthly forecasts for November 1979 thru October 1980. When Winters' model was used to predict demand historically, its average actual value divided by the forecast value (A/F) was close to 1. The standard deviation of the A/F values $(\sigma_{A/F})$ was .17. These measures of previous errors can be used to generate buffer stocks to handle larger than forecast demands. If one assumes that the A/F actual divided by forecast) values are approximately normally distributed, and that a 95% service level* is desired, the amount of buffer stock required in month t is

$$z_{.95}\sigma_{A/F}F_t.$$

*Defined as the probability of not stocking out in any given month.

**CHART 11-4.   Monthly Forecasts for
November 1979 through October 1980**

Month	Forecast
1979	
November	49,117
December	43,556
1980	
January	57,523
February	43,290
March	48,372
April	60,105
May	50,880
June	58,390
July	58,534
August	63,217
September	69,755
October	56,953

For example, for January this is

$$1.645(.17)(57523) = 16,086$$

Chart 11-5 shows the buffer requirements necessary to provide a 95% service level. Thus Carswell's problem is to determine how to meet the demands and buffer stock requirements given in Charts 11-4 and 11-5.

**CHART 11-5.   Buffer Stock
Requirements**

November	13,736
December	12,180
January	16,086
February	12,106
March	13,527
April	16,808
May	14,229
June	16,329
July	16,369
August	17,669
September	19,507
October	15,927

CHART 11-6. Costs and Initial Conditions at Carswell

Present production rate (units/day)	2585
Present inventory (units)	9245
Plant capacity without overtime (units/day)	4400
Manufactured cost/unit ($)	25.31
Direct labor as a % of manufactured cost	32
Wage rate ($/hour)	4.82
Annual inventory carrying cost (%/year)	37
Penalty rate for neg. inventory (%/month)	20
Hiring cost/employee ($)	570
Layoff cost/employee ($)	200
Labor efficiency (%) for:	
41–48 hours	75
48–56 hours	65
Overtime premium (%) for:	
41–48 hours	50
48–56 hours	50
New employee efficiency (%):	
First month	75
Second month	90
Third month	100

Month	Number of Production Days
November	15
December	19
January	22
February	21
March	21
April	22
May	21
June	20
July	22
August	21
September	21
October	23

Carswell had identified the relevant costs associated with hiring, layoff, and so on. These along with the production rate and inventory levels existing at the end of October 1979 are given in Chart 11-6.

Given any plan to satisfy the demands, it is possible to compute the costs associated with it. Chart 11-7 shows a summary of the minimal cost plan using linear programming. The solution involves laying off four workers in December and hiring 48 workers in May.

Now suppose as in the Carswell case that management feels strongly that a recession will depress the demand in the last part of 1980. Time

CHART 11-7. Linear Programming Solution for Aggregate Planning Problem

Month	Regular Production (units/day)	Overtime Production (units/day)	Total Production (units/day)	Seasonal Inventory	Number of Workers	Change in Workers
Nov.	2585.20	0.00	2585.20	-1,720	543	0
Dec.	2564.61	0.00	2564.61	5,008	539	-4
Jan.	2564.61	0.00	2564.61	0	539	0
Feb.	2564.61	0.00	2564.61	14,547	539	0
March	2564.61	0.00	2564.61	18,611	539	0
April	2564.61	0.00	2564.61	11,646	539	0
May	2737.61	0.00	2737.61	20,834	587	48
June	2772.19	0.00	2772.19	15,788	587	0
July	2795.25	0.00	2795.25	18,710	587	0
Aug.	2795.25	0.00	2795.25	12,883	587	0
Sept.	2795.25	0.00	2795.25	0	587	0
Oct.	2795.25	0.00	2795.25	10,918	587	0

Average seasonal (positive) inventory level = 10,745

Incremental Cost Analysis

Seasonal inventory costs	100,624
Overtime costs	0
Production level change costs	28,160
Negative inventory penalty costs	8,707
Cost of subcontracting	0
Costs associated with idle time	0
Total costs (sum of above)	137,491

series forecasting being simply an extrapolation of historical data does not account for this possibility. However, subjectively suppose management feels that demand may be 40% lower starting in June. Thus, the forecasts for June through October of 1980 can be revised downward as shown in Chart 11-8.

After revising the buffer stocks to reflect the new forecast, a linear programming solution for the aggregate planning problem can be found (see Chart 11-9).

With depressed demands in the latter part of 1980 the optimal plan calls for layoffs in December, February, May, and June. In comparing the solutions in Charts 11-7 and 11-9, one notes that there is no difference until February. With depressed demands a layoff of 38 in February should be implemented. Since the plans for the first 3 months are the

CHART 11-8. Revised Demands and Buffer Stocks for Carswell Cabinet

Month	Demand	Buffer Stock
June	35,034	9,797
July	35,120	9,821
August	37,930	10,607
September	41,853	11,704
October	34,172	9,556

CHART 11-9. Linear Programming Solution with Depressed Demands

Month	Regular Production (units/day)	Overtime Production (units/day)	Total Production (units/day)	Seasonal Inventory	Number of Workers	Change in Workers
Nov.	2585.20	0.00	2585.20	-1,720	543	0
Dec.	2564.61	0.00	2564.61	5,008	539	-4
Jan.	2564.61	0.00	2564.61	0	539	0
Feb.	2382.64	0.00	2382.64	10,725	500	-38
March	2382.64	0.00	2382.64	10,968	500	0
April	2382.64	0.00	2382.64	0	500	0
May	2300.05	0.00	2300.05	0	483	-17
June	1754.91	0.00	1754.91	4,496	369	-115
July	1754.90	0.00	1754.90	7,960	369	0
Aug.	1754.91	0.00	1754.91	6,097	369	0
Sept.	1754.91	0.00	1754.91	0	369	0
Oct.	1754.91	0.00	1754.91	8,339	369	0

Average seasonal (positive) inventory level = 4,466

Incremental Cost Analysis

Seasonal inventory costs	41,824
Overtime costs	0
Production level change costs	34,800
Negative inventory penalty costs	8,706
Cost of subcontracting	0
Costs associated with idle time	0
Total costs (sum as above)	85,330

same, Carswell can hold off on making any decision until February based on the possibility of a downturn in 1980.

SUMMARY

This chapter has discussed how time series forecasting can be used for planning. A key point was that applying time series forecasting to historical demands allows one to develop a probability distribution of errors, which can be useful in future planning.

REFERENCES

1. Box, G. E. P. and G. M. Jenkins, *Time Series Analysis Forecasting and Control*, Holden-Day, San Francisco, 1976.

2. Brown, R. G., *Smoothing, Forecasting and Prediction of Discrete Time Series*, Prentice-Hall, Englewood Cliffs, NJ, 1963.

3. Carswell Cabinet Company (A), University of Virginia Case, UVA-OM-268, Darden School, written by L. Shepley Herman and Robert D. Landel, 1980.

4. Mabert, Vincent, *An Introduction to Short Term Forecasting Using the Box-Jenkins Methodology*, American Institute of Industrial Engineers, Atlanta, Georgia, 1975.

5. Makridakis, S., S. C. Wheelwright, and V. E. McGee, *Forecasting: Methods and Applications*, 2nd ed., John Wiley, New York, 1982.

6. Wheelwright, S. C. and D. G. Clarke, "Corporate Forecasting: Promise and Reality," *Harvard Business Review,* November-December, 1976, pp. 40-68.

7. Winters, P. R., "Forecasting Sales by Exponentially Weighted Moving Averages," *Management Science*, vol. 6, no. 3, 1960, pp. 324-42.

CHAPTER

12

ECONOMETRIC METHODS FOR MANAGERIAL APPLICATIONS

A. AYKAÇ

INSEAD, European Institute of Business Administration

A. BORGES

INSEAD, European Institute of Business Administration

I. WHY USE ECONOMETRIC FORECASTING?

There seems to be a preconception among many users of forecasts, as well as forecasters, that econometric forecasting requires sophisticated skills in mathematics, economic theory, and statistics and therefore is best left to the specialists. There is some benefit to be derived from having specialized skills, but this is hardly the distinguishing feature of applied econometric work.

The most obvious differences among various forecasting techniques lies in the extent to which the forecaster is forced to articulate and formalize his or her views on the phenomena being forecasted and the procedures utilized. In principle, the use of econometric techniques in forecasting is the most demanding in terms of such articulation and formalization. At one extreme, expert opinion takes into account several determinants of the variable being forecasted, but the way in which these determinants interact and their respective weights are generally poorly articulated and sometimes inconsistent.* Time series methods, on the other hand, formalize the procedures involved but generally leave out all additional information except that which is contained in the series to be forecasted.

For example, if one were interested in forecasting the sales of cars one could ask industry experts and average out their opinions, but then one would have no way of finding out what might have gone wrong since the source of errors cannot be tracked down due to a lack of articulation. On the other hand, one could use any one of a number of time series methods, say a simple moving average of the past 6 months' sales. In this case a considerable amount of precious information is just not being explicitly incorporated—one would expect things like prices, incomes, credit conditions, general economic climate, and so forth, to influence car sales. The advantage of econometric techniques lies precisely in that such influential variables can be explicitly taken into account in a formal and consistent way. In addition, their individual effects may be disentangled from their combined influence.

The structure of this chapter is as follows: Section II describes the nature of the econometric approach with emphasis on the model and data. Section III considers the problem of interpreting and evaluating the estimates. Sections IV and V describe the use of econometric techniques for structural and policy analyses respectively and are followed by a concluding section.

II. THE NATURE OF ECONOMETRICS

Chart 12-1 schematically summarizes the nature of the econometric approach in general. Below, the major components of Chart 12-1 are discussed.

The Model

Through a process of formalization the actual phenomena are represented in the form of a *model*. This much abused word is nothing more than a scaling down of the "real world" to manageable proportions whereby the major variables affecting the process under consideration are singled out and their interrelationships spelled out. Let us say that one were trying to explain the sales of a particular company's products. After some reasoning, the conclusion is that sales $(S)_t$ is determined by the ratio of our price relative to the competition's price $(P/P_c)_t$, our adver-

---

*Recent research indicates more clearly that judgmental forecasts are more often than not, biased. See, for example, Hogarth and Makridakis[2] for an overview of such research and an extensive bibliography.

CHART 12.1. The Structure of the Econometric Approach[a]

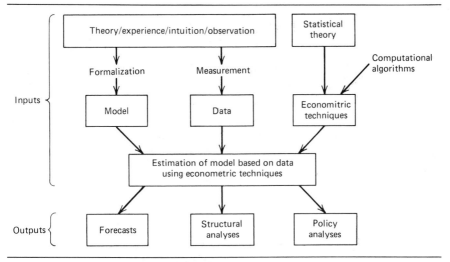

[a]Based on a similar diagram in *Intrilligator*.[3]

tising outlays relative to the competition's outlays $(A/A_c)_t$, and incomes $(I)_t$. This model can be written as:

$$S_t = a + b(P/P_c)_t + c(A/A_c)_t + d(I)_t + \epsilon_t$$

The parameters b, c, and d, which we do not as yet know, represent the weight to be assigned to the variables they correspond to in determining sales. The other parameter a and the "error term" ϵ_t are explicit recognition of the fact that this is just an approximation of "reality." If the model is a "good" one, these error terms will tend to be fairly small. If it is not a "good" model, then we have indications as to what to do to make it better.

An econometric model can be very simple or exceedingly complex. It can consist of a single equation involving, say, three variables, as in the sales equation presented above, or it can comprise several hundred equations and variables, as in the models used for macroeconomic forecasting (see Chapter 18). The optimal size of the model will depend on the ultimate objective of the end user(s); with an important tradeoff in model complexity between realism and manageability. There is a tendency to make it more and more complex, by adding variables and relationships, in an attempt to approximate reality as closely as possible. This quickly leads to unmanageable models, which are often impossible to implement, either because of computational difficulties or for lack of data, and which lose most of their usefulness since they become difficult to understand.

In deciding how complex a model should be, the uses of the model should be kept in mind. Let us consider the example given above of a simple model to explain the sales of a company's products. If its sole objective is to obtain accurate forecasts, then the criterion to add more variables should be their contribution to the explanation of the variation in the sales. This can be measured rather accurately, through certain econometric tests related to the goodness of fit (Section III). If, however, the model is to be used to test the sensitivity of sales to advertising outlays or to evaluate a policy of higher advertising outlays, then clearly A/A_c should be included. For these other purposes, the decision to include or exclude a variable is therefore based on different criteria; and, correspondingly, different econometric tests can be performed to determine the relevance of each variable.

The Data

The second ingredient in econometric work is *data*. Just as the process of formalization results in a model, the process of measurement results in a set of raw data. It is relatively easy to construct and manipulate models of any given size. Using the model, however, requires data on all of the variables included in the model, and they are often not available or not in the form desired.

Data, by definition, are quantitative expressions of the measurement of some object under study. This object, however, may be qualitative in nature. In many instances, for example, the marketing function requires measurements of how consumers "perceive" a certain product or how much they "like" this or that characteristic of the product—all attempts at quantification often put constraints on the tools which can be used to analyze such data; these constraints are very often erroneously overlooked. The implicit assumption that a number is a number and therefore all numerical measurements may be treated in a similar fashion may lead to important errors and misinterpretations. Different *scales* of measurement have different informational content. Traditionally, one distinguishes between *nominal, ordinal, interval,* and *ratio* scales.

For econometric work, the data have to be measured along an interval scale or better.* Fortunately, nearly all economic data meet this criteria. When one encounters such a problem, most likely in data relating to consumer preferences and behavior, one can either "massage" the raw data or use some proxy variable (the meaning of this is explained below) to circumvent the difficulty.

Finally, choices have to be made on such issues as whether to use real

---

*Strictly speaking this is true of any treatment of data that requires the use of averages or the calculation of standard deviations and so on and is not specific to econometrics.

or nominal quantities, total or per capita quantities, levels or first differences or percentage changes, seasonally adjusted or unadjusted data, and so on. Furthermore, the various series used must be compatible, for example, indices must have the same base year.

Time Series Versus Cross-Section Data

Time series data refer to a particular variable over time. The time period is usually a week, month, quarter, or year.

Cross-section data refer to a particular variable at a particular time but over different entities. These entities may be different countries, geographic regions, firms, industries, products, market segments, income groups, age groups, and so forth. For example, the measurement of sales over different age groups during 1980 would constitute a cross-sectional data base.

In some cases, cross-section and time series data may be "pooled" into a time-series of cross-section data.

In most cases cross-section and time series data will lead to different estimates of a model, and they are generally not comparable. Neither estimate is "wrong," but they serve different purposes. In general, time series data reflect short-run behavior while cross-section data reflect long-run behavior. Thus, for short-run forecasting purposes time series data would be appropriate, while for medium-term planning and structural analysis it may be more desirable to use cross-section data.

Proxy Variables. In many instances a conceptually specified variable in the model building stage cannot be measured or may simply be too costly to measure. In such cases one may be forced to find another variable which is a close substitute for the missing one. This substitute is called a *proxy variable*. The use of a time trend variable as a proxy for changing tastes or changing technology is a very common example. Other examples would be the use of cumulative output as a proxy for "experience" in explaining cost behavior, the use of concentration ratios as proxies for "imperfections" in markets, the use of the number of employees as a proxy for the "size" of a firm, and so on.

Dummy Variables. A special type of proxy variable is the so-called "dummy" variable. These allow the separation of information into discrete categories by assuming "dummy" values (0 or 1) for each of the categories. In general they are used to express qualitative data by an "either/or" situation: something happened or did not happen, an attitude was taken or not taken, a characteristic exists or does not exist, and so on. The typical example is that of accounting for war years. To do this, a dummy variable is created which has a value of 1 during the war years and 0 otherwise. Dummies also have been used to distinguish between periods where the investment tax credit was in effect and when it was not, periods where incomes policies were in effect and when they were not, periods when strikes were in effect, and so on; or to distinguish between more than two categories or situations.*

Problems with Data

Even when data can be found there are several problems one has to deal with.

1. *Accuracy.* All data are subject to measurement error. Not only are they inaccurate, but also the inaccuracies are not symmetric. Even in much used figures such as GNP, the margin of error may be as high as 15%. In other areas such as prices, the error is even greater. Measurements which seem relatively straightforward to take, such as counting the population, may involve errors of 1 or 2% in either direction (in the United States that corresponds to an error of about ±3 million people!). The same can be said of the records of firms, households, governments, and so forth. Some of these errors may be diminished by checking their source;† others may be dealt with through statistical means in the estimation process.

2. *Multicollinearity.* This refers to the tendency of data to move together in a highly correlated manner. This tends to pose certain statistical problems in treating the data, and there is very little that can be done about it. For purely forecasting purposes, provided the pattern of collinearity does not change, the problem is not serious. For policy purposes, however, it may lead to serious misinterpretation of the results obtained.

3. *Structural Changes.* In certain cases the data will include discontinuous changes such as wars, natural disasters, or a fundamental change in the nature of the process being studied. If the data are treated as if these effects did not exist, the interpretation of the results becomes exceedingly difficult and misleading.

The final input to econometric work is the software in the computer, or the techniques of estimation and inference. Although it is beyond the scope of this work to get into these techniques, it should be kept in mind that not all models can be estimated with any given technique. Luckily, however, the great majority of applied econometric work can be handled with the simplest, most straightforward techniques. Some standard texts are listed in the references.

---

*If there are n categories to distinguish among, it would take, at most, $n - 1$ dummy variables. The nth category would then be the "excluded" one, and the coefficients of the dummies included would be measuring the partial influence of those categories relative to the excluded one.

† See Morgenstern[6] for the classic treatment of errors in economic data.

The Managerial Uses of Econometrics

Chart 12-1 also summarizes the uses, or output, of econometric work. There are three general uses, as follows.

Forecasting is the use of a model whose parameters have been estimated from the relevant data to predict the values of a certain variable outside the sample of data actually observed.

Structural analysis is the use of the estimated model to derive information concerning the structure of the relationship being studied. This involves answering such questions as "given alternative formalizations, which one seems to be supported by the available evidence," "how sensitive is the variable of interest to changes in the other variables," and so forth. Although this is usually seen as the "scientific" purpose of econometrics, its managerial uses in everyday affairs are numerous. The responsiveness of demand to price changes in several different market segments and/or product lines, the responsiveness of sales to credit conditions, and the structure of costs are all aspects of structural analysis with important managerial applications.

Policy analysis is the use of the estimated model to "play out" different policies under alternative assumptions. It is thus an aid in choosing between various policy options. In its most common form, this implies the use of the estimated model to simulate the effects of differing policies, or the same policy under differing environmental conditions.

Although more will be said about these aspects below, it should be noted that once an econometric model is estimated for any given purpose, say forecasting, its use for other purposes is basically a free by-product. Thus, econometric techniques provide a managerial tool that surpasses, with little marginal effort, the purely forecasting interest.

III. INTERPRETATION AND EVALUATION OF ESTIMATES

The interpretation of the various parameters estimated is intimately linked to the model constructed. There are, however, various steps along the line (such as the model itself, the data, and the estimation procedure) where the true meaning of the parameters may become obscured.

Basic Indicators

The basic tools in extracting information of this nature are a set of "summary" statistics routinely generated by nearly all available econometric computer packages. Of these statistics, the most routinely used ones are the coefficient of determination (R^2, read "R squared"), the adjusted coefficient of determination ($\overline{R}^2$, read "R-bar squared"), the standard errors, and the Durbin–Watson statistic (DW). These statistics go a long way in clarifying issues before any more sophisticated techniques may become necessary.

The R^2 measures the extent to which movements in the dependent variable are being explained by the estimated model, that is,

$$R^2 = \frac{\text{variation explained by the equation}}{\text{total variation of the dependent variable}}$$

Thus it takes on values ranging from a low of zero to a high of one, the higher the R^2 the more variability being explained. However, the R^2 can legitimately be used for comparing the relative performance of two alternative models only when the dependent variables are the same. Also, since the R^2 will go up as more independent variables are added on, whether they are relevant or not, it is useless in cases where the number of independent variables is not the same. It is also useful to keep in mind that R^2 values tend to be high using time series data and low when using cross-section data.*

Correcting the R^2 for the number of independent variables gives an analogous statistic, the $\bar{R}^2$. This measure can decrease when a new variable is added to the equation, and it can also become negative. Thus it cannot be interpreted as the proportion of variance explained. However, for forecasting purposes, an equation with a higher $\bar{R}^2$ will have a smaller variance in the error of prediction. In the case of structural or policy analysis, on the other hand, the formulation with the highest $\bar{R}^2$ may not be the most desirable. It is quite possible that discarding a conceptually relevant variable may increase the $\bar{R}^2$ but bias the other parameter estimates, in which case the structural (or policy) analysis would be less intelligible. We shall examine an example below.

The standard errors of the estimated parameters provide an indication as to their "precision." In principle, the smaller the standard errors are, the more precise the estimates. This does not necessarily imply that we have estimated the "correct" value of a parameter—one can get a very precise estimate which is biased. It is conventional to report the standard errors as part of the regression equation by enclosing them in parentheses below the respective estimates. The major use made of the standard errors is testing to see if the parameters estimated are significantly different from zero. This is done by calculating a so-called "t statistic":

$$t = \frac{\text{parameter value}}{\text{standard error}}$$

---

*In orders of magnitude, while R^2's around 0.5 would generally be acceptable with cross-section data, they would be expected to be around 0.9 with time-series data.

In practice, the rule of thumb is that if the calculated (absolute) t value is greater than or around two, the parameter is taken to be significantly different from zero.

For example, if we had a model relating changes in real wages to changes in real wages lagged one period and changes in payroll taxes, putting these in logarithmic form and estimating the parameters with data between 1962 and 1978 for France gives:

$$CW = 0.054 + 0.313CW_{-1} + 0.819CI - 0.149CI_{-1} - 0.645CT$$

$$(0.011) \quad (0.143) \quad\quad (0.216) \quad\quad (0.233) \quad\quad (0.120)$$

$$\bar{R}^2 = 0.8304 \quad\quad\quad\quad DW = 1.616$$

To test which of these parameters are different from zero, we compute the t values by simple division to get:

Constant	4.19
CW_{-1}, change in wages lagged	2.19
CI, change in inflation	3.79
CI_{-1}, change in inflation lagged	-0.64
CT, change in taxes	-5.38

Thus all of the variables, except lagged changes in inflation, have significant effect on wages since we can reject the hypothesis that their coefficients are zero.*

The DW statistic provides an indication as to the existence of correlation between the residuals or error terms. It can range between zero and four and has an expected value of two if the residuals are independently distributed. Therefore, as a rule of thumb, if DW is around two we would tend to reject the existence of correlation in the residuals. The DW statistic should not be used if there is a lagged dependent variable among the explanatory variables because this will bias the DW toward two.† The interest of the DW lies in the fact that usually the existence of correlation in the residuals is indicative of a misspecification in the model. Thus although there are straightforward transformations of the data that will statistically correct for the effects of autocorrelation, these should not be used before the model is reviewed for possible oversights.

---

*Strictly speaking, one does not "accept" a hypothesis as correct but just fails to "reject" it.

†A modification of the DW exists for use in such cases. It is called the "h statistic" and is defined in all standard texts.

Modeling Problems

The most common problem encountered as a result of the modeling process is the inclusion of irrelevant variables or leaving out relevant ones. These "specification" problems lead to different results.

Leaving out a relevant variable will bias the estimates of all coefficients in the model. If the excluded variable is left out because of a lack of data and is replaced by a proxy variable this will also cause a bias but less of one. On the other hand, adding an irrelevant variable in the specification of the model will not cause any bias but will increase the variance of the estimated coefficients, that is, reduce their precision.*

Because there is no way of unambiguously knowing if a variable is being left out or erroneously included, one has to "feel" what is going on from the behavior of certain parameters. For example, in the wage equation discussed previously one may argue that gross domestic product should figure in the formulation as a proxy for economic activity and therefore the demand for labor. The estimated equation then becomes:

$$CW = 0.049 + 0.307CW_{-1} + 0.837CI - 0.135CI_{-1} - 0.636CT + 0.81CGDP$$

$$(0.025) \ (0.151) \qquad (0.236) \quad (0.250) \qquad (0.130) \qquad (0.332)$$

$$\bar{R}^2 = 0.816 \qquad\qquad DW = 1.699$$

The addition of this variable does not significantly alter our estimates of the other coefficients, whereas it does increase their standard errors; there is a drop in the $\bar{R}^2$, and the t value is 0.244 indicating that its coefficient is not significantly different from zero.† In this case the $CGDP$ variable is basically superfluous, and it may be excluded altogether.

On the other hand, one might conjecture that the oil crisis of 1973–74 caused some structural change in the labor markets although one cannot definitively put a finger on the mechanism of how this happened. The low DW (although biased toward two because of the presence of CW_{-1}) would support the view that there is some misspecification. Not knowing exactly what the variable is, one can create a dummy variable having a value of zero between 1962 to 1973 and unity between 1974

---

*If the left out (or irrelevant) variable is not correlated at all with the other variables, then these misspecifications will not influence the coefficient estimates.

†Some users of econometric techniques tend to discard variables with a t value below a certain size (usually below one). This is not recommended as a general rule. If dropping a variable significantly changes the coefficients of other variables, one has to revert to theoretical considerations of the model before dropping it— even if the $\bar{R}^2$ goes up.

to 1978, that is, the effect was not present prior to 1973 and was there afterwards.

Reestimating our original equation with a dummy variable (D) gives:

$$CW = 0.036 + 0.012CW_{-1} + 1.423CI + 0.286CI_{-1} - 0.516CT - 0.057D$$

$$(0.011) \quad (0.151) \qquad (0.266) \qquad (0.234) \qquad (0.103) \quad (0.019)$$

$$\overline{R}^2 = 0.897 \qquad\qquad DW = 2.0015$$

As can be seen in Chart 12-2, with the addition of the dummy variable, the other coefficients have changed significantly, the standard errors have changed (in some cases significantly), the $\overline{R}^2$ has gone up, and the DW is exactly two. The new t values are:

Constant	3.27
CW_{-1}	0.08
CI	5.35
CI_{-1}	1.22
CT	−5.01
D	−3.00

First we note that the dummy variable is definitely picking up a significant effect, and the only other change is that CW_{-1} has become insignificant. Under these conditions, we would be inclined to think that our initial formulation left out an important variable which tended to bias our estimates. At this point, it would be best to go back to the drawing board and reformulate the model.

Remember that the estimated coefficients represent the effect of the respective variables with all other included variables kept constant. This is why a constant term should always be included in an estimated equation even if it does not seem to make obvious sense conceptually. There will always be some, albeit minor, variables left out whose collective influence should be accounted for, and there will always be some error of approximation due to the linear equation used for estimation. The constant term will pick up the average of such influences and allow for "cleaner" estimates of other coefficients. In some cases, it will have a straightforward interpretation also. For example, in estimating cost functions, the constant term can be validly interpreted as the fixed costs in an operation.

Forecasts of Econometric Models

Once a model has been estimated in its final form, forecasting with it is fairly straightforward. The values of the exogenous variables are multi-

CHART 12-2. Comparison of the Use of Different Variables in Estimating Wage Behavior

	$\bar{R}^2$ / DW	Constant	Change in Wages Lag 1	Change in Inflation	Change in Inflation Lag 1	Change in Taxes	Change in GDP	Dummy
Model I	0.8304 / 1.616	0.054 (0.011)	0.313 (0.143)	0.819 (0.216)	-0.149 (0.233)	-0.695 (0.120)	— / —	— / —
Model II	0.816 / 1.699	0.049 (0.025)	0.307 (0.151)	0.837 (0.236)	-0.135 (0.250)	-0.636 (0.130)	0.081 (0.332)	— / —
Model III	0.897 / 2.0015	0.036 (0.011)	0.012 (0.151)	1.423 (0.266)	0.286 (0.234)	-0.516 (0.103)	— / —	-0.057 (0.019)

plied by their respective (estimated) coefficients and summed up. This will give us a point estimate of the forecasted dependent variable. However, relying on this point forecast would be an incorrect use of econometrics in forecasting. Provided that the procedures have been correctly followed, this point estimate will be equal, in expected value, to the variable(s) being forecast. This does not mean that it will turn out to be the actual value observed. We can, however, put a range around this expected value so that we are, say, 95% sure that the observed value will be within these limits. Also, it must be forgotten that each regression equation has an error term added on to it. Practically speaking, this would amount to what can be called an "add factor" whereby information of a punctual nature not incorporated into the model may be taken into account to modify the model's forecast. Finally, as will be seen below, the estimated model may be used to analyze the expected effects of variations in the explanatory variables on the forecasted figures.

IV. STRUCTURAL ANALYSIS

Once an econometric model has been specified and estimated it can be used for purposes other than forecasting. The structure of the model and the values of its parameters can provide much useful information about the phenomenon that the model represents. Structural analysis consists in extracting this information by algebraic manipulation of the model and by the utilization of certain concepts. The usefulness of structural analysis in managerial application is critical. Any firm stands to gain from a better knowledge of the "structure" characterizing its market, its industry, or the economy as a whole. Some examples can illustrate the potential of structural analysis. Let us return to the equation explaining the sales of a company's products:

$$S_t = a + b \left(\frac{P}{P_c}\right)_t + c \left(\frac{A}{A_c}\right) + d(I)_t + \epsilon_t$$

and let us assume that S_t is sales in volume. Then clearly the coefficient b should be negative since one expects sales to decrease when price increases. However, knowing the value of b, not just its sign, may be quite important for management, since higher or lower values may lead to quite different commercial policies. Suppose, for simplicity, that the price demanded by competitors, P_c, is assumed fixed in the short run; and that, in order to increase revenues, management is trying to choose whether to raise or to lower prices, P. Clearly, if the value of b is very large in absolute terms an increase in price will lead to a very substantial decrease in volume of sales, and revenue will decrease. If, on the other hand, b is small in absolute value, the decrease in volume of sales following a price increase will also be small, and revenue will go up. This type of information is very well conveyed by the concept of elasticity.* In this example, the elasticity of sales with respect to price (still assuming P_c constant) is

$$\frac{\dfrac{\Delta S}{S}}{\dfrac{\Delta P}{P}} = \frac{b}{P_c}\frac{P}{S}$$

where Δ indicates change. Since the company's as well as its competitor's prices are known and current sales are also known, if an estimate of b can be obtained the elasticity can be computed. Then, if its value is, say, -2, a 1% increase in price will decrease the volume of sales by 2% which more than offsets the price increase and, as a result, leads to lower revenues. If, however, its value is $-.5$, a 10% increase in prices, for example, will decrease sales only 5% and revenues will go up.

Structural analysis can provide particularly rich information in the case of dynamic models. When the interdependence between variables depends on the passage of time, it becomes quite useful to distinguish between short-run and long-run consequences of a change in an exogenous variable. To keep matters simple, let us return to the single equation model describing company sales. But let us extend it to include, as an explanatory variable, sales in the previous year. That is, the model becomes

$$S_t = a + b\left(\frac{P}{P_c}\right)_t + c\left(\frac{A}{A_c}\right)_t + d(I)_t + e(S)_{t-1} + \epsilon_t$$

which shows that sales depend on, among other things, how much the company sold in the previous period (S_{t-1}), reflecting certain specific dynamics of the market such as, for example, consumer habit formation. Now an increase in advertising outlays relative to the competition's still has an impact on sales equivalent to c units per unit increase A/A_c.

---

*An "elasticity" is the percentage change in one variable relative to a percentage change in another, or other things being held constant. For example, the response of demand to a change in price would be given by the price elasticity of demand, that is,

$$\epsilon p = \frac{\%\ \text{change in quantity}}{\%\ \text{change in price}} = \frac{\Delta Q/Q}{\Delta P/P} = \frac{P}{Q}\cdot\frac{\Delta Q}{\Delta P}$$

And the elasticity of sales in the current period with respect to the company's advertising outlays is still given by

$$\frac{\dfrac{\Delta S}{S}}{\dfrac{\Delta A}{A}} = \frac{c}{A_c}\frac{A}{S} \qquad \text{short term}$$

But this is only a short-run elasticity. In the long run one must take into account that if sales increase in the current period, then sales in the next period will also be higher, because of the dynamics of the market. Indeed, after the full long-term impact of this increase in advertising outlays has been felt, the final change in sales is captured by the long-run elasticity:

$$\frac{\dfrac{\Delta S}{S}}{\dfrac{\Delta A}{A}} = \frac{c}{1-e}\frac{A}{A_c S} \qquad \text{long term}$$

which, as expected, is larger than the short-run elasticity since e is less than 1.* There is, therefore, a difference in a dynamic model between the long-run and short-run impacts of changes in an exogenous variable. And the knowledge of these impacts is of obvious interest in many practical situations.

These variables are sometimes beyond the control of the firm or they can be part of the policy instruments in a firm's strategy—such as advertising outlays. In both cases, the benefit of having a quantified indicator of the impact of a change in these variables cannot be overemphasized.

V. POLICY ANALYSIS

A good econometric model is above all a representation of reality. It simplifies many aspects, it omits most details, but it concentrates on what is essential. As such, it can be used to describe what would happen if certain actions were taken, what would be the likely impact on a particular firm, or market, or economy of a change in one policy or

---

*Recall that the parameters of the model are the weights of each variable in the explanation of sales; clearly sales in the previous period cannot have a weight of more than 100% in the explanation of sales in the current period.

another. In other words, an econometric model can be used to perform a certain type of experimentation which cannot be conducted in the real world. This is called *policy analysis*.

A policy consists in the efficient utilization of certain instruments available to managers in order to achieve certain targets. For example, if a particular volume of sales is set as a target, managers can typically use price cuts or advertising campaigns to reach it. In order to determine the best combination of these two instruments it is important to know the links among prices, advertising outlays, and sales. This is where the econometric model becomes quite useful.

In the terminology of econometrics policy targets are dependent variables. Instruments, on the other hand, will be independent variables. Other independent variables exist, however: those which describe the environment in which the firm (or the market, or the economy) operates and over which managers do not have control. The structure of the model represents the link between targets and instruments, given the environment—or scenario—of the problem.

The model describing company sales,

$$S_t = a + b \left(\frac{P}{P_c}\right)_t + c \left(\frac{A}{A_c}\right)_t + d(I)_t + \epsilon_t$$

can be quite useful to analyze a policy of sales expansion through increased advertising outlays. The scenario for the analysis will be given by certain forecasts of incomes, prices (if they are not being used as an instrument), and the competition's advertising outlays (assuming they do not react to an increase in the company's own outlays). Then, with the estimates for the parameters a, b, c, and d it is possible to compute what level of advertising is necessary to achieve the target volume of sales.

Most cases of policy analysis are a great deal more complex, which makes the usefulness of the model even clearer. First, there is a distinction between short- and long-run policies. If, instead of a certain sales target for the coming year, the company sets a sequence of targets for the next 10 years, then the model should be used to determine the necessary path of advertising outlays. If the model has certain dynamic features this can become much less obvious than in the simple example given above.

Next, policy analysis becomes rather more difficult—and important— if uncertainty is taken explicitly into account. Each policy move can be determined given a certain scenario, that is, given certain values for the variables over which the firm has no control. But a scenario cannot be predicted with full certainty. For example, in our case of a sales target, the company should take into account that incomes may increase faster or slower, depending on macroeconomic policy; or that competitors may or may not increase their own advertising outlays. This problem is often dealt with by analyzing policies under different scenarios and choosing the best option for each scenario. If one policy is always the most efficient in every case, then it is said that a dominant strategy exists and the problem is solved. But often this is not the case, and choosing becomes difficult. The next step consists in attaching probabilities to each scenario and performing the analysis in terms not only of the targets to achieve but also of the risk of failure. For this type of policy analysis, a reliable econometric model is often an indispensable tool.

Finally, policy analysis is almost never as simple as the manipulation of a unique instrument to achieve a unique target. In most cases firms have more than one objective and must necessarily use more than one instrument. Often two or more objectives are incompatible, and certain tradeoffs must be made. Or, alternatively, policy must be conducted within certain constraints. For example, a company may want to maximize its sales under the constraint that profits do not drop below a certain level. Or another company may want to maximize its growth and simultaneously increase dividends paid out to stockholders. In these cases, the complexity of the choice is quite apparent, and the econometric model shows its maximum usefulness.

Two main approaches exist in multitarget policy analysis. One consists in the careful definition of the objective function of the firm. This requires that not only targets be specified very precisely, but also that the various tradeoffs among conflicting objectives—defined in terms of weights in the objective function—be established. Then the econometric model provides the link between the objectives and the investments, and the choice of the optimal policy becomes a problem of mathematical programming. Although the optimization problem may still be difficult, especially if targets are defined dynamically—such as, for example, maximizing discounted cash flow over a 10 year period—standard techniques exist that can be applied to most cases (see, e.g., Intrilligator[4]). The most frequent difficulty with this approach is the precise definition of targets and tradeoffs that is necessary to determine an objective function.

Alternatively, policy analysis can be conducted through simulation: instruments are attributed certain values, and the impact of these values on the targets is computed through the model. Then the choice of policy is based on the analysis of its global impact on all targets. Clearly, no formal definition of the tradeoffs among conflicting targets needs to be made: it can remain implicitly in the minds of the decision makers. The simulation of each policy simply provides the managers with the necessary information for a decision. If the model is accurate, the simulation results should correspond to what would have happened if the policy had been enacted: this type of information is ideally what decision makers would like to have.

Although the concept of simulation is simple, its implementation can again become quite complex. In most cases scenarios have to be defined and various simulations performed for each policy. Also, if the stochastic elements of the phenomenon are important, they can be included in the simulation, increasing the richness of the analysis. This is done by generating random numbers obeying a certain probability distribution, which is assumed to describe well the stochastic components of the problem, and adding these numbers to the appropriate equations each time the model is solved. Then each policy can be judged not only in terms of the targets defined, but also in terms of the impact of random disturbances.

In more or less complex cases, with or without a precise definition of targets and tradeoffs and including or not including stochastic elements, policy analysis can provide extremely rich information for business managers. It is clearly a quite useful byproduct of econometric modeling.

VI. CONCLUSION

What we have tried to do in this chapter is to point out that econometrics is not just a collection of techniques used by economists in testing abstract theories. It is a tool, and in some instances the only tool, that can provide managers with crucial inputs to their decisions and their possible outcomes.

For a long time managers have thought that econometric methods are mainly used for forecasting purposes and so they have been compared with other forecasting techniques. The debate on the relative usefulness of econometric methods in forecasting still continues.[8] Although it is not our intention to enter into such a debate here, we would like to make these points:

1. Often the alternatives considered to the use of econometric techniques are not logically distinct ones. It is well known, for example, that extrapolations on trend are just special cases and that ARIMA models for individual variables are logically implied by structural econometric models.

2. Comparing the forecasting accuracy of different methods relies, basically, on the difference between the point predictions made and the observed value of the variable to be predicted. As pointed out previously, however, the point prediction is but an expected value, and there is a calculable variation around this value. It is not at all obvious whether,

when such variation is taken into account, the forecasting techniques being compared yield significantly different results.

3. To the extent that economic time series change slowly and the other variables that effect the behavior of the variable being forecasted are not expected to change significantly, it is difficult for a "causal" econometric model to outperform the simpler ones *in the short run*. However, in the medium and long term, forecasts from econometric models have greater accuracy compared to the other approaches.

Our argument here has been that econometric methods go much beyond the purely forecasting applications. The structural and policy analysis possible with these techniques are probably of much greater use to managers than short-term forecasts. Using available information efficiently in quantifying the structure of the environment in which managers have to operate will have obvious benefits in the strategic thinking that goes on in a firm. The ability to "act out" the most likely outcomes of various alternative policies or to answer "what if" type questions will aid in clarifying problem areas before the fact.

It is precisely in such areas that econometric techniques have not been sufficiently exploited for managerial purposes.

REFERENCES

1. Dhrymes, P., *Introductory Economics,* Springer-Verlag, New York, 1978.
2. Hogarth, R. and Makridakis, S., "Forecasting and Planning: An evolution," Forthcoming in *Management Sciences.*
3. Intrilligator, M., *Econometric Models, Techniques and Applications,* Prentice-Hall, Englewood Cliffs, NJ, 1978.
4. Intrilligator, M., *Mathematical Optimization and Economic Theory,* Prentice-Hall, Englewood Cliffs, NJ, 1971.
5. Johnston, J., *Econometric Methods,* 2nd ed., McGraw-Hill, New York, 1972.
6. Morgenstern, O., *On the Accuracy of Economic Observations,* 2nd eds., Princeton University Press, Princeton, 1963.
7. Rao, P. and Miller, R. L., *Applied Econometrics,* Wadsworth, Belmont, CA, 1971.
8. "Symposium on Forecasting with Econometric Methods," *Journal of Business,* vol. 51, October 1978.
9. Theil, H., *Principles of Econometrics,* John Wiley, New York, 1951.

CHAPTER

13

JUDGMENTAL AND BAYESIAN FORECASTING

SAMUEL E. BODILY

The Colgate Darden Graduate School of Business Administration
University of Virginia

Often it is necessary to form a forecast judgmentally before any data are available and then to revise the forecast in stages as observations are made. Bayesian revision is a method for developing a *revised* forecast by combining empirical data with forecasts made *prior* to the empirical observations. Both the prior and the revised forecasts are expressed as probability distributions of an uncertain quantity or a yet-to-be-observed outcome.

This chapter describes Bayesian methods of forecasting and their application. The encoding of judgmental forecasts as probability distributions, which is useful in its own right as a method of forecasting, is discussed first. Then the procedures for combining the prior probability distribution with data are presented. The Bayesian approach is more than a statistical technique; it is a philosophy of inference and the use of information that can be combined with other methods of estimation. Some ways the Bayesian approach has been incorporated into other forecasting methods (e.g., exponential smoothing) are discussed at the end of the chapter.

JUDGMENTAL PROBABILITY

Forecasters routinely make judgments based on background knowledge and experience. Feelings are often expressed in qualitative terms such as saying a future event is "unlikely," "probable," or "quite likely." The language of probability allows one to quantify in more meaningful terms a forecast and the extent of the uncertainty relating to it. This section describes how to express and to elicit from an individual two types of probability forecasts: (1) *discrete* probabilities or forecasts of the chances that specific outcomes (such as rain today) will occur and (2) *continuous* probability distributions which specify the chances that an uncertain quantity (such as the amount of annual rainfall) will be at or below certain levels. Probabilities elicited from an individual represent that person's beliefs about the future; the probabilities will differ among individuals, even experts.

Discrete Outcomes

A loan officer has before her an application for a new loan. She has been asked by the credit review board of her company to forecast the applicant's ability to pay off the loan. A procedure for eliciting subjective probabilities for discrete outcomes using this example is described below.

1.   Identify the set of possible outcomes. In forecasting the repayment of a loan, the outcomes might be labeled "repayment" and "default." The outcomes must be defined so that they are *mutually exclusive*, that is, so that no more than one of the outcomes can occur. The set of outcomes must also be *collectively exhaustive*, meaning that all possibilities are included, that is, one of the outcomes must occur. In some cases an outcome called "other" is needed as a catchall category. Often it is sufficient to include the negative of the primary outcome, for example, the outcomes for a weather forecast may be "rain" and "no rain." Outcomes may be numerical; for example, if a loan has four payments the outcome might be defined as the borrower making zero, one, two, three, or four payments.

2.   Assign probabilities to outcomes. The probability of each outcome must be 0 or 1.0 or lie between 0 and 1.0, and the sum of the probabilities of the outcomes must be exactly 1.0. One device often used to aid the elicitation of probabilities is a reference lottery. Chart 13-1 shows one type of reference lottery, a fair probability wheel. The wheel is spun and the player wins a given amount if the pointer ends up in the shaded area. The portion of the wheel that is shaded is adjustable between 0 and 100%. The following dialogue illustrates how you might use such a device to obtain probabilities from the loan officer:

> You: Our problem is to forecast whether this loan will be paid off. You have a lot of information and a great deal of experience to use in making a forecast. To help you ex-

CHART 13-1. Reference Probability Wheel with Adjustable Win Probability for Calibrating Repayment Probability

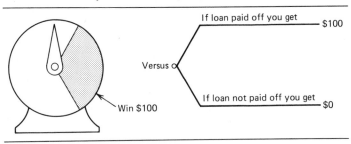

press your judgment in terms of probabilities, I will give you some concrete choices. This reference wheel provides us with objectively determined outcomes. Think of spinning the wheel. If the pointer ends up in the shaded area then you will win a prize. It doesn't matter what the prize is—let's make it $100. If the pointer does not end up in the shaded area, you get nothing. Now I want you to compare the reference wheel lottery with a lottery based on the outcome of this loan, keeping the prizes the same and assuming the prizes would be awarded at the same time in the future. If the loan is repaid then you get $100; if not, you get nothing. I'm going to ask you a series of questions where you choose between the reference wheel lottery and the loan lottery. As it is, I have the wheel set so that the shaded area is 30% of the wheel. Which lottery would you choose?

Forecaster: Well, since I would like to have that $100, I would take the loan gamble, since there is greater than a 30% chance that it will be repaid.

You: O.K. Fine. Suppose I set the reference wheel so that 95% of the area is shaded, and I ask you to choose between the loan lottery and the reference lottery?

Forecaster: That's an easy decision, too. I'd clearly take the reference wheel. This applicant has substantial debt now, and the economy being what it is, I'd say the chances that the loan will be repaid must be lower than 95%.

You: Let me set the reference wheel to 75%; which lottery do you take now?

Forecaster: This is a little harder, but I'd go with the loan.

You: What if I set the reference wheel to 80%?

Forecaster: That's closer but I'd still go with the loan. If you set the reference wheel at, say, 90%, though, then I really couldn't choose. The lotteries would then be equivalent, in my judgment.

You: That tells me then that you assess the probability that the loan will be repaid at .90.

The mental process for setting a probability in this dialogue is much like judging the length of an object by calibrating it against a more familiar object of known length. Although the probability is a personal judgment, it is often based on the informal processing of quantitative data. In this case, the forecaster may have mentally listed the loan applications that were similar to this one, considered how many of these were repaid, then adjusted the percentage to account for special characteristics of this particular loan.

The dialogue could be repeated for any number of outcomes. At the end it is not unusual for the probabilities of the outcomes to sum to more than 1.0. If so, the forecaster must reconsider her judgments and restate them so they then add to one.

Continuous Quantities

There are many instances when it is necessary to forecast a quantity that does not have just a few discrete outcomes. Annual rainfall or dollar sales of a corporation are just two examples of forecasted quantities that may take on any value in a continuous interval. Even when the quantity truly has discrete outcomes (e.g., the prime interest rate which is set usually in increments of one quarter of a percent), it may be simpler to treat the forecast as though it were a continuous quantity.

A convenient way to express probabilities for continuous quantities involves *fractiles*. Suppose, for example, that a meteorologist is forecasting annual rainfall. Since there are so many possible outcomes it doesn't make sense to speak of the probability of any one outcome. Instead, probability statements are generally made about intervals in which the outcome may lie, for example, the probability that rainfall will be greater than 25 inches but no greater than 30 inches. The p *fractile* is the level such that the probability is p that the uncertain quantity will be less than or equal to this level. Thus the statement "the .5 fractile is 40 inches" is equivalent to stating that "it is equally likely that rainfall will be above or below 40 inches."

The complete set of fractiles of an uncertain quantity is easily displayed with a cumulative distribution function curve. This is a plot of p on the vertical scale and the p fractile on the horizontal scale. Chart 13.2 shows a cumulative distribution function (CDF) for an uncertain quantity that is normally distributed. Note that the curve is steepest in the center where the quantity is most likely to fall and that in the lower and upper regions the fractiles are farther apart.

CHART 13-2. Cumulative Distribution Function for a Normal Distribution with Mean 600 and Standard Deviation 25

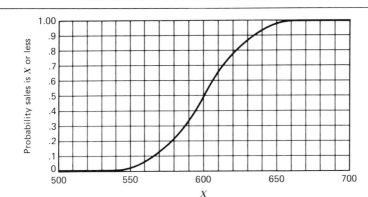

The most common way to assess the CDF is the *interval splitting method*. The steps of this method are illustrated below where a production manager forecasts the proportion of defective items produced by a new manufacturing process:

1. Determine low and high extremes. Suppose the production manager sets the range for proportion of defective items at 0 to 25%. This could be verified by asking him for the series of events that would lead to outcomes outside this range. There either must be no such path of events or the probability of any such path must be zero. The extremes provide two points on the cumulative curve: the lower bound has cumulative probability 0 and the upper bound is the 1.0 fractile.

2. Split the outcome interval into the two equally likely parts by identifying the .5 fractile or median. A question to elicit the .5 fractile is "Considering all possible levels of proportion defective in the interval 0–25%, where would you slice the interval into two equally likely pieces?" If the manager's response is "3.6%," then a point of the cumulative distribution curve could be placed at the .5 level above 3.6% (see Chart 13-3).

3. Split each interval into two equally likely parts by identifying the quartiles. Splitting the interval from 0 to 3.6% into two equally likely parts gives the first quartile (or the .25 fractile), and the third quartile results from splitting the interval from 3.6 to 25%. Let us say the quartiles are 1.5% and 7%. A consistency check can now be made with the question "Is it equally likely for the quantity to fall in or outside the interval 1.5–7%?" If the answer is no, some adjustments must be made in the assessed fractiles

CHART 13-3. The Quality Control Manager's Cumulative Distribution Function for Proportion Defectives from a New Manufacturing Process

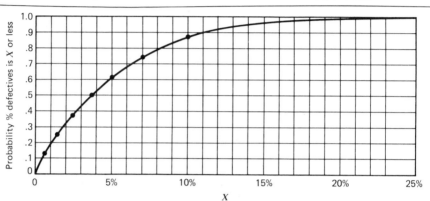

since the probability that the quantity lies between the .25 fractile and the .75 fractile is by definition one-half.

4. Continue the interval splitting until enough points have been obtained; plot the points and fair a line through the points. Chart 13-3 shows the plot of the octiles (splitting all the quartile intervals) and the curve drawn through them. The number of points to get for the curve depends on the accuracy desired and the degree of precision with which the fractiles can be specified. For many situations the quartiles are sufficient. Since more accuracy is generally desired in the tails of the distribution, the quartiles may be supplemented by some extra points in the low and high regions, for example, the .10 fractile and the .90 fractile.

An alternate procedure is to use the interval splitting method as a consistency check after assessing and fitting several arbitrarily chosen fractiles. This may avoid biases in some of the later responses due to fixations on the median. Additional references on judgmental probability assessment are given at the end of this chapter.[7,13,15]

A common phenomenon is that people who feel they know very little about an uncertain quantity will place the fractiles very close together, implying that they can forecast with high accuracy. They are then often surprised by the actual outcome. For example, in experiments with students it is typical to find that for almanac type questions (such as U.S. egg consumption or the number of whales harvested in Antarctica) 25% of the true answers fall outside the range from the .01 fractile to the .99 fractile. The advice: spread out the fractiles, especially the extreme ones.

A few simple ideas can improve judgmental forecasts. It may help to

**CHART 13-4. Examples of Uses of Judgmental Forecasts
with Selected References**

Competitive behavior	Pricing, advertising, bidding
Financial markets	Interest rates,[10] security prices[14]
Financial results	Return on investment, cash flows, cash requirements
Legal risks	Litigation results and damage awards[2]
Medical decisions	Results of various treatments[1]
Oil exploration	Discovery success,[3] amount of reserves
Political environment	Expropriation risk,[11] legislative risk
Sales	Consumer goods,[a] freight[b]
Weather	Mean temperature, rainfall,[17] high and low temperature[12]

[a]Reference 7, p. 17.
[b]Reference 7, p. 23.

decompose the problem: divide and conquer.[*,11] Thus to forecast egg consumption, one might judge population and consumption per person separately and then judge the distribution of egg consumption as the product of these two quantities. Or to estimate the likelihood of rare events such as nuclear power plant failure one may diagram the sequence of occurrences necessary to have the overall event, estimate the separate probabilities for each of these occurrences, and then multiply these probabilities. A method which uses decision trees to structure various scenarios that affect a forecast (e.g., a sales forecast) and to compute the probability of such an effect is given in Harwood et al.[†,7]

Judgmental assessment improves with practice and training. In general, a panel of forecasters will be more accurate by combining their expertise than by working alone. There are many ways to combine forecasts from individuals to get a group forecast. One approach, the Delphi process [**] is based on anonymous responses and controlled feedback of aggregate forecasts in a repetitive process. The group forecast is the median of the individual forecasts at the last round of discussion.

Some of the many examples of the use of subjective forecasts are summarized in Chart 13-4. One published application[10] is the forecast of interest rates at Morgan Guaranty Bank. Twice a month corporate and divisional officers meet to discuss and then forecast the 90-day interest rate for certificates of deposit. Experience has been that the mean of the probability distribution obtained by this group is closer to actuals than the prevailing rate available on the day the forecast is made.

*See p. 298 in reference 8.
†See p. 14 in reference 7.
**See p. 12 in reference 7.

REVISING PROBABILITIES USING EMPIRICAL OBSERVATIONS

After a forecast has been made, empirical observations are often taken and then a new forecast is made. Ideally, the new forecast will incorporate both the new empirical information and the *prior* probability distribution (i.e., the forecast made before the empirical observations). This section describes Bayesian methods for revising the prior to account for new information. Although in many of the examples the prior is judgmentally assessed, it need not be. It might instead be a probability distribution obtained from historical data. It should be evident that the term "prior" is defined relative to the current time. Thus the revised probability distribution calculated now may serve as the prior distribution when further revisions are made after collecting more observations.

"Flipping" the Tree

In an example given early in the chapter, a loan officer judgmentally assessed the probability at .90 that a certain loan would be paid off. Now the loan officer receives some more information about the loan. In particular, she has on her desk an envelope containing a credit-worthiness rating from an independent credit rating service, which simply declares the loan applicant either "safe" or "risky." The loan officer is now thinking about how to revise her forecast to account for the rating. Of course a "safe" rating would cause her to raise her probability forecast that the loan would be repaid, and a "risky" rating would cause her to lower it, but she isn't sure of the amount of the change. The rating service had told her of their experience with applicants like hers. Their records showed that of 900 similar applicants who received and eventually paid off their loans, 800 had been given a "safe" rating. On the other hand 40 out of 100 that had defaulted had also been given the "safe" rating by the rating service.

Bayesian revision for discrete outcomes can be carried out for this problem by "flipping" the probability tree, as follows:

1. Draw a probability tree based on the information as given, including on the tree the prior probability and the *likelihood* of the outcomes of additional information. Chart 13-5 shows the probability tree with the outcome of the loan preceding the outcome of the rating service. Next to each branch of the tree is the probability for that branch. The term "likelihood" is a general one, applying to the probability of a particular empirical observation, conditional on a given prior outcome.

2. Compute the joint probabilities, where joint probability equals the prior multiplied by the likelihood. In Chart 13-5 the joint

CHART 13-5. Probability Tree for the Information Used by the Loan Officer

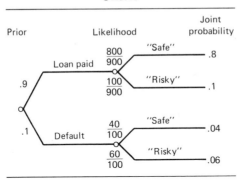

probabilities have been computed; for example, the probability that the loan will be paid off *and* the applicant is rated "safe" is .9 (8/9) = .8.

3. Draw the probability tree in reverse order and assign joint probabilities to the proper end points. While the tree in Chart 13-5 shows the loan officer's current information, what she would like are revised probabilities conditional on the credit-worthiness rating. Thus she needs the probability tree reversed as shown in Chart 13-6. That tree shows the sequence of possible events she faces as she opens the envelope with the credit-worthiness rating and then observes the outcome of the loan. That tree also shows the joint probabilities for each path through the tree, which were

CHART 13-6. Reversed Probability Tree for Computing the Loan Officer's Revised Probabilities

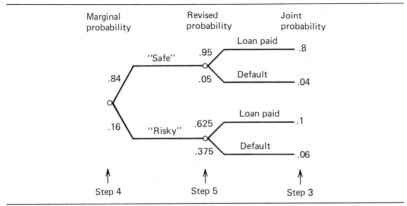

taken from Chart 13-5 and assigned to the appropriate end points of the reversed tree (e.g., the "safe"–default path of Chart 13-6 has the same joint probability as the default–"safe" path of Chart 13-5).

4. Calculate the appropriate "marginal" probabilities for the empirical outcomes by *summing* joint probabilities. The probability that the applicant is rated "safe" (.84) shown in Chart 13-6 was computed by adding the joint probabilities (.80 and .04) of the two paths in the tree that go through the "safe" branch. This is called the *marginal probability* and defines the chances that when the loan officer opens the envelope, she will read "safe."

5. Determine the revised probabilities by dividing each joint probability by the associated marginal probability. If the rating turns out to be "safe" then the revised probability is .8/.84 = .95. On the other hand, if the rating is "risky," then the probability the loan is paid is .1/.16 = .625.

The procedure just described could be carried out with more than two outcomes for the empirical observation or for the ultimate event being forecasted. If $O_1, O_2, \cdots, O_n$ are the possible outcomes for the event being forecasted and E is a possible outcome for the empirical observation, then Bayes's formula, an equivalent expression of the five steps given above for flipping the tree, is given by

$$Pr(O_i|E) = \frac{Pr(E|O_i)}{\Sigma_i [Pr(E|O_i)Pr(O_i)]}$$

where $Pr(O_i)$ = the prior probability of outcome O_i,
         $Pr(E|O_i)$ = the probability of observation E given outcome O_i, that is, the likelihood, and
         $Pr(O_i|E)$ = the revised probability of outcome O_i.

Note that the summation in the denominator is equivalent to $Pr(E)$, the marginal probability of observation E.

Revision of Forecasts for Continuous Uncertain Quantities

When the item being forecast is a continuously ranging uncertain quantity rather than a discrete outcome, Bayesian revision of the forecast is harder. As in the tree flipping procedure, the approach is to multiply prior probabilities by likelihoods and then normalize by dividing by the marginal, but with the large number of possible outcomes, a computer is generally needed to carry out the calculations. Fortunately, the revision can be carried out easily if the prior and the likelihood pair up in a convenient way into what are known as "conjugate families" of distributions. A *family* of distributions is one in which all member probability distributions differ only in the values of certain parameters. The normal distribution, for example, is really a family of distributions which differ only in their mean and variance (the two parameters of this family). A *conjugate* family is one in which the revised probability distribution belongs in the same family as the prior distribution. When working with conjugate families, the probability forecast can be revised simply by revising the parameters of the family. This revision can be done easily without a computer, even when it is carried out repetitively. In this section, three commonly occurring conjugate families are described: the normal-normal, the beta-binomial, and the gamma-Poisson. The first element in each hyphenated name refers to the family in which the prior belongs, and the second describes the family for the likelihood (or, in the other words, the type of sampling process assumed).

The Normal-Normal Conjugate Family

The normal sampling process is perhaps the one most commonly found in practice. We have all seen numerous applications of the familiar bell-shaped curve: educational and psychological tests, sales volume of products, quality control, and so on. Here it is assumed that the empirical data consist of n independent observations from a normal distribution where the variance (the square of the standard deviation) is known and the mean is not known in advance but has a normal prior distribution. Bayesian revision can then be carried out using the following results:

If n independent observations are made of a normally distributed uncertain quantity having known variance, var, and sample mean, m, and if the prior distribution of the population mean is normal with mean m' and variance $var' = var/n'$, then the revised distribution is a normal distribution with mean m'' and var'' given by

$$m'' = \frac{n'm' + nm}{n' + n}$$

$$var'' = \frac{var}{n''} \qquad \text{where } n'' = n' + n$$

Throughout this section, parameters are marked with a prime (') if they apply to the prior distribution and with a double prime ('') if they apply to the revised distribution. The prior and revised variance are both expressed in terms of the variance of the sampling process using n' and n'', which are interpreted as the effective sample sizes of the prior and revised distributions. Thus, for example, if $n' = 10$, the uncertainty expressed in the prior distribution is equivalent to the uncertainty present in 10 observations. The effective sample size of the revised distribution is just the sum of the effective sample size of the prior and the number of observations. Thus the revised distribution will never be more dispersed than the prior. Note that the revised mean is simply the average (weighted by the sample size) of the prior and sample means. These are conceptually straightforward and intuitively appealing results that are widely applicable.

Example: *Sales Forecasts.* A wholesaler of chemical fertilizers is replacing an existing fertilizer with a new product. His years of experience with other fertilizers gives him a basis for judgmentally forecasting the average sales of the product to a customer. His prior distribution is expressed by the normally distributed curve shown in Chart 13-2, which has a mean of 600 tons and a standard deviation of 25 (therefore, a variance of $25^2 = 625$). His years of monitoring sales leads him to believe that the typical fluctuation in a customer's purchases is normally distributed with a standard deviation of 50 tons ($var = 2500$). To improve the accuracy of his forecast he randomly selects 10 customers to use in a sample test. The average order for the 10 customers turns out to be 660 tons. Then the following calculations would provide him with a revised distribution for the average amount of sales to a customer:

$$n' = \frac{var}{var'} = \frac{2500}{625} = 4$$

$$n'' = n' + n = 4 + 10 = 14$$

$$m'' = \frac{n'm' + nm}{n' + n} = \frac{4(600) + 10(660)}{14} = 643 \text{ tons}$$

$$var'' = \frac{var}{n''} = \frac{2500}{14} = 178.6$$

Thus the prior distribution with mean 600 and standard deviation 25 is updated using the sample data to a revised mean of 643 and a revised standard deviation of $\sqrt{178.6} = 13.4$. Note that the dispersion in his revised forecast is lower than the dispersion in either the judgmental prior or the empirical observations used alone (and hence the accuracy is higher).

A major advantage of Bayesian methods is this ability to combine judgmental and empirical data in a statistically correct way to improve forecasting. Again, the revised forecast can now be used as the prior if further empirical observations are taken. Each time more information is added and the probability distribution revised, the weight placed on the original judgmental forecast is diminished, as it should be. In this example where the effective sample size for the prior, n', is 4, the effect of the prior on the revised forecast would be negligible if the number of empirical observations were large. If 100 companies were sampled, for example, then the revised distribution would be about 4% due to the prior and 96% due to the empirical observations.

The Beta-Binomial Conjugate Family

The beta-binomial revision process applies only if the quantity of interest is some proportion p, a number between 0 and 1. For example, p might be market share, the proportion of potential customers approached by a special promotion who will buy your product, or the proportion of defectives from a production process.

The primary assumptions underlying binomial sampling are (1) n observations are randomly taken and r of them are found to possess some particular property (e.g., r defectives in n random observations of items from a production process); (2) each observation is independent of the other observations; and (3) the probability of observing the particular property is a constant p. It is as if a large number of balls are placed in an urn, of which a fraction p are specially marked. A sequence of n balls is drawn from the urn, and each ball inspected for the special marking; after each ball is examined it is placed back in the urn and the balls are mixed up.

The beta family of probability distributions is used to specify a prior on p. A rich selection of shapes is available in the beta family; some examples are shown in Chart 13-7 (note that this is a relative frequency curve, not a cumulative probability curve). Two parameters, r' and n', determine the beta distribution; the mean is $p = r'/n'$ and the variance is $p(1 - p)/(n' + 1)$. When $p = 1/2$, the distribution is symmetric, but various nonsymmetric forms are possible with the tail on the left or the right as shown in Chart 13-7.

Some statistics books* give tables for fractiles of the beta distribution or approximations for computing them. These could be used for selecting the parameters r' and n' to best fit a judgmental prior. Later in this chapter a method is given for selecting the parameters of a prior using the mean and variance of a judgmental cumulative distribution function curve.

---

*See reference 8, for example.

CHART 13-7.   Examples of Relative Frequency Curves for the Beta Distribution

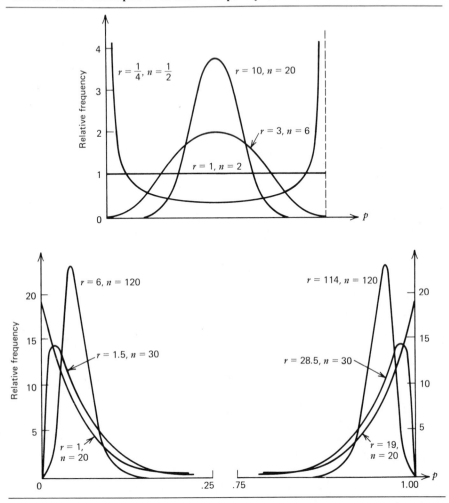

The principle result for the beta-binomial conjugate family is:

If the prior distribution of p is a beta distribution with parameters r' and n', and the sampling is binomial with r successes in n trials, then the revised distribution is a beta with parameters r'' and n'' where

$$r'' = r' + r \quad \text{and} \quad n'' = n' + n$$

Example: *Quality Control.*   Let's return to the production manager who judgmentally forecasted the proportion of defectives in his production process. It turns out that his prior distribution for p (shown in Chart 13-3) fits the beta very well if $r' = 1$ and $n' = 20$. (The relative frequency curve corresponding to this cumulative distribution is one of those shown in Chart 13-7.) Now the production manager randomly samples 100 items for defectives, finds five are defective, and wishes to revise his forecast. The situation appears to fit the requirements of binomial sampling described above: observations are independent, and items are equally likely to be defective. To revise his distribution, the production manager needs simply to compute

$$r'' = r' + r = 1 + 5 = 6$$
$$n'' = n' + n = 20 + 100 = 120$$

Then his revised distribution for the proportion defective is beta with parameters 6, 120. (Note the relative frequency curve for this distribution is also one of those shown in Chart 13-7.) This distribution has a mean of $6/120 = .05$ and a variance of $.05(.95)/121 = .0004$, compared to the same mean of $.05$ and a variance of $.0023$ in the prior. Interestingly, the empirical observations do not change the production manager's mind about the center of the distribution for p, but they do greatly reduce his uncertainty about it as can be seen by comparing the prior and revised relative frequency curves in Chart 13-7.

The Gamma-Poisson Conjugate Family

The final conjugate family we shall discuss is based on the Poisson model of sampling. This model is appropriate for sampling the number of occurrences of a particular type of event in a length of time (or unit of distance) when the arrival process satisfies certain properties. In particular the Poisson model requires that an arrival can occur at any time, that two arrivals cannot occur at the same time, and that the probability of a given number of arrivals in a specific interval does not depend on the number that arrive in any nonoverlapping interval nor the time (or location) where the interval begins. Examples of cases where the Poisson model is usually a good model are the number of telephone calls coming into a switchboard in a given period of time, the number of defects per square foot of a bolt of cloth, or the arrivals of customers to a bank teller.

The family of prior distributions that goes naturally with the Poisson distribution is the gamma family. A rich family like the beta family, the gamma family has two parameters r' and t'. The mean of the gamma is r'/t' and the variance is r'/t'^2. This is the distribution of the arrival rate of the Poisson process.

If the prior distribution of the arrival rate of a Poisson process is gamma distributed with mean r'/t' and variance r'/t'^2, and if the sample consists of r arrivals in time t, then the revised distribution is gamma with mean r''/t'' and variance r''/t''^2 where

$$r'' = r' + r \quad \text{and} \quad t'' = t' + t$$

The revision calculations are identical to those for the beta-binomial. The differences are in the assumptions of the sampling process. The binomial sample consists of the number of successes in n *discrete* trials, while in the Poisson there is continuous monitoring of arrivals. The parameter t' of the prior distribution reflects the effective amount of sampling time expressed by the prior; it's size relative to t determines the weight given to the prior in determining the revised distribution.

Example: *Forecasting Shipments Using Firm Orders.* In order to set his production schedule, a manufacturer needs to forecast the number of future shipments of a certain product that will be needed at a certain time in the future. Based on previous experience he has estimated a prior probability distribution for the rate at which orders will arrive for shipment at a future date. He feels that a gamma distribution with $r' = 10$ and $t' = 2$ (mean arrival rate is 5) provides a reasonable fit to his prior and that orders arrive in a Poisson manner. He then collects 3 month's worth of data on the number of orders for shipment at the future date; 45 orders are received. Doing the revision calculations he gets:

$$r'' = r' + r = 10 + 45 = 55$$
$$t'' = t' + t = 2 + 3 = 5$$

The revised mean is $55/5 = 11$, and the revised variance is $55/25 = 2.2$. This is the distribution for the arrival rate for the future. Using this distribution to estimate the number of orders he will receive before the shipment date and combining it with the firm orders he has already received will give him an estimate for the total orders he will need to ship at the future date.

Bayesian revision is relatively easy for the three conjugate families we have described. Bayesian methods can be used for any general statistical model, but the calculations are beyond the scope of this discussion. It should be stressed that the applicability of the three conjugate families depends on the applicability of each one's particular sampling model (i.e., normal, binomial, or Poisson) and on the ability to fit the prior distribution into the required family of distributions. In some situations none of the sampling models is appropriate. In others, the sampling model may be justified, but no member of the prior family of distributions fits the assessor's prior judgments. These factors serve to reduce the opportunity for using these methods, but not their power when they are justified. Further discussion and examples of Bayesian methods can be found in the references.[7,16]

Fitting Priors

For each of the three conjugate families we have described, it is easy to select the parameter for the prior if we know the mean and variance. But we may not know these values; in particular we may have assessed the prior using the fractile method and have only the cumulative distribution curve. In this case the mean and variance can be calculated from the fractiles. One approximate method is to read off the .05, .15, ..., .95 fractiles and then calculate

$$\text{mean} = \frac{.05 \text{ fractile} + .15 \text{ fractile} + \cdots + .95 \text{ fractile}}{10}$$

$$\text{variance} = \frac{(.05 \text{ fractile})^2 + (.15 \text{ fractile})^2 + \cdots + (.95 \text{ fractile})^2}{10} - \text{mean}^2$$

Alternatively, the prior might be selected by searching for the parameters that best fit the quartiles. Of course it is always appropriate to validate (using the tables for the beta, normal, or gamma) that the subjective cumulative curve fits the model of the prior closely.

BAYESIAN TIME SERIES MODELS AND ECONOMETRICS

Any discussion of Bayesian forecasting would be incomplete without mention of some of the work that has been done in applying Bayesian concepts to time series analysis and econometrics. Harrison and Stevens[5,6] have developed a general Bayesian approach that includes conventional methods, such as linear regression, exponential smoothing, and linear time series models, as special cases. The specifics of the approach are beyond the scope of this chapter, but the essential characteristics are that it relies on a parametric model of the time series where the parameters are specified probabilistically. Starting from a judgmental prior on the parameters, a sequential model specifies how the parameters change over time. The method allows uncertainty as to the underlying model itself and incorporates subjective judgments on the model structure.

This approach has been applied successfully in a number of settings, including the forecasting of cider in the United Kingdom[9] and fashion

CHART 13-8. Some Examples of Applications of Bayesian Forecasting

Discrete	Continuous			Bayesian Time Series	Bayesian Econometrics
	Normal-Normal	Beta-Binomial	Gamma-Poisson		
Loan repayment	Dollar sales	Defective rate	Customer arrival rate	Consumption	Macroeconomic models
Investment outcomes	Quality levels	Market share	Demand rate	Fashion sales	Effects of regulation
Product performance	Psychological properties	Advertising reach	Error rates	Economic variables	Behavior of markets
Product quality			Pace of innovation		
Market response			Technology adoption		
Interest rates					
Prices					
Competitor response					
Oil exploration					

forecasting for a mail order company.[4] It is especially useful in time series where there are sudden changes, a short data history, and the user of the method has information not contained in the time series.

Another area where Bayesian methods have been employed is econometrics. Zellner[18] presents the introductory mathematics which at times can be involved. This is a relatively new area of research with a good potential for application that is currently only in its developing stages.

SUMMARY

Methods for preparing forecasts that combine prior judgment with empirical observations have been described and illustrated. Procedures for assessing judgmental probabilities have been given for two situations: (1) when forecasting a yet unobserved discrete outcome and (2) when forecasting the level of a continuously ranging uncertain quantity. Bayesian revision of the prior probabilities in the first case are easily carried out by flipping the probability tree or using the equivalent Bayes formula. In the second case easy hand calculations are possible only when certain conjugate families of distributions apply to the prior and the sampling process behind the empirical observations. These are the normal-normal, beta-binomial, and the gamma-Poisson families. Many opportunities exist where Bayesian methods will enable the forecaster to improve the accuracy and believability of his or her forecasts by combining the judgmental approach with the statistical approach. Some illustrations are summarized in Chart 13-8, but only the creativity of the forecaster bounds the range of potential application.

REFERENCES

1. Betaque, N. E. and Anthony Gorry, "Automating Judgmental Decision—Making for a Serious Medical Problem," *Management Science*, B17, April 1971, pp. 421–34.

2. Bodily, Samuel E., "When Should You Go to Court?," *Harvard Business Review*, May-June 1981, pp. 103+.

3. Davis, J. C., "Estimation of the Probability of Success in Petroleum Exploration," *Mathematical Geology*, vol. 9, no. 4, 1977, pp. 409–49.

4. Green, M. and P. J. Harrison, "Fashion Forecasting for a Mail Order Company Using a Bayesian Approach," *Operational Research Quarterly,* 24, no. 2, 1973, pp. 193–205.

5. Harrison, P. J. and C. F. Stevens, "A Bayesian Approach to Short-term Forecasting," *Operational Research Quarterly,* 22, no. 4, 1971, pp. 341–62.

6. Harrison, P. J. and C. F. Stevens, "Bayesian Forecasting," *Journal of the Royal Statistical Society,* 38B, 1976, pp. 205–47.

7. Harwood, David L., Elliot S. Grossman, and Earl L. Bailey, *Sales Forecasting,* The Conference Board, New York, 1978.

8. Holloway, Charles A., *Decision Making Under Uncertainty: Models and Choices,* Prentice-Hall, Englewood Cliffs, NJ, 1979.

9. Johnston, F. R. and P. J. Harrison, "An Application of Forecasting in the Alcoholic Drinks Industry," *Journal of the Operational Research Society,* 31, 1980, pp. 699–709.

10. Kabus, Irwin, "You Can Bank on Uncertainty," *Harvard Business Review,* May–June 1976, pp. 95+.

11. Mancini, Louis, Jan Meisner, and Emanuel Singer, "Assessing Uncertain Ventures Using Experts' Judgments in the Form of Subjective Probabilities," *Omega,* vol. 9, no. 2, 1981, pp. 177–187.

12. Peterson, Cameron R., Kurt J. Snapper and A. H. Murphy, "Credible Interval Temperature Forecasts," *Bulletin of the American Meteorological Society,* vol. 53, October 1972, pp. 966–70.

13. Spetzler, Carl S. and Carl-Axel S. Stael von Holstein, "Probability Encoding in Decision Analysis," *Management Science,* vol. 22, no. 3, November 1975, pp. 240–358.

14. Stael von Holstein, Carl-Axel S., "Probabilistic Forecasting: An Experiment Related to the Stock Market," *Organizational Behavior and Human Performance,* vol. 8, August 1972, pp. 139–58.

15. Vatter, Paul A., Stephen P. Bradley, Sherwood C. Frey, Jr. and Barbara B. Jackson, *Quantitative Methods in Management,* chap. 5, Irwin, Homewood, IL, 1978.

16. Winkler, Robert L. and William L. Hays, *Statistics: Probability, Inference and Decision,* Holt, Rinehart & Winston, New York, 1975.

17. Winkler, Robert L. and A. H. Murphy, "Evaluation of Subjective Precipitation Probability Forecasts," *Proceedings of the First National Conference on Statistical Meteorology,* American Meteorological Society, Boston, 1968, pp. 148–57.

18. Zellner, Arnold, *An Introduction to Bayesian Inference in Econometrics,* John Wiley, New York, 1971.

CHAPTER

14

MONITORING AND ADJUSTING FORECASTS

C. D. LEWIS
Management Centre
University of Aston

In any practical forecasting situation, from time to time, forecasts can and do go out of control. This chapter discusses why, in real life situations, forecasts do go out of control and details the techniques that can be used to detect such out of control situations. Failure to detect out of control forecasts can lead to all types of problems, since in such situations the organization's goals are based on fiction rather than fact.

Having detected that forecasts have gone out of control, it is essential that the reason that caused that out of control situation to occur be established prior to corrective adjustments being made. The nature of the reason causing an out of control situation to occur will determine what corrective action should be taken to bring the forecasts back into control. The implementation of monitoring and adjusting schemes for forecasts obviously involves a cost. Whether the cost of such a scheme can be justified can only be established if the benefits of the scheme outweigh the cost. Such benefits will depend on the nature of the product being forecast, and thus a suitable categorization scheme for products also has to be established.

WHY FORECASTS GO OUT OF CONTROL

Most of the forecasting methods discussed in this handbook assume that what has happened in the past will be continued into the future.

Thus, existing data are used initially to establish a forecasting model which in retrospect would have performed well on those data. Subsequent to this "fitting" procedure, it is assumed that the forecasting model shown to perform well with existing, known data will also be expected to perform well when forecasting future, unknown data.

Obviously such forecasting methods cannot be expected to perform well when sudden discontinuities, or structural changes, occur in the data. In practice such changes can and do occur for a variety of reasons. Some of the reasons causing such changes in sales and demand data in particular are:

A change in imposed tax levels or rates, which can either stimulate or depress sales or demand.

A labor dispute which if it occurred to a competitor might stimulate or depress sales whereas if it occurred to a customer might depress sales.

Recession or booms in the economy.

The imposition of an artificial budgeting period such as the "financial year" or a sales year initiated by the release of a new car registration letter or number. This again can either stimulate or depress sales.

CHART 14-1. Out of Control Situation Caused by a Sudden Increase in Demand

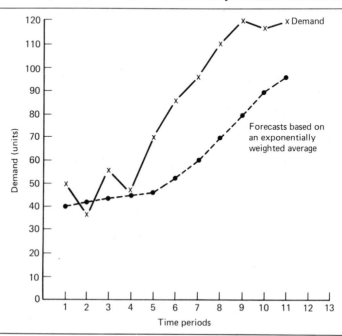

The effect of marketing promotions and so on will also effect sales and demand.

All the above situations, and many others, could cause sudden changes in the basic level of demand or sales for a product or service. If the size of such an induced change is significant, such a change would obviously invalidate the premise that what has happened in the past will be continued into the future. When this happens, it is apparent that any forecast based on previous data can go out of control. This is illustrated in Chart 14-1, which shows what would happen if an exponentially weighted average forecast (in practice one of the most commonly used forecasting methods—see Chapter 11) were to be used when a sudden upward change in the data occurred. From this figure it is apparent that the forecast is totally erroneous and that predictions produced subsequent to the change are meaningless.

The remainder of this chapter will be concerned with dealing with out of control situations as typified by Chart 14-1.

MONITORING FORECASTS

Graphical Methods of Detecting When
Forecasts Go Out of Control

Cumulative Sum of errors (CUSUM)

One of the problems of detecting when forecasts go out of control is that a sudden change that may have caused an out of control situation may not be apparent because of the naturally high degree of random variation (noise) that often occurs in industrial and commercial data. In such situations it is essential that the camouflaging effect of this noise should be removed to reveal the true situation. Consider the sales data depicted in Chart 14-2. Here it would appear that the average level of sales is approximately constant at 250 over the 60 week period involved. However, in reality a sudden change occurs in the data in the thirtieth week when the average level changes by 8% from 250 to 270. The reason that the reader cannot subjectively identify this change in average level is that it is obscured or camouflaged by the random variation or "noise" in those sales data.

One method of removing the camouflaging effect of the noise present in the data is to evaluate the *cumulative sum of errors* known as the CUSUM. This is done by establishing a reference level, which in this case could be the assumed average sales level of 250, and then evaluating the errors or differences of the individual data values from this

CHART 14-2. Noisy Data with an Apparent Average Value of 250

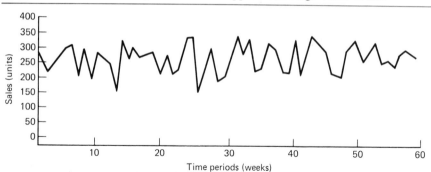

reference. This will produce a series of positive and negative errors, which can then be cumulated to produce the CUSUM.

If the CUSUM were to be formed using 250 as the reference value, and were the true average indeed 250, one would expect the plot of the CUSUM to remain horizontal—simply because the effect of the positive and negative errors would be approximately equal and opposite and would, therefore, cancel out. Examination of the CUSUM plot for these data, using 250 as the reference value (Chart 14-3), shows that the CUSUM does indeed remain horizontal up to the thirtieth week, thus confirming that the average value during that time was indeed 250. After the thirtieth period, however, one cannot fail to see that the CUSUM no longer remains horizontal but starts to climb steeply. This must mean that the positive errors exceed negative errors, indicating that the reference value must now be below the actual average and one can assume therefore that an upward change must have occurred. Since the rate of climb of the CUSUM plot must be an indication of by how much positive errors exceed negative errors cumulatively, then measurement of this rate of climb must indicate the actual size of change. In this case the rate of climb is 20 units per period, indicating that the size of the change is 20 and, hence, the average level of demand after week 30 must be 270 units.

The Use of V-Masks with CUSUMS

While the use of CUSUM presentations is most useful for subjectively highlighting changes or discontinuities in data, for consistent detection of changes of a certain magnitude and particularly the timing of such changes the method needs to be extended. Chart 14-4 shows the CUSUM plot for the out of control forecasting situation depicted earlier in Chart 14-1. Superimposed on this CUSUM plot is a V-mask whose pivot is placed b periods ahead of the current or most recent point on

CHART 14-3. CUSUM Plot for Noisy Data with Reference Value Set Equal to 250 (Chart 14-2)

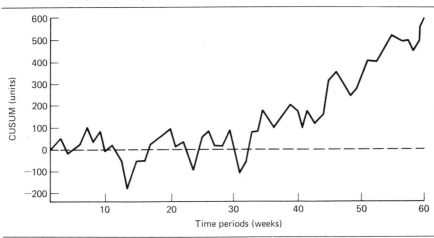

CHART 14-4. Illustration of V-Mask Being Applied to CUSUM Plot to Detect Step Increase in Demand

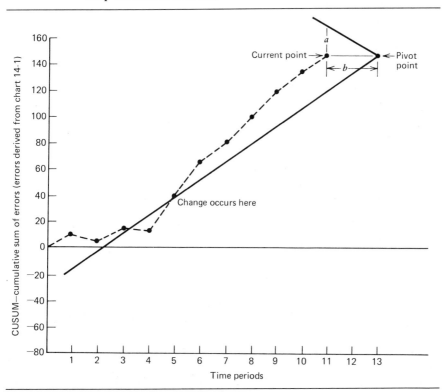

the CUSUM plot, and angled at a/b units per time period. The basis of this V-mask/CUSUM test is that if the CUSUM plot is cut by the lower limb of the V-mask an upward change in the original data is inferred, whereas a downward change is detected when the upper limb of the V-mask cuts the CUSUM plot. In either case the change is assumed to have taken place where the cut occurs. The sensitivity of the test, and hence the magnitude of the change it detects, is controlled by the V-mask parameters a and b. The narrower the angle of the V-mask the more sensitive the test. In practice, having decided what size of change it is required should be detected, the parameters a and b can then be adjusted accordingly, and the construction of a plastic or perspex mask also allows the method to be easily implemented. In this case the change is detected as starting at period 5, which corresponds well with the actual situation in Chart 14-1.

Automatic Methods of Detecting When Forecasts Go Out of Control

In many situations, graphical methods of detecting changes in data, which could cause forecasts subsequently to go out of control, are neither practical nor appropriate because of the large number of products or items involved.

In such situations automatic monitoring methods suitable for computer application are needed. Two such methods are now described.

The Automatic V-Mask/CUSUM Test

The V-mask/CUSUM test described in the preceding section can be expressed[3] in a form suitable for computer implementation using these two equations:

$$D_t = \text{Min}\left(D_{t-1} ; a\right) + \left(\frac{a}{b} + e_t\right)$$

and

$$R_t = \text{Min}\left(R_{t-1} ; a\right) + \left(\frac{a}{b} - e_t\right)$$

where a and b are the V-mask parameters, e_t is the current or most recent forecasting error, and Min $(D_{t-1} ; a)$ is interpreted as meaning take the value of D_{t-1} (the previous value of D_t) or a (the V-mask parameter), whichever is the smaller.

The test is interpreted such that if either D_t or R_t goes negative a change is detected which started in the preceding period when whichever value (D_t or R_t) became less than a. If D_t goes negative, a reduction

CHART 14-5. Computations for Automatic V-Mask/CUSUM Test Where $a = 20$ and $b = 2$.

Period t	Demand d_t	Forecast f_t	Error e_t	$\frac{a}{b} - e_t$	Min $(R_{t-1}; a)$	R_t	$\frac{a}{b} + e_t$	Min $(D_{t-1}; a)$	D_t
1	80	90	-10	20	20	40	0	20	20
2	110	90	20	-10	20	10	30	20	50
3	105	90	15	-5	10	5	25	20	45
4	95	90	5	5	5	10	15	20	35
5	68	90	-22	32	10	42	-12	20	8
6	74	90	-16	26	20	46	-6	8	2
7	71	90	-19	29	20	49	-9	2	-7

in the average value of the original data can be assumed, whereas when R_t goes negative an increase can be assumed. Chart 14-5 shows the application of this test to some demand data where the forecast is fixed at 90 and the V-mask is defined by $a = 20$ and $b = 2$. From Chart 14-5 it can be seen that a downward change is detected in period 7 when D_t goes negative and that this change occurred in period 5 when D_t became less than $a = 20$.

The Smoothed Error Test

While the V-mask/CUSUM test is very powerful in detecting small changes of average values in time series data, it is relatively cumbersome to implement and, therefore, has not gained as widespread an acceptance as the test to be described in this section—the smoothed error test. Indeed there are few computer forecasting packages that do not include this particular monitoring system.

The smoothed error test as proposed by Trigg[7] is simply defined by three equations, such that:

$$\bar{e}_t = \alpha e_t + (1 - \alpha) \bar{e}_{t-1}$$
$$MAD_t = \alpha |e_t| + (1 - \alpha) MAD_{t-1}$$

$$T_t = \frac{\bar{e}_t}{MAD_t}$$

where α = an exponential smoothing constant, often 0.1 or 0.2;
e_t = again the current or most recent forecasting error and $|e_t|$ its absolute value;
$\bar{e}_t$ = the current smoothed (or average) error;
MAD_t = the mean absolute deviation (evaluated as the exponentially weighted average of the *absolute* errors—which when mul-

tiplied by a factor of 1.25 can be used as an estimate of the standard deviation of the original data; and

T_t = a tracking signal whose value can only range ±1.

The larger the value of the tracking signal, the more likely a change has occurred in the data being monitored. Chart 14-6 indicates the confidence one can assume in the hypothesis that a change has occurred when using forecasts based on exponentially weighed averages[1] for corresponding values of α and tracking signal. In practice many systems highlight items as out of control if the tracking signal exceeds 0.7 which, if α = 0.2, would infer changes were detected at a 99% level of confidence. Conventionally, forecast errors are defined as demand or sales minus forecast (i.e., positive errors indicate underprediction and negative errors overprediction); and if this convention is adhered to, positive values of the tracking signal indicate an *increase* in the average value of the data being monitored and *negative* values, a *decrease*.

Chart 14-7 numerically details the application of the smoothed error test for 13 monthly demand values where forecasts are based on an exponentially weighted average u_t defined as

$$u_t = \alpha d_t + (1 - \alpha)u_{t-1}$$

d_t being the current or most recent value of monthly demand.

In this example initial values of $\bar{e}_{t-1}$ and MAD_{t-1} are set equal to $u_{t-1}/10$ and $u_{t-1}/50$ to avoid spuriously high values of the tracking sig-

CHART 14-6.   Tracking Signal Values when Forecasts Are Based on
Exponentially Weighted Averages

Cumulative Probability (%)	Tracking Signal				
	$\alpha = 0.1$	$\alpha = 0.2$	$\alpha = 0.3$	$\alpha = 0.4$	$\alpha = 0.5$
70	0.24	0.33	0.44	0.53	0.64
80	0.29	0.40	0.52	0.62	0.73
85	0.32	0.45	0.57	0.67	0.77
90	0.35	0.50	0.63	0.72	0.82
95	0.42	0.58	0.71	0.80	0.88
96	0.43	0.60	0.73	0.82	0.89
97	0.45	0.62	0.76	0.84	0.90
98	0.48	0.66	0.79	0.87	0.92
99	0.53	0.71	0.82	0.92	0.94
100	1.00	1.00	1.00	1.00	1.00

CHART 14-7. Fully Expanded Forecasting Schedule

		Jan.	Feb.	Mar.	April	May	June	July	Aug.	Sept.	Oct.	Nov.	Dec.	Jan.
This month's demand	d_t	60	70	55	80	90	65	70	75	60	80	90	100	95
Last month's forecast for this month	u_{t-1}	70.00*	68.0	68.4	65.7	68.6	72.9	71.3	71.0	71.8	69.4	71.6	75.2	80.2
α × this month's demand	αd_t	12	14	11	16	18	13	14	15	12	16	18	20	19
(1 − α) × last month's forecast for this month	$(1-\alpha)u_{t-1}$	56.0	54.4	54.7	52.6	54.9	58.3	57.0	56.8	57.4	56.6	57.2	60.2	64.2
This month's forecast for next month	$u_t = \alpha d_t + (1-\alpha)u_{t-1}$	68.0	68.4	65.7	68.6	72.9	71.3	71.0	71.8	69.4	71.6	75.2	80.2	83.2
This month's forecasting error	$e_t = d_t - u_{t-1}$	-10.0	2.0	-13.4	14.3	21.4	-7.9	-1.3	4.0	-11.8	10.6	18.4	24.8	14.8
α × this month's forecasting error	αe_t	-2.0	0.4	-2.68	2.85	4.28	-1.57	-0.25	-0.79	-2.36	2.11	3.69	4.95	2.96
(1 − α) × last month's smoothed error	$(1-\alpha)\bar{e}_t$	1.00*	-0.80	-0.32	-2.40	0.36	3.71	1.71	1.16	1.56	-0.64	1.17	3.88	7.06
This month's smoothed error	$\bar{e}_t = \alpha e_t + (1-\alpha)\bar{e}_{t-1}$	-1.00	-0.40	-3.00	0.45	4.64	2.14	1.46	1.95	-0.80	1.47	4.86	8.83	10.02
α × the modulus of this month's forecasting error	$\alpha|e_t|$	2.0	0.40	2.68	2.85	4.28	1.57	0.25	0.79	2.36	2.11	3.69	4.95	2.96
(1 − α) × last month's mean absolute deviation	$(1-\alpha)MAD_{t-1}$	10.00*	9.60	8.0	8.54	9.11	10.71	9.82	8.05	7.07	7.54	7.72	9.12	11.25
This month's mean absolute deviation	$MAD_t = \alpha|e_t| + (1-\alpha)MAD_{t-1}$	12.00	10.00	10.68	11.39	13.39	12.28	10.07	8.84	9.43	9.65	11.41	14.07	14.21
This month's estimate of standard deviation	$\sigma_t = 1.25\,MAD_t$	15.0	12.5	13.4	14.1	16.7	15.3	12.6	11.0	11.8	12.1	14.3	17.6	17.7
Trigg's tracking signal	$T_t = \bar{e}_t/MAD_t$	-0.08	-0.04	-0.28	0.03	0.34	0.17	0.14	0.22	-0.08	0.15	0.42	0.62	0.70

α = 0.2; * = estimate.

nal T_t at the start of the analysis. The *positive* tracking signal of 0.7 in the last month indicates that one can assume with 99% confidence (since $\alpha = 0.2$) that an *upward* change had occurred and that forecasts, as a result, would be likely to be out of control. The reader can readily verify this by examining the demand and forecast figures.

Implementation of Smoothed Error Monitoring Method

It has already been stated that once an out of control situation has been detected—due, invariably, to a change in the average level of demand or sales—it is essential to establish the underlying reason causing that change. This is usually done by marketing or sales personnel whose specialized knowledge is essential in such situations. To ensure that only a specified number of items are highlighted as out of control at any one time, the value of the smoothed error tracking is usually used to *rank* items in order rather than to establish levels of confidence in the hypothesis that a change has occurred.

Since indiscriminate use of the smoothed error tracking signal can cause wild fluctuations in the number of items notified as out of control, the following procedure[4] overcomes this, assuming a computer can be used.

1. Decide how many items which, if indicated out of control, sales and marketing staff can cope with (i.e., N).

2. Decide an overall level of confidence for all items.

3. Exclude items indicated as out of control in the last two to three periods.

4. Calculate the smoothed error tracking signal value for all remaining items and find those which exceed the overall limit.

5. Of those items in step 4, list in order of priority the top N.

The above approach will ensure that sales and marketing staff are not asked to investigate items for which a causal explanation as to why an out of control situation might have occurred is unlikely to be discovered. Those items notified as out of control under step 5 will be those whose forecasts are most out of control, for which a causal explanation will nearly always be found. At times of severe recession or market downturns, when *most* items would be notified as out of control using the above procedure, to maintain control and detect those items more out of control than most, it would be necessary to raise the specified level of confidence (step 2) considerably.

ADJUSTING FORECASTS WHEN OUT OF CONTROL
SITUATIONS HAVE BEEN CONFIRMED

When a monitoring scheme for forecasts confirms an out of control situation, it is obviously necessary for some form of corrective action to
be taken. In practice, not only will forecasts themselves have to be corrected, but also the functions and activities that are derived from those
forecasts such as loading schedules, stock levels, and so on.

There are several approaches to correcting forecasts, and the methods
available can be broadly classified as manual, semiautomatic, and automatic. The implementation of these methods of forecast correction will
now be discussed in detail, together with a discussion of for which type
of product each is appropriate.

Manual Methods of Correcting Forecasts

The identification by a forecast monitoring system that an out of control situation has occurred is generally an indication of a recent change
in the pattern of the data being forecast. Before any correcting action
can be taken, it is essential that the cause of that change be identified.
The departmental responsibility for identifying the cause of such changes
will vary depending on the individual organization, but more often than
not marketing and sales personnel will need to be involved. Having identified the cause of a change which has resulted in a product's forecast
being out of control, it is necessary to specify:

The size of the change.

When the change started.

For how long the change is likely to be sustained.

The implications of the change to the various organizational functions.

Changes can generally be regarded as permanent (at least for the fore-
seeable future) or temporary.

Where the change is assumed to be permanent, the forecast must be
manually adjusted to the new expected level of demand as shown in
Chart 14-8. Where the change is assumed to be temporary, not only
must the forecast be manually adjusted at the onset of the change; but
the duration of the change must also be identified and the forecast
manually adjusted for a second time back to the prechange level, when
the end of the change is assumed to occur, as is shown in Chart 14-9.

CHART 14-8. Improved Forecast Derived from Manual Interruption and Sales Intelligence When Change Is Assumed to Be Permanent

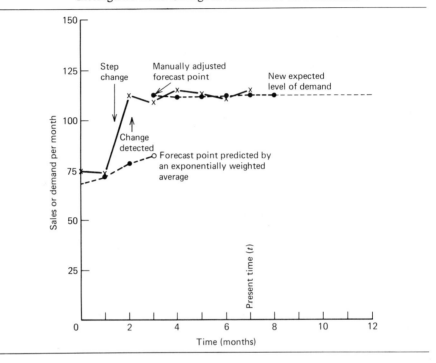

Semiautomatic Methods of Correcting Forecasts

Where it is known in advance that an out of control situation is likely to occur, it may be decided that rather than using a relatively labor-intensive manual system of correction, a semiautomatic method might be just as effective and certainly cheaper to implement. This is particularly true when a new product is launched and for an initial settling-in period forecasts are expected to be greatly in error. In such situations many companies have adopted a policy of increasing the sensitivity of the forecast for this initial phase. This is achieved quite simply, with forecasts based on an exponential smoothing method, by initially using a high value of α, the exponential smoothing constant. The effect of this can be seen in Chart 14.10 where for the first four periods the value of α has been set at 0.5, which has improved the forecast response considerably compared to the forecast using the more orthodox value of 0.2. After the initial settling-in period it is essential that the value of the exponential smoothing constant α is reduced to avoid the forecast responding erroneously to the occasional, one off, extremely high (or low) data value known as an impulse.

CHART 14-9. Improved Forecast Derived from Two Manual Interruptions and Sales Intelligence When Change Is Assumed to Be Temporary

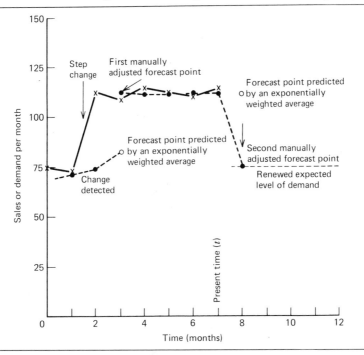

Automatic Methods of Correcting Forecasts

For products which are continually subject to changes or discontinuities, because of market promotions and so forth, it may be necessary to use a forecast that is automatically adjusted to respond to change situations. This automatic adjustment of the forecast can be achieved by altering the inherent sensitivity of the forecast to produce what is often referred to as an *adaptive* forecast. The description of a particular adaptive forecasting model which has gained widespread acceptance now follows.

Adaptive Response Rate Forecasting

Subsequent to Trigg's proposal in 1964 of a smoothed error tracking signal (as described earlier in this chapter), in conjunction with Leach in 1967 an adaptive response rate forecasting model of the form

$$u_t = |T_t|d_t + (1 - |T_t|)u_{t-1}$$

CHART 14-10. Improved Response of Exponentially Weighted Average Forecast with Semiautomatic Adjustment of α

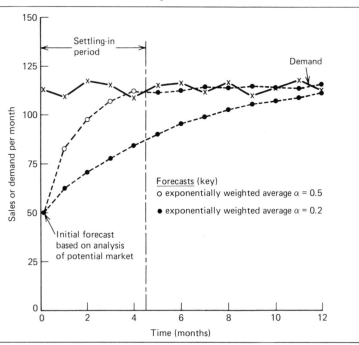

was proposed, where u_t and u_{t-1} are the current and immediate past values of an exponentially weighted average and $|T_t|$ is the absolute value of the smoothed error tracking signal as defined previously.

Using this forecasting model, when a change in the data being forecast occurs, relatively large forecasting errors are produced and hence a large tracking signal. Since the absolute value of the tracking signal has now replaced α (the exponential smoothing constant) for this adaptive response rate model, in such change situations the sensitivity of the forecast is thus increased, and in this form it will rapidly react and "home in" to the new (post change) level. After the "homing in" phase, when the forecast is essentially back in control and forecasting errors again are relatively small and of both positive and negative polarity, the value of the tracking signal is automatically reduced and hence so is the sensitivity of the forecast. This, in theory, is exactly what is required of the forecast if it is to avoid erroneous responses to single period impulses. However, as can be seen in Chart 14-11, the adaptive response rate forecast using $|T_t|$ as the exponential smoothing constant unfortunately always overreacts to single period impulses simply because at that time the current value of $|T_t|$ is increased, typically to a value of the order of

CHART 14-11.   Improved Response of Delayed Adaptive Response Rate

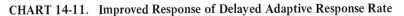

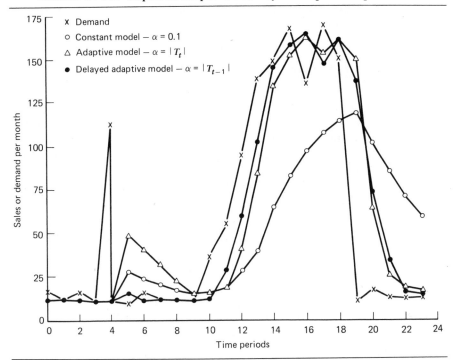

Time periods

0.4, and produces a subsequent forecast which is approximately 0.4 times the value of the impulse too high. This effect can be overcome by using $|T_{t-1}|$ rather than $|T_t|$ for α, in which case the forecast now becomes

$$u_t = |T_{t-1}|d_t + (1 - |T_{t-1}|)u_{t-1}$$

The improved response of this delayed version of the model in terms of its lack of response to a single period impulse is also shown in Chart 14-11 and is due to Schone.[6] The improved response of this model also to the subsequent step change, as depicted by Schone in this diagram, although technically possible rarely occurs. One can hardly claim an improved lack of response to a single period impulse and an improved response to a step change whose first value is, in effect, a single period impulse!

The adaptive response rate forecasting model described here has gained widespread acceptance as a forecasting method with automatic sensitivity adjustment, but because the values of the tracking signal values of this model differ considerably compared with nonadaptive systems (where α is fixed) it is *not* possible to monitor adaptive response rate forecasts using published tracking signal values such as those shown earlier in Chart 14-6.

ALLOCATION OF FORECAST MONITORING
AND ADJUSTING METHODS

The choice of which of the forecast monitoring and/or adjusting methods described in the previous section should be used must depend on the item or product being considered. Essentially the costs of implementing the proposed scheme or method must be more than offset by the savings directly attributable to the increased control of the forecasts and the resulting increased control of the operating systems based on those forecast. Obviously for cheaper items or products, the costs of such monitoring and adjusting schemes are unlikely to be justified.

ABC Analysis

A categorization scheme of an organization's items or products which can very conveniently be used to associate forecast monitoring and adjustment schemes is the well-known Pareto or ABC analysis. For those unfamiliar with this approach, it has been found that in most organizations if an item or product's importance is associated say with annual turnover value, a small proportion of those items will represent a large proportion of annual turnover value and a relatively large proportion of those items will only represent a small proportion. Conventionally this relationship is used to divide items into three categories which in order of descending importance are A, B, and C. This Pareto or ABC relationship is shown in Chart 14.12.

A Items. These are the most important items and typically have an annual turnover value of more than 6 times the average for all items. They are relatively few in number (typically 10–20%) and represent the major portion of annual turnover items (typically 70–80%). For these items it is essential that a sophisticated monitoring scheme such as the smoothed error method be employed so that changes in sales or demand are detected, subsequently investigated, and corrective action taken.

B Items. These are relatively important items and usually are more numerous than A items (typically 20–30%). For these items, whereas it is important that changes do not cause forecasts to be permanently out of control, it is often not possible to justify—on cost grounds—a sophisticated monitoring scheme with its associated subsequent manual intervention. These items, therefore, are very often suitably controlled

CHART 14-12.   **Allocating Forecasting Methods to Products Using ABC Analysis**

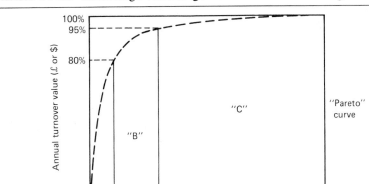

using automatic methods of forecast correction such as the delayed adaptive response rate scheme proposed earlier.

C Items.   Accepting that all items are to some degree important, C items are relatively unimportant compared with A and B class items. They are the most numerous (typically 60–70%), have an average turnover value of less than half the average for all items, and only represent a small proportion (typically, 5–10%) of the organization's annual turnover value. In cost terms it is often difficult to justify forecasting for these items at all, let alone an associated monitoring scheme. Indeed many organizations do not even maintain records for these items, preferring to maintain control by having a surplus. This works on the basis that to hold a 20% surplus on those 70% of items representing 5% in annual turnover terms is only an overall surplus of 1%, which is generally assessed to be less than the cost of implementing a recording and forecasting scheme to gain tight control. Where the traumatic move to a nonrecording system for C items is more than the organization can take, an adaptive response rate scheme such as that proposed for B type items is perhaps most appropriate.

As an example of how this type of ABC analysis might be used in the selection of a forecasting approach, Chart 14-12 indicates criteria that might be used in forming these three categories and the following guidelines indicate how a forecasting method might be selected:

1. A items—few but valuable. Forecast with most sophisticated non-adaptive method feasible and monitor.

2. B items—less valuable than A but more of them. Use adaptive forecast—no monitoring.

3. C items—cheap but numerous. No formal forecast—assess annually.

CONCLUSION

This chapter has attempted to describe the problems that can occur when previously well-behaved forecasts go out of control due to unforeseen structural changes in the data being analyzed. The early detection of such changes is obviously essential, and where large numbers of items are involved it is apparent that quantitatively based techniques suitable for computer implementation must be used.

The smoothed error method and the CUSUM method of monitoring are the most widely used quantitatively based monitoring systems currently available. The smoothed error method, the more widely used of the two, was specifically developed for monitoring forecasts and is incorporated in the majority of forecasting computer packages. It is easily interpreted and offers the possibility of automatically adjusting forecasts when changes in data do occur. The method has one minor drawback in that it does not specify exactly when a detected change occurred. The *CUSUM* method is generally more complex than the smoothed error method and certainly more expensive to implement. It does, however, possess the distinct advantage of specifying the timing of changes.

With the ever-increasing storage of data within computer systems, it is becoming increasingly important if management are to retain any "feel" for the data on which most of their decisions are based, that automatic, quantitatively based monitoring systems which are able consistently to detect changes in those data, be introduced.

REFERENCES

1. Batty, M. "Monitoring and Exponential Smoothing System," *Operational Research Quarterly*, vol. 20, 1969, p. 319.

2. Box, G. E. P. and G. M. Jenkins, "Some statistical aspects of adaptive optimization and control," *Journal of the Royal Statistical Society (B)*, vol. 24, 1962, p. 297.

3. Harrison, P. J. and S. Davies, "The use of cumulative sum (CUSUM) techniques for the control of routine forecasts of produce demand," *Operations Research*, vol. 12, 1964, p. 325.

4. Lewis, C. D., *Demand Analysis and Inventory Control,* Gower Publishing, Farnborough, United Kingdom, and Lexington Books, Lexington, MA, 1975.

5. Lewis, C. D., "The Use of a Computerised V-Mask to Identify Small Changes in Process Means," *Quality Assurance*, vol. 6, 1980, p. 3.

6. Schone, R. "Viewpoints," *Operational Research Quarterly,* vol. 18, 1967, p. 318.

7. Trigg, D. W. "Monitoring a Forecasting System, *"Operational Research Quarterly*, vol. 15, 1964, p. 271.

8. Trigg, D. W. and D. H. Leach, "Exponential Smoothing with Adaptive Response Rate," *Operational Research Quarterly*, vol. 18, 1967, p. 53.

15

AN INTEGRATED APPROACH TO MEDIUM- AND LONG-TERM FORECASTING

The Marketing-Mix System

RUDOLF LEWANDOWSKI
Marketing Systems

INTRODUCTION

Forecasting methods in current use often suffer from three major deficiencies. First, they are too complex to be understood by the average user; second, they involve a number of unrealistic assumptions which greatly hinder practitioners who use them; and third, they do not integrate into a single model extrapolative and explicative variables.

The purpose of this chapter is to describe an approach to medium- and long-term forecasting that aims to correct the above problems. This approach was developed by the author and introduced into continental Europe, where it is now widely used. It remains, however, little known in the Anglo-Saxon world, since up to now the author's writings have been confined to the German and French languages (see Lewandowski[2,3]).

The basic components of the marketing-mix approach to medium- and long-range forecasting, as will be described in this chapter, are: (1) the combination of extrapolative and explicative variables into a single model; (2) the integration of the medium- and long-term elements into a single model; and (3) the development of a realistic system that can be used by practicing managers who have an interest in forecasting.

It should be emphasized that this approach is practice oriented and empirically developed, its main aim being to help practicing managers make forecasts in a more efficient and effective way. For this reason, it does not comprise highly sophisticated mathematical formulas, and as such it is hoped that the reader of this handbook will gain a clearer understanding of—and thus be able to improve upon—his medium- and long-term forecasting functions.

THE INTEGRATED SETUP

There are two approaches to the study of the long term. The first of these is simply extrapolative, whereby some variable of interest is considered by itself and its trend is analyzed and then extrapolated in order to predict the future. Such an approach is both "blind" and "fatalistic"; however, in practice, it has been found to produce satisfactory results. This has been observed for individual products as well as larger market segments, or even whole technologies. While such trends were initially thought to be linear, during the 1960s logistic or S-curves were introduced to improve observation of the long-term behavior of the variable to be forecasted. It is today widely accepted that only nonlinear trends can adequately predict future patterns. The problem still to be solved, however, is which of the many existing nonlinear trends represents the best choice.

The second approach is the study of the causal factors that influence certain events, and then forecasts are made along the lines that if "a" happens, then "b" will follow. This sort of causal approach, although it works very well in the physical and natural sciences, has severe limitations in the economic and business environments. On the other hand, it is imperative to establish a method of ascertaining how changes in one variable will affect the others; hence there is a need for the development of some kind of explanatory models which will facilitate the interpretation of what actually happens in reality, and also help to provide more accurate forecasts. These models will be referred to as "explicative" in this chapter, meaning that their aim is to provide a clearer understanding of the factors affecting the future of a company, without necessarily going so far as to say that there may be causal relationships between the various elements comprising the explicative model.

A third alternative is to combine the two approaches above into an integrated set up that will include both exploratory trends and explicative variables. Up to now, according to the forecasting literature, this procedure has not been successfully attempted, even though its potential benefit is obvious.

**CHART 15-1. The Four Types of Integrated
(Long-Term and Medium-Term) Forecasting Models**

	Medium Term	
Long Term	Extrapolative	Explicative
Extrapolative (eq. Time Series)	Ld-Md	Ld-Mx
Explicative (eq. Causal)	Lx-Md	Lx-Mx

Key: Ld—Long-term extrapolative setup.
Lx—Long-term explicative setup.
Md—Medium-term extrapolative setup.
Mx—Medium-term explicative setup.

Another important element affecting the behavior of long-term trends is the influence of medium-term changes. In this respect, it is impossible to separate the medium and the long term; for example, a significant price increase forecasted for the medium term will inevitably affect long-term trends. Furthermore, cyclical fluctuations will affect longer term developments and must therefore also be incorporated into the long-term model. Chart 15-1 shows the four possibilities of forecasting models.

The Long-Term Extrapolative (Ld), Medium-Term Extrapolative (Md) Setup: Ld-Md

This is a purely extrapolative setup as both the long-term and the medium-term only allow for temporal developments which are not explained by incorporating explicative variables.

The analysis of such models is therefore automatic and relatively simple to carry out since it can be performed entirely with computer programs, particularly with regard to determining the extrapolative functions and their parameter optimization. The degree of explaining for the medium or long term with such functions can, however, only be mediocre.

The Ld-Md setup is only of interest where a large number of products have to be analyzed by a limited staff.

The Long-Term Extrapolative (Ld), Medium-Term Explicative (Mx) Setup: Ld-Mx

The long-term setup here is of an extrapolative nature, while that of the medium term attempts an explicative explanation of medium-term development. When the law contained in Ld is well adapted to the market development, which is the case for time series with comprehensive material from the past, and for products in the consumer goods sector, the medium-term analysis is not distorted and can provide excellent results. This setup concentrates more on an economic analysis and less on a long-term model construction.

The Long-Term Explicative (Lx), Medium-Term Extrapolative (Md) Setup: Lx-Md

This setup aims at a comprehensive explanation of the medium- and long-term development using explicative models. However, the explicative part of the model is oriented mainly for the long term, while the medium term is defined by an extrapolative model.

The Long-Term Explicative (Lx), Medium-Term Explicative (Mx) Setup: Lx-Mx

This setup aims to provide a comprehensive explanation of both the medium and the long term. However, due to its lack of extrapolative trends, it has not been adopted into the approach described in this chapter. A typical situation of this type would be a set of simultaneous equations, that is, an econometric model.

Although the development of such models is extremely difficult, only this type of setup ensures the formation of actual explicative systems with satisfactory operational reliability.

The purpose of the integrated approach described above is (1) to separate medium- from long-term influences and to determine their specific consequences; (2) to forecast each of the consequences separately; and (3) to eliminate as far as possible economic distortions caused by fluctuations from long-term trends.

THE METHODOLOGY OF THE INTEGRATED SETUP

In order for a practical system to be developed, the approach must provide for the possibility of combining the major elements of the medium and the long term, together with extrapolative and explicative characteristics. The purpose of this section is to illustrate how this can be achieved

A series of nonlinear growth functions exists which can be used to describe long-term developments. These are the following:

The exponential function with saturation level.

The symmetric-logistic function.

The Pyatt function.

The Gompertz function.

The Weblus function

The semilogarithmic function.

The von Boguslawski function.

The choice of the most appropriate of the seven functions listed above is, however, difficult. To avoid this problem, the functions have been classified into two groups (see Lewandowski[2]) known as "first and second order generalized logistic functions." The user is thereby able to let a computer program choose from these generalized logistic functions one which best fits the data. The two classifications of functions are as follows:

Generalized
logistic functions
of the first order
$\left\{\begin{array}{l}\text{symmetrical-logistic}\\\text{exponential}\\\text{von Bertalanffy}\\\text{Böhm}\end{array}\right.$

Generalized
logistic functions
of the second order
$\left\{\begin{array}{l}\text{Gompertz}\\\text{Johnson}\\\text{exponential}\end{array}\right.$

Some users may wish to look at long-term trends using one of the two generalized functions; such an approach, however, is somewhat simplistic in that it tends to disregard the medium term. The approach of this author therefore provides for the integration of medium-term economic fluctuations with the generalized logistic functions. In addition, lag effects can be incorporated into the system so that the influence of the medium term can eventually be eliminated, in such a way that long-term trends can be studied and correctly extrapolated.

The advantage of a simple extrapolative approach is that it is easy to implement, being a more or less automatic procedure, and can be used when forecasts are required for large numbers of products. It does, however, fail to take into account explanatory variables, which have an undeniable influence on the medium and long term. In order for this important integration to be achieved, generalized logistic functions of the third, fourth, and fifth order (see Lewandowski[3]) can be introduced by the user.

Equation (15-1), for example, presents a third order generalized logistic function.

$$P_t = \frac{P_0^*}{1 + e^{a - bt - cY_t + d \cdot Pr_t - f \cdot \Delta_t}} \tag{15-1}$$

where

$$Y_t = \text{private consumption at period } t,$$
$$Pr_t = \text{relative market price at period } t, \text{ and}$$
$$\Delta_t = \text{economic variable which specifies the price-}$$
income relation, which in turn is defined by

$$\Delta_t = \Delta Y_t - \Delta Pr_t$$

As can be seen, this model comprises both S-curve type trends and explicative variables such as private consumption, relative market prices, and price–income relations.

APPLICATION FOR THE CAR MARKET IN THE FEDERAL REPUBLIC OF GERMANY

The following description outlines the use of the generalized logistic function of the third order for determining the development of new registrations in the Federal Republic of Germany. The model employs the following four explanatory variables:

$X1$ = Nominal wages and salaries

$X2$ = Inflation rate

$X3$ = Car repair costs

$X4$ = New models launched on the market in a period of six months

Taking into account the above four variables, and assuming a logistic trend-growth function model (15-2) was developed and empirically tested for new car registrations in the Federal Republic of Germany. We have:

$$P_t = \frac{P^*}{1 + e^{a - bt + c \cdot Y_t + d \cdot \Delta Pr_t + e \Delta MP_t}} \tag{15-2}$$

where

P^* = the potential market level,
P_t = the current market performance,
$Y_t = X1_t / X2_t$ (i.e., Y_t is an inflation-adjusted index of wages and salaries),
$$\Delta Pr_t = \sum_{i=0}^{\infty} \lambda (1 - \lambda)^i Pr^*_{t-i} \text{ (i.e., changes in prices, allowing for time lags),}$$

where

$$\lambda = 0,3$$
$$Pr_t^* = (X3_t - 3,0)^2 + 9,0 \quad \text{and}$$

$$MP_t = \lambda \cdot X4_t + \lambda(1 - \lambda)X4_{t-1} + \lambda(1 - \lambda)^2 X4_{t-2} + \cdots$$
$$= \sum_{i=0}^{\infty} \lambda(1 - \lambda)^i MP_{t-i}$$

This type of model, therefore, allows the market development to be followed, with the aid of S-shaped functions, that is, incorporating saturation levels, as well as four economic variables. It has been found, however, that the model did not perform satisfactorily during the periods from 1963 to 1965, 1968 to 1970, and 1973 to 1976.

The first two periods represented a boom phase in the development of the car market in the Federal Republic of Germany, whereas the third phase was marked by a recessive development following the energy crisis. The model described here does not appear to be as suitable for the analysis of large cyclical fluctuations as for the description of "normal" business conditions.

A GENERALIZED LOGISTIC FUNCTION OF THE FOURTH ORDER (GLF4)

The fundamental idea of the GLF4 is based on the work proposed by Bonus.[1] The major difference of GLF4 is in the definition of the saturation level. Bonus has formulated the following model:

$$P_t^* = \frac{P_0^*}{1 + c \cdot Y_t^{-\alpha}} \tag{15-3}$$

that is, the potential market level P_t depends on the income level Y_t of private households.

If the Bonus model of the potential market evolution is incorporated into the definition of logistic growth, the following equation is obtained:

$$P_t' = b \cdot P_t(P_t^* - P_t) = b \cdot P_t \cdot \left(\frac{P_0^*}{1 + c \cdot Y_t^{-\alpha}} - P_t \right) \tag{15-4}$$

The solution of this equation is:

$$P_t = \frac{P_0^*}{1 + e^{-b \cdot t} + d \cdot Y_t^{-\alpha}} = \frac{P_0^*}{1 + A_1 e^{-b \cdot t} + A_2 \cdot Y_t^{-\alpha}} \tag{15-5}$$

where

P_0^* = maximum saturation level of the market, that is, the maximum attainable level of P_t,

$A_1 e^{-bt}$ = rate of the logistic growth of the market expansion, and

$A_2 Y_t^{-a}$ = influence of the explicative variables Y_t.

It is quite obvious, however, that market developments do not only depend on one single variable. An application of the model with income and price variables will therefore now be considered.

The GLF4 can be modified as follows, to allow for the income and price variables:

$$P_t^* = \frac{P_0^*}{1 + C\, Pr_t^\beta \cdot Y_t^{-\alpha}} \qquad (15\text{-}6)$$

Thus, the influence of the price and income variables is accounted for in multiplicative form, which appears to be more appropriate than an additive representation of these two variables.

The solution of equation (15-6) is:

$$P_t = \frac{P_0^*}{1 + A_1 \cdot e^{-bt} + A_2 Y_t^{-\alpha} + A_3 Y^{-\alpha} Pr_t^\beta} \qquad (15\text{-}7)$$

The term C can also represent an environmental variable for the medium term—for instance, the change in personal income (ΔX_t). This case is presented in Chart 15-2.

Although the differences between the fundamental structures of equations (15-2) and (15-7) are relatively small, the growth hypotheses defined according to (15-7) are more realistic and lead to a better description of actual market developments.

Although the ideas described in this and the preceding section had been applied for many years, it was found that in unfavorable situations (1966–67, 1974–75) the market development was only partially explained by the models; this was also the case for the pronounced upswing in the years 1969–70 and 1976–77.

Thus, while a relatively high forecasting accuracy was achieved for the period from 1955 to 1965, with an average deviation of 3%, this was no longer the case from 1966 onwards.

The generalized logistic function of the fourth order permits a better approximation of medium- and long-term analysis and forecasting by breaking down the most important factors influencing the market; but it does have several deficiencies. On the other hand, it was found that such functions exhibited a high degree of forecasting reliability,

CHART 15-2. Economic Significance of the Growth Components of GLF4

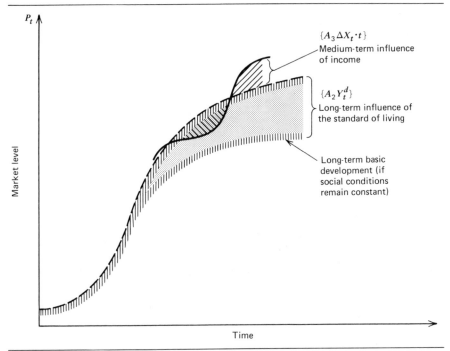

which became particularly clear when comparisons were made with purely extrapolative methods. For instance, forecasts made in 1975, using logistic functions, underestimated the actual demand level by about 25%. This underestimation will rise to about 35% for the year 1985, while the generalized logistic function of the fourth order will show a deviation of about 10%. Needless to say, however, an attempt to improve the GLF4 has been made, resulting in the GLF5 which is described in the next section.

THE GENERALIZED LOGISTIC FUNCTIONS OF THE FIFTH (GLF5) ORDER AS A GENERAL FORECASTING SETUP

The GLF5 differs from the previously described generalized logistic functions of the third and fourth order in that it has a more flexible structure, which applies not only to the long term but also to the medium-term component (see Lewandowski[3]). The GLF5 can be termed a function generator, incorporating all aspects and models of the medium and long term so far described. Chart 15-3 shows a schematic presentation of GLF5.

CHART 15-3.   The Generation of GLF5

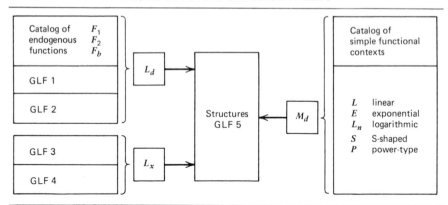

The application of the generalized logistic functions of the fifth order is vital within the framework of medium- and long-term forecasting. These functions describe not only generalized extrapolative models (with the aid of generalized logistic functions of the first and second order), but also generalized explicative models of the GLF3 and GLF4; furthermore, they also can be expanded to incorporate even more diverse situations than those so far encountered.

Criticism has been raised concerning the considerable complexity involved with GLF5. However, in the opinion of this author, the extraordinary possibilities of GLF5 have been overlooked. Its practical implementation by a large number of companies in recent years has proved that the technical difficulties arising from the application of specific systems of GLF5 can be kept to a minimum, while the quality of the analyses and forecasts could be considerably improved.

As applications have shown, the generalized logistic functions of the fifth order can become real explicative and operational systems which permit strategic corporate alternatives to be simulated and studied.

In order to easily generate these explicative models, the forecasting system *MARKET* was developed. This was done on behalf of about 20 international companies. The purpose of the system was to forecast the medium term and the long term for both sales and financial forecasting.

CONCLUSIONS

Even though there might be some difficulties with implementing the integrated setup described in this chapter, it is believed that it represents a unique and practical tool of market research for the analysis and forecasting of variables of interest.

The approach allows forecasters:

To find the significant variables of market reactions.

To determine the time lag effects for each variable.

To define the explicative concepts which characterize the market and consumer behavior.

To describe the functional relationships among the explicative concepts and the market and consumer behavior.

To describe the long-term trends by isolating medium-term influences.

The term "integrated" is appropriate to the setup described here in that the various market and consumer reactions form an integrated relationship, both in the medium- and long-term sector.

It is believed that the integrated setup is currently the only one that enables the real explicative market structures to be determined, and as such it represents a real corporate model for simulating and forecasting market conditions.

It is important to emphasize that the generalized logistic function of the fifth order permits us to measure and understand changes in trend. This is extremely important and cannot be done by the "classical" forecasting methods.

The degree of accuracy of the approach depends on the requirements of the analysis, the amount of data available, and the specific industry or company. However, the division of the total market can be easily interpreted using the principal variables concerned. In this way, the user can go to a much greater depth if he or she so desires.

Because of the repeated use of the forecasting system *MARKET*, there have been several papers describing specific applications; for example, see Lewandowski and Stöwsand,[7] Lewandowski and Faber,[4] Lewandowski and Faber,[5] Lewandowski and Rouas,[6] and Lewandowski.[3]

All of these models can incorporate both economic variables and internal factors related to marketing strategy dealing with the medium and long term.

REFERENCES

1. Bonus, H., *Die Ausbreitung des Fernsehens,* Diss. Bonn, 1967.
2. Lewandowski, R., *Prognose- und Informationssysteme, Band I,* Berlin, 1974.
3. Lewandowski, R., *Prognose- und Informationssysteme, Band II,* Berlin, 1980.
4. Lewandowski, R. and W. Faber, Analyse- und Prognosesysteme für den Papiermarkt, Marketing Report, *Papiermarktforschung Band I,* Hamburg, 1979a.
5. Lewandowski, R. and W. Faber, "Practical Setups of Market Modeling and

Forecasting," *Journal of the European Society for Opinion and Marketing Research,* vol. 7, no. 5, September 1979, pp. 192–201.

6. Lewandowski, R. and J. Rouas, The Application of Long and Medium-Term MMIS, Information Systems in Action, Esomar, Amsterdam, 1980.

7. Lewandowski, R. and H. Stöwsand, "Marketing Models for Use in Practice—A Criticism of Conventional Methods and a Practical Solution. It won't work here;" Ama/Esomar Conference, New York, 1979.

PART

3

FORECASTING
CHALLENGES

16

FORECASTING AND THE ENVIRONMENT: THE CHALLENGES OF RAPID CHANGE

ALAN R. BECKENSTEIN

The Colgate Darden Graduate School of Business Administration
University of Virginia

Rapid changes in the economy and other elements of a firm's external environment occurred during the 1970s. The impact of these events on standard forecasting techniques has been poorly understood. It is the purpose of this chapter to outline the impact of environmental change on forecasting techniques within the context of the total forecasting system of a corporation.

The relationship of environmental change to forecasting systems is addressed first. A survey of environmental factors and their impact is then presented. Performance measures are the subject of the third section. Finally, a general approach to incorporating environmental influences in forecasts is offered.

ENVIRONMENTAL CHANGE AND FORECASTING SYSTEMS

When managers forecast—and even when they choose not to formally —they make implicit hypotheses (assumptions) about the "environment" of their forecast. Consider the following example. Company X has decided to forecast its sales by relating them in a regression model to Real Gross National Product (RGNP). Because the sales of the company are affected by the economy, and the business cycle in particular, a causal model has been chosen.

What is the "environment" of this forecasting system? The *environment of a forecast* is the set of factors not explicitly accounted for by the forecasting system itself. In the most general sense, the environment contains an infinite number of factors. More realistically, it contains all of the factors known in practice to influence the variable being forecast, but which are not formally incorporated in the forecasting model. For company X, the environment includes those factors other than real GNP that affect sales.

Forecasting techniques tend to be quantitatively complex, but qualitatively simple. Managers almost always employ a larger set of factors in thinking about how to forecast sales than do model builders in formal development of a forecasting system. Three obstacles exist to dissuade a model builder (or a manager) from incorporating all relevant environmental information in a formal model: (1) the cost of modeling, (2) a lack of (or high cost of) precise data, and (3) the absence of truly definitive historical experience from which the differential effects of separate variables can be isolated.

Forecasting experts are trained how to search for the most cost-effective model. They necessarily sacrifice realism for usefulness. They cannot work with too many variables or too much complexity so they scientifically establish priorities. Where statistical indicators indicate little value added relative to cost from more complexity, the forecaster stops.

Managers are trained to be sensitive to a wide range of factors in the business environment, an activity referred to as *environmental scanning.* While qualitatively complex, scanning lacks the rigor of statistical forecasting methods for calibrating precise effects. Usefulness is sacrificed for the realism and flexibility that broad-gauged scanning offers.

If scanning and formal model building were independent activities, we could combine the two and achieve an ideal balance of realism *and* usefulness. The balance is more complicated, however. When change in the environment is rapid—and formal models encounter poor performance—scanning should be the basis for revamping the formal model to embrace the source of environmental change. This requires a two-pronged effort of more formalized scanning and more realistic models. Communication among scanners and model builders is essential. Each must understand the philosophy of the other to facilitate a meaningful contribution. Short of that a communications gap arises which manifests itself (1) to managers as a failure of techniques and (2) to modelers as "noise" in the environment which managers claim to understand only ex post facto.

The true state of affairs is that modelers make *premises* about the environment. Some of the premises are recognized explicitly, such as through explanatory variables that were either ignored or performed poorly at the margin during stable times. Others can be identified only by the managers/scanners. To the extent that early identification and continuous tracking of more promising environmental variables takes place, adaptation of forecasts to rapid change can be facilitated. The modelers' rigor must be applied to the scanners' ideas, and the scanners' ideas must be applied to the modeler's formal system.

Consider the following illustrative scenario about company X. Through 1971 a regression model explaining companywide sales with real GNP performed well both statistically and as a general guide to individual product line performance. During the 1973–75 period, sales were affected by a number of unusual changes in the environment. The environmental changes and their impact on company X's model are summarized in Chart 16-1.

Accelerated inflation, an inventory cycle, and the business cycle each affected the performance of forecasting models and the scanning of managers. The usefulness of the sales–RGNP relationship was lessened because the sacrifice in realism became too great. In other words, environmental change altered the choice of how much complexity to build into formal models while rendering some aspects of scanning efforts so useful as to demand more precise analysis.

The experience of company X was fairly typical during the 1970s.[2] Before considering how to solve the problem, in the next section we shall present a broader survey of the impact of environmental change on forecasting.

ENVIRONMENTAL FACTORS IN FORECASTING

The remaining chapters in this section of the handbook deal with how to forecast when particular environmental characteristics dominate. For example, business cycles present particular problems requiring technical solutions. Political risk might warrant the use of especially flexible methods. Consumer products, industrial products, and services have separate forecasting traditions based largely on different characterizations of environmental influences. The time horizon of forecasting is similarly affected by the nature of environmental change.

Environmental factors, which are common to most forecasting systems, can be classified as economic, organizational, competitive, technological, and demographic. Several are discussed below to provide an exposition of the impact of environental factors in forecasting. While no attempt to be exhaustive is intended, a number of prominent factors are discussed in each subsection that follows.

CHART 16-1. 1973–75 Environmental Changes and Their Impact on Company X

Change	Impact on Company X
Accelerated inflation	Sales measured in dollars grew more rapidly than unit sales causing the former to be misleading.
	Impact on model: regression line was tilted upward to account for inflation as inflationary experience was employed in reestimating the regression.
	Intelligence from management: declining unit sales conflicted with forecasts of inflated dollar sales from the model.
Inventory cycle	The model underestimated sales during 1973 and early 1974 when customers were hoarding inventory. It overestimated sales during late 1974 and 1975 when inventory levels were being reduced.
	Intelligence from management: the sales force understood the timing of the inventory cycle, but did not know how to adjust the model's output to account for it.
Business cycle	The explanatory variable (real GNP) accounted for the cycle in a crude way, but was imperfect for several reasons:
	1. Real GNP was not as accurate an indicator as other more related components of GNP. Previously, there had been no improvement in the model from paying attention to the difference.
	2. Forecasts of real GNP became more inaccurate causing the sales forecast to become more unreliable.
	3. Sales of various products sold by company X were acyclical. The total sales forecast became inadequate for more specific decisions.
	Intelligence from management: the impact of the cycle was understood at product levels, but no ability to reconcile that information with a total dollar sales forecast existed.

Economic Factors

Economic premises are often made in forecasts. For example, the fundamental choice of forecasting sales in units or dollars involves an assumption about *inflation*. Consider the contrast in the time

CHART 16-1. Company X Sales in Dollars and Units (1965–80)

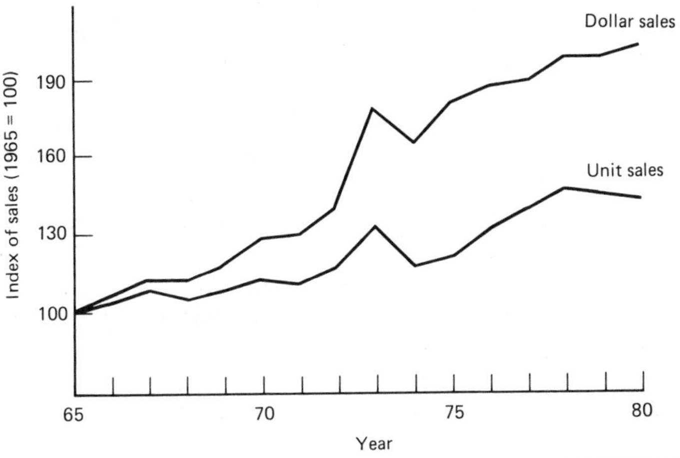

series plots (in Chart 16-2) of the dollar and unit sales for company X. The entire difference between the two variables is inflation in the average selling price of X's products. Forecasting techniques would certainly diagnose the two time series differently given no information about the specific form of the difference. It is reasonable to assume that the elimination of known causes—in this case inflation—from a time series will lead to greater forecasting accuracy.

Why does a simple point, such as adjusting for inflation, require explication? Forecasting models developed during periods of low inflation rates had no need to concern themselves with inflation. Historical fit was not improved by forecasting in units. A premise was therefore made about inflation when the dependent variable, dollar sales, was chosen. A manager who recognized that premise was in a better position to react to acceleration in inflation rates than if the role of inflation was ignored. The problems faced by company X (see Chart 16-1) could have been ameliorated by a company prepared to face the problem early.

Inflation does not affect all industries and all products in the same way. One problem this creates is that the variables chosen for forecasting may become inappropriate. The appropriate focus for forecasting may switch from the company's sales to the divisions' sales, the product line, the style, the geographic area, or to the customer class. The level of specificity of variables to be forecast is commonly referred to as an *aggregation* problem.

Generally speaking, the desired level of aggregation decreases when inflation—and other environmental forces as well—change more rapidly. This occurs for two reasons: (1) management needs information for decisions that often differs for different disaggregated variables, and (2) forecasting accuracy might be improved by focusing on the more specific behavior of disaggregated variables. The benefits of disaggregation must be weighed against the increased cost of forecasting more variables.

One of the most crucial economic premises made in forecasting models—especially those developed during the period from World War II through 1971—was that the *business cycle* did not exist. While most managers recognized the impact of a business cycle on their performance, there was rarely a premium to be paid for formal analysis of the impact of the business cycle. Relating variables blindly to time, without examining the true underlying phenomena, was sufficient for many purposes until the 1970s.

It is now understood that the practice of ignoring business cycles was developed during a period that was a historical accident. In most industrialized nations, the period from 1946 to 1971 was characterized by expansion of both the economy and the population. Those nations strongly subject to the vagaries of international trade were more attentive to economic factors in forecasting. Countries such as the United States, with large and growing domestic markets, could affort to forecast with models accounting for only the major trends. The cost of more detail or precision in measurement was rarely worth the small incremental benefits.

How exactly does a business cycle affect the choice of what and how to forecast? The most important effect is in placing a premium on forecasting turning points. Managers who can more confidently predict a turning point in their sales can usually make anticipatory decisions that improve performance at the margin.

Managers can rely less on standard measures of forecasting accuracy when turning points become important. Mean squared errors or mean absolute deviations might become considerably less important than the profit improvement from anticipating turning points. The latter is much less definable and is less susceptible to being measured in a "quick and dirty" formula which an analyst can employ on the computer. Measurement problems do not relieve managers from the obligation to forecast even if that requires closer communication and understanding between manager and staff analyst/forecaster.

The differential effects of a business cycle on sectors of an economy are well documented.[2] Like inflation, more frequent and pronounced business cycles imply the need for more disaggregated forecasting. A natural corollary to this principle is that planning should focus on the differential impact of the business cycle on various business segments. If Detroit is affected differently than Atlanta, marketing strategies might be varied accordingly. If higher priced items are affected more or less than lower priced items, a number of tactical decisions are available to managers. Forecasts should be designed to aid the disaggregated decision making.

Products with different characteristics are affected differently by a business cycle. Consider two products sold by an automobile manufacturer: (1) passenger automobiles and (2) replacement parts for passenger automobiles. How might sales of autos and auto parts differ over a business cycle?

Automobiles are a durable consumer product. Their purchase can generally be postponed during an economic downturn. The logical consequence of a slump in auto sales is an increase in the sales rate of replacement parts. As the average age of the stock of autos in use increases, the demand for repair parts increases. The very same information about the state of automobile sales could be used to improve accuracy in forecasting replacement part sales.

Had we observed only the aggregate variable, sales of automobiles and parts, we would have observed a deceptively more stable variable. However, we would not have understood the true market phenomena. Also, we would have been denied the opportunity to enhance decision making about autos and parts separately.

Variable definition is a topic whose importance is enhanced by economic change. Most analysts pay little attention to the differences in forecasting orders, sales, production, and shipments. During a business cycle, important differences in these variables occur. Orders and sales tend to vary from historical relationships during an economic downturn when orders are canceled more frequently. In general, the more cyclical a product, the more advantageous it is for a producer to maintain a backlog of orders that can be managed to accommodate both cyclical and stochastic fluctuations.

Production and sales will also react differently during a cycle as optimal inventory levels change. Often rapid inflation will interact with this relationship as larger finished goods inventories (for producers) and raw material inventories (for purchasers) become desirable as a hedge against inflation.

During the 1973–75 recession in the United States, an *inventory cycle* accompanied the business cycle and inflation. As related elsewhere,[2] an inventory cycle can cause traditionally strong relationships —such as sales and real GNP—to perform poorly in forecasting. The need to define variables accurately becomes critical (1) to avoid being deceived by the fluctuations observed, (2) to facilitate adjustment techniques that can compensate for the large errors of traditional models, and (3) to minimize the impact on forecasting during subsequent stable periods of the variations in historical data caused by the inventory cycle.

Forecast variables that are affected by *international trade* face a very complex environment. Obviously sales to other nations belong

CHART 16-3.   Recent Events in the International Economy
and Their Impact on Forecasting

Event	Impact
Freely floating exchange rates which have been volatile	Domestic and imported goods have had fluctuating costs relative to one another. In many cases, prices and profit margins of competing products have had large changes. Sales of individual manufacturers can therefore become more difficult to forecast. Sales by domestic manufacturers versus all sales can vary dramatically. Prices of raw materials traded become difficult to forecast.
Changes in the timing of various national business cycles	When business cycles coincide, the impact on total sales of worldwide markets differ. When the cycles differ greatly, the problem of forecasting where sales will be strongest becomes important. (In 1974-75 the cycles coincided in many countries.)
Changes in barriers to trade	When quotas or tariffs change, so does the environment for forecasting. Frequently, past observations have had limited value because of the environmental differences.

in this category. Domestic products that face significant competition from imports are similarly affected. Market definition becomes more important when the international environment is dynamic. The difference between worldwide sales, domestic sales, apparent consumption, sales by domestic producers, import sales, and so on can spell the difference between successful and unsuccessful forecasting. As is the case with other economic changes, careful international variable definition is less important under stable conditions, but it becomes crucial when rapid change occurs.

Chart 16-3 lists some changes in the international economy during the last decade and their impact on forecasting in a company. It would be useful to be able to suggest accurate methods for forecasting the international economic phenomena themselves. There are world econometric forecasting models, and the large banks forecast important events qualitatively. But this is an area of forecasting subject to great inaccuracy. Therefore the exercise of responding to the impacts listed in Chart 16-3 is often one of reaction and flexibility rather than precise accuracy.

Demographic Factors

One common premise implicit in many forecasts is the continuing growth of population. In the United States, as well as in most other industrialized nations, population grew steadily during the post–World War II period. More importantly, the age distribution of the population shifted dramatically as the postwar "baby boom" segment matured, reached child bearing age, and did not follow traditional patterns of when to bear children and how many to bear.

Many products and services are affected by the demographic shifts mentioned above. Some products, such as jeans, appeal primarily to only a segment of the population. As the postwar generation reaches middle age, will they continue to wear jeans? If not, jeans manufacturers will face a dwindling domestic market because of population shifts.

The shift of population geographically–to the "Sun Belt" in the United States, for example–is another environmental trend. This might affect sales of certain climate-related products. It might also alter the competitive positions of specific firms.

Forecasting models have typically ignored demographic factors for several reasons. First, the changes have manifested themselves slowly. In contrast, most time series models incorporate a relatively short history. Second, the improvement in forecasting performance from incorporating demographic factors is small for reasons related to the first point. Third, models already disaggregated by age class or geographic region are not common. Marketing research models are the major exception. It would be unusual to disaggregate only for demographic reasons unless radical shifts demanded such an approach. Therefore, the effects of disaggregated demographic changes could bear fruit in forecasting only if they could dominate a decision to disaggregate forecasts.

Organizational/Competitive Factors

The strategy of an organization, and therefore its approach to competition and the organizational implementation of that approach, can be considered part of a firm's forecasting environment. In a short- to intermediate-run forecast, changes in strategy can certainly affect variables to be forecasted. In a long-run forecast, the impact of corporate strategy on forecasting is less clear because the purpose of the forecast is to help shape strategic alternatives.

The effect of strategic variables on forecasting performance is as complex as the subject of corporate strategy itself. The purpose of this section is only to outline some common effects so as to sensitize the reader to the general issues. These effects can be broken down into two aspects of strategy: organizational and competitive.

Companies organize in such a manner as to implement their corporate strategy.[5] Differences in organizations–because they embody differences in strategy–create differences in how and what to forecast. As companies encounter environmental change, their strategies and hence their organizations frequently adapt. Predictable changes in the forecasting needs of managers are the likely result.

To illustrate, consider a company that is organized functionally with the marketing function dominating management attention. Forecasting is typically related to the budgeting process and to the review of annual performance. A relatively short time horizon is employed. Goal setting frequently is the objective of forecasting. Top management obtains a forecast independent of the marketing managers and sales force to better evaluate their input to the goal setting negotiation process and to allocate budgets.

The company later encounters a more hostile environment which requires greater adaptation of individual business strategies. Decentralization occurs and division general managers with profit responsibility replace marketing managers as the key decision makers. The purpose of forecasting changes. Accuracy becomes more important than goal setting. A longer time horizon becomes appropriate. Communication among general managers and forecasting specialists becomes more critical. Often the later become expendable.

The overwhelming conclusion is that organizational change frequently changes the entire basis for forecasting. A system that churned out forecasts the same way in both environments would likely fail. It would either generate the wrong type of forecasts or would not be used by managers. Forecasting systems must be tailored to the organization in which they are employed.[5] The organization is therefore a critical element of the forecasting environment.

Competitive factors can have equally profound effects on forecasting. Premises about competitors' responses are often implicit in most forecasts. A sales forecast that ignores changes in the responses of competitors or in the marketing strategy of the subject company itself risks significant sources of error. Changes in the nature of competition can occur due to changes in a number of factors. Some of these factors are the supply and demand balance, the number and size of competitors, the stage of the product life cycle, and technological change.

Frequently changes in competitive factors are not amenable to quantification in a forecasting system. They are nonetheless important premises that must be understood and checked as a source of error.

Other Factors

In particular industries other sources of the environment can dominate forecasting. These include technological change, product characteristics (durable versus nondurable, luxury versus nonluxury), and the quantity and quality of information, among others. The factors discussed in this chapter are meant to exemplify, but not exhaust, the sources of environmental change. All important sources should be treated with the same care methodologically.

FORECASTING PERFORMANCE AND ENVIRONMENTAL CHANGE

One reason forecasting systems often fail is the employment of poor measures of performance. This statement is doubly true when environmental change is rapid. The well-known concept of a periodic audit[8] should be employed in all forecasting systems; it offers guidance to the rapid change situation. (See Chapter 32.) The costs and benefits of forecasting will, as always, be the basis for selecting criteria for the frequency of reestimating models or reselection of the best forecasting technique. Earlier it was established how environmental change alters those costs and benefits. More specifically, it was demonstrated how specific environmental changes could generate errors. It is the task of this section to offer specific error measurement techniques as a guide to periodic audit of the entire system.

The most common approach to forecasting performance measurement is *historical fit*. All historical data are employed in estimating the parameters of the forecasting model, and then such measures as mean squared error (MSE) or mean absolute percentage error (MAPE) are calculated. Error measures have no critical value greater than which a model is unacceptable. A situational analysis of the cost of errors, often performed qualitatively, is the only means of judging acceptable standards.

The task often ignored is to perform a *post-audit on forecasting errors* to judge their source. With a noncausal model, the post-audit is not very scientific. One can compare errors to past values, search for a pattern of error, or attempt to explain errors according to environmental change. With a causal model, the ability to ascertain the causes of errors becomes a more formal and necessary task.

How specifically is a post-audit to be performed? The major difference from historical fit is that a post-audit measures the accuracy of the true forecasts. The standard measures of error, such as MAPE and MSE, can be applied to true forecasts as readily as they are applied to historical fit. The error value associated with a forecast n months ahead is the typical measure.

When the environment is dynamic, true forecast measures will exceed their counterparts in historical fit. The MSE of a forecast will differ from the MSE of fit for two reasons: (1) the model itself is not a perfect predictor of the future, and (2) the environmental premises of the model are invalid. For the example of company X, a regression model in which X's sales were regressed against RGNP had the following sources of error: (1) the sales–RGNP regression line did not have a perfect explanatory relationship, (2) the forecasts of RGNP were not accurate, and (3) many other forces in the environment affected sales.

An appropriate post-audit would compare fit error measures and forecast error measures and also attempt to explain each individual time period error qualitatively. Common sense and scanning should lead to some conclusions about the need for revising the model. If forecasts are more erroneous than fit, then three alternatives exist:

1. If a systematic rationale for forecast error exists, the forecasting system should be augmented to account for that influence.

2. If the reasons for large errors are unusual, nonrecurring events, no changes in models are necessary.

3. If the environmental change renders the forecasting system obsolete, wholesale redesign of the system is in order.

ADAPTING THE FORECASTING SYSTEM
TO ENVIRONMENTAL CHANGE

Various aspects of environmental change and forecasting have been discussed in this chapter. Although the topic treated is very broad, it is nevertheless useful to offer general prescriptions for adapting forecasting systems to environmental change. Seven prescriptions, and examples of some, are offered below.

Prescription 1: Careful Variable Definition. Both the variables being forecast and any explanatory variables should be defined accurately so that environmental influences do not destroy their validity.

Example: Company X should forecast unit sales rather than dollars. They should not substitute data on orders or production for units sold. They might also consider whether a component of RGNP, such as disposable personal income, might be a better explanatory variable.

Prescription 2: Aggregation/Disaggregation Alternatives. The level of aggregation should be considered carefully. An investment in more disaggregated forecasting may yield premiums during turbulent periods. The sources of environmental change should be examined for disaggregation implications.

Example: Company X could consider replacing total corporate sales forecasts with product line forecasts, each perhaps broken down by customer class.

Prescription 3: Consideration of Causal Models. Where noncausal models have achieved poor results during rapid change periods they should possibly by replaced by causal models that are better understood. That would facilitate the employment of scanning information when models require revision.

Example: Companies using simple time series models for forecasts of a time horizon longer than 2 months should consider regression models.

Prescription 4: Explicit Listing of Premises. The premises employed in a forecasting system should be listed explicitly. Both model builders and managers/scanners should participate in this process.

Example: The environmental factors listed in this chapter, among others, should be reviewed as candidates for premises.

Prescription 5: Premise Tracking System. A formal system of tracking the environmental factors deemed most important to the validity of forecasting system premises should be established.

Prescription 6: Broad Performance Measures. Performance measures of true forecasts should be employed. The various sources of error should be determined jointly by model builders and managers/scanners.

Example: For company X, the errors encountered in 1973–75 should have been examined, and the environmental factors listed in Chart 16-1 should have been uncovered through that process.

Prescription 7: Periodic Audit/A Plan for Change. The periodic audit should explicitly evaluate environmental premises and encompass a contingency plan for the forecasting system when various environmental scenarios are experienced. Ideally, this activity should manage the balance between environmental scanning and formal models. It should be made explicit that premises are made deliberately and that scanners and modelers complement one another. Most importantly, a plan should exist detailing the roles of the various parties and recognizing the alternative shocks to the system that could occur and how they will lead to adaptations in the system.

REFERENCES

1. Ascher, W., *Forecasting: An Appraisal for Policymakers and Planners,* Johns Hopkins University Press, Baltimore, 1978.
2. Beckenstein, A. R., "Forecasting Considerations in a Rapidly Changing Econ-

omy," in *Forecasting,* S. Makridakis and S. Wheelwright, eds., TIMS Studies in Management Science, North-Holland, Amsterdam, 1979.

3. Houthakker, H. S. and L. D. Taylor, *Consumer Demand in the U.S., 1929–70: Analyses and Projections,* Harvard University Press, Cambridge, MA, 1966.

4. Kami, M. J., "Planning in Times of Unpredictability," *Columbia Journal of World Business,* Summer 1976, pp. 26–34.

5. Lorange, P. and R. F. Vancil, *Strategic Planning Systems,* Prentice-Hall, Englewood Cliffs, NJ, 1977.

6. Makridakis, S., "Forecasting, Planning, and Strategy: Some New Directions," in *Long Range Planning* (to be published).

7. Pindyck, R. S. and D. L. Rubinfeld, *Econometric Models and Economic Forecasts,* McGraw-Hill, New York, 1976.

8. Wheelwright, S. and S. Makridakis, *Forecasting Methods for Management,* 3rd ed., Wiley-Interscience, New York, 1980.

17

LIFE-CYCLE FORECASTING

SATINDER K. MULLICK

GREGORY S. ANDERSON

ROBERT E. LEACH

WARD C. SMITH

Corning Glass Works

Life-cycle analysis as a marketing tool has been steadily growing in importance over the last two decades. While early uses of the concept were qualitative, efforts have been made recently to quantify the life cycle for many product classes. Life-cycle terminology has been incorporated in planning matrices in many companies. "Embryonic," "growth," "mature," and "aging" are the most common classifications used by many corporations. Substantially more rapid growth has occurred through the use of mathematical modeling, particularly with the availability of simplified computer programming techniques. For example, observations of a medical instruments business over several years indicate that modeling life cycles for this activity could lead to a different business perspective, including some important insights into product management.

Misjudgment about life cycles can be extremely costly. For example, the light truck market took off like a hula hoop, and Dana Corporation, a manufacturer of frames and other steel component parts, paid a major price for that misjudgment because they did not forecast the life cycle properly. The concept of the life cycle can be applied to a particular product model, to the product line that attempts to cover the spectrum of features and pricing to fit all the elements of a market segment, or to the market need itself. Each has a life cycle with longevity generally in the stated order. The study of each of the life-cycle elements of such a business is valid. The product life cycle offers a convenient focus for our purposes.

THE LIFE-CYCLE STATES

Normally, there are five stages in the life cycle of a successful product: product development, testing and introduction, rapid growth, steady state, and phasing out. However, to encompass another aspect of forecasting that relates indirectly to the product life cycle, we shall include another stage: the initial preproduct or technology development stage, which embraces the rapidly growing field of technological forecasting. Chart 17-1 summarizes these six states, the typical decisions made, and the main forecasting techniques suitable at each stage. The remainder of this chapter contains a brief, introductory discussion of these six stages.

The typical decisions and shape of the life-cycle curve in Chart 17-1 are mainly representative of durable goods. While nondurable goods and services also have life-cycle curves that contain the same major phases, the shapes of the curves will differ, and the values (costs) of the decisions will change. Furthermore, the components of the curves are different: the durable goods life-cycle curve components consist of purchases represented by new orders, multiunit owners, and replacement sales; the nondurable goods and most services curves consist of initial buyers and repeat buyers. The values (costs) of the decisions will frequently be less for nondurable goods than for durable goods, although the ultimate costs of overstocking will be higher for nondurable goods because of the shorter phasing out period.

Some forecasting is required at all stages, but the amount and complexity are a function of the dollars involved in the decision.

FORM OF THE LIFE CYCLE

Chart 17-2 shows three distinct cycles in the dominant energy source— a wood burning cycle, a coal burning cycle, and a petroleum and natural gas cycle.

The form and the length of the life cycle are highly variable from

CHART 17-1. Types of Decisions Made over a Product's Life Cycle, with Related Forecasting Techniques

Stage of Life Cycle	Preproduct	Product Development	Market Testing and Early Introduction	Rapid Growth	Steady State	Phasing Out
Typical decisions	Allocation of R&D Distribution system needs Personnel needs Acquisitions	Amount of development effort Product design Business strategies	Optimum facility size Marketing strategies, including distribution and pricing	Facilities expansion Marketing strategies Production planning	Promotions specials Pricing Production planning Inventories	Transfer of facilities Marketing effort Production planning
Forecasting techniques	Delphi method Progress functions Panel consensus Trend analysis Historical analogy Technical monitoring Sociopolitical monitoring	Delphi method Historical analysis of comparable products Priority pattern analysis Input-output analysis Panel consensus Technical monitoring Learning curve	Consumer surveys Tracking and warning systems Market tests Experimental designs Analogy Sales	Statistical techniques for identifying turning points Tracking and warning systems Market surveys Intention to buy surveys Substitution theory Trend analysis	Time series analysis and projection Causal and econometric models Market surveys for tracking and warning Life-cycle analysis Trend analysis Technical monitoring Sociopolitical monitoring	Slope characteristic Statistical tracking and market research Historical analogy and regression analysis

CHART 17-2. Life Cycle of Dominant Energy Source

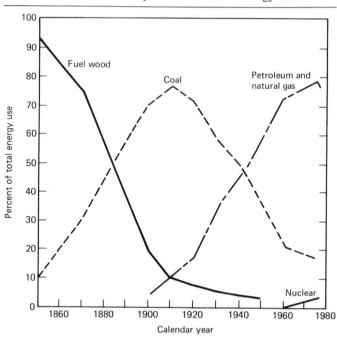

industry to industry. They are a function of social, political, technological, and managerial influences.

For example, renewal, segmentation, innovation, and repositioning have been used successfully at Corning Glass Works to alter the life cycle of several products.

In late 1976, Pyrex[R] brand clear ovenware was a mature to aging business with heavy price competition. Consumers viewed it as a commodity, with no gift purchasing. The decision to market Pyrex[R] with attractive serving baskets created a gift image and an entirely new segment. The business was totally incremental, with no loss in the basic clear business.

In 1978, Corning Medical's Model 175 Blood Gas Analyzer was suffering price competition from a lower performance, lower cost product. Corning's Model 165/2 was nearing the end of its life cycle, with sales dropping off sharply. The new Corning Model 168, with features and price comparable to the competitor, was introduced in late 1978. This allowed the upward repositioning of the 175 and the downward repositioning of the 165/2. This move increased profitability in both the Model 175 and the Model 165/2, as well as providing a successful new product.

Stage 1. Preproduct Development

Before a specific new product concept emerges, there are usually sociological, political, or technological developments that make the new product possible or necessary. The forecasting objective, prior to product development, is to determine when a new product will be possible or needed or required by legislation and what the characteristics of these products will be.

Here are the major forecasting questions in the preproduct stage.

When is a particular technology most likely to be developed to the stage that products are feasible and marketable?

When will social and political pressures force a change in a product or require a new one?

What are the potential sales opportunities that will emerge from this technology or new product requirements?

What will the characteristics of these markets be?

What events must occur for technological breakthroughs or for legislation to force new products or changes in existing products?

A recent review of glass and competitive materials indicated the trend line of available properties from various materials since 1900. This information using trend extrapolation is now predicting yet to be invented properties. Corning's marketers can now anticipate new competition or envision new product concepts even before the inventions have been made.

The above questions should be answered for the manager to make decisions relating to (1) how much R&D effort should be expended in technological development, (2) what extent the company will participate in a new or expanding industry, (3) what type of distribution system will be needed to sell the new products and when it should be available, and (4) the personnel and facility requirements associated with the business. These are some of the same questions and decisions that arise during the product development stage. But they must be considered in at least a macro way at this stage so that preliminary work can be undertaken if long lead times are necessary in preparing for product introduction (e.g., obtaining a research capability and establishing a reputation in a business). Corning made many of these assessments in the 1960s when we decided to enter the medical business. More recently we assessed the impact of genetic engineering and related biotechnology in light of higher energy cost forecasts, and as a result we have committed Corning to building a technical and commercial capability in this area.

An analysis of technical and technoeconomic trends can frequently help identify a product opportunity long before the economic significance of a research accomplishment is seen. A rough idea of the technical or economic advantage of a new product can provide clues as to its viability while it is still at a concept stage. Once a product concept has been identified, qualitative techniques, such as the Delphi method or panel consensus, are often utilized.

The primary basis for such forecasts is expert opinion, although historical analogies should be used as cross-checks when possible. This type of forecasting will cover periods up to 20 years into the future.

The dramatic increase in social and political influence on the innovative process makes the consideration of these inputs an increasingly important task. Programs to systematically monitor social and political change can frequently spot new or radically changed product requirements while they are still off on the horizon. Corning's ability to successfully market Celcor^R automotive substrates was a direct result of recognizing coming automobile emission standards.

A common objection to much long-range forecasting is that it is virtually impossible to predict with accuracy what will happen several years into the future. We agree that uncertainty increases when a forecast is made for a period of more than 2 years. However, at the very least, the forecast and a measure of its accuracy enable the manager to know his risks and to choose an appropriate strategy from those available. As a minimum, it is also advisable to consider expert opinions and judgments in an objective rather than in a subjective way.

Stage 2. Product Development

In the early stages of product development, the manager wants answers to questions such as these:

What are the alternative growth opportunities to pursuing product X?

How have established products similar to product X fared?

Should we enter this business; if so, in what segments?

How should we allocate R&D efforts and funds?

How successful will different product concepts be?

How will product X fit into the markets 5 or 10 years from now?

Forecasts that help to answer these long-range questions must necessarily have long horizons themselves.

Systematic market research is, of course, a mainstay in this area. For example, priority pattern analysis can describe the consumer's preferences and the likelihood that he or she will buy a product; thus this can be of great value in forecasting (and updating) penetration levels and rates. But there are also other market research tools, which will be used according to the state of the market, the product concept, and whether the product will compete in a clearly defined and basically established market, or in an undefined and new market.

While there can be no direct data about a product that is still a gleam in the manufacturer's eye, information about its likely performance can be gathered in several ways, provided that the market in which it is to be sold is a known entity.

An examination of relevant technical parameters and their history can highlight the relative technical advantage of a new product. This advantage should be similar to other successful new products in the market.

Frequently, the most critical element of a new product is price. Knowing in advance the lowest price that can be offered while still coining satisfactory returns can be vital knowledge. An examination of the learning curve of a new product, even though still in development, can provide a good source of early price information.

Another approach is to compare a proposed product with competitive products and rank it on quantitative scales for different factors. This is called *product differences measurement.* Another and more formal approach is to construct disaggregate market models by splitting out different segments of a complex market for individual study and consideration. An alternative method of forecasting sales or profits for a new product in a defined market is to compare it with an "ancestor" that has similar characteristics, such as color television versus black and white television.

Even within a defined market, it will be necessary to determine whether the total market is elastic or inelastic, that is, will it continue its historic growth rate or will the new product expand the size of the total market?

When the market for a new product is weakly defined and the product concept may still be fluid, few data are available and history is not relevant. This has been true for modular housing, pollution measurement devices, time-shared computers, and educational learning devices. The Delphi method or other "expert opinion" techniques and market research are most applicable here, with input–output analysis in combination with other techniques occasionally being of value. As a caution, expert opinion can be very wrong. Many "experts" in the business machine market passed up the opportunity to commercialize the xerographic machine.

Stage 3. Testing and Introduction

Before a product can enter its (hopefully) rapid growth stage, the market potential must be tested and the product introduced—and then more market testing may be advisable. At this stage, management needs answers to these questions:

What shall our marketing plan be, that is, which markets should we enter and with what production quantities?

How much manufacturing capacity will the early production stages require?

As demand grows, where should we build this capacity?

How shall we allocate our R&D resources over time?

Significant profits depend on finding the right answers to these questions. Therefore it is economically feasible to expend large amounts of effort and money on obtaining good forecasts in the short, intermediate, and long range. Based on such a short- and long-term forecast for cancer research funding, Corning built a new plant to make tissue culture labware with the planned capability to double capacity in four increments. This meant Corning's profits were much higher than if we had built a second plant several years later.

A sales forecast at this stage should provide three points of information: (1) the date when rapid sales will begin, (2) the rate of market penetration during the rapid sales stage, and (3) the ultimate level of penetration or sales rate during the steady-state stage. The date when a product will enter the rapid growth stage is hard to predict 3 or 4 years in advance (the usual horizon). A company's main recourse is to use statistical tracking methods to check on how successful the product is being introduced, along with routine market studies to determine if there have been any significant changes in the market and sales rate.

Although statistical tracking is a useful tool during the early introduction states, there are rarely sufficient data for statistical forecasting. Market research studies can naturally be useful, as we have indicated. But, more commonly, the forecaster tries to identify a similar, older product whose penetration pattern should be similar to that of the new product, since overall markets can and do exhibit consistent patterns. As discussed earlier, the relative technical and economic advantage of the new product should be similar to other successful introductions.

When it is not possible to identify a similar product, a different approach must be used. For the purpose of initial introduction into the markets, it may only be necessary to determine the minimum sales rate required for a product venture to meet corporate objectives. Analyses like input–output, historical trend, and technological forecasting can provide a base for estimating this minimum. Also, the feasibility of not entering the market at all, or of continuing R&D right up to the rapid growth stage, can best be determined by sensitivity analysis of yearly profit and loss, income, and cash flow statements.

To estimate the date by which a product will enter the rapid growth stage is another matter. This date is a function of many factors: for example, the existence of a distribution system, customer acceptance of or familiarity with the product concept, the need met by the product, and significant events (such as color network programming).

Stage 4. Rapid Growth

When a product enters this stage, the most important decisions relate to facilities expansion. These decisions generally involve the largest expenditures in the life cycle (except major R&D decisions). Here commensurate forecasting and tracking efforts are justified.

Forecasting and tracking must provide the executive with three kinds of information at this juncture:

Firm verification of the rapid growth rate forecast made previously.

A hard date when sales will level to "normal" steady-state growth.

For component products, the deviation in the growth curve that may be caused by characteristic conditions along the pipeline such as, for example, inventory blockages.

Intermediate and long-range forecasting of the market growth rate and of the attainment of steady-state sales require detailed marketing studies, intention to buy surveys, and product comparisons.

When a product has entered rapid growth, there are generally sufficient data available to construct statistical and possibly even causal growth models, although the latter will necessarily contain assumptions that must be verified later.

The sales of most products follow some form of an S-shaped curve, and quantitative methods can help to establish the parameters of the curve. One of the most useful such techniques is substitution theory.* Where a new product must displace an older one, it is possible to make a reliable prediction of the displacement rate with a small amount of

*J. C. Fisher and R. H. Pry, "A Simple Substitution Model of Technological Change," Report No. 70-C-215, General Electric Company, Schnectady, NY, June 1970.

data (5% maximum penetration) and little mathematical rigor. However, special care must be used if adoption requires that a large capital investment be written off. Corning has applied this tool in looking at color TV's substitution for black and white TV. We expect this approach will apply as Corning's optical wave guides begin to replace copper cable in the decade ahead.

Simulation is also an excellent tool for these circumstances because it is essentially simpler than the alternative of building a more formal, more "mathematical" model. Simulation bypasses the need for analytical solution techniques and for mathematical duplication of a complex environment and allows experimentation. Simulation also indicates to the forecaster how the pipeline elements will behave and interact over time—knowledge that is very useful in forecasting, especially in constructing formal causal models at a later date.

This knowledge is not absolutely "hard," of course, and pipeline dynamics must be carefully tracked to determine if the various estimates and assumptions made were indeed correct. Statistical methods provide a good short-term basis for estimating and checking the growth rate and signaling when turning points occur.

One main activity during the rapid growth stage, then, is to check earlier estimates; if they appear incorrect, the forecaster should compute as accurately as possible the error in the forecast and obtain a revised estimate. In some instances, models developed earlier will include only "macroterms"; in such cases, market research can provide the information needed to break these terms down into their components.

Stage 5: Steady State

In planning production and establishing marketing strategy for the short and intermediate term, the manager's first considerations are usually accurate estimates of (1) the present sales level and (2) the rate at which this level is changing. The forecaster thus must make two related contributions at this stage:

1. He should provide estimates of trends and seasonals, which obviously affect the sales level. Seasonals are particularly important for both overall production planning and inventory control. To do this, he needs to apply time series analysis and projection techniques, that is, statistical techniques.

2. He should relate the future sales level to factors that are more easily predictable, or have a "lead" relationship with sales, or both. Therefore, he needs to build causal models. Building permits are a good lead indicator for major appliances. At this point in the life cycle, sufficient time series data are available

and enough causal relationships are known or suspected from direct experience and market studies so that the forecaster can indeed apply these two powerful sets of tools.

Also important at this stage is the application of preproduct forecasting techniques to competing and technical alternatives. Predicting the rate at which your own product will be displaced can provide important planning information and help to identify research goals.

An often ignored alternative is to consider more aggressively altering the life-cycle pattern.

Traditional design strategy in the medical instruments market has been to approach each product model as an ultimate statement of the product need rather than as one of a series of statements that supports a changing need throughout a changing technology. It is easy to slip into project oriented rather than need-maintenance oriented management. This leads to a design philosophy that stresses a monolithic approach. It is a one-time statement with a maximum of features and state-of-the-art technology. It attempts to jump 7 years ahead to allow time for other commitments and does not consider the customer's ability to absorb multiple new and simultaneous changes. In its attempt to be self-contained, this approach locks the user on the outside, both physically and in understanding. Such a design does not lend itself to the composite life-cycle strategy.

The composite life-cycle (or business maintenance) strategy requires a companion design strategy to be successful. It must seek the flexibility that allows replacement of a module containing rapidly changing technology. It must recognize that certain desirable features can be added later, perhaps when the customer is more receptive. It recognizes that design and marketing are interactive and dynamic over product life. Such a design strategy requires new disciplines and therefore is not easily accepted. If the need maintenance approach described expands market share by adjusting to or even shaping a particular need, a second aggressive attack on the life-cycle pattern is the adaptation of the product to meet new needs. A screw compressor designed to compress and transport air and other gases can be adapted to transport confectionary sugar, even cement. By changing its seals and adding a bit of water, it becomes a vacuum pump. And where did it come from originally? Actually, it started life as an internal combustion engine. For each new market segment defined, the effective product life cycle is altered.

When one begins to creatively alter life cycles two questions arise, "When does a product life cycle become a business life cycle?" and "What are the limits to the definition of a product?" Many products by intent, or good fortune, serve multiple needs. Another insight which would seem to contradict the multiple need strategy is the observation that technologies survive products and that market needs survive technologies. The elegant complexity of business and markets is that activity expansion is practical in either or both directions. The expansion and pyramiding of life-cycle elements is descriptive of business growth. The key to profitability is maximizing the elements of synergy that exist for variations of the product, and at all functional levels of the business.

It is evident that a product life-cycle forecast is valid until someone makes a fundamental change. That change can be an image change, a feature addition, a price change, or even an alteration in accessibility. As creative as we are, we still forecast from past experience. When a company, which dominated a particular instrument market, went from distributor sales to direct sales, five competitors arrived to supply the distribution vacancy. The influx of new thought led to a new level of instrument design and performance. A decade later, when steady state was again reached, the unique image created by departure into a vertical dimension, as opposed to a horizontal dimension, again significantly altered market share. Each time this occurs, one is surprised at the significance of the departure from prediction. Equally surprising is what can constitute a fundamental change.

Stage 6. Phasing Out

Virtually all products go through a final phasing out stage, whether it lasts only a few months, a few years, or extends for as long as 10 or 20 years. Most product analysis is concerned only with estimating or establishing the S-shaped curve and not in determining when the plateau or gradual growth will turn down. This can result in lost profits because of inventories that must eventually be scrapped, inability to phase in the excess capacity with new product requirements, and excessive marketing effort for a dying product.

The most important questions to answer in this stage are: When will the decline or phasing out begin? And how long will it last? Answers will aid in decisions relating to marketing strategies (promotion efforts, pricing, and when to withdraw the product), production scheduling and inventory control, and facilities planning. Three basic approaches are normally taken to answer the foregoing questions:

1. Trend projection techniques and primarily the slope characteristic method can help to make good forecasts for the entire life cycle, including prediction of the downturn point and duration of the phasing out stage.

2. Historical analogies can be used to determine the overall pattern of the life cycle, and regression analysis (or some similar technique) can provide estimates of the parameters of the overall

curve, using product characteristics and differences as the independent variables.

3. Good tracking and warning tools, such as the Census Bureau X-11 (Shiskin routine), can identify turning points, and market surveys and other techniques can then be employed to determine the reason for the turning point. That is, is it temporary because of competitive moves, or is it a long-term market trend? Tracking techniques can also be used in the first two approaches to determine the correctness of the assumptions and models.

Perhaps the least amount of effort in forecasting is normally expended in this area, although there are significant rewards for good forecasts here. Forecasts for phasing out products with short life cycles, such as cereals and apparel, are particularly crucial. One cannot discuss life-cycle forecasting and its relevant decision processes without observing that large established companies, which are most likely to apply such skills, have not distinguished themselves in the area of diversification into new products and businesses. Success seems more likely to favor the newcomer to the business scene. This phenomenon is associated with the inability of the established company to utilize forecasting techniques without applying that company's own intrepretation—adjusting input and output data in ways that validate the status quo. Typical examples might be the defining of a market segment in terms of an existing product capability rather than in terms of market need. The result is a product activity that fits available resources, but one that is short lived.

Another variation of such selective forecasting involves the recognition that elements of the established business exist in a diversification product opportunity. Attempts to satisfy the market need are hopelessly bound up in the need to satisfy internal culture. In one such situation, a high technology company purchased an exclusive position with a unique product. Two internal requirements took precedence. First, the product housing was an item manufacturable by the established company. Utilization of this part or some cost-reduced variation of it was mandatory and effectively limited more creative approaches in second generation products. Second, development resources were directed at associated segments of the acquired market opportunity rather than at the optimization of the acquired business. This satisfied the need to bring into play the company's high technology resources but proved irrelevant to market need. In such opportunities, the market may be correctly forecast, but cultural adjustments lead to product life cycles that are shortened prematurely. The forecasting techniques are not invalid, but the tendency for input–output data to pass through a "status quo" filter can create a disastrous result.

AN EXAMPLE: TV GLASS ENVELOPE DEMAND FORECASTING

When TV was being conceived in the 1940s, it was not clear whether the glass envelope being used today (glass panel and glass funnel) would be the final choice.

There were alternative systems and materials. One system used a metal funnel and a sagged glass faceplate. This system was used for awhile, and over a million black and white TV sets were actually sold. Corning Glass Works worked on the alternate system using glass panels and funnels for many years before convincing the industry to opt for the system now in use. Corning Glass Works was not involved in the metal funnel system. If that system had prevailed, Corning Glass would not have enjoyed the worldwide growth opportunity and leadership in the TV industry.

When color TV was conceived, several forecasters assumed that black and white TV would fade away. In reality, the cost of small black and white TV's was reduced sharply, and a new multiple set market was created. Thus the demand for glass envelopes has grown at a good rate for over three decades.

Of course there were some who thought that color TV would replace black and white by 1960. They did not understand the dynamics involved in solving all the problems. Color TV demand finally took off in 1965, and all the major networks (NBC, CBS, ABC) went full blast

CHART 17-3. Household Saturation (U.S. TV Sets)

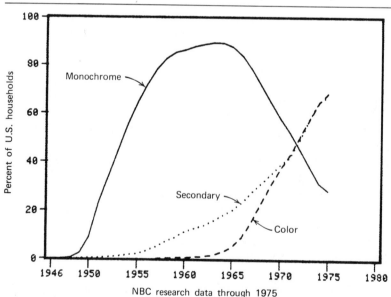

NBC research data through 1975

CHART 17-4.   U.S. TV Set Sales to Dealers

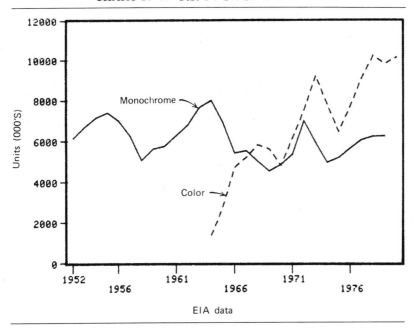

EIA data

to color programming to prevent losses in advertising income. (See Charts 17-3 and 17-4.)

Glass envelopes are now being used in video games and video terminals. The overall worldwide demand for glass envelopes has grown very well as new markets are identified.

A couple of technologies or concepts have threatened the system using glass envelopes, but innovations and cost reductions have kept the competitive system from taking over.

Projection TV systems remain a major threat.

SUMMARY

The types of decisions made throughout the product life cycle vary considerably, according to payoff implications and the need for forecasting accuracy. It is therefore apparent that the types of techniques used throughout the product life cycle will change over time, and new methods should be introduced as the need for new forecasts arises. Since data availability also differs significantly over time and affects the selection of the forecasting technique, the value and effectiveness of a particular technique cannot be precisely stated without considering its specific application.

BIBLIOGRAPHY

Chambers, John C., Satinder K. Mullick, and Donald D. Smith, *An Executive Guide to Forecasting,* John Wiley, New York, 1974. This book expands on the well-known *Harvard Business Review* article, "How to Choose the Right Forecasting Technique," July-August 1971. It is full of interesting real world examples and applications. Well-known input–output models are compared. A bibliography for forecasting and market research techniques is also included for new practitioners.

Smith, Ward C., "Product Life-Cycle Strategy: How to Stay on the Growth Curve," *Management Review,* a publication of American Management Association, January 1980. This article relates sales growth to resource allocation for medical instruments. Executives and practitioners should find this article very stimulating.

CHAPTER

18

FORECASTING RECESSIONS

ROBERT L. McLAUGHLIN
President, Micrometrics

Every few years a severe shock, called "recession," strikes the economy. The minimum requirement for recession is at least two quarters of negative real GNP, although there are more important ways to measure them. The most useful definition of recession is that the economy must meet three criteria— known as the three "D's"—duration, diffusion, and depth. In effect, for the economy to be in recession, the decline must have (1) a *duration* long enough to be at least as long as the shortest past recession, (2) a wide *diffusion* through the economy, and (3) a *depth* at least as severe as the shallowest recession on record.

There have been 10 *slowdowns* in the U.S. economy since World War II. Seven of these were severe enough to be recessions. Three of the slowdowns did not get that bad. During the postwar period from 1947 through 1980, the economy has grown an average of about 3.5% per annum in real (i.e., excluding inflation) terms. We can generalize, then, that when we operate above 3.5% the economy is in a growth period. When it is less than 3.5%, the economy is in a slowdown. If growth goes below zero (and fulfills the three D's), the economy is in recession.

RECESSION: ULTIMATE FORECAST CHALLENGE

Most of those who forecast do so because of the need to make decisions. And, if recessions represent an ultimate challenge to the forecaster, the truth is that one must forecast *any* time there is a decision to make. Decisions cannot be made for the past; they can only be made for the future. Consequently, whenever a decision must be made, a forecast—implicit or explicit—must also be made in support of that decision. Forecasting is decision support.

It is always difficult to forecast; it has never been easy. But the *maximum* problem of prediction is the forecasting of recession. And one of the most difficult recessions to forecast was that of 1980. It was literally in the fall of 1977 that economists began predicting the end of the business cycle expansion that had begun in April 1975. It was not officially ended until January 1980. In effect, forecasters—most especially, those who had to forecast in support of calendar year budgets—experienced three extremely difficult years, forecasting under the cloud of recession. One may *think* one only has to incorporate recession into the forecast every few years, but the period 1977 through 1980 proved how wrong is this insight.

The average *peacetime* business cycle from 1854 through 1980 (there have been 23 of them) has lasted 47 months— measured from peak to peak. Five peacetime cycles since World War II have averaged 49 months in duration. In the 65 years from 1854 through World War I, the average expansion was only 51% of the average business cycle. Between the two World Wars, this figure—in spite of the Great Depression—increased to 58%. Since World War II and the Keynesian revolution, the U.S. economy in peacetime has been in expansion over 80% of the time. Chart 18-1 records the distribution of quarterly percentage changes in the postwar period from the second quarter of 1947 through the third quarter of 1980. Note that 82% of the 134 quarters exhibited positive growth percentages.) One is hard put to find bad news in these figures, particularly when we realize that the period prior to World War I is often described as the "good old days." The truth is that, back then, the U.S. economy was in recession half the time.

In March 1975 the severest recession of the postwar era troughed, and a new business cycle began the next month. It should not be surprising that in the fall of 1977 recession scenarios began to appear. Only three of the 23 peacetime expansions since 1854 lasted longer than 36 months, and only one of the three was postwar. So, with a strict statistical methodology, it was easy to predict a 1978 recession. If the expansion extended *beyond* June 1978, it would be the longest peacetime expansion since World War II—an event with a very low statistical probability. If ever a case had to be made to demonstrate that pure statistical inference could not be used to forecast recession, the 1980 recession is probably the best. (The *business* economist appears to be exonerated from this mistake, since a survey by the National Association of Business Economists in August 1977 produced a 1978 forecast for real GNP of +4.5%—the actual growth in that year turned out to be +4.4%. A year later, in August 1978, the survey produced a 1979 forecast of +2.5%—the actual growth in 1979 was +2.3%.)

CHART 18-1.   Quarterly Growth: Real GNP (Annual Rates)

-10%					
-9	//				2
-8					
-7	/				1
-6					
-5	///				3
-4	/				1
-3	/////				5
-2	/////				5
-1	/////	//			7
-0					
0	/////	////			9
1	/////	////			9
2	/////	/////	////		14
3	/////	/////	/////	/////	20
4	/////	///			8
5	/////	/////	//		12
6	/////	//			7
7	/////	/////			10
8	/////	//			7
9	/////				5
10	/////	/			6
11	/				1
12					
13	/				1
14					
15					
16					
17					
18					
19	/				1
20					
					134

Economists tend to agree that the monetary and the fiscal policies of the Federal government have an impact on production (i.e., GNP) about 6 to 12 months later and prices about 18 to 24 months later. Though the time relationships may be imprecise, most of our economic forecasting methods are in some way dependent on this proposition. Economists continue to develop methods to forecast the economy, but events continue to increase the problems. More and more, the U.S. economy is becoming interdependent with foreign economies and, inevitably, the forecasting problems grow more difficult.

The most popular methods of economic forecasting in recent years have included econometric models that have tended to accent Keynesian approaches (with particular reference to fiscal policies), monetarist methods in which the policies of the central bank have been most dominant, and the indicator approach, one of the oldest methods available. These can be briefly summarized.

1. The traditional *indicator approach* has employed a three-phase timing system—leaders, coinciders, and laggers— for analyzing, monitoring, and forecasting the national economy. The coinciders represent indicators whose timing at turning points tends to coincide with the timing of the economy itself. The leaders involve indicators whose timing at turning points tends to occur earlier than the economy, and the laggers occur later. The indicator approach has been particularly useful in monitoring where we *are* and in forecasting the short-term future (the next few months). The techniques of the indicator approach not only have been useful in monitoring and forecasting the economy, but also have been widely applied in the development of short-term *sales* forecasts.

2. The *econometric approach* is widely used by corporations in medium-term forecasts—those extending through the following year's budget period. This approach uses a system of equations to represent the whole economic process beginning with government policy. (They of course are also very useful for long-term capacity forecasts that extend out 5 to 10 years. They are weak in short-term horizons— that is, weekly and monthly—though the indicator approach adequately serves here.)

3. The *monetarist approach* has been available for some time, but since the Roosevelt period, Keynesian economics has flourished, putting monetarism into the shadows. About 15 years ago, when stagflation began to be prevalent in Keynesian societies, Milton Friedman led the "Chicago school" of monetarists as an alternative to Keynesian economics. The monetarists put primary emphasis on the monetary policies of the central bank, whereas the Keynesians put major emphasis on the fiscal policies (i.e., taxation and spending). Although monetarism results in different political results (conservative economics) than Keynesianism (liberal economics), it does *not* result in more "forecasting" techniques. The monetarists call for steady growth in the money supply, a tendency that results in limiting the amount of money in circulation. To put a lid on the amount of money fed into the economic system results in lower inflation, but also—it is claimed by nonmonetarists—lower employment. Although monetarists have not produced an elaborate forecasting technology, their political influence is great, and no economic forecast can be made without considering the monetarist view.

4. The *judgmental approach* is really the "all other" category. If we cannot clearly isolate an economic forecasting technique as eminating from one of the above three, we can loosely include it in the judgmental category. The judgmental approach relies on the three approaches above (not to mention others such as surveys, anticipations, and time series analysis). In effect, then, it represents all the techniques, the above three and many, many more.

The many techniques of forecasting the economy—especially as they relate to forecasting recessions—can be summarized by use of a "five-phase" timing spectrum. The indicator, econometric, and monetarist approaches can all be viewed together here.

A FIVE-PHASE TIMING MODEL

An economic system can be viewed as a mass of indices that peak and trough at different times. These thousands of economic processes— for convenience—can be roughly organized into five time phases from "beginning to end." These are shown in Chart 18-2. All five lines are quarterly percentage rates of change (at annual rates). The top three lines are stripped of inflation. Since the fourth line is composed of costs, some of its elements do include inflation. The fifth, and last, line *is* inflation, as measured by the general price index used to de- flate GNP. Each of the five lines is composed of many, many indexes.

As a monitoring system, the top line represents a *first cause* indi- cator, whose effects trickle downward from upper left to lower right— finally ending in prices, the *final effect.* In between is the traditional "indicator" system comprised of leading, coinciding, and lagging in- dicators. The trickle down effect can be seen best after the top line troughed in 1969. The large dots show the timing of peaks and troughs. The small dots at right show forecasts produced by the Wharton model. The stars at the top show the dates of presidential elections. The shaded areas represent recessions, as defined by the National Bureau of Eco- nomic Research.

Although the timing of the various lines is hardly precise, the ten- dencies from upper left to lower right are quite clear and have been long established by econometric studies. Needless to say, the most interesting of these five rates of change is the first one, since it repre- sents in a single line the summation of Federal government economic policies. It is these *fiscal* and *monetary* policies that cause effects to trickle downward.

It is important to point out that policy does not direct all results. Many times the government is *reacting* to forces beyond its control,

CHART 18-2.   A Five Phase Timing Model of the U.S. Economy

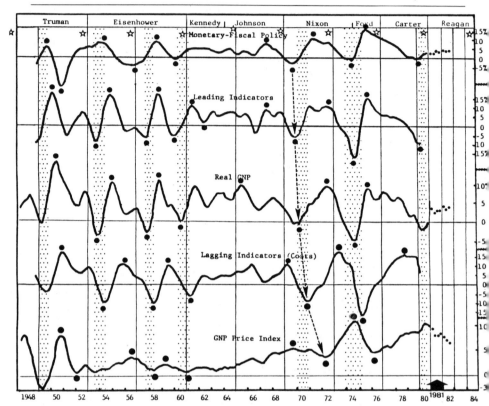

such as an OPEC oil price increase. It is not correct to imply that the government *causes* recession. Sometimes the policies do, but generally what happens to the economy, as depicted in the lower four lines, is a complex mixture of policy action and reaction.

The top line is composed of two components: fiscal policy and monetary policy. Each has equal weight in the index. The fiscal policy index is calculated by dividing government *expenditures* by government *receipts* (most of which are taxes). If in one period expenditures totaled $110 billion and receipts at the same time totaled $100 billion, the policy impact would be a 10% stimulus with the government putting $10 billion more into the economy than it took out. In the U.S. form of representative government, fiscal policy is heavily influenced by the Congress.

Monetary policy, on the other hand, is controlled by the Federal Reserve Board, a branch independent of the executive and legislative branches. Even so, the executive branch does appoint members to the Board. The intricate activities of the Federal Reserve are summarized in the policy line by the change in the money supply. It is well documented that a Federal Reserve policy action takes 6 to 12 months to have an impact on the economy—the middle of the five lines shown in Chart 18-2. It is also documented that the same policy action takes 18 to 24 months before finally affecting prices. This trickle down effect, with its imprecision and long time lags, cannot be fine tuned and that is one of the reasons why it is so difficult to manage the economic system.

Forecasting the behavior of the economy must start with trying to forecast government economic policy, with all its domestic politics and foreign influences on the system.

THE TRADITIONAL INDICATOR APPROACH

Back in the 1920s a method of forecasting the economy by timing indexes was developed by the National Bureau of Economic Research and, later, in the 1930s, the Bureau was requested by President Roosevelt to try to develop methods that would enable policy makers to *anticipate* economic activity. From these studies, the traditional "indicator" system was designed, and they are represented in the five-phase timing model by the three indexes in the middle: (1) "leading" indicators tend to peak and trough before the economy, (2) "coinciding" indicators—as represented by real GNP in the timing model—are those whose timing at peaks and troughs tends to roughly coincide with the timing of the general economy, and (3) "lagging" indicators tend to peak and trough after the general economy. Laggers perform the dual role of confirming turning points in the coinciders, as well as representing costs of doing business—such as interest rates and labor costs.

It is obvious that the so-called "leading" indicators lag the policy indicators in the top line. Consequently, in recent years, economists have considered both top lines as leaders. But the policy indicators have longer lead times. Long leaders are, inevitably, more difficult to handle. Leading indicators, representing the two top lines in the timing model, can be arrayed according to their timing at peaks and troughs. Such an array is known as an *indicator pyramid.*

INDICATOR PYRAMIDS

A device long used in logic is called a "straw man," in which a proposition or thesis is set up to see if it can be discredited. In economic forecasting, the straw man can be used to test for recession around business cycle peaks. (The opposite is the case *during* recession, in which the

CHART 18-3. An Indicator Pyramid

```
        1976                    1977                       1978
JFMAMJJASOND J FMAM J J AS OND J FMAM J J AS OND J FM
        H— — — — — — — — — — — — — — — — — — — — — — — — —
                           H — — — — — — — — — — — — — — —
                           H — — — — — — — — — — — — — — —
                              H — — — — — — — — — — — — —
                                   H — — — — — — — — —
                                       H — — — — —
                                          H — — —
                                            H— —
                                              H—
                                               H
                                               H
                                               H
```

straw man idea is used to test for an impending trough.) Since an economy can be viewed as thousands of economic processes—which we usually see in the form of indices or indicators—we can arrange lists of indicators according to timing just as was done with the five-phase timing model.

The indicator pyramid in Chart 18-3 is a list of leading indicators arrayed according to timing. It is called a pyramid for the simple reason that, if you tip your head to the right, it looks like one. In this pyramid, the Commerce Department's 12 official leading indicators are arrayed according to when they reached their highest levels (H) through March 1979, during the business cycle expansion that began in April 1975. Each minus sign represents a lower report issued since the high. The more minus signs that appear in the pyramid, the more pessimistic is the outlook. New highs at the right of a pyramid, then, represent optimism. (Note that the last three indices do not have any minus signs, signifying that the latest published figure *is* the high.) The indicator pyramid can be expanded into a much larger analytical model.

In Chart 18-4 there is an indicator pyramid containing 50 leading indicators. (These 50, along with others, are published each month in the government magazine *Business Conditions Digest,* often called *BCD*.) We can use this form of the pyramid to compare the configuration of highs in the current business cycle expansion to their *average* lead times before past recessions. This straw man tested a recession to begin in September 1979. (Note that a shaded area appears on the graph starting in October 1979.) The "chain of circles" trickling downward from upper left to lower right represents the *average mean* lead

CHART 18-4. A Recession Straw Man: Fifty Leading Indicators

A RECESSION STRAW MAN: FIFTY LEADING INDICATORS

Months Lead Time Before Past Recessions

Indicators	BCD#	Ave. Lead Time
Money Supply CHG (M2)	102	23.0
Money Supply CHG (M1)	85	18.3
Profits (with IVA & CCA)	80	18.3
Accession Rate	2	15.3
Housing Starts	28	12.8
Housing Permits	29+	12.8
Consumer Sentiment	58	12.7
Liquid Assets CHG	104+	12.3
Money Supply (M2: 1972$)	106+	12.0
Durable Unfilled Order CHG	25	11.8
Profitability % (Mfg.)	15	11.8
Money Supply (M1: 1972$)	105	11.3
Unemployment Claims	5	11.3
Price to Unit Labor Cost	17	11.3
Business Loans CHG	112	11.0
Stock Market	19+	11.0
Average Workweek	1+	10.8
Profitability % (Total)	22	10.8
Profits (1972$)	18	10.8
Cash Flow (1972$)	35	10.8
Sensitive Prices CHG	92+	10.8
Mortgage Debt CHG	33	10.5
Business Formation	12+	10.5
Overtime Hours	21	10.5
Quit Rate	4	10.3
New Businesses	13	10.0
Help Wanted Advertising	46	10.0
Layoff Rate	3+	9.8
Private Borrowing	110	9.3
Instalment Debt CHG	113	9.3
Capital Goods Orders	27	9.3
Residential Investment	89	9.0
Plant/Equipment Orders	20+	8.3
New Orders (Durables)	7	7.8
Inventories on Hand CHG	36+	7.8
Materials & Supplies CHG	38	7.7
Help Wanted Ads + Unemployed	60	7.5
Vendor Performance	32+	7.5
Instalment Loan Delinquency	39	7.3
Insured Unemployment Rate	45	6.8
New Orders (Consumers)	8+	6.0
Automobile Consumption	55	5.0
Inventories (Mfg/Trade)	31	4.8
Durable Unfilled Orders	96	4.8
Number Unemployed	37	4.8
Industrial Construction	9	4.8
Materials/Supplies on Hand	78	4.7
Business Inventories CHG	30	4.3
Goods Producing Employees	40	3.5
Unemployment Rate	43	3.5

O = Traditional Lead Time Before Past Recessions
H = Most Recent High In This Business Cycle
- = Lower Reports Issued Since High Level (H)
+ = 12 Official Leading Indicators

Shade Assumes Economic Peak In September

times for each of the 50 indicators, as measured before the preceding six recessions. You will see that the minus signs extend to the right through January 1980—the month the U.S. economy peaked and started into its seventh postwar recession. So you see this pyramid set with data at the moment the recession officially began.

The basic premise behind this straw man is this: if the economy is to peak in September 1979, then a lot of leading indicators should reach highs before then—otherwise they are not "leading" indicators. In pure theory, for a recession to begin in September 1979 the highs of the 50 leading indicators ought to trickle randomly down the chain of circles—half plotted before the chain and half after. As you examine this pyramid, shown with actual data plotted through January 1980, note the configuration of the highs (H). Only 16 highs are to the left of the chain—32% of the total of 50 highs. The other 68% of the indicators continued to improve, and you will see that they are either on or to the right of the chain. When two-thirds of the indicators go through to the right of the chain, the straw man is discredited. This pyramid discredits a September peak, because so many of the highs are to the right of the chain of circles.

All of this is easily said with 20-20 hindsight. It is quite another problem to deal with these events at the time they are occurring. The indicator pyramid, a relatively new analytical tool, was first used to test a trough in the U.S. recession of 1974–75. One of the main problems with using this analytical tool at peaks is that the pyramid signals *slowdowns,* but some slowdowns do not become recessions. Since leading indicators have an average lead time of almost a year, it is obvious that they peak and turn down before slowdowns, just as clearly as they do before those slowdowns that later become recessions. Therefore, it is easy to be misled into forecasting a recession, if the pyramid is the *only* forecasting method used. But it certainly should not be the only one. (An important incident occurred in 1976, when the pyramid began to show highs—at one point almost half the indicators had at least one minus sign. Although there is no evidence that anyone began to forecast a recession at that time, the very mild slowdown still appears in the graphs—particularly in employment, construction, and durable goods indices.)

Without doubt, the indicator pyramid is best used to analyze the current situation in light of periods before past business cycle peaks (or troughs, whichever the case may be). What the forecaster does is watch for patterns in the configuration of the highs that depart from normal (i.e., averages). When a situation develops that is out of the ordinary, the forecaster can separately analyze the key indicators in the list of 50.

The list of 50 leaders includes: (1) government policy indicators, the longest leaders; (2) the conventional factory indicators ("smokestacks"), which respond to the policies; and then (3) inventory leaders, which lead by the least amount of time before recessions. In Chart 18-4, you will note that the long leader highs at the top were randomly distributed before and after the chain of circles, meaning that policies were not discrediting the September straw man thesis. But now look to the middle (smokestacks) and see the highs to the right of the chain. That contradiction was explained by the collapse of the dollar in the summer of 1978, an event that made American-made goods cheaper relative to goods imported into the United States. In effect, the domestic/import mix was changed in favor of the domestic manufacturers. Thus, the optimistic character of the *middle* of the pyramid.

A MODEL OF AN AVERAGE RECESSION

A rather simple recession model can be developed by averaging past recession behavior. In other words, the character of the seventh post-war recession can be evaluated in terms of the average of the preceding six. In effect, the idea is to just add the six recessions together and divide by six. This yields an Average Recession Model (ARM) that enables one to analyze the current (seventh) situation. Once a recession is underway—a crucial assumption in the model—it is possible to track it by past standards.

As soon as the National Bureau of Economic Research announced (in June 1980) that the U.S. economy peaked in January 1980 and entered a recession, the first quarter of 1980 became the benchmark peak quarter and all six previous recessions were plotted together with a common peak. You see this in Chart 18-5, which shows an ARM model for the Industrial Production Index. The solid line in the graph proxies as an average recession, assuming the first quarter of 1980 as the peak. The dotted line superimposed on it represents the current (seventh) situation, plotted through the fourth quarter of 1980. The vertical bars represent the two-in-three probability values (given the standard deviations of past recession experiences). The two large dots show the traditional timing for this index at peaks and troughs in the past six recessions. The small dot, plotted in February 1980, shows the highest point reached in the seventh (current) situation. The index-ing calculations appear in the table below the graph.

As you can see, in the quarters following the peak, industrial pro-duction declined more sharply than average at first and then began to track closer to the average line. Needless to say, a forecaster moni-toring this graph can keep close watch on the severity of the current situation, relative to the many past recessions that are included in the model (solid line). The ARM model enables us to simulate some simple alternative forecasts quicly with a pencil and calculator. And the tech-nique is so simple that it can easily be adapted to *any* index. All one needs is enough history to average a few past business cycles. It is a decision making tool for forecasting the microsectors of the economy, that is, industries, companies, divisions, and product lines.

The weakness of the ARM model is that one must first bet on an extremely important assumption: the choice of the peak quarter. It was first used in August 1979 after real GNP in the second quarter of 1979 plunged. The first simulation used the first quarter of 1979 as 100—the benchmark. That is fine if that is what the historians later say *was* the peak. But they did not. Whenever real GNP declines decisively, the forecaster should set up the ARM model, as a simula-tion of events to come. But, as is always the case in virtually any economic model, such a simulation is based on assumptions. If the

CHART 18-5. Average Recession Model: FRB Industrial Production Index

Assumption: that the first quarter of 1980 is the peak quarter of a business

	A	B	C	D	E	F
Peak:	48.4	53.3	57.3	60.2	68.4	73.4
Trough:	49.4	54.2	58.2	61.1	70.4	75.1
Recession ending:	1949	1954	1958	1961	1970	1975
-8	—	86.4	94.9H	83.1L	91.7	84.9
-7	95.1	86.9L	97.1H	87.4	93.3	87.9
-6	95.1	88.9L	97.4H	91.5	94.8	90.0
-5	95.4	87.6L	97.1H	95.4	95.7	91.8
-4	98.1	90.3L	96.5	100.0H	97.0	94.7
-3	99.0	96.6	100.0H	96.0L	98.7	97.0
-2	100.0	98.6	101.0H	96.4L	99.1	98.4
-1	101.0	100.0	99.7	102.2H	100.4	99.4L
Peak	100.0	100.0	100.0	100.0	100.0	100.0
+1	96.8	95.3L	95.8	98.4	97.5	98.8H
+2	93.7	92.3	90.5L	96.0	97.0	99.7H
+3	93.9	91.9	88.9L	94.6	96.8	100.3H
+4	93.4	92.5L	93.6	98.4H	94.7	94.8
+5	98.3	95.0	97.9	101.5H	96.7	86.1L
+6	106.6H	100.2	102.1	104.9	97.7	86.9L
+7	115.1H	104.5	107.1	106.6	98.2	91.7L
+8	117.0H	106.1	102.7	107.6	99.8	93.9L
+9	119.5H	108.6	103.2	108.7	103.4	97.1L
+10	119.7H	109.0	109.5	109.6	105.8	98.9L
+11	117.0H	108.6	107.1	111.7	108.0	100.1L

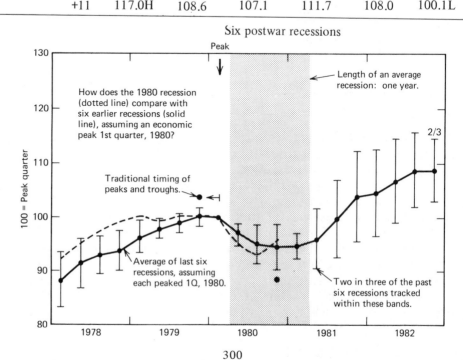

Six postwar recessions

Peak

How does the 1980 recession (dotted line) compare with six earlier recessions (solid line), assuming an economic peak 1st quarter, 1980?

Length of an average recession: one year.

2/3

Traditional timing of peaks and troughs.

100 = Peak quarter

Average of last six recessions, assuming each peaked 1Q, 1980.

Two in three of the past six recessions tracked within these bands.

1978   1979   1980   1981   1982

cycle expansion ending with the 1980 recession.

G 80.1 1980	H Average (4)	I Sigma (4)	J Average (6)	K Sigma (6)	L J + K Average Plus Hl	M J – K Average Minus Lo	N
92.5	87.7	3.6	88.2	4.9	93.1	83.3	
95.3	90.9	3.9	91.3	4.4	95.7	86.9	
97.2	92.9	2.5	93.0	3.3	96.3	89.7	
99.0	94.6	1.9	93.8	3.5	97.3	90.3	
100.0	96.6	1.4	96.1	3.3	99.4	92.8	
99.8	97.8	1.2	97.9	1.6	99.5	96.3	
100.1	99.0	.7	98.9	1.6	100.5	97.3	
100.0	99.8	1.4	100.1	1.5	101.6	98.6	
100.0	100.0	—	100.0	—	—	—	
95.1	97.1	1.1	97.1	1.4	98.5	95.7	
93.1	94.8	2.1	94.9	3.4	98.3	91.5	
95.7	94.3	2.0	94.4	3.9	98.3	90.5	
	94.1	.7	94.6	2.1	96.7	92.5	
	97.0	1.5	95.9	5.3	101.2	90.6	
	101.2	3.0	99.7	7.0	106.7	92.7	
	104.1	4.1	103.9	8.1	112.0	95.8	
	104.1	3.5	104.5	7.8	112.3	96.7	
	106.0	3.1	106.8	7.6	114.4	99.2	
	108.5	1.8	108.8	6.7	115.5	102.1	
	108.9	2.0	108.8	5.6	114.4	103.2	

Historical recession averages

assumptions are correct, the model will probably behave well. If the assumptions are not correct, the model will not be faithful to actual events. ARM is a simulation device. But like all simulators, it is correct according to its assumptions.

SUMMARY

Recession Forecasting is one of the most difficult of all forecasting challenges. In recent years, the entry into recession has also caused problems for those forecasting it. It is no accident that the Federal government—through its policies—is partly involved in recession, and most administrations try to prevent them. This has resulted in what has been called "gradualism," in which the economy is slowed down—

but not so slow that it turns negative. In the last three recessions, the economy has turned sideward toward the ends of the expansionary periods. The "horizontal" nature of these recent peaks has caused many premature forecasts of recession. In particular, the 1980 recession exhibited this zero economic growth for over a year before finally plunging down in the sharpest quarterly drop since World War II.

19

FORECASTING MACROECONOMIC VARIABLES

An Eclectic Approach

STEPHEN K. McNEES
Vice President and Economist
Federal Reserve Bank of Boston

NICHOLAS S. PERNA
Manager,
Economic Analysis
General Electric Company

I. WHY FORECAST MACRO VARIABLES?

Macroeconomic variables may appear irrelevant to practical decision making at the firm level. After all, no one sells the aggregate GNP or charges the Consumer Price Index (CPI) in exchange. Nonetheless:

> In a highly integrated economy, seemingly remote events spill over into individual markets of direct interest. For example, cost of living adjustments depend on the national, internationally determined CPI.

Sales depend not only on a firm's prices, production, and marketing strategies, but on the real disposable income of all consumers.

Macroeconomic variables describe the overall "economic climate" which in turn shapes consumer psychology and business attitudes. They also affect—and are heavily influenced by—government financial, expenditure, and tax policies.

Many of the most valuable forecasting techniques were originally developed for and have been extensively applied to predicting macroeconomic variables. This experience can serve as a guide to which forecasting techniques will be most helpful for handling the firm's forecasting problems.

The remainder of this chapter explores the practical art of macroeconomic forecasting. Section II describes and assesses the variety of available forecasting techniques such as time series analysis, econometric models, and business cycle comparisons. It also provides a catalog of forecast sources for the major macroeconomic variables. Section III focuses on *how* to forecast with an eclectic approach that permits the forecaster to utilize those techniques that he or she feels most comfortable with and to focus on those variables of greatest interest. A number of concrete forecasting examples, such as consumer spending and inflation, are covered in considerable detail.

II. FORECAST TECHNIQUES AND SOURCES

The *best* way to forecast depends on the interests of the forecast user and resources of the forecaster.

Current Period Estimation

A forecaster interested primarily in anticipating tomorrow's headlines can often rely heavily on underlying source data that are already available. For example, the GNP, its components, and their implicit price deflators are released quarterly. These estimates are based on monthly and weekly source data.* Even though an outsider cannot exactly replicate the Commerce Department's techniques, a fairly close estimate of preliminary GNP data can be made by careful study of actual monthly and weekly data.

*For a description of the data and their sources see reference 16, Tables 1 and 2, pp. 19–21.

Time Series Analysis

The simplest, least expensive way to forecast is with "time series"* techniques. There is evidence that this may be useful for projecting some macroeconomic variables, such as business inventories and state and local spending, and it may also have valuable microeconomic applications. Nevertheless, the approach has important limitations for most macroeconomic forecasting. It does not generally produce a rich, comprehensible, consistent story to accompany the numerical prediction. There is no assurance that the basic accounting identities (e.g., GNP must equal the sum of its components) are satisfied or that the results conform to economic "common sense" (e.g., unemployment will go up when real GNP falls). Time series equations cannot be used to conduct hypothetical ("what if") experiments and therefore do not adequately describe forecast risks and alternative outcomes. In short, even when it is accurate, the informational content of a time series forecast is low. However, the accuracy tends to deteriorate relatively rapidly as the forecast horizon lengthens because time series do not incorporate future (exogenous) influences known to affect future outcomes. A time series forecast would not, for example, be affected by an announced drastic change in government spending or monetary policy.

Econometric Models

Because well-constructed macroeconometric forecasting models would be capable of handling these problems, they have become the primary tool of most macro forecasters today.* As illustrated below, econometric relationships are an invaluable aid to forecasting several important macroeconomic variables, such as personal consumption expenditures and productivity.

As a practical matter, constructing a satisfactory formal macroeconometric model is an extremely challenging and relatively expensive undertaking. Immense theoretical and statistical problems—problems for which no general consensus solutions exist—confront the forecaster. Then, once the original model is developed, considerable resources must be devoted to updating, reformulating, and reestimating.

Finally, models do not forecast by themselves. At a minimum, the

---

*Those who wish to pursue the time series approach to economic forecasting are encouraged to refer to Nelson[11] or Pindyck and Rubinfeld (Part III, pp. 421–550).[14]

†Those not deterred by this warning are encouraged to refer to Pindyck and Rubinfeld (Parts I and II)[14] or Kuh and Schmalensee[6] for elementary expositions of the construction of multiequation macroeconometric models.

forecaster must provide projections of the future values of the exogenous variables required to solve the model (tax cuts, OPEC oil prices, federal housing support programs—to name a few). Even then, experience strongly suggests that the "first pass" model runs do not produce the most accurate forecasts. All econometric model forecasters have found it is necessary to adjust initial forecasts—often extensively. Most judgmental adjustments are made for one of two reasons: (1) the model has not been performing accurately recently, or (2) some external factor, not incorporated in the model, is expected to influence future events.*

Cyclical Comparison

Economic theory suggests certain variables that will influence the forecast, but typically it tells little about the *timing* of their impact—for example, whether their influence is instantaneous or spread out over time. Econometricians attempt to account for this by estimating lag patterns distributed over time. These estimated distributed lags, however, represent *average* historical experience, combining recessions and booms. Many observers have found enough regularity in past business cycles to segregate the historical data by phases of the business cycle. This procedure is particularly helpful for highly cyclical variables such as consumer durables and, as illustrated in example 2 below, housing starts and therefore residential fixed investment. Neither time series nor econometric methods have been very successful in predicting these variables. However, it can be difficult to match the phase of the current cycle with similar stages of previous cycles and to determine which past cycle is most like the current one.

External Forecasts

Macroeconomic forecasters can draw on a large body of published projections for help in formulating and evaluating their own. Among the most important sources (see Chart 19-1) are the following:

1. The median forecast of 11 variables from the *Business Outlook Survey* conducted quarterly by the American Statistical Association and the National Bureau of Economic Research.

2. Export and import forecasts published semiannually in the Organization for Economic Cooperation and Development's *Economic Outlook*.

3. Quarterly surveys of business capital spending plans, published quarterly in the *Survey of Current Business*.

*For supporting evidence, see McNees.[9]

CHART 19-1. Forecasting Techniques and Information Sources, by Variable

Macroeconomic Variable	Techniques	Sources
Personal consumption:		
Durable Goods	3, 4, 2	ASA/NBER
Auto Sales	3, 4	WARD'S
*Personal consumption, other	2	
Residential investment	3, 4	ASA/NBER
*Housing starts	3, 4	ASA/NBER
Business fixed investment	4, 2	BEA, ASA/NBER
Federal government purchases	4	BEA, ASA/NBER
State and local government		
purchases	1	
Exports	4, 1	OECD
Imports	4, 2	OECD
Change in business inventories	1, 3	
*Unemployment rate	2, 1, 4	CEA
*Productivity	2, 3	
*Compensation	2, 4, 3	BLS
GNP price deflator	4, 2	BLS, CEA
*Consumer price index	4, 2	USDA, USDE

Key to techniques: 1 = Time series methods
                             2 = Econometric relationships
                             3 = Cyclical comparisons
                             4 = External sources

*As illustrated in the following text.

Sources:

1. ASA/NBER: *Business Outlook Survey.* Published quarterly (March, June, September, December). Available from the American Statistical Association, 806 15th St., N.W., Washington, DC 20005. (202) 393-3253. Subscription price: $20/year.

2. OECD: *Economic Outlook.* Published semiannually (July and December). Available from OECD Publications and Information Center, Suite 1207, 1750 Pennsylvania Avenue, Washington, DC 20006. (202) 724-1857. Subscription price: $17.50/year.

3. BEA: *Survey of Current Business.* Published monthly by the Bureau of Economic Analysis of the U.S. Department of Commerce. Surveys of business capital spending plans for the current and two subsequent quarters appear in the March, June, September, and December issues. Budget information typically appears in the February issue. Available from the Superintendent of Documents, U.S. Government Printing Office, Washington, DC 20402. Subscription price (12 issues): $35/year by first class mail; $22/year by second class mail; single issue price: $1.90.

4. Ward's: *Ward's Automotive Reports.* Published weekly. Available from Ward's

Chart 19-1. Continued

Communications Inc., 28 W. Adams Street, Detroit, MI 48225. (313) 962-4433. Subscription price: $325/year including hardbound yearbook.

5. *Budget of the U.S. Government.* Published semiannually (January and July). Available from the Superintendent of Documents, U.S. Government Printing Office, Washington, DC 20402. Price: $5.00 for fiscal year 1981 budget.

6. BLS: *Monthly Labor Review.* Published monthly by the Bureau of Labor Statistics of the U.S. Department of Labor. Available from the Superintendent of Documents, U.S. Government Printing Office, Washington, DC 20402. Subscription price $18.00/year. Single issue price: $2.50.

7. CEA: *Annual Report.* Contained in the *Economic Report of the President.* Published annually in January. Available from the Superintendent of Documents, U.S. Government Printing Office, Washington, DC 20402. Price: $4.75 for 1980 report.

8. Department of Agriculture: *Agricultural Outlook.* Published 10 times per year. Available from the Superintendent of Documents, U.S. Government Printing Office, Washington, DC 20402. Subscription price: $19/year.

9. USDE: *Short Term Energy Outlook.* Published monthly by the Energy Information Administration of the U.S. Department of Energy. Available from the Superintendent of Documents, U.S. Government Printing Office, Washington, DC 20402. Price: $13/year. Single issue price: $4.00.

Note: Additional data sources are discussed in Chapter 28.

4. Information on automobile sales production, inventories, and pricing published weekly in *Ward's Automotive Reports* and several newspapers.

5. The *Budget of the U.S. Government* and the *Mid-Session Review of the Budget*, for projections of federal spending and tax policies and the underlying economic assumptions.

6. Periodic forecasts of food and energy prices issued by the U.S. Departments of Agriculture and Energy, reported in major newspapers.

7. In addition, many forecasters subscribe to at least one of the major commerical forecasting services.

An outside forecast can be used in a variety of ways to generate an independent forecast. The forecaster may want to use it "as is" for variables for which he has no special interest or forecasting expertise. More commonly, the outside forecast can, as illustrated below, be used as a "first pass" or starting point for generating an independent view.

The following section outlines briefly an eclectic, judgmental approach to macroeconomic forecasting techniques—time series modeling, cyclical comparisons, econometric regularities, and external information sources are all combined. The specific blend of approaches varies, depending on the forecast variable and horizon. It is judgmental in that it acknowledges at the outset that the forecaster will often choose to override his "objective technique" whenever new information or his or her own intuition suggest that things will turn out differently than they did in the past. A primary advantage of this approach is that a forecast "story"— the reasons behind and risks in the forecast—emerges from the interaction of the forecasting techniques and the forecaster's judgment.

A disadvantage of this flexible approach is that it is hard to describe succinctly. Several features cannot be taught but must be learned from experience. The remainder of this chapter is devoted to several concrete examples of how the eclectic, judgmental approach can be applied.

III. ECLECTIC FORECASTING: AN OUTLINE AND APPROACH

Chart 19-2 outlines an eclectic approach to forecasting GNP and other important macroeconomic variables. The task is divided into three stages: (1) the components of real GNP, (2) unemployment and productivity, and (3) compensation, profits, and inflation. Each stage is described briefly below, and several steps are illustrated in more detail in the following examples.

Components of Real GNP

It is helpful to start with the more "exogenous" components—those whose behavior is less closely tied to the current performance of the economy—and proceed toward the more "endogenous" variables whose behavior depends heavily on "everything else." Begin (step 1A) with exports and federal government purchases, where initial estimates can be taken from external sources. In addition, the relatively accurate Commerce Department survey of capital spending plans provides a good initial estimate of nonresidential fixed investment.

Next (step 1B), time series or autoregressive equations can provide a good starting point for short-term estimates of state and local government purchases of goods and services and changes in business inventories. It is necessary to reestimate these equations frequently and to modify the longer run forecasts with other information, such as the passage of Proposition 13 in California.

Then (step 1C) the ASA/NBER median forecast of housing starts and personal consumption expenditures for durable goods (PCD) can be analyzed using the cyclical comparison technique, described in example 2 below, to provide a rough guess about the frequency and amplitude

CHART 19-2. Bare Bone Diagram of A Eclectic Approach to A Macro Forecast

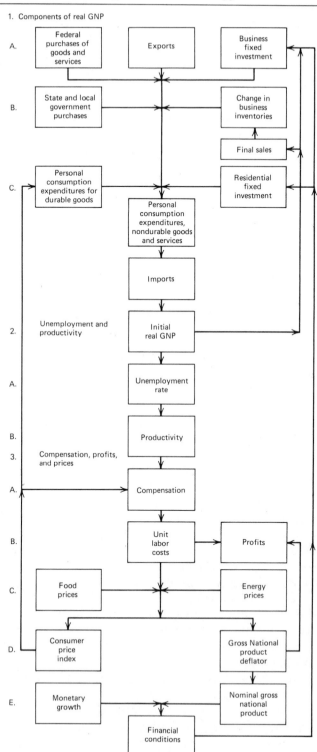

of the phase of the current cycle. These forecasts must be revised again to reflect prospective financial conditions and institutional changes.

Finally, (step 1D), an econometric relationship in conjunction with some external information can be used to produce a forecast of personal consumption expenditures for nondurable goods and services, as described below in example 1, and imports. Combining these steps produces an initial estimate of real GNP which should be used to go back and reassess the forecasts, especially those for business fixed and inventory investment. If these prospects are changed significantly, the whole process may have to be repeated until a consistent view emerges.

This process of a continuing series of iterations to insure consistency, both in the accounting and economic sense of the word, is common to all the stages of the forecasting process. While a computer could be used to achieve some consistency in milliseconds, a key feature of the eclectic approach is that forcing the forecaster to achieve consistency can sharpen his original insights.

Unemployment and Productivity

Compared with the first stage, forecasting unemployment (step 2A) and productivity (step 2B) are relatively straightforward, as explained in examples 3 and 4 below. However, once again, this stage may provide some insights that will call into question some of the forecasts generated in stage 1. No one promised that forecasting would be easy.

Compensation, Profits, and Prices

Integrating the "real" forecast with the "nominal" outlook for compensation, profits, and prices is the most challenging phase of forecasting. The procedure is illustrated for compensation and inflation in examples 5 and 6 below. Since the real spending decisions in stage 1 are acknowledged to depend on the rate of inflation, the results of stage 3 will probably require another pass at the preliminary forecasts generated in the earlier stages. In particular, the nominal GNP forecast combined with some assessment of the future course of monetary policy provides an important clue to prospective financial conditions. These conditions heavily influence consumer spending on durable goods and housing.

The stages outlined above and in Chart 19-2—starting with the *real* GNP and moving toward financial conditions—are probably the most appropriate approach for the production/sales decisions of nonfinancial businesses. Financial institutions and corporate treasurers would probably benefit from starting with the components of *nominal* GNP, combining these with monetary policy considerations to arrive at an impression of financial conditions, and turning then to prices in order to arrive at real GNP as a residual. More generally, the obvious rule is:

focus your primary attention on what you care most (and know most) about!

Example 1. Personal Consumption Expenditures: Judgmentally Modified Econometrics. The theory of consumer behavior is relatively well established: real consumer spending on services and nondurables goods (PCO) is related to its past value and some measure of income. Even though economic theory does not establish whether the effect of inflation would be positive or negative, a number of empirical studies suggest that consumption has been discouraged by inflation.

Theory also does not indicate which empirical measure of income is most appropriate. While several have been studied, they vastly complicate the forecasting process. As is often the case in forecasting, it is preferable to use a measure that is readily available (here, GNP) as a practical proxy for a theoretically ideal measure. In this case using GNP as an income measure does not reduce the accuracy of the forecast.

These considerations suggest the following econometric equation*:

$$PCO_t = -71.8 + .99 \, PCO_{t-1} + .09 \, \Delta GNP_t$$
$$+ .03 GNP_{t-1} - 3.7\% \, \Delta CPI_t \tag{19-1}$$

A forecast of PCO requires projections of the right-hand side's "explanatory" variables. Typically, the explanatory variables include some of the other variables being forecasted (in this case GNP) so that the forecast must be generated iteratively. The most convenient way to begin is with some easily obtainable projections, such as those released by the CEA or the median forecast from the ASA/NBER survey.

For example, using the CEA forecast available in early 1979 for 1979 GNP (2.2% growth) and the CPI (7.5%), the equation above implies that aggregate PCO would increase 4.1% in 1979, a large overestimate relative to the actual increase of 2.7%.

Much of the overestimate was due to incorrect forecasts of the explanatory variables in the equation. Using the actual values of GNP (1.0%) and the CPI (12.7%), the equation implies a 1.9% increase in PCO, an underestimate of what actually occurred. This shortfall is due partly to the influence of factors that the simple econometric equation ignores (and perhaps partly due to pure chance or bad luck!).

External factors were especially important in influencing the quarterly *pattern* of PCO. For example, the equation substantially overestimates

---

*The equation was fitted to real per capita data for PCO and GNP. Per capita predictions can be converted to aggregate predictions by using population projections —see reference 1. New Projections will be published in July 1981. For a more complete discussion of the derivation and estimation of this form of consumption function, see Kuh and Schmalensee (Chapter 3, pp. 31–49).[6]

actual consumer spending in the second quarter of 1979. The reason is now fairly obvious—the widespread gasoline shortages and lines. In this particular case, this negative factor was probably predictable in advance—the Iranian revolution occurred in late 1978. While some downward adjustment in the historical relationship was obviously necessary, the magnitude was (as is often the case) inevitably a matter of judgment. Since the disturbance was virtually unprecedented, econometric or time series modeling would have been of little help. The forecaster was forced to look back at the 1974 gasoline shortages and to gather anecdotal evidence in order to make an intelligent guess.

In the third quarter of 1979, PCO returned to the level that the historical econometric relationship indicated. However, in the final quarter of 1979 there was strong surge that the equation did not predict. A wide variety of possible reasons for the spending spree were advanced—consumer sentiment, inflationary expectations, increases in personal wealth (particularly capital gains on houses), rising tax and energy burdens, and even distortions in the data (see McNees[10]).

Although virtually no forecaster identified the relevant factor and assessed in advance the magnitude of its impact, such speculation is an integral part of forecasting. To the extent that a forecast error can be traced to a specific external factor (rather than to purely random noise), that information can be used to improve future forecasts. If the hypothesized influence is believed to be systematic, that factor can be incorporated into the explicit econometric forecasting techniques.

On the other hand, forecasting accuracy can suffer if a forecaster "overexplains" past errors. The procedure of adding a new factor to "explain" each new large error will quickly generate so many "explanations" that attention will be drawn away from those few factors that exert a systematic, stable influence on the forecasted variable. "Correction" of recent errors can make future forecasts *worse* as well as *better*.

The major point of this example is that a simple econometric relationship, such as that given above for PCO, *is* useful to achieve consistency with previous historical patterns but should be used only as a benchmark for judgmental adjustments. There is no reason to think that the future will only reflect the past (indeed there are many reasons to expect that it won't), so that accurate forecasts must try to incorporate new information not captured in previous data.

At the same time, the forecaster must recognize there are few occasions when a "new" factor that will exert a *systematic* influence in the future can be identified.

Example 2. Housing Starts: The Cyclical Comparison Approach. Housing starts, and thus residential investment, have undergone eight distinct cycles during the postwar period. (See Chart 19-3.) To the extent that the cycles exhibit regularity in their frequency and amplitude,

CHART 19-3. Postwar Housing Cycles

	Peak		Trough		Contractions		Expansions	
					Duration (Quarters)	Magnitude %	Duration (Quarters)	Magnitude %
8.	78:II	2.097	80:II	1.045	8	–50	?	?
7.	72:IV	2.424	75:I	.976	9	–60	13	115
6.	69:I	1.678	70:I	1.236	4	–26	11	96
5.	63:III	1.672	66:IV	.931	13	–44	9	80
4.	59:I	1.648	60:IV	1.185	7	–28	11	41
3.	54:IV	1.716	58:I	1.128	13	–34	4	46
2.	50:II	2.013	53:III	1.339	13	–33	5	28
1.	47:IV	1.525	49:I	1.168	5	–23	5	72

this regularity can be used to predict the timing and magnitude of future changes in housing starts.

For example, as of late 1975, it was clear that housing was in the up-swing stage of its cycle. Simply by assuming that the expansion would be identical to the *average* of previous cycles, one could have predicted that the expansion would last seven and a half quarters and rise to 1.8 million units. By late 1978, it was clear that housing starts had peaked and were entering the contraction phase. By assuming this contraction would be identical to the average in previous cycles, one could have predicted that the contraction would last nine quarters with a decline to 1.14 million units. This extremely simplistic approach would have somewhat underestimated the amplitude of the latest housing cycle and understated the length of the expansion, but it was a fairly accurate guide to the length of the contraction.

The cyclical comparison approach can lead to more accurate forecasts if the anticipated cycle can be more closely matched with one or more previous cycles. For example, the 1975–78 upswing could have been expected to be somewhat longer and stronger than average for several reasons. Housing demand was bolstered by the high rate of household formation as the baby boom came of age, by the sustained rise in home prices which led some home buyers to view their dwelling as a wise investment, and by the increased tax advantages of home ownership in an inflationary environment. On the other hand, it seemed unlikely that housing starts would rise to their all-time 1972 peak, since that episode was widely acknowledged to have been characterized by overbuilding in some regions. With this qualification, the insight that the 1975–78 expansion was more likely to resemble the 1970–72 experience than the postwar average would have led to a more accurate forecast of the expansion.

Housing activity, of course, cannot be predicted mechanistically from past cycles in isolation from the rest of the economy. Financial conditions—mortgage rates and credit flows to mortgages lenders—are very important. For example, after housing activity had leveled off in 1978 some forecasters believed that the contraction phase would be extraordinarily mild because the introduction of money-market certificates enabled mortgage lenders to compete successfully for funds. The first five quarters of the contraction *were* unusually mild, due either to this financial market innovation and/or to the demographic and financial factors supporting housing demand. In late 1979 and 1980 when interest rates rose to record levels, housing activity fell to slightly below its average trough level.

The moral of this story is that expenditures for long-lived items—houses, capital spending, and automobiles—are sensitive to financial conditions. In order to forecast these elements of spending, the cyclical comparison approach must be supplemented by an attempt to anticipate future financial conditions. Be forewarned that few forecasters have demonstrated the ability to accurately foretell financial conditions.

Example 3. The Unemployment Rate: Blending a Rule of Thumb with a Time Series Equation. Most forecasters use a simple rule of thumb, called "Okun's Law," to forecast the unemployment rate (Okun[12]). The rule of thumb relates the change in the unemployment rate, ΔUR, to the difference between the potential and actual growth rates of real GNP. The simple rule,

$$\Delta UR_t = 0.35 \, (\% \text{ change in potential GNP}_t - \% \text{ change in real GNP}_t)$$

tracked movements in the unemployment rate quite well over periods when the growth of potential GNP was stable.* In recent years, the slowdown in productivity growth has led to some uncertainty in estimates of the growth of potential GNP.† A prominent forecaster has noted that a time series equation picked up the slowdown in productivity more quickly than a forecasting model and its managers (Eckstein[2]).

One time series equation for forecasting the unemployment rate relates is simply to its three lagged values**:

$$UR_t = 0.35 + 1.73 \, UR_{t-1} - 1.03 \, UR_{t-2} + 0.24 \, UR_{t-3}$$

Until the estimates of potential GNP are improved, forecasters should use both approaches, using one as a cross-check on the other and leaning

---

*The coefficient of 0.35 which was obtained by trial and error rather than regression analysis, is expressed in annual terms. For quarterly changes it must be divided by four.

†See, reference 3 (pp. 72–76) and reference 4 (pp. 88–90).

**This formulation originally appeared in Sargent.[15]

more heavily on "Okun's Law" for long-term forecasts. Alternatively, the two approaches can be combined yielding the following relationship:*

$$UR_t = 1.432 + 1.27 \, UR_{t-1} - 0.789 \, UR_{t-2} + 0.203 \, UR_{t-3}$$
$$+ \, 0.014 \, (\text{potential GNP}_t - \text{real GNP}_t)$$

Prices, Profits, and Unit Labor Costs

Unit labor costs are a major determinant of the "core" rate of inflation and of movements in corporate profits and profit margins over the business cycle. Forecasting unit labor costs is a two-step process that involves projecting both compensation per hour and productivity. Productivity can be forecast with an econometric relationship driven only by real GNP. Compensation can be forecast either with an econometric wage equation or by an eclectic, "bottom-up" approach that adds together union wages, nonunion wages, fringe benefits, and payroll taxes.

Example 4. Productivity: An Econometric Relationship. Productivity, defined as the real output per hour of work in nonfinancial corporations or PROD, can be related to the annual rate of growth of real GNP (% ΔGNP), the change in the rate of growth of real GNP, and a simple time trend:

$$\% \, \Delta PROD = 3.1 + 0.11 \, \% \, \Delta \text{real GNP} + 0.33 \, \Delta(\% \, \Delta \text{real GNP}) - 0.08T$$

Like other cyclical variables, productivity depends on both the growth rate of GNP and changes in its growth rate. This equation provides an overly optimistic view of productivity performance. It does a better job when other cyclical variables such as the rate of capacity utilization, or causal factors such as the capital stock of research and development activity, are included. Like all of the equations presented here, it is intended as an aid in forecasting and does not attempt to unravel the causes of the mysterious slowdown in productivity.†

Example 5. Labor Compensation: Macroeconometrics or "Nuts and Bolts"

Macroeconometrics. The standard econometric approach links the growth in employee compensation (% ΔCOMP) to inflation (% ΔCPI) and variations in labor market conditions, as measured by changes in

---

*This formulation, along with an evaluation of the forecasting performance of the time series equation, originally appeared in McNees.[8]
†For some clues to unraveling this mystery see reference 5.

the unemployment rate, ΔUR. Estimated with annual data from 1955 to 1979, this equation,

$$\% \, \Delta COMP_t = 2.78 + 0.50 \, \% \, \Delta CPI_t + 0.24 \, \% \, \Delta CPI_{t-1} - 0.13 \, \Delta UR_t$$

overestimates compensation growth in 1979 by 1.5 percentage points, nearly twice its "normal" error. Two possible reasons for the overshooting are the impact of wage guidelines and the overstatement of inflation as measured by the CPI. With the personal consumption deflator, which treats home ownership differently, the 1979 error is cut in half.

"Bottom-up" Approach. An alternative, "bottom-up" approach to compensation forecasting adds together the components of total compensation—union wages, nonunion wages, fringe benefits, and payroll taxes.

Union Wages

Wages paid to workers covered by collective bargaining agreements consist of cost of living adjustments (COLAs), new settlements, and fixed (nonCOLA) deferred increases. The "average" COLA provision has a 0.6 "elasticity" with respect to increases in the CPI: a 10% increase in the CPI produces a 6% increase in wages (see Perna[13]). Escalator payments can be generated with an outside forecast of the CPI. New settlements can be estimated by examining the recent history of first year fixed increases with some modification for the government's current wage guidelines or the start of a new pattern. At the start of each year, the Bureau of Labor Statistics publishes estimates of the fixed increases in major contracts scheduled for the year. In 1979, this estimate was 5.1% (see Levin[7]).

The weight for each of the three components of union wages indicates the proportion of workers under collective bargaining agreements receiving each kind of increase during the year. In 1979, for example, about 60% of union workers were scheduled for deferred increases from previously negotiated contracts. However, these weights can add to more than 1 because many workers receive more than one type of increase in a year and the weights shift over the course of a 3-year collective bargaining cycle. A heavy bargaining year like 1979 has a higher proportion of first year increases and a smaller fraction of fixed increases from earlier contracts than 1981, a year with a light bargaining calendar.

Nonunion Wages

Nonunion wages tend to move like union wages, but exhibit greater sensitivity to variations in labor market conditions. More precisely, the difference between the growth of union wages and nonunion wages has varied systematically with the unemployment rate:

$$(\% \text{ change in union wages}) - (\% \text{ change in nonunion wages})$$
$$= -2.0 + 0.5 \text{ UR}$$

Total Wages

Chart 19-4 illustrates how estimates of union wages and nonunion wages can be combined and adjusted to yield an estimate of total labor compensation. Over the past 10 years, *compensation* has grown about one percentage point faster than *wages* because of increases in the cost of fringe benefits and payroll taxes. Since payroll tax increases vary from year to year, the exact adjustment would have to be explicitly estimated each year.

Using the CEA's CPI and UR forecasts for 1979, both the macroeconometric wage equation and the "bottom-up" approach accurately predicted the 8.8% increase in compensation per hour in 1979. Even though their predictions were perfect, the techniques were right for the wrong reasons! Based on the actual 11.3% increase in the CPI,* both approaches would have overestimated 1979 compensation growth by 1.5 percentage points, about twice their "normal" error. One reason for this overshooting may be the overstatement of domestic inflation as measured by the CPI. With the personal consumption expenditures deflator, which treats the costs of home ownership differently, the 1979 error would have been about normal. In addition, both approaches ignored the President's 1979 wage guidelines. Even if the techniques were valid for noncontrol periods, they would need to be adjusted for wage guidelines, if those controls were effective. Further research would be needed to sort out the relative importance of each of these reasons for the overshooting.

The macroeconometric approach can be combined with a CPI equation to produce a simultaneous wage and price forecast. The "bottom-up" approach provides some insights into the institutional features of the wage setting process. In practice, both procedures can fruitfully be employed to isolate the key factors underlying the numerical forecast.

---

*This is the year-to-year increase in the CPI (calendar year 1979 versus calendar year 1978). For December 1979 versus December 1978, the increase was considerably larger—13.3 percent. Whenever the inflation rate is accelerating, the December-versus-December increase will exceed the year-to-year rise. When inflation is slowing down, then the December-versus-December number will be smaller than the year-to-year.

CHART 19-4. A "Bottom-Up" Forecast of Labor Compensation in 1979

	Increase %	Weight	Contribution
a. *Union Wages*			
Cost of living adjustments[a]	4.9	0.45	2.2
First year settlements[b]	8.0	0.40	3.2
Deferred fixed increases	5.1	0.60	3.1
Union wage change			8.5%
b. *Nonunion:* Equals union plus/minus unemployment adjustments[a]			7.5%
c. *Average of union and nonunion wages*			7.7%
d. *Further adjustments*			
Add-on for fringes and payroll taxes:			1.0%
Labor compensation: per hour			8.7%

[a]Based on January 1979 CEA forecast.
[b]Assumed equal to previous year.

Quarterly Patterns

The preceding forecasts of productivity and compensation were all in terms of year-over-year percentage changes. In many situations, however, quarterly—rather than annual—forecasts are required. While the econometric equations can be estimated from quarterly data, the "bottom-up" approach to compensation is feasible only on an annual basis. There are, however, judgmental techniques available for translating annual forecasts—no matter how obtained—into a quarterly pattern.

In recent years, most of the quarterly variability of compensation has occured in the first quarter of the year (see Chart 19-5). The main reason for this is the legislated increases in Social Security tax liabilities which take effect at the beginning of each year; these can be forecast from data contained in the federal budget.

Productivity, on the other hand, has regular quarterly movements over the course of the several (or more) years that comprise the business cycle. The 1973–75 experience (see Chart 19-6) is fairly typical. Productivity began to falter shortly before the business cycle peak, fell during much of the recession, and then began to pick up again just before the bottom of the recession. Thus, a form of the cyclical comparison technique used above for housing can be used to fit quarterly patterns to the annual productivity forecast obtained from the economic equation.

CHART 19-5. Compensation Per Hour

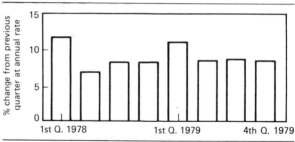

Example 6. From Unit Labor Costs to Prices. *Unit labor costs* are simply the ratio of compensation per hour and productivity, and their growth rate is approximately equal to the difference between the growth rates of the two factors. For example, in 1979, unit labor costs of non-financial corporations rose 9.4%, the difference between their 8.8% increase in hourly compensation and the 0.6 decline in productivity.

While current period unit labor costs are helpful for estimating current profits, prices are more closely tied to *standard unit labor costs*— compensation relative to average, long-term trend productivity. For example, unit labor costs rose at a 7.8% annual rate from 1976 through 1979, while the GNP deflator was rising at a 7.4% rate. Similarly, over the previous 3 years, the deflator rose at a 8.1% rate while unit labor costs were rising at an 8.4% rate. Even though the two series can deviate substantially for a quarter or even a year, the long-run link between the two is assured by the fact that compensation accounts for more than three-quarters of total costs (and income generated).

The CPI also moves very much like unit labor costs over a period of

CHART 19-6. Output Per Hour Nonfinancial Corporations

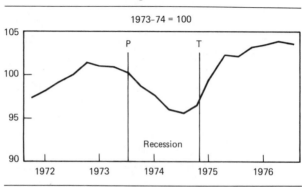

years. Its monthly or quarterly movements, however, are strongly influenced by volatile factors such as food and energy prices and mortgage interest costs. As shown in Chart 19-7, these three factors account for more than a third of the total CPI and can, as in 1979, be the most critical ones for forecasting the CPI.

IV. SUMMARY AND CONCLUSIONS

Business decisions place increasing reliance on explicit, quantitative forecasts of the overall economic environment—the expected future paths of the most important macroeconomic variables. The preceding discussion is intended to provide a brief description of the practical art of generating short-term forecasts of economy-wide variables.

- Among the major forecasting techniques—time series, cyclical comparison, econometric modeling, and "judgmental"—each has its own advantages and disadvantages. Consequently, most practitioners blend at least a little of each technique to arrive at the "best guess" forecast.
- External information—from other forecasters and from government agencies—is important for formulating a "personal" view on where the economy is heading. Bits and pieces of current, actual data are combined to estimate the initial starting point for what may unfold over the next year or more. An outsider's forecast is often used as a "first pass" to get the forecasting process started.
- Errors are a source of both annoyance and information to the forecaster. Sometimes past errors provide the first clue of an emerging new development in the economy. Other times, it is better to let bygones be bygones—creating an "instant theory" to "explain" past mistakes risks making future errors larger. Sometimes, as shown in the wage example, a forecast is "right for the wrong reasons."
- The most appropriate forecasting technique depends on the resources of the forecaster and the interests of the forecast user:
  - For the financial markets, current-dollar magnitudes are more important than real or constant-dollar components of GNP.
  - For highly cyclical variables such as housing and consumer durables, the cyclical comparison approach lends insight to questions of timing but careful attention to prospective financial developments is needed to gauge magnitudes and pinpoint turning points.
- Accuracy is of course the proof of the pudding in forecasting. However, most forecast users have additional requirements:
  - When "what if" questions must be answered, the forecaster will

CHART 19-7. The 1979 CPI: "Core" Plus "Special Factors"

(1) Component	(2) 1979 Weight (%)	(3) Forecast	(4) = (2) × (3) Contribution to Forecast	(5) Actual	(6) = (2) × (5) Contribution to Actual
Food	17.7	7.5[a]	1.3	10.0	1.8
Energy	10.3	14.5[a]	1.5	36.5	3.8
Mortgage interest costs	8.7	18.0[a]	1.6	35.0	3.0
Other ("Core")	63.3	8.0[b]	5.1	8.7	5.5
	100.0		9.5		14.1

[a]Inferred from CEA's *1979 Annual Report*, pp. 104–6.
[b]Assumed equal to unit labor cost forecast implied by CEA compensation and real GNP forecasts plus productivity equation in Example 4 above.

be drawn away from time series or even judgmental techniques toward concrete rules of thumb or formal econometric models.
– The choice between a standard econometric equation and the more laborious, judgmental "bottom-up" approach to compensation forecasting depends ultimately on how rich and detailed a story must accompany the forecast.

Just as a road map cannot tell you where you want to go, this brief outline cannot teach you how to forecast. On the other hand, once your forecasting destination has been fixed and your available means of transport have been assessed, it may help you avoid some wrong turns in the black-box maze of macroeconomic forecasting.

REFERENCES

1. Bureau of the Census, *Current Population Reports,* series p-25, no. 704, July 1977.
2. Eckstein, Otto, "Econometric Models for Forecasting and Policy Analysis: The Present State of the Art," *Proceedings of the American Statistical Association,* 1979.
3. *Economic Report of the President*, 1979.
4. *Economic Report of the President*, 1980.
5. Federal Reserve Bank of Boston, *The Decline in Productivity Growth*, Conference Series. no. 22, June 1980.
6. Kuh, Edwin and Richard L. Schmalensee, *An Introduction to Applied Macroeconomics*, North-Holland/American Elsevier, New York, 1973.
7. Levin, Beth A., "Scheduled Wage Increases and Escalator Provisions in 1979," *Monthly Labor Review*, U.S. Department of Labor, January 1979.
8. McNees, Stephen K., "An Empirical Assessment of 'New Theories' of Inflation and Unemployment," in *After the Phillips Curve: Persistence of High Inflation and High Unemployment*, Federal Reserve Bank of Boston, Conference Series no. 9, June 1978.
9. ____, "The 'Rationality' of Economic Forecasts," *American Economic Review*, May 1978, pp. 301–5.
10. ____, "The 1979 Consumer Spending Spree: New Era or Last Gasp?" *New England Economic Review*, May/June 1980.
11. Nelson, Charles R., *Applied Time Series Analysis for Managerial Forecasting*, Holden-Day, San Francisco, 1973.
12. Okun, Arthur, "Potential GNP: Its Measurement and Significance," *Proceedings of the American Statistical Association*, 1962.
13. Perna, Nicholas S., "The Contractual Cost of Living Escalator," *Monthly Review*, Federal Reserve Bank of New York, June 1974.
14. Pindyck, Robert S. and Rubinfeld, Daniel L., *Econometric Models and Economic Forecasts*, McGraw-Hill, New York, 1976.
15. Sargent, Thomas J., "Rational Expectations, the Real Rate of Interest, and the Natural Rate of Unemployment," *The Brookings Papers on Economic Activity*, vol. 2, 1973, p. 451.
16. *Survey of Current Business*, Bureau of Economic Analysis, U.S. Department of Commerce, January 1979.

CHAPTER
20
FORECASTING COUNTRY POLITICAL RISK

JOSÉ DE LA TORRE
The European Institute of Business Administration (INSEAD)

DAVID H. NECKAR
Political Risk Underwriter
Merrett Syndicates Limited
Lloyd's, London

FORECASTING COUNTRY POLITICAL RISK

Consider the following highly arbitrary list:

War between Iran and Iraq.
Turmoil in the Gulf States and in the Horn of Africa.
Racial unrest in South Africa, the U.K., and the Netherlands.
Revolution in Portugal and Nicaragua.
Labor strife in Poland and Italy.
Religious animosity in Ireland and India.
Military coups in Turkey and Bolivia.
Guerrilla activity in Angola and Malaysia.
The strain caused by refugees streaming into Thailand and Miami.

Political repression in Chile and the Philippines.

Civil war in El Salvador and Afghanistan.

Acerbic regionalism in Spain and Belgium.

Inner city clashes in the United States.

Dissidents in the Soviet Union and Argentina.

Terrorism almost everywhere.

There is no region, no country, no corner of the globe that is not touched by one form or another of social and political conflict. Conflict can lead to political change and this, in turn, may have significant adverse consequences on the economic environment in these and neighboring areas. For firms transacting business internationally, the implications are rather sobering.

In 1979, the world's stock of foreign direct investments (defined as those firms where 25% or more of the stock was under foreign control) approached a value of $500 billion. If other assets owned abroad by corporations, such as bank deposits, securities, inventories, and minority (less than 25%) interests, were added to this figure the total may very well reach $1000 billion. In addition, world trade amounted to more than $1400 billion in 1979. Given that a significant proportion of these figures would be exposed to loss at any point in time, the total capital value exposed to political risks is phenomenal.

Surely there is nothing new in this. Trade has been exposed to risks of this nature ever since the first caravans ventured across the Middle East. More recently, the history of expropriation of foreign investments is replete with examples such as Mexico's takeover of petroleum companies in 1938, Cuba after Castro, Indonesia under Sukarno, Lybia, Chile, Uganda, and so on. Large international companies have been coping with the consequences of political changes and social upheavals for years.

Ever since the collapse of the Shah's regime in Iran, however, where international companies found themselves with exposure to potential losses that may have exceeded $2 billion, the issue of political risk has gained both in importance and popularity. It is no longer acceptable simply to consider political uncertainty as just one more factor complicating the life of the international manager. The frequency of change and the size of the exposure have made it essential for most multinational enterprises to begin in earnest to assess and manage their political risks.

The term "country political risk" is an amalgam: "country" risk has tended to become a more defined term regularly employed by bankers, whereas "political" risk is widely and indiscriminantly used.

For example, country risk has been defined as: "the possibility that economic, political and social factors within a country might create a situation in which borrowers within a country would be unable to service and repay their debts to foreign lenders in a timely manner" (U.S. Comptroller of the Currency). Political risk, on the other hand, is generally applied in the context of events that are noncommercial and that lie outside the specific product/market or technological risks with which a given business is concerned. One could add that such political risks normally arise from the actions (or inactions) of governments.*

The first section below includes a general review of the main approaches to the question of assessing political risks. This is followed by a detailed examination of the problems involved in forecasting political risks as applied to the specific instance of expropriation of foreign assets. By doing this we hope to clarify the nature of the challenge which the topic poses, and provide some indication of the way in which forecasting techniques may be applied to meet that challenge.

I. THREE MAJOR APPROACHES

The problems associated with measuring the incidence of political risks in foreign countries have only become the subject of serious examination in comparatively recent times. The earliest approaches tended to focus on the impact of political risk on the foreign investment decision. In the last decade, and particularly following the 1973 oil crises, a number of studies have concentrated on the risks involved in international bank lending. None of these attempts, however, have been explicitly addressed to the problem of forecasting political change, although all are at least implicitly concerned with projecting some future outcome or with the possibility of change from an unstable

---

*To be more exact, political risk could be defined either in terms of government *actions* (e.g., direct interference with the conditions under which business operates or with the operations themselves) or in terms of political *events* which may or may not give rise to any governmental action. Second, it is important to distinguish changes that are gradual (and, presumably, predictable) and those which are sudden or discontinuous. Third, whatever the cause of change or its rate, further differentiation must be made between political events that directly impact business and those which, although highly unstable or disruptive, may not substantially change the business environment. Finally, a distinction must be drawn between political risk and uncertainty. Here we approach the crux of the issue: only through information and its assessment can uncertainty about a political environment and its potential impact on business be transformed into measurable and manageable risk. For a discussion of these definitions in more detail see Kobrin.[8]

present. Instead, the approach frequently adopted was to rank the perceived current level of political stability or instability, and thus infer a greater or lesser probability for change.

It may be useful to review these different approaches under three headings: empirical studies, political assessments, and quantitative models.

Empirical Studies

There are no comprehensive catalogues documenting the political events around the world that have had specific or discriminatory effects on international business, or of governmental interference on business activities. Since the range of events which are of potential interest is so broad and the impact of the changes in regulation or interference so variable, such an absence is not surprising. We do have available, however, a number of studies that have traced and attempted to analyze the history of expropriation, particularly with reference to the last 30 years. Three of the most notable studies are those by Truitt,[18,19] Hawkins et al.,[6] and Bradley.[1] They provide a useful starting point to illustrate the difficulty of gathering suitable data from which to draw prescriptive or normative conclusions.

Truitt considered the expropriation experience of British and U.S. investors since the conclusion of World War II, and he established that the extractive and service sectors were the most vulnerable to foreign government takeover, as illustrated in Chart 20-1. He derived from this a tentative framework for explaining expropriations and identifying the crucial variables affecting the propensity of the host government to expropriate, and the vulnerability of the foreign investment to such action.

A similar survey was that of Hawkins et al.[6] which examined instances of foreign takeovers of 170 U.S. affiliates during approximately the same period (1946–75) as Truitt had studied. They confirmed the vulnerability of firms in the extractive sector, and they also provided a breakdown of expropriations in terms of other criteria such as region and the nature of the takeover (see Chart 20-2). Among their findings were that most expropriations involved some form of compensation (however inadequate), and that the rationale behind most takeovers, although couched in the traditional left-wing rhetoric, was basically economic in nature. Most expropriations were directed at controlling an economic activity vital to the nation's economy, its external sector, or both.

A recent study by Bradley[1] examined the characteristics common to a sample of 114 affiliates of U.S. multinationals which had been expropriated by foreign governments during the period 1960–76. Four areas emerged as being significant. First, he cast doubt on the

CHART 20-1. Expropriation and Nationalization by Sector

Sector	Exproporiation and/or Nationalization Programs		Number of American and British Firms Taken	
Extractive				
Petroleum				
Integrated operations[a]	5		7	
Refining or distribution only	7		22	
Total petroleum		12		29
Plantation agriculture	3		3	
Mining	1		1	
Total extractive		16		33
Manufacturing	7		8	
Public utilities	5		3	
Service				
Trade[b]	5		12	
Commercial banking	7		22	
Insurance	6		131	
Misc. and unknown[c]			160	
Total service		18		325

Source: Truitt (p. 30).[18]
[a] Any petroleum investment except refining or distribution.
[b] Retail and export–import.
[c] Indicates that author is not sure how companies affected should be allocated between categories.

widely held notion that joint ventures, particularly with public institutions, reduce political risks. Technological sophistication was the second significant variable. Very high or very low levels of technological complexity seem to provide good insurance against expropriation. In the first case the local government is aware of its inability to duplicate the technology without the aid of the foreign firm; in the other, it appears simply not interested in getting involved. Third, Bradley's data show that affiliates which are highly integrated into a multinational system are less likely to be expropriated if cutting them off from the parent company would render them valueless. Finally, it appears that large, visible firms have a higher incidence of expropriation than small firms.

Political Assessments

General political assessments based on subjective data comprise the most widely practiced approach in dealing with country political

CHART 20-2. Summary Distribution of the Sample Foreign Takeovers of U.S. Firms, by Type of Characteristics and by Subperiod

	Entire Postwar Period		1946–70	1961–77	1967–71	1972–73
	Number	Percent				
		(percent of the total for the period indicated)				
Total—all industries and regions	170	100	12	22	79	57
By industry:						
Extractive	69	41	50	50	39	37
Financial	32	19	–	5	28	18
Manufacturing	51	30	–	27	27	40
Utilities	18	10	50	18	6	5
By region:						
Latin American	93	55	83	59	44	61
Africa	51	30	17	–	51	16
Middle East	14	8	–	32	4	7
Asia	12	7	–	9	1	16
By form of takeover:						
Expropriation	103	60	67	95	63	42
Intervention/requisition	25	15	–	–	14	25
Renegotiation of contract	20	12	–	–	8	25
Forced sale	22	13	33	5	15	8
By selectivity of takeover:						
Entire industry: mixed	21	12	33	–	8	19
Entire industry: foreign	68	40	42	68	38	28
Selected firms: no-industry specification	25	15	8	–	21	16
Selected firms within a specific industry	56	33	17	32	33	37
By political-economic circumstances:						
Leftist change in government	81	48	17	41	65	33
Right or center nationalist	7	4	17	–	6	2
Natural resource sovereignty	35	20	33	41	4	32
Mature and standardized product	47	28	33	18	25	33

Source: Hawkins et al. (p. 9).[6]

risks. They range from general surveys carried out by one- or two-man teams sent for specific on-the-spot assessment of local conditions, to the more complex ranking systems used by many banks. All of them rely almost exclusively on subjective assessments of a wide range of variables. Until very recently, most international firms limited their analysis of the political climate in a specific country to such occasions when a particular new investment was being considered. The assessment was geared to reach a go/no go decision based on present conditions concerning the relative attractiveness of the investment climate. If management perceived political risks to be high, the investment would be canceled or postponed, or, at best, a "risk premium" would be added to the financial calculations to account for the higher probability of loss. At no time was this exercise conceived as an ongoing proposition; unless a major catastrophe occurred, the country's political rating was unlikely to be reassessed.

In one of the earliest surveys of corporate practice in this area, Stobaugh[17] reported a prevalence for the "go/no go" or "premium for risk" methods involving little quantification or sophistication. Similarly, Root[15] showed the lack of systematic approaches to the appraisal of political risks by most U.S. multinationals, as did Marois[12] for French firms. What is perhaps more astonishing is that a survey of 193 U.S. corporations conducted by the Conference Board and reported in *Fortune* (Kraar[11]) showed that after the experience of a decade of political turmoil, less than half of them had any formal means for making political assessments. And even when such a formalized approach exists, as Kobrin[10] has shown, there is no guarantee that the output of the company's environmental assessment unit can be successfully integrated into the firm's strategic planning.

Some progress has been made, nonetheless, in handling subjective data about political trends in a systematic and prescriptive sense. One of the oldest methods is Professor Haner's BERI (for Business Environment Risk Index) system which collects judgments on 15 critical areas from a panel of experts located throughout the world. Using a standard Delphi technique, the panel's responses are collated, weighted, and incorporated into a composite index. The 15 criteria listed in Chart 20-3 can also be rearranged to highlight either political, operational, financial, or nationalistic factors in four subindices.

These and other similar techniques have the advantage of permitting rank ordering of different environments on a fairly comparative basis. They also allow for a significant degree of flexibility since the weights associated with the various criteria can be modified to suit different circumstances. However, the rankings can only be as good as the judgments which go into their components. Furthermore, they are basically static in nature, reporting conditions as they are now, with little reference to future risks. Implicitly, however,

CHART 20-3. Factors Assessed by BERI Panelists in Their Determination of the Level of Political Risk

1. Political stability
2. Attitude toward foreign investors and profits
3. Nationalization
4. Monetary inflation
5. Balance of payments
6. Bureaucratic delays
7. Economic growth
8. Currency convertibility
9. Enforceability of contracts
10. Labor costs/productivity
11. Professional services and contractors
12. Communications and transportation
13. Local management and partners
14. Short-term credit
15. Long-term loans and venture capital

Source: BERI Reports.

monitoring results of past ratings invites graphically the identification and projection of trends.

More complex and ambitious techniques have been developed by some of the major international banks which attempt to combine judgmental data with harder empirical information. Van Agtmael[20] reports on one of the earlier efforts in this direction. He suggested a two-scale process: an assessment of the priority the bank should assign to the country in question (a market measure), followed by an independent analysis of its credit-worthiness (the risk factor). Within the latter, in addition to the standard measures on debt servicing potential, foreign reserves, and the quality of the country's financial management, van Agtmael suggested a complex "political checklist" (see Chart 20-4) aimed at introducing a systematic approach to an area where "qualitative judgment is unavoidable."

An ambitious approach was proposed by Nagy.[13] He defines country risk as the size of the potential loss multiplied by the probability of its materialization. The net present value (NPV) of the expected cash flow from a typical loan serves as the basis for estimating the amount of the potential loss depending on whether the loss is by default, renegotiation, rescheduling, or blockage of funds transfer. Nagy's system is organized around five questions:

What is the likelihood that an adverse event will occur?

When is this event most likely to occur?

CHART 20-4. Political Checklist

I. Internal aspects

A. History
1. Time and mode of independence?
2. Record of stability.

B. Homogeneity
1. Sense of national duty?
2. History of conflicts between ethnic or religious groups?
3. Is there a dominant ethnic group or are groups of equal strength?

C. Form of government
if democracy
1. a. Strong opposition parties with radically different ideology?
   b. Effective government or chaotic situation?
   c. Corruption?
   d. Voting along ethnic lines?
   e. Is government sensitive to needs of population?

If military government
2. a. Widespread popular support or national liberation front?
   b. How strong is the army?
   c. Rivalries among army commanders?
   d. Underground opposition strong?
   e. Did military government follow ineffective, unpopular democracy?
   f. Does the regime have to rely heavily on repression or can it afford a certain degree of freedom?
   g. Do civil servants play a major role or are they alienated?
   h. What alternative power bases are there?
   i. Return to civil rule planned?

If one-man, one-party state
3. a. What if present leader dies?
   b. Are various ethnic groups represented in government?
   c. Is military large enough to be a major contender for power?
   d. Is civil service strong and independent?
   e. Is opposition effectively organized; does it have more stature?
   f. Are there specific interest groups opposing the regime?

D. Sources of potential unrest
1. Is there a suppressed minority group?
2. Are the students, intellectuals, civil servants, military, businessmen, or public opinion alienated from government?
3. Are there conflicts between the central government and traditional, regional centers of power?
4. Is strong foreign influence resented?
5. Is unemployment high?
6. Has the cost of living risen sharply without offsetting wage increases?

Chart 20-4. Continued

7. Is corruption widespread? Who are the victims?
8. Is there a sense that the government is unusually ineffective or that there is no economic progress?
9. Is economic progress confined to the center or purposely spread over the country as a whole?
10. Do the farmers own the land they till or are they mostly tenants with absentee landlords?
11. Is the economic gap between elite and the populace widening or narrowing?

E. Drastic political changes

1. Will a change in government or a coup lead to a drastic change in political orientation or economic chaos?
2. Is there any chance of a civil war?
3. Would a coup lead to political paralysis and a counterswing?
4. Would the next political regime be more/less likely to renounce or reschedule debt for political/ideological reasons?

II. External aspects

A. Danger of war

1. Is the area as a whole explosive or calm?
2. Are there major sources of conflict with neighbors?
3. Will a war seriously impair the economy?

B. Economic relations

1. Is there a threat of an effective economic boycott?
2. Are relations with major aid donors stable?
3. Are relations with World Bank and IMF healthy?
4. Are there plans for political agreements with major trade blocs for ensured access to major markets?
5. Does the country want to increase U.S. investment and trade?
6. Does the U.S. government have any leverage?

Source: Van Agtmael (p. 27).[20]

What is the probability that risk materializes from the event?

Specifically, how does this probability break down in terms of default, renegotiation, and so on?

When is the loss, irrespective of its form, most likely to occur?

By multiplying these various probabilities by the NPVs of the different outcomes and adding across years and outcomes, a "country risk factor" is obtained. Nagy put forward a checklist of relevant factors which bear upon these assessments and provides a framework for monitoring

CHART 20-5. Formation of Political System Stability Index (PSSI)

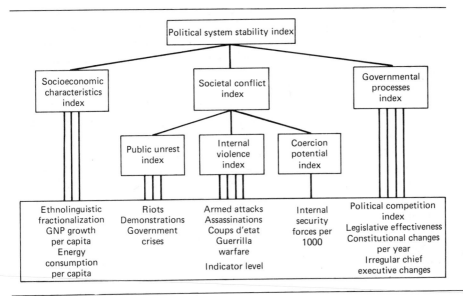

Source: Haendel et. al. (1975), p. 64.

critical assumptions upon which the judgments have been based in order to identify any sudden deterioration in the risk profile.

Quantitative Models

The last decade has witnessed a considerable increase in the application of quantitative techniques to the analysis of political conditions. Whether concerned with rank ordering of countries by different measures of stability or with econometric projections, the development of these models is the most significant step toward a true forecasting approach to political risk analysis.

Among the statistically based models, perhaps the best known is the "Political System Stability Index" (PSSI) developed by Haendel et al.[5] Its major advantage is that by measuring directly a series of discrete components of political risk, the resulting index is claimed to be free of any judgmental inferences or distortions (Chart 20-5).* The 15 underlying variables can all be measured directly (e.g., num-

---

*However, one cannot ignore the fact that the model is itself founded on a number of judgments and assumptions, for example, that "societal conflict" is adequately described by the components of "public unrest," "internal violence," and "coercion potential," or that, in their turn, these components are adequately measured by the raw data on riots, size of internal security forces, and so on.

ber of armed attacks in a year, defined as "an act of violent political conflict carried out by an organized group to destroy the power exercised by another organized group") from independent sources.

The Knudsen[7] "ecological approach" is based on the proposition that the presence of both a high level of national frustration and a visible foreign-owned sector will result in a high propensity to expropriate. The linking hypothesis is that whenever discontent is high, foreign investors serve as useful scapegoats to vent national frustrations. The key, obviously, is the measure of the level of frustration which Knudsen calculates as the gap that exists between the aspirations of the people and their welfare. Knudsen tested his model on data for 1968–71 and developed a classification of Latin American countries according to their propensity to expropriate which corresponded closely to later developments in the area.

Other more traditional techniques have been employed more recently on the same general problem. Rummel and Heenan[16] have employed multivariate analysis in order to "predict future political trends on the basis of current and historical information . . . and describe more fully underlying relationships affecting a nation state." Standard econometric techniques have also been attempted such as those developed by Feder and Just[4] and the Export-Import Bank of the United States.

Summary

These various methods share one unavoidable drawback: they are based on historical data that may be totally or partially irrelevant for future conditions. For example, recent high levels of political turmoil leading to a radical change in government may appear under the various quantitative indices as evidence of a high degree of political instability. While this may be undeniable for the immediate past, does it signify that instability will continue into the future? Or is the new government more likely to address the root causes of past instability and lead the nation to a new era of prosperity and tranquility? Obviously, no time series analysis can adequately answer these questions. Furthermore, to the extent that the data fed into the analysis are not entirely current, there will be a potentially significant gap between the last period for which data are available and current conditions. Given the rate of change of political and social phenomena in the less developed countries, and the difficulties (and commensurate delays) in generating reliable data in many of them, this is not an insignificant problem.

Haendel et al.,[5] for example, recognize these problems in the rankings generated by their model, and they provide a judgmental "confidence" factor for each ranking which reflects their qualitative appraisal of the data sources and their reliability. Rummel and Heenan[16] also state that "success is more likely when ... subjective and objective approaches are brought together in an integrated fashion"; and Kobrin[8] found that risk assessments based on the notion of instability tended to overstate actual risks to foreign investment and led to overly cautious policies. In the next section, we attempt to confront these problems by providing a comprehensive approach to measuring firm-specific political risks. It incorporates the lessons derived from various model building efforts with years of experience in assessing the potential for loss in hundreds of projects from many firms and throughout many countries.

II. A COMPREHENSIVE MODEL FOR ASSESSING POLITICAL RISKS

The political risks upon which we shall focus in this chapter are those related to the expropriation of foreign investments or assets, that is, the compulsory takeover of foreign assets by a host government with the implication of little or no compensation. In general, the "prompt, adequate, and effective" compensation called for by international law seems rarely to be paid by expropriating governments. But a firm operating in a given country needs to go beyond the question of what is the likelihood that its assets will be expropriated; it must be prepared to deal with whatever change in political conditions is forthcoming. The ability to predict an emerging situation before it is fully manifested is essential to any preparations required to survive it. It is this predictive ability that we believe can be enhanced through careful systematic analysis.

Chart 20-6 summarizes our approach; it consists of a total of 30 variables or composite factors that must be monitored on an ongoing basis. Those variables particular to the *country* in which the investment is located (or to be located) are examined first, followed by those pertaining to the investment or *project* itself, and each of the two elements have risks that are specific to themselves. The intention in the *country risk analysis* is threefold: establish some basic measures of reference, identify current trends and any potential break in the trends, and delimit the areas of concern that may harbor the seeds of potential threats to the investment. Such an analysis provides the backdrop against which the *project risk analysis* can bring into sharper relief the different features proper to the investment which either increase or diminish the risk.

Part I: The Country

It would be very difficult to provide an exhaustive set of questions for all the factors that should be considered under this heading; time

CHART 20-6.   Major Variables for Assessing Country Political Risk

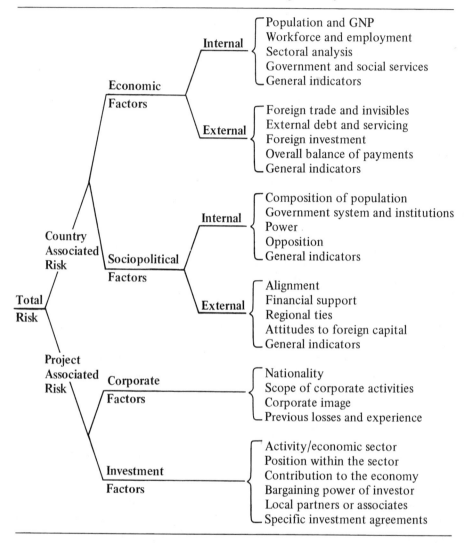

Economic Factors
- Internal
  - Population and GNP
  - Workforce and employment
  - Sectoral analysis
  - Government and social services
  - General indicators
- External
  - Foreign trade and invisibles
  - External debt and servicing
  - Foreign investment
  - Overall balance of payments
  - General indicators

Sociopolitical Factors
- Internal
  - Composition of population
  - Government system and institutions
  - Power
  - Opposition
  - General indicators
- External
  - Alignment
  - Financial support
  - Regional ties
  - Attitudes to foreign capital
  - General indicators

Corporate Factors
- Nationality
- Scope of corporate activities
- Corporate image
- Previous losses and experience

Investment Factors
- Activity/economic sector
- Position within the sector
- Contribution to the economy
- Bargaining power of investor
- Local partners or associates
- Specific investment agreements

Total Risk → Country Associated Risk, Project Associated Risk

and cost limitations make such an exercise futile. We divide the analysis into those factors that are predominantly economic and political, and then into those that are mostly internal to the country or related to its external relations. Such a division is obviously arbitrary as developments in one area of the economy or political life may have considerable consequences for the other variables under scrutiny. Therefore, the analyst must constantly be on the lookout for these ramifications and interdependencies and not be fooled by the apparent simplicity of the proposed structure.

A. Economic Factors—Internal

A reasonable starting point is an understanding of the basic components of the country's domestic economy. This means not only an analysis of what is produced, who consumes it, what levels of government involvement exist, and so forth, but also what changes in these various features are taking place, at what rate, and for what reasons. Typical points to watch are the state of the country's agricultural sector (e.g., percentage of population working in agriculture versus its contribution to total GNP) analyzed against the rate of urbanization and the level of unemployment. We may want to carry out this analysis under five separate headings.

Population and GNP.   Historical trends in the size of the country's population, the development of its economy, and its GNP per capita provide a first approximation of national welfare. When considered against the recent past, public pronouncements about expected growth rates indicate the potential disparity between the country's aspirations and its capacity to provide for its future development needs. Things to look for are, for example, relative growth rates of different GNP components, efforts at controlling population growth, and so on. Income distribution within the country and changes over time are useful clues to potential trouble. Countries which may appear stable and otherwise prosperous on the surface, such as Mexico or Venezuela, may look quite different in terms of risk if one observes that, for example in the case of Mexico, the percentage of national income going to the poorest 70% of the population has declined steadily since the late 1940s, when it oscillated around 34%, to about 28% in recent years. The implications for social discontent, even in a high growth economy, are evident.

Active Workforce and Employment Profile.   The size of the workforce, its distribution according to major economic sectors, as well as its geographic location will show what the country's productive human resources are and how and where they are deployed. It may also indicate disturbing trends, such as migration to the cities and growing masses of urban unemployed. Of significance here is the rate of economic growth required to create new jobs in particularly depressed areas and the levels of government spending for social services. The Brazilian experience provides a case in point for this type of analysis. Over the years 1960 to 1977 the percentage of the population living in urban areas has increased from 40% to 60%, that is, an increase of 40 million people in urban areas versus 3 million in the rural population.

Sectoral Analysis. This is probably one of the most straightforward elements in the analysis and must address such questions as:

What is the strength and diversity of the agricultural sector and is the country self-sufficient in food?

What are the country's major raw material resources; is it self-sufficient in energy?

How significant is the industrial sector; can it respond to the need to generate employment and foreign exchange?

What are the strategic sectors; are they controlled by the government or by foreign investors?

How large is the public sector; how efficient; is there a discernable trend to greater government involvement in the economy with a corresponding increase in its public accountability?

Government and Social Services. The absolute level of government expenditures should be examined against that of the private sector. The sectoral and geographic distributions of such expenditures need to be considered carefully to determine, for example, whether there are areas of obvious and urgent need (e.g., urban housing, health services, defense, etc.) and how these needs are being met. Furthermore, one should determine how public expenditures are being financed (e.g., external debt which may lay claims on future resources and their distribution) and the trends in terms of both revenue sources and major expenditure programs. The rigidity exhibited by either of these to changes in economic conditions is also a fundamental question. If revenues are highly volatile while expenditures consist mainly of inflexible social programs, any major disturbance to the system could result in severe political consequences. For example, the need to maintain substantial defense expenditures in Morocco and South Korea (in the former, for example, this item accounts for at least 40% of the government budget) places great strains on government finances—particularly if accompanied by problems in other key areas such as fluctuations in the price of phosphate or loss of exports markets at a time of recession.

General Indicators. It is also important to trace certain economic indicators such as the rate of inflation (both official and unofficial), the interest rate levels, the extent and growth of the government deficit, and so on; any major discontinuity in these series should be cause for concern and investigation.

At this stage of the process the analyst should have a reasonably clear picture of which economic variables are *critical* for continuity in the country's present development path, of the potential gaps between reality and aspirations, of the sensitivity of the economic system to a breakdown or failure in any of its critical links, of the chances that any such break might occur (or has already occurred), and of the inconsistencies that may exist between sectors or areas of the economy. The first set of questions should also involve the development of key measures of economic variables and performance, the observance of historical trends, and, most important, the discovery of any breaks in the various series. Assuming the how is possible, one might ask why these measures. Our objective is not economic analysis per se, but a search for what one might call the potential for trouble. If "what is likely to go wrong" follows Murphy's perfidious dictum, it is the political consequences that interest us, as these are ultimately the ones that may affect the safety of the investment.

B. Economic Factors—External

The reverse side of understanding a country's domestic economy must be an appreciation of its external payments position: what are its international obligations, their extent and their burden on the economy; what is the level of diversification of its export earnings and the exposure to changes in the prices of its key export commodities; to what extent it is dependent on imported oil, and so on. Again, five headings would be helpful in organizing the analysis of these issues.

Foreign Trade and Invisibles.   The essential items which the country needs to import and the products or services upon which it relies in order to pay for these are the main objective of this section. One must consider to what extent do imports consist of essential goods such as food, energy, or raw materials which are relatively price and income inelastic, and then one must assess the possibility of adverse price movements and their potential impact on the economy. In like manner, possible fluctuations in expected export earnings must be examined— whether caused by internal (e.g., crop damage) or external events (e.g., import restrictions in major markets). In addition, one should review the pattern of evolution of the country's overall foreign trade and its principal trading partners. What are the levels of dependency by commodity and by markets? How flexible is the external sector to respond to changing conditions? One critical area is the cost of oil: for a country such as Tanzania it represents over 50% of the country's foreign exchange earnings (earnings which are in themselves highly volatile). The same problem arises over Brazil's foreign trade account which is highly sensitive to the changes in prices of a few key agricultural products (coffee, soya beans, cocoa) on the income side, while being equally exposed to oil price increases on the payments side, since oil accounts for at least 50% of imports by value.

External debt.   Three essential elements should be treated here:

The level of the outstanding foreign debt (public and private), in both absolute terms and relative to GNP and exports.

Its maturity profile.

The level of debt service (including dividend payments on foreign investments) relative to national income and exports.

The figures must be weighed carefully against the level of foreign exchange earnings and the size and potential of the economy. If difficulties in servicing the debt are being experienced or are expected, the impact on domestic economic and political pressures must be evaluated, as well as the possibility and likely effects of transfer restrictions and import controls. Many recent examples of these types of problems come to mind: in Jamaica, the weight of external debt and chronic balance of payments difficulties became a major issue in the 1980 election which led to the defeat of Manley by Seaga. In the case of Brazil, the awesome overhang of foreign debt has already led to growing import controls and restrictions on foreign remittances—and there are signs of pressure building up to oblige foreign investors to convert their subsidiaries' foreign debt into equity.

Foreign Investment.   Countries which often shun external indebtedness as a solution to their exchange difficulties, turn instead to foreign investment on the twin assumptions that more real income is thereby generated to pay future claims and that dividend payments are cyclical and not likely to fall due in hard times. This, history has taught us, is not always the case. The size and importance of the foreign sector, its distribution by branches of economic activity, its diversification in terms of countries or origin, and so on are all critical elements to the analysis. They affect the probability that when all else fails a "nationalistic" government will point to the spectre of foreign ownership as the root of all evil. Over 70% of Nigeria's manufacturing sector was foreign owned in the late 1960s, which probably was a major force behind the indigenization program known as the Nigerian Enterprises Decree launched in 1974. Similarly, the fact that over 55% of Canadian industry was in foreign (predominantly U.S.) hands was the principal motivation for the creation of the Foreign Investment Review Agency in April 1974.

Overall Balance of Payments. To complete the examination of the country's external position the overall balance of payments should be reviewed with particular emphasis on trends in the remaining items in the capital account and on the level and changes in the country's reserves. In this context, the "Errors and Omissions" entry may provide revealing information about irregular capital flows and sudden surges in flight capital.

General Indicators. Lastly, the country's official and unofficial exchange rates and the spread and terms which its borrowers can obtain on the international capital markets should be monitored for clues of sudden changes in confidence levels, both external and domestic.

This set of questions serve an evident purpose: determine to what extent external constraints will dictate domestic economic policy. If there is a high degree of dependence and instability together with high debt-service payments, risks of inconvertibility and expropriation will rise commensurately. In Mozambique, shortly after the revolution, the government, faced with severe external payment difficulties, nationalized those enterprises that consumed significant amounts of foreign exchange. Likewise in Nicaragua, the grave shortage of foreign currency after Somoza's ouster has prompted the new revolutionary government to take control of the main sources of foreign exchange. A diversified export base, on the other hand, may reduce the potential for downstream economic impacts of disastrous proportions even when the economy may be highly export dependent as is the case with most island states in Asia.

C. Sociopolitical Factors—Internal

Composition of Population. The division of the country's population into its various ethnic, religious, tribal, or class components provides a useful starting point. The size of each component part, its geographic distribution, its political and social status, its share in the country's wealth, and its participation in key governing institutions should be examined in order to determine how well they fit together and how coherent is the whole social structure. A typical problem area for this kind of analysis is the Arab world where in some countries minority sects (Wahabites in Saudi Arabia, Alawites in Syria) hold the reins of power against a background of fundamentalist religious turbulence caused by the Shi'ite Moslem revolution in Iran, ethnic separatism, and traditional complications such as the problem of substantial numbers of expatriate workers. With regard to the latter, in countries such as the Gulf Emirates, Iran, and Kuwait, these noncitizen immigrants easily outnumber the local (and privileged) nationals. Similarly, there is the implicit tension in the Far East over the expatriate Chinese minorities: in Malasia, for example, the Chinese are notably more prosperous and successful than the Malays which has led to the government imposing restrictive Malasianization measures applicable to foreign investments.

System of Government and Institutions. The formal status and composition of the country's government and its institutions are important to the analysis since they provide the external "appearance" which needs to be grasped in order to understand how the system works or is meant to work. (The different "reality" of power is considered separately below.) A suitable framework should accurately describe the constitution, the deliberative, legislative, and executive functions, and the structure and nature of the political parties (should there be any). For example, unless one understands that a country such as Brazil is divided into states which elect deputies for the Bicameral National Congress, and also that each state has individually a governor appointed by the President, it is difficult to understand the significance of constitutional issues raised by the opposition. One has, as it were, to learn the political language of the country concerned within which the reality of power is played out.

Power. The external forms of the country's institutions will rarely reveal the effective structure of power therein. They should, however, provide an essential framework for its analysis and draw attention to areas of potential or actual conflict, or of unexplained obscurity. The type of questions one should ask here include: who actually makes the key decisions and what the principal sources of support are for the current government; how far it is either dependent on or closely associated with foreign capital; what role the armed forces and internal security apparatus play; who are the major beneficiaries of the status quo; who are the major losers; and so on. This is a particularly critical and difficult area of analysis since almost by definition the data are obscured or concealed. Perhaps here more than anywhere else, what is required is a great deal of skill in inferring from external observations and considerable judgment in the use of internal or local sources of information.

Opposition. Although earlier sections may have partially illuminated the question of the actual or potential alternative government, one should give specific attention to the issue of opposition to the status quo within the country. The basic questions which must be answered are what are the significant opposition groupings, whence did they draw their support, and how effective are they. Unfortunately, it is often extremely hard to obtain balanced information on these questions, and one must treat one's data extremely carefully in order to compensate for the inevitable biases that are inherent therein. One example of this problem was the now well-publicized and analysed incident at the Great Mosque in Saudi Arabia which was originally presented as an isolated minor incident involving a few religious fanatics. In order to obtain a proper appreciation of this event, one needed to be aware of the deep significance of the location, the shock which was felt by the other Gulf nations and the basic tribal tensions undermining the political system. The difficulty which the army and the national guard had in subduing this rebellion meant that it had more significance than the Saudies were prepared to admit, as confirmed by evidence of other linked disturbances elsewhere within the Kingdom which went largely unreported.

General Indicators. Data to be monitored include the level and frequency of strikes, riots or terrorists acts, the number of political prisoners, and the extent of official corruption. Incidents such as the Great Mosque affair should encourage one to check back through the analysis, question all assumptions, and review areas that show signs of breaking under the tension.

D. Sociopolitical Factors—External

Alignments. The best starting point is to establish how the country is aligned, what its position is on certain key global issues (e.g., apartheid, the Middle East, etc.), who its principal political allies are, and how dependent it is upon them. For example, if we take a "nonaligned" nation do we mean one that is nonaligned such as Yugoslavia or such as Cuba? Has the country signed a treaty of friendship with the Soviet Union as in the case of Syria or Afghanistan?

Financial support. Besides political allies one must also identify economic supporters of significance: both those who deliberately provide items such as aid, food, soft loans, and military supplies as well as those who are de facto important supporters by virtue of vital economic links. The support which America provides to Saudi Arabia is obvious, but the support which Syria receives from Saudi Arabia, Iraq, and Kuwait is less so—although the effect was quite clearly shown in 1980 when the Saudies induced the Syrians to step back from their confrontation with Jordan. The position of France in Africa is also interesting: by virtue of the CFA franc system the French government and treasury exercise considerable de facto influence over the French West African states—as well as some more obvious support such as military aid (e.g., in the Central African Empire).

Regional ties. The global alignment of the country must not make one overlook the country's relations with its immediate neighbors, including the existence of border disputes or external military threats. The question of whether nearby states are involved in supporting, harboring, or financing groups opposed to the government should also be addressed here. A particular problem country is Qaddafi's Lybia: engaged in regular border tension with Egypt to the east, it supports internal subversion in Tunisia to the west (incident in 1980) and direct military intervention to the south (Uganda and Chad). To the north, it has a point of influence and sporadic discord in Malta. In addition, Lybia has been involved in encouraging the Polisario in the Western Sahara dispute as well as in deestablishing attempts in Gambia, possibly Senegal, and the Central African Empire, not to speak of its general support of terrorist activities worldwide. A different case in point is Pakistan where we can find as complex an external position as may be found anywhere: once aligned with the United States and the West, but recently estranged from them; drawn unwillingly into the Afghanistan conflict and thus into confronting Russia, the principal support of its distrusted neighbor India; with the Chinese poking their heads round the door.

Attitude to Foreign Capital and Investment. The role that foreign capital plays should have become clear in the economic sections, and the government's (and the opposition's) attitudes toward it in the subsequent political section. The existence of an investment code is not an absolute guarantee of protection of investors' rights (e.g., Zaire nationalized a number of enterprises in 1974, some of which were "protected" by its investment code; Egypt's law 43 is worded in such a way that expropriation and nationalization can be justified). It does serve, however, as evidence that the government (at least the current one) has recognized certain rights of the investor. In this context China poses an interesting problem: it does not have an established system of commercial law as we know it in the West and, therefore, there is a risk, not so much of deliberate expropriation, but of difficulties arising out of misunderstandings caused by different interpretations of the general rights of investors and those of the government.

General Indicators. Finally, some useful indicators of the country's external position are its voting pattern at the United Nations, the existence of formal and active opposition groups in exile, and terrorist acts committed in third countries.

The progression from a system where foreign companies freely operate sales branches and wholly owned subsidiaries, to one where they must divest part or most of their shareholdings and export a significant portion of their output is now history in many developing and industrializing countries. The likelihood and speed with which these events may take place depend not only on the extent of foreign capital domination in key sectors of the economy, but also on whether or not the current government finds itself in a position where the sacrifice of foreign goodwill is the cheapest price for survival.

Part II: The Specific Project

The intention in this section is to identify the key features of the project itself and of the investor responsible for it, and to consider these as systematically as possible in the light of any particular problem areas which have been identified in the earlier analysis. One is concerned not simply with whether the investment or project is likely to be expropriated by a current government, but also with whether there are features proper to the project or the investor which may make it particularly vulnerable in the event of any change in the status quo.

A. Corporate Factors

Nationality. The actual (or perceived) nationality of the investing corporation will have a significant impact on the safety of the investments, depending on the relations which the host country has or has had with the investor's home country. Difficulties can arise from the vestiges of a colonial relationship or from previous support for an earlier government. The memories of its bitter struggle for independence still complicate Algeria's dealings with France, and the question of compensation for nationalized French interests has never been properly settled. An example of where this problem can arise suddenly and unexpectedly was the recent occasion when British companies in Saudi Arabia were put at risk as the result of the screening on U.K. television of a film entitled "Death of a Princess," a film which was judged by the Saudies to be particularly offensive. Yet, certain countries are able to maintain surprisingly good relations with difficult countries—witness the recent experience of Italian companies in Libya, although at the time of Qaddafi's accession they did suffer some losses. United States corporations in Latin America tend to be exposed to relatively higher risks than their European counterparts since they have inherited a historical role as symbols of support for repressive military regimes.

Scope of Corporate Activities. The type and geographic location of the corporations' activities worldwide may have a material influence on the level of risk: for example, trading with or investing in a nation that is hostile to or boycotted by the host government. Apart from the well-known boycott of Israel by Arab and Moslem countries, other complications can arise such as those that result from a company's dealing with South Africa. Nigeria is one of many Black African nations that have taken an exceptionally strong line against corporations that trade with South Africa.

Corporate Image. The investor's reputation or image is another possible source of risk. Corrupt payment scandals or a history of involvement in the financing of political subversion have left lasting scars on certain U.S. corporations which are still viewed by local governments (and opposition groups) with mistrust. Apart from the notorious example of ITT and the Allende regime in Chile, one may cite the United Fruit Company and its successors which are still trying to live down the reputation acquired in Central America in the 1950s, in spite of subsequent major changes in corporate policy and extensive public relations efforts.

Previous Losses. Careful scrutiny of the circumstances in the past which have led to expropriation or other political-type losses is essential. Apart from indicating what may be expected, it can show certain strengths—for example, if the investor managed to obtain proper compensation or retains a good working relationship in the country concerned. The nationalizations of oil companies in the Middle East and elsewhere appear to have taken place quite smoothly with reasonable compensation being paid and with the companies continuing to operate on the basis of management contracts. Gulf Oil managed to live through the revolution in Angola and emerged from it in a strengthened position. Certain banks, in an industry particularly exposed to nationalization, have fared better than others in obtaining reasonable terms from governments which are obliged to maintain good working relationship with international financial organizations.

B.   Investment Factors

Activity/Economic Sector. The first feature to establish is the significance of the sector in which the foreign enterprise is active, both in respect to the internal and the external economy of the country. In general, certain sectors such as those involving primary sources (mining, plantations, oil) are more likely to be nationalized. However, one must consider the relative level of foreign capital within the sector as well as the importance or political sensitivity of the sector to both government and opposition.

Position within Sector. The size of the enterprise relative to others (including those which are locally owned) within the sector affects the degree of monopoly or oligopoly power that a firm may exercise, thus making it a more or less suitable target for expropriation. Monopolies in sectors such as public utilities, railroads, electricity, and so on have historically been particularly vulnerable to nationalization. There may of course be occasions where a foreign investor is the only corporation capable of deploying the technology or resources for a given investment. However, it is usually only a matter of time before the government or a succeeding government requires the investor to give up or share part of its monopoly.

Contributions to the Country's Economy. It is essential to attempt to quantify the net benefits that the enterprise brings to the local economy. Positive contributions include capital invested or loans, technology, the hiring of local labor and the corresponding generation of income and tax revenues plus reinvested earnings if any, savings of foreign exchange through import substitution effects, and the support of local businesses. These are partially offset by dividends and capital repatriation, loan repayments, license fees and royalties, management fees, intercompany payables, transfer pricing, and additional imports required. The view that the host country will have of these costs and benefits may not correspond to that of the firm. It should be obvious that in terms of risks the former view is the important factor. A typical case of this dichotomy can be found in those industries that have been set up in low wage countries in Southeast Asia, North Africa, and the Caribbean to process goods for export markets. While foreign investors may consider that they are creating jobs that would not otherwise have existed and generating foreign exchange, local governments increasingly question whether reasonable wages are being paid and what the long-term benefits are for the local economy. This may lead to increasing demands that foreign companies make more substantial investments in production and transfer higher levels of technology.

Bargaining Power of the Investor. One must identify the real strength of the investor's inputs to the project in order to identify those that may be exclusive and difficult to replace such as spare parts, control of technology, or downstream processes and markets.

A widely cited example of an investor with enormous power in this respect is that of IBM, a corporation that has consistently refused to dilute its shareholdings in its foreign subsidiaries. In India, when put under pressure to cede part of its local affiliate to domestic interests, IBM chose to close down operations rather than comply. The large multinational oil companies have also exercised considerable strength from their control of refining and distribution networks, although there are indications that their relative power is declining in this repsect with the rise of national and independent oil companies.

Local Partners or Associates. The nature and identity of any local partners should be checked to determine whether they might in fact increase the risk: for example, eminent local figures closely associated with the government will only be an asset as long as the government lasts. In Nicaragua, in the aftermath of the Sandinista revolution, one of the first decrees issued concerned the nationalization of assets owned by the Somoza family and those closely associated with it in either the army or the administration.

Specific Investment Agreements with Host Governments. Lastly, one needs to examine any special agreements that have been entered into by the investor with the host government to consider whether or not they improve the risk. A typical problem area is that of oil or mining exploration and production agreements which frequently offer attractive tax concessions in order to attract investors, but which are very frequently renegotiated once the investor has become committed and is successful. The very favorable agreement negotiated between Rio Tinto Zinc's Australian subsidiary and the Papua–New Guinea government turned into a major contentious issue once production had started and copper prices climbed unexpectedly. A renegotiation of the agreement under difficult conditions made it possible for both parties to save face and continue operations. By assuring that social benefits accrue to the host nation over the duration of the project, and that these benefits are evident to all major political forces, the firm can have a major impact on how it is perceived and, therefore, on the likelihood that changes in economic or political factors would result in a higher probability of intervention.

III. CONCLUSION

No purely mechanical system could be expected to deal with the subtleties required in forecasting country political risk. Rough rankings of countries in terms of their relative political stability can and have been compiled using various quantitative techniques. But how good these are as predictors of future stability remains questionable. The fact that causality is not easily determined in political phenomena, that up-to-date information is difficult to obtain, and that stability itself is not necessarily a good measure of risk all contribute to the many doubts often expressed about such methods. Furthermore, the nature of the industry and of the investor and the timing of the project are critical variables that alter in a significant way the risk profile within the same set of economic and political conditions.

Yet, no human being could possibly master this complexity for more than just a handful of countries. Unaided by quantitative tools the political risk analyst would be drowned in a sea of information. Judgment can best be applied when the range of variables to consider has been reduced to a manageable set. Here lies the challenge for truly forecasting political risks. It requires first of all good measures of quantifiable variables that can be processed in a mechanic and efficient fashion. Second, it calls for many qualitative assessments of elusive trends such as levels of aspiration and frustration among diverse interest groups. Finally, it demands good judgment, above all, to mix these many inputs in a coherent manner and to spot, as Holmes, the dog that did not bark in the night.

REFERENCES

1. Bradley, David G., "Managing Against Expropriation," *Harvard Business Review,* July-August 1977, pp. 75–83.
2. *Business Week,* "Foreign Investment: The Post-Shah Surge in Political-Risk Studies," December 1, 1980, p. 69.
3. Eiteman, David K. and Arthur I. Stonehill, *Multinational Business Finance,* 2nd ed., Addison-Wesley, Reading, MA, 1979.
4. Feder, Gershon and Richard E. Just, "A Study of Debt Servicing Capacity Applying Logit Analysis," *Journal of Development Economics,* March 1977, pp. 25–39.
5. Haendel, Dan, Gerald T. West and Robert G. Meadow, *Overseas Investment and Political Risk,* Monograph Series No. 21, Foreign Policy Research Institute, Philadelphia, 1975.
6. Hawkins, Robert G., Norman Mintz and Michael Provissiero, "Government Takeovers of U.S. Foreign Affiliates," *Journal of International Business Studies,* Spring 1976, pp. 3–15.
7. Knudsen, Harald, "Explaining the National Propensity to Expropriate: An Ecological Approach," *Journal of International Business Studies,* Spring 1974, pp. 51–71.
8. Kobrin, Stephen J., "When Does Political Instability Result in Increased Investment Risk?" *Columbia Journal of World Business,* Fall 1978, pp. 113–22.
9. ——, "Political Risk: A Review and Reconsideration," *Journal of International Business Studies,* September 1979, pp. 67–80.
10. ——, "Organization and Institutionalization of the Environmental Assessment Process" (manuscript), Massachusetts Institute of Technology, October 1980.

11. Kraar, Louis, "The Multinationals Get Smarter About Political Risks," *Fortune,* March 24, 1980, pp. 86–100.

12. Marois, Bernard, "Assessment and Management of Political Risk: Practice of French Firms" (manuscript), paper presented at the Annual Conference of the European International Business Association, London, December 1979.

13. Nagy, Pancras J., *Country Risk: How to Assess, Quantify and Monitor It,* Euromoney Publications Ltd., London, 1979.

14. Robock, Stefan H., "Political Risk: Identification and Assessment," *Columbia Journal of World Business,* July-August 1971, pp. 6–20.

15. Root, Franklyn R., "U.S. Business Abroad and Political Risk," *MSU Business Topics,* Winter 1968, pp. 73–80.

16. Rummel, R. J. and David A. Heenan, "How Multinationals Analyze Political Risk," *Harvard Business Review,* January-February 1978, pp. 67–76.

17. Stobaugh, Robert B. Jr., "How to Analyze Foreign Investment Climates," *Harvard Business Review,* September-October 1969, pp. 100–108.

18. Truitt, J. Frederick, "Expropriation of Foreign Investment: Summary of the Post World War II Experience of American and British Investors in Less Developed Countries," *Journal of International Business Studies,* Fall 1970, pp. 21–34.

19. ——, *Expropriation of Private Foreign Investment,* Indiana University Graduate School of Business, Bloomington, IN, 1974.

20. van Agtmael, Antoine W., "Evaluating the Risks of Lending to Developing Countries," *Euromoney,* April 1976, pp. 16–30.

21. Walter, Ingo, "International Capital Allocation: Country Risk, Portfolio Decisions and Regulation in International Banking" (manuscript), New York University, undated.

22. Wilson, John O., "Measuring Country Risk in a Global Context," *Business Economics,* January 1979, pp. 23–27.

Other Sources

The principal country risk rating services are provided by Prof. Haner's BERI, Business International, and the World Political Risk Forecasts service of Frost & Sullivan, according to *Fortune,* March 24, 1980, p. 95. Some of these rating services have begun to prepare long-term projections on the various factors scored. No track record is yet available. For some pointed criticism of these methods see *Business Week,* December 1, 1980, p. 69.

There are many sources of data on political phenomena. Two widely used by Haendel, West, and Meadow are: Charles Taylor and Michael Hudson, *World Handbook of Political and Social Indicators,* 2nd ed., Yale University Press, New Haven, CT, 1972; and Arthur Banks, *Cross-Polity Time-Series Data,* MIT Press, Cambridge, MA, 1971.

Most major newspapers and business journals are replete with instances of interference resulting from government change, ranging from minor bureaucratic nuisances to outright expropriation. Also, major sources such as Business International and its various regional units, *Multinational Service* in Brussels, and Washington's *International Business Report* have made it a profitable business of tracking down and reporting trends and events which generally fall within the mantle of political risks. What is not yet available is any systematic analysis of these data along lines similar to the studies cited above.

CHAPTER

21

ENERGY FORECASTING

GUY DE CARMOY
Professor Emeritus
INSEAD

INTRODUCTION

Over the last decade, energy has become disproportionately expensive, when compared to other goods. The prospects of an oil shortage in the medium term and of actual exhaustion of oil and gas reserves in a few decades have become a major concern.

At a time when the primary sources of energy—that is, crude oil, gas, and coal—were abundant and cheap, there were in fact very few specialists in government circles, oil companies, and utilities who were actually concerned with energy forecasting. Today, however, this task merits serious consideration. It is an area that involves not only the producers of primary energy and electricity (the secondary form), but also the final users—the individual consumer and those in industry and transportation. Energy is a resource essential to the functioning of all branches of economic activity, and to the everyday life of individuals, and as such is an indispensable element of modern-day societies.

The demand for energy is in derived form, in that it depends on the demand for goods and services which require an energy input. The supply of energy encompasses each of the various factors involved in production, placing special emphasis on capital and technology. The objective of both users and producers of energy is to ensure that the supply and demand for energy are properly balanced. Governments, too, consider it their responsibility to contribute to this equalizing process. Energy has thus entered the field of domestic—and indeed international—politics, since considerable sums of money are involved in its purchase or sale.

The obvious questions of concern to business forecasters involve the future price and availability of energy. This chapter will deal with the needs for energy (and the resulting national policies), and the methods of forecasting energy supply and demand, including as appraisal of those in use today.

I. ENERGY NEEDS AND NATIONAL POLICIES

The future price of energy will be determined not solely by the economic elements of demand and supply, but also, for reasons stated above, by political factors. To better understand the question of energy availability and price forecasting, the following discussion should be considered.

Energy Demand and Supply

As already mentioned, the main areas of energy use are private households, industry, and transportation, whereas the suppliers of energy fall into two groups, primary energy producers and producers of electricity (i.e., the utility services).

Households consume a variety of energy products—fuel, oil, gas, electricity—for such purposes as heating, cooking, and lighting. In industry, energy can obviously be a significant item in the determination of manufacturing costs. The corporation concerned will compare energy efficiency, capital cost of equipment, and various fuel costs, and may thus substitute one source of energy for another—as a result of both the cost factor and technological innovation. Similarly, whatever the mode of transportation, energy is an indispensable input. All modes of transportation, individual or collective, with the exception of electrically powered railroads, constitute a captive market for petroleum products.

The role of utilities is to transform primary sources of energy—coal, oil, natural gas, and enriched uranium—into electricity, which will then be distributed to industry, commerce, and individual households. Utilities will compare both capital costs and those incurred in purchasing the different primary sources of energy. Due to lengthy lead times, long-term forecasting is particularly applicable to the utilities, in terms of both supply and demand. For example, the time required for the siting and construction of large power plants can be anything from 6 to 12 years, taking into account lengthy authorization procedures. (See Chapter 4.)

A further example is the development of a coal mine or an oil or gas field: it is an intensive operation, generally taking about 10 years. Technical difficulties such as location (e.g., offshore drilling), climate (permafrost), and distance add to both capital and operating costs and to the duration of the operation. Long-range planning and forecasting are thus of critical importance. Whereas reserves of coal are considerable, those of conventional crude oil (as opposed to oil sands) are limited. Oil companies are therefore concerned with two ratios. The first is the relationship of reserves to production. A ratio of say 10 to 15 to 1 should be maintained so as not to expose the producer to a sudden shortage. The second factor is the rate of recovery, which is currently in the 25% range. With the help of appropriate technology for secondary and tertiary recovery, the ratio can be improved.

Energy Pricing and Energy Elasticities

In a competitive economy, producers exploit deposits to maximize their economic gains. Consumers, on the other hand, determine, by means of rational economic decisions, "how much" and what type of energy they should consume.

Elasticity is "the responsiveness of the demand or supply of a commodity to changes in factors which influence that demand or supply" (Stobaugh and Yergin[10]). Two important factors are prices and incomes. *Price elasticity* is measured by the percentage change in energy demand (or supply), divided by the percentage change in price, all other things being equal. Similarly, *income elasticity* is measured by the percentage change in energy demand divided by the percentage change in income. A stiff increase in oil prices can cause a stagnation or fall in demand, as experienced in industrialized countries after 1974.

It was generally assumed in the affluent 1950s and 1960s that energy consumption increased in direct proportion to national income—that is, that the increase in demand was proportional to the increase in revenue. Under these particular conditions, the ratio between the two variables was close to 1 because there was no incentive to save energy. In the lean 1970s, however, it was observed that the increase in energy consumption could and should be less than the increase in revenue, which meant that the ratio was falling below 1. Although there was an incentive to save energy, its usage had become an ingrained habit, and consumption was thus not reduced in proportion to the rise in prices. The price elasticity of energy, therefore, tended to be low.

In a political system dominated by the industrialized countries associated in the Organization for Economic Cooperation and Development (OECD), and in a period of fast economic expansion, the price of oil was largely influenced by the more or less concerted strategies of the large oil companies. The oil "majors" held the concessions from the producing countries and controlled the markets of the consuming countries. The working of this oligopoly was easily compatible with the state regulations and taxes in both groups of countries.

The seizure of companies' assets and the fixation of prices by oil producing countries substituted a new type of oligopoly for the previous one. The new decision makers had complete mastery of both output and prices.

Noneconomic factors also entered the picture, which greatly added to the complexity of the price determination and energy availability problem.

National Policies of Oil Exporters

Price levels, elasticities, and the situation of reserves are of primary concern to the mapping of national energy policies, which differ according to the structure and prospects of the foreign trade in energy—this trade being essentially in oil, which is by far the largest traded commodity in the field of energy.

Oil-exporting countries, with the prospect of the gradual exhaustion of world oil reserves, can expect in the long term an increase in the constant dollar value of their national reserves. Tradeoffs have to be made between higher income in the near future and capital conservation in the long term. The accumulation of trade surpluses in currencies subject to depreciation, such as the dollar, is becoming less and less attractive, and has been a contributory factor in the decision of a number of the nations in the Organization of Petroleum Exporting Countries (OPEC) to opt for a long depletion rate, and therefore a limitation (if not reduction) in their current level of production and exports.

National Policies of Oil Importers

Industrialized countries have completely lost control of crude oil prices and, more recently, of the level of oil supplies. They can, however, take energy options in order to choose which energy consumption should be encouraged, at what pace, and with which substitution and conservation goals. But the effectiveness of planning will depend on the accuracy of forecasts, and the alternative scenarios adopted.

In addition, a major concern of the oil-importing country is to ensure that the balance of payment will not be running into a permanent deficit as a result of successive increases in the real price of imported oil.

The question is how to reduce the deficit in current payments.

1. One means is to increase the price of exports so as to improve the deteriorated trade balance. But oil producers may index the oil price on the price of imports from industrialized countries.

2. Another alternative is to increase the volume of exports, depend-
    ing on the absorption capacity of the oil-producing country and
    on the production capacity and technological ability of the in-
    dustrialized country.

3. A third possibility, in a long-term perspective, is to reduce con-
    sumption and increase investment with a view to promoting
    export industries and developing actions for energy conservation
    and substitution (Cotta[3]).

A reduction in consumption will have deflationary effects on the national income insofar as the industries are working for the domestic
market. An increase in oil prices will reflect on the cost of energy intensive goods and services and therefore on the general level of prices, and
it will have an inflationary effect on export prices. It can thus be seen
that governmental actions are limited and cannot simultaneously satisfy
all economic and political criteria.

The Global View

Energy is a complex system penetrating the whole range of economic
activities at both national and international levels. An upheaval in the
relative prices of energy vis-à-vis other products at home and abroad in-
duces government policy makers to reassess economic policies and trade
relationships. Furthermore, oil company executives are concerned about
questions of cost of production as well as the influence on consumption
caused by higher energy prices.

Energy resources should, theoretically at least, be sufficient to meet
the world consumption needs of the year 2000, which are expected to
be between two or three times higher than the 1980 level. However, the
growing needs for energy will have to be met more and more by coal
and nuclear-generated electricity, as oil and gas supplies will be gradually
reduced. It is hoped that new energy sources presently at the stage of
research and development will also become commercially valid—for
example, shale oil. Until new energy resources become commercially
feasible, however, oil imported by the OECD countries will be shipped
from the reserve-rich but politically unstable areas of the Middle East
and North Africa to the industrialized Western countries. It is expected
that the production from the OPEC countries will be gradually reduced,
while world demand for oil will be increasing; and non-OPEC oil production will not compensate for the difference between a growing demand and a declining supply.

Energy forecasting is an essential aid in terms of helping energy-
importing countries to define their strategies in light of the different
options available to them. It is these options that will eventually deter-

mine energy prices and availability and heavily influence companies' forecasts and strategies.

II. FORECASTING METHODS

The Energy Market in the Macro Economy

Energy prices are derived from the behavior of those involved with the demand for and supply of energy. Thus the energy market forms part of a general macroeconomic equilibrium. Industrial output represents the income effect for *energy consumed in industry*, aggregate consumption expenditure represents the income effect for *energy consumed in the domestic sector*, and both the industrial output and the consumer expenditure account for the *energy consumed in the transportation sector*.

These three sectors consume coal, gas, petroleum products, and electricity in amounts determined by income and price changes. Market factors such as the price of imported oil, relative fuel prices, national policies (e.g., taxes on energy), and regulations determine the share of each energy source in the short term. In the long term, price levels, technology, and the efficiency of fuel conversion lead to interfuels substitutions. Taking into account conversion losses in power generation of the energy sector proper, it is possible to evaluate the primary energy demand by source (Kouris[7]). Chart 21-1 illustrates the interdependencies involved.

Primary Energy Demand Projections

A good example of forecasting methodology is offered by the report on "World Energy Demand to 2020" presented to the 1977 World Energy Conference in Istanbul by the Energy Research Group from Cambridge University.[6]

The boxes on the top line in Chart 21-2 refer to the factors of energy demand in their historical perspective. Energy demand is a function over time of population growth and energy growth. The growth in energy consumption is related on the one hand to national income as mentioned above, and on the other hand to a variety of socioeconomic components, which include the degree of industrialization and urbanization. The pattern of consumption is largely determined by the nature and volume of domestic resources and by the physical and financial ability to resort to imported resources. The collection of data on past demand makes it possible to establish accurate historical energy balances and ratios.

The next requirement from forecasters is a set of assumptions. These appear in the boxes on the second line in Chart 21-2. Assumptions apply

CHART 21-1. A Model of the Energy Market[a]

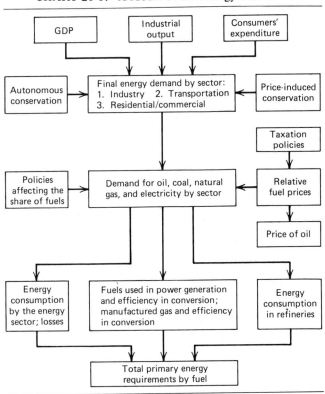

[a] Source: Kouris[7] p. 5.

to the rhythm of economic growth (high or low), price response (nil, normal, or strong, under different price elasticities), and to energy efficiency (e.g., introduction of a new technology improving the energy input–output ratio). These assumptions allow for the construction of models for primary energy, interfuel substitutions, and oil-specific demand, as shown on the third line. Assuming oil will be the primary source in short supply, it is advisable to consider the possibilities of energy substitution. In the present state of technology, there are two main substitutes for oil-fired power stations: coal and nuclear-generated electricity. But, for the time being, there is no substitute for oil in sea, road, and air transport. Hence the calculation of oil-specific demand. Energy substitutions can expand over time. Thus the breeder technology will enlarge the potential for nuclear energy. It is hoped that before the end of the century coal gasification and/or liquefaction will allow substitutions for some specific uses of natural gas and of petroleum products. Solar energy and nuclear fusion are still long-term expectations. Once

CHART 21-2. Energy Demand Methodology[a]

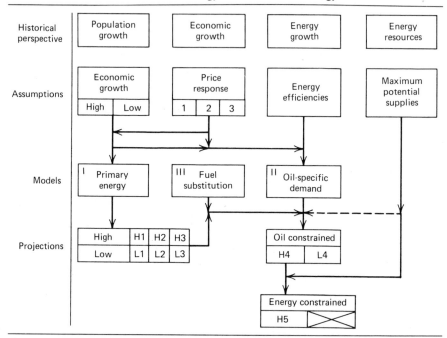

[a]Source: Ref. 6, p. 243.

the models have been chosen, the next task of forecasters is to make projections.

Chart 21-3 shows how forecasters have applied their projections of energy consumption to two assumptions: one of low growth (3% per year), and one of high growth (4.1%) of the world economy. Fast development projections for the developing regions were combined with alternative (high and low) assumptions for the OECD area. Both growth assumptions were then associated with assumptions on the price response and oil and energy constraints. Rules were established for fuel substitutions, taking into account the difference in convenience and cost to the user between one fuel and another, the world supply potential for different fuels in future years, and the factor of inertia restricting the rate of substitution in each of the final demand sectors.

The projections of the main scenarios are presented in Chart 21-3, which shows the different levels of primary energy demand in 2000 and in 2020, compared with the 1972 level (Energy Research Group[6]).

Primary Energy Supply Projections

The 1977 World Energy Conference attempted to draw up an inventory of the maximum technical capacity for the production of primary sources

CHART 21-3. Projections of World Primary Energy Demand[a]

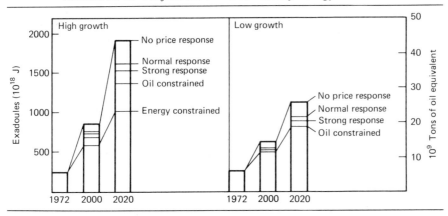

of energy if the most favorable conditions were met. Two cases are significant, the one on oil and the one on uranium. For each the forecasters had been using different methods.

The study on "The Limits of the World Oil Supply"[5] was entrusted to Pierre Desprairies of the Institut Français du Pétrole. It used the Delphi method, based on questionnaires sent to oil companies and independent experts and consulting firms. Each expert was questioned twice; the second answer was made in light of the first answers of the other experts, but the latter were couched in an anonymous form. The major finding was that the ultimate recoverable resources of conventional crude oil would amount to 240 Gt. It was assumed that the present recovery rate of 25% would be increased to 40% by the end of the century. The breakdown of the ultimate resources confirmed, in the view of the experts, the importance of the Middle East–North Africa area. On the question of the rate of future discoveries (new fields plus revaluation of old fields), the experts were relatively optimistic for the near future (around 4 Gt per year), and distinctly more pessimistic for the distant future when the rate of discoveries would not exceed the 1977 level of consumption (3 Gt). Chart 21-4 graphs the cumulative world discovery and production. It makes assumptions about the ultimate recoverable resources and their medium depletion rate. This allows two curves to be drawn: that of cumulative (past and future) discoveries, and that of cumulative (past and future) production. Both curves approach each other after the year 2025. As the rate of future discoveries slackens, the potential for future production is reduced. The conditions for reaching production capacity are quite stringent in terms of costs, progress in technology, and investment requirements (Desprairies[5]).

A study of the contribution of nuclear energy to the world needs

CHART 21-4. Cumulative World Oil Discovery and Production[a]

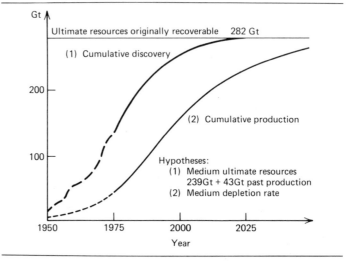

[a]Source: Ref. 6, p. 26.

from 1975 to 2020 was presented by the National Canadian Committee at the 1977 World Energy Conference.[8] The Committee made the general assumption that the share of electricity production generated by nuclear energy would follow an asymptotic trend to 50%. It then submitted five nuclear scenarios:

A. With light water reactors and no reprocessing
B. A 10-year delay in each region for the introduction of the breeder.
C. Base case with the introduction of the breeder first in Europe in 1987, and a few years later in the other industrialized countries.
D. Scenario with a more efficient breeder.
E. Scenario of the thorium cycle based on the high-temperature reactor, introduced in place of the breeder.

The demand for uranium is of course dependent on the choice of reactors: a choice linked to the mastery of technology and to sociopolitical factors. The demand obviously will be much lower in scenario C (base case) than in scenario A, which is based on the rejection of the breeder and of the related "plutonium economy." Chart 21-5 compares the impact of A and C scenarios on uranium demand.

Balancing Energy Supply and Demand

Forecasters generally handle energy demand and supply separately, and then they make subsequent comparisons and integrations. Such was the

CHART 21-5. Influence of the Breeder on World Uranium Demand[a]

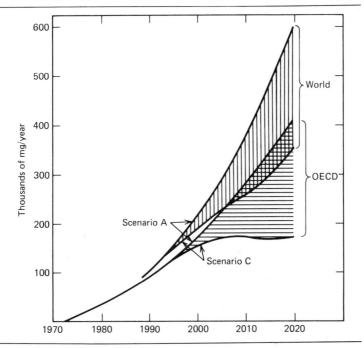

approach adopted by the Workshop on Alternative Energy Strategies (WAES) in its 1977 report entitled *Energy: Global Prospects 1985–2000*.[11] WAES followed a step-by-step approach based on a number of scenario variables: world energy prices (no change, rising, or falling), world economic growth (low or high), national policy response (vigorous or restrained), oil discovery production limits (high or low gross addition to reserves), and lastly, principal replacement fuels (coal or nuclear). Out of 48 possible futures, five scenarios were selected. Two integration procedures were then considered: (1) unconstrained integration, wherein no consideration was given to the availability of desired energy imports (such as oil), and (2) constrained integration, which forced the fuel mix to conform to global fuel availability. The first procedure was just a series of national summing-up processes, assuming that potential surpluses in any region (e.g., the Middle East) were available for export (e.g., to OECD countries), thus revealing prospective gaps and shortages. The second procedure was aimed at finding a means of closing the gaps in terms of required expansion of both the energy system and related costs. As some preferred fuels in a given area were perhaps in relative shortage, while others, less favored, were in relative surplus, major shifts in fuel use patterns were calculated in order to meet end-user demands (WAES[11]).

CHART 21-6. Ranges of Demand and Supply of Oil[a]

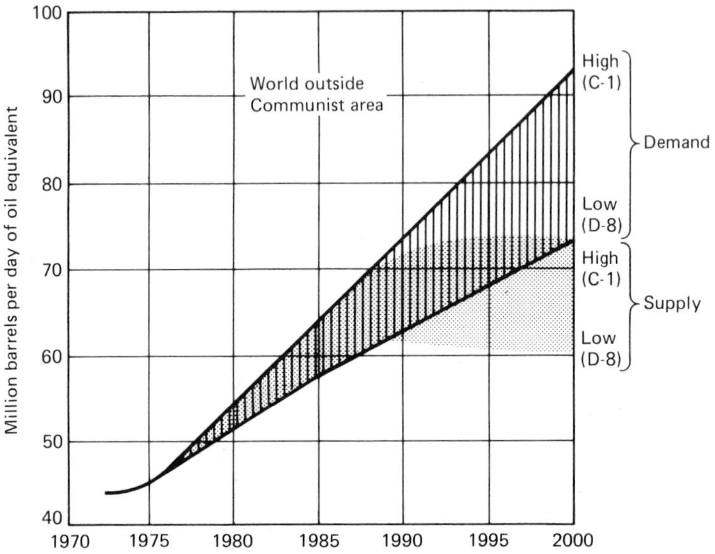

[a]Source: Ref. 11, Fig. 8.3, p. 237.

"The world oil problem, in simple terms, is the difference between desired oil imports and potential oil exports." WAES has calculated the range of demand and supply of oil for its selected scenarios. This range appears in graphic form in Chart 21-6. The lowest of preferred oil demand estimates are matched to the highest of potential oil supply estimates. In terms of quantity, the potential export volume of OPEC ranges between 38.7 mbd and 34.5 mbd, leaving the year 2000 with a prospective shortage of between 20.0 mbd for the high growth scenario C-1 and 15.2 mbd for the low growth scenario D-8 (WAES[11]).

Whatever the assumption, there is a mismatch between energy demands and supplies. The potential supply shortfall will not, of course, materialize. The oil market will balance itself through a combination of enforced conservation (such as rationing), reduced economic growth, higher oil prices, and possibly increased domestic supplies.

III. APPRAISAL AND APPLICATIONS

According to Clark,[2] the forecaster "does not try to describe the future, but to define the boundaries within which possible futures must lie."

The builders of energy models have to make a number of simplifying assumptions, which are of critical importance as they determine the results of the models (Stobaugh and Yergin[10]).

Projections and Realities up to 1978

Since 1973, energy predictions have been consistently more optimistic than the subsequent reality. This is particularly apparent in a comparative study of 78 energy projections to 1985 made under the aegis of the International Energy Agency (Brodman and Hamilton[1]). Projections of economic growth were revised downward as illustrated in Chart 21-7.

CHART 21-7. Projections of the Energy/Economic Growth Ratio (1970–1985 OECD)[a]

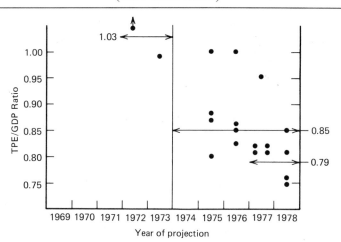

	Number of Projections	Mean
Pre-1974	2	1.03
1974–1978	22	0.85
1977–1978	10	0.79
Total	24	0.86

Year of Projection	Projections				
1972	1.06				
1973	0.99				
1974	0.78	0.80	0.85	1.0	
1975	0.80	0.87	0.88	1.0	
1976	0.83	0.85	0.86	1.0	
1977	0.81	0.81	0.82	0.82	0.95
1978	0.75	0.76	0.79	0.81	0.85

[a]Source: Broadman and Hamilton,[1] p. 4

Nonetheless, those made in 1977 and 1978 estimated an economic growth of 3.75% for the OECD area, a figure much too high in light of the economic climate in 1980.

The comparison of projections on OECD nuclear installed capacity reveals a rapid decline in expectations, from a mean of 531 GW in the pre–1974 projection to a mean of 271 GW in the 1977–1978 projections. The main reasons for this decline are stronger public opposition to nuclear power, increased regulatory requirements, uncertainty about the last phases of the fuel cycle, and cost escalation.

The projections for oil imports by the United States reveal a considerable dispersion, which reflects a variety of opinions on both the scope for increase of the U.S. indigenous oil supply, and the estimated effects of the administration's energy proposals. The estimates for oil imports of OECD Europe and Japan present a more compact grouping and a substantial spread between the pre–1973 and post–1973 estimates.

OPEC Production Prospects

It is only since 1973 that energy forecasters have made assumptions about the essential parameter—world demand for OPEC oil (including OPEC's own demand)—or, to put it another way, required OPEC production. The estimates spotted on Chart 21-8 are unconstrained demands by importers, with a view toward balancing world demand and supply.

The mean projection in world demand for OPEC oil in 1985 is set out at 1968.4 metric tons or 39.4 mbd. This figure is unrealistic.

The actual volume of OPEC exports was 29.8 mbd in 1979, as a result of the decision of Saudi Arabia and Iraq to step up their production and compensate for the fall in output of Iran. But a number of countries (Kuwait, Abu Dhabi, Algeria, Libya, Indonesia, Venezuela) have threatened to curtail their output in 1980 (Croll[4]). Their concern is to avoid unduly reducing their reserve/production ratio. The Arab Gulf countries have no incentive to invest massive revenues in dollars, thereby risking the depreciation of their financial assets. Thus a contraction, rather than expansion, of OPEC exports is to be expected in the short to medium term with further price increases.

Economic Implications

Any substantial increase in oil prices has serious implications for the economies of oil-importing countries. The first effect is a trade loss because the importing country has to pay more to the exporting country for a given amount of oil. The second effect is a reduction in demand for the goods and services of industrialized countries because the oil exporters do not immediately spend their incremented earnings. A third effect is an increase in domestic prices, and a fourth is a deterioration

CHART 21-8. Projections of World Demand for OPEC Oil in 1985[a]

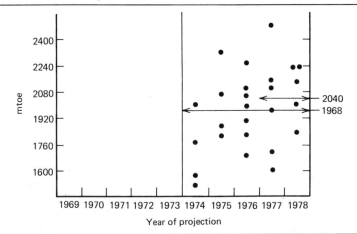

Year of projection

	Number of Projections	Mean
Pre-1974	0	
1974–1978	26	1966.4
1977–1978	11	2040
Total	26	1966,4

Year of Projection	Projections (in mtoe)						
1974	1515	1570	1775	2000			
1975	1805	1875	2070	2320			
1976	1695	1815	1905	1990	2055	2100	2250
1977	1605	1710	1964	2100	2140	2433	
1978	1830	2000	2145	2225	2230		

[a]Source: Broadman and Hamilton,[1] (p. 4).

of the trade balance. The OECD has estimated the effects of a 10% oil price increase in 1980 coming about after the sharp 1979 increase. The overall real income loss to the area would be 1% of GNP, adding half a percentage point to inflation.

The economies of oil-importing countries are thus constrained on four fronts: real resources, income, prices, and balance of payments. Price and income effects also have an impact on employment and investment. If governments engage—with the handicap of a long lead time —in a strong drive for energy conservation and substitution, then shifting income from consumption into investment will be required, which is an unpalatable prospect at a time of stagflation. The interlocking constraints are of such magnitude that they constitute a challenge to the stability and viability of the industrialized countries of the West.

The Political Dimension

The energy problem is presently at the heart of geopolitical competition. Industrialized countries lost economic and political control over the abundant oil reserves located in the Middle East at a time when their economic activity and the well-being of their citizens were even more closely linked to the growing use of cheap imported oil. Together with the ownership of the reserves, the control over price and the rhythm of production passed into the hands of producing states moving without transition from feudal to industrial societies. This resources-rich region is exposed to the rivalries of the superpowers. The risks of destabilization have grown in the recent past: revolution in Iran, rebellion in Saudi Arabia, recurrent troubles in both Yemens, Soviet occupation of Afghanistan, and war between Iraq and Iran. The power balance has shifted against the United States. The global security of the group of industrialized countries associated in the OECD is in jeopardy. The external political challenge is of the same order of magnitude as the domestic economic challenge.

Long-range energy planning should be conducted not exclusively in terms of technology and markets, but also in conjunction with macroeconomic and political forecasting. The main reason for the inaccuracy of the projections quoted above is that "in energy politics is a crucial factor, yet an explicit consideration of it is typically omitted in most formal models" (Stobaugh and Yergin[10]).

Company Action

The above analysis leads to one certain forecast: energy prices will rise in a framework of relative scarcity. The probability exists that these increases will be sporadic rather than gradual.

A company which is not in the energy business cannot have an impact either at a branch or national energy policy level. But its management should keep informed of overall developments and be engaged in specific actions at the company level.

Information on energy is available and widely circulated by governments, international organizations, and trade associations. Information on political and military events in key energy-producing areas such as the Middle East is widely circulated. Management should be on the outlook for news and comments. It cannot operate without up-to-date knowledge of the facts. The comments of the best experts and columnists must be taken into consideration. Management can no longer take refuge in a "business as usual" ivory tower.

So much for the general.

As for the specifics, action should be centered on energy conservation and substitution. Energy consumption can be reduced not only by seeking to contain obvious waste, but also be researching more efficient uses of energy. Considerable energy savings can be achieved in each of the sectors of transport, housing, and industry. New equipment for the improvement of auto engine efficiency, building insulation, waste heat recovery, and so forth, is on the market. Each company should detect which conservation measures are best adapted to its activities and should then carefully plan the related investments and amortize them over the duration of their economic life.

Substituting one source of energy for another is an important management decision, involving large capital outlay. It should be based on an in-depth analysis of government policy options, technological developments, and cost-effective comparisons.

In summary, sound energy management should become a part of the global strategy of the firm.

REFERENCES

1. Broadman, J. R. and R. E. Hamilton, *A Comparison of Energy Projections to 1985*, IEA Monograph 1, International Energy Agency, Paris, 1979.
2. Clarke, A. C., *Profiles of the Future*, 1973, quoted by S. Makridakis and S. Wheelwright, in *Forecasting, Methods and Applications*, 2nd ed., John Wiley, New York, 1982.
3. Cotta, A., *La France et l'impératif mondial*, Paris, 1978, PUF, pp. 78–96.
4. Croll, D. O., "Growth in a Year of Crisis," *Petroleum Economist*, January 1980, p. 6.
5. Desprairies, Pierre, "The Limits of the World Oil Supply," World Energy Conference, Istanbul, 1977.
6. Energy Research Group, Cavendish Laboratory, "World Energy Resources to 2020, World Demand to 2020," World Energy Conference, Istanbul, 1977. Published as "Resources Energétiques Mondiales 1985–2000" in *Editions Techniques pour la Conference Mondiale de l'Energie*, Paris, 1978.
7. Kouris, G. J., *Energy Modelling: The Economist's Approach*, paper presented at the IASA Conference on Large-Scale Energy Systems, Vienna, 1980, pp. 1–2.
8. The National Canadian Committee, "The Contribution of Nuclear Theory to World Energy Needs from 1975 to 2020," World Energy Conference, Istanbul, 1977.
9. *OECD Economic Outlook*, no. 26, December 1979, pp. 22–23.
10. Stobaugh, R. and D. Yergin, eds., *Energy Future*, Report of the Energy Project at the Harvard Business School, Random House, New York, 1979. Appendix, Limits to Models, pp. 236, 238, 264.
11. Workshop on Alternative Energy Strategies (WAES), *Energy, Global Prospects 1985-2000*, McGraw-Hill, New York, 1977. Pp. 57–66, 71–78, 238, 285.

CHAPTER

22

FORECASTING

Incorporating
Special Events and
Marketing Actions

RUDOLF LEWANDOWSKI
Marketing Systems

INTRODUCTION

There is a more or less constant need today for short-term predictions
to be made, to provide an insight into a multitude of possible future
scenarios. Furthermore, these forecasts are frequently required where
projections for extremely large numbers of items are involved. This high
demand for short-term predictions has necessitated the development of
an automatic procedure that provides analyses and forecasts in a mechanical and easily operated fashion. However, such a "black box"
approach suffers from the deficiency that for many users it is a source
of distrust, in that the actual way in which the system functions remains
beyond their understanding. A further disadvantage is that the mechanical approach cannot take into account such changes in the environment as those brought about by, for instance, sales promotions, special
events (e.g., unusual weather conditions), or competitors' reactions.
Existing forecasting systems have, for the most part, remained unable
to resolve the resulting paradox.

The purpose of this chapter, therefore, is to illustrate a short-term forecasting system, automatic in nature and mechanical in operation, which is nevertheless comprehensible to the user and provides results that can subsequently be easily interpreted.

The basis of the system is the "breakdown" of a time series into each of its components, and the facility is also extended to the user whereby he or she may intervene, as desired, to modify the quantitative forecasts. Such modifications can be carried out for any of the time series components and then will be applied automatically to each specified item. The system described in this chapter is oriented toward business enterprises and has been used for the last 10 years by almost 100 major European companies (see Lewandowski, pp. 259[5]).

SOME FUNDAMENTAL CONCEPTS

For short-term analysis and forecasting, the time series is broken down (as mentioned above) into the following major components:

Average: M_t

Seasonality: S_t

Influence of the variations in the calendar or climate: $S_t^{(c)}$

Influence of special actions: ψ_t

Influence of a correlated series: E_t

Random variable: ϵ_t

The forecast can now be expressed in the following functional form:

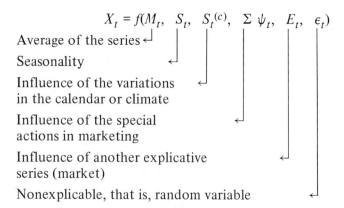

$$X_t = f(M_t,\ S_t,\ S_t^{(c)},\ \Sigma\ \psi_t,\ E_t,\ \epsilon_t)$$

Average of the series

Seasonality

Influence of the variations in the calendar or climate

Influence of the special actions in marketing

Influence of another explicative series (market)

Nonexplicable, that is, random variable

In most companies, even those which only market a limited number of products, there are usually a great many time series to be analyzed.

This is because analyses are carried out first in terms of the overall sales of a product, then according to the distribution of these sales, to their various regions, and so on, until the actual points of sale are finally reached. Furthermore, when forecasting for the short term, forecasts are required on a more frequent basis due to the short intervals of time between predictions.

Because of this large number of series to be analyzed, any manual intervention in the monitoring and forecasting processes becomes very difficult. In recent years, therefore, in order to allow automatic control, methods have been developed that no longer require the user to make complex and tedious manual adjustments. The approach described here is one such method.

INADEQUACIES OF FIXED PARAMETERS FORECASTING METHODS

The latest developments in control theory have resulted in an increased ability, as far as effective monitoring and automatic control of forecasting procedures are concerned. The following section presents some of the methods derived from the development of such forecasting/monitoring systems.

Whichever short-term forecasting system is chosen, a crucial problem remains the "optimal" definition of the method's parameters. In fact, in the 15 years since the first publication on the subject of exponential smoothing, many companies have had considerable difficulties, on the application side, in terms of how the best values of the model's parameters could be calculated. For example, the approach used for optimizing the parameters of the exponential smoothing methods assumes that the parameters remain constant throughout. Unfortunately, however, this approach is somewhat unrealistic.

Moreover, the computation of optimal parameters requires an enormous amount of time, and it is thus costly; hence even the introduction of larger, cheaper computers does not make the use of static exponential smoothing models any less problematic.

ADAPTIVE METHODS OF PARAMETER OPTIMIZATION

Adaptive forecasting methods have been developed to serve as a possible remedy for the deficiencies mentioned above, and the best known of these approaches are described in Chapter 14.

In parallel with the tracking signal investigations by Trigg and Leach,[7] a somewhat similar but more general method has been developed by the author (Lewandowski[3]).

The O.P.S.* approach is an offshoot from the tracking signal of Trigg and Leach, which acts as an indicator intended solely to control α_t. It not only introduces a dynamic concept into the definition of the tracking signal, but also, and most importantly, it adds the idea of supplementary filtering of random errors, by the introduction of a specific indicator—the standardized error.

O.P.S. also has been used for the control of a seasonality smoothing coefficient, β_t. This latter phenomenon, being unavailable to *any* other adaptive exponential smoothing models, is unique to the O.P.S. method.

As has already been shown, one of the two signals which enables the detection of irregularities in the filter system in the method of exponential smoothing is the average deviation signal, AWS. This signal is a major facet of the O.P.S. system, in that it allows the automatic control of the coefficients of exponential smoothing.

Here are the fundamental definitions:

$$AWS_t = \sum^{t} {}^*\epsilon_t / MAD_t$$

where

$$\sum_{t} {}^*\epsilon_t = (1 - \gamma_s) \cdot \sum {}^*\epsilon_{t-1} + \epsilon_t \qquad \text{(accumulated smoothed error)}$$

$$MAD_t = (1 - \gamma) \cdot MAD_{t-1} + \gamma \cdot |\epsilon_t| \qquad \text{(mean absolute deviation)}$$

where

$$\gamma = \gamma s_t = \gamma s_0 \exp - \frac{\epsilon_t^2}{MAD_t^2}$$

and

$$0 \leqslant \gamma \leqslant 1$$
$$0 \leqslant \gamma_s \leqslant 1$$

As can be seen, AWS is a function of ϵ_t, as are the two supplementary parameters γ and γ_s.

A system can now be studied whereby the smothing coefficient α_t can be developed as a function of the requirements of the forecast. Assuming that the value of α_t, at time t, can be expressed as follows:

$$\alpha_t = \alpha_0 + \int_0^t \Phi(\alpha_{t-1}, t, \epsilon_0, \epsilon_1, \ldots, \epsilon_t) dt$$

---

*O.P.S.: From the German "Optimale Parameter-Steuerung": optimal parameter control.

then

$$\Delta\alpha_t = k_1 \cdot \exp \frac{\Sigma_t^*(\Gamma_t^{(1)}\alpha_{t-1} + \Gamma_t^{(2)})}{MAD_{t-1}}^{\lambda_1} - k_2 \cdot \exp \frac{(\Gamma_t^{(1)}\alpha_{t-1} + \Gamma_t^{(2)})}{MAD_t}^{\lambda_2}$$

The interpretation of the forecasting deviations shows that two variables can be considered:

1. The deviation signal AWS, which rapidly detects the appearance of systematic errors and any irregularities in the system. As the value of AWS increases, that of the smoothing coefficient α_t becomes progressively inadequate, and thus ultimately too weak.

2. The normed error

$$NF_t = \frac{\epsilon_t}{MAD_t}$$

which permits the immediate recognition of random variations.

The two fundamental signals of the control system are (1) AWS, responsible for increasing the smoothing coefficient, and (2) NF, aimed at decreasing this coefficient.

The major advantages of the O.P.S. system are as follows:

1. It is not necessary to calculate the values α_t, β_t, and γ_t, all of which are valid *on average* for the entire past. The system determines the combination of α_t, β_t, and γ_t, which is optimal for *each period.*

2. The system is capable of rapidly adapting to any modification that is characteristic of the series, and it can also react more accurately to the concept of forecasting optimality.

3. Once the pair k_1 and k_2, corresponding to the stability criterion of the system's control, has been defined, it can be used as a standard and universal approach for dealing with any time series.

4. The calculation times of such a system are compatible with (or shorter than) those required by other exponential smoothing methods.

5. If it is known with certainty that forecasting errors are not inherent in the system, these systematic forecasting errors can be avoided over long periods. A useful interpretation of these errors can thus be obtained.

6. The system is more accurate than rival methods (see Chart 22-1). A study recently completed (Makridakis et al.[6]) has shown that

CHART 22-1. Comparison of the Various Methods

Model	Mean Deviation	Calculation Time
Chow	6.11	80
Trigg and Leach	4.82	55
Dobben de Bruyn	3.70	55
Lewandowski (O.P.S.)	3.26	100

Source: Lewandowski, p. 165.[4]

for micro series, the method of O.P.S.-FORSYS has been superior to that of other methods.

7. Rapid and reliable recognition of significant changes in the sales level is ensured—on average, two to three periods after the actual change, even when the random noise is very large.*

The *AWS* signal can serve as the basis of an efficient "early warning system," which is used widely in many practical situations.

MARKETING ACTIVITY AND SHORT-TERM FORECASTING

Whatever the effectiveness of the forecasting system employed, it must not be forgotten that such an automatic approach leaves aside a number of phenomena related both to the policy of the company itself, and to the behavior of the markets.

Thus, when a company producing detergents, for example, launches a sales promotion campaign for one of its products, the sales figures will be above the usual level for several months. Sales of most consumer goods are subject to similar fluctuations under the influence of various marketing campaigns, such as that mentioned above, or a temporary reduction in sales prices, various advertising campaigns, and so forth. Also to be considered is the negative influence of competitors' activities.

Finally, the economic environment itself is responsible for such events as changes in taxation, government measures concerning credit policy, social disturbances, strikes, and so on. All of these occurrences—which will be referred to as "special events" or "actions"—inevitably have a strong influence on "normal" sales. They disrupt the "average" trend, or seasonality, to such an extent that interpretation of the results as provided by classic forecasting methods proves to be extremely dif-

---

*The FORSYS approach is based on the O.P.S. method described in this section; it is a widely used system in Europe for the analysis and forecasting of time series.

ficult, if not totally impossible. It is essential that emphasis be given to this particular point.

Many product managers are incapable of determining the effects of marketing activities and special events. One of the primary reasons for this deficiency is that they lack the basic methodology necessary to tackle the problem. The results of a recent survey, where a considerable number of product managers were interviewed, indicated that 85% of them were unable to explain "ex post" large deviations in sales due to special events taking place during the previous 2 years. This value increased to 95% when managers attempted to explain deviations that occurred during a period in excess of 2 years. Whether the reason for this was that the person responsible had only just taken over the job and was unaware of the history of special events for that product, or whether it was simply the result of "slackness," the net result was still that a fundamental entity of information was lost.

Under these conditions, then, how can a sales series be correctly analyzed, with accurate forecasts being produced as a result?

Large fluctuations in sales levels must be dealt with specifically within the framework of short-term forecasting, for the following reasons:

1. A pertinent analysis of sales is too unreliable—if not altogether impossible to achieve—if such "semirandom" variations disrupt the fundamental fluctuations of the series.

2. In most cases, the disruptive events are the direct result of the activities of the company itself (e.g., temporary reduction in prices, sales promotion campaigns, actions taken on distribution channels, etc.). It is only natural, therefore, to measure the direct repercussions on sales, in order to carry out feasibility studies which will then permit the selection of appropriate marketing activities.

3. Practical experience shows that the history of those special events that have influenced time series is difficult to reconstruct: not only in terms of making a pertinent and numerical analysis of the series, but also because of the informative value of past experience that has been lost, owing to a lack of relevant documentation.

4. The forecasting value of a system is increased if such information is taken into account. The integration of special events into the forecasting process permits the different fundamental characteristics of the series (e.g., averages, trends) to be well qualified—an indispensable prerequisite for a good forecast.

Although most special actions are of a qualitative nature, the possibilities offered by present-day forecasting methods—for *quantifying* the effects of special actions—are illustrated in this chapter.

Taking into account the possible occurrence of various special events, by means of an integrated forecasting system, results in fact in a real short-term marketing information system which permits:

An extremely accurate analysis of past data.

A high degree of accuracy in the quantification of sales promotion campaigns.

An appreciable improvement in the quality of the forecasts.

REACTIONS OF THE MARKET TO SPECIAL ACTIONS

Below, we briefly explain the FORSYS approach for the integrated analysis of special actions (cf. Lewandowski[4,5]).

Assume that a market develops in line with the sales boom shown in Chart 22-2. In period t the product manager decides to temporarily reduce the retail sales price by 5% during the two periods that follow. Consumers, profiting from the special offer, then buy additional quantities of the product. The result of the price decrease is in fact twofold:

1. For well-known economic reasons, there is an increase in sales during the period of the price reduction.

2. There is a reduction in sales during the periods that follow those of price reduction. This is due to the accumulation of stocks by consumers when they were buying at the lower price.

It is useful to relate the increases or decreases in sales to those sales that would have been recorded if this special action had not taken place. Chart 22-2 illustrates the deviations of actual sales in relation to "normal" sales for each period since the introduction of the special action. The curve of the "normal" sales represents the actual dynamic behavior of the market, in relation to the specific effect of the special action.

DISCUSSION OF AN ACTUAL CASE OF
QUANTIFICATION OF A SPECIAL ACTION

The sales of a particular aperitif in a certain region of France were influenced by a promotion campaign (special action No. 7) in the spring of 1972. The product manager had estimated the influence on the market (sales to retailers) to be as follows:

First period (May 1972)—probable increase in sales, as compared with the norm: +35%.

CHART 22-2. Time Series with Special Action

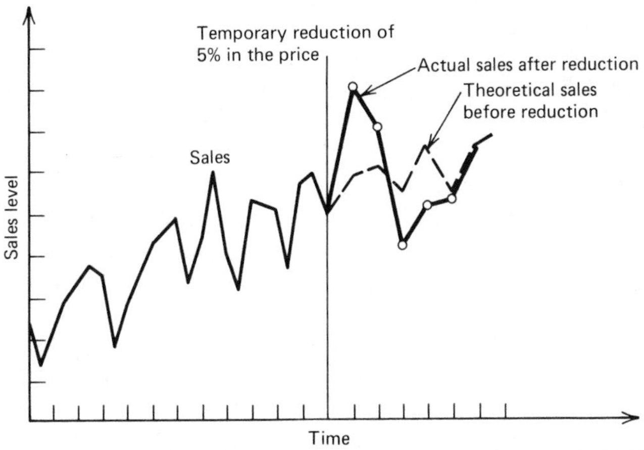

Second period (June 1972)—probable increase in sales, still influenced by the sales promotion campaign in the first half of this month: +5%.

Third period (July 1972)—destocking or decrease in orders, as compared with the norm (countereffect): –30%.

Fourth period (August 1972)—end of destocking, with a slight decrease in orders: –10%.

This scenario of reactions (see "Base Values" in Chart 22-3) illustrates that the process of quantification leads to a somewhat different "pro-

CHART 22-3. Example of Automatic Quantification of a Special Action by the FORSYS System

Table of the Analysis of Special Actions							
Type: 7 Period	Base Value	Value of the Special Action Before Each Implementation					
		0	1	2	3	4	5
1	35.0	38.2	38.0				
2	5.0	8.6	8.8				
3	–30.0	–16.4	–14.6				
4	–10.0	–5.6	–4.5				
5	0.0	0.0	0.0				
6	0.0	0.0	0.0				

Sales Promotion Campaign—Spring 1972

file" of this special action. Thus the system appears to detect a major increase in orders in the first two periods (see column 0 in the corrections made by the system—Chart 22-3). But what appears to be more significant is that the destocking foreseen by the product manager proves to be less than estimated: a total of –22%, as opposed to –40%. The quantification procedure therefore appears to signal a positive balance which is more favorable than had previously been envisaged.

If the product manager was to decide to reuse the same sales promotion campaign (i.e., No. 7), the system would propose a slightly different profile of the special action (see column 1 in Chart 22-3).

Considering, for example, the sales figures described previously for a brand of aperitif, it can be seen that a detailed analysis of the sales history permitted an accurate quantification of a certain number of special actions that had strongly influenced the market. Thus for the period July 1971 to April 1974 the market was influenced by seven different special actions. From Chart 22-4, which shows the synthesis of their respective effects, the following conclusions can be drawn:

1. Special action No. 6 (price increase in January 1972) led to major fluctuations in the sales level (up to +156%), which occurred over six periods from November 1971 to April 1972.

2. During certain periods the overlapping of special actions can be ascertained. While the initial effects of advance purchases by the retail sector, owing to the increase in prices announced for January 1972, were felt in November 1971, the influence of special action No. 1 (sales promotion aimed at retailers in September–October 1971) can still be observed. At the same time, in December 1972 the concurrent influence of special action No. 8 in its final phase, and of special action No. 9 in its initial phase, can be seen.

3. A detailed analysis of each special action enables measurement of the impact of repeated actions.

Consider special action No. 1 (sales promotion aimed at retailers) as an example. This special action has been launched several times in the past, and its quantitative analysis has provided the following information (see Chart 22-5):

1. The special action influenced three periods, with a positive impact on the first two periods, and a negative one on the third (effects of destocking).

2. Its total influence (balance) was highly positive, although slightly less so than initially estimated by the product manager. Thus an average influence of

$$(+8.3) \quad (+7.9) \quad (-4.3)$$

CHART 22-4. Synthesis of the Different Special Actions

						Retrospective Analysis of the Special Actions					

Month/Year	*	1	2	3	4	Special Actions Number 5	6	7	8	9	10
1 JL 71	*										
2 AU	*										
3 SE	*	8.5									
4 OC	*	7.7									
5 NO	*	-4.3					40.3				
6 DE	*	0.0					70.6				
7 JA 72	*						156.3				
8 FE	*						-41.5				
9 MR	*						-27.8				
10 AP	*						-13.6				
11 MA	*							38.2			
12 JU	*							8.6			
13 JL	*							-16.4			
14 AU	*							-5.6			
15 SE	*										
16 OC	*								15.3		
17 NO	*								10.6		
18 DE	*								-17.6	77.9	
19 JA 73	*								-5.0	-39.4	
20 FE	*									-30.8	
21 MR	*									-10.5	
22 AP	*										
23 MA	*		11.6								
24 JU	*		-13.6								
25 JL	*		-12.5								
26 AU	*		-3.5								
27 SE	*					38.6					
28 OC	*					69.6					
29 NO	*					-48.3					
30 DE	*					-14.5					
31 JA 74	*					-3.9					
32 FE	*										
33 MR	*										
34 AP	*										
35 MA	*										
36 JU	*										
37 JL	*										
	*										

is established, as compared with

$$(+10.0) \quad (+5.0) \quad (-5.0)$$

envisaged by the marketing department.

3. The values resulting from successive corrections of the special action, which are shown in columns numbered 1, 2, 3, . . . , permit an assessment of whether its repetitive use leads to a systematic change in its profile; in the case in question it seems that the reaction of the market to this special action is relatively stable.

CHART 22-5. Special Action: Sales Promotion Aimed at Retailers

Type	Base value	Value of special action before each implementation					
PERIOD		0	1	2	3	4	5

Type	Base value	Value of special action before each impiementatior					
PERIOD		0	1	2	3	4	5

Type	Base value	Value of special action before each implementation					
PERIOD		0	1	2	3	4	5
1	20.0	11.6	10.6	11.1	11.3	11.6	
2	10.0	-13.4	-15.0	-14.9	-14.3	-13.6	
3	-10.0	-12.5	-12.3	-12.1	-13.0	-12.5	
4	-10.0	-11.5	-13.1	-12.8	-12.3	-11.5	

.200 TABLEAU DE L'ANALYSE DES ACTIONS SPECIALES .200

Type	Base value	Value of special action before each implementation					
PERIOD		0	1	2	3	4	5
1	10.0	8.5	8.2	8.5			
2	5.0	7.7	8.1	7.7			
3	-5.0	-4.3	-4.2	-4.3			
4	0.0	0.0	0.0	0.0			
5	0.0	0.0	0.0	0.0			
6	0.0	0.0	0.0	0.0			

Sales promotion aimed at retailers
Sept.-Oct. 1971 and 1974

These specific outputs of the matrix of the special action comprise the fundamental instrument for the analysis and monitoring of various short-term sales promotion campaigns, and indeed for every product of the company.

ADDITIONAL REMARKS ON THE GENERAL IMPACT OF SPECIAL ACTIONS, AND THEIR SHORT-TERM EFFECTS

As shown above, the short-term influences of special actions are limited to a period of time that is less than 6 months. However, it must be admitted that certain special actions have not only a short-term effect, but in fact continue to exert an influence on the market for a period sometimes exceeding 1 year.

As Chart 22-6 shows, there are simultaneous effects:

1. A short-term effect (up to 6 months) which will be referred to as

CHART 22-6.   Temporary and Permanent Effects of a Special Action (S.A.)

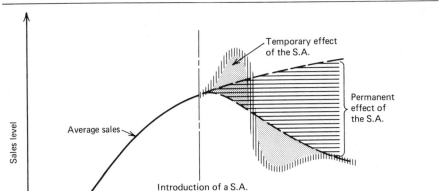

the *temporary effect* of the special action. This can be measured easily by a short-term forecasting system.

2. A long-term effect (exceeding 6 months) which will be known as the *permanent effect* of the special action. The extent and duration of such effects are generally difficult to measure—at least by short-term forecasting systems. This is why these permanent effects must not, in the opinion of this author, be taken into consideration in a short-term forecasting system.

CONCLUSIONS ON THE INTEGRATED TREATMENT OF SPECIAL ACTIONS

In summary, the following is a synopsis of the main points of the effects of special actions on forecasting systems:

1. Automatic consideration of special events or actions clarifies the extraordinary variations in sales that result from temporary changes in the purchasing behavior of the consumer. These changes are directly related to the special actions of the company or its competitors and, in principle, are independent of the changes in the characteristics of the series itself—such as average, trend, or seasonality.

   All too often, seasonality is badly quantified by so-called

classic methods, because they do not employ the concept of special actions. The result of this is a considerable reduction in the capabilty of the forecasting system used.

Experience has shown that the majority of time series relating to sales of consumer products demand an integrated treatment of special actions.

2. The evaluation of the impact of special actions on the market is an essential element in the analysis of the profitability of short-term marketing.

Experience proves that many companies launch sales promotion campaigns that have profitability rates that are too low, or even negative. The financial cost of certain special actions exceeds the profit gained from the increase in sales.

Moreover, the advantage of monitoring the effect of special actions is to bring to light those actions that are no longer viable —sometimes contrary to the opinion of sales managers. The average saving made by avoiding a repeat of the same mistakes fully justifies the investment involved in installing an adequate forecasting service.

Many product managers or sales directors would be surprised to hear the effective profitability of certain special actions which, even if they have borne fruit in the past, have subsequently lost their impact.

The dynamic analysis of special actions is an element of effective management of the short-term policy relating to sales promotion campaigns in marketing.

3. A better understanding of the effect of special actions permits a search for those actions that are best suited to attain fixed objectives in the short term.

This consequence of an integrated treatment of special actions leads to the planning of sales promotion campaigns in the short term for the company.

4. The introduction of marketing activity to an integrated forecasting system is a major element in the dynamic analysis of sales, and it constitutes a viable system of short-term marketing information. It does so by permitting, on the one hand, an effective dialogue between forcasting management and sales staff and, on the other hand, by providing in a quantitative and coherent form, a synthesis of various information on the market environment.

REFERENCES

1. Chow, W. M., "Adaptive Control of the Exponential Smoothing Constant," *Journal of Industrial Engineering,* vol. 16, 1965, pp. 314.

2. Dobben de Bruyn V, C. S., "Prediction by Progressive Correction," *Journal of the Royal Statistical Society*, B 26, 1964, pp. 113.

3. Lewandowski, R., "Ein voll adaptationsfähiges Modell zur kurzfristigen Prognose," *AKOR-Tagung*, Aachen, 1969.

4. Lewandowski, R., *Prognose- und Informationssysteme Band I*, Berlin, 1974.

5. Lewandowski, R., *La Prévision à Court Terme*, Paris, 1980.

6. Makridakis, S., et al., "The Accuracy of Extrapolation (Time Series) Methods: Results of a Forecasting Competition," *Journal of Forecasting*, Vol. 1, No. 2, 1982, pp. 1–38.

7. Trigg, D. W. and A. G. Leach, "Exponential Smoothing with an Adaptive Response Rate," *Operational Research Quarterly*, vol. 18, 1967, pp. 53.

CHAPTER

23

ANTICIPATORY ANALYSIS FOR NEW ENTRY STRATEGIES

JEAN-CLAUDE LARRÉCHÉ
INSEAD

INTRODUCTION

The long-term survival of a corporation depends on its ability to expand and renew its activities over time. Its two main axes for renewal and growth include primarily the introduction of new products and the penetration of new markets. These two types of actions are globally called *new entries*.

In a recent survey of 148 companies, Hopkins[16] found that on average 15% of the current sales volume of these companies was attributable to new products introduced in the past 5 years. Moreover, two-thirds of the executives responding in the survey stated that the dependence on new products would increase in the future. In terms of performance, the median failure rate was 33% indicating that, for half of the companies surveyed, more than one out of three new products did not meet management's expectations.*

Because of their importance for business and their inherent risks,

---

*Several other studies are reviewed in two excellent recent books on new product planning: Urban and Hauser[32] and Choffray and Lilien.[8]

new entry activities represent an area where the need for forecasting is critical. It is also, unfortunately, an area where the applicability of classical forecasting techniques is limited. One obvious difficulty in using classical forecasting techniques for a new entry is the lack of historical data. Another is that a new entry creates a disruption of the existing market equilibrium, thus invalidating the historical market or competitive patterns.

One can distinguish three types of new entry failures. A type 1 failure corresponds to a potential risk that had been anticipated, but was accepted as a reasonable business undertaking. A type 2 failure results from an event that could not be reasonably anticipated before the new entry. A type 3 failure is due to factors that were not correctly analyzed by management, although they could have reasonably been anticipated.

The third type of failure is the one that is most controllable and should be systematically reduced. It can be decomposed into two elements: an unsatisfactory breadth of analysis or an unsatisfactory depth of analysis, and these two sources of errors call for different corrective actions. In order to minimize the risk of not considering an influent factor, management should follow a comprehensive framework to review all facets of a new entry. On the other hand, a number of models are available or can be developed to analyze in depth critical problem areas.

The use of a comprehensive framework to systematically investigate the strategic implications of the future evolution of a market situation is termed an *anticipatory analysis*.* Although an anticipatory analysis may be performed in various circumstances, this chapter concentrates more specifically on the evaluation of new entry strategies. It will be assumed that a product-market opportunity has already been identified as being economically attractive. The issues of opportunity identification as well as preliminary technological and commercial feasibility studies will not be covered here.

A typology of new entry situations will first be described to put into perspective the various managerial problems that are regrouped under this generic title. A framework will then be presented that identifies the main aspects of an anticipatory analysis for new entries. Finally, some representative models more specifically used for new product planning will be discussed.

---

*A similar concept is the "prospective" approach (Godet[11]). The prospective approach tends, however, to be associated with a specific procedure while we use the expression "anticipatory analysis" to represent a general philosophy. This philosophy implies that one analyzes systematically the elements of a dynamic situation to anticipate its evolution, irrespective of the availability, form, or quality of available data. Instead of being constrained by existing quantitative data, as is the case in classical forecasting, anticipatory analysis encourages the extraction of information from the organization by raising appropriate questions.

A TYPOLOGY OF NEW ENTRY SITUATIONS

Research results on new entries are plagued with definitional problems. A new entry may at one extreme represent a major venture for a corporation and at the other extreme only a minor product line extension. In one case it may open a completely new industry based on a revolutionary technology, and in another case it may only be an imitation of well-established and fully tested competitive products. It is obvious that the resources and risks involved will be considerably different for these various types of new entries. The know-how of a corporation will also vary widely in these different cases, and a typology of new entry situations should illustrate the varying levels of information available for anticipatory analysis.

The concept of new entry can be classified by specifying *what* is new (a product or a market) and *for whom* it is new (for the industry at large or for a specific firm, market, or product). One can consequently organize new entries around five classifications*:

1. Is the product new for the industry?
2. Is the product new for the firm?
3. Is the market new for the industry?
4. Is the market new for the firm?
5. Is the product new for the market?

These five dichotomies would provide 32 types of new entries if they were totally independent. Some of them are, however, redundant: a product which is new for an industry must *a fortiori* be new for the firm and for the market. The 13 remaining feasible and mutually exclusive types of new entries are represented in Chart 23-1. At one extreme is the complete innovation corresponding to cell 1. A firm develops a product which is new for the industry and introduces it in a market from which the industry was absent. This is extremely rare as a single firm is usually unlikely to create a product *and* a market that are simultaneously new for an industry. The entries of Univac into computers, Xerox into reprography, and Polaroid into instantaneous photography are examples of a type 1 new entry.

At the other extreme, the firm is launching in a market in which it already operates a product which it has already introduced in other

---

*In this discussion, a market is considered to be a specific consumer group. An industry is a set of firms that have a similar technological basis or compete in some markets, although they may not always manufacture similar products or be systematically present in the same markets.

CHART 23-1. Typology of New Entries

Market \ Product	For industry: New / For firm: New	For industry: Exist / For firm: New	For industry: Exist / For firm: Exist	Product for market
New / New	1	4	9	New
New / New	2	5	10	New
Exist / Exist		6	11	Exist
Exist / Exist	3	7	12	New
Exist / Exist		8	13	Exist

markets. Competition has already introduced a similar product in this market. The firm may have delayed its introduction by oversight or to avoid cannibalization with its current product line. In this situation, the firm has a great deal of information: it knows the product, it knows the market, and it has already benefited from observing the market's reaction to competitive offerings. An example of such a new entry is the delayed introduction of a product in a less developed country.

The amount of information available varies significantly according to the type of new entry considered, and the typology provides a guide to systematically search for possible data sources: from other products of the firm in similar markets, from the same product of the firm in other markets, from similar competitive products in similar or other markets, and from similar markets served by competition with different products. Even in the best case, however, the information available to anticipate the outcome of a new entry will be less than when forecasting the sales of a given product already established in a specific market. It is thus particularly important to isolate all available information and to exploit it as much as possible, and this is the purpose of anticipatory analysis.

KEY ELEMENTS OF ANTICIPATORY ANALYSIS

Marketing is one of the major interfaces of the firm with its environment, and it requires consideration of a broad range of elements internal as well as external to the firm. A systematic analysis of these elements is becoming increasingly important as growth opportunities become less obvious and competition intensifies. This represents an irreversible evolution from perceptions inherited from the 1960s in which free spending was more characteristic of marketing than careful analyses. A marketing audit represents the integration of such systematic analyses (Kotler et al.[19] and Naylor and Wood[23]). Its purpose is to provide a diagnosis of a firm's market posture based mainly on historical data.

An anticipatory analysis, on the other hand, is primarily concerned with the future. This future will be affected by uncertain external factors and also by the actions of the firm, thus making anticipatory analysis more difficult than a historical marketing audit. The impact of a new entry strategy may be considerable. For instance, launching a new product at a low price may develop new segments of the market and result in a growth rate higher than the one which could have been projected on the basis of historical data. Furthermore, a strategy may result in competitive reactions, the effects of which are difficult to predict.

These different factors influencing the success of a new entry strategy lead to the definition of three components of anticipatory analysis:

1. *Projective Analysis.* Its purpose is to determine one, or several, probable schemes of the evolution of the situation assuming a simple extrapolation of past strategies. This projection would not consider a new entry contemplated by the firm.

2. *Proactive Analysis.* Assuming that competitors do not change their strategies, proactive analysis tries to anticipate the evolution of the situation for alternative strategies of the firm.

3. *Reaction Analysis.* The highest level of sophistication in the analysis consists in taking into account the reaction of competitors to the actions of the firm.*

The process of anticipatory analysis is represented schematically in Chart 23-2. Projective analysis is a direct extension of the marketing audit in the future. On the basis of the resulting projections, alternative strategies are formulated and their effects are evaluated assuming an unchanged behavior of competitors. This may lead to the cancellation, modification, or addition of alternative strategies. The remaining set of strategies is then evaluated taking into account possible reactions from competitors. This may again result in deletion, modification, and addi-

---

*The economists have in particular used reaction functions to study imperfect competition as in the Cournot and Stackelberg solutions (Henderson and Quandt, pp. 223-31[15]). Urban and Hauser use the expressions "proactive" and "reactive strategies" to reflect the degree of initiative of the firm compared to its competitors (Urban and Hauser, pp. 572-74[32]). Here, proactive and reaction analyses represent two different stages of an anticipatory analysis.

CHART 23-2. Marketing Audit and Anticipatory Analysis

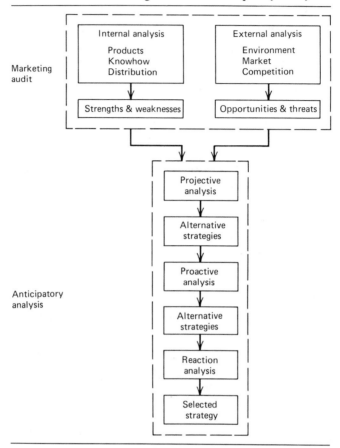

tion of alternative strategies. The end result of the anticipatory analysis is a systematic investigation of alternative strategies.

In each of the steps in the anticipatory analysis, the investigation involves four basic components: the firm, the environment, the market, and the competition. The relative importance of each varies over the phases of the analysis. Firm and market considerations are relatively important all through the analysis as they constitute the key components of the exchange relationship. Environmental factors will be considered mainly in the projective phase, while the relative importance of competitive issues will increase in the proactive and reaction analysis phases.

The key elements of an anticipatory analysis for new entries will now be briefly presented (see Chart 23-3). The resulting framework is not exhaustive, but it does isolate issues determining the success or failure of new entries.

CHART 23-3. Key Elements of an Anticipatory Analysis for New Entries

Environmental Analysis

Evolution of economic, sociocultural, technological, and legal environments
Impact of new entry or other firm's actions on the environment

Internal Analysis

Coherence with distinctive competence
Cost estimates: reliability and evolution
Resources available
Capacity to monitor and adapt

Market Analysis

Market projection
Market stability
Direct market posture elements
   Awareness
   Market positioning
   Product availability
Impact on primary demand
   New consumers
   New applications
   Increased usage
   Increased added value
Impact on selective demand

Competitive Analysis

Projection of current competitors' actions
   Competitors' objectives
   Competitors' resources
   Market gaps
   Competition intensity
New sources of competition
Impact of entry strategy on competitors
   Sales
   Market share
   Profits
   Emotional impact
Potential competitive reactions
   Marketing mix element level
   Product market level
   Product market portfolio level

Anticipatory Environmental Analysis

The importance of correctly anticipating the evolution of the environment is well illustrated by the diverging strategies followed by Sears, Roebuck and Company and Montgomery Ward between 1945 and 1955. After World War II, Montgomery Ward anticipated another great depression and consequently decided to limit its growth. On the opposite side, Sears anticipated a long period of prosperity and consequently decided to expand rapidly in metropolitan centers. While the two merchandisers were of somewhat similar size before the war, Sears was 3 times bigger than Montgomery Ward in 1955 and in a much better strategic posture. Had an important depression occurred, the relative performances of the two firms probably would have been inverted.

The issues to be covered in an anticipatory analysis include:

1. *Economic Environment.* What is the expected evolution of inflation, GNP growth, purchasing power, raw material costs and availability, interest rates, and demographics?

2. *Sociocultural Environment.* What is the expected evolution of life styles, values, and reference groups?

3. *Technological Environment.* What improvements can be anticipated in the design or manufacturing of existing products? What substitute products could emerge in the future?

4. *Legal Environment.* What laws are likely to be adopted in the future, especially in the areas of product safety, advertising, pollution, or energy conservation?

The main emphasis in anticipating the future evolution of the environment is undoubtedly on projective analysis. Although usually less significant, the proactive and reaction analyses should not be neglected as they may isolate important issues in some specific situations. In the proactive analysis, for instance, a strategy to penetrate a new country based on local manufacturing and job creations could develop goodwill with the local government and facilitate the entry. In the reaction analysis, potential unsolicited reactions to the new entry from various elements such as antitrust agencies or consumerist, religious, and cultural groups should be investigated.

Anticipatory Internal Analysis

Anticipatory internal analysis is primarily concerned with factors that could create changes in the firm's competitive advantage.

1. *Coherence of an Entry Strategy with the Firm's Distinctive Competence.* An ideal entry strategy is one that simultaneously fully satisfies

market needs, provides a clear and defendable competitive advantage, and is based on the distinctive competence of the firm. This ideal strategy is seldom feasible, and the decision is usually more one of degree: how far should the firm move from its area of competence to adequately satisfy market needs and keep a competitive advantage? The real issue is to explicitly consider this deviation in anticipating the outcome of the corresponding entry strategy.

In a projective phase, coherence of the entry strategy with the firm's current distinctive competence should be explicitly considered to systematically identify potential risks and the uncertainties which may exist in various estimates. In a proactive phase, the actions that the firm has taken, or could take, to decrease the risks associated with a deviation from its current distinctive competence should be explicitly analyzed. Such actions include, for instance, extensive product testing, market research, hiring of managerial talent with experience in the new area, consultancy, and appropriate selection of an advertising agency.

2. *Cost Behavior.* Cost estimates are crucial in the selection of an entry strategy. In a projective phase, one should consider possible changes in cost estimates due to environmental factors such as inflation on labor or raw materials, or stricter legal norms on product reliability or pollution standards. In a proactive phase, one should investigate the behavior of cost for alternative strategies and, in particular, the so-called experience effects. The Boston Consulting Group[4] has brought empirical evidence that in a wide range of products unit costs tend to decline by 20–30% everytime cumulative production of the product is doubled. This shows that substantial cost variations may result from different production levels and that these potential variations are particularly important at the time of the new entry.

3. *Resources Available.* In planning a new entry, resources are allocated according to the objectives set. More ambitious objectives will necessitate higher resources to be reached and may entail a higher perceived financial risk. In a study of 37 entries, Biggadike[2] has, however, found that projects with higher market share objectives tended to be more successful (see Chart 23-4). The percentage of entrants achieving their objective was 50% for those with market share objectives above 10% and only 32% for others. Entry on a large scale will result in lower costs and a higher efficiency which may in part explain these findings. Another reason is that a project to which higher resources have been committed will draw more management attention and care. Resources should consequently be concentrated on key entries, and one should systematically question the desirability of minor projects creating unnecessary dispersion.

The anticipatory analysis should also investigate why resources can become inadequate and whether their level of allocation can be adjusted when required. A new entry plan which is already extending the financial

CHART 23-4. Market Objectives and Achievement in First 2 Years of Entry

Share Objective	Number of Entrants	Achieved Objective	Missed Objective
Up to 5%	16	4	12
6–10%	3	2	1
11–15%	7	2	5
16–20%	5	4	1
More than 20%	6	3	3
	37	15	22

Source: Biggadike.[2]

capabilities of the firm is less likely to succeed if disfavorable, unexpected events do occur. An analysis of the business portfolio provides an anticipation of future cash flows (Day[10]), and the role of the new entry within this portfolio gives an indication of its priority in obtaining extra resources when required.

4. *Capacity to Monitor and Adapt.* A new entry creates a disturbance in a competitive market. To monitor market changes closely an information system needs to be set up where timeliness is more important than minute accuracy. A flexible organization, clear procedures, easy communications, and clear responsibilities are also essential to success.

Anticipatory Market Analysis

In an anticipatory analysis for a new entry, attention will be concentrated on the factors influencing the evolution of the market. A desirable step-by-step approach consists in making a projection of the market without the new entry, then considering the impact of alternative strategies for the new entry, and finally taking into account the full dynamics of the situation with reactions from, and counterreactions to, competition.

1. *Market Projection.* In the case of an entry into an existing market, a projection can be made of the market's evolution in the absence of the new entry as a basis for analysis. Such projection can in part be done through classical forecasting techniques although it should not be limited to a forecast of market size only. It also should include basic market elements such as the relative importance of the sources of growth, including new users, new applications, or more usage of the product; the relative growth of alternative market segments; the evolution of the

needs of these market segments; and the impact of these factors on the evolution of the market shares and profitability of the main competitors in the market, assuming a continuation of their current strategies.

2. *Market Stability.* The more stable a market is, then the more robust one can expect a projection of that market to be. On the other hand, the more unstable a market is, then the more opportunities that exist for new entries. The evaluation of the stability of a market is an important aspect of anticipating the outcome of a new entry strategy. It should consider consumers and distributors satisfaction and loyalty, potential technological changes, strengths of competitive postures, and entry costs.

3. *Direct Market Posture Elements.* The market posture of a product is ultimately determined by market share, sales, and profits. To anticipate the impact of a given entry strategy one should, however, first consider in depth the factors that are more directly under the influence of the firm: the brand and features awareness that the new entry will achieve; the market positioning of the new entry relative to consumer needs and competitive offerings; and the availability of the new product in distribution channels.

4. *Impact of Entry Strategy on Primary Demand. Primary demand* is the total demand for a product class. A new entry can in some circumstances develop this primary demand. This may in some cases be easier than gaining consumers away from the competition and will generate a less intensive competitive reaction. In the case of a completely new product creating a new product class, the development of primary demand is indeed the only avenue of expansion. There are, however, two broad issues to be considered in developing primary demand. The first is to identify the sources of primary demand which can be tapped with a new entry. The main sources to consider are new consumers, new applications, increased usage on existing applications, and increased added value per usage.

The second issue is the ability of the new entrant to keep the benefits of the additional primary demand that it has developed. There is ample evidence that efforts made by the smaller firms to develop the primary demand tend to benefit proportionally more to the market leader. This is obvious, for instance, when a firm makes potential consumers aware of the existence and benefits of a given product class; the consumers then discover that within this product class another firm provides a product better adapted to their need. The capability of the firm to retain the expansion of primary demand brought by its new entry will depend to a large extent on the three direct market posture elements previously discussed: awareness, market positioning, and product availability.

5. *Impact of Entry Strategy on Selective Demand. Selective demand* is the demand for a specific brand in a product class. An obvious objective of a new entry strategy is to gain selective demand. The demand for the new entry will be gained, at least partly, on competitors, unless it is obtained entirely from a development of the primary demand. Even in this unlikely case, competitors may not loose sales but will loose market share. All competitors will not be equally affected by the new entrant, and this will influence their individual reactions. It is consequently important to anticipate not only the level of selective demand for the new entrant but also how much market share has been transferred from each of the competitors and from cannibalization of existing offerings of the firm. The new entry will gain market share mainly from the brands that are positioned close to it, that is, those most similar to it in terms of product characteristics, price, or distribution outlets. It can consequently be said that through market positioning a firm does, to a large extent, choose its competition. For each alternative entry strategy, it is thus essential to anticipate the market position that will be achieved and the resulting pattern of competition.

Anticipatory Competitive Analysis

In the high market growth situation of the 1960s, a strategy formulated in the "absolute" to satisfy simultaneously the needs of the market and the objectives of the firm was to a large extent a sufficient condition of success. In the more competitive contemporary situation, the satisfaction of market needs is more than ever a necessary condition, but not a sufficient one. A market strategy will be effective only if it is also adequate relative to competitive actions, and competitive analysis has become increasingly important (Oxenfeldt and Moore[24] and Porter[26]).

Following a systematic approach, an anticipatory competitive analysis should contain: a projective phase investigating probable actions of existing and potential competitors in the absence of a new entry by the firm; a proactive phase considering the impact of new entry strategies on competitors; and a reaction phase analyzing potential reactions of competitors to new entry strategies.

1. *Projection of Current Competitors' Actions.* When planning a new entry into an existing market, one should anticipate that current competitors, even if they do not expect the new entry, are also in the process of planning their own future actions. A failure in anticipating actions simultaneously prepared by competitors may result in a reduced competitive advantage for the new entrant compared to what it expected, in excessive competition in some market areas, and at the extreme in a possible market obsolescence of the new entry before it is even introduced. Some of the factors to consider in order to anticipate the actions currently planned by competitors are their objectives and resources, the market gaps which they may try to fill, and current competition intensity.

2. *New Sources of Competition.* The new entry contemplated by the firm may also be exposed to the competition of other corporations which plan to enter the market in the future. These are firms that can base this new entry on a distinct competitive advantage and have the resources required to exploit it. They include, for instance, firms that: already have similar products in other markets, such as foreign competitors; already serve the market with other types of products; could penetrate the market by forward or backward vertical integration of their activities; could acquire an existing competitor in the market and provide him with additional resources or a new distinctive advantage.

3. *Impact of Entry Strategy on Competitors.* The impact of the new entry on competitors will depend on the relative importance of their increased sales due to the development of primary demand and of their current sales lost to the new entrant. The importance of this impact can be analyzed at four levels: sales, profits, market share, and emotions.

A new entry will result in a loss of market share for some competitors, even if their sales or profits increase due to the development of primary demand. A firm which is primarily concerned with its sales or profit level may not realize in the short run that its market share is declining. As a result, its competitors may gain a cost advantage which may considerably weaken its posture in the long run. This is one of the reasons why market share is increasingly seen as one of the most critical performance measures of the marketing-oriented firm (Buzzell et al.[5]). A new entry which gains its market share from the less marketing-oriented competitors is consequently less likely to generate strong reactions, especially if it does not reduce their sales or profits.

When a firm enters a market, it will also have an impact on competitors beyond sales, market share, and profits. This is an emotional impact due to the interpretation by the competitors of the firm's intentions and of their implications for the industry. For instance, the new entry of a specific firm in a market may be interpreted as a signal that this market has high potential, that prices are going to decline, that technology is going to be renewed, or that marketing investments should be expected to increase significantly. These interpretations may lead some firms to join the market, others to suspend additional investments in this market, and still others to fight off the new entrant beyond an economically reasonable level.

4. *Potential Competitive Reactions.* The analysis of the impact of the new entrant on the market and on the competition provides a number of indications of the possible retaliatory moves that the competition could undertake. In order to anticipate the main scenarios, these competitive moves can be systematically analyzed at three levels:

1. *The Marketing Mix Element Level.* Competitors may react directly against the distinctive advantage that the new entrant is

capitalizing on. They may, for instance, respond to an improved product by their own product enhancements, to a cheaper product by price cuts, and to high promotional investments by increasing their own promotional budgets.

2. *The Product Market Level.* Instead of responding to the new entrant on its own terms, competitors may choose to keep the initiative and react on other elements of the marketing mix. They may, for instance, react to an improved product by price cuts and to high promotional investments by increased allowances to distributors.

3. *The Product Market Portfolio Level.* Competitors may also be able to counterattack in another product market where the new entrant is more vulnerable. The existence of such a possibility depends on the interrelationships of competitors across product markets, but it should be anticipated by the new entrant.

MODELS FOR NEW ENTRIES

Given the strategic importance of new entries it is not surprising that a large number of models have been developed to assist managers in this area. The more representative of these models are presented here, and the emphasis is placed on the issues that they address in the context of a systematic anticipatory analysis. The progressive coverage of various elements can be illustrated by looking at the classes of models that have emerged over time: stochastic models, process models, aggregate models, and product positioning models.

Stochastic Models

Stochastic models attempt to estimate the long-term equilibrium market share of a product from the past purchasing behavior of consumers. This behavior is represented by a probablistic process which is the combined outcome of all factors influencing purchasing decisions. The nature and parameters of this probabilistic process are determined from data gathered in a market test or in the first months of introduction of the new product. This approach cannot consequently be of help in the early stages of the new entry planning process. Furthermore, it requires that successive purchases made by a representative group of consumers be observed over a relatively short period of time, and this limits its use to frequently purchased packaged consumer goods.

In this case, stochastic models are perfectly adapted to the type of data provided by consumer panels and are useful in forecasting the equilibrium market share on the basis of early sales results. Equilibrium market share is particularly difficult to anticipate judgmentally from early sales results of frequently purchased packaged consumer goods as sales will usually go through a peak and stabilize later at a lower level. This is due to the fact that the early growth comes from new triers of the product, and then new triers and repeat buyers combine to produce a high level of sales which declines as sales come from only repeat buyers. Stochastic models attempt to represent this phenomenon by operationalizing in different ways the general concept of brand loyalty. This can be achieved by separating explicitly repeat buyers from new triers, by distinguishing between different repeat classes, or by estimating the purchase probability of a brand given a purchase history for one individual.

Different types of stochastic models have been developed since the late 1950s.* The stochastic modeling approach is illustrated here by a brief description of STEAM, one of the most complete stochastic models (Massy[20] and Massy et al.[21]). It uses data gathered from a consumer panel in the first months following the launching of a new product to estimate the sales volume after the introductory period. The households belonging to the panel are divided into "depth of trial" (DOT) classes according to the number of times they have purchased the new product. Those who have never bought the product are in DOT class zero, those who have bought it once are in DOT class one, those who have bought it twice are in DOT class two, and so on. This separation of the population into DOT classes provides a higher homogeneity within each class in terms of experience and brand loyalty.

In each of these DOT classes, and on the basis of consumer panel data, the STEAM model determines the probability distribution of interpurchase times. This distribution can be used to compute the probability that a household in a given DOT class will buy the new brand within 1 week, 2 weeks, and so on. From these probability distributions, the STEAM model simulates the behavior of individual households and provides an estimate of future brand sales.

The results of one application of the STEAM model are shown in Chart 23-5. In this example, the model has been used on the basis of the consumer panel data gathered in the first 6 months after the launching of a new brand. Probability distributions were estimated from these data which allowed a simulation of individual households in order to forecast sales from 6 months to 3 years after the introduction of the new brand. While sales have increased regularly over the first 6 months, the model forecasts a decline and a stabilization of sales at a much lower

*For an excellent review of stochastic models, see Massy et al.[21] and Montgomery and Ryans,[22] from which this section draws.

CHART 23-5. Example of Application of the STEAM Model[a]

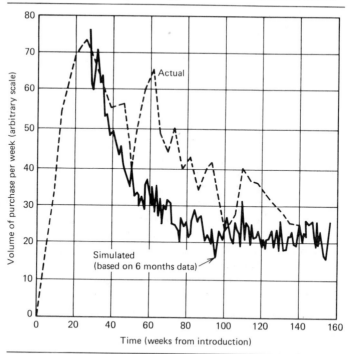

[a]Source: Massey et al.,[21] (p. 412).

level. Starting around week 50, the firm tried to stop the sales decline with an intensive promotional campaign. This was obviously not taken into account in the projections of the model and results in higher actual than predicted sales. Despite these additional marketing efforts, the sales of the new brand appear to decline inexorably toward the predicted equilibrium level. The analysis of repeat sales by the STEAM model has successfully detected the basic response to the product by the market which seems to be only temporarily affected by increased promotional investment.

By analyzing market dynamics in detail over a period of time stochastic models can project the long-run sales equilibrium level of a new brand as long as these dynamics do not change. Stochastic models require that data be available either from a market test or from the beginning of the introduction period. Consequently, they cannot contribute to the early phases of the new entry planning process and are mainly limited to frequently purchased consumer packaged goods. With some exceptions (Hartung and Fischer[14] and Horsky[17]), they merely provide a projection of market dynamics but do not make any provision for the influence that a change in the brand strategy would have on these dynamics.

Process Models

Process models explicitly consider that after the introduction of a new product, consumers go through different stages, from total ignorance of the product to its repeated purchase and strong brand loyalty. At a given point in time, different consumers will be in different stages in the consumption process. The transfer of consumers from one stage to the next is influenced by the marketing elements of the new entry strategy. This influence can be explicitly represented in the model, and the impact of alternative strategies on predicted sales can consequently be tested.

The best-known process models for new products are DEMON (Charnes et al.[7]), NEWS (Charnes et al.[6]), SPRINTER (Urban[31]), NEW-PROD (Assmus[1]), and TRACKER (Blattberg and Golanty[3]). The process modeling approach is illustrated here by a brief description of SPRINTER. This model has been designed to assist in the formulation of marketing strategies for new frequently purchased consumer products. It is based on the process of diffusion of innovation and decomposes the population of consumers into five classes according to the nature of their purchases. Consumers are considered to move from one class to another according to the process represented in Chart 23-6. For instance, consumers buying the new brand for the first time will move from the potential trial class to the preference class. When buying the new brand a second time, they will then move to the loyalty I class, and so on.

CHART 23-6. General Structure of the SPRINTER Model[a]

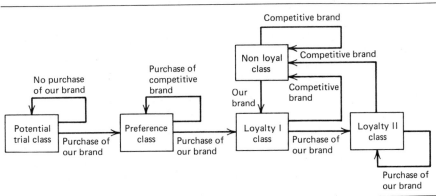

[a]Source: Urban,[31] (p. 311).

In each of these classes, the consumer behavior process is composed of five stages:

Awareness process

↓

Purchase intent process

↓

Search process

↓

Choice process

↓

Post-purchase process

The number of potential consumers moving from one stage to the next is a function of the marketing activities of the firm which include advertising, sampling, couponing, pricing, and distribution. The representation of this diffusion process is different for each class. For instance, advertising and promotion are particularly important in bringing a consumer to her/his first purchase of the new product, and their effects are modeled in detail in the potential trial class. After several purchases, consumers have a better knowledge of the product. Promotional activities are consequently represented in a more global fashion in the loyalty classes, while the effects of price on the purchase decision receive more attention.

Consumers are not simulated individually, and the "movement" of consumers referred to above is only figurative. The process is modeled at the level of the total number of consumers in each class. More than 500 equations represent the phenomena which ultimately determine the number of consumers buying the product in a time period and the resulting changes in the number of consumers in each class. The critical elements in these equations are response functions that describe the effects of marketing decisions. The estimation of these response functions, as well as of other parameters, requires an important data gathering program. For the introduction of a new brand, data are gathered in a market test through: a store audit; a consumers panel; awareness, attitudes, purchase intent, and product usage surveys; salesmen's reports; and advertising audits.

The SPRINTER model can be used to test alternative marketing strategies for a new product. In addition, the risk associated with the new brand can be evaluated by giving probability distributions for the input parameters and running a Monte Carlo analysis. Finally, the model provides an option to search automatically for the best strategy within a range of feasible decisions specified by the user.

The strength of process models is to explicitly consider the impact of marketing strategies on the outcome of a new entry. In addition, the detailed representation of the diffusion process provides a better understanding of market dynamics and a better diagnosis of potential problems at various levels: awareness, purchase intent, product availability, sales, profits, and so on. A potential drawback of process models lies in their strong data requirements. This is in part alleviated, however, by the fact that the modeled process can be represented in such a way that the model can accept judgmental inputs formulated by managers on the basis of their experience and of their knowledge of the new entry situation (see, e.g., Assmus[1]).

Aggregate Models

Aggregate models represent a situation at a global level in a single equation, or at least in a very limited number of equations. This is in fact the case with most classical forecasting techniques. The main purpose of such aggregate models is prediction, rather than explanation, and their explanatory power tends to be poor.

In the area of new entry planning, aggregate models are difficult to develop because of the lack of historical data. When an entry is planned in an existing market, classical forecasting techniques can obviously be used to predict the evolution of the total market size, assuming it will not be significantly affected by the new entry. However, aggregate models to predict sales or market share of a new entry are difficult to develop because of the lack of historical data. A notable exception, however, is the new product model developed at the N. W. Ayer advertising agency (Claycamp and Liddy[9]). The purpose of this model is to predict product performance before market introduction. A data base has been built by the advertising agency of N. W. Ayer from the introduction of 60 food products, household supplies, and personal care items. These data were gathered from consumer surveys, retail audits, commercial data services, and a panel of experienced marketing and advertising executives. The principle of this approach was to develop a model from this data base in order to draw lessons from past introductions and to forecast the performance of new brands in similar product classes. The missing history of a new brand was in a sense replaced by observations made on the past introductions of similar products.

The general structure of the model is composed of three stages, as

CHART 23-7.   General Structure of the AYER Model[a]

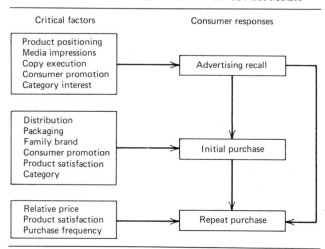

[a]Source: Cldyclamp and Liddy,[9] (p. 415).

illustrated in Chart 23-7: advertising recall, initial purchase, and repeat purchase. The marketing variables which have a major influence vary from one stage to the next. Advertising recall is mainly a function of the general product positioning and advertising. The initial purchase is mainly influenced by advertising recall, distribution, packaging, promotion, and consumer satisfaction with the product samples. At the repeat purchase level, price, product satisfaction, and purchase frequency become the critical factors. The response functions describing the influence of these marketing variables on advertising recall, initial purchase, and repeat purchase have been estimated from the data base. For instance, initial purchase of a new brand 13 weeks after introduction has been found to be best represented by:

$$
\begin{aligned}
\text{Initial purchase} = {} & -16 + 0.36 \ (\text{advertising recall}) \\
& + 0.19 \ (\text{distribution} \times \text{packaging}) \\
& + 9.25 \ (\text{family brand}) \\
& + 0.09 \ (\text{consumer promotion}) \\
& + 0.02 \ (\text{product satisfaction}) \\
& + 0.07 \ (\text{category usage})
\end{aligned}
$$

The model is used before the introduction of a new brand by first asking a group of experts from the agency and the firm to estimate the values of the independent variables (product positioning, media impressions, etc.) for a given new entry strategy. The expected values of advertising recall, initial purchase, and repeat purchase are then computed by replacing the independent variables by their estimated values in the three response functions.

This model has been tested on eight new entries to predict initial purchase 13 weeks after introduction. For seven out of eight entries, the actual initial purchases were within ± 10% of the predicted levels, and for five of them the predictive accuracy was within ± 5%. The eighth entry had achieved better than anticipated retail distribution, and its actual initial purchases were 13% higher than the predicted level.

This aggregate model takes into account a number of market factors which are under the direct influence of elements of the marketing mix, and consequently it can be used to test alternative marketing strategies. Its use is limited, however, to new frequently purchased packaged consumer brands which are similar to the products in the data base.

Product Positioning Models

None of the above models explicitly takes into account the characteristics of the new product. The impact of product characteristics is considered only globally, through variables representing product positioning and product satisfaction in the Ayer model, or implicitly in consumers' responses in other models.

More recently, a number of techniques have been developed which explicitly take into account the influence of product characteristics on consumer choice.* The purpose of these techniques it to guide market research and to provide a representation of the tradeoffs made by consumers in choosing a specific brand in a product class. An example of such a representation is given in Chart 23-8 for a beer market. It indicates that the two most determining characteristics for consumers in choosing between beer brands are perceived price/quality and lightness. In addition, it gives the position on these dimensions of four national brands and four regional brands (A–D). Finally, the numbers 1 to 9 correspond to the most preferred combinations of the two characteristics (or "ideal points") for nine market segments; the radius of the circle around each number is proportional to the size of the corresponding segment. For instance, the Miller and Hamms brands seem to be most preferred by segment 2, while Schlitz and Budweiser seem to be closer to the preferences of segment 1.

These techniques are the basis of some new product models such as LINMAP (Shocker and Srinivasan[27]), PERCEPTOR (Urban[30]), STRATOP (Pessemier[25]), and ASSESSOR (Silk and Urban[29]).

For instance, the purpose of the PERCEPTOR model is to help managers in the design, evaluation, and refinement of new frequently pur-

---

*For an excellent review of these techniques, see Green and Srinivasan[12] and Shocker and Srinivasan.[28]

CHART 23-8.   Example of a Perceptual Map[a]

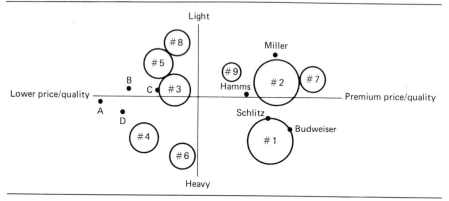

[a]Source: Johnson,[18] (p. 16).

chased consumer products. It is based on a series of market surveys which provide perceptual maps such as the one represented in Chart 23-8, but at different levels. In a first stage, a perceptual map is obtained representing the positions of existing brands and the ideal points of homogeneous market segments. This study provides a basis to analyze the current situation and to generate new product concepts. In a second stage, a new product concept is shown to a sample of consumers, and data are gathered to provide a new perceptual map which includes the perceived position of the new product concept. If the new concept appears to have a market potential, a third survey is made where the physical product is given to a consumer sample for actual use; this provides another perceptual map including the perceived position of the new product after usage.

In estimating the long-run market share of a new product, the PERCEPTOR model uses a classic decomposition between the effects of first trials and repeat purchases. The probabilities of trial and of repeat purchase are postulated to be a function of the squared distance between the positions of an ideal point and of the new brand. They are, however, estimated from perceptual maps gathered at different stages. The probability of trial function is estimated from the perceptual map obtained from consumers exposed to the new concept and from their stated purchase intentions. The probability of repeat purchase is estimated from the perceptual map obtained from consumers having actually used the product and from their stated intentions to repurchase the new product.

Like most new product models, PERCEPTOR provides an estimate of the expected market share of a new product. Being based on the positioning of the new brand relative to existing offerings and to the market needs, it also gives two critical inputs to the formulation of an entry strategy. First, it gives an estimation of the market share obtained by the new entry from each of the existing brands. This estimation of market share transfers is based on relative positions, and the closer the new brand is positioned to an existing offering the more impact it should be expected to have on its market share.

Second, the market share corresponding to alternative positioning strategies can be estimated. When the expected outcome of a positioning strategy is found acceptable, the product characteristics and marketing mix corresponding to this strategy can be determined. In this fashion, the model can guide the modification and improvement of a new product before its introduction.

CONCLUSIONS

New product or market entries are essential to preserve the long-term competitiveness and survival of a firm. The development of adequate entry strategies is also one of the most difficult areas of management as illustrated by the high failure rates reported in the literature. In order to reduce this risk of failure, a complete anticipatory analysis should be systematically performed with the following objectives:

1. Evaluating the factors influencing the future performance of an entry strategy.
2. Identifying improved entry strategies.
3. Providing a detailed knowledge of the situation and of potential threats so that strategies may be more readily modified after entry according to the course of events.

An anticipatory analysis for a new entry should systematically investigate the future evolution of the environment, the firm, the market, and the competition. This investigation should be performed at three levels. In an initial projective phase, the expected evolution of these key areas is determined, assuming that the firm will not undertake a new entry. In a proactive phase, the impact of alternative new entry strategies on the environment, the firm, the market, and the competition is evaluated. Finally, in a reaction analysis phase, the possible reactions of these elements are investigated. Such a systematic approach is necessary to avoid two major pitfalls. The first one is a basic implicit assumption that there is a predetermined evolution of the firm, the environment, the market, and the competition and that a new entry will insert itself naturally in this evolution. This reflects a total reliance on projective analysis and underestimates the direct impact or the reactions that a new entry may generate in a given situation. The second pitfall is the human tendency to select elements of the analysis that support a pre-conceived position on a particular problem. This is particularly likely in new entry decisions which may have significant organizational implications, and some aspects of the problem may remain hidden by default. Not only may this bias the decisions but, in addition, it may leave management unprepared when new events develop during the entry period.

Models have been developed over the last 20 years to assist managers in new entry decisions, and representative examples of these models have been presented. They differ widely in terms of the techniques that they used and the points in the planning process where they can make a contribution. What is more important, however, is to realize for which areas of an anticipatory analysis they can be most valuable and what are their current limitations. The purpose of a new entry model is to assist management in investigating in detail a subcomponent of the situation and in testing alternative strategies, given some simplifying assumptions. The responsibility of the manager lies in having a complete view of the elements influencing the new entry, through a systematic anticipatory analysis, and in exploiting models to get a better understanding of some aspects of the situation when feasible. Not only will this allow him to better appreciate the likely performance of a new entry strategy, but also, and maybe more importantly, it will help him to face new events when they emerge.

REFERENCES

1. Assmus, Gert, "NEWPROD: The Design and Implementation of a New Product Model," *Journal of Marketing*, vol. 39, January 1975, pp. 16–23.

2. Biggadike, Ralph, *Entering New Markets: Strategies and Performance*, Report No. 77–108, Marketing Science Institute, Cambridge, MA, September 1977.

3. Blattberg, Robert and John Golanty, "TRACKER: An Early Test Market Forecasting and Diagnostic Model for New Product Planning," *Journal of Marketing Research*, vol. 15, May 1978, pp. 192–202.

4. Boston Consulting Group, *Perspectives on Experience*, Boston Consulting Group, Boston, 1970.

5. Buzzell, Robert D., Bradley T. Gale and Ralph C. Sultan, "Market Share: A Key to Profitability," *Harvard Business Review*, vol. 53, no. 1, January–February 1975, pp. 97–106.

6. Charnes, A., W. W. Cooper, J. K. Devoe, D. B. Learner, L. Light, L. Pringle, and E. F. Snow, "NEWS Report: A Discussion of the Theory and Application of the Planning Portion of Demon," in *Models of Buyer Behavior* (Jagdish N. Sheth, ed.), Harper & Row, New York, 1974, pp. 296–309.

7. Charnes, A., W. W. Cooper, J. K. Devoe and D. B. Learner, "DEMON: A Management Model for Marketing New Products," *California Management Review*, vol. 11, no. 1, Fall 1968, pp. 31–46.

8. Choffray, Jean-Marie and Gary L. Lilien, *Market Planning for New Industrial Products*, John Wiley, New York, 1980.

9. Claycamp, Henry J. and Lucien E. Liddy, "Prediction of New Product Performance: An Analytical Approach," *Journal of Marketing Research*, vol. 6, November 1969, pp. 414–20.

10. Day, George S., "Diagnosing the Product Portfolio," *Journal of Marketing*, vol. 41, no. 2, April 1977, pp. 29–38.

11. Godet, Michel, *The Crisis in Forecasting and the Emergence of the "Prospective" Approach*, Pergamon Press, New York, 1979.

12. Green, Paul E. and V. Srinivasan, "Conjoint Analysis in Consumer Research: Issues and Outlook," *Journal of Consumer Research*, vol. 5, no. 2, September 1978, pp. 103–23.

13. Harary, Frank and Benjamin Lipstein, "The Dynamics of Brand Loyalty: A Market Approach," *Operations Research*, vol. 10, January–February 1962, pp. 19–40.

14. Hartung, Philip H. and James L. Fisher, "Brand Switching and Mathematical Programming in Market Expansion," *Management Science*, vol. 11, August 1965, pp. 231–43.

15. Henderson, James M. and Richard E. Quandt, *Microeconomic Theory*, 2nd ed., McGraw-Hill, New York, 1971.

16. Hopkins, David S., *New Product Winners and Losers*, The Conference Board, New York, 1979.

17. Horsky, Dan, "An Empirical Analysis of the Optimal Advertising Policy," *Management Science*, vol. 23, 1977, pp. 1037–49.

18. Johnson, Richard M., "Market Segmentation: A Strategic Management Tool," *Journal of Marketing Research*, vol. 8, February 1971, pp. 13–18.

19. Kotler, Philip, William Gregor and William Rodgers, "The Marketing Audit Comes of Age," *Sloan Management Review*, vol. 18, no. 2, Winter 1977, pp. 25–43.

20. Massy, William F., "Forecasting the Demand for a New Convenience Product," *Journal of Marketing Research*, vol. 6, no. 4 November 1969, pp. 405–13.

21. Massy, William F., David B. Montgomery and David G. Morrison, *Stochastic Models of Buying Behavior*, The M.I.T. Press, Cambridge, MA, 1970.

22. Montgomery, David B. and Adrian B. Ryans, "Stochastic Models of Consumer Choice Behavior," *in Consumer Behavior: Theoretical Sources* (Scott Ward and Thomas S. Robertson, eds.), Prentice-Hall, Englewood Cliffs, NJ, 1973, pp. 521–76.

23. Naylor, John and Alan Wood, *Practical Marketing Audits*, Associated Business Programmes, London, 1978.

24. Oxenfeldt, Alfred R. and William L. Moore, "Customer or Competitor. Which Guideline for Marketing?" *Management Review,* August 1978, pp. 43–48.

25. Pessemier, Edgar A., *Product Management: Strategy and Organization*, John Wiley, New York, 1977, Chapter 5.

26. Porter, Michael E., *Competitive Strategy*, Free Press, New York, 1980.

27. Shocker, Allan D., and V. Srinivasan, "A Consumer-Based Methodology for the Identification of New Product Ideas," *Management Science*, vol. 20, February 1974, pp. 921–37.

28. Shocker, Allan D. and V. Srinivasan, "Multiattribute Approaches to Product-Concept Evaluation and Generation: A Critical Review," *Journal of Marketing Research*, vol. 16, May 1979, pp. 159–80.

29. Silk, Alvin J. and Glen L. Urban, "Pre-Test-Market Evaluation of New Packaged Goods: A Model and Measurement Methodology," *Journal of Marketing Research*, vol. 15, May 1978, pp. 171–91.

30. Urban, Glen L., "PERCEPTOR: A Model for Product Positioning," *Management Science*, vol. 21, April, 1975, pp. 858–71.

31. Urban, Glen L., "SPRINTER Mod III: A Model for the Analysis of New Frequently Purchased Consumer Products," *Operations Research*, vol. 18, no. 5, 1970.

32. Urban, Glen L. and John R. Hauser, *Design and Marketing of New Products*, Prentice-Hall, Englewood Cliffs, NJ, 1980.

CHAPTER

24

FORECASTING FOR INDUSTRIAL PRODUCTS

DAVID WEINSTEIN
INSEAD

INTRODUCTION

Forecasting the sales of industrial goods is critically important for a great many organizations. Furthermore, within the firm, forecasting serves as a basis for production, finance, personnel, research and development (R & D), and other related activities. Even though industrial sales forecasting is no different from any other type of prediction—in theory, at least—the use of statistical forecasting methods in this respect is problematical. The majority of industrial sales forecasting activities remain intuitive, complex, and, quite often, highly political.

A review of the relevant literature and extensive field research, involving interviews with numerous managers, show that the likelihood of changing the present practice of industrial forecasting is low. Since personal objectives and, in turn, rewards for achievement are derived from the forecast, salesmen and executives are reluctant to "formalize" forecasting methods. Moreover, the present forecasting procedure provides for information exchange and performance review at various hierarchical levels. These discussions are regarded as an important byproduct of the forecasting process and as being vital for organizational perception of changes in the external and internal environments. Thus, the process itself is as important as the forecast, which explains why the managers interviewed felt that drastic changes in industrial forecasting practice were inconceivable.

Although they reject the use of statistical methods, managers are nevertheless not insensitive to the biases and gamesmanship in their present practices. But rather than drastically change their approach, they prefer to identify its weaknesses and make improvements wherever possible. In other words, they are willing to accept the weaknesses in their own system, since although a changeover to the "statistical alternative" may result in greater forecasting accuracy, the costs in doing so—in terms of existing benefits that would be lost by a change—are prohibitive. The challenge, then, is to help preserve the strengths of current practices and find remedies for issues that are problematic.

The purpose of this chapter is to identify these concerns and propose some practical solutions. In the following sections, the industrial sales forecasting process is identified more specifically. This stereotype facilitates the reader's understanding of both the concepts proposed and their applicability. The "universal weakness"—that is, concerns that are general for most industrial situations—is then discussed, and some practical help is proposed. A framework for analysis is subsequently provided, which is designed to identify and assess specific sources of bias in a given sales forecasting system.

THE TYPICAL FORECASTING SYSTEM

The typical forecasting system for industrial products has three major components: the salesforce composite subsystem, headquarters subsystem, and reconciliation subsystem.[13] The first two subsystems provide their respective inputs into the third, which then assesses both vantage points and combines them into a forecast. As can be seen by the solid lines in Chart 24-1, the process may be iterative. If the reconciliation subsystem fails to yield a forecast (whether by consent or by decree), further rounds of discussion will take place until a forecast is finally obtained. The dashed lines in Chart 24-1 represent informal flows of information and feedback which influence the inputs into the reconciliation subsystem. Explicit information (the solid lines) flowing from headquarters staff to the salesforce may include economic and industrial statistics, likely competitive development, capacity constraints, new product information, and promotional programs. Explicit information flowing from the salesforce to headquarters staff may include developments observed at the level of end users, tactical competitive moves (prices, promotion, etc.,), and manpower constraints. However, a great deal of implicit information flows between the three subsystems, which includes both formal and informal feedback—an example of the latter

CHART 24-1. The Typical Forecasting System for Industrial Products

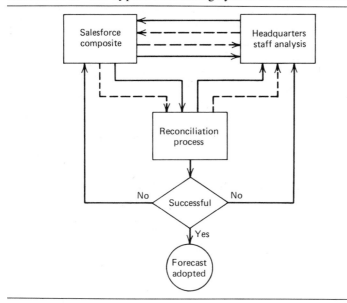

is the perceptual impressions from past experience of working members of other subsystems.

A distinction should be made between two forecasting situations in which the subsystems in Chart 24-1 play rather different relative roles: The strategic and tactical forecasts. The first involve new projects (e.g., new product or new territory), whereas the latter relate to an ongoing activity. Another distinction is that a "strategic" forecast usually implies a change in the allocation of resources (e.g., investment or divestments) and is long-term oriented (see Chapter 6 in this handbook). Tactical forecasting is generally under the control of headquarters and is derived from strategic scenarios and information such as (1) selected salesperson and executive opinion, (2) macrostatistical projection of useful variables (e.g., regional surveys of buying power or sales, by Standard Industrial Classification[3]), and (3) feedback from local test markets.

The role of the salesforce is rather limited where strategic forecasting is concerned, and the approaches adopted are more analytical, based on methods that are discussed both in this handbook and elsewhere.[1,5,22]. However, tactical forecasts are based on opinions of both headquarters staff and salespersons with field experience—all of whom are deeply involved in the sales process. The salesforce would usually rely on an intuitive approach yielding a "salesforce composite." This forecasting activity provides the basis for plans in production scheduling, finance, and other functions; and it also determines, to a large extent, personal objectives for the salesforce—that is, sales quotas. Achievement of the latter is the basis for personal evaluation, financial bonus, and stature in the organization, but at the same time, this encourages biases in forecasting—as discussed later in this chapter.

A brief discussion of the salesperson's role may be of some help in the assessment of the strengths and weaknesses of the "salesforce composite" in industrial marketing. The determinants of this role are the product and the market. The typical industrial salesperson deals with a mix of complex products and a restricted number of clients. The latter require not only different technical specifications and logistical services, but also, in this environment, a deep understanding of the client's business and organization. Thus the salesperson should be technically competent and have a good personal rapport with members of the customer organization. Reliance on the salesperson's intimate knowledge of his or her territory is indispensable in industrial marketing, and because of this invaluable experience, the salesperson's judgment is very influential.

There is evidence that the performance of statistical forecasting routines is superior to that of human judgment.[9,20,21,35] However, while the former would only detect and evaluate structural changes a posteriori, the salesperson may be able to identify such changes on a more timely basis—once enough evidence of impending change has been accumulated. More importantly, the salesperson's credibility vis-à-vis his or her superior is high, for the former is held personally responsible for his or her actions. For these reasons, the sales forecasting process for industrial products has resulted in a "bottom-up" procedure which is well rooted and difficult to change. One obvious strength of such a system is the benefit of the salesperson's alertness and ability to interpret phenomena he or she encounters in the field. Another advantage of the salesforce composite is the scrutiny to which the information is subject as it travels through the system via different parties each with his or her own vantage point. These two strengths are the basic reasons for the longevity of salesforce composites in the forecasting of industrial sales.

The remainder of this chapter is based on an investigation of numerous salesforce composites in a cross section of industries and countries.[13] The research methodology involves a careful analysis of the systems, based on three waves of interviews across numerous organizations,[18] thereby resulting in identification of the actual operating system.

ISSUES OF CONCERN

The salesforce composite is a product of human judgment. While Taylor (see Chapter 31) discusses in detail the problems it entails, in this chapter the primary concern is with the interaction between the individuals responsible for this judgment. Such interaction includes exchange of information, on the one hand, and negotiation and gamesmanship on the other. Clearly, since the sales forecast influences the outcome of the negotiations for objectives, and thereby various rewards, the parties will tend to introduce their own biases. The nature of such biases depends on the particular business, its reward system, the individuals involved, and the nature of their interaction. A systematic framework of analysis is proposed below, which helps the manager to identify and assess the problems specific to his or her own situation. However, three universal problems with industrial sales forecasting systems are considered first, and an attempt is made to provide some practical answers. These three issues are (1) expertise and contagion errors, (2) loss and distortion of valuable information, and (3) confusion between forecasts and objectives.

1. Expertise and Contagion Errors

The cornerstone of the forecasting process is the individual salesperson's experience and insight into his or her client's territory. The salesperson prepares a forecast on this basis, and discusses it with his or her superior, who will then prepare a more aggregate forecast, as a function of his or her own experience and observations of past forecasting errors by subordinates. The individual errors of judgment at every level are called "expertise" errors. Staelin and Turner[30] have shown that the smaller the "building blocks" of the forecast, the smaller the aggregate error, for at the territory level errors in different directions will mutually cancel.

The assumption in the above case is that every salesperson prepares a forecast independently. However, this is not always the case, since salespeople communicate with each other and are also exposed to common information provided by staff at headquarters and other sources. In particular, data on the macroeconomic outlook, capacity constraints, and promotional plans might be disseminated by corporate planners. This could cause a "contagion" error,[30] that is, a common forecasting error at individual territory level by all salespeople receiving the same information.

Since the design of sales territories is subject to other concerns, treatment of expertise errors by disaggregation is not always possible. Thus the salesperson's analysis can only be improved by training and consulting activities. The isolation of systematic individual biases, as will be described later, is also of considerable importance. These activities may be carried out on a continuous basis, within the interaction of the salesperson and his or her superior, in the form of evaluation of past forecasts. Furthermore, headquarters staff may provide periodic training programs or conferences which are aimed at reducing expertise errors.

Contagion errors should be considered in light of the common information that is disseminated. Consider, for example, the case of production capacity constraints when communicated to the salesforce. A common reaction by the salesperson is to try to change his or her sales mix in order to avoid negotiations with those responsible for allocation and possibly disappointing clients. Thus, the communication of capacity constraints may eventually cause overcapacity and restrict previous expansion plans based on strategic market potential. Contagion errors may be caused by pessimistic industry and economic forecasts, thereby creating "self-fulfilling prophecies." A similar effect may be caused by the "reputation" of other parties to the sale. For example, past problems of quality control or customer service may be extrapolated by the salesforce, causing a downward bias in the forecasts of the affected products.

Sensitivity to formal and informal information causing contagion error is essential. In discussing this problem with managers, it was noticed that the amount of formal attention to contagion errors varies. One practical approach is for every manager who collects subordinates' forecasts to aggregate them and communicate his or her perception of percentage contagion error and possible causes. As the process moves up the system, more evidence may be accumulated regarding contagion errors.

Another approach to the problem involves sequencing and experimentation. Corporations have been studied which require every salesperson and manager to provide an independent forecast before being exposed to common information; after exposure the person is allowed to correct his or her forecast. In one case, at a time when contagion errors were suspected to be serious, an organization withheld information from a sample of salespeople and managers in order to provide a "control" for these errors. This approach is clearly extreme, but it does show the amount of concern and effort that some firms are willing to invest.

2. Loss and Distortion of Information

A system of humans who are collecting, transmitting, transforming, and interpreting information is expected to filter and distort information. Senior executives, when interviewed, were content to "live with the problem," since too much information flowing directly to them would clutter their overview. However, the same executives complained that there are some data that salesforce composites lose. Retention of this data, they say, would improve decisions which are based on the sales forecast. More specifically, these concerns may be divided into three categories: absorption of uncertainty, loss of data for segmentation analysis, and loss of timely strategic information.

Absorption of Uncertainty

The end result of a salesforce composite forecast is usually a predicted value for future sales. Since this is the outcome of numerous deliberations, it is considered by the users (i.e., senior executives) to be fairly reliable. However, they also know that uncertainty is associated with the forecast, and awareness of the extent of such uncertainty is invaluable, because it is this factor that represents the risk of the strategy being pursued. This is important in two ways, for both overestimates and underestimates result in either real or opportunity costs which management has to take into consideration.

Three different approaches may be used to conserve risk information within the system: conditional forecasting, three-point forecasts, and key account reporting. Under the first approach, rather than submit forecasts, salespeople and their superiors present scenarios in which explicit assumptions are made about customer behavior and needs, competitive activity, environmental forces, and internal company resources. The combination of these variables into several possible scenarios allows management to assess the up or down side risk involved. The second approach requires the submission of three estimates (pessimistic, most likely, and optimistic), rather than a single sales figure prediction. There are two benefits of this approach, the immediate one being that the possible risk is determined by the range of variation. The second is the possibility of simulating various scenarios and obtaining the "risk profile" of the periods' sales using the Monte Carlo simulation. This profile would allow management to trade off reward and risk according to their risk preference.[16]

Finally, a "key account" approach might help ascertain the possible risk. Under this method, certain accounts are monitored closely, and their unexpected behavior is "flagged." Accounts in this category may be opinion-leading companies, or disproportionately large customers whose behavior may considerably influence sales. In order to utilize the information from such accounts, past experience must be accumulated before explicit extrapolations can be made.

Lack of Data for Segmentation Analysis

The forecasting system generally follows an ongoing segmentation based on past strategies (e.g., byproduct, geographic region, or end use). Due to changes in the competitive environment it is in the interest of product managers to study possible scenarios under alternative segmentation schemes (e.g., in terms of the account size, purchasing organization types, technology, etc.). As shown in Chart 24-2 the salesperson prepares a forecast by aggregating forecasts of individual accounts. In turn, his or her manager aggregates the forecast across the sales territories. Concern has been expressed, particularly by product managers, that after this aggregation they no longer have access to the raw data at a disaggregate level. However, unless they undertake a special research project, a study of the consequences of alternative segmentation schemes is impossible. If raw data by accounts were available on a timely basis, management could anticipate the emergence of new segments and act on it earlier than is presently the case. This problem may be solved by retention of account characteristics, sales records, and forecasts in a data bank accessible to management. The data would be collected from forecasting forms, call reports, and purchase orders which are periodically filled out by individual salespeople.

Although the principles behind such a data bank are simple, its successful utilization has several prerequisites. First, the notion of segmentation analysis and periodic forecasting by various segmentation schemes should be a "way of life" for managers, so that demand for the service will persist. Second, the salesforce should be motivated to provide the information periodically, since the resulting analysis would eventually be to their benefit. Finally, the proper infrastructure for building and maintaining this computer-based system should be available.

Loss of Strategic Information

Because industrial marketers rely heavily on salesforce composite forecasts, they take the risk of failing to detect certain strategic changes that might be taking place in the field. Two research experiments may be cited here. In one, the appearance of a new, significant, and competitive product was not reported by many salespeople who had been formally trained to do so.[26] In the other, information which salespeople obtained from their customers was not correct, and in fact, systematic changes in client perception had been taking place, with salespeople being unable to detect them.[14]

The measures companies may take to correct these flaws are mainly in the form of positive and constructive feedback to the salesforce, coupled with periodic training. Whereas rewards for especially valuable information may be offered, a system could also be designed to provide for the flow of qualitative information alongside quantitative forecasts. In other words, a "strategic observation" section may be required as an appendix to each quantitative forecast. This section would include the manager's observation and, in addition, significant subordinate observation. Clearly, some information will always be suppressed or distorted; however, the importance of this problem can be minimized by providing the format for reporting strategic observations and giving positive feed-

CHART 24-2. Steel Products Company: Annual Sales Forecast

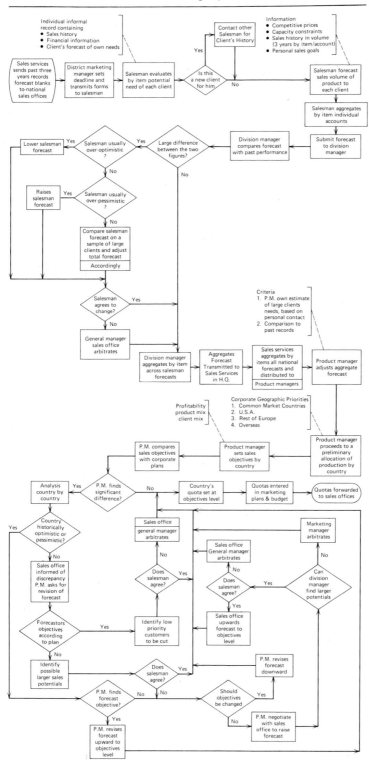

back when such information is actually transmitted. The more isolated and helpless the salesperson feels, the less motivated he or she will be to help the organization change in the face of phenomena the salesperson can actually observe in the field.

3. Confusion Between Forecasts and Objectives

The forecast is an integral part of the management system because it serves to set targets and objectives for the individuals concerned. However, as the literature shows, objective setting is a rather complex process.[24,25] The more related it is to the forecast, the more difficult it is to avoid bias in anticipation of objectives.[8,20] Furthermore, the greater the role of the individual in setting his or her own objectives, the higher the likelihood of his or her bias.[35] The amount of bias and its direction depend on the way objectives are used by the organization. In practice, then, an understanding of one's use of objectives would help identify the bias introduced by subordinates into their forecasts. The following represents a brief discussion of the three purposes of setting objectives, that is, to reduce fluctuation and ambiguity, to determine performance norms, and to provide motivation.[8]

1. *Reduction of Fluctuation.* This phenomenon generally takes place through the superior delegating and the subordinate committing himself or herself to a prespecified achievement. As the forecasting process makes its way up the system, more aspects of the external and internal environment are considered, and possible responses are given to various uncertainties. Moreover, the process of aggregation should cause a mutual cancellation of the "expertise effect" errors, thus smoothing out the forecast. Finally, related to this benefit is the opportunity for sharing opinions about the business, evaluation, and feedback.[6]

2. *Norms of Performance.* When both the subordinate and his or her superior know what is expected of them—each at their respective level —they can reduce their role ambiguity. Since in many cases good performance is rewarded, whereas failure may entail penalties, there is a need to determine precisely what is meant by "good performance."[12,32,33]

3. *Motivation.* The level at which an objective is set is in itself of motivating value. For example, a sales quota just above a salesperson's own estimation might stimulate him or her to work harder, whereas one set far beyond his or her abilities might be demoralizing. Likewise, given a progressive bonus structure, a target just under the salesperson's capability might be stimulating, whereas one set too low might result in complacency.[10,11]

Finally, the response of individuals to the objective setting process will depend on their culture and individual profile.[6,7] Furthermore, their forecasts will be affected by the nature of their interaction with others. In other words, the salesforce composite process is one of "rolling negotiations" (salesperson with his or her superior, and the latter with his or her own superior). The next section provides a framework for assessing some of the biases involved in the process.

FRAMEWORK FOR ANALYZING BIAS

The "bottom-up" nature of the process for industrial sales forecasting, coupled with the inseparability of forecasts and objectives, necessitates a need for negotiation at every interface in the system. Replications of studies of salesforce composite systems in the United States, Europe, and South America show that at every subordinate–superior interface, the process follows five steps[34] (see Chart 24-3).

1. Benchmark Forecast Preparation

The "benchmark forecast" is the individual's assessment, based on four types of input: (1) formal system inputs, (2) raw disaggregate forecasts, (3) information search, and (4) past forecasting experience. Once such a benchmark is determined, bias behavior and negotiation tactics enter the process.

Formal System Inputs. The individual communicates on a continuous basis with parties, in and out of the organization, who assimilate, transmit, and manipulate information.[28] The routing of this information, and its content, will depend on the organization's structure and the strategy it pursues. For example, multiproduct and multimarket oriented organizations usually use some form of matrix organization, with managers of products or markets relating laterally to the salespeople and providing strategic information.

Raw Disaggregated Forecasts. At every level, there is an input of disaggregate data that was compiled at an earlier stage. Salespeople will first obtain or perform forecasts for their largest clients or key accounts. Similarly, a sales manager will obtain forecasts for the salesperson reporting to him or her, as well as for the accounts the manager handles directly. The reason this category should be distinguished from the previous one is that it is used as a filter for the former, as shown in Chart 24-3.

Information Search. Interviews with numerous salespeople and their managers reveal that each individual searches for information beyond these formal organizational interfaces. The more experience an individual has, the larger his or her informal network of information. This may include colleagues in competing firms, professional associations, trade

CHART 24-3. The Rolling Negotiation Concept

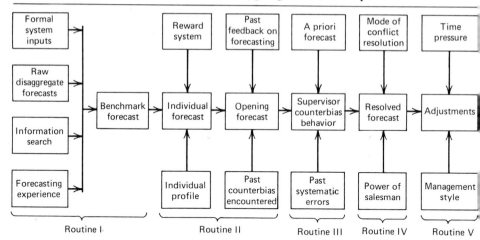

publications, and so on. The more uncertainty the individual faces, the more he or she will rely on such an informal search.

Past Forecasting Experience. The way the individual processes information also depends on his or her past experience with the procedure. On the one hand past forecasting performance bears on the process in terms of the size of past errors and their direction (however, "error" in this case is the difference between the benchmark forecast in the previous period and actual results, rather than the formally agreed forecast). On the other hand, the individual's formal training is also a part of the experience. Salespeople who receive such formal education may utilize certain information and methods quite differently from those who do not. This variance may be observed across different companies, as well as within the same organization.

2. Individual Bias Behavior

As we have seen above, three factors contribute to the individual bias that is applied to the benchmark forecast: the need for reducing fluctuations, norms of performance, and motivation. There are also two types of bias that influence behavior: income maximizing[31] and approval seeking.[8] Obviously the profile and experience of the salesperson will influence his or her behavior. Our investigations show that younger, inexperienced salespeople display greater optimism than their more mature and weathered counterparts.[19] Similarly, within multinational corporations, Italian forecasters, for example, were found to be more optimistic than their French colleagues. Finally, the initial forecast may

be used as an "opening position" in a negotiation process whose end result may be influenced by many nonmarket or customer-oriented
factors.

3. Superior Counterbias Behavior

When a subordinate or an executive submits a forecast to his or her
superior, the latter will naturally evaluate the prediction. The criteria
that he or she will inevitably seek are his or her own observations on
the territory or product in question. Variation between the subordinate
and superior's forecast will trigger a comparison of analyses and attempts
to reach a concensus on "what will happen." However, the superior also
inspects the submitted forecast from another vantage point: in terms of
past forecasts from this person. Thus, if the subordinate has shown signs
of overoptimism in the past, the superior will try to temper it, and vice
versa.

4. Resolution

Bridging the gap between a supervisor's and a subordinate's forecast
differs across companies and cultures. Concensus seeking has been observed in some companies, in comparison with downwards imposition
in others. Moreover, a systematic difference emerges according to the
role of the salesperson. The salesperson in industrial marketing is a
"boundary person" with his or her role extending to the organizations
of both his or her employer and clients.[29] This role gives the salesperson
power over the performance of his or her function. The more important
the role of the salesperson in the mix of marketing activities, the more
complex is his or her task and hence the greater is the power he or she
possesses.

5. Authorization and Adjustment

Following the resolution, any changes in objectives must be disaggregated
down to the individual salesperson level. Most companies interviewed
felt that concensus seeking is desirable; however, because the forecasting
process is rather time consuming, downwards imposition may have to
take place at some point in time. Some companies, once they impose
forecasts from the "top down," take steps to explain the forecasts provided and offer formal qualitative feedback, while others do nothing of
the sort.

This model of the interface between a subordinate and his or her superior during the forecasting process is of a "rolling" nature. It applies
to all interfaces as the process flows up the hierarchical system. The
framework is useful for analysis of the interface in relation to past

forecasting performance. Thus certain systematic deviations may be identified as a function of untempered pessimism or optimism. Similarly, the analysis may identify good quota negotiators (who minimize sales quotas in order to maximize their bonus) as a source of variance between sales forecasts and actual performance. Clearly, different sources of bias will play different roles in various industries, companies, cultures, and times. The role of this framework is to help both the superior and subordinate to analyze their past forecasting (either separately or together) with the help of a systematic agenda. Efforts to implement this model in quantitative estimation of bias for various individual situations are underway.

The Forecasting Manager

As a result of universal weaknesses, specific biases may be treated in a different way. Rather than consider the issues in isolation, the forecasting process may be seen as a clear organizational responsibility. Since forecasting errors, especially those caused by "contagion," are somewhat costly, minimizing them justifies an organizational investment. One corporation with which the author is familiar has appointed a "forecasting manager." The task of this executive is to improve the system, information flow, and training of salespeople, as well as to train managers in the use of forecasting methods—both statistical and intuitive. A major side benefit which has occurred in this case is the ongoing feedback to individual forecasters on the quality of their forecasts, which can thus point to personal biases. Another reaction reported in the literature[15] is the active reward to the salesperson for good forecasting performance. However, more experience is needed before these findings can be generalized for all organizations.

CONCLUSION

This chapter has shown that due to the importance of the *process* of forecasting in an industrial product's company, statistical forecasting methods are not practical or attractive to management. The salesforce composite system, which is actually the dominant method for short-term forecasts, contains numerous situation-specific biases as well as several universal weaknesses. Several ways of treating the weaknesses in order to minimize their effects have been proposed, together with a framework that models the interface, occurring at various levels, between the forecaster and his or her superior. This framework should help in the analysis of a particular situation and in the assessment of some of the biases present. Having observed numerous systems of industrial sales forecasting, the author is convinced that not all biases and weaknesses have been captured by his analysis. However, since the advantages of this forecasting practice override the weaknesses, it is felt that industrial forecasts are condemned to continue the struggle with this double-edged sword. If an organization attempts to correct weakness and continues its effort to treat biases systematically, then methods of improvement will emerge and the "faults" of using humans rather than statistical routines will be minimized.

REFERENCES

1. Armstrong, J. Scott and Michael C. Grohman, "A Comparative Study of Methods for Long-Range Market Forecasting," *Management Science*, vol. 19, no. 2, October 1972, pp. 211–21.

2. Ayal, Igal and Zvi Maimon, "Sales Demands on Security Brokers," *Industrial Marketing Management*, no. 7, 1978, pp. 161–69.

3. Barr, J. J., "SIC: A Basic Tool For Marketers," *in The Environment of Industrial Marketing* (Donald E. Vinson and Donald Sumplinpaglia, eds.), Grid, Inc., Columbia, OH, pp. 114–19.

4. Busch, Paul, "The Sales Manager's Basis of Social Power and Influence Upon the Salesforce," *Journal of Marketing*, vol. 44, Summer 1980, pp. 91–101.

5. Chambers, John C., Satinder K. Mullick and Donald D. Smith, "How to Choose the Right Forecasting Technique," *Harvard Business Review*, July–August 1971, pp. 45–74.

6. Churchill, Gilbert A., Neil M. Ford and Orville C. Walker, Jr., "Organizational Climate and Job Satisfaction in the Salesforce," *Journal of Marketing Research*, no. 13, November 1976, pp. 323–32.

7. Churchill, Gilbert A., Neil M. Ford and Orville C. Walker, Jr., "Personal Characteristics of Salespeople and the Attractiveness of Alternative Rewards," *Journal of Business Research*, 1979, pp. 25–50.

8. Cyert, Richard M. and James G. Morih, *A Behavioral Theory of the Firm*, Prentice Hall, Englewood Cliffs, NJ, 1963.

9. Dalrymple, Douglas J., "Sales Forecasting Methods and Accuracy," *Business Horizons*, December 1975, pp. 69–73.

10. Darmon, René Y., "Salesmen's Responses to Financial Incentives: An Empirical Study," *Journal of Marketing Research*, no. 11, November 1974, pp. 418–26.

11. Darmon, René Y., "Setting Sales Quotas with Conjoint Analysis," *Journal of Marketing Research*, vol. 16, February 1979, pp. 133–40.

12. Donnelly, James H., Jr. and John M. Ivanovich, "Role Clarity and the Salesman," *Journal of Marketing*, no. 39, 1975, pp. 71–74.

13. Farley, John U., James M. Hulbert and David Weinstein, "Price Setting and Volume Planning by Two European Industrial Companies: A Study and Comparison of Decision Processes," *Journal of Marketing*, vol. 44, Winter 1980, pp. 46–54.

14. Fouss, James H. and Elaine Solomon, "Salespeople as Researchers: Help or Hazard?" *Journal of Marketing,* vol. 44, Summer 1980, pp. 36–39.

15. Gonick, Jacob, "Tie Salesmen's Bonuses to Their Forecasts," *Harvard Business Review*, May–June 1978, pp. 116–23.

16. Hertz, David, *New Power for Management*, McGraw-Hill, New York, 1969.

17. Hogarth, Robin M. and Spyros Makridakis, "Forecasting and Planning: An Evaluation," *Management Science*, vol. 27, no. 2, 1981, pp 115+.

18. Hulbert, James M., John U. Farley and John A. Howard, "Information Processing and Decision Making in Marketing Organizations," *Journal of Marketing Research*, no. 9, February 1972, pp. 75-77.

19. Marvin A. Jolson, "The Salesman's Career Cycle," *Journal of Marketing*, no. 38, July 1974, pp. 39-46.

20. Lowe, E. A. and R. W. Shaw, "An Analysis on Managerial Biasing: Evidence from a Company's Budgeting Process," *The Journal of Management Studies*, vol. 5, February 1968, pp. 304-15.

21. Mabert, Vincent A., "Statistical Versus Salesforce Executive Opinion Short Range Forecasts: A Time Series Analysis Case Study," *Decision Sciences*, vol. 7, 1976, pp. 315-18.

22. Makridakis, Spyros and Steven C. Wheelwright, *Forecasting: Methods and Applications*, John Wiley, New York, 1978.

23. Minzberg, Henry, Dwen Raisinghani and André Théoret, "The Structure of Unstructured Decision Processes," *Administrative Science Quarterly*, vol. 21, June 1976, pp. 246-74.

24. Modig, Jan-Eric, "Forecasting Gamesmanship," *Managerial Planning*, September-October 1976, pp. 24-26.

25. Oliver, Richard L., "Alternative Conceptions of the Motivation Component in Expectancy Theory," *in Sales Management: New Developments from Behavioral and Decision Model Research* (Richard P. Bagozi, ed.), Marketing Science Institute, Cambridge, MA, 1978, pp. 40-63.

26. Robertson, Don H., "Sales Feedback on Competitors' Activity," *Journal of Marketing*, no. 38, April 1974, pp. 69-71.

27. Shapiro, Benson P., "Account Management and Sales Organization: New Developments in Practice," *in Sales Management: New Developments from Behavioral and Decision Model Research*, (Richard P. Bagozi, ed.), Marketing Science Institute, Cambridge, MA, 1978, pp. 265-94.

28. Simon, Herbert A., "Applying Information Technology to Organization Design," *Public Administration Review*, May-June 1973, pp. 268-78.

29. Spekman, Robert E., "Organizational Boundary Behavior: A Conceptual Framework for Investigating the Industrial Salesperson," *in Sales Management: New Developments from Behavioral and Decision Model Research* (Richard P. Bagozi, ed.), Marketing Science Institute, Cambridge MA, 1978, pp. 133-44.

30. Staelin, Richard and Ronald E. Turner, "Error in Judgmental Sales Forecasts Theory and Results," *Journal of Marketing Research*, vol. 10, February 1973, pp. 10-16.

31. Steinbrink, John P., "How to Pay Your Salesforce," *Harvard Business Review*, July-August 1978, pp. 111-22.

32. Teas, Kenneth R., John G. Wacker and R. Eugene Hughes, "Path Analysis of Causes and Consequences of Salespeople's Perceptions of Role Clarity," *Journal of Marketing Research*, no. 16, August 1979, pp. 355-69.

33. Walker, Orvill C., Gilbert A. Churchill, Jr. and Neil M. Ford, "Organizational Determinants of the Industrial Salesman's Role Conflict and Ambiguity," *Journal of Marketing*, no. 30, January 1975, pp. 32-39.

34. Weinstein, David, *Analysis of Salesforce Composite Systems*, paper presented at TIMS International Conference, Athens, July 1977.

35. Wotruba, Thomas R. and Michael L. Ludow, "Salesforce Participation in Quota Setting and Sales Forecasting," *Journal of Marketing*, vol. 40, April 1976, pp. 11-16.

CHAPTER

25

FORECASTING FOR SERVICE PRODUCTS

VINCENT A. MABERT
Indiana University

MICHAEL J. SHOWALTER
University of Wisconsin—Madison

I. SERVICE SECTOR

Service Trends

The service sector of the U.S. economy has grown from 54.7% in 1947 to 65.7% in 1975 as measured by current GNP dollars. This growth is largely a result of changes in the economy that have led to a more affluent middle class. The U.S. Department of Commerce, in a recent policy report, comments on this change (ref. 8, p. 12):

> The evolution of the United States into a services economy has significant implications for U.S. economic growth and for economic policy formation. Services are less cyclical than goods, growing less in booms, and falling less in recessions. Services tend to be more labor intensive and to use less capital equipment than manufacturing. Productivity increases have been slower in services, and price increases have generally been more rapid. The average size of service establishments tends to be small, and there has been less concentration of production into large firms than is the case in many manufacturing industries.

In many service industries, growth should continue to increase in the 1980s. Government, communications, and finance are three areas where significant growth will occur.

From all indications, a startling transformation has taken place in consumer markets. Spending for services now accounts for over two-fifths of the average consumer expenditure. Changing consumer demand patterns have not only increased the demand for existing services, but have also fostered the introduction of many new services. Important trends in consumer services include a growing emphasis on security, which has expanded the market for such services as insurance, banking, and investment; greater stress on health, which has led to an increasing demand for dental, medical, and hospital services; and the growth in the number of working women, which has led to greater demand for the services provided by restaurants, clothiers, and day-care centers.

Increased spending for business service has been even more impressive. Business service firms offer the twin advantages of a low overhead and a guarantee of expert assistance. Except for the largest companies, it is impossible to efficiently duplicate the service provided by such firms as A. C. Nielsen, Dun and Bradstreet, or Booz, Allen, and Hamilton.

Service Characteristics and Demand Forecasting

Due to the unique characteristics of services, the nature of forecasting service demand differs substantially from forecasting (physical) product demand. Most important is the fact that consumption and production of serivces occur simultaneously. Unlike a product which may be produced and inventoried to satisfy a future demand, services must be provided whenever the customer makes contact with the service organization or shortly thereafter. If this customer demand has not been anticipated (forecasted), it is quite possible that adequate capacity may not be available and that demand cannot be satisfied. On the other hand, a firm may anticipate a level of demand and provide sufficient capacity, but the demand may not materialize, resulting in underutilized capacity. Thus, demand forecasting accuracy has an impact on the organization's ability to provide customer service and at the same time effectively utilize productive capacity.

The intangible nature of a service creates some technical problems in developing demand forecasts. Whereas a product has a physical presence which can be accurately measured along several dimensions, the definition of a "unit of service" is far more difficult to quantify. The "quantity" of service received by a customer depends on the customer's expectations and needs. Due to the vagary of consumer behavior, the same set of activities may be provided to two customers, but the service (benefit) received will be different.

Much of the service demand forecasts must be specified in units of a critical input to the service system rater than in units of output. For example, a hospital may forecast demand for service in terms of number of patients admitted with the knowledge that each patient will require differing amounts of medical care and will receive differing levels of service; or, the U.S. Postal Service may forecast service demand in terms of number of letters to be received knowing that some will require more sorting than others and differing levels of service will be provided each letter (time interval until delivery). Thus, the emphasis on *what* must be forecast has changed. For products, the emphasis is on forecasting demand in terms of dollars or volume of *output* required from the manufacturing system; with services the forecast is of the dollars or volume of *input* which initiates the service output. These surrogate forecasts of service demand must be considered cautiously whenever management decisions are made based on them, since they may not accurately reflect the levels of productive capacity or service output actually required.

The product life-cycle concept applies to services as well as products. For those services which have a simple technology base and/or require minimal capital investment, the product life cycle becomes an important element in developing short- and intermediate-term forecasts of service demand. Most services are not patentable (although some services can be copyrighted) and are subject to copying by competitors. If the operating system to provide the services requires no new technology, competitors can quickly and easily provide the same service; or, if the underlying technology is labor intensive, new service organizations can easily enter the industry (i.e., real estate firms, business consulting services). Services with any of the above characteristics tend to experience a life cycle significantly shorter than the average life cycle for other services and most products. For such services, short- and intermediate-term demand forecasts must explicitly account for dominance of the life-cycle pattern on demand.

A final characteristic of services which may affect the forecasting of demand is the need for customer contact with the service system. If the customer must interact with the productive system to receive a service the proximity of the productive system to the customer becomes important. The potential demand for service is a function of the location of the service facility relative to a particular customer market. This results in demand forecasting activity that is service-facility specific. If customers in a market area cannot be attracted to a service facility, there is no need to forecast potential customer demand. A *product* can be expanded into other market areas on a regional or national basis simply by expanding the distribution system for that product. To expand the market area for a *service* that requires customer interaction, however, necessitates the addition of another service facility in the new market area. Thus, demand forecasting for service will tend to be service-facility focused, and total demand forecasts will be aggregated from the individual facility demand forecasts.

Demand Forecasting Requirements for Decision Making

Managerial decision making in service organizations is concerned primarily with the relationship between demand and capacity. As mentioned above, it is impossible to inventory services in advance of demand; therefore, management seeks to make decisions regarding demand and capacity that maintain an equilibrium between them. Any imbalance between demand and capacity is undesirable from an efficiency perspective, since imbalance results in either unsatisfied (lost) demand or underutilization of capacity. Thus, management centers its attention on the problems of (1) managing the demand for services, (2) managing the capacity of the service organization, or (3) managing both demand and capacity. Although management could most effectively achieve balance by modifying both demand and capacity simultaneously it is unlikely that they influence both equally. Generally, management has greater control over the capacity level in both the long range and short range. The degree of control exercised over demand for services may vary considerably from one organization to another depending on the strength of an organization's marketing program and the nature of the market environment. Similar to "physical" products, demand for services may be viewed as controllable by the organization over the long range but may be relatively uncontrollable in the short range. The latter is the period when it is most difficult to achieve balance in service products organizations.

Solving this balance problem generally requires a considerable variety of informational inputs. One type of input commonly required to solve these problems is some forecast of future demand. It should be expected that the same form of forecasted demand data would not be suitable to analyze and evaluate each problem situation. In reality, the nature of the forecasted demand information requirements will differ substantially from one setting to another. It is expected that each forecast must emphasize different *components* of demand to facilitate good decision making.

Problems relating to the management of demand for services can be classified as either *demand identification* or *demand manipulation* problems. Demand identification problems focus on the determination of market opportunities for the service organization. Market opportunities include unsatisfied demands for existing services as well as unsatisfied demands for which the organization currently provides no service. Chart 25-1 presents a matrix of components of forecasted demand information required to analyze each of these demand identification problems.

The second category of demand problems relates to the need for demand manipulation. It is likely that there may not be sufficient demand to efficiently operate the service organization's productive capacity. A variety of techniques could be used by management to

CHART 25-1. Components of Forecast Demand Information for Decision Making

	Service Life Cycle	Market Share	Location of Demand	Average Demand	Maximum Demand	Minimum Demand	Trend of Demand	Seasonality of Demand	Pattern of Demand Variability
I. Demand identification									
A. Market opportunities									
1. New markets		X[a]		X			X		
2. Existing markets	X	X			X				
B. Service opportunities									
1. New services	X	X		X	X				
2. Existing services	X	X		X	X				
II. Demand manipulation									
A. Services mix packaging		X		X	X	X			
B. Services pricing	X	X		X					
C. Services backordering					X			X	
D. Services adv./promo.		X				X	X		
E. Services substitutibility		X		X		X			X

[a] The marked categories specify those components of forecasted demand information that must be explicitly recognized and measured.

modify market demand in the short run, such as service mix packaging, pricing, back ordering, advertising/promotion, and service substitution. The problem facing management is to determine the potential for these techniques to modify demand. Chart 25-1 identifies those components of forecast demand information considered essential to determine the relative impact of each demand manipulation technique.

Decision making regarding capacity management in a service organization can be similarly classified as either capacity identification or capacity manipulation. Capacity identification problems focus on determining what capacity additions, deletions, and/or modifications are required to satisfy future market requirements. These capacity identification problems focus on determination of the facility(s) size (in terms of input/output rate), the location of the facility(s), and the process technology(s) to be utilized at each facility. Chart 25-2 presents a matrix of the components of forecast demand information required to analyze each of these capacity identification problems.

If management is not able to manipulate demand to maximize efficiency of the service organization, it may be necessary to modify capacity of the productive system in order to balance demand and capacity for optimal efficiency. The capacity manipulation classification includes those techniques that management can use to modify capacity in the short-run such as hiring/firing employees; employing full-time, part-time, and/or temporary employees; reassigning employees among different tasks; use of overtime; and subcontracting another service organization's capacity. The problem for management is to determine the potential of these techniques to modify capacity to achieve a balance of demand and capacity. Chart 25-2 identifies the critical components of forecast demand necessary to determine the relative value of each capacity manipulation technique.

No attempt has been made to identify what specific forecasting techniques should be used to generate forecast demand information for use in evaluating each problem. For a given problem there may be a number of equally acceptable forecasting methodologies. By definition, an acceptable forecasting methodology is one that adequately represents the *components* of demand necessary to provide analysis of the specific area of interest to management.

In the next sections, a forecasting structure is presented and illustrated with case study examples. At this point, you will see how various techniques can assist in the forecasting problem.

II. FORECASTING SERVICE PRODUCTS

Structuring Forecasts

The prediction of future events requires that a structure be formulated to depict the forecasting occasion. There are two terms that need to be

CHART 25-2. Components of Forecast Demand Information for Capacity Decision Making

	Service Life Cycle	Market Share	Location of Demand	Average Demand	Maximum Demand	Minimum Demand	Trend of Demand	Seasonality of Demand	Pattern of Demand Variability
I. Capacity identification									
A. Facility(s) size	X[a]		X		X		X		
B. Facility(s) location		X	X	X					
C. Facility(s) technology	X			X				X	
II. Capacity manipulation									
A. Labor force size				X			X	X	X
B. Labor force composition			X	X		X		X	X
C. Labor force task reassignment flexibility									X
D. Labor force overtime					X			X	X
E. Subcontracting					X		X	X	X

[a]The marked categories specify those components of forecasted demand information that must be explicitly recognized and measured.

435

clearly defined: market demand and sales forecast. These two concepts are not the same and have unique implications. Kotler (ref. 6, p. 99) defines them as:

> *Market demand* for a product/service class is the total volume which would be bought by a defined customer group in a defined location in a defined time period under defined environmental conditions and marketing effort.

> *Sales forecast* is the expected level of company sales based on a chosen marketing plan and assumed environmental conditions.

In a macro sense, market demand attempts to measure all potential sales, while company sales forecasting represents a micro activity. Whether an analyst views a forecasting problem from a macro or micro perspective may depend upon his or her assigned mission. For example, McDonald's Corporation planners are concerned about the trends (demand identification) in consumer eating patterns and would attempt to forecast market demand for different types of food service that might be implemented (demand manipulation). However, a unit manager would execute a micro sales forecast to determine material and work force requirements on a day-to-day basis (capacity manipulation). This would involve both demand identification and manipulation. Identification would recognize the normal daily traffic, while manipulation could reflect the presence of a coupon promotion program currently in effect.

This example highlights another issue in forecasting, and that is the appropriate forecast horizon. In many situations, long-range forecasts tend to be estimates of market demand while short-range forecasts deal with company or division/unit sales forecasts. The long-range versus short-range forecasts reflect two extremes on the forecasting continuum. Generally, the long-range forecast attempts to account for the actions of many market forces, such as competition, consumer awareness, political and economic conditions, and technological trends. In the short range, the forecasting problem focuses mainly on the marketing efforts of the organization and does not account in an explicit way for macro factors like technology and political conditions.

Forecasting procedures range from simple approaches to highly sophisticated statistical methods. There are three data base sources for systematic forecasting:

1. Past behavior or historical data.
2. Current behavior.
3. Future intentions.

The development and implementation of a good forecasting system may rely on a combination of all three of these items rather than just one. Also, the system may rely on a number of techniques such as regression and exponential smoothing.

Forecasting Practice

A small survey was conducted of 17 service organizations in Indiana to determine the techniques and the data sources utilized in forecasting a variety of requirements. Ten of the respondents were financial institutions (banks and savings and loans) and the remaining organizations were academic institutions.

Chart 25-3 presents the information collected for the financial institutions. The sample covers large to small organizations based on assets and number of employees. The exhibit indicates that a variety of data sources are used, mostly relating to business and economic activity. All use their forecasts for budgeting, and the larger ones also use forecasts for portfolio management. Larger institutions use computers for forecasting, while there is no trend apparent as to the number of individuals involved in the forecasting function. Most forecasting is on an annual and/or quarterly basis. Some longer range forecasting is present for four of the 10 surveyed.

Chart 25-4 presents the results for the academic institutions. Again, the size of the schools varies from 32,000 to 1100 students. A variety of data sources are used. They mostly relate to demographic information on population. Time series analysis is very popular as a technique in this area. A broad range of uses are presented such as facility planning, budgeting, curriculum design, placement, and faculty sizing.

This group of 17 organizations may not be a representative sample, but it does indicate a number of aspects that we have discussed. First, there is no single technique that can be universally applied to the forecasting needs of the service organizations. Second, the data base requirements vary substantially. Some firms are very sensitive to economic activity, while others react to population factors. Third, forecasts are used for a variety of functions from budgeting to work force sizing. And fourth, the organizational commitment has no patterns. In some cases it is highly centralized, with a well-defined group responsible for forecast creation. In other cases, it is decentralized, with major departments/divisions executing this function.

Forecasting is a unique activity for each organization, and any attempt to provide an optimal approach would be foolish. Rather, a broad structure based on forecast horizon and demand dynamics is suggested. The next two sections illustrate the complexity of forecasting service products.

III. LONG-RANGE FORECASTING

Long-range forecasts are critical inputs for the strategic planning in any organization. Very few services lend themselves to easy forecasting. In some cases, demand may be rather stable in pattern, and competitive

CHART 25-3. Financial Institutions

Size Assets (Millions $)/ Employees	Techniques Used	Input Variables	Forecast Uses	Time Range	Computerized	Number of People
2296/2480	Simulation Regression External sources	Prime rate Economic indicators	Portfolio management Budget	3–5 years Yearly Quarterly	Yes	4
1900/2135	Regression External sources	Prime rate Economic indicators	Portfolio Budget	Yearly Quarterly	Yes	3
320/240	Regression External sources	Prime rate Economic indicators	Portfolio Budget	Yearly Quarterly	Yes	5
280/280	Time series	Historical economic indicators	Budget	3 years	Yes	2–3
270/300	Regression Time series	Prime rate Economic indicators	Portfolio Budget	Yearly Monthly	Yes	2–3
225/275	Time series	Historical data Economic indicators	Portfolio Budget	5 years Yearly	—	5
175/170	Time series	Historical data Economic indicators	Budget	3–5 years Yearly	—	2–6
104/130	Time series	Historical data Economic indicators	Budget	Yearly Quarterly	—	5
70/170	Time series	Historical data Economic indicators	Budget	Yearly Quarterly	—	5
20/45	Time series	Historical data Economic indicators	Budget	Yearly Quarterly	—	5

CHART 25-4. Academic Institutions

Enrollment	Employee(s)	Techniques Used	Input Variables	Forecast Uses	Time Range	Computerized	Number of People Involved
32,000	5,400	Time series Some regression	No. of H.S. grads. Individual trends Retention rates	Budgeting Facility plan	10 years 2 years Yearly	Yes	All admin.
30,000	10,000	Regression Executive opinion	Birth rates College going rates Economic data	Facility plan Budgeting Faculty planning	10 years 2 years Monthly	Yes	All admin.
17,108	2,500	Time series Trend analysis	Census figures Live births	Financial & facility plan.	10 years 5 years 2 years	Yes	6–12
11,000	4,000	Time series Regression	Census data, Number of H.S. graduates	Facility plan. Budgeting Cash flow plan.	5 years 2 years	Yes	4
6,500	3,000	Time series Jury Planned size	Census data National trends Private education costs	Faculty plan. Curriculum Size/facility	4–8 years facilities 2–3 years budget	For control only	All admin.
4,300	700	Time series	Birth rates Proj. number of 18-year-olds Government stats.	Income-budget Faculty plan Curriculum	10 years 3 years Yearly	No	7–10
1,100	150	Time series Company representatives	Govt. statistics (from Center for Technical Assessment)	Faculty plan. Recruitment Academic prog./placement Budget	10 years 5 years	Yes	9

relationships nonexistent, as exhibited in public utilities. However, in a vast majority of markets, demand is not stable from year to year, and sales forecasting becomes a critical factor in the firm's success.

The long-run forecast helps chart the course an organization will take in positioning itself in the marketplace. Major decisions on new service products, equipment and facility acquisitions, and manpower planning evolve from the long-run forecasts. For example, electric utilities now require a 10-year lead-time to bring generating capacity on-line. This long lead time requires extensive advance planning if enough capacity is to be available without overbuilding.

Long-run forecasting can be executed in highly dynamic or relatively stable markets. *Highly dynamic* market forecasting involves identifying a market need/want (segmentation), matching the service delivery system to the need/want (competitive edge), and then making the market aware of the available service (advertising/education). One quickly sees that this forecasting situation is intimately involved with the market planning effort of the firm, and a greater emphasis on demand manipulation exists.

On the other hand, *stable* market forecasting implies little or limited effort expended to influence/educate the market about the service. Rather, stable market forecasting assumes that fundamental demand already exists for the service (i.e., electric power, waste disposal, health care, etc.), little service differentiation is present, and advertising/education have minimum impact on consumer behavior. Thus demand identification is the focus that becomes an input to capacity manipulation. Let us look at two case studies of long-range forecasting that involve both identification and manipulation of demand and capacity.

The Ministry of Tourism of the Turks and Caicos Islands wanted to know the potential of their islands as a vacation spot and how to attract more visitors in the highly dynamic leisure-time market. A program was conducted involving six phases.[9] First, a task force gathered all available historical data on previous visitors to the island, studying the embarkation and disembarkation documents completed by every nonresident visitor to the island during the most recent 18-month period. Second, the information was analyzed to determine the geographic and demographic composition of previous visitors. A profile of previous visitors was established and was used to determine travel behavior with reference to: geographic origin, sex, time of year, average length of stay, purpose of visit, and method of transportation. These facts were analyzed to establish an 18-month pattern, with particular emphasis placed on identifying patterns within the peak or off-peak seasons.

Third, historical visitor profiles were developed to target the prospective audience. Three potential markets were identified: the seasonal island travelers, owners and operators of private aircraft, and scuba divers. Fourth, advertising campaigns were targeted for metropolitan markets, four of which were determined to be highly seasonal (New York, Detroit, Boston, and Washington, D.C.) and four of which were determined to be relatively nonseasonal (Miami, Tampa, Jacksonville, and Orlando). Markets with additional potential were then identified for similarities in the profile. Fifth, results of the program were measured through a continuing arrival survey.

Finally, the results of the research are being used to modify existing efforts in charting future programs with the greatest potential. The results of this program have been quite successful. Since the program was introduced in 1977, the number of nonresident visitors to the island has increased by approximately 85% from 6500 in 1977 to approximately 12,000 in 1978.

Thus, one quickly sees that the success of forecasting market potential for services is intimately involved in the nature of the service being utilized and the identification of the target market. The forecasting function is clearly linked with identifying customers' wants (demand identification), making the customer aware of available service (demand manipulation), and delivering quality service (capacity management).

The second case study involves a more mature market. Stable market forecasting occurs in markets where the service is homogeneous, well established, and experiences little volatility. Utilities (electric, gas, water, disposal, phone, etc.) are examples of a stable market service. In most cases the forecasting task focuses on demand identification rather than manipulating demand through an extensive marketing plan. This is not to say that market planning does not exist. The market plan, however, has minimal influence in changing consumer behavior since stable markets are generally saturated and exhibit little base for predicting future behavior for capacity decisions. Often statistical procedures like regression and time series analysis are used to analyze historical data to determine patterns, relationships, and trends.

The forecasting of peak power consumption for Duke Power[4] illustrates the stable market forecasting system, where decisions on long-range capacity are critical. The historical total power consumption is divided into two parts: base load (BL) and weather responsive (WR) usage. The base load represents the system requirements influenced by general public and economic activities, but excluding weather effects. The weather response usage in the summer represents a tremendous increase in demand due to air conditioning. However, this weather response effect lasts for a short period. Knowing the base load and weather response consumption is important in capacity planning so that "brown-outs" are minimized.

The daily summer consumption data were analyzed. Scatter plots of degree-hours between noon and 4:00 P.M. were examined to identify unusual characteristics and outlines. With the data screening completed, regression was used to estimate the relationship of power consumption and weather effects. The model is

$$MW = a + b \text{ (deg-hour)} \qquad (25\text{-}1)$$

where MW = actual peak power consumption for the particular summer afternoon and

deg-hour = weighted difference from 67°F between 12:00 noon and 4:00 P.M.

Using equation (25-1), a was interpreted as the base load for that year. The weather-related component was the product of b times the 20-year average value of degree-hours for a particular day. This approach was applied on the summer months data for 12 years (1963–74) to obtain the base load and weather-effect relationships over that period. These data became the bases for projecting future levels of each component. A trend line was fitted to each component to reflect the appropriate growth rate to obtain a forecast. Chart 25-5 illustrates the overall approach.

However, blindly using the trend projections may be inappropriate. At this point the forecaster must use judgment, since future behavior does not always follow past experience. With energy conservation becoming an important issue in the early 1970s, Duke forecasters recognized some adjustment was necessary. To account for this trend, all future forecasts were modified by the ratio of actual 1974 to forecasted 1974 consumption. This modification reflects the conservation activities taking place at that time.

These case studies illustrate two different approaches to long-range forecasting. The forecasting of tourism business required both demand identification and manipulation. Identification in this case involved profiling vacationer characteristics and island services. With identification completed, manipulation involved promotional activities in user markets to attract vacationers. On the other hand, Duke's approach was to identify demand and forecast future consumption levels with regression. No attempt was made to explicitly manipulate demand in planning for coming years. Duke will manipulate capacity to satisfy expected demand.

IV. SHORT-RANGE FORECASTING

The short-range forecasting problem presents an extremely challenging area for services. Since services cannot be readily inventoried, the service delivery system must match supply and demand. In those situations where appointment systems or customer backlogging are possible, the

CHART 25-5. Long Range Forecasting of Load Requirements at Duke Power Company

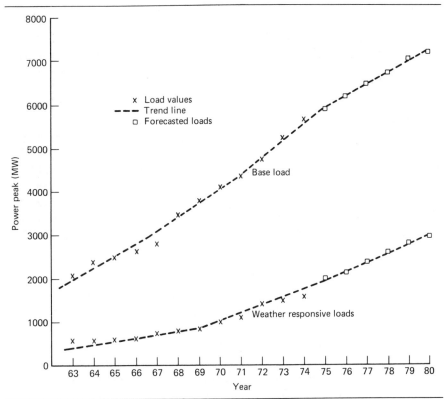

matching problem becomes easier. However, the appointment system is the exception rather than the rule. With demand randomly occurring, the service delivery system must intentionally overstaff to provide a reasonable level of service. Determining the appropriate level of staff influences the service level, operating costs, and profitability of the organization.

Short-range forecasting occurs at the operating unit level. Generally, capacity manipulation is the primary focus, like determining expected traffic for staffing needs for a branch bank or fast food establishment. At this point, the forecast horizon may be a day or week, and the forecast interval may be an hour or less. Telephone operator[3,5] and flight crew scheduling[1] are two decision areas that utilize very short planning horizons and intervals.

The market forces present may yield either a dynamic or stable forecasting situation. The dynamic situation requires that the forecasting system respond to rapidly changing events like promotional programs and new service introductions. In such a setting, there is less reliance on historical information and more weighting of managerial judgment for forecast generation. The Burger Chef FAST System (Forecasting and Labor Scheduling Technique) illustrates the dynamic short-range forecasting activity in the fast food industry.

FAST is a transaction-based (as opposed to sales-dollar-based) forecasting system which relies on a moving average of customer transactions for the past 10 weeks (excluding exceptional days) to forecast transactions for the week, day, and hour. This forecast is then converted to a work force schedule by day and hour.

A forecast of total expected transactions for the week is determined by the unit manager. Historical transaction levels are reviewed with a major concern for transactions 1 year ago on the same week and last week's transactions. This provides an indication of seasonal swings and current trends. A third factor considered by the unit manager is exceptional events occurring during the week near the unit. Such things as special coupon programs, fairs (county and state), school activities, and so on, all can have an impact on demand. The weekly forecast is entered into the FAST program, and an hourly labor schedule for the entire week is produced.

Chart 25-6 illustrates one day (Thursday) of the weekly report for one unit. In the upper-left corner, management's expected weekly transactions are displayed. Based on historical daily patterns, using the 10-week moving average model, this figure is then broken down into expected transactions by day and percentage of total weekly demand for Thursday. The remainder of this report provides information regarding expected hourly transactions, the work force needed, and a summary of labor standards.

At Burger Chef, the unit manager is an integral part of the forecasting function. He or she reviews historical demand to provide a base estimate. This base may then be modified to reflect exceptional conditions that may be present during the coming week. In this situation the unit manager accounts for the dynamics of the fast food market when making the forecast. Other service industries experience more stable demand patterns which influence the type of forecasting system. In such a setting, greater reliance on a mechanical system is possible, as illustrated by the following Chemical Bank case study.

At Chemical Bank,[2] the short-range forecasting system concentrates on the paper flow problem of the back office. The operations group is under pressure to meet deadlines for transit checks—checks drawn on other banks and cashed at Chemical Bank. Before checks can be sent to the Federal Reserve or correspondent banks for collection, they must be encoded, proofed, microfilmed, sorted, and bundled. Transit checks missing the appropriate dispatch time mean lost availability to the bank.

CHART 25-6. Daily Forecast Prepared By Burger Chef FAST System

| REPORT ID 8771501 | DIST: 32 AREA: 030 | BURGER CHEF SYSTEMS INC. | AREA MGR: J.D. HAYMAN | DAY |
| RUN DATE 07/06/79 | FOR PERIOD 04 WEEK 4 | HOURLY LABOR SCHEDULE | WESTERN INDIANA DIST. | 5 |

RESTAURANT 0875 WALNUT STREET   THURSDAY   GRILL

WK FORECAST TRAN 4,229
DAILY TRANS 660
DAILY % OF WK 15.6%
AVG DAILY TRANS 625

	07	08	09	10	11	12	01	02	03	04	05	06	07	08	09	10	11	12	01
TRANS PER HR	0	0	0	1	29	109	149	74	38	32	34	43	46	32	31	31	11	0	0
% PER HR	.0	.0	.0	.1	4.4	16.5	22.6	11.2	5.8	4.9	5.1	6.5	7.0	4.8	4.7	4.7	1.7	.0	.0
UNITS/TRANS	.0	.0	.0	.8	2.9	3.1	3.1	3.0	2.5	2.3	3.0	3.6	3.2	3.0	3.0	2.8	2.4	.0	.0
TOTAL UNITS/HR	0	0	0	1	84	338	462	222	95	74	102	155	147	96	93	87	26	0	0
CREWING:																			
FRONTLINE	.0	.0	.0	.0	1.1	2.9	3.7	2.0	1.3	1.2	1.2	1.4	1.5	1.2	1.1	1.1	.5	.0	.0
DINING ROOM ATTEND	.0	.0	.0	.0	.0	.0	.0	.0	.0	.0	.0	.0	.0	.0	.0	.0	.0	.0	.0
DRIVE THRU	.0	.0	.0	.0	.0	.0	.0	.0	.0	.0	.0	.00	.0	.0	.0	.0	.0	.0	.0
DRINK DRAWER	.0	.0	.0	.0	.0	.0	.0	.0	.0	.0	.0	.0	.0	.0	.0	.0	.0	.0	.0
COORDINATOR	.0	.0	.0	.0	.0	.0	.0	.0	.0	.0	.0	.0	.0	.0	.0	.0	.0	.0	.0
BACKLINE	.0	.0	.0	.0	.9	3.0	3.5	2.0	1.0	.8	1.1	1.5	1.4	1.0	1.0	1.0	.3	.0	.0
HRLY TOTAL	.0	.0	.0	.0	2.0	5.9	7.2	4.0	2.3	2.0	2.3	2.9	2.9	2.2	2.1	2.1	.8	.0	.0

DAILY TOTALS:

TOTAL HRS	38.7/50.0
FOOD PREP	2.7
OPEN/PORTER	3.5
CLOSE	3.0
SCHEDULED HRS	47.9/60.0
ALLOWED MANHES	66.0
STO MGMT ADJ HRS	8.0 PER

Therefore, the determination of the appropriate staffing level (capacity manipulation) requires good forecasts.

A variety of projection methods, such as three-parameter exponential smoothing and the Box–Jenkins approach, were investigated as predictors of daily volumes and proved inadequate. Projection techniques assume that the time series behavior is equally spaced over time. That is, all changes in the workload level occur at equally spaced intervals. For example, those individuals conducting weekly or biweekly transactions have behavior patterns that are equally spaced in time because they occur every five or 10 operating days. However, the banking environment is more complex, since many individuals' transactions are controlled by calendar dates, which are not equally spaced over time due to the unequal number of days in a month. Also, the presence of holidays provides additional influences that affect daily volumes. To overcome the deficiencies of the projection techniques, an alternate approach using regression was investigated; it was subsequently implemented for management's use.

An initial investigation indicated that week day, calendar day, month, and holidays all had an impact on workloads. These four classifications of variables were identified as potentially important in predicting daily volumes at Chemical Bank. They were obtained through data analysis and experience. The authors stress that experience and familiarity with the banking industry were important in identifying the potential variables in the model. This was especially true with the new holiday variables. For example, the presence of a federal holiday caused increased workloads before and after the holiday.

A multiple regression model was developed as the most appropriate method to model daily volumes for the variables identified. The identified variables represented temporal effects that reflect behavior shifts between one period and another. Therefore, a series of dummy zero-one variables were required that were turned on and off for the appropriate day being predicted. Two years of daily data were used to estimate the model, given by:

$$\hat{V}_t = \alpha_0 + \alpha_1 x_1 + \alpha_2 x_2 + \cdots + \alpha_n x_n \qquad (25\text{-}2)$$

where $\hat{V}_t$ = volume forecast for day t, measured in pounds of checks,
$\quad\quad \alpha_0$ = estimated constant,
$\quad\quad \alpha_i$ = estimated coefficient for impact of event type i, and
$\quad\quad x_i$ = A zero/one variable indicating the absence/presence of event i (i.e., Monday, third month, day after Christmas, etc.).

To keep the model current, it is updated once a month. The most recent month's data are added to the master data set, while the oldest data are removed. The coefficients are then reestimated. The model utilizes

CHART 25-7. Shift Scheduler Output

Shift Start–Stop	Type of Employee	Shift Schedule for 77/12/5 No. of Employees	Empl. Hrs.	Hrs. Avail. for Work	Machine Hrs.
3:00–10:30	Part-time	4	30.0	25.4	24.4
4:00–10:30	Part-time	47	305.5	254.0	243.9
4:00–9:00	Part-time	33	165.0	147.3	141.5
Total		84	500.5	426.8	409.7

Time Period	Work Left from Prev. Per.	New Work Avail.	Total Work	Total No. Exp.	Capacity	Work Left Over	Capacity Excess or Shortage
1:00–1:30	0	24,090	24,090	0	0	24,090	−24,090
1:30–2:00	24,090	4,087	28,177	0	0	28,177	−28,177
2:00–2:30	28,177	5,884	34,061	0	0	34,061	−34,061
2:30–3:00	34,061	15,451	49,512	0	0	49,512	−49,512
3:00–3:30	49,512	16,408	65,920	4	2,096	63,824	−63,824
3:30–4:00	63,824	21,046	84,870	4	2,088	82,782	−82,782
4:00–4:30	82,782	3,855	86,637	84	43,092	43,545	−43,545
4:30–5:00	43,545	3,623	47,168	84	48,216	0	1,048
5:00–5:30	0	44,992	44,992	84	44,100	892	−892
5:30–6:00	892	41,832	42,724	84	44,436	0	1,712
6:00–6:30	0	26,815	26,815	84	44,100	0	17,285
6:30–7:00	0	51,515	51,515	84	44,016	7,499	−7,499
7:00–7:30	7,499	70,213	77,712	84	43,848	33,864	−33,864
7:30–8:00	33,864	54,676	98,540	84	42,168	56,372	−56,372
8:00–8:30	56,372	22,380	78,752	84	41,412	37,340	−37,340
8:30–9:00	37,340	20,350	57,690	84	40,740	16,950	−16,950
9:00–9:30	16,950	10,349	27,299	51	23,919	3,380	−3,380
9:30–10:00	3,380	7,450	10,830	51	24,123	0	13,293
10:00–10:30	0	6,349	6,348	51	24,684	0	18,336

Total volume predicted (in pounds):	1,421
Total volume predicted (in items):	461,364
Total cost:	2,359.61

approximately 30 of the 54 variables identified. In general, the model has provided R^2's around .85, with only minor shifts from that value.

The daily forecasts are then converted to expected half-hour arrivals at the bank using historical arrival percentages. The half-hour forecasts are used as input to a mathematical programming model to determine the appropriate full- and part-time staff. Chart 25-7 illustrates a typical report, showing the number of workers, work hours, work flow, and productivity.[7]

For both case studies, demand identification and capacity manipulation are the primary concerns of management. Both illustrate that forecasting at the operating unit level utilizes a short horizon and interval for planning requirements. When demand is relatively stable, greater reliance on mechanical techniques is possible, as shown at Chemical Bank. However, when demand dynamics are great, more human judgment is present in generating the forecasts of demand.

V. CONCLUSION

This chapter has focused on the forecasting of service products, describing the demand and capacity interaction present in service organizations and the wide variety of approaches that can be taken to generate the forecasted demand. We saw that in stable market environments, formalized techniques, like regression, are used for both long- and short-range forecasting. The forecast focus in stable markets is on demand identification, with management prepared to manipulate capacity. On the other hand, in dynamic markets demand manipulation and human judgment become more important for forecasting.

It is clear that no single technique or set of rules will guarantee good forecast performance. The forecasting system must be tailored to the specific setting and linked into other organizational activities like marketing plans and the data collection system. In this way the forecasting system can adapt and provide useful information.

REFERENCES

1. Baker, E., L. Bodin, W. Finnegan, and R. Ponder, "Efficient Heuristic Solutions to an Airline Crew Scheduling Problem," *AIIE Transactions,* vol. 11, no. 1, March 1979, pp. 37–41.

2. Boyd, K. and V. A. Mabert, "A Two Stage Forecasting Approach at Chemical Bank of New York for Check Processing," *Journal of Bank Research,* vol. 8, no. 2, Summer 1977, pp. 101–7.

3. Buffa, E., M. J. Cosgrove and B. J. Luce, "An Integrated Work Shift Scheduling System," *Decision Sciences,* vol. 7, no. 4, October 1976, pp. 620–30.

4. "Duke Power Company–Revised," Intercollegiate Case Clearing House, Case #9-677-147, Soldiers Field, Boston, MA, 1977.

5. Keith, E., "Operator Scheduling," *AIIE Transactions,* vol. 11, no. 1, March 1979, pp. 37–41.

6. Kotler, P., *Marketing Management,* Prentice-Hall, Englewood Cliffs, NJ, 1967.

7. Mabert, V. A., R. Fairhurst and M. A. Kilpatrick, "An Encoder Daily Shift Scheduling System at Chemical Bank," *Journal of Bank Research,* vol. 9, no. 3, Fall 1979, pp. 173–80.

8. "U.S. Services Industries in World Markets," U.S. Department of Commerce Report, Washington, DC, 1976.

9. Yesavich, P. C., "Where on Earth are the Turks and Caicos Islands," *Resort Management,* September 1979, pp. 22–24.

CHAPTER

_____ 26 _____

LONG-TERM FORECASTS
AND WHY YOU WILL
PROBABLY GET IT WRONG

WILLIAM PAGE
Science Policy Research Unit
University of Sussex

INTRODUCTION

The track record of many long-term forecasts has been pretty dismal and, despite the efforts currently going into long-term forecasting, the underlying approaches remain as before, and so offer little reason for thinking they will produce better results.

This chapter briefly documents the difficulties of long-term forecasting methods, compares their past and present performance, and shows why it is so hard to remedy past methodological weaknesses. In order to be specific, two areas—population growth and metal supply and demand—are used to illustrate the arguments made.

Although there is little hope of increased accuracy in long-term forecasts, it still seems sensible to:

1. Avoid trusting any particular forecasting method, regardless of how convincing it or its results may appear to be.

2. Think seriously about the true significance of recent events; seemingly important events can ultimately prove trivial, and vice versa.

3. Look for reasons why your forecast is likely to be wrong.

4. Look for the implications of their being wrong.

Are long-term forecasts to be trusted, or are they wrong sufficiently often that forecasters are under an obligation to warn users against taking them too seriously? This paper concludes that forecasts have been proved right when they have been pretty vague (especially in the metals field), or when one gives marks to forecasts that proved right but for the wrong reasons (especially in the population field); but that most forecasters who tried to identify anything but the crudest long-term trends generally got it wrong; and, perhaps equally important, they virtually always missed important factors and developments that time showed to be among the most important.

If the forecasting methods that are used today were substantially different from those used in the past, then these findings would be of historical interest only. As it is, this chapter argues that current techniques are essentially the same as those used in the past; the use of computers, for instance, may change the appearance of what is going on, but does little to change the reliance upon judgments of which trends are worth analyzing and which are trivial, and which relationships merit most scrutiny.

OVERALL SUCCESS RATES

Although the aim of a forecaster may not be to predict the future accurately (it may be to warn of possible problems or opportunities, and thus to change the otherwise foreseen future), it is clear that many of the forecasters of the past had accuracy as one of their objectives, and this is the dimension concentrated on in the present chapter. Although there are cases where, for instance, warnings of possible problems were the focus, one usually finds the forecaster then trying to identify ways of living with the problem (such as living with seriously reduced supplies of mineral resources), rather than ways of eliminating the problem; in this case, it suggests they really believed that running out of minerals was virtually unavoidable.

A hindsight review of long-term forecasts for the supply and demand for nonferrous metals,[11] going back to 1910 and up to the mid-1960s, identified around 90 exercises that looked ahead at least 3 or 4 years, and sometimes a few decades, and which between them contained 372 checkable specific forecasts; three major studies are discussed separately. Overall, 68% of these 372 forecasts have been proved correct by time; 84% of those concerned with price were correct and, at the other extreme, 52% of those looking at precious metals (those that looked at precious metal prices come into both categories).

This is surely an impressive record, and one which is improving: 56% of the 132 specific forecasts published up to 1939 have proved right, as against 75% of the 240 published since then. It is impressive if one ignores the vagueness of many of these forecasts, and the view that the prewar world was much less stable (and thus that much harder to foresee). Examples of "correct" forecasts include:

1910: Chile and Peru may become important copper producers[5]; given the deposits then being found, this was almost a statement of the obvious; no details of quantities or timing were attempted.

1937: The use of zinc alloys in die casting "doubtlessly will expand greatly"[12]; again, a seemingly safe statement, given the vagueness of "greatly."

1940: "A continuation of the upward trend in the consumption of purchased scrap is anticipated in the next decade"[7]; but what of tonnages, prices, which metals, and so on?

1959: "It seems inescapable that there must be a steadily, and probably rapidly, rising demand" for most materials.[2]

As an example of a wrong forecast, this one from 1926 can be cited: "Exhaustion of the known reserves [of many metals] workable at present costs and yields may be quick and disastrous; conservation is a real necessity."[3] What actually happened was that "known reserves" expanded manyfold, so that conservation was not a "real necessity."

Three large exercises did quantify many of their anticipations, and usually got it very wrong. Perhaps the most important was the 1952 Paley Commission in the USA,[14] which looked ahead to the 1970s. For the USA, only 11 (16%) of 70 checkable forecasts of supply or demand were within the range 80–120% of what we now know to be the actual figures as 48 have proved to be overestimates; only 10 of the 51 for other market economies were within this range, and 39 of that 51 were underestimates. If the forecasts of change are taken, rather than of absolute levels, then the outcome has been even more disappointing.

Moving now to population forecasts, we can cite the remarkable accuracy of long-term projections of the U.S. population size during much of the last century. A projection published in 1815[13] was still almost right on for 1860 (31.4 million versus 31.8 million) and was right on for all the intervening decades. Another, published in 1843,[13] erred by only a few per cent over the next 50-odd years—the actual U.S. population in 1900 was put at 76.0 million by the census, and between 74 and 80 million by this 1843 forecast. Other examples can be quoted.

How was this degree of accuracy achieved? Almost certainly it was through the luck of having a real world that developed smoothly. Over the decades starting with 1810, U.S. population grew at 33.3% (total, 1810–20), 34.4%, 32.6%, 35.7%, and 35.3%; thereafter, the rate declined, but again in a relatively smooth manner. Thus events in the real world were most sympathetic to these forecasters, although much of the growth in the second half of the last century was due to immigration rather than to births less deaths (and massive immigration was not well anticipated). This is analogous to the point we made about postwar metal forecasts existing in a more stable world than their prewar predecessors.

Since then, history has been fooling population forecasters (in the United States and United Kingdom, at least). In general, the opposite to what they expected has happened to population size. A British forecast by Honey[6] expected U.K. population size to decline by 14% between 1931 and 1971; it grew by 25%. Male and female life expectancies were actually around 69 and 72 years respectively in 1971, not 62 and 66; there were 49 births per 1000 women aged 15–19 in 1971, not the anticipated 33.9. Countless other authors and forecasts could be cited, but much is summed up by one of the most eminent demographers of the prewar era, P. K. Whelpton:

> Mankind is somewhat more handicapped in its efforts to prolong life than to prevent births. A perfect application of the best-known methods of contraception would accomplish the latter end, but science has not yet indicated how all the present inhabitants of this earth may secure everlasting life.[15]

Strictly speaking, he may have been absolutely right; in practice, it is the opposite situation that mankind has been facing.

LESSONS FROM THE PAST

Whelpton was not an ignoramus unaware of theory, data, or method and putting forward generally denounced views; he was a leader in his field, with the weight of much of history, contemporary evidence, and his peers on his side. The same goes for the Paley Commission on materials, as indeed it does for most of the forecasters whose work has been covered implicitly or explicitly in this review; respectable professional bodies and publishers are unlikely to print work that does not conform to such standards. Yet the conclusion must be that long-term forecasters have a pretty poor track record on what they have forecast.

Neither have they done well on what they did not forecast—on major events that have gone more or less unanticipated. American demographers did not anticipate massive immigration to the United States, and improvements in those things that increase life expectancy have generally been underestimated.[4,9] Mining forecasters have had little if anything to say about some developments that time showed to be crucial influences on the industry—the Great Depression, World War II, nationalization in developing countries, environmental protection, or the energy crisis. In some senses, these developments all had their origins outside the narrowly defined mining industry, and in broader social and political spheres.

It is very difficult to say what has gone wrong (and thus, how to put it right), because any explanations that one can come up with either run against the evidence, or else are difficult to test because of a lack of information.

One might think that our predecessors were a little naive in their ambitions and did not realize the magnitude of the task facing them. Maybe, but it is hard to square this with such statements as this from 1914: "Prognostication is now recognized as a difficult profession."[1]

Was their information base or theory particularly poor? At times, it certainly was (e.g., American demographers during much of the last century often had little to go on). However, it is hard to sustain this as a generalization; demographers and metal forecasters of the 1930s had a wealth of data to draw on and, while they no doubt would have liked more, that often applies today. Theory must have improved to some extent, but the comparison with prewar theory is probably not as marked as might be expected; many of the forecasters whose work we have examined suffered from no lack of theory, much of it very similar to that in use today. The collection of 90-odd metals forecasts were analyzed in terms of their use of very simple apparent methods (e.g., apparent assertions of principles), explicit models (linking together a number of variables), and intermediate methods (extrapolation, curve fitting, etc.). Perhaps surprisingly, more of the studies published before 1940 used explicit models than of those published after 1940 (around 10% as against 5%), and the same is true for intermediate methods (35% against 20%). Whelpton, Honey, and others were in no theoretical vacuum.

Even relatively complex mathematical models were used by population forecasters, usually with little success (contemporary users, please note). Two Americans, Raymond Pearl and Lowell Reed, acquired a reputation for this game. They generated mathematical equations describing population growth over time by studying some animal and then some human populations; they often achieved "excellent" fits. However, they modified their equations[13] when the 1940 U.S. census diverged slightly from a forecast they made in 1922 (actual, 131.2 million; forecast, 136.3 million). Since then, their 1922 forecasts have become wider off the mark—and their revised forecasts, even more so (e.g., 1970 actual, 203.2 million; 1922 forecast, 167.9 million; revised after 1940 census, 160.4 million). One lesson to be drawn from this

and other applications of mathematical models in population forecasting is that, regardless of how well an equation fits past and present
data, the real world is capable of breaking away from the trend in the
future. The degree of conviction of the mathematical analyst does little
to help his or her accuracy, even if it helps the analyst to sell his or
her wares.

Broadening out from this specific point, it can be argued that present-
day forecasting methods are substantially similar to prewar methods.
While this is clearly not true of such aspects as computing power, be it
for handling a relatively straightforward equation or a complex computer model, it is true of the fundamental approaches. Forecasters then
and now have to decide which parameters and relationships are important, and what kind of future they imply, and it is dangerous to assume
that modern tricks have eliminated this fundamental intellectual input.
Many modern methods, such as sophisticated statistical projections,
cross-impact matrices, Delphi, or even computer models can certainly
be useful tools but, as shown by Pearl, Reed, and others, they do not
substitute for intellectual input.

One specific weakness of past forecasts, especially those for metals,
does emerge: they failed to anticipate major forces for change (e.g.,
nationalization or environmental protection) whose roots lay in broad
social and political spheres. This suggests that contemporary forecasters might be wise to search for future sources of such change outside the narrow confines of their main topic of interest. However, as
discussed below, a good imagination can come up with falsehoods as
well as truths concerning the future.

Some of the population exercises point to another conclusion: do
not get too carried away by recent events, because they may not be too
significant. U.K. population projections produced by the Government
Actuary/Office of Population Censuses and Surveys are frequently
revised in the light of short-term trends, and consequently they have
fluctuated markedly. One reason Honey expected contraceptive practices to greatly reduce the U.K. birth rate was that the Church of
England had just withdrawn its objections to them; this event was
perhaps given a significance it did not have. Again, one can sympathize
with the authors of *Resources in America's Future*[8]; while preparing
their section on aluminum, eight car producers moved to aluminum
engine blocks; the seven who then moved back to cast iron did so after
the report had been published.

This question of which contemporary events are significant and
which are trivial has often caused problems, and hindsight offers little
guidance on how to handle it; sometimes, forecasters missed the significance of trends that they dismissed as short-term fluctuations. A hypothetical 1960 forecaster who warned about forthcoming concern over
the environment would have been taking a risk, perhaps a big risk, of

being ignored, and thus of doing himself little good. But events would have proved him right. He might have found equally sound (or unsound) pointers toward a move against mining (foreign or locally owned) in developing countries; certainly, pointers in this direction are there to be found.[10] However, events so far would have proved him wrong on this. There is no obvious way for the present forecaster to know if any current warning of Third World hostility against mining will ultimately show his wisdom and perception, or simply show his inability to understand the industry and ability to waste the time of any reader or client he had.

WHAT TO DO

On the evidence presented here, there may be an argument for long-term forecasters (in demography and metals, at least) to be more cautious as to how their forecasts should be presented. There is certainly a need to warn about the uncertainty contained in their forecasts and the poor predictive record of similar past forecasts. Apart from reasons related to professional vested interests, there is a counter-argument to be found in the view that, without professional forecasters, people who make decisions must then make their own long-term forecasts which can be even less accurate. It is unfortunate that the track record of the profession (full-time or part-time forecasters) is not impressive; obviously, it is inescapable that investors in a mining and smelting project would ideally like to know how much metal they could sell and at what price (given their best efforts on both counts), and that builders of schools would like to know how many children they should be catering for. On the other hand, accuracy is not the most important characteristic of predicting the future. Often forecasting the direction of change in long-term trends can be as important.

If the accuracy can now be provided by long-term forecasters, it would be interesting to know which are the real breaks with history that gives them such new-found ability. If accuracy cannot be provided, it should be made clear to the users of forecasts; this is probably not best done by giving ranges of estimates (because even they have proven wrong in the past), but by openly admitting the problem and, to the extent possible, drawing attention to developments that might upset the forecasts that are presented. Most importantly, however, long-term forecasters should attempt to provide clear and sensible assumptions so that alternative future scenarios can be developed. It must be remembered that even though accuracy is an important factor, it is by no means the only benefit obtained by long-term forecasting.

Finally, a great deal of emphasis should be shifted from forecasting the future to better understanding the present since many signals which are currently available can provide considerable clues for forthcoming changes in trends and patterns in the environment. These signals, however, are often ignored since the emphasis is on forecasting rather than monitoring. After all, it should be remembered that the future, even the long term, begins with the present.

REFERENCES

1. Anonymous, "The Future of Copper Prices," *Mining and Scientific Press,* 8 August 1914, p. 203.
2. Anonymous, "Sunny Days for Copper," *Mining Journal,* January 1959, p. 57.
3. Bain, H. F., "Future demand for metals," *Mining and Metallurgy,* October 1926, pp. 411–15.
4. Cole, H. S. D., et al: *Thinking About the Future,* Sussex University Press, 1973.
5. Douglas, James, "The Future of Copper," *Mining and Scientific Press,* 8 January 1910, p. 87.
6. Honey, F. J. C., "The Estimated Population of Great Britain, 1941–71," *Journal of the Institute of Actuaries,* vol. 68, no. 3, 1937, pp. 324–47.
7. Hordan, L. (ed), "Previews of Tomorrow's Metallurgy," *Mining and Metallurgy,* September 1940, pp. 430–31.
8. Landsberg, Hans, L. Fischman and J. Fisher, *Resources in America's Future,* Johns Hopkins, Baltimore, 1964.
9. Page, William, "Population Forecasting," *Futures,* April 1973.
10. Page, William, "Mining and Economic Development: Are They Compatible in South America?" *Resources Policy,* December 1977.
11. Page, William and Howard Rush, *Long-Term Forecasts for Metals: The Track Record, 1910–1960s,* Occasional Paper 6, Science Policy Research Unit, University of Sussex, April 1978; summarized in *Futures,* August 1979, and in *Uses and Abuses of Forecasting* (T. G. Whiston, ed.), Macmillan, London, 1980.
12. Parsons, A. B. and S. St. Clair, "Outlook for World Consumption of Metals and Fuels," *Mining and Metallurgy,* April 1937.
13. Peterson, William, *Population,* Macmillan, London, 1961.
14. The President's Materials Policy Commission (Chairman: William S. Paley), *Resources for Freedom,* 5 vols., U.S. Government Printing Office, Washington, DC, June 1952.
15. Whelpton, P. K., "The Future Growth of the Population of the United States," in *Problems of Population* (G. H. L. F. Pitt-Rivers, ed.), Kennikat Press, New York, 1932.

CHAPTER

27

EVALUATION
OF FORECASTS

BERT STEECE

University of Southern California

INTRODUCTION

Given the wide range of forecasting models available, the ability to evaluate the performance of these models is essential. Our purpose is to set forth general criteria which address three relevant questions of model evaluation:

1. What measures of forecast accuracy are available?
2. Should a given model be modified to improve forecast accuracy?
3. What criteria other than accuracy need to be considered in selecting a forecasting model?

Our discussion is organized as follows. We begin with a discussion of the relationship between model fitting and forecasting accuracy. Because accuracy is such an important attribute of any forecasting model, we discuss several measures of forecast accuracy. We then discuss model criticism techniques, which focus on improving the forecast accuracy of a given model. Lastly, since accuracy is not the only attribute that should be considered in evaluating alternative forecasting models, we discuss other important evaluation criteria.

THE RELATIONSHIP OF MODEL FIT TO FORECASTING

Ample evidence exists to suggest that a model which fits historical data well does not necessarily forecast well. Thus, it makes little sense to judge the accuracy of a forecasting model in terms of its ability to fit historical data. Unfortunately, this has been the predominant criteria employed in evaluating the accuracy of a forecast model and in selecting among alternative models. We propose to judge a model in terms of its ability to forecast well in a post-sample sense. That is, the goodness of the model is judged not in terms of how well it fits historical data, but how well it forecasts data not used in estimating the model.

A reasonable way to proceed with a post-sample evaluation is to split the data into two sets. The first set of data, called *estimation data*, is used to estimate model coefficients. The remaining data points, called the *prediction data*, are used to measure the forecast accuracy of the model. Some authors refer to data splitting as cross validation.

A variety of data splitting strategies are available. The appropriateness of a particular strategy is dependent on the number of available data points and the length of the forecast horizons. A popular strategy is to use half the sample data to estimate the model and the other half to measure forecast accuracy. Another strategy, double cross validation, splits the data into two subsets. A model is estimated from the first subset and tested on the other subset; we then repeat the procedure with the second subset serving as the estimation data and the first subset serving as the prediction data. An incalculable number of other strategies exist.

MEASURES OF FORECAST ACCURACY

In order to assess the performance of alternative forecasting models, a criterion for forecast accuracy is required. The relevant concept to be considered here is the error loss function. We assume that for every forecast error e_t, there is an associated loss $\ell(e_t)$. In principle, as noted by Granger,[5] we can employ any particular error loss function.

Unfortunately, the specification of an error loss function is usually shrouded with difficulties. For example, the loss associated with forecast errors may be notional rather than real since decisions may not be made as a result of the forecast. In situations where forecasts lead to decisions, the potential consequences of specific errors may be too diverse or complicated to quantify. Given these difficulties, we usually adopt the loss functions implied by common measures of forecast accuracy.

How critical is the choice of a loss function? The answer to this question depends on the objectives. If the objective is simply to rank order alternative models, Granger and Newbold[6] show that the choice of a loss function is not too crucial. On the other hand, if the objective is to measure the extent to which one model is better than other alternative models, the specific form of the loss function is crucial. Steece and Wood[13] provide an illustration of the measurement of comparative accuracy when a particular loss function has been specified.

Summary Measures

The measure most frequently adopted is the root mean square error (RMS):

$$RMS = \sqrt{\frac{1}{m} \sum_{t=1}^{m} e_t^2}$$

where e_t is the forecast error at time t and m is the number of observations in the prediction data set. We prefer RMS to the mean square error since RMS has the same units of measurement as the realized series and is thus easier to interpret. The implied loss function for RMS is quadratic; in other words, the loss associated with an error increases in proportion to the square of the error.

A disadvantage of RMS is that it is an absolute measure, dependent on the units of measure. Relative root mean square error (RRMS) is similar to RMS except that it is dimensionless. RRMS is given by:

$$RRMS = \sqrt{\frac{1}{m} \sum_{t=1}^{m} \frac{e_t}{z_t}^2}$$

where z_t is the realized series. Problems may arise if z_t is near zero. In addition, RRMS suffers from a bias favoring forecasts that are below the realized value. We can demonstrate this by looking at extremes; a forecast of zero can never be off by more than 100%, but there is no limit to errors above the realized value.

A third measure of forecast accuracy is mean absolute error (MAE):

$$MAE = \frac{1}{m} \sum_{t=1}^{m} |e_t|$$

MAE is appropriate whenever the loss function is linear and symmetric.

Brown[2] shows the approximate relationship between MAE and RMS to be:

$$MAE = 1.25 \ RMS$$

Thus, as mentioned earlier, if our objective is to rank order alternative models, the choice between MAE and RMS is not crucial.

Mean absolute percentage error (MAPE) is given by:

$$MAPE = \frac{1}{m} \sum_{t=1}^{m} \left| \frac{e_t}{z_t} \right|$$

MAPE is similar to MAE except that it is a relative measure. As with other relative measures, MAPE suffers from a bias favoring forecasts that are below the realized values. Problems may arise when z_t is near zero.

Theil's U Coefficient

Theil's U coefficient is frequently cited in the literature as a measure of forecast accuracy. Unfortunately, there is some confusion about the coefficient because Theil proposed two different coefficients at different times, under the same symbol.

Theil[14] first defined a statistic measuring the accuracy of the forecasts by:

$$U = \frac{\sqrt{\sum\limits_{t=1}^{m} e_t^2}}{\sqrt{\sum\limits_{t=1}^{m} z_t^2} + \sqrt{\sum\limits_{t=1}^{m} p_t^2}}$$

where p_t is the forecast for z_t. This statistic is bounded between 0 and 1, with 0 being a perfect forecast. Unfortunately, the U coefficient does not provide a good ranking of forecasts. Granger and Newbold (ref. 6, pp. 39–40) give the following example as an illustration. Suppose that

$$z_t = \alpha z_{t-1} + a_t \qquad 0 \leqslant \alpha < 1$$

and consider the predictor:

$$p_t = \beta z_{t-1} \qquad 0 \leqslant \beta \leqslant 1$$

Granger and Newbold show that the limit of U^2 tends to $1 - [2\beta(1 + \alpha)]$ $/(1 + \beta^2)$ which is minimized for $\beta = 1$ rather than for the optimal value of $\beta = \alpha$. This problem arises with any measure of forecasting accuracy that is not a simple function of mean square error.

Because of the problems associated with the U coefficient, Theil[15] suggested an alternative definition:

$$U_1 = \sqrt{\frac{\sum\limits_{t=1}^{m} e_t^2}{\sum\limits_{t=1}^{m} (z_t - z_{t-1})^2}}$$

where e_t represents the one step ahead forecast errors. We observe that U_1 represents a comparison of the sum of squares of the one step ahead forecasts with those of a random walk (naive) model. When U_1 equals unity, the random walk model is as good as the model being evaluated. If U_1 is less than unity, the model being evaluated is better than the random walk model. On the other hand, if U_1 is greater than unity, there is no point in using the model being evaluated since the random walk model produces better results.

Unlike the first measure introduced by Theil, U_1 provides a proper ordering of alternative models. Consider the example by Granger and Newbold which we discussed earlier. U_1^2 approaches $(1 - \alpha)^2 + (\beta - \alpha)^2$ in the limit which is minimized for the optimal value $\beta = \alpha$. Leuthold et al.[8] illustrate the use of the U_1 coefficient in evaluating alternative forecasting models.

The Coefficient of Determination

In regression applications, the coefficient of determination (R^2) is one of the most frequently quoted fitting statistics. The coefficient of determination is generally defined as the percentage of variation of the "dependent" variable, z_t, that is explained by the forecasting model. Recently, Nelson[11] and Pierce[12] have extended this concept to time series models.

Given our earlier admonition about the relationship between model fitting and forecasting, we remind the reader that our interest focuses on the post-sample coefficient of determination as opposed to the more frequently quoted fitted R^2. The post-sample coefficient of determination is given by:

$$R^2 = 1 - \frac{\sum\limits_{t=1}^{m} e_t^2}{\sum\limits_{t=1}^{m} (z_t - \bar{z})^2}$$

where $\bar{z}$ is the post-sample mean of z_t. We observe that R^2 provides a comparison of the sum of squares of the one step ahead forecast errors of a model with those of the mean model. The mean model simply uses the mean of the data as the forecast. R^2 ranges from 0 to 1 with a value of 1 indicating that the forecasted values are perfectly correlated with the realized values. Hosking[7] and Nelson[11] discuss the use of R^2 to test hypotheses about the forecasting model.

MODEL CRITICISM

Model criticism focuses on the question of whether or not there is approximate concordance between the model in its current form and the data. If the data and the model are discordant, then the iterative cycle of model specification, estimation, and criticism is repeated until a suitable model is found. We introduce three techniques for model criticism: (1) a test for structural stability, (2) Theil's decomposition, and (3) a test for information content.

A Test for Structural Stability

By comparing the forecasts of a model with the realized values of the prediction data set, we can determine whether or not the structure of the model is stable over time. This comparison can be accomplished graphically. However, we must exercise extreme caution in interpreting our graph since successive forecasts from the same time origin are positively correlated.

Because this correlation gives a false impression of possible discrepancies, Tiao et al.[16] have developed a formal statistical test for structural stability. If the model is structurally stable, then the set of m subsequently realized values in the prediction data set will not differ significantly from the set of m forecasts made from time origin t. As demonstrated in their paper, a test of this hypothesis is obtained by referring

$$Q = \sum_{i=1}^{m} \frac{a_i^2}{\sigma^2}$$

to a chi-squared distribution with m degrees of freedom. Q is the standardized sum of squares of the one step ahead forecast errors $a_1, a_2, \cdots, a_m$. If the model is not stable over time, we expect Q to be inflated since the forecast errors will be larger than expected. Thus, large values of Q cast doubt on the hypothesis of structural stability. Since σ^2 is not known in practice, a closer approximation might refer

$\hat{Q} = \sum_{i=1}^{m} a_i^2/\hat{\sigma}^2$ to an F distribution with m and $n - p$ degrees of free-

dom, where p is the number of model parameters. However, when m is large, this refinement makes little difference.

Theil's Decomposition

We assume that the realized series has mean and variance:

$$E(z_t) = \mu \qquad V(z_t) = \sigma^2$$

Theil (ref. 15, p. 34) shows that the expected squared forecast error can be decomposed as follows:

$$E(z_t - p_t)^2 = (\mu_p - \mu)^2 + (\sigma_p - \rho\sigma)^2 + (1 - \rho^2)\sigma^2 \qquad (27\text{-}1)$$

where p_t is the predictor series, μ_p and σ_p^2 are respectively the mean and variance of p_t, and ρ is the correlation between p_t and z_t. We note that the expected squared forecast error is minimized whenever the following conditions are satisfied simultaneously: (1) $\mu_p = \mu$, (2) $\sigma_p = \rho\sigma$, and (3) ρ is maximized.

The sample analogue of the expected square forecast error is the mean square prediction error (MSE):

$$\text{MSE} = \frac{1}{m} \sum_{t=1}^{m} (z_t - p_t)^2$$

Thus, the sample analogue of equation (27-1) is

$$\text{MSE} = (\bar{p} - \bar{z})^2 + (s_p - rs)^2 + (1 - r^2)s^2 \qquad (27\text{-}2)$$

where $\bar{p}$ and $\bar{z}$ are the sample means of the predictor and realized series, s_p and s are the sample standard deviations, and r is the sample correlation between the two series. We now divide equation (27-2) by MSE and obtain the following three quantities:

$$U^M = \frac{(\bar{p} - \bar{z})^2}{\text{MSE}}$$

$$U^R = \frac{(s_p - rs)^2}{\text{MSE}}$$

$$U^D = \frac{(1 - r^2)s^2}{\text{MSE}}$$

Theil calls U^M the bias proportion, U^R the regression proportion, and U^D the disturbance proportion.

For an optimal forecast, U^M and U^R should not differ significantly from 0 and U^D should be close to 1. If we consider the regression

$$z_t = \alpha + \beta_{p_t} + \epsilon_t$$

then U^M is 0 when $\hat{\alpha} = 0$ and U^R is 0 when $\hat{\beta} = 1$. If we plot the predicted values against the realized values, the spread of the values around the line of perfect forecasts $z_t = p_t$ yields information on possible forecast model inadequacies. U^M, U^R, and U^D summarize this information.

Theil (ref. 15, p. 29) shows that MSE can be decomposed into a second set of quantities:

$$U^M = \frac{(\bar{p} - \bar{z})^2}{\text{MSE}}$$

$$U^S = \frac{(s^p - s)^2}{\text{MSE}}$$

$$U^C = \frac{2(1 - r)s_p s}{\text{MSE}}$$

Theil calls U^M the bias proportion, U^R the variance proportion, and U^C the covariance proportion. Although it has been common practice to report the decomposition of MSE into U^M, U^S, and U^C, Granger and Newbold[6] show that a meaningful interpretation of U^S and U^C is impossible.

Test for Information Content

One method of assessing the relative information content of alternative models is to combine them into a linear composite of the form

$$z_t = \beta_1 p_{1t} + \beta_2 p_{2t} + \epsilon_t \tag{27-3}$$

where p_{1t} is a set of one step ahead forecasts computed from one model and p_{2t} is the corresponding set from another model. The weights β_1 and β_2 are estimated by ordinary least squares. Since β_1 and β_2 sum to approximately unity for unbiased forecasts, we can express equation (27-3) as follows:

$$z_t = \beta p_{1t} + (1 - \beta)p_{2t} + \epsilon_t$$

We note that a test of the proposition that p_{1t} and p_{2t} are unbiased is provided by the hypothesis that $\beta_1 + \beta_2 = 1$.

Nelson[10] demonstrates that the probability limit of the least squares estimate β is unity if the forecasts from model one subsume all of the information present in the forecasts from the second model. In general, where neither forecasting model subsumes the other, the least squares estimate of β is

$$\hat{\beta} = \frac{s_2^2 - s_1 s_2 r}{s_1^2}$$

where s_1 and s_2 are the sample standard deviations of the forecast errors and r is the sample correlation between the two sets of errors.

Consider the comparison of an econometric model, p_{1t}, with an ARIMA model, p_{2t}. If the composite equation demonstrates that information from the ARIMA model significantly improves a given variable's forecast from the econometric model, we conclude that the econometric model fails to efficiently utilize the larger information set available to it. Given the inefficient use of information, two approaches appear reasonable. First, the forecaster needs to carefully examine the specification of the model. A second approach is to employ the forecasts computed from the linear composite equation. For a discussion of linear composite forecasting, we refer the reader to Cooper and Nelson.[4]

OTHER CRITERION FOR EVALUATION

Thus far, our discussion has focused on the criterion of accuracy. While accuracy is obviously an important attribute of any forecasting model, accuracy is not the only attribute that should be considered in the evaluation of alternative models. Other important evaluation criteria include the characteristics of the information set, the time horizon of the forecast, and the cost of application.

The characteristics of the information set are important because they limit our search for alternative models. These characteristics include (1) the length of the series, (2) the pattern of the data, and (3) the type of forecasting relationship. There are three types of forecasting relationships: (1) single series, in which the series is forecast only from its own past; (2) noncausal, in which the series is forecast from other series which are not really causal but may help to predict; and (3) causal, in which the series is forecast from other series which are causally related. A given model can effectively handle only certain characteristics. For example, simple exponential smoothing models are not effective with seasonal data nor are they effective when linear trend is present. Similarly, ARIMA models require at least 50 observations and are not appropriate when the structure of the data generating process is changing over time.

The time horizon of the forecast also limits our search for alternative models. Some models are appropriately employed for short-range forecasts while other models are more appropriate for medium- to long-range forecasts. For example, exponential smoothing models are appropriate for short-range forecasts; decomposition models and Box–Jenkins models are usually better than smoothing models for medium-range forecasts. Econometric models tend to perform well when the time horizon is medium- to long-range.

The cost of application is a key attribute for any forecasting model. The cost of application is very much dependent on the level of sophistication and generality of the model. Usually, the more sophisticated and general a model is, the higher the cost of application.

In selecting a forecasting model for a given situation, the forecaster is frequently compelled to make a tradeoff between higher cost of application and perhaps a lower level of accuracy or a model that may not fit the particular situation quite as well. Unfortunately, the tradeoff between cost and accuracy is complicated by the fact that more sophisticated models are not always more accurate than simpler and usually less costly models. Certainly, there are many situations where sophisticated models outperform simpler models. However, several studies have concluded that this is not always the case (see ref. 3; ref. 4, pp. 1–32; ref. 9; ref. 10, p. 915). As an example, in comparing econometric and ARIMA forecasting models, Nelson (ref. 10, p. 915) concludes that "the simple ARIMA models are relatively more robust with respect to post-sample predictions than the complex FRB-MIT-PENN models."

CONCLUSIONS

The difficulty that confronts the forecaster is the lack of a single criterion for judging the appropriateness of a forecasting model in a given situation. We have mentioned several criteria whose tradeoffs need to be carefully considered before a model is selected. The relative importance of the various criteria is a value judgment and is dependent on the situation to be forecast and the forecaster's experience with the various models.

REFERENCES

1. Box, G. E. P. and G. M. Jenkins, *Time Series Analysis, Forecasting and Control*, Holden-Day, San Francisco, 1976.
2. Brown, R. G., *Smoothing, Forecasting, and Prediction*, Prentice-Hall, Englewood Cliffs, NJ, 1963, pp. 282–83.
3. Clearly, J. P. and D. A. Fryk, "A Comparison of ARIMA and Econometric Models for Telephone Demand," *Proceedings American Statistical Association*, 1974, pp. 448–50.
4. Cooper, J. P. and C. R. Nelson, "The Ex Ante Prediction Performance of the St. Louis and F.R.B.-M.I.T.-PENN Econometric Models and Some Results on Composite Predictors," *Journal of Money, Credit and Banking*, vol. 7, 1975, pp. 1–32.
5. Granger, C. W. J., "Prediction with a Generalized Cost of Error Function," *Operational Research Quarterly*, vol. 20, 1969, pp. 199–207.
6. Granger, C. W. J. and P. Newbold, "Some Comments on the Evaluation of Economic Forecasts," *Applied Economics*, vol. 5, 1973, p. 37.
7. Hosking, J. R. M., "The Asymptotic Distribution of R^2 for Autoregressive Moving Average Time Series Models When Parameters Are Estimated," *Biometrika*, vol. 66, 1979, pp. 156–57.
8. Leuthold, R. M., J. A. MacCormick, A. Schmitz and D. G. Watts, "Forecasting Daily Hog Prices and Quantities: A Study of Alternative Forecasting Techniques," *Journal of the American Statistical Association*, vol. 65, 1970, pp. 90–107.
9. Makridakis, S. and M. Hibon, "The Accuracy of Forecasting: An Empirical Investigation," *Journal of the Royal Statistical Society* A, vol. 142, 1979, pp. 97–145.
10. Nelson, C. R., "The Prediction Performance of the F.R.B.-M.I.T.-PENN model of the U.S. Economy," *American Economic Review*, vol. 62, 1972, p. 910.
11. Nelson, C. R., "The Interpretation of R^2 in Autoregressive Moving Average Time Series Models," *American Statistician*, vol. 30, 1976, pp. 175–80.
12. Pierce, D. A., "R^2 Measures for Time Series," *Journal of the American Statistical Association*, vol. 74, 1979, pp. 901–10.
13. Steece, B. M. and S. D. Wood, "An ARIMA-Based Methodology for Forecasting in a Multi-Item Environment," *TIMS Studies in the Management Sciences*, vol. 12, 1979, pp. 167–87.

14. Theil, H., *Economic Forecasts and Policy*, North Holland, Amsterdam, 1958, p. 32.
15. Theil, H., *Applied Economic Forecasting*, North Holland, Amsterdam, 1966, p. 28.
16. Tiao, G. C., G. E. P. Box and W. J. Hamming, "Analysis of Los Angeles Photochemical Smog Data: A Statistical Overview," *Journal of the Air Pollution Control Association*, vol. 25, 1975, p. 271.

28

SELECTING AND USING EXTERNAL DATA SOURCES AND FORECASTING SERVICES TO SUPPORT A FORECASTING STRATEGY

TIMOTHY A DAVIDSON
Consultant
Temple, Barker & Sloane, Inc.

JEANNE L. AYERS
Research Assistant
Temple, Barker & Sloane, Inc.

INTRODUCTION

Once an organization has recognized that quantitative forecasts are needed to serve as a base-line foundation to the planning and control process, attention often turns to the acquisition of external data and expert forecasting services. Only the largest organizations attempt to rely solely on in-house staff dedicated to data collection and mathematical modeling. It is difficult to imagine an industry in today's economy whose destiny is self-contained—a microeconomy whose dynamics are not in the least influenced by events, strategies, and evolutionary trends emanating from the outside. If such a condition existed, long-term sales and market forecasts could be accurately determined without outside help. Because the dynamics of one industry are affected by(and affect) those of others, the forecasting task cannot be treated parochially. The economic forecasting industry and many syndicated data services have emerged in answer to this need.

In 1963, a handful of major American firms in quite dissimilar markets (Esso, GE, IBM, Bethlehem Steel, and John Deere) recognized the advantages of working with a national economic model and engaged Lawrence Klein and the Wharton Economic Forecasting Associates (WEFA) to provide such a service. Klein's model was based on the pioneering work of Paul Samuelson in the 1940s. These early patrons were among the first to draw practical benefit from a series of mathematical equations which represented an input–output model of the U.S. economy. By the mid-1970s, Data Resources Incorporated, Chase Econometrics, and WEFA had established a profitable practice providing services to large American industrial organizations. Each of these firms had its own complex national economic model as its raison d'être, and each produced notably different projections.

Significant advances in economic modeling techniques and in survey methods coupled with the utilization of the computer have contributed to the growth of this industry since the early 1970s. Several newly formed forecasting service firms are directing products and services toward the small- and medium-sized organization. Competition and wide-scale use of computerized data delivery systems via timesharing networks promise to provide forecasting services to firms who could not afford such luxuries in the 1970s.

This chapter illustrates the multiplicity of data and forecasting services available to large and small organizations having recognized needs for better planning. It provides guidelines for choosing and using such products and services effectively.

DEVELOPING A FORECASTING STRATEGY

Normally, organizations will decide they want a forecasting system when they observe large deviations from plan, year after year. They observe that some items are out of stock while others are hopelessly overstocked. The short-range production schedule contains more last-minute changes than not. Inventories and service staff are at the wrong geographical location for the demand. The cost of poor planning becomes very evident to the financial controller, to the operations manager, and to the marketing/sales director, resulting in the establishment of a task force to suggest some systematic changes.

After cursory examination of an organization's planning/scheduling process, the task force often finds that different parts of the organization are using forecasts for demand which are:

Prepared informally and independently.

Are heavily laced with judgment.

Have little relationship with past patterns of demand.

Have not received consensus approval by a managerial committee.

Are not periodically reviewed and modified when conditions change.

Many of these deficiencies can be resolved with procedural improvements such as the establishment of a single company forecast and a permanent forecast review committee. Such a committee's responsibilities include the production, review, and distribution of one demand forecast to be used in marketing, manufacturing, and financial planning throughout the organization.

It soon becomes evident that the periodic production of forecast values for each key item is a greater challenge than the procedural deficiencies. It is at this point that the task force recognizes the need to examine both quantitative as well as judgmental forecasting approaches.

Quantitative forecasting is based on a mathematical model of the patterns of demand for an item and/or the relationships between explanatory variables and the demand. In the consumer goods industry, manufacturers can sometimes develop sales forecasts based solely on the patterns of trend, seasonality, and cycle which are evidenced in a product's shipment history. These period-to-period changes reflect the purchase behavior of the wholesaler and/or the consumer. More accurate forecasts of a product's sales can often result from the examination of the mathematical relationship between causal (or explanatory) variables such as price, advertising expenditures, and trade promotion discounts.

PREREQUISITES FOR QUANTITATIVE FORECASTING

Before long, the forecasting task force realizes that to proceed with quantitative forecast model development the organization will need:

Historical data for the items under study.

Forecast data for the causal model inputs.

Technical know-how in statistical forecasting.

Computer programs for time series analysis or for causal model building.

Computer terminals with access to a time sharing computer.

If forecasts are to be systematically generated on a regular basis over a long time, and if the above requisites are available with existing resources, the organization can proceed to develop an in-house system. Such a solution approach minimizes out-of-pocket costs and provides greater control. More frequently, firms look to outside services to provide one or more of the prerequisites and continue to use those services until equivalent in-house resources are provided. The extent to which company resources are expended on the development of a forecasting system should be proportional to the savings derived from the use of better forecasts. That is, successful forecasting should lead to lower costs or greater profits.

The benefits clearly depend on what is being forecasted. For example, reducing inventory safety stocks due to better forecasts can free capital which can then be invested elsewhere. Better forecasts of receipts and disbursements may reduce the need to borrow short-term funds and thus reduce interest expense. If the benefits of forecasting can be expressed in monetary terms, the future stream of benefits and costs can be discounted to obtain the present value of the project. The expected benefits should also be weighted by the probability that they will be achieved. Even precise forecasts will not assure a company a benefit such as cost savings or greater profits. They only have the potential to do so providing that management responds wisely to their signals. When the benefits are nonmonetary, a subjective estimate of benefit values is necessary.

Similarly, the cost of producing forecasts depends on what is being forecast and the accuracy required. In general, the costs include the expense of developing models and computer systems, the costs of data acquisition and storage, and the computer (time-sharing) costs. New users of forecasting systems often underestimate the data acquisition costs and the costs of administering and maintaining the effectiveness of a forecasting system.

With the problem identified and the potential benefits quantified, the task force needs to draw up specifications which define the extent of the forecasting effort.

The level of detail (e.g., regional versus national forecasts), the time horizon, the desired accuracy needed to return the expected benefits, the speed of forecast production and its frequency all need to be specified prior to the development of quantitative models or data systems employing the forecasts.

PUBLISHED FORECAST DATA

Forecasts of macroeconomic variables like population, GNP, personal income, and so on are produced and published by government and private data sources to help organizations in long-term planning. The following U.S. government sources provide macroeconomic forecasts free to the public:

U.S. Bureau of the Census: *Current Population Reports* (Series P-25) contains demographic projections such as population by age, sex, race, and income.

Bureau of Labor Statistics: *Monthly Labor Review* provides national, industry, and occupational projections of the labor force.

U.S. Bureau of Economic Analysis: *Population and Economic Activity* (1972) for the United States and Standard Metropolitan Statistical Areas (SMSA's) contains historical data and projections for population, income (household and per capita), earnings by industry, and production indices for selected industries. *Area Economic Projections* (1974) contains projections of population, employment, personal income, and earnings by industry for states and regions, Bureau of Economic Advisors (BEA) economic areas, SMSA's, and non-SMSA portions of BEA areas.

U.S. Industrial Outlook contains brief trends and a 10-year outlook for over 135 industries.

Private organizations, like the following, produce macroeconomic forecasts of demographic and economic measures at little or no cost to the public:

The Conference Board, *Guide to Consumer Markets,* New York. This provides statistics and graphs on consumer behavior in the marketplace. Projections of population, employment, income, expenditures, production and distribution, and prices are included.

National Planning Association, *National and Regional Economic Projection Series,* Washington, DC. This long-range forecasting service analyzes and projects population, employment, personal income, and personal consumption expenditures for the United States, states, and SMSA's.

Sales and Marketing Management, *Survey of Buying Power.* Contains short-range projections and growth rates for population, households, effective buying income, and retail sales for states, counties, and SMSA's.

Business International's *Forecasting Studies.* Cover trends and key indicators; contain some non-U.S. forecasts.

Commodity Research Bureau publishes demand, supply, and price level forecasts of all major commodities.

Business Week features in their first issue each year a forecast entitled "Industrial Outlook," projecting major industry trends in the coming year.

Trade journals produce short-term forecasts for their industry focus, such as *Electronics'* "World Market Forecasts," *Oil and Gas Journal's* "Forecast/Review," and *Iron Age's* (Chiltons) "Annual Metalworking Forecast."

For a complete list of published forecasts, see *Business Forecasting in the 1980s,* a selected annotated bibliography compiled by Lorna Daniels of Baker Library at Harvard Business School, Boston, MA. This book provides a list of books and articles providing general forecasts as well as the sources of forecasts on specific subjects. In addition, most libraries now have fee-based computerized data retrieval services which can do literature surveys and data searches for published forecast sources.

The major advantage of using published sources is the low cost. The labor required to search, transcribe, and validate the forecast data somewhat offsets the low cost. More important is the fact that these macroforecasts are usually not specific enough for an organization's routine forecasting needs.

DATA SOURCES

All quantitative modeling is based on the examination of historical data collected and arranged in time sequence with the oldest first and the most recent last. Such data are called time series data. Good quality time series data contain no inconsistencies, gaps, or errors. The published forecast data discussed earlier can be thought of as the extrapolations of historic data series into the future. The major premise of all quantitative modeling is that the patterns and relationships that have occurred in the past will remain in the future.

Most organizations require microeconomic forecasting models specific to their industry segment, their company, or their own product/service. The first and foremost data source needed for microeconomic modeling is the organization's own record keeping system. Company records of shipments, financial records of manufacturing, distribution, and selling costs, and other data (such as price discounts, advertising expenditures, etc.) from the core of the management information database which underlies a forecasting system. The validity, the span, and the consistency of the company source data will have a definite bearing on its utility in the development of forecasting models.

When causal modeling is found to be important (e.g., multiple regression modeling of sales demand), then data from external sources are likely to be used for the independent variables. The major sources of external data are the U.S. government, periodicals and journals, trade associations, syndicated data sources, and forecasting service organizations. Of these, the government is the largest source of both demographic and economic information.

Perhaps the most important tools for a forecaster are the various indices to government publications. The most comprehensive index to U.S. government source data is the *American Statistics Index: A Comprehensive Guide and Index to the Statistical Publications of the United States Government,* a Congressional Information Service annual with monthly supplements. This publication indexes every statistic put out by the federal government. It covers social, economic, demographic, and natural resources and some technical/scientific data. Publications are indexed by subject and name, by economic, demographic, and geographic category, by title, and by agency report number. A list of other important indices follows in the bibliography for this chapter.

U.S. GOVERNMENT SOURCES

Major sources of government data the forecaster will find useful include:

U.S. Bureau of the Census which conducts dicennial censuses of population, housing, agriculture, business (retail, wholesale, and service trade), manufacturers, mineral industries, transportation, construction and governments (at both state and local level). This bureau also produces current reports on population estimates and projections, population characteristics, distribution of consumer income and consumer buying intentions, retail and wholesale trade, construction, manufacturing activity and commodity production, foreign trade (exports, imports), housing vacancies and housing characteristics, state and local government finances, employment, and service trades. Most census data are available on computer tape or punched cards.

U.S. Bureau of Labor Statistics collects, processes, analyzes, and disseminates data relating to employment, unemployment, the labor force, productivity, prices, family expenditures, wages, industrial relations, and occupational safety and health.

Bureau of Economic Analysis produces estimates of national income, gross national product, and related series; estimates of income distribution, input–output accounts, and anticipated business investment; analyses of business trends, balance of international payments, and foreign investments and foreign transactions of the U.S. government.

Federal Reserve System and the Department of the Treasury provide financial and business statistics such as the money supply, interest rates, federal finance, securities, credit, and bank and savings institution statistics. International data on liabilities to and claims on foreigners, exchange rates, and trade are also given.

Other useful government publications are detailed in the bibliography of this chapter.

In addition, individual states and local governments can provide regional and local data. Unfortunately, very little consistent data are available from other countries although the United Nations has made strides in securing macroeconomic measures of its member nations.

PERIODICALS AND JOURNALS

In addition to periodicals such as *The Wall Street Journal, Business Week, Forbes, Fortune,* and so on, which keep managers abreast of the most current data and trends, many trade journals such as *Chain Store Age, National Petroleum News,* and *Datamation* publish annual statistical surveys, which are often valuable data sources for the subject industry. To find the names of trade journals arranged by industry, check *Standard Rate and Data Service: Business Publication Rates and Data* or the *Standard Periodical Directory.*

TRADE ASSOCIATIONS

Most industries and markets have some sort of trade association representing them. These associations often act as data collection agencies and publish an assortment of macro statistics covering the trade or industry as a whole. Access to this data may be restricted, however, to association members. A list of major trade associations can be obtained in:

U.S. Department of Commerce's *Directory of Trade Associations: Fact Book.*

Directory of National Associations of Businessmen.

The Yale Research Company's *Encyclopedia of Associations.*

Examples of useful trade association publications include:

Electronic Market Fact Book from the Electronic Industry Association.

Department Store and Specialty Store Merchandising and Operating Results, National Retail Merchants Association.

Annual Statistical Report from the American Iron and Steel Institute.

SYNDICATED SOURCES

Statistics are also published by commercial organizations. Fairchild Publications is one example of a firm that publishes a variety of books containing data on such industries as clothing, appliances, and textiles. Financial data such as stock prices, trading volumes, dividends, company earnings ratios, bond yields, and information relating to credit can be obtained from:

Dun and Bradstreet, Inc., *Dun's Census of American Business.*

Moody's Investors Services.

Standard and Poor's Corporation Statistical Service.

The Fortune Directory by Time, Inc.

Much of this data can be accessed from computerized databases such as Standard and Poor's *Compustat, Value Line,* and Dow-Jones' *News Retrieval Service.* A complete list of data base suppliers for all kinds of data, historical as well as forecast, can be found in:

Computer Readable Databases: A Directory and Data Source Book, 9th ed., by Martha Williams, Knowledge Industry Publications, White Plains, NY, 1979.

Directory of Online Databases (Quarterly), Cuadra Associates, Inc., Santa Monica, CA.

Many market research firms sell data on a subscription basis. The data provided by these organizations is sometimes subjective when dealing with consumer preferences. Other syndicated data suppliers report product movement in specific market areas or through certain channels of distribution (outlets). Much of this market research is based on a sampling (versus a census) of the population and therefore requires certain demographic adjustments to project full market size. Prominent syndicated data firms include:

Market Facts, Inc., NPD Research, Inc., National Family Opinion (NFO), and Market Research Corporation of America (MRCA) for consumer panels and mail survey.

A. C. Nielsen Company and Audits and Surveys, Inc. for retail store audits and product tracking services.

Selling Areas-Marketing, Inc. (SAMI) and Pipeline for audit services covering warehouse withdrawals,

Predicasts, Inc., which abstracts short- and long-range forecast statistics for basic economic indicators and industry forecasts from the news media, periodicals, and journals.

FORECASTING SERVICE ORGANIZATIONS

When in-house statistical forecasting, economic modeling, and system development staff talent is not available, an organization may turn to forecasting service firms for help in establishing forecasting models and a forecasting system. Certain of these organizations maintain large macroeconomic models of the U.S. economy and provide historical data and forecasts to their clients for a fee.

There are many advantages to using such services. They often forecast variables that are not available from other sources. Their forecasting specialists produce unbiased forecasts of variables which may have already been forecast by the government or trade associations. Many of these organizations will carry on specific research and micro-forecasting work for a client firm. Considerable energy is spent on providing data that are current, correct, and easy to access by the client via time-sharing computer terminals. The major disadvantage is that these services are often expensive. They may involve an annual subscription fee as well as time-sharing computer charges.

By the end of the 1970s, three firms emerged as leaders in economic forecasting: Data Resources, Inc. (DRI), Chase Econometrics, and Wharton Economic Forecasting Associates, Inc. (See Chapter 19 for examples of this approach.) Each uses an input–output (econometric) model of the U.S. economy consisting of from 800 to 1000 equations. Included are factors such as interest rates, housing starts, consumer debt burden, auto sales, plant utilization rates, and business investment. The differences in their macro-forecasts are largely due to judgmental input of certain exogenous factors such as the Federal Reserve Board's monetary policy, the possibility of legislative changes in taxes or industry regulations, or the possibility of foreign actions such as war or OPEC price changes. Frequently the results of their models are published for several scenarios; the user then decides which one he or she will adopt as most likely.

Merrill-Lynch Economics Inc., a subsidiary of the big brokerage firm, is a newer and smaller player in the economic forecasting industry. The Merrill-Lynch approach creates a macro-model of the economy by aggregating the effects of individual industry macro-models.

On average, no forecasting service firm does any better or worse in forecasting than the others. Most client firms believe that they do better than their own in-house staff. It is wise to conduct a rigorous comparative analysis when considering the use of these agencies as some do far better than others in dealing with the dynamics of a particular industry. For an interesting comparison of the accuracy of the forecasts produced by the major services, see Stephen McNees, "The Forecasting Record for the 1970s," published in the September/October 1980 issue of the *New England Economic Review*. This article would help a financial organization select Wharton due to its track record in projecting interest rates in the turbulent late 1970s.

The major difference in the four services is their ancillary products. Wharton, for example, is known for its international model, Chase for its metals service, and DRI for its model of the chemical industry. Thus, managers may well base their decision on what service to engage on the basis of the special products and services they need. However, in order to obtain the specialized services, a client must subscribe to the use of the basic macro-model offered.

Other firms engaged in macro/micro economic forecasting include Evans Econometrics, Strategic Information, the General Electric MAPCAST Group, the National Bureau of Economic Research, and Citibank Economics. Academics at the following schools also produce similar data: University of California at Los Angeles, The University of Michigan, Georgia State University, The University of North Carolina, Kent State University, and Claremont College.

Other economic consulting firms offer more tailor-made services to organizations in need of forecasting know-how. These specialized services include:

Developing and programming computerized forecasting systems.

Doing one-time forecast modeling projects.

Providing a complete forecasting system on a continuous basis with computer-to-computer linkages.

Providing computer software and hardware facilities and technical support staff.

Economies of scale and staff specialization in devising and implementing forecasting models give economic consulting firms the ability to develop forecasting systems in less time and at lower costs than if the same-quality job were done by in-house staff. This is especially true for small- or medium-sized firms that cannot afford the staffing costs for a forecasting department. Arthur D. Little, Booz, Allen & Hamilton, and Temple, Barker & Sloane, Inc. are examples of consulting organizations that provide microeconomic modeling and forecasting system development services. Several directories of business consultants are listed in the bibliography.

The most important factors in choosing among alternative consulting firms include their forecasting experience in your industry, their responsiveness to client needs, the quality of peripheral support services (like computer programs and their availability on time-sharing computers), their educational programs, and their ability to communicate with management on technical subjects without losing sight of practical solutions.

SOFTWARE AND SERVICE BUREAUS

Most recognized forecasting approaches are in the public domain. The theory behind them is published in numerous texts and papers. If an organization chose to, it could commission its programming staff to reproduce promising forecasting approaches for use on in-house computers. Most organizations find it more economical to use software products of one or more forecasting modeling methods on publicly available time-sharing computers or on their in-house computer to develop models. The following are examples of such software products: SIBYL/RUNNER Interactive Forecasting from the Applied Decision Systems division of Temple, Barker & Sloane, Inc.; BETA from the Econo-scope Group Inc.; FUTURSCAN from the Futures Group; FLEXICAST from Health Products Research, Inc.; LAECON from Lochrie and Associates; and EPS from Data Resources, Inc.

CONCLUSIONS

Forecasting services will continue to expand to serve a market of medium- to small-sized firms in the 1980s, resulting in the integration of macroeconomic-, industry-, corporate- and product-level models. Managers will have the ability to measure the impact of industry outlook models on their own marketing mix models. They will be able to utilize pro forma financial planning devices to determine the impact of a given macro-forecast scenario on their own balance sheet and income statements. The development of regional and localized data and forecasts, and improved international forecasting, will allow the assessment of business strategy at local, national, and worldwide levels.

Economic demography will become a primary forecast tool. With the 1980 census, it is possible to show maps of population distribution on office terminals. Managers will be able to examine county-by-county breakdowns by income, age distribution, population density, and rate of growth. The question that remains to be answered is whether, with more accurate and timely information made available to them, managers will be able to make better (more profitable) decisions.

BIBLIOGRAPHY

Indices and Guides to Data Sources

National

Androit, John, ed., *Guide to U.S. Government Publications,* McLean, VA. Documents index (every 18 months). Indexes statistical publications of the U.S. government by title and originating agency.

Monthly Catalog of U.S. Government Publications, Superintendent of Documents, U.S. Government Printing Office (USGPO), Washington, DC (monthly). Index of materials published by the Superintendent of Documents. Publications indexed by author, title, subject, and series or report number.

Wasserman, Paul, ed., *Statistical Sources: A Subject Guide to Data on Industrial, Business, Social, Educational, Financial and Other Topics for the United States and Internationally,* 5th ed., Gale Research Company, Detroit, MI, 1977. Updated periodically. Provides a selected listing of key statistical sources organized by subject or country.

Bureau of the Census Catalog, U.S. Bureau of the Census, Washington, D.C. Contains a descriptive list of Census Bureau publications arranged by subject.

Encyclopedia of Business Information Sources, Gale Research Company, Detroit, MI. Listing of information services on detailed subjects and industries arranged alphabetically by subject.

Measuring Markets: A Guide to the Use of Federal and State Statistical Data, U.S. Industry and Trade Administration, Washington, DC, 1979.

Statistical Reference Index, Congressional Information Service, Washington, DC. Guide to American statistical publications from sources other than the U.S. government such as trade and professional organizations.

Statistics Sources, 6th ed., Gale Research Company, Detroit, MI.

Regional

U.S. Bureau of the Census, *Directory of Federal Statistics for Local Areas: A Guide to Sources,* USGPO, Washington, DC, 1976.

Directory of Federal Statistics for States: A Guide to Sources, USGPO, Washington, DC, 1967. Includes publications with data for the state level only. Arranged by subject.

Index of Urban Documents, Greenwood Press, Westport, CT (published quarterly). Covers annual publications of major cities and their counties in the United States. Arranged by subject and area.

Encyclopedia of Geographic Information Sources, 3rd ed., Gale Research Company, Detroit, MI, 1978.

Directories of Business Consultants

Consultants and Consulting Organizations Directory, Gale Research Company, Detroit, MI. A three-volume set providing a reference guide to concerns and individuals engaged in consultation for business and industry, cross indexed by subject and location.

Association of Management Consultants: Directory of Membership and Services, Milwaukee, WI.

Directory of Management Consultants, 1977 ed. Consultants News, Fitzwilliam, NH.

Institute of Management Consultants: Directory of Members, New York, NY.

Resources: Useful Data Sources

Bureau of the Census

Statistical Abstract of the United States
Historical Statistics of the United States

Social Indicators, provide a comprehensive compilation of industrial, social, political, and economic statistics in the United States

Census of Agriculture

Census of Business

Census of Construction Industries and Current Construction Reports

Census of Governments and Current Government Reports

Census of Housing and Current Housing Reports

Census of Manufacturers and Annual Survey of Manufacturers

Census of Mineral Industries

Census of Population and Current Population Reports

Census of Retail Trade

Census of Wholesale Trade

Census of Selected Service Industries

Census of Transportation

County Business Patterns

Enterprise Statistics

Foreign Trade Series on Imports and Exports

Current Industrial Reports

County and City Data Book

Bureau of Labor Statistics (BLS)

Handbook of Labor Statistics. This is one of the most useful government tools for forecasters. It makes available in one volume all of the major series done by the BLS including such topics as GNP, national income, labor force, employment, productivity, prices, and unions.

Monthly Labor Review

Survey of Consumer Expenditures

CPI Detailed Report

Wholesale Prices and Price Indices

BLS Handbook of Methods of Surveys and Studies

Chartbook of Prices, Wages, and Productivity

Employment and Earnings Statistics for the United States

Bureau of Economic Analysis

Survey of Current Business and its supplement

Business Statistics

U.S. Industrial Outlook

Business Conditions Digest

Regional Employment by Industry 1940–70

Other Government Sources

U.S. President, Economic Report of the President

Federal Reserve Bulletin

Economic Indicators, Council of Economic Advisers
Handbook of Basic Economic Statistics
Historical Chartbook, U.S. Board of Governors of the Federal Reserve System
Statistics on Income: Corporation Income Tax Returns, IRS
Yearbook of Industrial Statistics, New York, U.S. Statistical Office
Treasury Bulletin
The Budget of the U.S. Government
Social Security Bulletin

PART

4

MANAGING THE FORECASTING FUNCTION

29

FORECASTING, PLANNING AND STRATEGY

What Needs To Be Forecast

CHARLES H. KAPPAUF
J. ROBERT TALBOTT
Business Marketing Development
American Telephone & Telegraph Co.

INTRODUCTION

This chapter approaches the question of what needs to be forecast from the standpoint of examining the dynamics of a business and the decision processes that require forecasts in order for the business to be successful. In order to understand these dynamics, three basic methods for determining what are the most significant items to be forecast are discussed:

Ask corporate decision makers.

Ask the forecast users.

Examine each forecast situation by using influence diagrams, decision analyses, or similar tools.

This chapter also discusses the conditions that are necessary in order for a forecast to be worth the effort to produce it. These include the following:

A decision actually will be made based on a forecast, that is:
1. There are alternatives available.
2. The parties controlling the decision expect to use the forecast.
3. There is determination to make a decision.

The impact of the decision will be of more than routine significance.

In some instances forecasts are important simply for their role in integrating various aspects of the business (as distinct from decision making).

All of the above assume that forecasts can be separated into those that have high significance in their impact on the business and those that do not. The experiences of the authors and others suggest that such distinctions can be made.

This chapter includes a go/no go checklist as a practical guide for determining when a forecast is worth an appreciable amount of effort. Examples are given of actual corporate situations indicating forecast variables that were of critical importance to a particular business. The importance of multiple scenarios in forecasting is also discussed. Finally, a survey of current forecast practice is summarized indicating the items forecast, their uses, and their frequency. Observations are given regarding this survey. The most important of these is that most businesses typically do not pay sufficient attention to their most important variables. We conclude that it is essential for businesses to consciously select what to forecast, that there are structured ways to do this, and that the consequences are rewarding.

OVERVIEW

The Dynamics of Understanding the Business and Deciding What to Forecast

Every action that a human takes assumes something with respect to the future. Accordingly *everything* is forecast. The practical problem of course is to identify the degree to which each forecast is consciously made and the relative effort associated with each one.

The authors have conducted or have access to various surveys covering a wide range of business forecasters. Many of these sources are confidential. The authors believe them to be a broad and reasonable representation of medium to large North American corporations.

Our surveys confirm that even the largest firms bring a specific conscious effort to only a small percentage of the items that are forecast. The others are forecast by simple, mechanistic means, by assumptions and/or are derived from inputs by more consciously developed forecasts, or are assumed directly. It is obviously important that some forecasts are more important than others. The familiar 80/20 rule obviously has relevance. Ways to select this small percentage effectively will be discussed.[1]

It is both demonstrable and intuitively obvious that identifying key forecast variables is rewarding. In spite of this there is little evidence to suggest that most companies have systematic processes for determining where to direct their forecasting activities in terms of maximum effectiveness. However, there are examples of apparent successes, structured processes are available, and the results can be rewarding particularly in terms of the insights they give to key decision variables. (A variable is key if its likely values would significantly change the decision that it affects.)

Forecasts exist only to serve as inputs to the decision processes. Consequently, all of the answers to the questions of what to forecast come from analyzing decisions and decision processes.

There is a dynamic relationship between understanding the business and deciding what to forecast. It is relatively unimportant which comes first. It is important to recognize that each can help the other and that one of the functions of forecasting is to feed information to managers about changes in the dynamic relationships among both internal and external variables.

Some businesses have derived a reasonably comprehensive appreciation of the key variables that lead to a proper understanding of their own business. Therefore, they have a proper understanding of what the key forecast items are. For example, airlines cite seat miles and capacity as being the most important forecast items. Similarly, basic metals producers cite raw material availability and price as key forecast items. Other forecasts are, in effect, derived from these and can be more mechanistic, as illustrated later in this chapter.

In this chapter we concentrate on the high leverage forecasts since that leads to the highest payoff. Procedures for identifying those forecasts that have the maximum impact on the business are discussed.

Three Basic Methods for Determining What to Forecast

There exist processes and methods for consciously searching for the most effective items to forecast, in both specific and general situations. This chapter discusses three basic methods for determining what to forecast and provides a go/no go checklist for specific forecasts.

The three basic search methods are:

Situational analysis.

Ask the user, that is, the decision maker.

Refer to the practices of others.

Each of these has both pros and cons.

Other factors important in determining whether to proceed in specific cases include acceptance of the forecast, resources available, and whether you have the option to refuse! All of the above are discussed later.

CONDITIONS NECESSARY TO MAKE
ANY FORECAST WORTHWHILE

A Decision Is to Be Made

The first condition is that a decision is actually to be made (see Chart 29-1).

Anticipation is the basis for all business or corporate action; therefore decision making is the basis for any business being concerned about predicting the future. There is no other valid reason for a corporation to concern itself with either formal or informal perspectives about the future.

No decision can be made without the possibility of alternative actions. In the absence of alternatives the forecast is a nonevent. Consequently, alternative actions must be available and open for consideration.

Finally, forecast resources, management attention, and a decision structure must be present. Probably the most important resource available from the forecast standpoint in any corporation is management time and interest. Those responsible for using and/or approving the forecast must be available and willing to evaluate the usefulness and consequences of the forecast. The forecast must also be presented consistent with the decision maker's thought processes and objectives.

CHART 29-1. The Purpose of Forecasting Is to Provide Input to a Decision Process

Recognized	Business objectives	
need	Information (assumptions, forecasts)	Decisions
for	Attention and decision mechanism	
decision	Operational plans (alternatives)	

The above is true at all levels of the organization and at all levels of detail with respect to forecasts.

The Impact of the Decision is Significant

The second condition necessary to make a forecast worthwhile is that the impact of the decision is significant.

For purposes of simplification, we will assume that there are two and only two basic types of forecasts. One set of these consists of those items that have high leverage with respect to their impact on the corporation. The second set obviously are those that have low leverage. This chapter concerns itself principally with the process by which one decides which forecasts have high leverage.[11,16] The point is not to say that all other forecasts require no attention at all, but rather to say that the variability of the result is far less important to the business than those with high leverage. These other items can be "forecast" in a relatively mechanistic way. Hogarth and Makridakis[8] have found abundant evidence that such approaches work well in these circumstances anyway. Examples of the low leverage item might include short-term stock levels for certain parts that are easily obtained on short notice. High leverage decisions fit no obvious pattern because they can be either strategic or operational, long or short term, and related to revenue, expense or capital. Examples we are aware of include a 1-year change in promotional efforts in one city,[14] interfiber competition in a 5-quarter forecast of textiles,[4] and the impact of California's Proposition 13 on short-term sales in the state and local government market.[12] Examples pointing to the value of successfully identifying key variables come from the product management area where a study by Fogg indicated a ratio of 40 projects needed to produce one market success.[5] Further, Cooper has found that forecast items were crucial in 70% of product failures.[2]

Other examples show that corporate strategy may point to forecasting needs. A simple example of corporate strategy determining the focus for forecast importance is that of market size and price structure. For instance suppose it is corporate strategy to grow in its market and to do so by pricing below its major competitors; it is then quite obvious that it is important to forecast the total market, the cost trends of competitors, and the costs of producing one's own product. For another example, if it is corporate strategy to find and exploit new technology, then it is obvious from a forecast standpoint that the important item to forecast is the timing of the availability of the new technology, the length of its life cycle, and any constraints to its introduction, for instance government approval.[7]

The Forecast Is Necessary to Integrate Multiple Activities

A different reason for forecast importance is its role in integrating multiple activities.

Planning discontinuities are often caused by organization size and specialization.

The very nature of the modern large organization presents integration challenges to such corporations. For instance, many businesses are functionally organized so that new products are handled by one or-organization and existing products by still another. Hall has called this "uncertainty introduced by others in the same organization."[6] The integration of planning with respect to the impact of one function or organization on the others can properly be handled through the development of related forecasts. Chart 29-2 illustrates this.

SPECIFIC FORECASTS: MAKING GO/NO GO DECISIONS

To decide whether or not to proceed with a specific forecast consider the conditions described above and use the checklist in Chart 29-3. Note specifically that this approach applies only to forecasts with significant leverage. Other low leverage forecasts should be provided as necessary using simple processes such as smoothing or analogy.

The answers to the questions 1-7 in Chart 29-3 should all be "yes" if you are to proceed with the forecast. This process puts forecast management in a position to know only whether it wants to proceed with a forecast or not. Obviously, actually refusing to prepare a forecast may be dangerous to one's general well-being. However the go/no go decision can at least be understood and on its own terms. (The authors prefer to presume a rational environment.)

As mentioned above, we are concerned here primarily with high leverage forecasts. Forecast organizations may often turn out many forecasts that have little real leverage. The proper action in this situation of course is to routinize those forecasts so that maximum resources are

CHART 29-2. The Chain of Forecasts

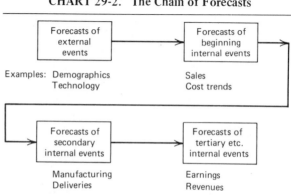

CHART 29-3. A Go/No Go Forecast Checklist

1. Does the forecast lead to an identifiable decision?
2. Is the outcome of the decision significant, that is, important in terms of reward or absence of penalty?
3. Is it possible for the decision to be impacted, that is, are there any alternative actions?
4. Is the decision within the firm's planning horizon?
5. Will the forecast be used/believed? (Specifically, does the decision maker want it?)
6. Can the forecast be ready in time for the decision?
7. Is the forecast feasible concerning input and methods?
8. Do you have the option to refuse to provide the forecast?

available for items of greatest importance, that is, high leverage forecasts.

LOOKING FOR THE MOST IMPORTANT ITEMS TO FORECAST: A STRUCTURED APPROACH

To be most effective, forecast organizations should be consciously and routinely examining their business to search for the most important items to forecast. It is a rare function in any business that can be really effective without planning for its own work—forecasting is certainly no exception.

To accomplish this, forecast organizations should use specific methodologies for determining which items are highly leveraged and which ones are not. This is done by developing relationships between the forecast items and the criticalness of the variance with respect to the future of the business.

There are structured ways for performing such analyses. Some of these are analytic, and some of them are surveys of users or of comparable organizations. They are discussed below.

Structured Approaches for Deciding What to Forecast

The first method we shall discuss is to ask the decision experts, that is, ask senior management or senior analysts in the firm. Their experience and intuition can often point simultaneously to both understanding how the firm works and, therefore, what should be forecast. There are limitations to this, of course, because of biases from the past carrying over to the future, a limited perspective from an organizational standpoint, and so on. Work by Hogarth and Makridakis[8] shows that some of these limitations are relatively serious. However, this approach can be effective and often is an excellent starting point.

A second and more comprehensive method of determining the important forecast items is to conduct a survey of the users of the existing forecasts. Again, this is relatively quick and inexpensive and can provide valuable insight into the advantages and disadvantages of the existing forecasting information within the firm. It has some of the same disadvantages as mentioned above with respect to bias, perspective, and so on. However, by interviewing users from different organizations one can at least gain insights into some of the biases. For specific methodology see Talbott.[15] A supplement to this approach is to survey the users in others businesses. See examples later in this chapter. Also see references.

Although the above approaches are useful, structured analyses and modeling for each situation are by far the best ways to determine what forecast variables really have high leverage. This approach may be the most expensive, but there are shortcuts to using it as will be described below. The literature is full of discussions of these techniques. (See Chapters 2, 5, and 9 for some examples.) Brief descriptions of the basic variations follow.

1. *Influence Diagrams.* This is the best way to begin and requires the least formal effort. In its simplest form an influence diagram is a systematic schematic showing what decisions and outcomes are affected by what variables and by other decisions. Such diagrams usually can be easily developed and can be "modeled" by subjective evaluation of the degree of impact of particular variables and decisions on the ultimate decision to be made. The most significant variables are the ones to forecast, of course.

2. *Decision Trees.* This is a more elegant and more structured version of an influence diagram. The chief difference is that decision trees require a sequential relationship to be shown, that is, each decision must be positioned with respect to all prior decisions in terms of which comes first. As in the case of influence diagrams, decision trees can be drawn on a simplified basis but can also require months of effort to do properly, particularly if there is a complex set of events and decisions and if probabilities are to be developed. As a matter of practice, if manufacturing decisions or new product decisions or financing decisions are generally the same, but only applied to different products or different points in time, a limited number of decision trees might be applicable to multiple situations.

3. *Other Models.* These can be built to actually test the impact of specific variables on the firm. (Models, if you will, would include the influence diagrams and decision trees mentioned above.) Models built in

order to develop a planning process, for instance a new product, often permit a forecaster to determine the impact of the forecast on key decisions by using them in a what-if mode. Analytical forecasting models themselves can isolate key variables.

4. *Sensitivity Analyses.* These can be made using the models just referred to or can be developed in a more modest and subjective fashion. It is often useful to make some effort to determine the variation in an input, the degree of which would change the decision itself in some fundamental way.

5. If the relationship between the forecast and decision making is not understood then it is almost impossible to effectively evaluate what to forecast. The appropriate action under these circumstances of course is to implement one of the structured approaches discussed above. See Chart 29-4.

In summary, any or all of these tools can be used to assist a forecaster in determining the probable impact of a variable, that is a forecast item, with reference to its impact on corporate decisions. Caution: it is generally not realistic to assume that some total system can be developed which would uncover all of the key variables for a particular firm. Therefore, the processes described above must be used in an eclectic fashion.

Multiple Scenarios: Part of Deciding What to Forecast

Since the forecasting process is one of describing our present perception of future events and structuring them in such a way as to make better decisions, it is important to recognize the decision risks associated with multiple outcomes. Accordingly, forecasters should determine when to prepare and present multiple scenarios. A recent survey by The Conference Board[10] indicates that this is seldom done in practice.

We suggest a sensible test for deciding when to use multiple scenario

CHART 29-4. Test to Determine Readiness to Select What to Forecast

Cause and effect well understood?

If yes: Complete forecast algorithm.
        Select key forecast outputs.
        Select key forecast inputs.
        Concentrate attention on key inputs.

If no: Analyze to improve understanding.

criteria. Such a test can be performed by answering the following questions.

1. Would it help the decision in a significant way if multiple scenarios were presented?

2. Is there an outer limit in either direction as to how much change in a key variable would change the decision?

3. Is the proposed decision so robust as to preclude the need for evaluating other possibilities?

Level of Detail Is Important in Determining Forecast Items

The processes discussed above apply equally at any level of aggregation or disaggregation, although it is usually best to begin a structured analysis at the strategic level. For example, consider the forecasting of short-term sales by product and territory and market by component. Normally these are not high leverage and can be derived by disaggregating a national forecast of average configurations. However, a proper situation analysis may show that one territory or one market is crucial to overall strategy and results. For example, the average price may not reveal great sensitivity, but that same price may be very sensitive to a specific territory or market segment.

Expected Accuracy and Go/No Go Decisions

Forecasts are sometimes not made simply because the item to be forecast is considered to be unpredictable. This is not appropriate. Hogarth and Makridakis[8] have reviewed many studies and concluded that often the most significant variables are the least predictable. See the use of sensitivity analyses above.

When to "Forecast" an Assumption

Assumptions are normally made to provide starting points, to provide commonality to a multiple user, and/or to avoid making a forecast. To deal with assumptions in doing situational analyses treat them equally with forecasts. Refer to Chart 29-2.

Forecast management should consciously decide when to forecast and when to assume. These criteria may be helpful:

Assumption impact on the decision.

Effort required to forecast rather than assume.

Authority to forecast rather than assume.

Decision makers should be clearly informed about what has been assumed so that they can review their "comfort index" with respect to the assumptions.

CURRENT PRACTICE

Objective Is Insight

One of the objectives of this handbook is to give first-hand knowledge as a self-development opportunity to those who are new in the field. In addressing the question "What Needs to be Forecast?", one way to obtain first-hand knowledge is simply to ask other people in the forecasting arena what they are forecasting.

How We Assessed Current Practice

We asked a two-part question: (1) identify in generic terms several of the important item(s) forecast by your corporation and (2) discuss the use and importance of these forecast items. We gathered answers to this question by drawing on (1) responses obtained from surveys which we have conducted and on (2) responses obtained from talking informally with personal and professional contacts.

Examples of High Leverage Forecasts

From our assessment of current practice, we have selected some examples that we feel are indicative of companies that seem to have effectively matched forecasting effort to corporate need.

Example 1. Industry sales of major appliances are forecast by product line. This includes refrigerators, freezers, ranges, dishwashers, clothes washers and dryers, compactors, and disposals. The input to this forecast is a forecast of housing completions, income, and inflation. The output from the industry sales forecast is used to forecast company sales and to help make pricing, promotion, and investment plans. The forecasts are done quarterly for 2 years and annually for 10 years.

Example 2. The U.S. macroeconomic environment and major industries are forecast twice a year. One forecast is annual for 5 years. This is used as input to the strategic planning process. The second forecast is quarterly for 8 quarters. This is used as input to a budget forecast. The budget forecast is used as: (1) a tool for forecasting financial results and (2) a standard against which management performance is measured. Along with the budget forecast a working capital forecast is prepared on a quarterly basis; it is used to monitor trends in working capital positions.

Example 3. Company unit sales volumes in each of 20 product lines are forecast quarterly for 1 year and annually for 5 years. This represents 95% of corporate revenues. The 1-year period forecast is used for (1) production scheduling for shift planning and materials purchasing, (2) inventory planning, and (3) budgeting. The 5-year period forecast is used for facilities and financial planning.

Example 4. Future energy demand, fuel availability, and penetration of energy supply technology are forecast over a period of 40 years. These forecasts are used for energy facilities planning. The planning horizon is 8–12 years prior to completion plus a 30–40 year useful life.

Example 5. A major bank forecasts (1) general economic conditions and interest rates, (2) regulatory changes and other environmental factors, and (3) loan and deposit categories. The first set of items are used to develop budgets, asset and liability management policies, and funds management policies. The second set of items are forecast because banking is a highly regulated industry and these items significantly affect the business of the bank. The third set of items are forecast not only for budgeting in asset and liability management but also for issues such as having adequate resources to satisfy demand without being overstaffed.

Example 6. A respondent from the airline industry suggested seven important categories of forecast items. Here are some of them. The amount of earned revenue is forecast by month for each of the various types of airline fares available during the forecast period. The forecast is used to assess the profitability of the various fare offerings and alternative pricing strategies. A forecast is made of the monthly volume of passengers boarded at each city in the airline's route system. This forecast is done 3 times a year for a 1-year period. It is used to establish budget and staffing requirements for each city and forms the basis for a performance measurement system.

Example 7. An aluminum producer forecasts U.S. demand for wrought and cast aluminum products by product and market for a 10-year period by quarter. This forecast is used to develop marketing plans and revenue forecasts. Aluminum ingot supply worldwide is forecast by region by year for 5 years. Its primary use is for facilities planning, but it is also used as input to the demand forecast.

Example 8. A company in the pulp and paper industry forecasts technology change. Trends in technological parameters, such as paper machine speed and capacity, are followed and projected into the future. In addition, substitutions of one technology for another are followed and extrapolated. These forecasts are made to ensure that the developments in their laboratory are in the forefront of the technology and to attempt to determine what technology will be needed in the future.

Example 9. A fertilizer manufacturer forecasts sales by product, by sales area, and by sales channel on a yearly basis. Their production facility is limited, and therefore the forecast is used to (1) schedule plants to optimize output and (2) allocate materials to sales people.

Example 10. An automobile insurance company forecasts the average costs and number of claims of various automobile insurance coverages such as property damage, bodily injury, and collision damage. The forecast is used to set today's rates for insurance coverage which must cover expenses of future claims.

Example 11. A textile manufacturer forecasts all major markets and market sectors in which the company's products are sold. This forecast is used to assist in market share analysis and projections and to anticipate likely demand. This company forecasts sales volumes on a monthly, quarterly, and annual basis. The monthly forecasts are used for short-term operating decisions such as monthly sales targets, production planning, finished goods inventory planning, and raw material purchasing. The quarterly forecasts are used to update budget, corporate profit, and cash flow projections. The annual forecasts are used for long-term strategic planning.

Summary of What Others Do

From our assessment of current practice, we have identified three important characteristics of the forecast activity: (1) the forecast item itself, (2) the use of the forecast, and (3) the frequency of the forecast item. We compiled our responses according to these three characteristics, and we categorized them according to 12 general kinds of forecast items, eight general uses of the forecast, and four frequency classes.

The three forecast activity characteristics and their corresponding categories are shown in Charts 29-5, 29-6, and 29-7. Each is accom-

CHART 29-5. Forecast Item

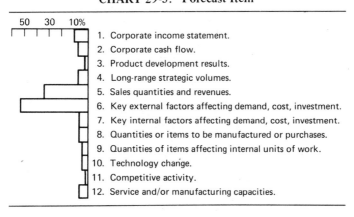

50   30   10%

1. Corporate income statement.
2. Corporate cash flow.
3. Product development results.
4. Long-range strategic volumes.
5. Sales quantities and revenues.
6. Key external factors affecting demand, cost, investment.
7. Key internal factors affecting demand, cost, investment.
8. Quantities or items to be manufactured or purchases.
9. Quantities of items affecting internal units of work.
10. Technology change.
11. Competitive activity.
12. Service and/or manufacturing capacities.

CHART 29-6. Use of the Forecast Item

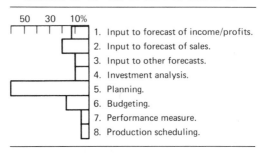

panied with a bar chart which gives the percentage of responses that fell into each category. No claim is made that this makes a statistically significant sample. However, we believe it to be a reasonable representation of the forecast activity of medium to large North American corporations.

From our responses, two forecast frequencies/uses stand out. These are (1) a quarterly forecast for 1 or 2 years, which is used for budgeting, and (2) an annual forecast for 5 or 10 years, which is used for strategic planning.

Observations About Current Practice

There is a danger in playing follow the leader, but asking others what they forecast reveals what they consider important. Therefore, the value of this compilation comes from learning what others do and do not do, and on this basis evaluating one's own needs.

Note, for example, the relatively large percentage of responses that forecast key external factors affecting demand, cost, and investment. On the other hand, there is only a small percentage of responses that forecast technology change and competitive activity. This does not seem to correspond with their strategic importance, and therefore it indicates an important omission in current forecast practice.[2,3]

CHART 29-7. Frequency of the Forecast Item

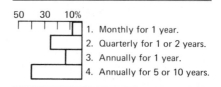

SUMMARY

It is essential for businesses to consciously select what to forecast. Those that do so will find a select few variables that significantly affect decisions of major importance to the business. There are structured ways to examine individual forecasts and to search for important but unidentified ones. Some businesses have achieved success in this area, but the majority seem to be unaware of this potential.

REFERENCES

1. Balthasar, J., S. Boschi, and R. Menke, "Calling the Shots in R&D," *Harvard Business Review,* May-June, 1978, p. 151.

2. Cooper, W., "Why New Industrial Products Fail," *Industrial Marketing Management,* vol. 5, 1975, p. 315.

3. Doyle, D., "Marketing Planning in the Multiproduct Firms," *Industrial Marketing Management,* vol. 4, 1975, p. 574.

4. Fella, S., "Forecasting in a Cyclic Environment," *Proceedings of the 1979 Marketing Conference of the Conference Board.*

5. Fogg, R., "New Business Planning: The Internal Development Process," *Industrial Marketing Management,* vol. 5, 1976, p. 179.

6. Hall, W., "Great Planning Disasters," *Futures,* February 1980, p. 45.

7. Hayes, R. H. and R. Schmenner, "How Should You Organize Manufacturing?" *Harvard Business Review,* January-February 1978, p. 105.

8. Hogarth, R. M. and S. Makridakis, "Forecasting and Planning: An Evaluation," *Management Sciences,* vol. 27, No. 2, 1981, pp. 115ff.

9. Howard, R., L. Matheson, and W. Miller, eds., *Readings in Decision Analysis,* SRI, Menlo Park, California, 1977.

10. Hurwood, D. L., E. S. Grossman, And E. L. Bailey, *Sales Forecasting,* Conference Board Report 730, New York, 1978, p. 178.

11. McKenney, J. and P. Keen, "How Managers' Mind Work," *Harvard Business Review,* May-June 1974, p. 79.

12. Michalak, W., "Sales Forecasting Techniques," *Proceedings of the 1979 Marketing Conference of the Conference Board.*

13. Schoeffler, S., "Nine Basic Findings on Business Strategy," *The Strategic Planning Institute,* 1977.

14. Schifeta, L., "New Sales Management Tool: ROAM," *Harvard Business Review,* July-August 1967, p. 59.

15. Talbott, J. R., "Managing the Forecasting Function," *Proceedings of the Second International Conference–Forecasting, Analyzing, and Planning for Utilities,* 1977.

16. Talbott, J. R., "Managing Uncertainty: Facing Reality," *Proceedings of the Third International Conference–Analysis, Planning, and Forecasting,* 1980.

BIBLIOGRAPHY

Fella, S., "Practical Pointers and Caveats on Short-Term Forecasting," *Proceedings of the 1979 Marketing Conference of The Conference Board.*

Holloway, C. *Decision Making Under Uncertainty,* Prentice-Hall, Englewood Cliffs, NJ, 1979.

Raiffa, H., *Decision Analysis,* Addison-Wesley, Reading, MA, 1970.

CHAPTER

30

INTEGRATING
FORECASTING
AND DECISION MAKING

WILLIAM REMUS
University of Hawaii

MARK G. SIMKIN
University of Nevada

INTRODUCTION

All organizations must monitor and respond to the environment. Some variables in the organization's environment need only be monitored, but crucial environmental variables need to be both monitored and their future values predicted. Forecasting these crucial variables gives management the lead time to make decisions and plan. A good forecast allows an organization to take advantage of opportunities and avoid pitfalls in the environment through timely decision making.

The purpose of this chapter is to identify those characteristics of forecasts that make them useful for decision making purposes and to illustrate the role that these characteristics play in common forecasting/ decision making settings. To illustrate characteristics, consider the following story.

Freddie Falsepoint was the statistical analyst for the telephone company in Metro City. It was November. When his boss, Pete "Piles-

CHART 30-1.   Freddie Falsepoint's Memo to Peter Hardgrove

Date: December 15, 1985

Memo To: Mr. Peter Hardgrove, Manager
                   Marketing Services

From: Frederick Falsepoint, Analyst

Re: Sales Forecast for 1986

Demand for telephone products has been strong during the last few years, and it is expected that this trend will continue into the future, at least for the near term. Undoubtedly, the strength of this demand is in large part attributable to the excellent work of our customer representatives and the ability of our inventory staff to keep our installers supplied with equipment. In view of the large number of items carried by our company, this is no small achievement.

Given the items identified above and the present inflationary experience of the country, total sales next year are projected to be $X.Y million. Naturally, this projection is subject to statistical error which makes this forecast uncertain. Thus, an updated forecast will be provided at a later date.

It-On" Hardgrove asked for a sales forecast for the coming year, Freddie thought to himself: "Just what I need—another project." Thus, Freddie delayed the project with the excuse that he "needed more data" in order to make a good forecast. As the end-of-the-year deadline approached, however, the marketing vice president began to ask for the forecast. With the vice president on his back, Pete finally ordered Freddie to prepare the forecast and have it to him by the next morning.

Freddie had less than 8 hours and even fewer ideas. Thus, in the end Freddie took last year's sales figure, multiplied it by the inflation rate, and a small 4% upward adjustment, and called this result his forecast of corporate sales. Completing his forecast, Freddie drafted the memo illustrated in Chart 30-1. Freddie chuckled over the last phrase since he knew that the earliest he would probably get around to the next update was sometime next December—if that early! However, the forecast was finished, the boss was satisfied, and the only thing that remained was the Christmas shopping. . . .

THE GUIDELINES

What did Freddie do wrong? Just about everything! Even common sense would identify a number of pitfalls in the story above. However, to be specific, consider the guidelines for preparing decision-oriented forecasts outlined in Chart 30-2. From a review of these guidelines, it is apparent that Freddie Falsepoint did a miserable job. Let us examine these guidelines point by point.

The first point is that the forecast be timely. Although it would appear that Freddie's work satisfies this criterion, just the opposite is probably the case. Often, a manager must make a decision well in advance of the forecast period. For example, inventory reordering must be planned with enough lead time to allow for shipment. Similarly, budgets must be prepared for supervisory reviews long before the fiscal year in which they will be used. Since Freddie's forecast is just 2 weeks short of the planning year, it is unlikely that it will be of much use for the near term.

The second guideline is that the forecast be expressed in the dimensional units needed by the decision maker, and the third guideline requires that these units be at the appropriate level of disaggregation. Freddie's work violates both these requirements. If the telephone sales forecast is used by inventory control staff, for example, the forecast should be in *units of equipment* rather than *dollars*. Further, both the installers and the inventory control staff will want to know how many units of each type of telephone equipment will be sold in the coming year. For a forecast to be useful for decision making purposes, the trans-

---

CHART 30-2. Guidelines for Integrating Forecasting and Decision Making

---

Preparation

1. Forecasts must be timely.

2. Forecasts must be in the units appropriate for the decision.

3. Forecasts must be disaggregated to the degree required by the decision makers.

4. Forecasts should be detailed enough to show seasonal or other cyclical variations. Forecasts of quarters or even months are generally more useful than a simple annual forecast.

5. Forecasts should include not only the most likely value but also the best-case and worst-case values.

6. Forecasting assumptions and limitations should be clearly spelled out in an appendix.

Distribution

7. Forecasts should be "blessed" by top management.

8. Forecasts should be distributed in an easily-understandable report to all appropriate managers.

9. Forecasts should be regularly updated and distributed.

---

lation of dollars into disaggregated units should be done by the forecaster as a natural part of the forecasting process.

The fourth guideline points out that many forecasted variables have seasonal patterns. When forecasts are made on a quarterly or monthly basis, these patterns become apparent and can be used to improve the decision making process. In Freddie's case, the pattern of sales may be used to set the best times to order equipment and the pattern of orders over the year. Also, the pattern of sales may predict cash flow surpluses or times when additional financing may be needed. Freddie's forecast fails to help with these crucial problems.

The fifth guideline suggests that forecasts should indicate not only the most likely value, but also the best case value and the worst case value. Freddie's forecast is only a point estimate and therefore does not follow this suggestion. One reason why the inclusion of best case and worst case values is desirable is because forecasting itself is an inexact art rather than a precise science. A forecast which includes a range of potential values calls attention to this property and gives the decision maker an indication of how much uncertainty the forecaster attaches to the forecast. Often, this range is computed statistically as a *confidence interval*, in which the range includes, say, 95% of all likely forecast outcomes. If a 95% figure is chosen, the range is said to be a *95% confidence interval*. If a 95% confidence interval results in too wide a range (e.g., a sales forecast between –1000 and +4000 units), it is possible to compute a narrower range at lower probability.

Another reason why it is desirable to provide forecast ranges rather than point estimates is because many decision making processes are not based on the most likely outcome, but rather on best case expectations or worst case expectations. For example, to assure adequate supplies of telephone equipment, the inventory control staff of the company may want to purchase enough equipment for the high-order sales projections. On the other hand, where large investments in plant and equipment are involved, a conservative decision maker may want to base the decision on the worst case portion of the forecasting range. Finally, the best, worst, and most likely projections permit a manager to devise strategies that are flexible enough to take advantage of the best case if it arises while preparing the company to survive the worst case.

When forecasting ranges are not provided to management but the decision making process calls for them, it is reasonable to expect managers to create their own. Often, this creative process is subverbal and perhaps even subconscious. There is nothing inherently wrong with such creative processes as long as the resultant range estimates are reasonable. When judgmental methods result in unreasonable ranges, however, suboptimal decisions may result. For example, this may mean overstocking inventory because management was overly optimistic in its sales estimates, or it may mean a failure to capitalize on a given opportunity because management's worst case projections of the project's potential were too low. In either case, bad decisions result from a lack of vital forecasting information. The provision of forecasting intervals may help avoid such trauma.

Looking back to Freddie Falsepoint's memo, we see that he failed to provide any forecasting intervals although he did state that his projection was "subject to statistical error." For the situation at hand, however, the uncertainty in the forecast is not attributable to the (naive) statistical method which was used to create the forecast, but rather to the natural doubt surrounding any projection about future business behavior. The use of the word "statistical" in Freddie's memo has been used for sheer subterfuge. Because most managers are not particularly conversant with statistical methods and are therefore not prepared to discuss the drawbacks of statistical methodology, there is little doubt that Freddie will get away with his statement despite the fact that it is nonsense.

The sixth guideline advises the forecaster to provide background information about his or her forecast(s). Managers tend to distrust forecasts that magically appear and that provide little in the way of explanation about how the forecast was constructed or the crucial assumption made by the forecaster. Forecasts increase in usefulness when managers are informed about the limits of the forecast—especially, the conditions under which the forecast would no longer be valid. Thus, our sixth guideline suggests that the forecaster explain assumptions, explain limiting conditions, and so forth, in a straightforward way.

Freddie's memo failed to provide explanations about his forecast, but we are not required to make the same mistake. Perhaps the easiest way to make critical information available to the decision maker regarding the forecast is to summarize it in an appendix. This appendix is more desirable than footnotes because (1) the appendix can more fully document the forecasting assumptions and procedures and (2) the appendix can state more clearly what a decision maker needs to know in order to use the forecast(s) intelligently. Thus, the appendix should briefly explain in easy to understand terms how the forecasts were derived, what assumptions were made in the course of their construction, and what conditions limit their use. Just having this information in some obscure, jargon-filled, technical memorandum will not overcome managerial resistance, and certainly will not support the decision making activities for which the forecast was intended.

In spite of the many talents of the forecaster and the many hours of work that might have been expended in behalf of a particular forecast, there is no assurance that the decision makers receiving the forecast will use it. Where the forecaster is employed in a little-understood corporate staff department, for example, there may be a tendency for the manager to dismiss the forecast as "uninformed" or "unofficial." For this reason, it is desirable that forecasts be "blessed" by top management in order to lend credibility to the forecast and encourage its use for planning purposes. Thus, in Freddie's case, the memo should have been written by the Marketing Vice President, not Freddie.

The mechanisms for obtaining the blessings of top management will differ from situation to situation and from company to company. The price for the blessing may be adjustments to the forecast or it may be formal review by a committee. Armstrong[1] points out that adjustments to a forecast usually do not improve the accuracy of the forecast. In fact, he found some evidence that the adjusted forecasts are less accurate.[2] But the bottom line is that adjustments to forecasts are often essential if the forecasts are to be used.

When the forecast is formally approved and released for use, there are still the two dangers that (1) it will not be distributed to those who need it and/or (2) it will not be in the right form for decision making purposes. To overcome the first problem, the forecaster should take the time to find out who might require the forecast and make sure that these individuals receive copies of all relevant reports. Our friend, Freddie, has washed his hands of this problem by simply directing his memo to his immediate boss. Such action is irresponsible.

To overcome the second problem, the forecaster should personalize the forecast so that it directly meets the decision maker's informational needs. This may mean disaggregating the forecast, converting the units of the forecast, and so on. The problem of distribution and the problem of constructing useful forecasts are intimately related issues and should be considered as a set. This is the eighth guideline: forecasts should be distributed in an easily understandable report to all appropriate managers.

At last we come to the problem of updating forecasts. Bad forecasting methodology is much worse than an inaccurate forecast because the former is controllable whereas the latter usually is not. Updating a forecast is a vital part of the forecasting function. Thus, as new data become available, the forecast must be updated and redistributed. Presumably, these updated forecasts will be more accurate and therefore more useful to the decision makers. Freddie is not planning on updating his forecast until he is told to do so. We all lose by such an attitude because valuable information will not be communicated and a vital task will go unfinished.

THE GUIDELINES APPLIED TO
FAMILIAR BUSINESS ACTIVITIES

In this section we consider some familiar business activities and examine how our forecasting guidelines apply in particular settings. Our purposes here are (1) to discuss the importance of the forecasting function in each business setting, (2) to make clear how the forecasting function ties in with the decision making activities of those individuals involved in each setting, and (3) to illustrate which of our guidelines are particularly important in each instance. Space does not permit an exhaustive review. Therefore, we have focused our attention on the following areas: (1) inventory control, (2) personnel planning, (3) cash flow analysis, (4) budgeting, (5) tax planning, and (6) resource allocation.

Inventory Control

The decision to replenish stock is often based on either an observance of low existing levels of inventory or on some inventory policy. Perhaps the most common inventory model in use today is the economic order quantity (EOQ) model, which requires a forecast of period demand—for example, a 1-year forecast of demand—in order to compute the order amount. Where inventory demand for certain products is fairly uniform throughout the year, the use of such mechanical forecasting methods as moving averages or exponential smoothing may provide a reasonable estimate of future demand, and therefore enable the decision maker to compute such ancillary information as order quantity, reorder point, and time of inventory cycle automatically with a computer program. However, for products whose demands are seasonal or volatile, for products requiring considerable lead time for deliveries, and for products requiring the use of in-house production for replenishment, advanced planning may require a more sophisticated forecast of future usage.

The guidelines for integrating forecasting and decision making are especially applicable to forecasting for inventory control. The forecast must be timely to provide sufficient lead time for ordering. The forecast must be in units of product rather than in dollars. Also, the forecast must be disaggregated since each different product in inventory is controlled separately.

Where seasonality is involved in product demand, constructing a forecast which is detailed enough to show seasonal fluctuations is very important. If it is assumed (as EOQ does) that demand is consistent throughout the year when in fact it is not, suboptimal inventory strategies must necessarily develop. Unfortunately, computerized inventory control systems often are based on this latter assumption. The result can be shortages during periods of high demand and/or the investment of dollars in excess inventory during periods of low demand. In either case, an accurate forecast of the demand pattern can lead to a more cost-effective inventory policy.

Inventory forecasts that include not only the most likely value but also the best and worst case values are especially useful in inventory planning and control. Firms emphasizing customer service may wish to stock on the high side of the forecast range to assure adequate stocks for future demand or to qualify for quantity discounts. Forecast ranges are also useful when negotiating with suppliers for such things as terms of contracts, delivery dates, options, and so forth.

Inventory forecasts are not especially interesting to top management, but inventory forecasts should nonetheless have the approval of top management if they are to be the basis of further decisions. Moreover, because inventory decisions have important implications for marketing staff, accounting personnel, and perhaps production workers, inventory forecasts should be distributed in an easily understandable report to all managers affected. Sometimes this may lead to controversy—for example, when marketing personnel disagree with the number of units of a particular product expected to be sold. However, to the extent that such controversy may lead to a more realistic forecast, such instances may actually result in positive outcomes.

Inventory forecasts should be updated regularly, especially where seasonality or other fluctuations have an important bearing on inventory disbursement behavior. Such updates not only enable managers to revise their expectations, but they also enable forecasters to track their forecasts during the course of a given planning year.

Personnel Planning

Personnel planning involves the projection of future levels of employment for various categories of workers within the organization. The military services are particularly important users of personnel planning models because of their need to project the effects of various recruitment policies, enlistment policies, promotion policies, and retirement policies. In the private sector, large organizations like Xerox, IBM, and General Motors use personnel planning models for much the same purposes, except that the ranks of the military are replaced with managerial levels of the business firm.

The personnel forecast projects employee levels years into the future; a 1-year forecast is usually inadequate. The forecast is expressed in numbers of individuals in the various employment categories rather than in salary dollars as may be found in the budget. The degree of disaggregation is also important because individuals are to be matched with jobs in individual departments. Thus, a forecast by division is usually inadequate for decision making purposes except perhaps at the highest managerial levels of the organization.

Unless the organization participates in a highly seasonal industry (e.g., agriculture or automotive manufacturing) it is usually not necessary to forecast employee levels on a month by month or quarter by quarter basis. A year by year forecast may be sufficient. However, those organizations embarking on substantial expansions or contractions in their work forces would obviously be exceptions to this general rule.

The imprecision in the timing of new hires, promotions, and retirements leads to a degree of uncertainty surrounding any personnel forecast. Therefore, these forecasts should include not only the most likely value but also the best case and the worst case values. The forecasting range can then serve as input for budgeting purposes, for retirement planning purposes, for cash flow analysis purposes, and so forth.

Where personnel forecasting is involved, it is important to identify in great detail in an appendix what methodology and assumptions were used. Was the personnel forecast first made at a very aggregate level and then disaggregated, or vice versa? Was input from the various division or department managers obtained? Was a Markov chain model applied or present employee levels extrapolated in some way? These are the type of questions that should be answered in the appendix.

Inasmuch as personnel levels affect such a large part of the business organization, it is also important that personnel forecasts receive the blessings of top management. To some extent, this blessing is inherent in the plans themselves: presumably, the forecasts reflect the intentions of top management to expand or contract specific organizational operations, and therefore the forecast merely extrapolates the effects of such plans on corporate employment. However, it is one thing to suggest that this natural connection exists and quite another to state that the projections are reasonable to the decision makers at the top. Thus, the acquisition of top management's blessing is needed to make this link explicit.

Finally, we come to the question of updating forecasts. Here, there is likely to be some latitude. It is usually not necessary to update the forecast too quickly: once or twice a year would probably be sufficient. It is much more important that the forecast be updated (and distributed) whenever important changes in the external environment of the organization or the internal policies of the organization dictate.

Cash Flow Analysis

Cash flow analysis attempts to forecast the dollar receipts and expenses of an organization in one or more business years. If the cash inflows and cash outflows were uniform across the year, little forecasting would be required, and little decision making would be involved. In many businesses, however, the various types of revenues and expenses have substantially different patterns. This leads to cash surpluses during some periods and cash deficits in others. With good forecasting and cash management practices, these cash flow problems can be handled efficiently.

Forecasts for cash flows are usually made by disaggregating cash expenditures and revenues. Each disaggregated cash category is then analyzed separately. Some categories such as repayments of loans are uniform across the year and can therefore be projected with a fair amount of certainty. Other categories, such as the sales of some product lines, have substantial seasonal variations. Usually, revenues are disaggregated at least to the degree that products or services with differing seasonal patterns are separated. Then each subcategory is forecast separately. When the cash expenditures and revenues are recombined, the company's cash flow position in coming weeks and months can be predicted. The financial manager will then minimize the cash deficits by rescheduling discretionary payments; he or she also arranges financing of the remaining deficits and the investment of the surpluses in short-term, interest-bearing financial instruments.

In organizations with large revenues and expenses, small variations between the forecasted and actual cash flows can lead to major financing problems. Thus, it is very helpful to provide worst case and best case forecasts also. This will allow the cash manager to plan for contingencies.

Inasmuch as cash flows usually vary with alternate assumptions regarding corporate activities, it is vital that the forecaster make such assumptions explicit in an appendix. For example, revenue items which are forecast using a projected level of corporate business should be identified as uncertain items with a given degree of variability. Similarly, business expenses which will be incurred only if a contract is signed or a bank loan is approved should be called to the reader's attention in the appendix.

In most businesses, cash flow forecasts are used as critical planning documents. Therefore, it is important that cash flow forecasts be approved by top management. Since the likelihood of close managerial scrutiny is high with cash flow forecasts, it is equally important that the forecast be written in an easily understood report and distributed to all appropriate managers in a timely fashion. A highly technical forecast will not only be unintelligible to the busy executive, but it will also reflect poorly on its source.

Barring major business disruptions, forecast error is reduced with subsequent updates. The update function is particularly crucial for cash flow forecasts since even short-term illiquidity represents a major problem to the business entity, and moderate-term cash surpluses will result in unproductive asset resources. Thus, cash flow forecasts should be updated frequently to provide adequate planning tools for cash management activities.

Budgeting

An organization must decide how best to use its funds to accomplish its objectives, and an organization must monitor the expenditure of these funds to assure a measure of control in the daily operations of its business. The process of budgeting enables the business organization to both plan and monitor its costs and revenues and therefore accomplish both these control objectives in an efficient manner. The corporate budget usually is prepared shortly before the beginning of each fiscal year. However, the amount of planning and preparation which must be done before a budget can be formalized is such that the forecasting and detailed analysis involved are performed months in advance of the budget's start date.

There are four common types of budgetary systems:

1. Cost-center systems.

2. Revenue-center systems.

3. Profit-center systems.

4. Investment-center systems.

With cost-center budgeting, only costs need be forecast in preparing the budget. With revenue-center budgeting, only revenues need be forecast. With profit-center budgeting, both costs and revenues need be forecast. Finally, with investment-center budgeting, both revenues and investment assets must be forecast.

It is not uncommon for an organization to use different budgeting systems for different functional departments or for different managerial levels. For example, at lower managerial levels, the forecasting effort is usually limited to different types of costs and a cost-center budgeting system. At top management levels, however, a revenue-center approach is most often used in which both costs and revenues must be forecast in the budgetary process. In all cases, the forecasts must be prepared in dollars and must be prepared well in advance of the fiscal year in which they will be used.

Usually, budgeting is done for one fiscal year, although 2-year budgets, 5-year budgets, and even 10-year budgets are also commonly prepared. Near-term budgets must detail revenues and expenditures for each of the 12 months of the fiscal year. This means that both revenues and costs will show seasonal variations as required.

Most budgets should be prepared on a disaggregated basis. Thus, such items as salaries, supplies, travel, advertisements, and so forth are forecast separately. Like costs, revenue components such as sales, cash acquisitions from divestment of stocks, bonds or land, loan repayments, and so forth, are forecasted individually, especially where such revenue items are earmarked for special projects such as new plant acquisition.

The budgetary assumptions (i.e., aggregate forecasts of crucial variables) are to be blessed by top management with the distribution of the budget. In reality, a number of problems occur which affect the forecasts. Often, there is so much paper work in the budgetary package that the assumptions and limitations of the budget are not clear. Similarly, the best case and worst case values in the forecasts may not be provided. These characteristics violate our guidelines and should be avoided.

The budgetary process does not stop when each element of the organization has prepared its budget and obtained top management's approval.

The budget is regularly updated on a monthly basis or quarterly basis throughout the fiscal year. Actual revenues and expenditures are compared with budgeted values and actions taken to correct activities deemed out of control. The forecasts are updated and used to revise the budgets for the coming months. With a good computer-based accounting system and good forecasting practice, the budget can be an extremely valuable tool in the decision making processes of the organization.

From the foregoing discussion, it is apparent that cash flow analysis and budgeting are closely related. Usually, budgeting is designed to plan the use of funds so their expenditure can be controlled. Cash flow analysis attempts to predict surpluses of funds (and ways to invest them) and temporary deficits (and ways to get funds to cover them). If everything came in as budgeted, and revenues/expenditures occurred simultaneously with sales/purchases, cash flow analysis and budgeting would be quite similar. Difference in time patterns, however, cause differences between the numbers yielded by the two processes. Also, the processes differ because different people are involved. Financial analysts do cash flow analyses while managers budget.

In some organizations the questionable practice of obtaining next year's budget by taking last year's budget and making small adjustments to it is utilized. The amount of adjustment is proportional to the anticipated growth in revenue. Clearly, this approach fails to use the power available from good forecasts and avoids the crucial examination of how funds should best be allocated.

Tax Planning

The money that an organization pays in taxes is money that could be used for more productive purposes. Therefore, an organization must plan carefully to avoid paying unnecessary taxes, and this involves forecasting.

When an organization completes the budgeting process as outlined in the preceding section, the budget can be translated into a *pro forma* income statement. This statement, in turn, can be used to forecast the organization's tax liability. Steps can then be taken to reduce taxes.

The most careful tax planning involves a reiterative, simulation process in which the effects of alternative courses of action are examined for their effects on tax liability. The relative advantages and disadvantages of alternative tax treatments, accounting policies, and depreciation schedules are similarly examined in order to reach policy decisions with regard to tax planning efforts. In effect, therefore, tax planning requires an entire series of forecasts—one for each possible set of conditions—and the decision making process that results is contingent on the tax liabilities that are output from these efforts.

One source of tax shelter for company dollars is the investment tax credit and accelerated depreciation associated with new equipment. To fully evaluate this decision, a manager must be able to project the maintenance costs as the old equipment ages, project the need for this kind of equipment in the future, project the increased cost of equipment if the company waits to replace it, and project the worth of any increased efficiency and effectiveness of the new machine. This formal analysis requires forecasts to be made. Usually, the forecasting methodology is naive, but there is often enough data to make better forecasts of these crucial factors.

In the latter case, the projections are *not* often made by the forecasting department but instead by management scientists, operation researchers, or industrial engineers. Yet, some of the same guidelines apply. The projections must be timely, that is, done in time so that equipment can be procured this tax year. The projections must be disaggregated to the level of a single machine of a particular type. The analysis must reflect best and worst case projections, and the forecasting methods/limitations must be clearly spelled out. The whole analysis package will then go to the appropriate manager for the decision. The package should be easily understood by all and updated if projections change. Seasonal variations usually do not affect these kinds of decisions.

Resource Allocation

In one sense, resource allocation is just like budgeting in that both are concerned with the use of organizational resources in a timely, efficient manner. As we use the term here, however, resource allocation differs from budgeting to the extent that (1) resource allocation deals with one-time decisions such as physical acquisitions of plant and equipment, (2) resource allocation makes use of newly acquired assets, or soon to be acquired assets, as opposed to the use of operational revenues, and (3) resource allocation often results in sunk costs.

Decisions involving resource allocation problems with the characteristics identified above are usually made with cost benefit analysis. Basically, the idea is to compute the tangible and intangible costs of a given project and compare these values with the tangible and intangible benefits resulting from the project's implementation. In theory, any project should be considered worthwhile as long as the cost–benefit ratio is less than 1. In reality, the imprecise nature of the analysis is such that conservative managers prefer to see after-tax ratios of 1:2 or before-tax ratios of 1:4 before embarking on a given project.

Cost–benefit analysis can also be used to decide among several competing projects. In such cases, a separate cost–benefit ratio is computed for each project, and the inverses of these ratios are then used to rank these projects in descending order. All projects with cost–benefit ratios greater than 1 can be pursued; or, given budgetary restrictions, the projects can be chosen for implementation starting from the top of the list and continued until the budgetary limit is reached.

Forecasting is intimately related to cost–benefit analysis because both costs and benefits must be projected into the future before the final cost–benefit ratio can be computed. As in other areas, the accuracy of the forecast is very important since the ultimate decision to go ahead with a project or not relies directly on the cost–benefit ratio computed from the analysis. However, adherence to the guidelines outlined above is of equal importance in assuring usable figures and good documentation. In the paragraphs below we examine the application of these guidelines in greater detail.

The application of our first guideline—that forecasts must be timely— should be clear from the fact that the cost–benefit analysis cannot proceed until both costs and benefits have been projected into the future. Moreover, some projects are available for only a limited period of time— the use of optioned land, for example—and these are obvious examples of resource allocation decisions requiring a timely forecasting component. The timeliness of the forecast is critical in allowing the decision maker to examine the consequences of alternate forecasting assumptions and, therefore, to ultimately make a decision on the desirability of the project itself.

The second guideline—that forecasts be in the units appropriate to the decision—requires that both costs and benefits be expressed in dollars. Tangible costs are already expressed in dollars, and intangible costs (e.g., environmental pollution or exposure to personal injuries) are often calculated in dollar terms through the use of conversion factors. Benefits are usually less easily expressed in dollars and are often highly dependent on the assumptions of the forecaster. This is one reason why it is critical to include an appendix with the forecast to make such assumptions clear and to enable the decision maker to examine these assumptions in greater detail if desired.

The requirement that the forecast be disaggregated relates to the comments above. Certainly, costs must be forecast separately from benefits. Usually, it is also desirable that the various cost and revenue components of a given project be disaggregated as well. This may not only make the forecaster's job easier but will also make clear how important each item is expected to be in the overall analysis. The larger the component, the more accuracy (in absolute terms) is desired in the forecast for that component.

It is usually not necessary that the forecasts for a cost–benefit analysis include seasonal detail. For large projects involving investment in fixed assets, for example, yearly projections are sufficient. However, it is important that the forecast project the number of years in the useful life of the investment and that the assumptions regarding the choice of figures in this matter be stated explicitly as part of the forecast's appendix.

The requirement that the forecasts should include a range of values (best case and worst case projections) is very important in cost–benefit analysis because of the uncertainty that surrounds any long-term forecast and because of the magnitude of the investment that rests on the decision resulting from the analysis itself. Clearly, if even worst case projections of costs and benefits result in a favorable cost–benefit ratio, management will have more confidence in pursuing a given project than if only the best case outcome produces this favorable ratio.

It is also important that the forecasts attendant with cost–benefit analysis be blessed by top management. As noted above, the forecasts are the inputs to the analysis which follows, and this is an area in which top management will have a critical interest. Moreover, since senior managers themselves will most likely be making the decisions resulting from the analyses, it is clear that the forecaster must have the managers' confidence if the task of evaluation is to proceed smoothly.

The distribution of the forecasts made for cost–benefit analyses will necessarily be limited. Line managers and middle-level managers are not likely to require such forecasts, for example, and updating is similarly unimportant for one-time investment decisions involving sunk costs. However, where reevaluations of existing projects are involved or zero-based budgeting techniques are used, annual updating may be required.

SUMMARY

Where forecasts are used as inputs to aid decision making activities, it is important that the forecast be oriented to this purpose. In this chapter we have identified nine characteristics of forecasts that make them useful for managerial decision making. These characteristics deal with the dimensions of (1) timeliness, (2) decision making units, (3) level of aggregation, (4) seasonality, (5) forecast ranging, (6) explanatory appendices, (7) top–management approval, (8) distribution, and (9) updating. The closer a forecast adheres to the guidelines involving these items, the more useful the forecast is likely to be for decision making purposes.

The latter part of this chapter illustrated the application of the guidelines to the following exemplary business activities: (1) inventory control, (2) personnel planning, (3) cash flow analysis, (4) budgeting, (5) tax planning, and (6) resource acquisition. Here our objectives were to discuss the importance of the forecasting function in familiar decision making settings, to make clear how the forecasting function and the decision making function are related in each situation, and to emphasize those guidelines presented earlier that are particularly important to forecasting in each business setting.

REFERENCES

1. Armstrong, J. Scott, "Evidence on the Value of Experts in Forecasting: The Seer-Sucker Theory," Working Paper No. 79-035, Wharton School, University of Pennsylvania, 1979.

2. ____, *Long Range Forecasting*, John Wiley, New York, 1978.

BIBLIOGRAPHY

Armstrong, J. Scott, *Long Range Forecasting,* John Wiley, New York, 1978.

Delbecq, Andre L., Andrew H. Van de Ven and David H. Gustafson, *Group Techniques for Program Planning,* Scott, Foresman, Glenview, IL, 1975.

Ewing, D. E., *The Human Side of Planning*, Toronto, Macmillan, 1969.

MacCrimmon, Kenneth R. and Ronald N. Taylor, "Decision Making and Problem Solving," *in Handbook of Industrial and Organizational Psychology* (Marvin D. Dunnette, ed.), Rand-McNally, Chicago, 1976, pp. 1397–453.

Mockler, R. J., *Business Planning and Policy Formulation*, New York, Appleton-Century-Crofts, 1972.

Murphy, Alan H. and Robert L. Winkler, "Subjective Probability Forecasting: Some Real World Experiments," *in Utility, Probability, and Human Decision Making* (Dirk Wendt and Charles Vlek, eds.), D. Reidel, Dordrecht, 1975.

Sackman, H., *Delphi Critique: Expert Opinion, Forecasting, and Group Processes,* Lexington Books, Washington, DC, 1975.

Slovic, Paul., Baruch Fischhoff, and Sara Lichtenstein, "Behavioral Decision Theory," *Annual Review of Psychology,* Annual Reviews, Inc., 1977, pp. 1–39.

Spetzler, C. S. and Carl A. S. Stael von Holstein, "Probability Encoding in Decision Analysis," *Management Science*, vol. 22, 1975, pp. 279–300.

Swalm, Ralph O., "Utility Theory: Insights into Risk Taking," *Harvard Business Review*, vol. 44, 1966, pp. 123–31.

Vroom, Victor H. and Philip W. Yetton, *Leadership and Decision-Making,* University of Pittsburg Press, Pittsburg, 1973.

Wheelwright, Steven C. and Darral G. Clarke, "Corporate Forecasting: Promise and Reality," *Harvard Business Review*, November–December 1976, p. 40.

Winkler, Robert L., "Probabilistic Prediction: Some Experimental Results," *Journal of the American Statistical Association,* vol. 66, 1971, pp. 675–85.

Woods, Donald H., "Improving Estimates that Involve Uncertainty," *Harvard Business Review*, vol. 44, 1966, pp. 91–98.

CHAPTER

31

ORGANIZATIONAL AND BEHAVIORAL ASPECTS OF FORECASTING

RONALD N. TAYLOR
Faculty of Commerce and Business Administration
University of British Columbia

This chapter highlights common behavioral and organizational difficulties in forecasting and proposes solutions for these difficulties. Although little research on behavioral and organizational phenomena has been done in the context of forecasting, much of the research on decision making, judgment, and planning is relevant to forecasting. Forecasting can be viewed as a key component of decision making; it involves the estimation of the exogenous events that may occur and how they will affect the outcomes of implementing a decision. Similarly, research on the judgment of probability of events is relevant to forecasting. Forecasting also can be related to research on planning, but forecasting should be carefully distinguished from planning. *Forecasting* involves anticipating future events; *planning* is concerned with devising courses of action to achieve desired objectives. Hence, forecasting provides an input to the planning process.

The four behavioral and organizational difficulties in forecasting discussed in this chapter are (1) coping with bounded rationality, (2) improving probabilistic judgments, (3) stimulating creativity in innovative forecasts, and (4) facilitating implementation of plans. The latter topic is included in this treatment of forecasting since the research literature

CHART 31-1.   Checklist for Improving Forecasts by Considering Organizational and Behavioral Aspects

Blocks to Good Forecasting	Organizational and Behavioral Aspects	Strategies for Improving Forecasts

Highly complex forecasting situations	Cognitive strain	1. Organize information for forecast
		   a. chunking
		   b. optimum level of aggregation
		2. Decompose forecast
		   a. factor forecast
		   b. segment forecast

Highly uncertain forecasting situations	Biased probabilistic judgments a. representativeness b. availability c. anchoring and adjustment d. overconfidence	1. Improve assessment of subjective probabilities 2. Bootstrap 3. Decompose current state and change 4. Index level of uncertainty 5. Use amalgamated forecasts
Unstructured situations requiring innovative forecasts	Stimulating creativity in forecasts	Brainstorming
Acceptance and implementation of plans	Resistance to plans and planning activity	1. Use participation 2. Use Nominal Group Technique 3. Use Delphi technique

demonstrates that a basis for effective implementation of plans can be developed during the preceeding planning activities—including forecasting. A checklist summarizing these four blocks to good forecasting, the organizational and behavioral aspects related to these forecasting difficulties, and strategies for improving forecasts by overcoming these blocks in shown in Chart 31-1. The issues included in Chart 31-1 are discussed in this chapter.

COPING WITH BOUNDED RATIONALITY IN FORECASTING

Research has demonstrated dramatically the extreme limitations in human cognitive abilities. Consider the view of human cognitive ability expressed by Shakespeare: "What a piece of work is man. How noble in reason, how infinite in faculties. . . ." This idealistic position has been contrasted with conclusions emerging from research on cognitive limitations[30] and with Simon's[26] statement that "The capacity of the human mind for formulating and solving problems is very small compared with the size of the problems whose solution is required. . . ." In this section the implications of human cognitive limitations for forecasting are discussed.

Bounded Rationality and Cognitive Strain

Beginning with a classic study by Miller[20] which concluded that the human mind can retain only a very small amount of information in short-term memory, the evidence indicating the severe limitations in human information processing ability has accumulated. Simon's[27] notion of bounded rationality acknowledged the inadequacy of the human mind for coping with the overwhelming information richness of the complex decision situations that typically occur in organizations. *Bounded rationality* means that decision makers exhibit rationality only within their artificially constrained perception of a complex decision problem. Decision makers attempt to compensate for their limited abilities by constructing a simplified model of the problem and by behaving rationally within the constraints of the model.

Cognitive strain figures importantly in producing bounded rationality. *Cognitive strain* is a breakdown of a decision makers cognitive processes when the informational demands of a problem exceed his or her information processing capacity (i.e., information overloading). The existence of bounded rationality and cognitive strain have been well documented. Both experimental research in the laboratory and studies of actual organizations have shown that bounded rationality and cognitive strain are widespread in administrative decisions made in such contexts as natural resource management, military tactics, governmental policy, and business.

In an effort to understand why cognitive strain occurs, the psychological attributes of decision makers which predispose them to cognitive strain have been investigated.[17] A key variable underlying cognitive strain—risk taking propensity—also is central to the process of forecasting. The risky situation to which an individual high in risk-taking propensity tends to expose himself or herself involves uncertainty about outcomes and the possibility of losses (including opportunity losses) of resources. The research literature reports several measures of risk-taking propensity—psychological tests, the mean variance criterion, and empirically derived utility functions.

One of the most promising measures is the use of empirically derived utility functions: this method has been used to help businesspeople understand their own and other's attitudes toward risk. Spetzler[31] found that top managers of a company varied greatly in the risk-taking propensity indicated by their utility functions. In contrast, Swalm[33] found that most managers in a large company exhibited very risk-averse utility functions. Rather than using a more risk neutral strategy, which would be better for their company when small percentages of its resources were at stake, he found that managers tended to be inappropriately risk-averse. Obtaining such information about risk-taking propensities of managers permitted the organization to correct this limitation by encouraging risk-averse managers to take more risks.

Organizational units also suffer from a phenomenon similar to bounded rationality. Research on communication networks indicates that, for the complex tasks typically found in organizations, highly centralized networks are inappropriate. It appears that the large information load inherent in complex tasks tends to overload the information processing ability of any single person in the network. This suggests that the information processing activities involved in most organizational decision making would be performed most effectively when shared among relevant organizational members.

Aids for Coping with Bounded Rationality in Forecasting

Based on the literature on cognitive processes of decision makers, two strategies for coping with bounded rationality in forecasting have been developed and are widely used. One approach involves organizing information in a manner helpful to a forecaster; the other approach takes the form of decomposing the forecasting task to reduce its complexity.

Organize Information Input for Forecasts

To reduce the cognitive demands on forecasters in processing information, a meaningful way to organize information may be provided (chunking), or information may be appropriately arranged prior to its receipt by a forecaster (optimum level of aggregation). Simon[28] suggested "chunking" to assist decision makers in interpreting a complex array of stimuli by effectively organizing the information it contains. Grouping the information into meaningful chunks, or categories, and ordering the categories in importance may increase information processing capacity. For example, as a manager receives reports from operating units, he or she may cognitively arrange the information they contain in terms of actual or anticipated decision problems (e.g., labor shortages, equipment maintenance). This process is consistent with the research literature on humans as active information handlers; that is, rather than attempting to remember "facts" they organize information in a way that has meaning for them.

Partitioning information into the optimal level of aggregation prior to its presentation to a forecaster has been suggested as a way to improve information processing efficiency. [18] Detailed information (e.g., store-by-store sales) may be needed for some decisions, but using aggregated information (e.g., regional sales) reduces information load. The general rule is to provide information at a level of aggregation that is most suitable for the forecast. One should be careful to provide aggregated information only when it is appropriate, since it may be very difficult to disaggregate information.

Decompose the Forecasting Task

The most frequently used strategy for overcoming bounded rationality in forecasting involves decomposing a complex problem to bring it within the bounds of a forecaster's cognitive ability. As Raiffa[24] has stated, the intent of decomposition is to divide and conquer. A complex problem is decomposed into simpler problems, the simpler problems are analyzed, and the analyses of the simpler problems are pasted together with logical glue to reconstruct the complex problem. Decomposition methods fall roughly into two classes: (1) factoring complex problems into components and (2) segmenting the complex unit for which the forecast is desired into simpler subgroups and forecasting separately for each subgroup.

1. *Factoring Complex Problems.* Factoring a forecasting task into complex components, which may in turn be factored, reduces information load in complex forecasting situations. Delegation of forecasting activities is a salient example of problem factoring. Factoring allows division of labor and specialization when the parties involved in forecasting have differing capabilities, and it permits forecasting activities to be carried out by individuals or groups in parallel. Of course, breaking up a forecast into subtasks is useful only when few interrelationships exist among the subtasks. When many interrelationships exist, the advantages of factoring clearly are outweighed by the coordination difficulties. Hertz[11] has described the application of factoring in making capital budgeting forecasts; the problem was factored to get forecasts about the parts—then the parts were synthesized to get an overall forecast.

An example of decomposition by logically sequencing subforecasts is provided by a study in which forecasts were made in two forms—direct and decomposed—for questions that differed in level of uncertainty.[3] A question of intermediate uncertainty level asked the subject to estimate how many packs of Polaroid color film were used in the United States in 1970. The decomposed form of the question led the subject through a logical sequence of steps to arrive at the estimate: (1) How many people lived in the United States in 1970? (2) What was the average family size? (3) Cameras were owned by what percentage of the families?

(4) What percentage of the cameras were Polaroid cameras? (5) How many packs of film were used in the average Polaroid camera? (6) Color films comprised what percentage of the Polaroid films used? The decomposed version yielded more accurate forecasts for all questions asked in the study, and the superiority of decomposition was greatest in the highly uncertain estimates.

Forecasting also can be improved by decomposing according to causal chain to assess simultaneous causality. Rather than treating a forecasted variable as a direct function of the causal variables, one can describe the causality in greater detail by exploring causal chains using simultaneous equations. Although the number of equations can become prohibitively large, the overall approach is easy to grasp. Results from the first equation are used to input to the second equation; results from the second equation are used to input to the third equation, and so on. This approach organizes the problem into more manageable pieces.

In decomposing a complex organizational problem it is possible to simplify the problem by developing a model. The challenge is to build a model that can be more easily manipulated than the complex system, yet which includes the aspects of the system that have the greatest implications for the forecast. Simon[28] suggested that complex organizational problems should be decomposed into the semi-independent components corresponding to their functional parts. The use of "decomposable matrices" is based on his view of complex systems as containing a hierarchy of levels in which the operation of the system at each level can be specified by describing its component functions. Most practical forecasting problems meet the conditions for "nearly decomposable" systems in that the interactions among subsystems exist, but tend to be weak. Hence, decomposable matrices can be used to analyze forecasting systems.

When done appropriately, the use of decomposable matrices can simplify the forecasting task with little loss of relevant information. The informational requirements of the forecast can be brought closer to the cognitive capabilities of the forecaster by ignoring weak interactions among subparts belonging to different components of the system for which the forecast is to be made. Strong interactions, however, should be taken into account in the forecast. For example, while it is not necessary to observe the interaction of each member of one organization with each member of another organization to understand the interface between the two organizations, it may be necessary to observe the relationships between top executives of the two organizations.

Simon has suggested that factoring should be the basis for designing organizational decision processes of the future.[29] One organizational structure proposed to increase capacity to process information—the use of lateral, self-contained authority structures[9] —is based on the principle of decomposition. This frequently used structure involves decomposing the broad decisions facing an organization and assigning components to self-contained decision units (e.g., product divisions). Although these decision units are hierarchically arranged in organizations, the lateral structures are equally important. Decentralizing the forecasting activities (and perhaps the forecasting specialists) in this manner offers several advantages: (1) the output diversity required of a single forecasting unit is reduced since there is less need to share information across decision units, (2) less coordination and scheduling within each unit are needed, and (3) the information sources and forecasters are brought closer together, thus reducing information distortion and loss produced by long communication chains. Moving forecasting down in organizations to a point closer to where information upon which the forecast is based originated reduces the extent to which "uncertainty absorption" occurs. Uncertainty absorption refers to a false sense of security that information tends to acquire as it is transmitted up an organizational hierarchy.

A major weakness with this approach, of course, is that the forecasts must contain components that are sufficiently independent to make forecasts originating from these components feasible. If the components are highly interconnected and a forecast of one unit is highly dependent on forecasts made by other units, this strategy would not be appropriate. Another weakness is that while less coordination is required within units, coordinating the resources and outputs across forecasting units may be extremely difficult.

In general, factoring is suitable when the forecasting task is complex, uncertainty is high, components are relatively independent (or relationships among them are known), and/or the parties to the forecast have different abilities or information which permit specialization and division of labor.

2. *Use Segmented Forecasts.* In complex, or highly diversified, organizations, segmented forecasts can be developed independently for each organizational unit (or authority structure); then, the segmented forecasts can be amalgamated. Where the segments are independent, equally important, and information on each segment is good, segmented forecasting is appropriate. If the segments are not independent, at least it is necessary to be able to accurately measure the relationships among them.[2]

IMPROVING PROBABILISTIC JUDGMENTS

Forecasting attempts to reduce uncertainty by acquiring information about courses of action that may be taken and the consequences of these actions. Yet, it frequently is difficult to accurately determine the likelihood of decision outcomes. Generally, forecasters would prefer to base estimates on objectively determined historical indicators or trends.

The literature from psychology—where the issue has been called statistical versus clinical prediction—shows that statistical methods clearly are superior to clinical methods, in situations where statistical methods can be used. Statistical predictions require that a number of similar (repetitive) decisions be made, and the future is judged on the basis of past experiences. Unfortunately, it appears that the more important the forecast, the less likely it is that objective methods will be used.[2] Instead, forecasters rely on subjective judgments regarding the likelihood of events, and estimates based on subjective judgments have proved to be highly inaccurate. This section examines the biases in probabilistic judgments that have been identified in the research literature and suggests ways to improve subjective judgment of probabilities. For further information regarding the judgmental aspects of forecasting see the chapter by Bodily (Chapter 13) in this handbook.

Biases in Probabilistic Judgments

Much research has been directed toward determining the cognitive processes (heuristics) underlying inaccuracies in judging probabilities. Laboratory studies have identified three major heuristics that can seriously distort the subjective judgments of probabilities: representativeness, availability, and anchoring.

"Representativeness" pertains to the probability that an event will be generated by a given process or that an object will belong to a given class.[13] It appears that the representativeness heuristic is used by attempting to determine the degree of similarity between an object and a class of objects, that is, the degree to which the object is representative of the class. This heuristic is supported by research demonstrating that subjects tend to regard small samples as more accurate and reliable than they actually are (the law of small numbers) and to neglect population base rates in judging probabilities.

The "availability" heuristic[37] can lead to judgmental biases in which an event is judged likely or frequent if it is easy to imagine or recall relevant instances. For example, frequent events tend to be easier to recall than examples of less frequent events. Similarly, likely occurrences are easier to imagine than unlikely ones. While availability is often a valid clue for the assessment of frequency and probability, reliance on it may produce systematic biases if it also is affected by factors that are not related to likelihood (e.g., familiarity, emotional saliency, and recency).

"Anchoring and adjustment" involves setting a natural starting point (anchor) and shifting this point to reflect the implications of additional information. The shift is found in most instances to be imprecise and insufficient.[38] In one study, subjects were asked to predict the percentage of African nations in the United Nations. A starting point was set by spinning a wheel of fortune in the subject's presence; then the subject was asked to revise the number upward or downward to obtain his or her answer. It was found that the randomly determined starting point strongly influenced the estimates. Subjects starting with 10% made predictions averaging 25%; but subjects starting with 65% made predictions averaging 45%. Apparently, the anchor can be based on very little information, and people are loath to change their minds in the face of additional evidence. In a study of employment interviewing, for example, it was found that decisions to hire or reject an applicant were made rapidly (often within 5 minutes), and information obtained after this point had little bearing on the decision.

Another general finding from research outside the laboratory is that people tend to be optimistic in their judgments. Kidd,[14] for example, reported that engineers were optimistic in predicting the time required to overhaul electric generators. The estimated time to complete a project was generally about 60% of the time actually required, even though the projects were well underway when the time estimates were made. Similarly, Copeland and Marioni[6] found an overestimate of earnings that averaged 15% in analyzing 6-month forecasts in 49 companies.

Aids for Improving Probabilistic Judgment

Since probabilistic judgments are widely used in forecasting, it is important that they be improved. Five methods for increasing the accuracy of probabilistic judgments are discussed here: (1) improving assessment of subjective probabilities, (2) decomposing current state and change, (3) bootstrapping, (4) indexing level of uncertainty, and (5) using amalgamated forecasts.

Improve Assessment of Subjective Probabilities

A number of methods for eliciting subjective probabilities of events related to forecasts have been developed,[23,16] but no single method has been found to be the best." One difficulty is that the cognitive processes involved in probability assessment are poorly understood. One of the more promising techniques is the use of a "probability wheel" as a reference point.[32] This wheel has two adjustable sectors, one blue and the other red. One use of the wheel is to ask an individual to bet either on a fixed event (e.g., next year's production will not exceed a given level) or on the blue sector. The amount of blue in the wheel can then be varied until the subject becomes indifferent between the probability shown on the wheel and the probability of not exceeding the given level of production. The proportion of blue in the wheel is assigned as the probability of the event.

In obtaining probability assessments for decision analysis, the Decision

Analysis Group at Stanford Research Institute has recommended that probabilities be elicited by several techniques; that the problem be carefully structured; that biases which may distort judgment be minimized; and that personal interviews, rather than computer-interactive techniques, be used with clients unaccustomed to judging probabilities. Methods frequently used for obtaining judgments include interviews and surveys (e.g., by mail or telephone). The literature on behavioral science research methods contains much information about these methods and their uses; Tull and Albaum[36] provide a useful discussion of survey research, and Bouchard[4] discusses interviewing. Although the training of probability assessors appears to hold considerable potential for improving the assessment of subjective probabilities,[1] improvement due to training has not been clearly demonstrated.

Bootstrap

A useful objective method for improving probabilistic judgments is bootstrapping. This approach assumes that decision processes used by people can be made explicit and that the forecaster can lift himself up by his bootstraps. When each decision is complex and a number of similar decisions are to be made, it is possible to build a simple regression model of forecasting behavior which can be used routinely in future decisions. The bootstrapping notion reflects a general finding that a regression model frequently can do better in making predictions than the original decision maker can (e.g., in predicting which applicants for admission to graduate school will be successful). Kunreuther has discussed when the regression model should be used in production planning and when it should be contravened.[15]

Decompose Current State and Change

Forecasts can be aided by decomposing the forecast into current state and change components and then considering each component separately. This is similar to the base rate problem in psychology. Making the forecaster aware of the importance of base rates should reduce the impact of the representativeness bias mentioned above. It also should make apparent any serious difficulties in measuring the current state—a consideration that frequently is overlooked in forecasting. Morgenstern[22] has described the difficulties in measuring current states in economics; Hedlund et al.[10] have discussed base rate issues in predicting which mental patients are dangerous, and Thompson[35] has pointed out the importance of considering current states in weather forecasting. To illustrate the importance of carefully assessing base rates, consider that it has been estimated that 40% of the errors in 1-year forecasts of the U.S. GNP are due to errors in measuring current GNP.[5]

Index Level of Uncertainty

Forecasting can be improved by choosing relevant and reliable information. To cope with uncertainty absorption—the tendency mentioned above for information to take on a spurious aura of certainty as it is transmitted through an organization—it has been proposed that an "uncertain index" value be assigned by the originator of the information before information is transmitted.[43] This indexing of uncertainty (or reliability) would permit forecasters to select information and weigh its importance for forecasts judiciously.

Use Amalgamated Forecasts

The reliability and validity of forecasts can be improved by using a number of judges in amalgamated forecasts. The evidence in support of amalgamated forecasts is impressive. As long as judges have a minimum level of expertise, amalgamated forecasts are better than the average quality of the individual forecasts that were amalgamated. For example, accuracy in forecasting football scores was found to be almost as good for the amalgamated forecast as for the best judge[42]; and, when "expert" forecasts of the United States GNP were made, the group amalgamation was superior to 62% of the judges.[44] Winkler[41] examined different weighting schemes for amalgamating predictions of football scores and found that the ways in which the judgments were amalgamated made little difference in the accuracy of the amalgamated forecasts. The important feature was the use of multiple judges in arriving at the forecasts.

STIMULATING CREATIVITY IN INNOVATIVE FORECASTS

Innovative forecasting typically requires solutions to future-oriented problems. To be creative, the solutions must be original (statistically improbable or infrequent), relevant, and practical. A major perceptual block to innovative forecasting is functional fixedness, which inhibits the transfer of a response from an ordinary use to an unusual use.[34] The usual laboratory setting for studying functional fixedness is the candle problem, in which it has been found that using a box to support a candle is easier to solve if the box is empty. Much of the research on functional fixedness has concerned the impact of various features of the decision problem (e.g., labeling the box) or hints in reducing the extent of functional fixedness. In an accounting application, methods for dealing with functional fixedness as accountants attempted to adjust to a change in accounting methods have been discussed.[12]

Brainstorming is a widely used method for stimulating creativity that is relevant for improving innovative forecasts. It can be used by groups, or by individuals working alone during at least part of the exercise. Although brainstorming provides little structure to guide the group in developing creative solutions to problems, a series of rules are given to encourage free expression of ideas. The rules are: ideas are expressed freely without considering their quality, group members are encouraged to modify and combine previously stated ideas, and a moratorium is placed on the evaluation of ideas until all ideas have been listed. Much research has been directed toward evaluating brainstorming and the conditions under which it is most effective in stimulating creativity. One of the major conclusions is that having individuals work alone while developing lists of ideas generally produces more creative ideas.

FACILITATING IMPLEMENTATION OF PLANS

Surveys of difficulties in use of forecasting methods (e.g., see ref. 40) indicate that forecasts frequently fail due to implementation problems. In this section the behavioral and organizational bases for resistance to plans and planning activities are examined; and participation of subordinates in planning, the Delphi technique, and the Nominal Group Technique are suggested as aids in implementing plans.

Resistance to Plans and Planning Activity

"Probably the most universal difficulty arises from people's fears of planned change . . . almost all ambitious plans are intended to produce new patterns of thought and action in the organization. However, as has been said innumerable times, people resist change—or, more accurately, they resist *being* changed by other people."[8] There are many reasons for resistance to change, ranging from fear of change, threat of being manipulated, conflicting interests, constrained freedom of choice in work activities, and failure to see the value in planning, to increased workload due to planning activities. Resistance can take the form of either open hostility or covert sabotage of the planning effort. Even the best designed plans will fail if those who must carry them out refuse to do so.

Considering the values and needs of those involved in planning is important in implementing plans. The values and needs of all participants, not just top management, should be accomodated to the greatest extent possible if plans are to guide the behavior of all members in an organization. Whenever possible, implementation of plans can be facilitated by building in values and objectives that are shared by those who must carry them out. There also is a motivational basis for involving the implementors in the planning process. Goal setting has been found to motivate performance, and self-set goals tend to be more highly motivating than are goals set by others. The more people in organizations participate in the objective-setting process, the greater is their motivation to achieve them. This is the basis of the Management by Objectives (MBO) program in which subordinates are asked to set their own work goals in conjunction with their superiors.

Aids to Implementing Plans

Resistance to planning generally has been dealt with by properly introducing the planning system, by educating those who implement plans regarding the values of planning, and by rewarding organizational members for their planning activities (financially or otherwise). In addition, the involvement of those who must carry out plans in the initial stages of planning—including forecasting— is valuable both in improving the quality of planning decisions and in assuring the acceptance and implementation of the resulting plans.

Use Participation

A survey of how large companies manage overall organizational change showed that a participative approach was used in all the successful changes studied.[21] In contrast to the authoritative approach (where plans are dictated by higher management) and the delegated approach (where piecemeal plans are developed by lower level managers), the participative or shared approach allows both direction from higher management and some measure of discretionary action by those affected by a change. Building on prior research, Vroom and Yetton[39] have proposed a procedure by which decision urgency, resources of subordinates, agreement of subordinates with organization goals, and need for acceptance of a decision are analyzed through a participation tree. The analysis yields strategies that guide a decision maker in the degree to which he or she should involve subordinates and the form the involvement should take. Given sufficient lead time, opening up the planning process for participation of those who are expected to implement the plans may be advisable when they can constructively contribute relevant information and/or when it is important that the plans be accepted by these people.

Little is known about the manner in which implementors contribute to planning decisions (the decision activities that occur in the participative meetings, content, interactions among group members, quality of the decisions, etc.). Limited evidence indicates that the effectiveness of participation of subordinates in planning decisions depends on the nature of the subordinates, as well as on the type of decision problem. The effects of participation are mediated by personality of the subordinate; those with an authoritarian personality and a low need for independence have been found to react positively when little participation is used.[19]

The participation approach can create difficulties if too many people are involved and if considerable time and effort are devoted to solving minor problems. In complex, important planning problems, however, participation offers considerable assistance for the effective implementation of plans.

Use the Nominal Group Technique or the Delphi Technique

Both the Nominal Group Technique (NGT) and the Delphi are strategies that can be used to involve organizational members in planning decisions. They are more highly structured than is participative management and generally are focused on the solution of a specific problem.

The NGT[7] is a group meeting in which members seated around a table silently and independently list their ideas on the topic being considered, take turns in suggesting ideas to the group, discuss the combined list of ideas, and vote on priorities. The group decision is the pooled outcome of the votes. The Delphi technique,[25] developed for technological forecasting, uses interaction among group members to integrate the opinions of experts about a particular subject, but it attempts to remove the dysfunctional aspects of face-to-face communication (e.g., powerful members dominating the discussion). Typically, the procedure involves isolating the participants from one another and presenting them with a series of questionnaires in which their opinions and reasons are solicited. The information is consolidated and circulated anonomously to each member of the group after each round.

Although some features of these two techniques have been criticized (e.g., the simple questionnaires used in Delphi), the evidence has shown that, for about the same cost, they are superior to conventional discussion groups in quality of the solutions generated. And all three methods produce similar benefits from involving organizational members in planning decisions. Choosing between NGT and Delphi for planning decisions depends on the feasibility of physically bringing group members together and the urgency of the solution. When group members cannot be assembled at one location, use Delphi; when the solution is urgent, use NGT.

CONCLUSIONS

Forecasting is essential to the effective management of complex, interdependent organizations—and, indeed, to the functioning of society. Yet, the behavioral and organizational difficulties that thwart effective forecasting are formidable. This chapter has attempted to highlight some of the common behavioral and organizational difficulties in forecasting, to analyze the processes underlying these difficulties, and to suggest solutions based on this analysis. It is hoped that this approach will help to bring relevant theory and research to bear upon the solution of practical forecasting problems.

REFERENCES

1. Alpert, Marc and Howard Raiffa, "A Progress Report on the Training of Probability Assessors," unpublished manuscript, 1969.

2. Armstrong, J. Scott, *Long Range Forecasting*, John Wiley, New York, 1978.

3. Armstrong, J. Scott, W. B. Denniston, and M. M. Gordon, "The Use of the Decomposition Principle in Making Judgments," *Organizational Behavior and Human Performance*, vol. 14, 1975, pp. 257–63.

4. Bouchard, Thomas J. Jr., "Field Research Methods: Interviewing, Questionnaires, Participant Observation, Systematic Observation, Unobtrusive Methods," in *Handbook of Industrial and Organizational Psychology* (Marvin D. Dunnette, ed.), Rand McNally, Chicago, 1976.

5. Cole, Rosanne, "Data Errors and Forecasting Accuracy," in *Economic Forecasts and Expectations: Analysis of Forecasting Behavior and Performance* (Jacob Mincer, ed.), National Bureau of Economic Research, New York, 1969.

6. Copeland, Ronald M. and R. J. Marioni, "Executive Forecasts of Earnings per Share versus Forecasts of Naive Models," *Journal of Business*, vol. 45, 1972, pp. 497–512.

7. Delbecq, Andre L., Andrew H. Van de Ven and David H. Gustafson, *Group Techniques for Program Planning*, Scott, Foresman, Glenview, IL, 1975.

8. Ewing, D. E., *The Human Side of Planning*, Macmillan, Toronto, 1969, p. 44.

9. Galbraith, Jay, *Organization Design*, Addison-Wesley, Reading, MA, 1973.

10. Hedlund, James W., Ivan W. Sletton, Harold Altman, and R. C. Evanson, "Prediction of Patients Who Are Dangerous to Others," *Journal of Clinical Psychology*, vol. 29, 1973, pp. 443–54.

11. Hertz, David B., "Risk Analysis in Capital Investment," *Harvard Business Review*, vol. 42, 1964, pp. 95–110.

12. Ijiri, Y., R. K. Jaedicke and K. E. Knight, "The Effects of Accounting Alternatives on Management Decisions," in *Research in Accounting Measurement* (R. K. Jaedicke, Y. Ijiri and O. Nielson, eds.), Chicago, American Accounting Association, 1966, pp. 186–99.

13. Kahneman, Daniel and Amos Tversky, "Subjective Probability: A Judgment of Representativeness," *Cognitive Psychology*, vol. 3, 1972, pp. 430–54.

14. Kidd, John B., "The Utilization of Subjective Probabilities in Production Planning," *Acta Psychologica*, vol. 34, 1970, pp. 338–47.

15. Kunreuther, Howard, "Limited Knowledge and Insurance Protection," *Public Policy*, vol. 24, 1976, pp. 227–61.

16. Ludke, Robert L., Fred F. Strauss and David H. Gustafson, "Comparison of Five Methods for Estimating Subjective Probability Distributions," unpublished manuscript, 1976.

17. MacCrimmon, Kenneth R. and Ronald N. Taylor, "Decision Making and Problem Solving", in *Handbook of Industrial and Organizational Psychology* (Marvin D. Dunnette, ed.), Rand McNally, Chicago, 1976, pp. 1397–453.

18. Marschak, Jacob, "Remarks on the Economics of Information," *Contributions to Scientific Research in Management*, W.D.P.C., Los Angeles, 1959.

19. Melcher, A. "Participation: A Critical Review of Research Findings," *Human Resource Management*, vol. 15, 1976, pp. 12–21.

20. Miller, George A., "The Magical Number Seven, Plus or Minus Two," *Psychological Review*, vol. 63, 1956, pp. 81–97.

21. Mockler, R. J., *Business Planning and Policy Formulation*, Appleton-Century-Crofts, New York, 1972.

22. Morgenstern, Oskar, *On the Accuracy of Economic Observations*, Princeton University Press, Princeton, NJ, 1963.

23. Murphy, Alan H. and Robert L. Winkler, "Subjective Probability Forecasting: Some Real World Experiments," *in Utility, probability, and Human Decision Making* (Dirk Wendt and Charles Vlek, eds.), D. Reidel, Dordrecht, 1975.

24. Raiffa, Howard, *Decision Analysis*, Addison-Wesley, Reading, MA, 1968.

25. Sackman, H., *Delphi Critique: Expert Opinion, Forecasting, and Group Processes*, Lexington Books, Washington, DC, 1975.

26. Simon, Herbert A., *Models of Man*, John Wiley, New York, 1957, p. 198.

27. ____, *The New Science of Management Decision*, New York University Press, New York, 1960.

28. ____, *The Sciences of the Artificial*, M.I.T. Press, Cambridge, MA, 1969.

29. ____, "Applying Information Technology to Organization Design," *Public Administration Review*, May–June 1973, pp. 269–77.

30. Slovic, Paul, "From Shakespeare to Simon: Speculations—and Some Evidence—About Man's Ability to Process Information," unpublished manuscript, 1972.

31. Speltzler, C. S., "The Development of a Corporate Risk Policy for Capital Investment Decisions," *IEEE Transactions on Systems Science and Cybernetics*, SSC-4, no. 3, Sept. 1968, pp. 279–300.

32. Spetzler, C. S. and Carl A. S. Stael von Holstein, "Probability Encoding in Decision Analysis," *Management Science*, vol. 22, 1975, pp. 340–58.

33. Swalm, Ralph O., "Utility Theory: Insights into Risk Taking," *Harvard Business Review*, vol. 44, 1966, pp. 123–31.

34. Taylor, Ronald N., "Psychological Aspects of Planning," *Long Range Planning*, vol. 9, 1976, pp. 24–35.

35. Thompson, Philip D., *Numerical Weather Analysis and Prediction*, Macmillan, New York, 1961.

36. Tull, Donald S. and Derald S. Albaum, *Survey Research: A Decisional Approach*, Intext, New York, 1973.

37. Tversky, Amos and Daniel Kahneman, "Availability: A Heuristic for Judging Frequency and Probability," *Cognitive Psychology*, vol. 5, 1973, pp. 297–32.

38. Tversky, Amos and Daniel Kahneman, "Judgment under Uncertainty: Heuristics and Biases," *Science*, vol. 185, 1974, pp. 1124–31.

39. Vroom, Victor H. and Philip W. Yetton, *Leadership and Decision-Making*, University of Pittsburg Press, Pittsburg, 1973.

40. Wheelwright, Steven C. and Darral G. Clarke, "Corporate Forecasting: Promise and Reality," *Harvard Business Review*, November–December 1976, p. 40.

41. Winkler, Robert L., "The Consensus of Subjective Probability Distributions," *Management Science*, vol. 15, 1968, pp. B61–B75.

42. ____, "Probabilistic Prediction: Some Experimental Results," *Journal of the American Statistical Association*, vol. 66, 1971, pp. 675–85.

43. Woods, Donald H., "Improving Estimates that Involve Uncertainty," *Harvard Business Review*, vol. 44, pp. 91–98.

44. Zarnowitz, Victor, *An Appraisal of Short-Term Economic Forecasts*, Occasional Paper No. 104, National Bureau of Economic Research, New York, 1967.

32

THE FORECASTING AUDIT

J. SCOTT ARMSTRONG
Wharton School, University of Pennsylvania

This chapter provides a step-by-step checklist to help you conduct an audit of your organization's forecasting procedures. The checklist might help to identify ways to improve forecasting within an organization. It might also be valuable to directors to ensure that adequate steps are being taken to prepare the forecasts in an organization.

Before examining the checklist, imagine the following scene in the boardroom of a large corporation called Ajax.

Chairperson: The next thing on the agenda is to hear Mr. Raft, our Chief Executive Officer, describe the forecast for our company.

Raft: Today, I present to you the annual forecast for our firm. It covers the next 5 years.

We take this forecasting task seriously. Top management was actively involved. As they are the ones who use the forecasts, it was appropriate that they also be involved in making the forecasts.

Our industry is characterized by rapid change and a turbulent environment. In view of this, we realize that

Robin Hogarth, Robert Fildes, and Spyros Makridakis provided useful comments on earlier versions of this chapter. Support for this paper was provided by IMEDE, Lausanne, Switzerland.

historical data provide a poor guide to the future. Rather, it is necessary to be forward looking and to use our judgment. As a result, the members of our top management team spent many hours in meetings with me to prepare these forecasts.

In the final analysis, forecasting is more of an art than a science; nothing can currently replace experience and good judgment. Therefore, we sought out the best judgment. We hired one of the top economic consultants and obtained his opinions on the economic future of our firm.

We sought to use the best possible method to prepare the forecasts. As I mentioned, it was essentially a judgmental procedure that we used. But we also examined the output from some highly sophisticated computer methods. Of course, we used our judgment to modify the results from these computer methods.

The judgmental procedure we used with our management team also helped to achieve commitment to the forecasts. Since those concerned have agreed, we intend to meet these forecasts!

Our most important need was to obtain more information. We spent much time and money this year to seek out whatever data were needed. This required that we obtain data from all areas of the company. In addition, we subscribed to one of the most prestigious econometric services so that we would have early access to their short-range macroeconomic forecasts.

Before presenting the forecasts, some comment about last year's forecast is in order. Sales and profits at Ajax were lower than we had forecast. Actually, we had been quite optimistic in our forecast. Also, the growth in the economy leveled off due to government policies. So the results were not surprising, after all.

The forecasts for the next 5 years are provided in the tables of the report before you. Overall, we forecast a growth in dollar sales of 12.5% for next year with an increase in profits of 16%. We believe that these figures will improve in years 2 through 5. During that time we forecast annual growth of 15% in sales and 20% in profits. Roughly half of the increase will be due to inflation and half to the growth in unit sales. These forecasts provide our best assessment of the future. We are confident of the forecasts.

For the rest of the meeting, I suggest that you examine the forecasts. They are provided in detail in the report— covering our eight major product areas for our three major geographical markets for each of the next 5 years. We believe you will find these forecasts to be reasonable and realistic.

(A long discussion of the forecasts followed. Numerous questions were raised and answered. The board concluded unanimously that the forecasts were reasonable.)

What is wrong with the Ajax meeting? Many things. My study of forecasting problems over the past 20 years has led to some guidelines for good forecasting. I tried to violate as many guidelines as I could in the Ajax case. Perhaps you would like to reread the Ajax description to see how many things you believe to be wrong.

 Take Five Minutes to Analyze Ajax

PITFALLS IN FORECASTING . . . AND SOLUTIONS

To examine the pitfalls, I will refer to the Ajax case. After listing each pitfall, suggestions are made to correct the pitfall. Some of these solutions will seem counterintuitive. If it contradicts your experience, do do not change your mind; instead, decide what information you need before changing. A set of references (end of this chapter) is provided in case you would like to pursue certain points. You might also agree with some of the solutions. In that case, ask yourself what actions you should take.

Pitfall 1: "Top Management Made the Forecast"

Top management is likely to be biased toward a favorable view of the future (e.g., McDonald[24]). They find it difficult to use evidence that is unfavorable. The reward system in the company could bias their forecasts. Furthermore, their success over the years has given them a great deal of confidence in their own judgment. In addition, top management time is expensive.

Solutions. The obvious solution is to eliminate top management from direct involvement in the forecasting process. Management should be used primarily as a source of information about what plans the company will follow. Their plans and opinions would be used as *inputs* in developing the forecasts.

Pitfall 2: "The Forecasts Are Based on Judgment"

Surveys of corporate forecasting practices agree with what most of us suspect: the important forecasts usually are made judgmentally. In a survey of 52 manufacturing firms, Rothe[30] found opinion-based techniques to be the most popular forecasting method, with 96% of the organizations using this approach. The use of judgment seems to be especially prevalent in forecasting for strategic decision making.

Although experts are good at telling how things are now, they are not good at forecasting *changes*. The farther one goes into the future, the less emphasis should be placed on judgment. This recommendation contradicts common sense; however, the limited research to date supports such a conclusion (Armstrong[5]).

Solutions. Decrease the use of judgmental methods, especially for the long-range forecasts. Judgment can be used as a source of data, but it should not be used to analyze the data. For analysis, reliance should be placed on methods such as extrapolation or econometrics (ref. 1, pp. 363–72*).

If it is not possible to eliminate judgmental methods, much can be done to improve them. The use of data banks and presentation techniques are helpful (see solutions to Pitfall 10). Structured procedures for collecting and analyzing subjective forecasts provide another approach (see solutions to Pitfall 3).

Pitfall 3: "We Spent Many Hours in Meetings to Obtain These Forecasts"

Organizations frequently develop their forecasts in meetings. This is based partly on a belief that there is safety in numbers. That much is true. When using experts to make forecasts or to provide inputs to forecasts, use at least three experts, or, better yet, use six to 10 experts; seldom would you need more than 20 (Libby and Blashfield[20] and Hogarth[14]). Larger groups are helpful when the experts have relevant knowledge yet differ among one another, when uncertainty is great, and when the cost of errors is high.

The negative aspects of meetings are that they often consist of people with similar viewpoints and they are frequently conducted with little structure. This can lead to conformity among the group members. You can get "one opinion 6 times" when you have a six-person meeting, especially when the boss is present. This is an inefficient way to use each member's information.

Solutions. Use a number of experts, but obtain independent contributions from each expert. Preferably, the group is heterogeneous so that people have different viewpoints on the problem. Structured tech-

---

*Further descriptions and evidence on many of the points in this chapter are provided in my book, *Long-Range Forecasting* (Armstrong[1]).

niques, such as the developmental discussion (Maier and Maier[23]), can be used to reduce conformity in group meetings. For developmental discussion, the group leader prepares for the meeting by decomposing the problem so the group can work on it. During the meeting the leader provides an opportunity for all group members to participate, especially those with minority opinions; helps the group avoid evaluation; and does not add his/her own ideas. Or you can simply eliminate the meeting by using questionnaires or Delphi. The Delphi technique calls for distributing more than one round of questionnaires to the same group of experts. They receive an anonymous summary of the group responses from their previous round, and they answer the same questionnaire a second time. Johnson[15] presents an example of the use of Delphi for a long-range market forecast at Corning Glass Works. Linstone[22] provides an advocate's view of Delphi, while Sackman[33] presents a skeptic's viewpoint.

Pitfall 4: "We Hired the Best Expert"

The use of the "best" expert provides reassurance to top management. The more prestigious and more expensive the expert, the greater the reassurance. Unfortunately, this reassurance in the forecasts is unjustified. Findings from extensive research on experts has led to a surprising conclusion: we do not know how to identify experts who will provide better forecasts of *change*. This applies whether expertise is based on self-assessments, education, experience, or previous accuracy (Armstrong[5]).

Solutions.   Some minimum level of expertise is required in the subject area of the forecast. Typically, however, this minimum is achieved quickly. For example, psychology students in their first course have been found to be as accurate in judging others as are psychologists with many years of experience. The implication is interesting and valuable: select *cheaper* experts. Use part of the savings to hire additional experts, and take an average of their forecasts.

Pitfall 5: "We Used the Best Method"

Typically, uncertainty exists about which forecasting method is the best. Despite this, management often feels that one method must be best.

The selection of the one best method is risky. For one thing, you might choose incorrectly. Furthermore, even though a method may be best in principle, mistakes may occur in the use of the method.

Solution.   Be eclectic. Instead of devoting the budget to the one best method, spread it among two or three reasonable methods. Preferably these methods should differ substantially from one another. That is, they should use different information, and they should process the information in different ways. This procedure will reduce the *reliability* of the selected methods. However, if the final forecast is based on an average of the forecasts from each method, it will yield a modest gain in accuracy (ref. 1, pp. 263–68). More importantly, it helps to avoid big errors due to mistakes.

A variety of forecasting methods are available. Most forecasting methods can be described in terms of five categories: judgment, bootstrapping, extrapolation, econometrics, and segmentation. These classifications are based not on the type of data but on *the way in which the data are analyzed:*

1. *Judgment* means that the data are analyzed in one's head. This includes structured judgmental techniques such as questionnaires or Delphi.

2. *Bootstrapping* means that the judgmental rules have been formalized into an objective process. This can be done either by asking the forecaster to describe the forecasting procedure or by inferring the rules from a statistical examination of a set of forecasts.

3. *Extrapolation* methods use only the data on the variable to be forecast. They do not assess causality, but merely project the data using a mechanized procedure. Typical ways to extrapolate include regression of the variable against time, moving averages, and exponential smoothing.

4. *Econometric* methods use causal relationships in a formal way. These relationships can be estimated by a variety of techniques, but most common is the use of regression analysis.

5. *Segmentation* methods try to identify segments of similar decision making units. Separate forecasts are then made of the population and behavior of each segment. The segment forecasts are then added.

Numerous sources provide detailed descriptions of forecasting methods (e.g., Wheelwright and Makridakis[39]). Guidelines on which methods are most appropriate for which situation are provided in reference 1 (pp. 358–89).

Pitfall 6: "Highly Sophisticated Methods"

Surprisingly, relatively simple methods are as accurate as highly sophisticated methods. For example, a review of published studies (Armstrong[2,3]) found simple econometric methods to be as accurate as complex econometric methods. Simple methods are also easier to understand, less expensive, and less prone to errors.

The advantage of complex methods is that almost everyone loves a rain dance. To acquaint you with this phenomena, a summary is provided here of the "Rainmaker Theories":

Rainmaker Theory Number One. "What rain?" The rainmaker gets so involved with the dance that he sometimes forgets that he has to make rain.

Rainmaker Theory Number Two. "Yes, I know it didn't rain—but didn't you like the dance?" The successful rainmaker is the one who can convince the client that he really did not want rain—he wanted to watch the dance.

Rainmaker Theory Number Three. "Who cares why it rains?" The science of rainmaking evolves into the science of rainmaking dances.

Who can blame management if they have hired the best rainmakers to perform their forecasting dances?

Solution.   Use relatively simple methods. A good rule of thumb is that the method be simple enough so it can be understood by the user. To test understanding, the users should be able to calculate the forecasts by hand. Another, less stringent, test is that the user should be able to describe the method to someone else.

Pitfall 7: "Objective Forecasts Were Revised by Judgment"

Forecasters, and sometimes users of forecasts, make subjective adjustments to the forecasts from objective methods. These subjective adjustments are likely to make the forecasts less accurate (Harris[12] and Kelly and Fiske[17]). This is important where change is large. Research in economic forecasting has yielded different results: subjective adjustments have yielded mixed results here. It appears that for short-range economic forecasts, subjective adjustments have often helped. My hypothesis is that the gain from judgment, in improving the estimate of the current situation, may outweigh the poorer forecasts of changes (which are small in the short run). Support for this is provided in McNees.[27]

Solution.   Experts often have useful information to contribute. In particular, they have good information about the current situation. They also know about plans for the future. The most effective ways to use this information are to make subjective estimates of current status and to make *inputs* to the model that forecasts change. Another way to use experts is to obtain subjective and objective forecasts of change and then to average these. It seems risky, however, to revise forecasts subjectively after they have been obtained from an objective method; this often reduces accuracy.

In the event that judgment is used, it should be identified. A record should be made of the size of the adjustment and of the forecast error without the adjustment.

Pitfall 8: "We Will Meet Our Forecast"

Ajax failed to distinguish between the forecast and the plan. The forecast tells what will happen, given of the organization's environment, capabilities, and plans. A plan is a written set of actions that the organization will try to follow. People in an organization should work to meet their plan: that is, to carry out their various marketing, production, and financial strategies. It is the plan, not the forecast, that should provide motivation for action. Ajax should try to meet the plan, not to meet the forecast.

Solutions. Two separate documents should be prepared, one to describe the plans and the other to provide forecasts for each set of plans. You could start with the plans and develop forecasts for each plan. The forecasting and planning processes interact, but they should each be treated separately.

If the forecast is not satisfactory to management, they should change the plan, not the forecast. The latter is analogous to changing the weather forecast in order to make your picnic a success.

Pitfall 9: "We Need More Information"

Obviously we need *some* information to make good forecasts. Surprisingly, however, we quickly reach the point where "more information" adds little value. This conclusion has little intuitive appeal, but it is drawn from a substantial amount of research. This is especially true when making judgmental forecasts because the human mind is not capable of handling large amounts of data (Goldberg[10]). Also, it is likely that the user will use irrelevant information if it is provided (Kahneman and Tversky[16]). Objective methods make better use of large amounts of data, but even here additional data produce only modest gains (ref. 1, pp. 175–78 and 189–93; ref. 19, Chapter 5).

The situation is not much different if one means "better" instead of "more" information. Improvements in the quality of the data beyond a modest level have not been shown to produce more accurate forecasts. This holds even for econometric models (Denton and Oksanen[8] and McDonald[25]). For example, the accuracy of *unconditional* short-range forecasts, those where the causal variables were forecast, has been found to be equal to the accuracy for *conditional* short-range forecasts, where the values used for the causal variables were known (ref. 1, pp. 218–19, 241, and 378).

Solution. It is popular to say that we want more information. This often leads to an expensive search and delays decisions. Usually, the problem is that we make poor use of the information that is already available. Forecasters should limit the budget for information and allocate more to methods for analyzing and using the existing information.

Pitfall 10: "Used Data from All Areas of The Company"

The implication from the Ajax forecasting process is that management seeks the data they need when they make their forecast. A danger with this approach is that the search for data may be done simply to support management's beliefs. This process of seeking "confirming evidence" is even common among scientists, who are presumably trained to look for disconfirming evidence (Armstrong[4]).

Solutions. The creation of a "central data bank" will help to overcome the biased use of data. The organization should decide in advance what types of data might possibly be relevant for each type of strategic decision. One way to do this would be to ask key managers what information would help to make better forecasts. Another approach is to take an inventory of the information that is currently being used by the company in preparing forecasts. Still another approach is for the professional forecaster to decide what information would be useful. The important information would be collected routinely and stored in the central data bank (which could be a computer, a chart room, a file drawer, or a notebook). Unfortunately, one defect of this approach is that for any given decision, the data bank will also contain much *irrelevant* data. This suggests that the central data bank should not be large; otherwise managers can find irrelevant data to confirm their beliefs.

The presentation of the historical data is also important if the data are used as an aid to judgmental forecasts. Tables can be presented in simple ways. Even better, graphs can be constructed. The graphs can display long historical trends to help overcome the problems that experts have in that they weight the latest information too heavily. Some caution is needed, however, when dealing with situations involving rapid exponential growth (growth by a constant percentage per year). Recent research suggests that judgmental forecasts greatly underestimate such growth. The suggestions for dealing with such problems are counter-intuitive:

1. Observe the data at less frequent intervals (Wagenaar and Timmers[38]).

2. Use an inverse representation of growth (e.g., to forecast population density, use square miles per person rather than people per square mile). For some reason, people are better able to forecast exponential growth when it is expressed as a decreasing function Timmers and Wagenaar[37]).

Most cases, however, do not involve rapid exponential growth.

Pitfall 11: "We Used an Econometric Service for Short-Range Forecasting"

Ajax subscribed to an econometric service. They were not alone in their belief that econometric services provided more accurate short-range forecasts: sales by econometric services have grown dramatically in recent years (Shapiro[35]). Surprisingly, the promise of econometric forecasts for short-range forecasts has not been fulfilled. It is not for lack of study. Rather, econometric methods have not produced significant improvements in accuracy in comparison with judgmental or extrapolation methods (Armstrong[2,3]). Furthermore, no significant differences in accuracy have been found among the various econometric forecasting services (McLaughlin[26] and Hatjoullis and Wood[13]).

Solutions. Reduce or eliminate expenditures for short-range forecasts from econometric services. Alternative sources of macroeconomic forecasts, such as extrapolations or surveys of business economists, are available at low cost. Some are free.

Pitfall 12: "I Knew It Would Happen"

According to Winston Churchill, "The most essential qualification for a politician is the ability to foretell what will happen tomorrow, next month, and next year, and to explain afterwards why it did not happen." This qualification is also useful to corporate forecasters.

We deceive ourselves when we look back on our forecasts. Our subconscious does much of this deception. We are seldom surprised by the outcome, no matter how different the outcome was from our prediction. To demonstrate this, Fischoff and Beyth[9] asked people to make predictions of political and social events. After the events occurred, these people were asked to recall what predictions they had made.

Often they remembered incorrectly what they had predicted: they remembered predicting the true outcome even when they had predicted otherwise. When they had written their predictions and could see that they were incorrect, they rationalized what they wrote, claiming: "Yes, I wrote that, but I really knew it would happen the way it did."

Solutions. Rationalizing that "we knew it would happen" may help us to survive in organizations, and it helps us to get through life without changing our beliefs. Nevertheless, we can take steps to deal with this problem of discarding information that conflicts with our forecast. One step is to determine *in advance* what forecasts would be "surprising." The simplest way to do this is to provide forecasts with upper and lower bounds. Statistical confidence intervals can be calculated from objective methods. Williams and Goodman[40] showed how confidence intervals, calculated from a short-range forecast of changes in the number of telephones in service, provided good estimates of the precision of the forecasts (90% of these forecasts were inside the 95% confidence intervals).

Subjective estimates can also be used to obtain the upper and lower bounds. Estimates by a single expert are unlikely to be accurate (Lichtenstein, Fischoff and Phillips[21]). However, if a number of experts are used, their average confidence levels will have some validity. More importantly, they will define what outcomes would be surprising to management.

If upper and lower bounds had not been previously established, all is not lost. False outcomes can be prepared and presented to unsuspecting experts who could be asked if the outcomes were surprising. The true outcomes could then be provided. A similar approach helped to reduce "hindsight bias" in Slovic and Fischhoff.[36]

Pitfall 13: No Analysis of Previous Accuracy

The CEO did *not* provide a quantitative appraisal of the accuracy of the previous forecasts. A formal assessment might be useful in identifying the most appropriate forecasting methods. It can also be useful in identifying whether the forecasts are being used properly. For example, Griffith and Wellman,[11] in a retrospective study of forecasts for six hospitals, found that when the forecast disagreed with management's prior beliefs, the forecasts were ignored.

Solution. Present, in graphical form, the accuracy of the methods that were used to make forecasts for the past year as well as for previous years. Where possible, examine the methods to determine whether the differences among them are statistically significant.

Pitfall 14: "Our Best Assessment of The Future"

Ajax provided its "best assessment of *the* future." Who could quarrel? You can. Who among us does not believe in Murphy's Laws—a basic one being, "If something can go wrong, it will." The problem is that much uncertainty exists about the future. Changes might occur in the environment (e.g., the government imposes tariffs on your products) or in your organization's capabilities (e.g., your factory burned down). Alternatively, you might fail to meet your plan (e.g., people in the organization were not committed to the plan, or the plan might not have been within the capability of the organization).

Solutions. Rather than providing *the* forecast, provide forecasts for a set of *alternative futures.* These forecasts should cover different possibilities for the organization's

- environment,
- capabilities, and
- plans.

Especially important are the forecasts dealing with unfavorable environments. Management can then make contingency plans in light of these forecasts for alternative environments. This helps keep the organization open to change.

Pitfall 15: "We Are Confident of These Forecasts"

Read the following sentence. "FINISHED FILES ARE THE RESULT OF YEARS OF SCIENTIFIC STUDY COMBINED WITH THE EXPERIENCE OF YEARS."

Now count aloud the number of times that the letter F appears in that sentence. Count them only once; do not go back and count them again. Record your answer here: _____ . Now state your confidence in your answer on a scale from 0%, meaning that you are sure you are incorrect, to 100% meaning that you are sure you are correct. Record your answer here: _____ .

Most people feel confident of their answers. A convenience sample of 50 Wharton MBA students reported an average confidence level of about 91% for the letter-F test. The confidence levels were not related to accuracy. For the 34% who had the correct answer (which is 6), the average confidence level was 87%. For the 66% who had incorrect answers (which ranged from 2 to 5), the average confidence level was 93%. The letter-F test illustrates that ratings of self-confidence by individuals are of such poor validity that one should assume them to be worthless for predictions of a single event (for evidence on this, see Pickhardt and Wallace[29]).

When experts work on forecasts, they typically gain confidence in those forecasts. This gain in confidence has little relationship to accuracy, especially when the task itself provides little feedback (Oskamp[28] and Ryback[32]). Confidence by forecasters falsely reduces anxiety for those who use the forecasts. For an illustration, consider the Ford Motor Company, where 800 stylists predicted unanimously that the Edsel would appeal to prospective purchasers (Baker[6]). They were wrong, of course.

Solutions. Be skeptical of subjective assessments of confidence made by experts—or by yourself. Look for objective assessments (ref. 1, pp. 167–68, 221–22, 245, and 268 describe ways to obtain these). As mentioned above, the best way to assess confidence is to see how well a given forecasting method has done in its previous forecasts.

Interestingly, a better assessment of confidence can be made if the forecaster concentrates on reasons why the forecast would be incorrect. As shown in Koriat, Lichtenstein and Fischhoff,[18] and Cosier,[7] the examination of contradictory reasons for a given prediction will lead to a better assessment of the uncertainty surrounding that prediction. This procedure helps to remove the optimistic bias. (This also provides a remedy for Pitfall 1, where top management made the forecast.)

Pitfall 16: No Mention of Costs

No mention was made of the costs of the forecasts. Quite often firms spend too little on forecasting; other times they spend too much. But, according to a survey of 52 firms by Rothe,[30] few firms keep track of their expenditures on forecasting.

Solutions. Ideally, firms should continue to increase expenditures on forecasting as long as they obtain a good rate of return on this investment. In practice, the benefit is not easy to determine. On the other hand, large departures from good practice might be spotted. Schnee,[34] for example, showed that spending on weather forecasts in the United States is much larger than the potential savings that might result, even if one were to have perfect forecasts.

Keep a separate budget for forecasting. Furthermore, some general guidelines might be established. One rule of thumb (from ref. 1, pp. 432–38) is that the expenditures on forecasting should not exceed 2% of the sales volume. This might be adjusted in light of the situation (e.g., lower budgets for large companies).

USING THE CHECKLIST

The Ajax board members were asked to examine the forecasts. But board members are no better than other experts in judging whether the forecasts are reasonable. Nor is it clear what would be unreasonable as a forecast. Perhaps the board members would judge how "favorable" the forecasts are, rather than how reasonable they are.

Rather than giving extensive concern to the forecasts, the board members should concentrate on the forecasting process. Is the forecasting process reasonable in this situation? The Forecasting Audit Checklist (Chart 32-1) can help in the examination of the forecasting process. (The numbers in the checklist correspond to the pitfalls.)

The purpose of the checklist is to improve the forecasting process rather than to identify errors. Therefore, the board should agree on an auditing process well in advance of the forecast review. For example, the Forecasting Audit Checklist (or a modified version) could be pro-

CHART 32-1. Forecasting Audit Checklist

Forecasting Methods	No	?	Yes
1. Forecast independent of top management?	——	——	——
2. Forecast used objective methods?	——	——	——
3. Structured techniques used to obtain judgments?	——	——	——
4. Least expensive experts used?	——	——	——
5. More than one method used to obtain forecasts?	——	——	——
6. Users understand the forecasting methods?	——	——	——
7. Forecasts free of judgmental revisions?	——	——	——
8. Separate documents prepared for plans and forecasts?	——	——	——
Assumptions and Data			
9. Ample budget for analysis and presentation of data?	——	——	——
10. Central data bank exists?	——	——	——
11. Least expensive macroeconomic forecasts used?	——	——	——
Uncertainty			
12. Upper and lower bounds provided?	——	——	——
13. Quantitative analysis of previous accuracy?	——	——	——
14. Forecasts prepared for alternative futures?	——	——	——
15. Arguments listed *against* each forecast?	——	——	——
Costs			
16. Amount spent on forecasting reasonable?	——	——	——

vided to management so they will know what questions the board would like to address next year. It will do little good to surprise management.

I suggest a four-step procedure for the audit meeting. These steps are listed here with reference to the checklist:

1. *Assess the methods without the forecasts.* Most of the discussion should focus on the methods. Which forecasting methods were considered, and which ones were used? The auditor is in a good position, as an outsider observer, to say whether the methods are reasonable. (See checklist items 1 through 8).

2. Given that the methods are judged reasonable, *what assumptions and data were used in the forecast?* (This step may be difficult to separate from the previous step.) One role of the auditor is to judge whether all relevant factors have been examined. In particular, the auditors might help to ensure that key environmental factors have been assessed. (See items 9 through 11.)

3. *An assessment should be made of uncertainty.* This should include upper and lower bounds for each forecast, contingency forecasts, previous accuracy, and the arguments *against* each forecast. Interestingly, in a study on long-range metals forecasts, Rush and Page[31] found that while 22% of the 27 forecasts published from 1910 to 1940 made explicit references to uncertainties, only 8% of the 63 studies from 1940 to 1964 did so. In other words, the concern over uncertainty *decreased* over time. (See items 12 through 15.)

4. Finally, an *assessment should be made of costs.* (See item 16.)

Management could use this four-step procedure as the agenda for the meeting.

SUMMARY

The Ajax case was presented to illustrate forecasting pitfalls in an organization. Numerous steps can be taken to improve on this approach. Some of these steps, not intuitively obvious, were drawn from research. Other steps were obvious and were included because they are sometimes forgotten.

The "forecasting audit checklist" consists of 16 questions to ask about the forecasting process, assumptions and data, uncertainty, and costs. These questions can generally be answered by a "yes" or "no." Scores for this checklist can range from 16 yes's to 16 no's. A score of 16 yes's indicates that reasonable steps are being taken to obtain forecasts for the organization; it provides an ideal to work toward. A score of 16 no's indicates gross negligence. The Ajax Corporation scored 16 no's. In other words, Ajax was as bleak a picture as I could imagine in terms of forecasting procedures.

The major point is to select *some* checklist for evaluating the forecasting process. You could use the checklist provided here, or you could adapt it to your situation.

An advantage of concentrating on the forecasting process rather than on the forecast is that the process can be improved over time. This will help to improve forecasts in the future. When one looks only at the forecasts, there is little hope for progress. Like the old Chinese proverb says: "Give a man a fish, and you feed him for a day. Teach a man to fish, and you feed him for a lifetime."

REFERENCES

1. Armstrong, J. Scott, *Long-Range Forecasting: From Crystal Ball to Computer.* Wiley–Interscience, New York, 1978a.

2. _____, Forecasting with Econometric Methods: Folklore vs. Fact," *Journal of Business*, vol. 51, 1978b, pp. 549–64.

3. _____, "Econometric Methods and Science Court," *Journal of Business*, vol. 51, 1978c, pp. 595–600.

4. _____, "Advocacy and Objectivity in Science," *Management Science*, vol. 25, 1979, pp. 423–28.

5. _____, "The Seer-Sucker Theory: The Value of Experts in Forecasting," *Technology Review*, vol. 83, June/July 1980, pp. 18–24.

6. Baker, Henry G., "Sales and Marketing Planning of the Edsel," *in Marketing's Role in Scientific Management*, American Marketing Association, Chicago, June 1957, pp. 128–44.

7. Cosier, Richard A., "The Effects of Three Potential Aids for Making Strategic Decisions on Prediction Accuracy," *Organizational Behavior and Human Performance*, vol. 22, 1978, pp. 295–306.

8. Denton, Frank T. and E. H. Oksanen, "A Multi-Country Analysis of the Effects of Data Revisions on an Economic Model," *Journal of the American Statistical Association*, vol. 67, 1972, pp. 286–91.

9. Fischhoff, Baruch and Ruth Beyth, "I Knew It Would Happen: Remembered Probabilities of the Once-Future Things," *Organizational Behavior and Human Performance*, vol. 13, 1975, pp. 1–16.

10. Goldberg, Lewis R., "Simple Models or Simple Processes? Some Research on Clinical Judgments," *American Psychologist*, vol. 23, 1968, pp. 483–96.

11. Griffith, J. R. and B. T. Wellman, "Forecasting Bed Needs and Recommending Facilities Plans for Community Hospitals: A Review of Past Performance," *Medical Care*, vol. 17, 1979, pp. 293–303.

12. Harris, J. G., Jr., "Judgmental versus Mathematical Prediction: An Investigation by Analogy of the Clinical vs. Statistical Controversy," *Behavioral Science*, vol. 8, 1963, pp. 324–35.

13. Hatjoullis, G. and D. Wood, "Economic Forecasts—An Analysis of Performance," *Business Economist*, vol. 10, Spring 1979, pp. 6–21.

14. Hogarth, Robin M., "A Note on Aggregating Opinions," *Organizational Behavior and Human Performance*, vol. 21, 1978, pp. 40–46.

15. Johnson, Jeffrey L., "A Ten-Year Delphi Forecast in the Electronics Industry," *Industrial Marketing Management*, vol. 5, March 1976, pp. 45–55.

16. Kahneman, Daniel and A. Tversky, "On the Psychology of Prediction," *Psychological Review*, vol. 80, 1973, pp. 237–51.

17. Kelly, E. Lowell and D. W. Fiske, "The Prediction of Success in the VA Training Program in Clinical Psychology," *American Psychologist*, vol. 5, 1950, pp. 395–406.

18. Koriat, Asher, Sarah Lichtenstein and Baruch Fischhoff, "Reasons for Confidence," *Journal of Experimental Psychology: Human Learning and Memory*, vol. 6, 1980, pp. 107–18.

19. Laughhunn, D. J., *On the Predictive Value of Combining Cross-Section and Time-Series Data in Empirical Demand Studies*, Bureau of Economic and Business Research, University of Illinois, Urbana, 1969.

20. Libby, Robert and Roger K. Blashfield, "Performance of a Composite as a Function of the Number of Judges," *Organizational Behavior and Human Performance*, vol. 21, 1978, pp. 121–29.

21. Lichtenstein, Sarah, B. Fischhoff, and L. D. Phillips, "Calibration of Probabilities: The State of the Art," *in Decision Making and Change in Human Affairs*, (H. Jungermann and G. de Zeeuw, eds.), Reidel, Dordrecht, Holland, 1977.

22. Linstone, Harold, *The Delphi Method: Techniques and Applications*, Addison-Wesley, Reading, MA, 1975.

23. Maier, Norman R. F. and Richard A. Maier, "An Experimental Test of the Effects of 'Developmental' vs. 'Free' Discussions on the Quality of Group Decisions," *Journal of Applied Psychology*, vol. 41, 1957, pp. 320–23.

24. McDonald, Charles L., "An Empirical Examination of the Reliability of Published Predictions of Future Earnings," *Accounting Review*, vol. 48, 1973, pp. 502–10.

25. McDonald, John, "An Analysis of the Significance of Revisions to Some Quarterly U. K. National Income Time Series," *Journal of the Royal Statistical Society: Series A*, vol. 138, 1975, pp. 242–56.

26. McLaughlin, Robert L., "The Forecasters' Batting Averages," *Business Economics*, vol. 3, May 1973, pp. 58–59.

27. McNees, Stephen K., "An Evaluation of Economic Forecasts," *New England Economic Review*, November/December 1975, pp. 3–39.

28. Oskamp, Stuart, "Overconfidence in Case Study Judgments," *Journal of Consulting Psychology*, vol. 29, 1965, pp. 261–65.

29. Pickhardt, Robert C. and John B. Wallace, "A Study of the Performance of Subjective Probability Assessors," *Decision Sciences*, vol. 5, 1974, pp. 347–63.

30. Rothe, James T., "Effectiveness of Sales Forecasting Methods," *Industrial Marketing Management*. vol. 7, 1978, pp. 114–18.

31. Rush, Howard, and William Page, "Long-Term Metals Forecasting: The Track Record 1910–1964," *Futures*, vol. 11, 1979, 321–37.

32. Ryback, D., "Confidence and Accuracy as a Function of Experience in Judgment-Making in the Absence of Systematic Feedback," *Perceptual and Motor Skills*, vol. 24, 1967, pp. 331–34.

33. Sackman, Harold, *Delphi Critique: Expert Opinion, Forecasting, and Group Process*, Heath, Lexington, MA, 1975.

34. Schnee, Jerome E., "Predicting the Unpredictable: The Impact of Meterological Satellites on Weather Forecasting," *Technological Forecasting and Social Change,* vol. 10, 1977, pp. 299–307.

35. Shapiro, Harvey D., "The Battle of the Economic Forecasters," *Institutional Investor,* vol. 14, February 1980, pp. 103+.

36. Slovic, Paul and B. Fischhoff, "On the Psychology of Experimental Surprises," *Journal of Experimental Psychology; Human Perception and Performance,* vol. 3, 1977, pp. 544–51.

37. Timmers, Han and Willem A. Wagenaar, "Inverse Statistics and Misperception of Exponential Growth," *Perception and Psychophysics,* vol. 21, 1977, pp. 558–62.

38. Wagenaar, Willem A. and Han Timmers, "The Pond-and-Duckweed Problem: Three Experiments on the Misperception of Exponential Growth," *Acta Psychologica,* vol. 43, 1979, pp. 239–51.

39. Wheelwright, Steven C. and S. Makridakis, *Forecasting Methods for Management,* 3rd ed., John Wiley, New York, 1980.

40. Williams, W. H. and M. L. Goodman, "A Simple Method for the Construction of Empirical Confidence Limits for Economic Forecasts," *Journal of the American Statistical Association,* vol. 66, 1971, pp. 752–54.

CHAPTER

33

THE FUTURE OF
FORECASTING

SPYROS MAKRIDAKIS
INSEAD

STEVEN C. WHEELWRIGHT
Graduate School of Business, Stanford University

No book on forecasting can avoid looking at the future of the forecasting field itself. As with any forecasting task, this requires examining the past, interpreting the present, and predicting the future. The chapters of this handbook have provided the reader with a variety of material dealing with the present state of the forecasting art, the areas where forecasting can be successfully applied, the difficulties involved in such applications, and the challenges facing those who select a career in forecasting or participate in or manage aspects of the forecasting function. While these chapters have dealt primarily with the current environment and current practice, there are several questions that need to be addressed over the longer term.

Where is the field of forecasting going?

Where will the new opportunities for improving the forecasting function arise?

Where will the new challenges and major problems develop?

How can study of the future help executives make better decisions in the present?

These and related questions are addressed in this concluding chapter, following a brief historical perspective on forecasting methods and practices.

FORECASTING: A BRIEF HISTORICAL PERSPECTIVE

Before the 1950s, there was little or no systematic business forecasting. Although some methodologies, such as regression and time series decomposition, were available, their applications were limited to leading economics departments in academia and to large government bureaus. Serious widespread application of such techniques was severely hampered by a lack of timely data and the tediousness of the required computations.

In the mid-1950s, two major breakthroughs occurred that dramatically changed the forecasting field. The first was the introduction of a broad range of *exponential smoothing techniques.* Initially, these were employed rather timidly by the military, but then they gradually spread to business organizations. The biggest advantages of these methods—which were empirically based and practically oriented—were their simplicity in concept and their ease of computation. For the first time, the door was opened to a group of methods of considerable practical value that could be used easily, even with the mechanical calculators of the time. It's unfortunate that while such methodologies had significant appeal to practitioners, most academics and professional forecasters thought that such simple methods could not be sufficiently accurate to deserve serious attention. It has taken almost 30 years to recognize that exponential smoothing methods—simple and unsophisticated as they may be—do very well in comparison with many of their much more sophisticated competitors. (See Makridakis and Hibon[9] and Makridakis et al.[10])

Although exponential smoothing methods are extremely easy to use, requiring only a few equations and relatively few arithmetic calculations, in the 1950s they were still difficult to apply on a grand scale. If forecasts were needed for several thousand items, an enormous amount of work was required to maintain data files, make the required computations, and simply transcribe the results. Fortunately, a second major breakthrough in the 1950s overcame many of these problems. That was the introduction of the computer, which allowed not only exponential smoothing but a host of other forecasting methods to be used on a much more continuous basis. Subsequently, the computer has revolutionized the applicability of forecasting methods in general and has caused exponential smoothing models to be widely used in both business and government.

Since the initial work on smoothing methods in the 1950s, a number of variations and extensions of such techniques have been developed. Most notable of these are Brown,[3] Holt,[7] and Winters.[12] More recently, adaptive parameter exponential smoothing techniques, which allow smoothing methods to be used in a more mechanical and automated mode, have been developed. In these newest techniques, the user need not specify the parameter values for the exponential smoothing model. Rather, they can be computed and updated automatically.

Not long after smoothing methods began to gain attention in the mid-1950s, *decomposition methods* began to gain some attention. Prominent in this group was the Census II method developed by Julius Shiskin at the Census Bureau of the U.S. government. While these decomposition methods had little statistical underpinning, they had significant intuitive appeal to practitioners (see Chapter 10).

As computer power became cheaper and its availability more widespread during the 1960s, the door was opened for more statistically sophisticated forecasting methods. Such techniques as econometric methods became practical and were used to quantify and test econometric theory with empirical data. Within a decade, the field of econometrics developed as a profession in its own right, and by the early 1980s it represented a market of several hundred million dollars a year.

During the 1950s and 1960s, academicians were still searching for a unifying theory of forecasting. An approach to forecasting that incorporated many of the elements of such a theory finally became a reality with the work of Professors George Box and Gwilym Jenkins.[2] The Box–Jenkins methodology, as it became known, provided a systematic procedure for the analysis and forecasting of time series that was sufficiently general to handle virtually all empirically observed time series data patterns. A significant boose was given to the popularity of the method when several comparative studies of forecasting methods showed the Box–Jenkins approach to be at least as accurate as econometric approaches (see Armstrong[1]).

A variation of the autoregressive/moving average (ARIMA) method developed by Box and Jenkins also emerged in the mid-1970s. These were the adaptive parameter ARIMA methods (see Harrison and Stevens[5] and Makridakis and Wheelwright).[11] By the late 1970s, more efficient approaches for modeling ARIMA processes were being developed by people like Parzen.[12] One of the difficulties associated with the early ARIMA modeling approaches had been their statistical sophistication, which made them difficult for nonspecialized practitioners to understand. Since management tended to be unwilling to accept forecasts gained from methods that represented "black boxes," it was not until more efficient modeling methods that aided interpretation of model results were developed in the late 1970s that these ARIMA techniques gained widespread use.

On the qualitative side, technological forecasting methods became very popular during the 1960s and 1970s. Such methods as the Delphi approach and the Cost Impact Matrices approach were in use in a number of organizations by the early 1980s. These qualitative or technological forecasting approaches attempted to deal with the long-term trends in variables where the historical data and patterns necessary to apply statistical forecasting approaches simply were not available or didn't apply. Concurrently, considerable effort was expended in the marketing field on the topic of new product and new market forecasting which shared this lack of historical data.

One of the most interesting developments in the field of forecasting in the late 1970s was the realization that forecasts alone are useless until applied for planning and decision making purposes. Several studies pointed out that organizational problems would frequently block the use of forecasts, even when such forecasts could demonstrate highly accurate performance over time. During this same period, several studies identified the individual behavior characteristics that could block use of "proven" forecasting approaches. These studies, often of a multidimensional psychological nature, indicated that management revisions of forecasts were often based on wishful thinking, biased illusions, and political influence, rather than on objective reality. (See Hogarth and Makridakis.[6])

One conclusion of this historical review of forecasting is that a number of parallel avenues have been developing over the past 30 years. Of importance to this chapter is how those developments will continue or change in the future and the impact they will have on the practice of forecasting for management.

It is the editors' opinion that three important factors will have a major impact on the future of forecasting. The first and most crucial is the forecaster. Important questions include: How does he or she arrive at a forecast? How certain does he or she feel about the future? How are these forecasts incorporated into the planning or decision making processes of the organization? The second factor is the external environment to which the forecasts apply. This environment seems to be undergoing an increasingly rapid rate of change. Important questions include: Can the forcaster keep pace with such changes? Can such changes be predicted? What will their influence be on forecasting accuracy? A third factor is internal development within the forecasting field that will affect the ability of forecasters, and the methodologies they apply, to predict the future. Important questions here include: Is there a need for more forecasting methods? Will forecasting accuracy improve as more sophisticated methods and better data become available?

The next three sections deal with each of these factors in turn. The intent is to discuss their influence and importance for the future of forecasting and to provide the editors' views on these issues, in the hope that they might serve as a reference point for challenging the individual reader's views and the development of thought in the forecasting field.

THE INTERNAL MILIEU OF THE FORECASTER

For more than a decade, psychologists have been gathering mounting evidence that human judgment exhibits serious limitations and is affected by a number of biases. One striking finding reported by such psychologists is that simple quantitative models perform as well or better than human judgment under repetitive conditions (see Dawes[4]). This finding is of major significance to forecasters and organizations seeking to utilize effective forecasting. The evidence is such that these biases and limitations can no longer be ignored. Those involved with forecasting must begin to understand how their predictions are affected by judgmental biases and what their information processing limitations are in order to be able to develop the most effective forecasting procedures in the future.

Two simple examples can be used to illustrate the impact of such biases. The first comes from Armstrong (Chapter 32). In the example the reader is asked to look at a single sentence to record the number of "F's" found in the sentence and the confidence that he or she has as to the correctness of that number. The sentence used is: "FINISHED FILES ARE THE RESULT OF YEARS OF SCIENTIFIC STUDY COMBINED WITH THE EXPERIENCE OF YEARS."

While it is interesting that the majority of readers cannot accurately count the number of "F's" in this sentence (the correct number is 6), what is more important is the confidence that people have in their answer, independent of its correctness. Armstrong found that there was no correlation between the confidence level given and the correctness of the answer. In his data, 34% of the participants recorded the correct answer and, on average, they had an 87% confidence level that were correct. For the 66% who had incorrect answers (ranging in value from 2 to 5), the average confidence level was 93%. Unfortunately, many decisions are taken on the basis of how certain those involved are about their forecast of the outcomes. Given that perceived certainty can be so exaggerated and be independent of the accuracy of the forecast, it becomes important to ask basic questions about judgmental approaches to assessing future outcomes.

Another illustration is provided in Chart 33-1, which presents the annual sales of a 4-year-old product line. The assignment in this example is to prepare a forecast for future values of annual sales. One of the authors has asked this question on many occasions while teaching forecasting classes to both MBA's and executives. Invariably, both audiences come up with forecasts based on a continuation of the pattern shown in

CHART 33-1.   Sales (in thousands of units) of "Electrack"

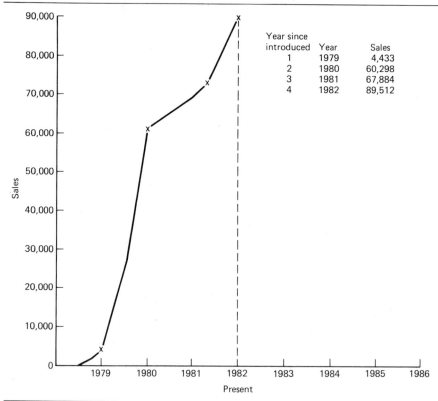

Year since introduced	Year	Sales
1	1979	4,433
2	1980	60,298
3	1981	67,884
4	1982	89,512

Chart 33-1. Interestingly, however, the data that make up this exhibit are the first four numbers from a table of random numbers. The tendency of management audiences to see a pattern where none in fact exists is what psychologists refer to as "illusory correlations" (see Langer[8]). Again, the question for the reader is the frequency with which forecasts are made, assuming that patterns do exist where there is no statistical evidence that such is the case.

Additional examples of this sort are cited in Chapter 31 by Taylor, who deals in some detail with the range of judgmental issues that face forecasters. One of the things that will be critically important in the future, and that the editors think must be addressed in the forecasting field, is methods by which the extent of such bias can be reduced or eliminated. The editors firmly believe that, while it will take time, forecasters will eventually understand enough about human biases and limitations to be able to design procedures that minimize their dysfunctional effect on forecasting or, alternatively, to find procedures that will unbias such forecasts. Consistency in forecasting seems to be a crucial factor for avoiding biases; hence the utilization of formal models will need to be increased in the future, since formal models obliged forecasters to be consistent.

Finally, there are important political issues involved with forecasting and the role of the forecaster. Events related to the 1973 oil embargo and to subsequent changes in Middle Eastern countries are just a few examples of the impact that political change can have on forecasts (see Chapter 20 by De La Torre and Neckar). While the authors doubt that accurate forecasts of political events are likely to be in the offing, other approaches to compensate for these sources of uncertainty may develop. For instance, forecasters may be asked to predict the amount of uncertainty in such fields as a useful input to management, rathern than simply predicting the outcome.

THE EXTERNAL ENVIRONMENT

Since its introduction in the 1950s, the computer has played an important role in all types of forecasting applications. The editors believe that new developments in computers in the coming decade will provide considerably broader opportunities for the field of forecasting. Accompanying the steadily increasing power and decreasing cost of computers have been parallel developments relating to data storage and memory devices. The issue of computers in forecasting is shifting from gaining access to computer power and data storage to best utilizing those resources and capabilities. The editors believe that in the future the job of forecasting will be facilitated by efficient, easy-to-use computer programs and software packages. They will be mainly interactive; they will cover the full range of forecasting methodologies; and they will be packed in a form that provides a convenient interface between formal forecasting methods and judgmental inputs.

Concurrent with computer developments has been the development of data communication networks that make possible almost instantaneous receipt and transmission of large volumes of data. Such data communication capabilities are becoming commmplace; coupled with advancements in computer technology they create large interconnected networks with major implications for forecasting. It is becoming increasingly easy, for instance, to gain access to specialized data banks and to retrieve a variety of types of information in a matter of seconds. From the point of view of the forecaster, the question shifts from where to locate appropriate data to how to develop systems that can routinely scan such data to discover changes in trends, patterns, and relationships. Undoubtedly one of the biggest future challenges facing forecasters, this question will have a significant impact on the performance and relevance of forecasting.

During the 1970s and the early 1980s, many business observers and economists seem to feel that the worldwide business environment was becoming increasingly competitive. If that trend continues, organizations will be faced with situations in which successful forecasting, effective planning, and appropriate strategic analyses will be a necessity for survival in an increasingly hostile environment. However, if information becomes available simultaneously to all competitors, additional challenges and problems will be created. To a certain extent, forecasting the future will be the equivalent of trying to predict the stock market. Information about the stock market is disseminated so fast that anyone interested can obtain such information in a matter of minutes. The consequence is that all information is continuously discounted. The end result is that the stock market cannot be predicted. At any point in time, it is equally likely that the stock market (as a whole, or for any given stock) will go up or down. At the same time, it is easy to understand that, although it is not possible to predict the stock market, anyone who fails to keep continuously informed will soon find himself or herself at a disadvantage compared to those who have better information. Similarly, if the competitive information needed for worldwide business organizations is readily available to all, obtaining that information becomes a minimum defensive move rather than an offensive strategy.

Finally, organizations will be operating in a faster changing, and technologically more advanced, environment. Both of these characteristics create difficulties for forecasting and increase the level of uncertainty that must be handled. The editors believe that two aids to dealing with such uncertainty will be the widespread dissemination of planning models capable of answering "if . . . then" type questions and role playing or business games which will allow managers and executives to experiment, in a laboratory-type situation, with how the future might behave and its implications for their organization.

CHANGES IN THE FIELD OF FORECASTING ITSELF

The editors believe it unlikely that many changes will take place in the methodologies applied in forecasting, at least within the next decade. A large number of methods are already available. The need is for consolidation and improvement of these methods, rather than for totally new developments. Attention is likely to focus on gaining a better understanding of existing methods and the conditions under which forecasting accuracy can be increased with them. Similarly, understanding how forecasting affects planning and strategy formulation, and procedures that more fully utilize existing knowledge about the future, will be the focus of attention.

The editors believe that in the future there will be several specialized forecasting services to provide economic, industry-wide, and sectoral forecasts. As argued previously, these forecasts will be available to everyone, which will eventually shift the burden of organizational forecasting back to the forecasters themselves. These forecasters will not only have to deal with internal organizational variables in forecasting, but also will need to assess the validity and accuracy of numerous externally provided forecasts.

Finally, the organizational and human problems that often hinder the implementation of forecasting need to be better understood so actions can be taken to make managers less resistant to the use of formalized forecasting methods and more prepared to understand their implications and usage in planning and strategy. As is becoming increasingly clear, this is no small task, owing in part to the tendency to adjust quantitatively based forecasts, which often leads to a decline in forecasting accuracy. As psychologists turn more of their attention to the specifics of forecasting situations, significantly improved approaches for handling this area should be developed.

SUMMARY

The editors foresee an increasingly important role for forecasting. However, they do not believe that forecasting will become easier or necessarily more accurate in the future. Organizations will have little choice but to utilize formal forecasting methods to a much greater extent than they have in the past, accepting their weaknesses and limitations, and recognizing that managers themselves cannot do any better. Moreover, the field of business forecasting will have to be enlarged to include such areas as political forecasting, energy forecasting, technological forecasting, and related fields. Because of the importance of these areas to several other aspects of business forecasting, development of procedures that systematically incorporate these at the firm level into planning and strategy will be essential.

Finally, planners, strategists, and decision makers will need to understand and accept that forecasting the future does not eliminate uncertainty, no matter how much time or money is spent. Learning to live with uncertainty and finding more effective ways to assess its impact on future plans and strategies will be a major challenge to both forecasters and managers.

REFERENCES

1. Armstrong, J. S., "Forecasting with Econometric Methods: Folklore versus Fact," *Journal of Business,* S1, 1978, pp. 549–600.
2. Box, G. E. P. and G. M. Jenkins, *Times Series Analysis, Forecasting and Control,* Holden-Day, San Francisco, 1969.

3. Brown, R. G., "Exponential Smoothing for Predicting Demand," presented at the Tenth National Meeting of the Operations Research Society of America, San Francisco, November 16, 1956.

4. Dawes, R. M., "Shallow Psychology," *in Cognition and Social Behavior,* (J. S. Carroll and J. W. Payne, eds.), Erlbaum, Hillsdale, NJ, 1977.

5. Harrison, P. J. and C. F. Stevens, "Bayesian Forecasting (with Discussion)," *Journal of the Royal Statistical Society B,* vol. 38, 1976, pp. 205–247.

6. Hogarth, R. M. and S. Makridakis, "Forecasting and Planning: An Evaluation," *Management Science,* vol. 27, no. 2, (February, 1981), pp. 115+.

7. Holt, C. C., "Forecasting Seasonality and Trends by Exponentially Wieghted Moving Averages," Office of Naval Research, Research Memorandum No. 52, 1957.

8. Langer, E. J., "The Illusion of Control." *Journal of Personality and Social Psychology,* vol. 32, no. 2, 1975, pp. 311–28.

9. Makridakis, S. and M. Hibon, "Accuracy of Forecasting: An Empirical Investigation," *Journal of the Royal Statistical Society A,* vol. 142, part 2, 1979, pp. 97–125.

10. Makridakis, S., R. M. Hogarth and M. Hibon, "The Accuracy of Time-Series Methods: The Results from a Forecasting Competition," INSEAD Working Paper, 1981.

11. Makridakis, S. and S. C. Wheelwright, "Adaptive Filtering: An Integrated Autoregressive-Moving Average Filter for Time-Series Forecasting," *Operational Research,* Q., vol. 28, 1977, pp. 425–37.

12. Parzen, E., "Forecasting and Whitening Filter Estimation," in *Forecasting Volume 12,* S. Makridakis and S. C. Wheelwright, eds., TIMS/North-Holland, Amsterdam, 1979, pp. 149–66.

13. Winters, P. R., "Forecasting Sales by Exponentially Weighted Moving Averages," *Management Science,* vol. 6, 1960, pp. 324–42.

GLOSSARY OF
FORECASTING TERMS*

ABSORPTION OF UNCERTAINTY (24): Risk information as the forecast process travels through the organization.

ACCURACY (27): The most commonly used criterion for evaluating the performance of alternative models. Accuracy measures the correctness of the forecast as measured against actual values.

ADAPTIVE FORECASTING MODELS (22): Models whose parameters are not fixed within the whole range of data. That is, the parameters of these models vary when new information becomes available. The advantage of these models is that the user does not have to estimate optimal parameters initially; rather, these parameters are modified (i.e., adapted) as new information becomes available.

ADMINISTRATIVE CONTEXT (6): Organizational structure and processes (e.g., reward mechanism, communication climate, procedures) that provide the context within which strategic decisions are made.

A/F RATIO (11): The actual demand divided by the forecasted demand; a measure of forecast error that is useful when forecast errors tend to get systematically smaller or larger as actual demand gets larger.

AGGREGATE MODEL (23): Model representing a situation at a global level in a single equation, or at least in a very limited number of equations.

---

*This glossary provides operational definitions used by the contributing authors. The number following each term is that of the handbook chapter for which the definitions are included so that the reader can understand the breadth of usage of the term.

AGGREGATE PLANNING (11): The task of developing a strategy—such as changing the workforce size, subcontracting, producing constant amounts, and using inventory to accommodate fluctuations in demand, and so on—in order to meet demands over the next 6 to 18 months.

AGGREGATION (16): The combined measurement of two or more distinct phenomena with a single variable. For example, total company sales is an aggregate of sales of the company's various products.

ALPHA (8): See Exponential Smoothing, Constant.

AMPLITUDE (19): In describing a cyclical variable, the quantitative change between the peaks and troughs of the cycles.

ANTICIPATORY ANALYSIS (23): Use of a comprehensive framework to systematically investigate the strategic implications of the future evolution of a market situation.

ARIMA (9): Abbreviation for autoregressive (AR) integrated (I) moving average (MA), the name of a broad class of time series models.

ARIMA (5): A powerful set of autoregressive integrated moving average models which have displayed impressive predictive ability in financial forecasting applications.

AUTOCORRELATION (9): The lag k autocorrelation of a time series of n observations is the correlation between the value at time t, say Z_t, and the value at time $t - k$, say Z_{t-k}, calculated over pairs of times $(k + 1, 1)$, $(k + 2, 2)$, . . . , $(n, n - k)$ exactly as one would calculate the correlation of two distinct variables X and Y.

AUTOCORRELATION FUNCTION (5): The autocovariance coefficient measures the covariance between a time series and itself displaced by k time units. The autocorrelation coefficient is the autocovariance coefficient divided by the process variance. The autocorrelation function, or correlogram, is simply a plot of the autocorrelations across all k time units.

AUTOCORRELATION FUNCTION (9): Collection of individual autocorrelations from lags $k = 1, 2, 3, . . . ,$ up to some chosen maximum lag. Used to identify a model for a time series.

AUTOMATIC ARIMA MODELING (9): Often a misnomer (some would say always a misnomer), intended to suggest internalization in the computer of model identification through interpretation of autocorrelation functions, partial autocorrelation functions, and so on.

AUTOREGRESSION (19): In time series analysis, dependence of a variable on its own past values.

AUTOREGRESSION (9): A typical element of many time series models wherein a value at time t, say W_t, may be suggested to be associated with previous W series values, say $W_{t-1}, W_{t-2}, . . . , W_{t-p}$, in the case of pth-order autogression.

AVERAGE COMPONENT OF DEMAND (8): See Level of Component of Demand.

AWARENESS (23): Index representing the percentage of consumers in a given market who can recall the name of a brand (brand awareness) or its specific features (product feature awareness).

BAYES'S THEOREM (13): A formula for calculating revised probabilities on the basis of prior probabilities and empirical observations originally shown by the Reverend Thomas Bayes.

BENCHMARK FORECAST (24): A forecast based on objective data inputs prior to personal bias and negotiation.

BETA-BINOMIAL (13): A conjugate family where the prior and revised forecasts are in the beta family of probability distributions and sampling is binomial.

BIAS (27): Term used to indicate the discrepancy when the magnitudes of forecast errors in one direction exceed those in the other direction; also referred to as Systematic Error.

"BOTTOM UP" (24): A process initiated at the bottom of the hierarchy in the organization.

BOX–JENKINS METHODS (11): The most sophisticated of all time series techniques, capable of handling any pattern of demand.

BOX–JENKINS PHILOSOPHY (9): The logical process suggested by George E. P. Box and Gwilym M. Jenkins for building a parsimonious time series model from observed data through iterative steps of identification, estimation, and diagnostic checking.

BUSINESS POLICY (6): Field of study of the top management task, including, in particular, strategic thinking and overall organizational design.

CAPACITY IDENTIFICATION (25): The determination of capacity additions, deletions, and modification to meet demand.

CAPACITY MANIPULATION (25): Short-run decisions that modify capacity; for example, staff schedules.

CARRYING COSTS (3): Costs that range over obsolescence, damage, warehousing, and investment; should certainly be no less than economic cost of capital.

CAUSAL MODEL (27): A model that assumes that the variable to be forecast exhibits a cause/effect relationship with one or more variables.

CAUSAL MODELING (28): Development of a forecasting model that quantifies the relationships between the variables thought to cause change in an item under study (the dependent variable).

CENSUS (28): A method of data gathering that attempts to audit all parts of the population under study. See Sampling for an alternative approach.

CENSUS II METHOD (10): An elaborate decomposition method designed by the U.S. Bureau of the Census and used worldwide for deseasonalizing.

CHANGES IN TREND (15): Disruptive events affecting the long-term evolution of a given market or product, particularly after some important event has taken place in the economic, social, or marketing environment. After the 1973–1974 oil crisis, changes in trends caused intricate problems in forecasting, since it had become very difficult to define true long-term growth.

CLASSICAL DECOMPOSITION (10): A simple method of separating trend, cycle, and randomness.

COINCIDING INDICATOR (18): An economic indicator whose peaks and troughs tend to coincide with the timing of the general economy.

COMPANY FORECAST (2): A company's estimated sales, in units and dollars, for an item, given a price and a marketing strategy.

COMPANY POTENTIAL (2): The *maximum* that a company could sell at a given price, irrespective of the capacities of its production and marketing facilities.

COMPETITIVE POSTURE (6): Position chosen by a company vis-à-vis direct competition; for example, innovative leader, passive follower, competing only in certain segments of market.

COMPUTER SEARCH (8): A technique that employs heuristic procedures to attempt to identify desirable values for a mathematical function that does not exhibit well-behaved mathematical properties.

COMPUTER SEARCH, DIRECT SEARCH (8): A computer search technique for multivariable problems that uses two types of "moves." The first type, an exploratory move, changes one variable at a time and examines the impact on the function value. At the end of a set of exploratory moves, the "pattern" of exploratory moves that yielded improvements is used to *simultaneously* change all variable values in the direction indicated. This process is repeated until a local optimum for the function is reached.

COMPUTER SEARCH, GRID (8): A computer search technique that defines a set of uniformly spaced values for the search variable(s) and computes the objective function value for every combination, selecting the set of values yielding the most desirable result.

CONJUGATE FAMILY (13): A family of probability distributions with the property that a prior selected from the family combined with the appropriate sampling process gives a revised probability distribution in the same family.

CONSERVATION (21): The purpose of energy distribution is to spare energy resources, either by improving the efficiency of the production process or by reducing the waste in consumption.

CONTAGION EFFECT IN FORECASTING ERRORS (24): The part of the forecasting error relating to having been influenced by common information such as forecasts of GNP.

CONTINGENCY PLANNING (6): Preparation of plans for environmental conditions that are not "most likely" but for which the firm wants to be ready; also called "what-if" planning.

CONTROL THEORY (8): A body of mathematical theory used for analyzing both the transient and steady-state behavior of physical or managerial control systems.

CONTROL THEORY (22): A branch of engineering that uses the idea of feedback to correct for deviations from objectives. Examples of control theory applications are thermostats and automatic pilots. Ideas or concepts from control theory are widely used in forecasting (e.g., adaptive forecasting models, Kalman filters, adaptive filtering, etc.).

CONVERGENCE (19): In forecasting, the equality of a forecast produced by an iteration to the forecast of the same variable used going into the iteration. For example, if a forecast of GNP is used to generate forecasts of components of GNP, convergence is achieved when the sum of the component forecasts equals the forecast of GNP used to produce them.

CORRELATED SERIES (22): Forecasting models cannot predict perfectly real data. The difference between the actual and forecasted values is called the error. Theoretically, these errors are random. In several cases, however, they are not. If they are not, they are called *correlated series*.

COST (27): The most important elements of the cost of generating forecasts are model development costs, computer costs, and model maintenance costs.

CROSS VALIDATION (27): A test of model validity. The sample data are split into two subsets: an estimation data set and a predictor set. The first subset is used to estimate the model parameters. The second subset is used to test the forecasts generated from the model. Many strategies exist for splitting the data into two subsets.

CUMULATIVE DISTRIBUTION FUNCTION (CDF) (13): A curve showing the probability distribution of an uncertain quantity, where x is displayed on the horizontal and the probability that the uncertain quantity is x or less is displayed on the vertical.

CYCLE (10): A recurring sequence of expansion and depression periods. Business cycles are common phenomena, but they vary in length and magnitude.

CYCLICAL COMPARISON (19): A technique for forecasting variables that show some regular cyclical behavior. The technique involves judging where in the cycle the variable currently stands and which previous cycle(s) the current cycle most closely resembles.

CYCLICAL COMPONENT OF DEMAND (8): Long-run changes in the demand pattern associated with general business and economic cycles.

CYCLICAL VARIABLES (19): Variables that show a tendency to rise and fall regularly over time. A variable is considered more highly cyclical the greater and more well defined the increases and decreases over time.

DATA SPLITTING (27): See Cross Validation.

DECOMPOSITION METHODS (11): Approaches that seek to break the underlying pattern of a time series into cyclical, seasonal, trend, and random components. The components are analyzed individually, extrapolated, and recombined to obtain forecasts.

DELPHI (5): A forecasting technique developed by scientists at the Rand Corporation. It offers a systematic and rational means of obtaining the relevant intuitive insights of experts.

DEMAND IDENTIFICATION (25): The determination of market opportunities and demand levels.

DEMAND MANIPULATION (25): The use of various programs to influence demand.

DEMOGRAPHIC (28): Data that relate to characteristics of the population (e.g., age, sex, family, size, education, etc.).

DEPLETION RATE (21): The time horizon at which a given reserve of fossil fuel will be exploited. The depletion rate will be high in the case of accelerated exploitation and low in the case of slow exploitation of the reserve.

DIAGNOSTIC CHECKING (9): The time series model building step where the estimated errors of a model are examined for independence, zero mean, constant variance, and so on.

DIFFERENCE (9): A transformation of a time series Z of n observations creating a new time series W by taking, for a difference of order s, $W_t = Z_t - Z_{t-s}$, $t = s + 2, \ldots, n$. Differences are employed to achieve stationarity. They are associated with the term "integrated."

DISTINCTIVE COMPETENCE (6): The unique set of strengths that differentiates a firm from all its competitors.

DISTRIBUTED LAGS (19): A way of describing the way the influence of a variable is spread over time. The distribution of influence is assumed to follow a particular mathematical form, the details of which may then be estimated using statistical techniques.

DIVERSIFICATION (6): A direction of growth of the firm that leads it into new markets (or market segments) and new technologies or manufacturing processes.

DOUBLE CROSS VALIDATION (27): A method in which the data are split into two subsets and a model is estimated on the first subset and tested on the other subset. The second subset is then used to provide estimates, and the resulting model is tested on the first subset.

DOUBLE EXPONENTIAL SMOOTHING (8): A method that takes a single smoothed average component of demand and resmooths it a second time so as to allow for estimation of a trend effect.

DYNAMIC MARKET FORECASTING (25): A service in which many factors influence the timing and level of demand.

"EARLY WARNING SIGNAL" (22): This signal allows the rapid monitoring of changes and determines when systematic errors are taking place.

ECONOMETRIC MODELING (28): The development of forecasting models using quantitative measures, often implying the use of the multiple regression technique.

ECONOMETRIC MODELS (5): A forecasting approach that employs a collection of causal relationships to describe the forecasting environment. In many cases econometric models transform the forecasting problem to that of predicting exogenous rather than endogenous variables.

ECONOMETRIC MODELS (27): Models that assume that an economic system can be described, not by a single regression equation, but by a set of simultaneous equations. Thus, the methodology allows for mutual dependence among the variables. For example, not only do wage rates depend on prices but prices also depend on wage rates.

ECONOMETRICS (18): An economic planning and forecasting model-building method that combines the disciplines of economics, statistics, and mathematics. It has been particularly useful to liberal economists as a planning tool. It is, therefore, used by Keynesian economists more than by monetarists, who are opposed to Keynesian principles. An econometric model of an economy is a small version of the real thing and is used to simulate various policy scenarios to see the effects of changed taxes, different monetary policies, and so on.

ECONOMETRICS (19): The quantitative examination of economic trends and relationships using statistical techniques, and the development, examination, and refinement of those techniques.

ECONOMIC ORDER QUANTITY (3): An amount of product to procure at one time in order to minimize the sum of the modeled "costs" taken into account.

ELASTICITY (21): The responsiveness of the demand or supply of a commodity to changes in factors that influence that demand or supply. Price elasticity is measured by the percentage change in energy demand (or supply), divided by the percentage change in price, all other factors being constant. Income elasticity is measured by the percentage change in energy demand divided by the percentage change in income.

EMPIRICAL (19): Based on investigation of actual occurrences. Empirical studies contrast with theoretical studies, in which hypotheses are produced by the application of mathematics and logic to a set of assumptions. Empirical and theoretical results are usually used in interaction with one another.

ENERGY BALANCE (21): The energy situation of a given area presented schematically in the form of a balance between demand or domestic consumption on the one hand, and supply or domestic production plus net imports on the other hand.

ERROR (8): The difference between an actual and forecasted value computed by subtracting the forecasted value from the actual value.

ERROR COST FUNCTION (27): Assigns a cost, $l(e)$, to the effect of an error of size e. The most frequently used functional form of the error cost function is quadratic; this form assumes that the effect of an error is proportional to the square of the error.

ENVIRONMENTAL SCANNING (16): The process of seeking information about the numerous aspects of a firm's environment that affect its current and future activities.

EX ANTE FORECAST (27): A forecast that uses only information available at the time of the actual forecast.

EXOGENOUS (3): The category of variables that are determined outside the (forecast) model.

EXOGENOUS FACTORS (28): Factors that occasionally alter the economic environment one is attempting to model. An OPEC price hike might be considered an exogenous factor if one were studying the U.S. chemical industry.

EXPERIENCE EFFECT (6): The effect whereby, for most manufactured products, the value added component of cost declines by 20–30% every time cumulative production output doubles.

EXPERTISE EFFECT IN FORECASTING ERRORS (24): The part of the forecasting error relating to one's own independent evaluation of one's sales territory.

EXPLICATIVE MODELS (15): Models that define the criteria that consumers or the market perceive as important; for instance, not only the annual increase in salaries but also the real increase above some weighted moving average of the last few years.

EXPLICATIVE OR EXPLANATORY VARIABLES (15): Variables that explain part of the overall fluctuation of what we attempt to forecast. For instance, if price or advertising changes, then these will affect sales. Thus, the variable price or advertising is called explicative or explanatory since it explains part of the behavior in sales.

EXPONENTIAL SMOOTHING (8): A method to systematically revise the estimates of forecast model coefficients by using each successive actual observation as it becomes available. The revisions are done in such a way as to assign exponentially decreasing weights to older historical observations.

EXPONENTIAL SMOOTHING, ADAPTIVE (8): An exponential smoothing operation that allows for the adaptation of forecast model coefficients at a *variable* rather than a fixed rate to allow greater responsiveness to shifts in a time series.

EXPONENTIAL SMOOTHING, CONSTANT (8): The fraction of the current error used to adjust the forecast model coefficient in the exponential smoothing operation.

EXPONENTIAL SMOOTHING, CONSTANT, INDIVIDUALIZED (8): A value or set of values for exponential smoothing constants that have been computed for the particular time series in question.

EXPONENTIAL SMOOTHING, CONSTANT, ROBUST (8): A generally recommended set of values for the exponential smoothing constants intended for use with all of a set of time series.

EXPONENTIAL SMOOTHING OPERATION (8): The basic operation by which all model components or coefficients of an exponential smoothing forecasting system are revised. It states: new estimate = old estimate + fraction of the error. The error is understood to mean the most recently observed value.

EX POST FORECAST (27): A forecast that uses some information beyond the time of the actual forecast.

EXTRINSIC FORECAST (3): A class of forecasts that is based on relationship(s) to other, usually external, variable(s).

FAST (25): The Burger Chef forecasting and labor scheduling system.

FAST-BREEDER REACTOR (FBR) (21): Reactor of the second generation, colloquially known as the "breeder," that produces more fissile material (i.e., plutonium, an artificial element), than it consumes.

FEEDBACK (3): The use of error measure(s) in generating subsequent estimates so as to damp next error(s).

"FLAGGING" (24): Drawing one's attention to the unexpected behavior of an account.

FORECAST (3): An estimate of the future based on the past, as opposed to (subjective) prediction.

FORECAST (11): An estimate of what value the quantity to be predicted will actually take.

FORECAST BASE (19): The latest actual values of a variable when a forecast is made.

FORECAST HORIZON (19): The distance into the future of the time period forecasted. Forecasts of 1 year have a 1-year forecast horizon.

FORECAST HORIZON (11): The length of time into the future for which forecasts must be prepared.

FORECAST INTERVAL (3): The time horizon over which a forecast is made, including delivery and review time.

FORECAST REVIEW COMMITTEE (28): A 6- to 10-person group of an organization's staff that meets periodically to develop, adopt, modify, and disseminate the approved forecasts for an organization.

FORECASTING EQUATION (8): A mathematical function that specifies how the model coefficient values are to be combined to produce a forecast.

FORECASTING HORIZON (27): The length of time into the future for which forecasts are prepared.

FORECASTING SERVICE FIRMS (28): Any of a group of commercial organizations that produce macro-forecasts, provide consultative advice on the meaning of the forecasts, and offer other peripheral services for their subscribers.

FORECASTING SYSTEM (11): A collection of subsystems that contains analysis of past history, calculation of a forecast, monitoring of the forecast, and the application of managerial judgment.

FORECASTING TASK FORCE (28): A group of from 3 to 10 staff members whose job is to recommend a plan to improve (or establish) a formal forecasting process for an organization.

FORCING (8): A technique for causing a particular computational result in forecasting systems. The most common use is to "force" individual item forecasts to combine to equal an overall aggregated value.

FREQUENCY (19): In describing a cyclical variable, the amount of time separating equivalent periods of adjacent cycles.

FUEL CYCLE (21): The four successive stages involving the use of uranium as a fuel: the mining of uranium ore, the enrichment of uranium, the retreatment of irradiated fuels, and the disposal of waste.

FUNCTIONAL FORM (27): A mathematical statement of the relationship among the variables in a model. For example, the most frequently used functional form for the error cost function is the quadratic form.

GAMMA-POISSON (13): A conjugate family where the prior and revised forecasts are in the gamma family of probability distributions and sampling satisfies the requirements of the Poisson probability model.

GENERALIZED LOGISTIC FUNCTIONS (15): Forecasting functions that include all major logistic functions and allow the user to select the one that best fits the data.

GENERALLY ACCEPTED ACCOUNTING PRINCIPLES (GAAP) (15): The rules that certified public accountants must follow in the generation of external financial statements. These rules affect the time series properties of financial data.

GOAL (11): An estimate of what one would like to happen; a target to aim for.

GROWTH FORMULA (6): $g = [R = (R - i) (D/E)] (1 - d) (1 - t)$

where g = average annual growth rate in sales and assets

R = normal return on assets (i.e., profit before interest and taxes over net assets)

i = average cost of debts

D/E = debt/equity ratio

d = dividend payout

t = tax rate.

HIGH-TEMPERATURE REACTOR (HTR) (21): A reactor of the second generation using thorium as fuel.

HISTORICAL FIT (16): The degree to which the values generated by a forecasting model approximate the actual history of the variable. Measures of historical fit help answer the question, "How accurate is my model?"

IDENTIFICATION (9): The time series model building step where patterns in summary statistics from the observed data, such as autocorrelation functions, partial auto correlation functions, and so forth, are associated with a potential model for the data. (This definition bears no relationship to the usage of the same word in the economics literature.)

IMPULSE (8): A type of input signal used in control theory to investigate the response of a control system. It is a single large deviation in either a positive or negative direction from what would normally be expected.

INCOME SMOOTHING (5): The potential manipulation of actual financial transactions or the manner in which the transactions are reported so that certain management objectives are attained.

INDICATOR APPROACH (18): A method for analyzing, monitoring, and forecasting the national economy by indicators arranged according to their timing at peaks and troughs of the business cycle. Loosely, the approach includes leading, coinciding, and lagging economic indicators. (In recent years, the approach has been widened to a five-phase system that includes government policy as a *first cause* indicator and inflation as a *final effect* indicator.)

INDICATOR PYRAMID (18): An economic tool for analyzing economy performance. A long list of economic indicators is arrayed according to the indicator's timing at peaks and troughs of the general economy. Those with the longest lead times before recessions signal possible turns in the general economy.

INDIFFERENCE CURVES (3): Each is a line of constant value for a performance measure, defining various combinations of two other variables whose several value pairings define the constant result.

IN-HOUSE (COMPUTER) SYSTEMS (28): Any data processing system of programs and procedures performed on computer equipment owned and managed by internal staff (versus outside service bureaus).

INITIAL CONDITIONS (8): A set of computational procedures for deriving the values of all necessary model parameters for a forecasting system from a set of historical data.

INTEGRATED (9): A typical element of many time series models wherein one or more differences of the time series is included in the model. (The original series may be recreated from the differenced series by a process of "integration"—actually summation in the typical discrete environment.)

INTEGRATED APPROACH (15): Definition of the market evolution for the medium term with consideration of long-term influences.

INTEGRATED FORECASTING MODELS (15): Four types of models resulting from combinations of extrapolative and explicative elements, together with the medium and long term. They are:

Ld—Long-term extrapolative setup.

Lx—Long-term explicative setup.

Md—Medium-term extrapolative setup.

Mx—Medium-term explicative setup.

INTERVENTION MODEL (9): A time series model that allows one to represent the effects of identifiable isolated events, such as strikes, wars, boycotts, price changes, and so on, through one or more "dummy" time series assuming only 0–1 values corresponding to times of nonoccurrence or occurrence of the event.

INTRINSIC FORECAST (3): A class of forecasts that is some transformation of a historical time series.

INVENTORY BUFFER (3): The safety stock carried in addition to working inventory to cushion against stockouts.

ITERATION (19): In forecasting, one generation of variable forecasts. If new forecasts of previously forecasted variables are produced, several iterations may be necessary to achieve convergence.

JUDGMENTAL ADJUSTMENT (19): A change in a forecast made on the assumption that the forecasting technique being used does not take into account all available information. For example, the forecaster may believe that historical relationships or trends have changed, or the forecaster may foresee special events that will cause temporary deviations from the historical norms.

JUDGMENTAL FORECASTING (28): The practice of developing forecasts based on the intellectual experience of the staff, with little or no formal analysis of quantitative data.

KEY ACCOUNT (24): A customer whose demand fluctuations have an important impact on total sales.

KEYNESIAN ECONOMICS (18): The policies of Alfred Lord Keynes, the English economist. Under these policies, an economy can go into deficit in hard times (with government spending more than it receives in taxes). But in good times, these deficits must be offset by surpluses. It is rarely followed in practice. Usually governments do not pursue in the surplus periods, and inflation results. Still, the basic Keynesian thesis represents a good mechanism for running an economy. Unfortunately, in free economies, legislatures seldom have the discipline to increase taxes as needed to produce surpluses.

KEY SUCCESS FACTORS (6): The elements of a company's strategy that have the strongest causal link to success in a specific business; for example, brand name, low cost.

LAGGING INDICATOR (8): An economic indicator whose peaks and troughs tend to occur later than those of the general economy. They are used (1) to confirm the turns in "coinciding" indicators and (2) as cost indicators whose purpose is to monitor the costs of doing business.

LEADING INDICATOR (18): An economic indicator whose peaks and troughs during the business cycle tend to occur sooner than those of the general economy.

LEAD TIME (21): Delay between the first exploration of a given reserve and the startup of operations after the feasibility study, mine development, and plant construction.

LEARNING CURVE (3): The demonstrable theory that a constant percentage reduction in variable performance time occurs with successive experience doublings.

LEVEL COMPONENT OF DEMAND (8): The long-run average of the stable component of demand. It is the base value in relation to which the other components are defined.

LIFE CURVE (3): A portrayal of the fraction of total demand that can be expected to occur over various (usually equal) intervals during which demand is nontrivial.

LIGHT-WATER REACTOR (LWR) (21): Electricity is produced from the fission of uranium in a reactor. The reactor of the first generation in most common use is the light-water reactor using enriched uranium as fuel and either pressurized or boiling water as moderator.

LIKELIHOOD (13): The probability of a certain empirical observation, conditional on a certain prior outcome.

LOGISTIC FUNCTIONS (15): Nonlinear growth curves that include a saturation level, usually following a steep growth. There are many types of logistic curves, such as S-curves, the Gompertz function, the Pyatt function, and so on.

LONG-RANGE PLANNING (6): Process of preparing plans for a "long" time period, typically 3 to 10 years; not identical with strategic planning.

MACROECONOMIC VARIABLES (19): Variables describing economic conditions in terms of the sum of actions of a large number of economic agents, usually the sum for the nation as a whole. For example, Personal Consumption Expenditures is a macroeconomic variable, being the sum of all consumer expenditures of all individuals in the United States.

MACROECONOMIC VARIABLES (28): Key items such as interest rates, employment percentages, population, GNP, and so on, which are seen to affect all of the industries within a national economy.

MACRO FORECASTING (25): Forecasting aggregate demand over long time horizons.

MACRO-STATISTICAL PROJECTIONS (24): A forecast of major economic indicators that are frequently used as proxy for the economic climate of business activity.

MARGINAL PROBABILITY (13): The probability of an event, unconditional on any other event.

MARKET CAPACITY (2): The number of *units* of a product or service that could be absorbed by a market at a given time irrespective of prices of products or the marketing strategies of suppliers.

MARKET POTENTIAL (2): The expected sales, expressed in the quantity of product and the dollar volume, of an entire industry, given a known mix of products, prices, and market strategies.

MEAN (13):   The average of some data or an uncertain quantity.

MEAN ABSOLUTE DEVIATION (MAD) (3):   The arithmetic mean of the absolute values of deviations from a distributor's mean. About 0.8 of the standard deviation for the normal distribution.

MEAN ABSOLUTE PERCENTAGE ERROR (MAPE) (16):   The average value of the absolute value of errors expressed in percentage terms.

MEAN SQUARED ERROR (MSE) (16):   The average value of all error values squared. This measure places a penalty on larger errors that is more than proportional. An error twice as large enters the MSE calculation as a quantity 4 (2^2) times as large.

MICROECONOMIC VARIABLES (28):   Items such as industry segment size, company sales, revenue, or product shipments that are keys to the planning process of an organization.

MICRO FORECASTING (25):   Forecasting at the operating unit level; for example, daily demand.

MODEL (19):   A description of a relationship or set of relationships among economic variables, usually in the form of arithmetic equations. Using a model, historic relationships among variables may be used to produce forecasts of some variables from forecasts of others.

MODEL CRITICISM (27):   Focuses on question of whether or not there is approximate concordance between the model in its current form and the data. If some aspects of the data seem to be discordant with respect to the model, then the model needs to be modified in an attempt to alleviate the deficiencies.

MONETARISM (18):   A school of economic thought that puts maximum emphasis on the monetary policies of the Federal Reserve Board in running the U.S. economy. Monetarists believe in a steady rate of increase in the money supply in order to prevent inflation. Monetarist economists also tend to be of the conservative, laissez faire philosophy of not interfering with the economic processes dictated by a free market.

MOVING AVERAGE (9):   A typical element of many time series models wherein a value at time t, say W_t, may be suggested to be associated with previous random error series values, say $a_{t-1}, a_{t-2}, \ldots, a_{t-q}$, in the case of qth order moving average behavior.

MOVING AVERAGE (10):   An average value of several periods (2, 3, 4, or as chosen) that is repeated from period to period. It smooths the data.

MULTIPLE TIME SERIES MODEL (9):   A times series model that involves a simultaneous equation structure, and thus permits all series involved to be dependent (or endogenous, or output) series, that is, series that can be simultaneously forecast.

NAIVE MODEL (27): A model that uses the most recent available data as the future forecast.

NONSTATIONARY (9): Loosely used as a description of a times series that has no fixed mean level. (More strictly, refers to nonconstancy of all moments of a time series, or even its probability distribution over a fixed small number of time periods.)

NORMAL-NORMAL (13): A conjugate family where the prior and revised forecasts are in the normal family of probability distributions and sampling is normal.

NUCLEAR FUSION (21): An energy-producing process based on the reaction of deuterium and tritium, isotopes of hydrogen; both at present and for years to come, the process is in the research stage.

OBJECTIVES (6): In the broadest sense, the results that the management (or owners) of a firm want to achieve with a firm; often more narrowly defined as level of growth, profit, and so forth.

PARSIMONIOUS MODELS (5): Certain relatively simple time series models that have been demonstrated on quarterly earnings data. The process by which these models are generated circumvents the most time-consuming and subjective phase of Box-Jenkins modeling.

PARTIAL AUTOCORRELATION (9): The lag k partial autocorrelation of a time series W is essentially the estimated coefficient of W_{t-k} in the regression of W_t on $W_{t-1}, W_{t-2}, \ldots, W_{t-k}$. Partial autocorrelations are useful in determining appropriate autoregressive lags.

PERIODIC AUDIT (16): The act of reviewing on a regular basis the decisions of what model parameters to choose, which technique to employ, what to forecast, and so on.

PLAN (11): A chosen course of action that is often based on a forecast; however, a plan may not equal a forecast.

POST-SAMPLE EVALUATION (27): An evaluation of the model using the prediction data set. See Cross Validation.

PRIMARY DEMAND (23): Total demand for a product class.

PRIMARY ENERGY (21): (a) Energy derived from direct combustion of nonrenewable fossil materials such as coal, oil, and natural gas and from uranium fission. (b) Hydroelectricity, using kinetic energy as opposed to combustion (see Secondary Energy).

PRIOR (13): Forecast given before taking some empirical observations.

POLICIES (6): The functional components of strategy, that is, marketing policy, manufacturing policy.

POSTERIOR (13): Forecast given after taking and incorporating some empirical observations; a revised forecast.

PROACTIVE ANALYSIS (23): Analysis anticipating the impact of alternative strategies on the future evolution of a situation.

PROCESS MODEL (23): Model explicitly representing the consumption process as an evolution of consumers through different stages.

PRODUCT POSITIONING MODEL (23): Model explicitly taking into account the relative positioning of products on specific attributes.

PRO FORMA FINANCIAL PLANNING (28): The evaluation of plausible scenarios by simulating their effect on the organization's familiar balance sheet and income statement, often through the use of a time-sharing computer program.

PROJECTIVE ANALYSIS (23): Analysis of the future evolution of a situation by assuming an extrapolation of past strategies.

QUANTITATIVE FORECASTS (19): Forecasts in which a numerical value for a variable is produced. Quantitative forecasts are in contrast to qualitative forecasts, in which only a general statement about future conditions is made; for example, "GNP will rise sharply."

QUANTITATIVE MODELING (28): The development of a forecasting model using statistical methods that analyze numeric data representing the historical records. See Econometric Modeling.

RAMP (8): A type of input signal used in control theory to investigate the response of a control system. It constitutes the introduction of a trend component (positive or negative) into an input function that did not previously contain such a trend.

RANDOMNESS (10): The component of a time series that is lacking a pattern. It is referred to as the *noise* or *error* of the series since it cannot be forecasted.

RANDOMNESS (NOISE) (8): The unexplained variations in a time series.

RANDOM VARIABLE (23): A numerical quantity that can take values within a certain range. Random variables are used in forecasting to predict some factors of interest by assuming quantitative model.

RANDOM WALK MODEL (27): See Naive Model.

REACTION ANALYSIS (23): Analysis anticipating the strategic reactions of the elements of a situation to alternative actions.

REALISM IN FORECASTING (16): The degree to which a forecasting system employs all known influences on a variable. Perfect realism is typically an undesirable state to achieve in a forecasting system because of the high cost of achieving it.

RECESSION (18): When the U.S. economy turns negative. The minimum requirement for recession is at least two quarters of negative *real* (i.e., adjusted for inflation) growth. It must have a duration at least as long as the shortest recession on record, a wide diffusion throughout the economy, and a depth at least as deep as the shallowest recession on record.

RECONCILIATION OF FORECASTS (24): The use of forecasts prepared by various sources to extract one final forecast.

RECOVERY (RATE OF) (21): The share of the reserves of a given field that can actually be extracted during the time of exploitation. The use of new extraction techniques can improve the rate of recovery, thus adding to the exploitable reserves.

REGRESSION METHODS (11): Techniques that attempt to use historical data to develop a relationship between demand (dependent variable) and a set of independent variables. Forecasts are then made by specifying values for the independent variables and using the developed relationships.

RELATIVE FREQUENCY CURVE (13): A picture of a probability distribution where an uncertain quantity is displayed on the horizontal axis and relative frequency is displayed on the vertical axis.

RELATIVE MARKET SHARE (6): Market share of the firm measured either against market share of the market (segment) leader, or against an average of several major competitors. There is strong empirical evidence that high relative market share correlates with high profitability.

RESERVES (AS OPPOSED TO RESOURCES) (21): Resources: All known or unknown quantities of fossil materials, exploitable or not. Reserves: *Known* resources of the same materials that are exploitable at existing conditions of costs (including production, transport, and transformation).

ROBUSTNESS (3): The property of producing almost the same result over a wide range of varying conditions—implying insensitivity to measurement errors.

ROLLING NEGOTIATIONS (24): A process by which salespersons negotiate their aggregate results with their own superiors and so on.

SALES FORCE COMPOSITE (24): A forecast prepared by the sales force as a result of observations and customer contact.

SALES GOALS (2): A hoped-for sales level for a company, a division, or a product.

SALES QUOTA (2): A goal that has been broken down into smaller units, such as a region, a district, or a specific representative's territory to provide a management objective.

SALES QUOTA (24): A sales objective that the salesperson or executive agrees to achieve, usually used as a basis for performance approval.

SAMPLE SIZE (13): The number of samples in a survey.

SAMPLING (28): A method of data gathering where only a small portion of the population is studied (versus the census approach). Care has to be taken when the results of a sampling audit are projected to the full population.

S-CURVE OR FUNCTION (15): Characterized by a slow start, a steep growth, and a saturation in sequence. Widely used in forecasting sales of new products or introduction of new techniques. Part of a general category of growth curves called logistic.

SEASONAL COMPONENT OF DEMAND (8): Systematic variation about the level component of demand through a seasonal period of relatively short duration (1 year, e.g., when monthly data are used).

SEASONALITY (5): A tendency for a data set to repeat itself or exhibit periodic behavior over a specified time interval. It is a pervasive factor in the modeling of quarterly earnings data.

SEASONALITY (10): The component of a time series that occurs repeatedly from year to year (or other periodicity). It is caused by "seasonal" need or availability, and it does not affect the prevailing direction taken by the series.

SEASONALITY (11): Condition when a systematic pattern occurs in the time series data, for example, when demand during the winter is consistently low while summer demand is consistently high.

SECONDARY ENERGY (21): Electricity is a secondary form of energy when it is derived from the combustion of one of the fossil fuels (coal, oil, natural gas), or from uranium fission. The term "primary electricity" applies to hydroelectricity, using kinetic energy as opposed to combustion or fission (see Primary Energy).

SEGMENTATION (24): The disaggregation of the market or customer body to smaller homogeneous groups allowing simultaneity of more "tailored" marketing activities.

SELECTIVE DEMAND (23): Demand for a specific brand within a product class.

SELF-SUSTAINABLE GROWTH (6): The level of annual sales growth that a company can finance out of retained earnings and without changing financial structure and dividend policy.

SERVICE LEVEL (3): Any of a number of indicators of the amount of demand routinely satisfied by finished goods (inventory) (e.g., percentage of orders filled, percentage of units filled, percentage of dollars filled, etc.)

SHADED AREA (18): In economic forecasting and analysis, areas of graphs that indicate periods in which the U.S. economy is in recession. The shade follows the peak month (high point in the business cycle) and ends in the lowest month (trough). Expansionary periods are unshaded.

SHARED EXPERIENCE (6): Exists when the experience effect applies to activities (e.g., manufacturing or distribution) that are shared by different end products.

SLOWDOWN (18): When the U.S. economy experiences at least two quarters of growth less than the traditional average growth rate of

+3½% per annum. (If the growth turns *negative* for at least two quarters, the slowdown then meets the minimum standard for recession.)

SMOOTHED VALUES (22): Averaged values obtained by using any of the exponential smoothing models. They are called smoothed because randomness has been eliminated through the smoothing process. So these values do not fluctuate widely but they are closed.

SMOOTHING CONSTANTS (11): Constants with values between 0 and 1 that control how quickly values change.

SOFTWARE PRODUCTS (28): Computer programs that have been developed and tested for general distribution and use (versus company-specific application programs); they are purchased, leased, or licensed from the author. Care is taken in the development of software products to insure the widest applicability to a broad range of uses.

SOLAR ENERGY (21): A blanket term covering a diverse set of renewable energy technologies that can be divided into three major groups: thermal applications, fuel from biomass, and solar electric. All forms of energy, including the deposits of fossil fuels formed in past geological ages, are derived from the sun.

SPECIAL EVENTS OR ACTIONS (22): Unusual circumstances (such as extremely bad weather, strikes, big promotional campaigns, price wars, etc.) that cannot be dealt with directly by forecasting models. These events must be dealt with on a judgmental basis so that their influence can be incorporated into forecasting. The process of dealing with these events is termed "special actions."

SPECIFICATION ERROR (27): One caused by either the incorrect choice of a functional form or the failure to include variables in the model.

STABLE MARKET FORECASTING (25): Predicting demand in a saturated or mature market.

STANDARD DEVIATION (13): Square root of variance, a quantity often used to measure the amount of dispersion exhibited by an uncertain quantity or by some data.

STANDARD INDUSTRIAL CLASSIFICATION (24): A convention for classifying business activities that provides a framework for classifying secondary statistical and economic data.

STATIONARITY (5): Characteristic of a process with a joint distribution that is invariant with regard to displacement in time. Time series data must either exhibit stationarity or be capable of being transformed to this state.

STEP (8): A type of input signal used in control theory to investigate the response of a control system. It constitutes the shifting of the level component of demand to some new higher or lower value which then continues for some time into the future.

STOCHASTIC MODEL (23): Model representing market behavior in a probabilistic fashion.

STOCKOUT COSTS (3): Costs that an organization chooses to use to represent the potential opportunity loss; they can be inferred by analyzing actual current behavior in inventory control.

STRATEGIC BUSINESS UNIT (6): A set of product/market activities for which one homogeneous competitive posture can be defined; an SBU does not necessarily exist as an organizational entity.

STRATEGIC FORECAST (24): Long-term oriented forecast, taking into account new and structural development.

STRATEGIC MANAGEMENT (6): An approach to management that combines strategic thinking about competitive posture with planning of organizational capability.

STRATEGIC PLANNING (6): The systematic process of determining a company's competitive posture, technological and market scope, and resource allocation patterns. The minimal elements that have to be present in strategic planning are: a critical questioning of explicitly understood present strategy, a search for opportunities and threats in the environment, a resource audit, and the consideration of alternative strategies.

STRATEGIC PORTFOLIO (6): A classification scheme for the various strategic business units of a diversified firm according to relative competitive posture and attractiveness of business environment. Specific a priori recommendations regarding business strategies and corporate strategy can be derived from the strategic portfolio.

STRATEGIC SEGMENTATION (6): The process of identifying segments of an overall market with the purpose of finding segments in which the firm can achieve such meaningful and lasting differentiation of its products or services from competitors that it can earn higher margins.

STRATEGIC WINDOW (6): The—typically limited—time period during which a particular constellation of competitive forces provides the firm with an opportunity to gain a lasting improvement in its competitive posture.

STRAW MAN (18): An old tool of logic in which a proposition is stated and then attempts are made to discredit it. If it can be discredited, then the expected result is not a very likely possibility. A popular use of the "straw man" is to assume an impending recession. If it is likely to occur, then many leading indicators should peak and turn down. If they do not, the assumption of impending recession is discredited.

STRUCTURAL CHANGE (5): A major intervention in the time series properties of a data set. Some event of significance has permanently altered the process by which the data are generated.

STRUCTURAL STABILITY (27): Property of a model for which both the model parameters and the functional form are constant over time.

SUBSTITUTION (21): Of different sources of primary energy for one another for heating purposes or for production of electricity. Road and air markets are captive markets for oil products. Nonetheless, synthetic fuels derived from coal or tar sands could be substituted for these products at a price. Thus substitution is limited by cost and technology considerations.

SURVEY OF BUYING POWER (24): Periodic surveys of economic activity (number of employees, sales volume, etc.) that help estimate market potentials.

SYNDICATED DATA (28): Data that have been gathered, compiled, verified, published, and distributed for sale by a commercial organization to interested parties.

TACTICAL FORECAST (24): A short-term oriented forecast assuming no major structural changes.

TIME HORIZON (28): The farthest extent an organization needs to project a forecast. For example, a time horizon of 4 to 6 quarters may be needed for forecasts prepared for financial planning and resource allocation purposes. A forecast time horizon of 2 to 4 weeks may be satisfactory for production scheduling.

TIME SERIES (9): An ordered sequence of values of a variable observed at equally spaced time intervals.

TIME SERIES ANALYSIS (5) (19): A forecasting technique in which the future behavior of a variable is predicted from its past behavior.

TIME SERIES ANALYSIS (28): The branch of quantitative forecasting where data for one variable are examined for patterns of trend, seasonality, and cycle. Several univariate forecasting methods are available to the time series analyst.

TIME SERIES FORECASTING (9): A quantitative forecasting approach in which a principal emphasis is placed on the reasoned utilization of time-lagged data (i.e., historical data) in forecast development. Time series, or multiple time series simultaneously, depending on the specific forecasting problem.

TIME-SHARING (28): The operation of a digital computer where several computer terminals may be simultaneously operating their own separate programs. Time-sharing computer programs (versus batch programs) often are conversational with the terminal user.

TOP DOWN (24): A process initiated at the top of the hierarchy in the organization.

TRACKING SIGNAL (8): A computed value to alert the forecaster that biased forecast errors or large forecast errors or a combination of the two are being observed. It implies the need for manual intervention in nonadaptive forecasting systems.

TRANSFER FUNCTION MODEL (9): A single equation, multiple series time series model wherein one dependent (or endogenous, or output) time series is to be forecast as a function of one or more independent (or exogenous, or input) time series, and (potentially) the dependent series' own history. It is presumed that the dependent series does not influence subsequent values of the independent series.

TREND (10): The prevailing average tendency of a series, often expressed as the average growth over a time period.

TREND (11): Condition when a time series shows a consistent increase or decrease over time.

TREND COMPONENT OF DEMAND (8): The per period change in the level component of demand.

TREND CYCLE (10): Statistically speaking, what is left in a time series when seasonality and randomness have been removed. It incorporates both the average growth of the series (the trend) and the deviations from it due to the business cycle. The trend cycle is what has to be forecasted.

TRUE FORECASTS (16): Forecasts that are made with complete uncertainty about future events including explanatory variables.

UPDATED FORECASTS (9): Revisions of the original forecasts in the light of data that become available subsequent to the time period in which the original forecasts were made.

USEFULNESS IN FORECASTING (16): The degree to which a cost-benefit tradeoff is favorable in forecasting. An extremely useful forecasting system would be one that explains most of the variations in the forecast variable with a simple low-cost model. Usefulness and realism are not synonymous.

VARIANCE (13): The average squared deviation from the mean of some data or of an uncertain quantity; a measure of variability or dispersion.

WINTERS' THREE-FACTOR METHOD (11): An exponential smoothing technique proposed by Peter Winters which can be used when the quantity being forecast displays linear trend or seasonality.

INDEX